NATIONS AND MEN

An Introduction
to International Politics

Third Edition

NATIONS AND MEN

An Introduction to International Politics

Ivo D. Duchacek
The City College of the City University of New York

℗
THE DRYDEN PRESS
Hinsdale, Illinois

For
Henri Roque,
L'Homme à Cheval

Copyright © 1975 by The Dryden Press
All Rights Reserved
ISBN: 0-03-089496-4
Library of Congress Catalog Card Number: 74-6848
Printed in the United States of America
5678 090 987654321

Preface

Nations and Men: An Introduction to International Politics is a concise introductory text in international politics that seeks to provide today's students with the essential tools for analyzing how nations interact. It avoids utopian thinking and false analogies with domestic politics and analyzes the world as it is and as it can be expected to be in all probability in the last decades of the twentieth century. The focus is on why nations and men act as they do and not on how they should act. Further, an effort has been made to "rehumanize" international politics by concentrating on the problems of individual and group perceptions and misperceptions and on the role of ideologies and moral considerations in the decision-making process. In view of the complexity and limited predictability of international decisions—national leaders are often certain only of their uncertainty—the study of international politics should always be a lesson in humility. I hope *Nations and Men* does not fail in this requirement.

The text is divided into fourteen chapters grouped into four major sections: Part I deals with the territorial fragmentation of humanity into nation-states, the causes and effects of nationalism, and external consequences of internal cleavages—ethnic, racial, political, ideological, economic, and social. The discussion of national self-determination leads to the analysis of the concept of national self-preservation. In this context Chapter 4 examines the concept of national interest, whose meaning is usually a matter of inconclusive controversy in terms of national goals and means of attaining them.

Part II focuses on the decision-making processes, especially on the human factor in international politics. Chapters 5 and 6 examine the frailty of human judgment when national leaders comparatively evaluate national capabilties and intentions in the light of the available, never complete, information. The controversial question of the role of ideology as an operational code in the conduct of foreign policy is dealt with in Chapter 7; that chapter also includes a case study of interpenetration of communism and nationalism—a consequence of grafting a supranational doctrine onto the existing system of nation-states.

Part III describes some of the potential restraints on national freedom of action. Chapter 8 deals with the role of moral considerations in decision making and includes various case studies, ranging from Munich, Dresden, and Hiroshima to My Lai. Chapters 9 and 10 examine the impact of international law and international organizations, including the United Nations, on the behavior of nations and their leaders. The theory and practices of functionalism, pacific settlements of disputes, collective security, and peace-keeping operations are included in Chapter 10.

Part IV concentrates on major techniques that interacting nations tend to consider in order to solve or shelve their conflicts of interests or to promote their cooperation. Chapter 11 examines the probability of nuclear wars and the frequency of conventional local and regional wars, including internationalization of internal conflicts. The general practice of interference in an interdependent world and political manipulation of economic relations affecting the Poor and newly rich Oil Worlds are analyzed in this framework. A short discussion of game theory is included. Chapters 12 and 13 analyze signaling and balancing techniques, ranging from the promotion of messianic doctrines to conventional and nuclear arms races and alliances; discussion of nonalignment and the continuous efforts to reduce the armament race to a lower level complete the major themes of these two chapters. Chapter 14 examines the assumptions, limits, and promises of diplomatic negotiations, including tacit bargaining and hostile competition without violence.

Nations and Men begins with an analysis of those phenomena with which the student has some familiarity: the territorial dimension of local and national politics, ethnonational sentiments, and transnational links. Then, step by step, more complex concepts are developed and conceptual controversies presented so that, in due time, the student is encouraged to think critically, conceptualize, generalize, and handle such approaches as are offered by macrolevel or microlevel analyses, decision-making theories (including organizational and bureaucratic models), individual perception, cognitive dissonance, tacit bargaining, strategies of conflict, and international law. Theories and models are woven into specific case studies; concrete examples are taken from ancient, modern, and contemporary history. Since the students who will use the text are generally too young to remember much about the Korean War, the two Cuban crises, and the controversies concerning the war in Vietnam, these and other recent crises, including the fourth Arab-Israeli war of 1973 and the Cyprus crisis of 1974, are briefly identified. Fuller description is, of course, given of such more distant events as the Hiroshima and Dresden raids, the Soviet-Nazi Pact, and the Munich agreement, which has become part of current terminology and is often used as a shorthand label, readily understandable by statesmen and the mass media that argue about the wisdom or folly of appeasement, summit diplomacy, and the foresight or blindness of national leaders. In 1962, for instance, the Chinese press described the solution of the Cuban missile crisis as a "Munich in the Caribbean," leaving many a contemporary American student (and probably many a Chinese peasant) puzzled as to the reasons for the sudden emergence of the city of the Olympic Games in the Caribbean waters.

The third edition of *Nations and Men* features the illustrative documents that characterized the first and second editions. Users of the book have found them helpful (and asked for more) in familiarizing students with the exact jargon, tone, flavor, and terminology of original political statements, treaties, or scholarly definitions. The documents are directly related to the analyses contained in the text and range from the UN study of multinational megacorporations, the Brezhnev Doctrine, and the 1974 Arab-Israeli disengagement accord to the vitriolic anti-Soviet editorials in the *Peking Review*, the text of the Soviet-American agreement on a "hot line," and the Sino-American statement of 1973 recording disagreement on the subject of Taiwan and other matters. All of these documents—forty-four altogether—are clearly distinct from the text.

The third edition is also enlivened by various diagrams as well as political cartoons that tend to illustrate the old Spanish proverb that the world is a comedy for those who think and a tragedy for those who feel.

Although the text was entirely reorganized and portions of all chapters were thoroughly rewritten to permit addition of new materials and elimination of those portions of the book which the users of the second edition have found unhelpful, the third edition retains the basic features of the previous edition. It remains a relatively short but wide-ranging text that permits the instructors to branch out into their field of current interest and research with assurance that the more general aspects of international politics have been covered in the text.

At the end of each chapter the user will find suggestions for the use of the volume of readings intended to accompany the text, *Discord and Harmony: Readings in International Politics*, edited by the author. This reader brings together selections that juxtapose analyses written by prominent scholars and various political statements and descriptive case studies. The reader is divided into fourteen chapters. Among the scholars and statesmen whose analyses or opinions are reproduced in the reader are: Graham T.

Allison, Richard J. Barnet, Kenneth E. Boulding, Karl von Clausewitz, Karl W. Deutsch, Rupert Emerson, Amitai Etzioni, Richard A. Falk, Frantz Fanon, Philip Green, John H. Herz, Stanley Hoffmann, Ole R. Holsti, Fred Charles Iklé, Herman Kahn, Vladimir I. Lenin, Charles Burton Marshall, Mao Tse-tung, Hans J. Morgenthau, Arthur M. Schlesinger, Jr. (on the Bay of Pigs fiasco), J. David Singer, Theodore C. Sorensen, and Robert F. Kennedy (on the Cuban missile crisis), Kenneth N. Waltz, and Max Weber. The Soviet-Nazi cooperation of 1939-1941 is illustrated by excerpts from the Nazi secret archives.

The changes in the third edition of *Nations and Men* reflect the critiques and suggestions offered by the users of the second edition; they have proved extremely helpful and deserve my sincere thanks. While preparing the third edition I also received a detailed critical review of the second edition from Professor John H. Herz of the City College of New York; his careful scrutiny led to a substantial reorganization of the text. I am greatly indebted to him. In addition, I received specific suggestions concerning various chapters in the book: Professor Benjamin Rivlin of the City University of New York commented on segments dealing with the Third World and the political manipulation of international economic relations; Professor Walker Connor of the State University of New York (Brockport) commented on the chapter on nationalism; Professor Henry Pachter of the City University of New York offered suggestions concerning the chapter on ideology and imperialism; and Professor Milton M. Silva of Juniata College suggested various changes in the overall organization of the text. Their contributions are greatly appreciated.

My particularly warm thanks go to Professor Robert G. Wirsing of the University of South Carolina, who reviewed the completed manuscript of the third edition in painstaking detail. His constructive critique and the various suggestions he made concerning matters of fact, emphasis, interpretation, and organization have been followed with great appreciation and gratitude. In the final phase I received systematic and imaginative editorial assistance from Ms. Nancy Clemente which is here gratefully acknowledged.

New York,
December 1974

I.D.D.

Contents

ix

Introduction

The fundamental precondition for understanding relations among nations is the study of the world as it is and not as we wish or pray it to be; our impatience with our imperfect world cannot daydream out of existence the harsh facts of life and human nature. A reform or a plan for a more humane and rational future, to be successful, must begin with a systematic analysis of exactly what is to be reformed.

In the study of politics the term "facts of life" has a very broad range. It includes not only the physical environment with its limitations and opportunities but also plans and efforts to alter it; not only the present and the history that has shaped it (even though the impact of history and its lessons for our time are so variously interpreted) but also plans for the future, both noble and ignoble; not only the usual human behavior but also the exceptional. Political ideology, religious creed, rational analysis, irrational impulses, perverse concepts, and even wishful thinking may all become "facts of life" in politics when they gain organized support and become triggers of political action. What seems unrealistic or impractical today may prove feasible and practical tomorrow—for better or worse. This is what pacifism, internationalism, socialist humanism, and many other "isms," including fascism, hope for. Humanism and plans for a peaceful world compete with inhumanism and plans for a violent world for the support of individuals and nations.

In the study of international relations, neither utter pessimism nor easy

1

optimism is warranted. A systematic study of international politics will reveal that human beings often act egoistically, irrationally, and destructively, whether they act as individuals or as members of groups, tribes, nations, or ideological movements. We should not be too optimistic about the perfectibility of humanity.

On the other hand, human beings have proved their capability of using reason and of acting with intelligence, foresight, and occasionally even generosity. Individual and group past and present behavior does not preclude a different and better (but, of course, also worse) behavior in the future. Prenuclear history, ancient or recent, may prove to be an unreliable guide to human and national reaction to the unique challenges of the nuclear and technetronic age.[1] Some observers express the hope that for the first time in human history, world unity is within reach; they believe that the very destructiveness of modern weapons will prevent their use and that mutual terror will impose unity and humanism on the divided world. The American writer and philosopher Lewis Mumford, in *The Human Way Out*, writes:

> Those who hold, as a final axiom of life, that politics is the science of the possible presume to know in advance the limits of human potentiality. . . . Who is so brash as to fix in advance the limits of human imagination and inventions, of human intelligence and sympathy . . . [and] predict, with confidence in his own ineffable wisdom, what is or is not possible under circumstances that mankind has never faced before? . . . Our business is not to masquerade as providence by laying down in advance what is possible. Ours is the humbler task of recognizing what is necessary. . . . If we dare to speak and act on behalf of the human race, as brothers helping brothers, who will oppose us?[2]

Perhaps we should not be too pessimistic—even though we may be tempted to respond to Mumford's question and emphasis on brotherly love by pointing to nationalists and other Cains.

The mixture of idealism and cynicism, reason and irrational impulses, enlightenment and narrow-mindedness, egoism and altruism, parochialism and ecumenism, the tendency to destroy and the zeal to construct—all this, history and the present confirm, is *human*. In studying international politics we should constantly bear in mind that we deal not with abstract entities but with human beings, organized in and generally identified with their territorial communities.

Notes

1. Zbigniew Brzezinski coined the term "technetronic" to describe the postindustrial age of electronic computers and automation in his book *Between Two Ages: America's Role in the Technetronic Era*. New York: Viking, 1970.

2. Lewis Mumford, *The Human Way Out*. Wallingford, Pa.: Pendle Hill, 1958, pp. 5-8.

Part I
NATIONS

Territorial and Ethnic Fragmentation of Humanity

1
The Territorial Dimension of International Politics

Ideally, humanity is one and indivisible. In fact, however, it has been divided for millennia into fiercely competing clans, tribes, cities, churches, factions, interest groups, political parties, ideological movements, empires, nations, and territorial states. For the past three hundred years, the most durable and most efficient unit to which individuals and groups give their effective allegiance and with which they most unconditionally identify themselves has been the *territorial state*, often also called the *nation-state* or *national state*. It is the largest politically organized community that, "when the chips are down, effectively commands men's loyalty, overriding the claims both of the lesser communities within it and those which cut across or potentially enfold it within a still greater society."[1] Despite the growing awareness of worldwide interdependence, the mass movement of goods, people, and ideas, and the unifying compulsion of modern technology that makes both global destruction and global construction possible, most people still primarily feel and act as members of their territorial nation-states. A state is still considered a more efficient instrument than any alternative for coping with people's collective problems: it protects them against external dangers (or so they believe), maintains internal peace and order, and, taking up the collective challenges of modern economy, technology, and ecology, provides people with

5

economic progress, social security, cultural advancement, group identity, and eventually, as they hope, with a cleaner environment.[2]

The territorial states are the principal actors on the international scene, and their contacts, cooperation, competition, and conflicts are the core subject of the study of international politics.

In addition to the states there are also other actors on the world scene; their roles have so far remained less decisive than those of national governments. Four categories of such secondary actors may be identified:

1. Intergovernmental coalitions, alliances, ideological blocs, and universal permanent organizations, such as the United Nations or Universal Postal Union, represent organized aggregates of territorial states. These international collectivities are usually endowed with some permanent common institutions and, occasionally though rarely, they demonstrate a collective will and capacity to act jointly on the world scene. Chapter 10 of this book will deal with them in more detail.

2. Political dissidents and opposition groups are taken into account internationally for the simple reason that they direct their efforts toward unseating the existing political authority by election, subversion, or violence and so becoming the new national leadership. If their prospect of achieving this goal is realistic or deemed so by foreign governments, legitimate as well as illegitimate opposition groups, as "governments of tomorrow," may play a significant international role long before their accession to power; some of them, especially revolutionary factions, often establish contacts with foreign governments for the purpose of asking for and receiving verbal, material, or military support. Examples are: guerrilla movements, liberation armies, exiled political groups, competing factions in authoritarian systems and also legitimate or subversive opposition parties in democracies. (Chapters 3 and 11, which deal with methods of foreign interference in domestic affairs, will examine the potential and actual international roles of domestic opposition and dissidence in greater depth.)

3. Ethnic, racial, linguistic, or religious groups appear as important actors on the international scene whenever they significantly challenge the central territorial authority by the threat or actuality of rebellion or territorial secession from the existing state. Foreign governments have often entered into cooperative compacts with such potential nation-states. (Chapter 3 will focus on such groups in connection with the principle of national self-determination.)

4. Functional interest groups whose transnational activities affect the foreign policy of their own national government and domestic as well as foreign policies of their host governments necessarily influence politics among nations. Examples of such nongovernmental bodies whose influence and budgets may overshadow many a nation-member of the United Nations are: international labor, agricultural, and professional organiza-

tions and, even more important, multinational manufacturing, extractive, commercial, and banking megacorporations (see Document 1.1).

In this chapter, we will be primarily concerned with the structure and attributes of the principal actors on the international scene, the territorial states.

NATION-STATES

Today the human race is divided into some 140 territorial states. Political authority everywhere is clearly territory-bound. Well-protected national boundaries indicate the limits of each of the 140 national government's territorial control and coercive power. Within the nation-states, internal boundaries determine the extent of administration and control exercised by subnational units of authority: towns, counties, cities, provinces, regions, or, in the American federal terminology, states—the fifty components of the federal nation.

Singly, the 140 nation-states own and administer their portions of the world; collectively, they influence the whole of it. No inhabited place has escaped direct or indirect control by territorial states. The colonies, protectorates, and dependencies that still remain in Africa, Asia, Latin America, the Caribbean, and the Pacific represent administrative extensions of territorial states, mostly West European. High seas and outer space do not belong to any state. The free exploration of and traffic in the high seas and outer space (even though it is not yet clear exactly where they begin) are more or less regulated by tacit and a few written agreements among nations.

The number of territorial components into which humanity has been divided varies with time and according to the different criteria we may use. The United States can be counted as one territorial unit if our criterion is that of a constitutional monopoly to determine and conduct the nation's foreign policy. In terms of territorial authority with respect to internal affairs, the United States may for some purposes be counted as an aggregate of over fifty units (fifty states, Washington, D.C., Puerto Rico, and several dependencies, including the Virgin Islands, Samoa, Guam, and the Pacific Trust Territory) or as an aggregate of over 38,000 units of local government (if we ignore well over 50,000 school and special districts). Internationally and in the United Nations, however, the United States is counted as one national state with one vote in both the Security Council and the General Assembly.

The Soviet Union is counted as one nation with a great-power (that is, veto-power) status in the Security Council, but as a three-unit aggregate endowed with three separate votes in the United Nations General Assembly (the Soviet Union as a whole and two of its fifteen major components:

DOCUMENT 1.1

A UN STUDY ON MULTINATIONAL CORPORATIONS: MAXIMIZERS OF WORLD WELFARE OR DANGEROUS AGENTS OF IMPERIALISM?

The term "multinational corporation" is employed in the [UN] report to cover all enterprises which control assets—factories, mines, sales, and other office—in two or more countries. Under this definition multinational corporations are responsible for most foreign direct investment. . . .The typical multinational corporation is large-size, predominantly oligopolistic, firm with sales running into hundreds of millions of dollars and affiliates spread over several countries. Another relevant feature is that most parent companies of the multinational corporations are located in the developed countries. . . . Eight of the 10 largest multinational corporations[1] are based in the United States. The United States accounts for more than half of multinational corporations having total annual sales of more than $1 billion. . . .Although the network of multinational corporations is world wide, the bulk of their activities is located in the developed market economies. Over two-thirds of the estimated book value of foreign direct investment is located in this area where the advanced economic level and similarities in institutional and social structures have facilitated the spread of the multinational corporate system. Although the developing countries have received only about a third of the total estimated stock of foreign direct investment, that is, only half as much as the developed countries, the presence of foreign multinational corporations in the developing countries is generally of greater relative significance, since their economies account for much less than half of that of developed market economies. . . . The general conclusion that many multinational corporations are bigger than a large number of entire national economies remains valid. Thus, the value-added by each of the top ten multinational corporations in 1971 was in excess of $3 billion—or greater than the gross national product of over 80 countries.

From Department of Economic and Social Affairs, UN Secretariat, *Multinational Corporations in World Development*. New York: UN Publication ST/ECA/190, 1973, pp. 6-26 *passim*.

1. The top ten in terms of sales in billions of dollars are: (1) General Motors (U.S.)—28 billion; (2) Exxon (Standard Oil, N.J.) (U.S.)—18 billion; (3) Ford (U.S.)—16 billion; (4) Royal Dutch/Shell (Holland-England)—12 billion; (5) General Electric (U.S.)—9 billion; (6) IBM (U.S.)—8 billion; (7) Mobil Oil (U.S.)— 8 billion; (8 and 9) Chrysler (U.S.)—7 billion; Texaco (U.S.)—7 billion; and (10) Unilever (Holland-England)—7 billion. The big ten are then followed by such multinationals as I.T.T. (U.S.), 11th; Philips (Holland), 15th; Volkswagen (Germany), 17th; Nippon Steel (Japan), 20th; Nestlé (Switzerland), 29th; Fiat (Italy), 49th; Renault (France), 54th; British-American Tobacco (England), 69th; and Campbell Soup (U.S.), 209th. The last in the list is Iowa Beef Processors (U.S.) 211th, with sales of $1,015 million in 1971.

the Soviet Ukraine and Soviet Byelorussia); according to the Soviet Constitution the Soviet Union is composed of fifteen union republics (among them the Ukraine and Byelorussia) that, in turn, are territorially subdivided into autonomous ethnic republics, autonomous ethnic regions, and autonomous ethnic districts as well as into administrative provinces and districts.

The People's Republic of China, which is a unitary, nonfederal state, is treated internationally as one unit, with one vote in both the Security Council and the General Assembly of the United Nations; according to the Chinese Constitution China is divided into five major non-Chinese ethnic autonomous regions and about fifty minor ethnic autonomous areas in addition to twenty-one administrative provinces and three national cities. Then there is the strange case of Taiwan (Formosa), the seat of the anticommunist regime of Chiang Kai-shek. In the United Nations Taiwan and its government were treated as legitimate representatives of China until 1971, when Taiwan was expelled and the communist regime of the People's Republic of China was seated as a permanent member in the Security Council and General Assembly. Nevertheless, in subsequent years Taiwan, although no longer a member of the world organization, has continued to be treated as a sovereign nation by the United States and a few other nations that, despite frequent protestations from Peking (see Document 14.2), maintained diplomatic or consular relations with the Nationalist government in Taipei.

A recent study tried to establish a definitive list of territorial units of authority relevant to the study of international and comparative politics.[3] Even when the researchers limited their study to territories with at least 10,000 inhabitants, there were difficulties. An exception had to be made for the Vatican, whose diplomatic impact through numerous international contacts and through its nuncios (ambassadors) residing in various countries is far greater than that of many a territorial state. The list naturally included all the members of the United Nations, nonmembers such as Switzerland, which refused to join on account of its strict interpretation of neutrality, and some of the divided countries (such as North and South Vietnam, North and South Korea, and West and East Germany, both of which became UN members in 1973). The list also included the remaining colonies and dependencies that may be viewed as potential territorial states and future members of the United Nations, for instance the Portuguese colonies in Africa: Mozambique, Angola, and Guinea-Bissau with Cape Verde. On November 2, 1973, the United Nations General Assembly recognized the liberation forces in Bissau as forming a new nation, engaged in a struggle "to expel the Portuguese forces of aggression" from its territory. The resolution expressed "welcome to the accession to independence of the people of Guinea-Bissau, thereby creating the sovereign state of the Republic of Guinea-Bissau." The resolution was adopted with 93 votes for, seven against and thirty abstentions. The resolution also condemned the Portuguese government's policy of perpetuating its illegal occupation of certain sectors of Bissau, not yet liberated by the rebel forces. More important for the future of Guinea-Bissau than the favorable vote in the United Nations was the military *coup d'état* in Portugal (April 25, 1974), whose military leaders seemed committed to a liberal solution of Portugal's imperial presence in Africa (Guinea-Bissau, Cape Verde Islands, Mozambique, and Angola). Recognition by the United Nations of a nation not yet fully sovereign but in the process of attaining independence is not unprecedented: the Philippine Commonwealth, one of the original members of the United Nations, deposited its ratification on October 11, 1945, although its independence was formally proclaimed only on July 4, 1946.

The "definitive" list mentioned above also included various quasi-independent units or protectorates such as Andorra (controlled jointly by France and Spain), Liechtenstein (controlled by Switzerland), Monaco (under France), San Marino (under Italy), Sikkim and Bhutan (controlled by India), and several units of a controversial status such as Puerto Rico and some island kingdoms, sheikdoms, and chiefdoms.

As noted previously, in terms of political and financial clout, some multinational megacorporations affect politics among nations more significantly than four-fifths of the territorial units on the above list. On the other hand, as the energy crisis of 1973-1974 amply demonstrated, a few of the microstates that had barely made the above list (such as Abu Dhabi and Qatar) proved able to give all Western major powers and Japan chills: literally as well as economically. Their rich oil deposits more than compensated for their insignificance in terms of population or sophisticated weapon technology.

National Differences

Territorial states differ from one another in many important ways: in their size, number of inhabitants, intensity of internal cohesion, geographical-strategic vulnerability, natural resources, degree of economic and technical dependence on others, military strength, dominant ideology, history and its ensuing traditions, anxieties and prejudices, national goals and methods of political action, political and economic systems, and the degree, form, and intensity of relations to other nations and to international organizations.

These differences are often abysmal. They help to explain why the human race, divided as it is into territorial components, rarely thinks and acts uniformly. The ecumenic concept of a collective interest of humanity is often evoked only to conceal parochial national egoism. About two-thirds of the human race live and think under conditions of extreme poverty, illiteracy, and ill-health, expending too much energy in a strenuous struggle for food for excessively growing populations and against the rigors of intemperate climates. Over one-third of humanity live and think under conditions of relative prosperity, security, literacy, hygiene, and a temperate climate. This area is sometimes inaccurately referred to as the underpopulated and well-developed "northern" part of the world. It encompasses Canada and the United States (which with 7 percent of the world's population have a 40-percent share of the world's income), Western Europe (including northern Italy and Austria), the northern tier of East Central Europe (East Germany, Poland, and Czechoslovakia), and the Scandinavian countries. Despite geography, Australia and New Zealand could be added to the well-developed "North."

The gap between the North and the underdeveloped and overpopulated "South" is considered by some observers as potentially more dangerous than the current tension between ideological blocs and among territorial states. Sixty-eight percent of the world's population live in Asia, Africa, and Latin America; their share of world income amounts to a mere 15 percent. In consumption of total world production of raw materials, statistics show the share for the United States to be 50 percent, all the other developed countries 45 percent, and the rest 5 percent. The gap has not narrowed but is actually increasing, mostly because the uncontrolled rise of populations in the emerging countries cancels out the increases in industrial and agricultural production. A cartoon dipicting the hunger of the world's South (see Figure 1.1) was used in 1969 as a main theme in a campaign in favor of a United States crash program for population stabilization by means of birth control. A full-page advertisement in the *New York Times* by the Campaign to Check Population Explosion claimed "Hungry Nations Imperil the Peace of the World ."[4]

In such a context the economic power, technological achievements, and high standard of living in the United States make this country a yardstick of comparison but also a natural target of envy, suspicion, and hatred. During the 1973 worldwide energy crisis,partly caused by the Arab embargo on oil in the wake of the fourth Arab-Israeli war and partly resulting from decades of wasteful overuse of natural resources, the executive director of the United Nations Environment Program, Canadian oil expert Maurice F. Strong, noted:"Two hundred million Americans use more energy for air-conditioning alone than China's population of seven hundred million for all purposes. I believe it is highly questionable whether any country has a permanent right to a disporportionate share of the world's resources."[5]

Because of the rising world population, the world demand for food has been increasing since the late 1960s by approximately 30 million tons a year. The statistics indicate that the average North American (a person from the United States or Canada) consumed nearly a ton of grain a year in the early 1970s (about 100 pounds of it in the form of beer and whisky), while the average person in poor countries consumed about 400 pounds of

FIGURE 1.1
THE WORLD'S SOUTH

Drawing by Bruce Shanks; © 1966 Buffalo Evening News, Inc.

grain a year. One politically important dimension of the developing world food crises is that that the United States and Canada now control a larger share of the world's exportable supplies of food grains than the Middle East does of oil. As James Reston put it, "the main question is what the United States and Canada will do about it."[6]

In 1972 a special international commission conducted a survey of education throughout the world for the United Nations Educational, Scientific and Cultural Organization (UNESCO) in Paris. Its study concluded that "in the education race, as in the march to economic progress" attempts to narrow the gap between the developed North and underdeveloped South "have all failed." In 1968, according to the commission, developed nations spent more than $120 billion on education; developing nations less than $12 billion. Yet the industrial nations have only one-third of the world's population and only one-fourth of its young people. In North America, the Soviet Union, and Europe more than 95 percent of the children of primary-school age were attending school in 1968, in the Arab states 50 percent, and in Africa only 40 percent.

Transnational Similarities

National territorial boundaries do often separate significantly different economic, administrative, and belief systems, but this does not mean that territorial states and nationalism have eliminated profound differences among men within a national community or that they have eradicated similarities and affinities transcending national boundaries. Not all members of a national community can ever think alike, even though their rulers so often claim they do. Humanity, split into nations, is also split within nations by ideological, religious, class, professional, and individual differences. No territorial community, even the most totalitarian, has ever succeeded in becoming monolithic.

Nor do all members of a territorial community differ in their habits, thoughts, acts, and goals from other individuals and groups in other nations. Not only fashion in clothes, taste in art, and mode of life but also political ideals and methods of political action have always moved freely across national or imperial boundaries. A Hindu might today long for a shiny new Cadillac or a color television set as any American might; on the other hand, an American might long to escape his time and place for a Hindu-like contemplation. While some young Americans are dreaming about gurus or drugs in Nepal, Nepalese youngsters are rushing to American movies in glorious Technicolor and then dreaming about Los Angeles, of all places. Thanks to mass media, the transnational movement of ideas and politics is today much more rapid and universal than it was, let us say, at the time of the Apostles. A Buddhist monk in Saigon who expressed his political protest through self-immolation by fire has had his tragic counterpart as far away as Prague, where the Czech student Jan Palach set himself afire in protest against the Soviet occupation of his nation in 1968. Many American protest techniques, including the occupation of university buildings, mishandling of deans, and "pornopolitics," have now become almost universal and may be witnessed in Athens, Tokyo, Madrid, Berlin, Teheran, and Dakar. Many foreign languages have already adopted such American terms as "picket," "sit-in," "teach-in," "streaking," "mill-in," and "sleep-in" as part of their acceptable vocabulary. (Indeed, all modern languages are repositories of cross-cultural influences.)

The phenomena of transnational migration and sharing of ideas, concepts, terms, and methods of action have been easily overinterpreted by wishful thinkers. We should not be prematurely carried away into an illusion of an already emerging supranational community or universal brotherhood. In the late 1960s how much did the American protest movements against the United States involvement in Vietnam, the outdated structures of the American colleges, and the military-industrial complex really have in common with the simultaneous Spanish, French, Dutch, Japanese, West German, Iranian, Italian, Catholic Irish, and Czechoslovak ferments, despite the identical age bracket and the similarity of methods? Although the protest movements in both East and West attack their respective establishments, Western protesters often seem to glorify what their Eastern counterparts try to topple (see Figure 1.2).

Even when there is a common ideology that links up several national or subnational groups in a supranational movement or organization, experience indicates, as we shall see in more detail in Chapter 7, that in practice universal concepts and themes rarely succeed in escaping the embrace of nationality and territoriality. Incantations of supranational ideology often conceal but cannot obliterate the reality and strength of nationalism.

FIVE ATTRIBUTES OF STATES

Despite many profound differences among territorial states in terms of their power and goals, several attributes common to all can be identified. For the purpose of our study we shall focus on the following five characteristics: (1) inhabited territory, (2) government, (3) sovereign equality, (4) external recognition, and (5) recognition from within or internal cohesion.

Inhabited Territory

A territorial state as a spatially delineated, permanently inhabited area is separated by more or less clear boundaries from other similarly constituted and similarly defined territorial communities (see Document 1.2). Interterritorial boundaries are very visibly marked on maps by thick lines and on mountain ridges and fields by signs and posts. Control over the penetrability of state frontiers is expressed by a variety of means: military, police, and administrative controls; tariff controls; passport and visa requirements; immigration and customs officers; coast and frontier guards;

FIGURE 1.2
DUTCH VIEW OF YOUTH PROTESTS

Demonstrations . . . in East

. . . and West

Drawing by Behrendt in *Algemeen Handelsblad*, Amsterdam, 1968.

DOCUMENT 1.2

TERRITORIALITY: AN ORGANIZATIONAL NECESSITY OR ANIMAL INSTINCT?

It is perhaps the most striking single characteristic of the national state as an organization, by contrast with organizations such as firms or churches, that it thinks of itself as occupying, in a "dense" and exclusive fashion, a certain area of the globe. The schoolroom maps which divide the world into colored shapes which are indentified as nations have a profound effect on the national image. . . . The territories of nations are divided sharply by frontiers carefully surveyed and frequently delineated by a chain of customs houses, immigration stations, and military installations. We are so accustomed to this arrangement that we think of it as "natural" and take it completely for granted. . . . The territorial aspect of the national state is important in the dynamic of international relations because of the *exclusiveness* of territorial occupation. This means that one nation can generally expand only at the expense of another; an increase in the territory of one is achieved only at the expense of a decrease in the territory of another. This makes for a potential conflict situation.

From Kenneth E. Boulding, "National Images and the International Systems," *Journal of Conflict Resolution*, 3 (June 1959), 123-124.

One aspect of every nation's self-image is the equation of national identity with possession of a certain piece of territory; a nation's self-image has been identical with the territory occupied, directly or as colonies.

From Jerome D. Frank, M.D., *Sanity and Survival*. New York: Random House, 1968, p. 107.

Birdsong takes place when and if the male gets his territory. . . . Only when he finds that perch which will be the advertisement of his territorial existence—his alder, his gate, his willow bough—does the will to sing enchant him. Birdsong from the female is unquestionably an announcement of sexual readiness. But it occurs in response to the male's announcement of territorial readiness. . . . Territoriality—the drive to gain, maintain, and defend the exclusive right to a piece of territory—is an animal instinct approximately as ancient and as powerful as sex. . . . Nationalism as such is no more than a human expression of the animal drive to maintain and defend a territory. It differs from the social territoriality of the primate only to the degree of man's capacity to form coalitions.

From Robert Ardrey, *African Genesis: A Personal Investigation into the Animal Origins and Nature of Man*. New York: Atheneum, 1961, pp. 49-50, 172-173.

---

fortifications; and in some areas censorship of mail, jamming of foreign broadcasts and television, electrified barbed wires, police dogs, watchtowers, radar, mine fields, and Chinese or Berlin walls. Unlike family, caste, religion, or pressure groups, the collective interest or "spirit" of a state has a very concrete territorial dimension. Rupert Emerson emphasizes that a nation, with its double basis of soul and soil, is "characteristically associated with a particular territory to which it lays claim as the traditional national homeland. The emotional and intellectual tie in the minds of men is buttressed by a location in space which anchors the nation with permanence on the face of earth."[7] (The case of a state whose government has temporarily lost control over both its territory and its people will be considered later.)

The portion of the inhabited surface of the earth that belongs to any one nation and is organized by it as a territorial state is, as noted above, only more or less clearly defined. There is still doubt about the exact line of demarcation of state boundaries in inhospitable, sparsely populated areas where a nomadic way of life prevails: for instance, in the southern part of the Arabian peninsula, between Ethiopia and Somalia, and in central Asia. From such indefinite boundaries curious controversies arise. In 1962 the People's Republic of China claimed that it had been building a strategic road through the Indian province of Ladakh for several years without the Indian government ever taking notice and protesting the Chinese works on what New Delhi claimed was Indian sovereign territory. When Indian troops were sent to reassert the Indian sovereignty over the territory, a Sino-Indian armed class ensued. Chinese military superiority resolved the dispute, for the time being, in favor of China's claim that the territory was Chinese and that it had only temporarily become part of India as a consequence of the British conquest of southern Asia. A similar dispute resulting from an ill-defined boundary led, in 1965, to an armed skirmish between 30,000 Indian and Pakistani troops in an inhospitable area known as Rann of Cutch, off the Arabian Sea. The dispute was submitted to binding arbitration by a special three-man commission comprised of a Swede appointed by the United Nations secretary-general, a Yugoslav appointed by India, and an Iranian appointed by Pakistan. After eighteen months of investigations, the dispute was finally resolved on July 4, 1969, when India and Pakistan signed a series of maps delineating the new border. India received 3200 square miles of the territory and Pakistan received 350 square miles, including some high ground of possible strategic value.

In other instances even a clearly drawn national boundary may be the subject of an unresolved interstate controversy. Smoldering boundary disputes exist between India and China over the MacMahon line, between India and Pakistan over Kashmir, between Pakistan and Afghanistan over the Pushtoo region, between Israel and the Arab States over every square yard of the Israeli territory, between Guatemala and Honduras over the Belize region, between Ecuador and Peru, Chile and Bolivia, Bolivia and Paraguay (a dispute that led to war from 1932 to 1935), Guyana and Venezuela, and China and the USSR over some areas near the Amur River in the Far East and in the region of Chinese Turkestan (Sinkiang) in central

Asia. With regard to the line dividing Russian Turkestan from Chinese Turkestan, for example, the Chinese maps "had been drawn with the boundaries several hundred miles to the west of the present location, thus including a large part of the [Pamir] plateau within Chinese Sinkiang,"[8] while the Soviet maps included the same areas within Moslem Soviet Asia. In 1964, China raised not only the old question of the precise delineation of controversial Sino-Soviet boundaries but also the broader problem of the return of some former Chinese territories that had been wrested from the Manchu Empire in the eighteenth and nineteenth centuries by the expansionist Russian Empire and then kept by its allegedly antiimperialist successor, Soviet Russia. Any claim that is recorded on an official map for future action but is not pressed further for the time being was once defined by Nehru as a "cartographic aggression."

In 1969 the Soviet-Chinese boundary dispute moved from maps and penmanship to the Siberian scene and the actual use of guns. It was finally inflated into a big propaganda issue. In March 1969, near Nizhni Mikhailovka in the Soviet Far East, Soviet and Chinese military units clashed over disputed Damansky Island (called Chenpao [Treasure] Island by the Chinese), claimed by both. The island is located in the middle of the Ussuri River, which forms part of the frontier between Communist Russia and Communist China. In international law, boundary lines along streams that serve as international boundaries are usually drawn along the middle of the main channel ("thalweg" in international legal terminology). But the main channel may shift during flooding, or there may be controversy over which branch is the main channel. The Ussuri River, subject to flooding in the spring, is a capriciously meandering stream that frequently shifts its channel, abandoning old river branches and forming new islands and sandbanks. A caprice of a meandering stream dividing two friendly nations is rarely a problem; between two hostile nations it can become a highly explosive issue or a welcome pretext for settling larger accounts. The Ussuri River became the border between czarist Russia and imperial China under the Peking Treaty of 1860, by which the Chinese Empire ceded (under duress, according to Communist China) all the land west of Ussuri to Russia. Both the Soviet and the Chinese governments exploited the clash to further dramatize their current political conflict. Mass rallies were organized in both countries, and a bitter press campaign was supposed to whip up an appropriate nationalist frenzy (see Document 1.3). Later China and Russia somewhat reduced the tone of their mutual recriminations and agreed to try to reach an agreement by means of direct diplomatic negotiations.

Although many international boundaries remain controversial for a considerable length of time, the neighbors usually have to recognize, however reluctantly, that line at which one nation's effective authority ends and that of the other nation begins. The United States, which in the 1950s did not formally recognize the existence of the mainland Chinese government and

DOCUMENT 1.3

A SINO-SOVIET BORDER CLASH

On March 2, 1969, the Soviet revisionist renegade clique sent armed soldiers to flagrantly intrude into Chenpao Island on the Ussuri River, Heilungkiang Province, China, and killed and wounded many frontier guards of the Chinese People's Liberation Army by opening up with cannon and gun fire on them. This is an extremely grave armed border provocation carried out by the Soviet revisionists, a frantic anti-China incident created by them and another big exposure of the rapacious nature of Soviet revisionism as social-imperialism. . . . Our frontier guards repeatedly warned the Soviet revisionists' frontier troops. But it produced no effect. Only when they were driven to the end of their forbearance were our frontier guards compelled to fight back in self-defence, giving the intruders who carried out the provocations well-deserved punishment and triumphantly safeguarding China's sacred territory.

We warn the Soviet revisionist renegade clique: We will never allow anybody to encroach upon China's territorial integrity and sovereignty. We will not attack unless we are attacked; if we are attacked, we will certainly counter-attack. Gone forever are the days when the Chinese people were bullied by others. You are utterly blind and day-dreaming if you think you can deal with the great Chinese people by resorting to the same old tricks used by tsarist Russia. If you continue making military provocations, you will certainly receive severe punishment. No matter in what strength and with whom you come, we will wipe you out resolutely, thoroughly, wholly and completely.

Down with the new tsars! Down with Soviet revisionist social-imperialism!

From *Jen-min Jih-pao (People's Daily)*, Peking, March 4, 1969.

The Chinese Government has consistently held that the Sino-Soviet boundary question should be settled peacefully and that, even if it cannot be settled for the time being, the status quo of the border should be maintained and there should definitely be no resport to the use of force. There is no reason whatsoever for China and the Soviet Union to fight a war over the boundary question.

The Chinese Government declared solemnly on many occasions that at no time and under no circumstances will China be the first to use nuclear weapons.

But at the same time China will never be intimidated by war threats, including nuclear war threats. Should a handful of war maniacs dare to raid China's strategic sites in defiance of world condemnation, that will be war, that will be aggression, and the 700 million Chinese people will rise up in resistance and use revolutionary war to eliminate the war of aggression. . . .

From *Hsinshua* Agency, October 7, 1969.

which recognized even less its sphere of influence in the Far East, was made keenly aware during the Korean conflict of the point at which the effective military control—and strategic sensitivity—of mainland China began. For it was the American crossing of the 38th parallel that led to the

Chinese intervention in Korea in November 1950. The Arabs, who for a quarter of a century had not recognized the political and legal existence of the state of Israel, were similarly made aware of the location of the military boundary of Israel, and vice versa. In matters of national boundaries, effective military control may be more meaningful than any jurisdictional yardstick. Maps, speeches, legal documents, and historical claims may present one version, the guns of the frontier guards another. History in particular is a debatable guide for the settlement of boundary disputes. How far back into history should one go or could one go in presenting a boundary claim? In the name of historical precedent, Spain could claim the whole of the Western Hemisphere, the Moslems could claim the whole of Spain and the southern part of France up to the Loire River, Czechoslovakia could claim part of Poland and the Baltic coast, and the People's Republic of Mongolia could claim all the land conquered by Genghis Khan. In the middle of the Suez crisis of 1956, extremist Israeli groups, elated over the military victory against the Egyptian forces in the Sinai peninsula, put forward a claim to restore the biblical boundaries of Israel, although the Bible does not seem to include a detailed map of the Middle East area. As a result of the 1967 war Israeli territorial control was extended to the whole of the Sinai peninsula, the Golan heights, and the Jordanian part of Jerusalem. The gun emplacements rather than the Bible seemed to be the decisive factor. In October 1973 Arab guns and missiles, supplied by the Soviet Union, challenged the 1967 territorial expansion. A costly Arab-Israeli war and near-atomic confrontation between the Soviet Union and the United States followed, proving the old lesson that a territorial arrangement imposed on, rather than diplomatically negotiated with, the adversary can rarely prove durable. Neither the Bible nor missiles can guarantee interterritorial peace; while a freely negotiated boundary agreement appears to be a better guarantee, such agreements have not in the past and cannot now be viewed as inviolate: subsequent challenges by either side as a consequence of internal political upheaval or generational changes may upset them. One example of agreement on the inviolability of highly controversial boundaries is the decision of the Organization of African Unity in 1963 mutually to respect the intra-African state boundaries as obtained at the time of the achievement of independence, that is, boundaries that had been originally established by colonial conquest. This principle was extended to Asia when in the following year it was endorsed by the conference of all nonaligned nations in Cairo.

Government

Control over a more or less well-defined territory reflects the effectiveness of the central political authority, that is, of the government. By "government" we mean the agency which, in Max Weber's words, successfully claims a monopoly of the *legitimate* use of coercive force within a given territory. "The political authorities, only they, have some generally accepted right to utilize coercion and command obedience based upon it," notes a recent study. It adds: "Force is legitimate where this belief in its justifiable nature exists."[9]

National government is usually composed of three or four distinct branches: the executive, the legislative, the judicial, and a career civil service. In international politics the executive branch of government and the diplomatic sector of its permanent administrative service appear as the decisive actors and spokesmen of the nation, however influenced or circumscribed they may be by the legislators or judges.

The existence of, and the need for, a central superior authority reflects the individual incapacity of people to ensure domestic order, external security, and collective welfare. In order to achieve these goals people have always delegated regulatory, police, and defense powers to a group of leaders. In many cases people have failed to prevent undesirable leaders from assuming such powers. But at the heart of even the most brazen usurpation of power there is always a basic need to establish authority.

Some of the functions of governments have changed over the centuries, but many of these changes are less drastic than is usually assumed. Priorities in the efforts to "insure domestic Tranquility, provide for the common defence, promote the general Welfare . . . ," in the words of the United States Constitution, have varied under the impact of the international situation, internal developments, or prevailing social or economic concepts. At all times, all governments, manorial or royal, medieval or modern, have been concerned with more than just making, interpreting, and enforcing laws and defending the territory against external enemies. Central authority has always participated in the shaping of the economic and social life. This was so even in the period of economic liberalism when the general belief was: that government governs best that governs least. At that time, for instance, the United States government was expected to keep the peace, subsidize shipping, build roads, maintain tariffs, and grant homesteads to settlers. Prior to the twentieth century it was often proclaimed that freedom and legal order were the preconditions for welfare to be achieved by an unhindered competition and free enterprise. Today, often the reverse is assumed—that welfare is the cause rather than the result of domestic tranquility.

The services rendered and the control exercised by the central authority over a given territory and the people who inhabit it make the state the highest secular authority; it is the state that gives legal recognition and protection to an individual or withdraws both, making him a prisoner or a second-class citizen, or causing him to emigrate and seek protection and recognition in a new territory and by a new government. An individual is subject to the authority of a state because, and only because, he finds himself on its territory as a result of birth, naturalization, or circumstance. There is no "no-man's land" between states; as soon as one leaves the territory of one state he crosses into the sovereign domain of another. An idealist may proclaim himself a citizen of the world, or a person may be deprived of his citizenship; yet whether a citizen of the world or stateless, a "man without a country" cannot help living on a territory and under the authority of a territorial state.

Sovereign Equality

Common to all states is their mutually accepted claim—and fiction—that they are sovereign, equal, and independent. Article 2, paragraph 1, of the United Nations Charter proclaims: "The Organization is based on the principle of sovereign equality of all its Members."

The combination of sovereignty and equality is not fortuitous. Despite great differences in actual power, size, and wealth, nations consider one another legally equal because, in principle, all are equally sovereign—that is, supreme within their own territories. No nation has the right to perform governmental acts on the territory of another nation without the latter's permission or authorization. Legally, no nation is superior or inferior to another. Even the United Nations cannot discharge any function on national territory against the will of the nation concerned. Article 2, paragraph 7, of the Charter says:

> Nothing contained in the present Charter shall authorize the United Nations to intervene in matters which are essentially within the domestic jurisdiction of any state or shall require the Members to submit such matters to settlement under the present Charter; but this principle shall not prejudice the application of enforcement measures under Chapter VII.

In this connection many authors consider the physical terms "impermeability" and "impenetrability"[10] of sovereign nations to be largely synonymous with equality, sovereignty, and independence.

For example, the United Nations peace-keeping forces in the Middle East, on Cyprus, and in the Congo could "penetrate" the boundaries and exercise their functions on the territories of the parties concerned only with their consent and only for so long as their consent continued to be given. The frontiers of a sovereign state can legitimately be penetrated against its will only by war or by military sanctions authorized by the United Nations; the very purpose of war or military sanctions is to break or curb the sovereign will of a target nation by the penetration of its territory and resulting intervention in its domestic as well as external affairs. Legally speaking, the wall of sovereignty can be breached only by the will of a nation or by the breaking of its will.

The term "sovereignty" antedates the United Nations by some three hundred years. The origin of the concept and term is monarchical. The French word *souverain* (sovereign) actually means a supreme ruler not accountable to anybody, except perhaps to God. The term began to be used with reference to those kings and princes who had succeeded in asserting their central legislative, administrative, and tax-collecting power in two directions: against the universal aspirations of the Roman popes and emperors and against the local authority of feudal and manorial lords. "The chief mark of sovereignty," wrote Jean Bodin in the sixteenth century, "is the power to give law to all the citizens." This medieval definition is still adhered to today by all states, whether communist, fascist, dictatorial, or democratic, and whether old or newly established.

The principle of the equality of great and small powers is proclaimed in Article 18 of the United Nations Charter, the section that gives each member of the General Assembly one vote. Decisions on important matters are to be made by a two-thirds majority of members present and voting. Therefore, in the General Assembly the principle of one nation, one vote, whether the nation is large or small, is fully recognized (see Document 1.4). This affirmation of the principle of sovereign equality in the General Assembly is, however, largely emptied of its contents by the provision that only the Security Council can make a *binding* decision: the General Assembly can debate and recommend—that is, authorize—but it can never order an action. Making binding decisions is the sole domain of the primary organ of the United Nations, the Security Council, in which all substantive decisions must be made by an affirmative vote of nine members out of fifteen, including the concurring votes of the five permanent members, the "Great Powers." The negative vote of one single Great Power nullifies a decision even if made by a majority of fourteen to one. Here the towering superiority of the "Big Five" in relation to all the other members of the organization is proclaimed despite the Charter's solemn provision concerning the equality of all nations, small or large. The Charter cannot bridge the gap between the fiction of equality and the fact of inequality. It embodies both the myth and the reality, and this is why it contains an inner contradiction that it cannot solve.

While nations proclaim their sovereignty—that is, "the supreme authority to give and enforce law within the national territory, singly and collectively with regard to all its inhabitants"—in actual fact nations are less self-justified, less self-sufficient, and less self-contained than their proud assertions of independence and sovereignty suggest.

Sovereignty and independence are legal assertions and political ideals; traditionally they have been expressed in absolute terms. The rhetorical claim that a sovereign nation is accountable only to itself for its decisions and actions is, in fact, quite relative, that is, relative to the superior or inferior power and dynamism or passivity of other nations. Some analysts also claim that international concern for human rights, ecology, and technological and social progress has substantially diminished modern nations'

DOCUMENT 1.4

TWO EQUAL AND SOVEREIGN MEMBERS OF THE UNITED NATIONS

Characteristic	Maldive Islands	The United States
Former status	British colony	British colony
Independence	July 25, 1965	July 4, 1776
Area	115 sq. mi. (19 atolls, containing 877 inhabited islands)	3,615,211 sq. mi.
Population	110,000 (est. 1972 by UN)	204,600,000 (1970 census)
Votes in the UN General Assembly	One	One

capacity to go it sovereignly alone. Independence is often a subject for solemn speeches, proclamations, and constitutional preambles; inter-dependence, and quite often dependence, is the reality. Chapter 11 will deal in more detail with a gamut of measures that nations have been using in order to pierce or lower the walls of national sovereignty. In addition to war, whose very purpose often is to destroy another nation's sovereignty or transform its independence into dependence, there are other strategies that may attain similar results by means short of war. In the political arena such techniques include subversion, external support of domestic dissidence, psychological warfare, and other forms of interference. In the economic sphere, there is a very broad spectrum of techniques, ranging from rewards and lures (such as economic aid) to blackmail and punitive operations such as tariff, currency, and credit manipulations, embargoes, boycotts, blockades, and more or less subtle neoimperialist permanent controls. They are examined on p. 432.

External Recognition

Whenever a new state appears on the map of the world or whenever a new revolutionary regime takes over the government of an established state, we observe how the leaders of these new governments literally rush to have their legitimacy confirmed by recognition by at least the most important members of the international system (today generally symbolized by membership in the United Nations). The mutual recognition of states usually results in the establishment of consular and diplomatic missions, embassies, or legations. After the Congress of Vienna at the end of the Napoleonic wars in Europe, the term "embassy" was reserved for the diplomatic missions exchanged between great powers only; diplomatic missions between small powers or between great and small powers were called legations, and their heads were called ministers plenipotentiary and envoys extraordinary. The difference between embassies and legations has tended to disappear since World War II. Most of the missions are now called embassies, irrespective of their power status.

Is the diplomatic recognition of a state an essential condition for its existence? Some legal authorities maintain that only an act of international recognition brings a state into legitimate and legal existence. Whatever the legal arguments may be, there are some states that are deficient in every attribute of a state *except* that of international recognition. Their boundaries are unclear and contested since in many cases they have been drawn to suit the economic and strategic interests of colonial conquerors; the boundaries cut across tribal, lingual, or ethnic territories and are therefore not recognized as valid by either inhabitants or their neighbors. Their governments, trying to build a nation, do not exercise effective control over the entire territory, and their internal cohesion—their consensus and feeling of being one nation—is almost nil. In many new states, only a thin stratum of the governing elite feels itself to be representative of the new nation; within their boundaries, allegiance to a tribe or linguistic group still takes precedence over allegiance to the nation. Yet even when the reality of such a territorial state is debatable on the national stage, it is a significant and recognizable unit internationally. Robert C. Good has pointed out:

> Viewed from within, a new nation seems evanescent . . . it is riven with divisions: it lacks a tradition of common institutions and an awareness of the commonweal; indeed, its "public" constitutes a bare fraction of the population, for most of its citizens are oblivious to their membership in a national community. However, in its external relations, the reality of a new nation . . . finds expression. Membership in the United Nations, recognition by foreign governments, and attendance at international gatherings confirm its existence . . . . Disputes with the former metropole [Algeria versus France; Egypt versus England; Indonesia versus Holland; the Congo versus Belgium] underscore even more emphatically the substance and cohesion of the new state.[11]

According to prevailing theories, a state exists and has rights under international law even though it may not be recognized by any other nation. The Convention of the Rights and Duties of States, adopted at the Inter-American Conference held at Montevideo in 1933, proclaimed:

> *Article 3* The political existence of the state is independent of recognition by other states. Even before recognition the state has the right to defend its integrity and independence, to provide for its conservation and

prosperity, and consequently organize itself as it sees fit, to legislate upon its interests, administer its services, and to define the jurisdiction and competence of its course. . . .

Article 6 The recognition of a state merely signifies that the state which recognizes accepts the personality of the other with all the rights and duties determined by international law.

The authoritative *Digest of International Law*, published by the U.S. Government Printing Office and edited by F. H. Hackworth, former member of the International Court of Justice, defines the state as "a people permanently occupying a fixed territory, bound together by common laws and customs into a body politic, possessing an organized government, and capable of conducting relations with other states." Theoretically, a state capable of conducting relations with other states may decide to conduct none and live in total isolation. In fact this does not happen, since it is in the interest of a state to be recognized and so enter into legitimate economic and political relations with other states. Of course, every new state that has established itself as an independent sovereign entity may be without external contacts for a day or two while awaiting diplomatic recognition. In cases of former colonies, the former colonial master usually grants the diplomatic recognition first, often coupled with sponsorship of the new state's application for United Nations membership.

Diplomatic recognition of one national government by another is distinct from universal recognition of the principle according to which a territorial state is the appropriate and legitimate form of political, administrative, and ideological organization for every national community that wishes to have, and is *able* to establish and maintain, its own territorial state. Diplomatic recognition applies this general principle to a concrete situation. For the new state or new government, the recognizing state assesses (1) ability to exercise internal authority, (2) ability to accept and discharge international obligations, and (3) legitimacy. (The last is a very controversial yardstick since the recognizing state may twist criteria to fit its own preferences and aims.) Following such an assessment, diplomatic recognition is usually expressed in the form of a reciprocal exchange of diplomatic and consular missions. Diplomatic recognition does not imply any endorsement of the recognized government's ideology or internal and external policies. Governments and states that intensely dislike and distrust each other still maintain more or less correct diplomatic contacts (Franco's Spain and Communist East Germany in 1973, for instance). Before World War II, nazism in Germany, fascism in Italy, and aggressive imperialism in Japan did not prevent the United States, the Soviet Union, France, or England from maintaining their embassies in Berlin, Rome, and Tokyo. Only on the eve of a declared war or in the wake of an undeclared war are diplomatic relations severed, ambassadors and their staffs repatriated, and care of the diplomatic buildings transferred to neutral or friendly nations for the duration of hostilities. The ethnic identity and the right of a state to exist are not challenged when disapproval of its policy has reached a point of irreconcilable enmity or war; the withdrawal of diplomatic contacts is directed at the existing government of the state. Very often the state that has withdrawn its diplomatic recognition insists on professing its friendship toward the nation, people, and state while proclaiming its irreconcilable hostility toward the existing government. Both the People's Republic of China and the United States made such a distinction in their respective attitudes with regard to each other's peoples and existing political leadership before their government-to-government relationship was more or less normalized in 1971-1972.

One Nation, Several Governments   Sometimes governments lose control over some or all of their territories to a foreign enemy in an international war or to an internal enemy in a civil war. This may lead to more than one internationally recognized government and complex problems of conflicting simultaneous diplomatic recognition. This happened to several European governments during World War II. As a consequence of the Nazi-Soviet collaboration, from 1939 to 1941 the eastern half of Poland, the three Baltic states of Estonia, Latvia, and Lithuania, and the Rumanian provinces Bessarabia and northern Bukovina were occupied and annexed by the Soviet Union. As a result of the Nazi conquest, Czechoslovakia and Poland in 1939, Norway, Denmark, Holland, Luxembourg, Belgium, and France in 1940, and Yugoslavia and Greece in 1941 all had their territories occupied or pro-Nazi puppet governments imposed on them. While the Axis powers recognized either the disappearance of these states or the imposition of pro-Nazi governments on them (the loss of its two provinces by Rumania and the Italian conquest of Albania were politically and legally complex affairs), the Allies continued to treat these nations' exiled governments in London as if they were states endowed with all their rights and duties in behalf of their subjugated nations. Without people or territories they were not really states but governments that had been recognized as representing their states as they had existed before and might exist again after an Allied victory. It was in that period of temporary suspension of direct contacts between governments and their states that the United States, the Soviet Union, and the United Kingdom granted the diplomatic representatives of these governments-in-exile the rank of ambassadors, until then reserved only for the representatives of the great powers. At a time when the governments-in-exile could exercise effective control only over that portion of territory represented by their rented rooms in London hotels (transformed into prime ministers' offices, chancelleries, and military headquarters, and as such endowed with the right of exterritoriality by the permission of the host English government), the raising of their legations to embassy rank may appear to have been nominalistic fantasy. Perhaps it was; but in the middle of the war the gesture was viewed as an important morale booster and a solemn reaffirmation of the Allied goal ultimately to restore these states, nations, and governments to their pre-Nazi status. These states actually had two sets of governments recognized as legitimate by the opposite sides in the war: the governments-in-exile were recognized by the Allied powers, and the puppet regimes ruling in the national capitals were recognized as legitimate governments by Germany, Japan, and Italy. At a certain point, Poland actually had three internationally recognized governments: one recognized by the Western powers in London, another recognized by the Soviet Union in Moscow, and the third, the Nazi military government, in actual control of Poland.

Such simultaneous international recognition of different governments representing the same nation and state also occurred in 1940 with regard to France. Nazi Germany, fascist Italy, Japan, and many nonbelligerent states, including the United States, recognized the government of Marshal Pétain in Vichy, while the British government granted recognition to a Free French National Committee in London headed by General de Gaulle.

Other examples of simultaneous external recognitions of two rival governments within the same nation by different groups of states were the Soviet and Western recognitions of two governments, communist and anticommunist, for Korea, Vietnam, Germany, and China. While initially after World War II the divisions imposed on these four countries by a combination of external and internal forces were deemed very provisional by all concerned, a quarter of a century later, in the early 1970s, their divisions moved from the category of explosive controversies into temporarily unalterable facts of life. Peking's very strong opposition to any international recognition of Taiwan as a "second China" (see Document 14.2 for the Chinese Communist statement on this subject) did not include a Chinese Communist threat to use force for the purpose of reunification.

As for the Nationalist Chinese government in exile on Taiwan, one difference between it and the European governments-in-exile during World War II should be noted. Unlike the European governments that in 1939-1940 completely lost control of their national territories, the Chinese Nationalists have continued to control and develop their fraction of the national territory, an island-province with a population of almost 12 million. Although "rump" China is only a microscopic morsel of the Chinese mainland with its 750 million people (1 billion by the year 2000), it is still a large state by African standards for instance. Taiwan's population would rank it seventh of thirty-four independent African countries plus the few remaining colonial possessions. In economic terms Taiwan maintains one of the world's fastest economic growth rates—12 percent in 1972; in the same year the value of Taiwan's exports exceeded the value of Mainland China's exports by more than half a billion dollars, and the Taiwanese had a standard of living (measured by per-capita income) roughly four times higher than that of the mainland Chinese.

In civil wars the incumbent governments and the insurgents simultaneously claim authority over the same nation and state. Severance of diplomatic relations, traditional in international wars, sometimes has an exact counterpart in civil wars, especially when their duration and outcome may significantly affect the important interests of outside powers. A withdrawal of recognition from the existing government and diplomatic recognition of the insurgents, permitting military and economic aid to the rebels, has become one of the very frequent forms of foreign interference in the domestic affairs of a nation split asunder by an internal war. During the Spanish Civil War (1936-1939), the democratic states—France and England in particular—continued to consider the republican government of Spain and its socialist, democratic, communist, and anarchist supporters the legitimate spokesmen of the nation-in-crisis, while the fascist powers, Germany and Italy, gave early recognition to Generalissimo Franco and substantial aid to his rebel forces. Franco's final victory over the republican forces removed his opponents not only from the domestic scene but also, after World War II, from the international scene.

The absence of diplomatic recognition and regular diplomatic missions does not exclude other forms of contacts and negotiations. Between 1955 and 1968, for example, the United States and the People's Republic of China while not diplomatically recognizing each other, conducted diplomatic negotiations through their respective ambassadors accredited to the communist government of Poland. Over 130 such meetings were held in that period. When in 1971 President Nixon's security advisor Henry A. Kissinger made his first trip to Peking to negotiate with Mao Tse-tung and Chou En-lai, there were no diplomatic relations between Peking and Washington; they were still not established in 1972 when President Nixon paid an official visit to China. Subsequently, a representative mission of China in Washington and a U.S. mission in Peking were established; except for the name, both missions had all the usual functions and immunities of embassies. Other examples of constant contacts without diplomatic links were the relatively regular contacts between the North Korean and American officers at Panmunjon on the 38th parallel in Korea and the 1968-1973 negotiations between North Vietnam and the United States in Paris; the latter finally led to the formal cessation of hostilities and an uneasy peace in Vietnam. Such semidiplomatic contacts have often led and may in the future again lead to regular diplomatic relations. Another form of partial recognition is the grant of an *observer* status by the United Nations (*e.g.* Vatican). In some cases such a status anticipates future full membership; West Germany (until 1974) and the Palestine Liberation Organization (since November 1974) are examples.

Recognition from Within: Internal Cohesion

The effectiveness of a territorial government in external and internal affairs is intimately linked with the intensity of support and cooperation it receives from most of the people most of the time. We say "most of the people," since there is no nation or state in the world in which some groups or individuals would not feel occasionally or permanently alienated from and opposed to the government or state whose citizens they are.

The stability and perceived legitimacy of a territorial state are therefore linked with its capacity to represent, satisfy, and identify with a territorial community. By territorial community or territorial interest group we mean an aggregate of individuals and groups who are aware of their bonds of identification with each other, regardless of their social, ethnic-cultural, or ideological differences, as well as conscious of their links with the past, present, and future of their territorial-political organization. As we shall see in more detail in Chapter 3, sometimes territorial communities emerge and assert themselves as highly cohesive bodies *before* they can establish their own states. At other times cohesive territorial communities emerge a long time *after* the establishment of a territorial system; some of the existing, relatively homogeneous national communities were originally forced into cohesion, but, over centuries, the imposition from above finally produced habit and the fact of cooperative cohesion.

A frequently used term for cooperative cohesion and effective allegiance to a territorial state on the part of its inhabitants—allegiance based on habit, feelings, and rational satisfaction—is *nationalism*. The term, as currently used by both scholars and the mass media, poses some problems; so, of course, do several other terms related to nationalism, such as "nation" (Is there a white-black-Hispanic-American nation or only a state? Is there a German-French-Italian-Swiss nation?), "nationality" (often used to denote citizenship rather than ethnic-cultural identity), and "ethnonationalism," which is of recent coinage and represents a useful concept in analyses of multinational or polyethnic states. At this point it should be stressed that nationalism, as a set of feelings, attitudes, and behaviors, may be directed toward the existing state in two ways: if directed *positively*, it corresponds to our concept of internal cohesion and recognition of the usefulness and legitimacy of the state; if directed *negatively*, its aim may be either substantial internal reform of the existing state or secession from it, as is frequently the case in territorial systems, empires, or states composed of more than one ethnic group. The next two chapters will deal with nationalism as an integrative force, nationalism as a disintegrative force, and the effects of both on international relations.

Notes

1. Rupert Emerson, *From Empire to Nation*. Cambridge, Mass.: Harvard University Press, 1960, pp. 95-96.

2. A more detailed treatment of "Political Man: A Territorial Animal" may be found in Ivo D. Duchacek, *Comparative Federalism: The Territorial Dimension of Politics*. New York: Holt, Rinehart and Winson, 1970, pp. 1-45.

3. Bruce M. Russett, J. David Singer, and Melvin Small, "National Political Units in the Twentieth Century: A Standardized List," *American Political Science Review*, 57:3 (September 1968), 932-951.

4. *New York Times*, February 23, 1969. Five years later, the same newspaper published some frightening statistical projections concerning the population explosion in South Asia: India's population increased by 21.6 percent from 1951 to 1961, and it increased by 24.7 percent in the subsequent decade (1961-1971). The 1972 census in Pakistan showed a population of 65 million with a population growth rate of 3.1 percent per year. Pakistan's population is expected to double, before the year 2000. Bangladesh's population was about 75 million in 1974; the density of its population was one of the highest in the world, 1300 people per square mile, only 8 percent of whom lived in cities. With a population growth of roughly 3 percent a year, the population density in Bangladesh by 1997 is expected to be 2600 people per square mile. Clarence Maloney, "The Ghost of Malthus in South Asia," *New York Times*, February 14, 1974.

5. *New York Times*, November 21, 1973.

6. *New York Times*, July 7, 1974.

7. Emerson, *From Empire to Nation*, p. 105.

8. W. A. Douglas Jackson, *The Russo-Chinese Borderlands*. New York: Van Nostrand, 1962, p. 3.

9. Gabriel A. Almond and G. Bingham Powell, Jr., *Comparative Politics: A Developmental Approach*. Boston: Little, Brown, 1966, p. 18.

10. Hans J. Morgenthau, *Politics among Nations*, 4th ed. New York: Knopf, 1967, pp. 301-305.

11. Robert C. Good, "State-Building as a Determinant of Foreign Policy in the New States," in Laurence W. Martin (ed.), *Neutralism and Non-Alignment*. New York: Praeger, 1962, p. 7.

Additional Readings

Additional readings on the subject of territoriality may be found in *Discord and Harmony: Readings in International Politics,* edited by Ivo D. Duchacek and published by Holt, Rinehart and Winston in 1972. Analyses of territoriality by Kenneth E. Boulding, Robert Ardrey, John H. Herz, and J. David Singer constitute Chapter 1, "The Territorial Dimension of International Politics, pp. 3-20.

2
Nationalism

There is no generally accepted definition of nationalism, yet most political leaders and analysts seem to agree that nationalism is still the single strongest political force, stronger than the supranational ideologies or universalistic themes of our technological and interdependent age. One of the authorities on the history of nationalism, Hans Kohn, defined nationalism as

> a state of mind permeating the large majority of a people and [that] claims to permeate all its members; it recognizes the nation-state as the ideal form of political organization and the nationality as the source of all creative cultural energy and of economic well-being.[1]

More sadly, another historian, Arnold J. Toynbee, defined nationalism as a "state of mind in which we give our paramount loyalty to one fraction of the human race—to a particular tribe of which we happen to be tribesmen."[2]

Why is it so? Why has people's loyalty to their nation and state so often prevailed over other commitments or considerations?

This chapter will examine the following three clusters of possible answers to this question:

1.   One reason for the mass identification of the people with their nation and state is the *duty* and *habit* of serving the same territorial authority; people frequently derive important advantages from their manifested loyalty and obedient behavior.

2.   Another reason for nationalism is the people's exposure to and acceptance of the same *way of life* and general *culture*.

3.   The third reason for nationalism is *contact with alien groups*, especially if they are or are assumed to be hostile; this factor can actually raise the intensity of nationalism to the *n*th power (if we use mathematical terminology).

The preceding three groups of inducements, complexly intertwined, have in fact often produced a high degree of national cohesion. Nevertheless, they cannot guarantee a monolithic national unity. Many territorial states are marked by hostile internal fragmentation that affects or reflects the external fragmentation of mankind into nations. Ethnic and ideological dissent within nation-states and its linkages with international politics will be further analyzed in Chapter 3. In this chapter our focus is on nationalism as a fundamental loyalty in feeling and in behavior that individuals and groups manifest toward their geographically delineated political system, that is, their territorial nation-state.

SHARING THE SAME TERRITORIAL AUTHORITY

"Among the most important experiences that can unite a group," notes Leslie Lipson, "is that they share the same unit of government."[3] A state may predate a nation (Chapter 3 will deal with the contrary process: when a nation predates a state); a national cohesive community may be created, as it were, from above, that is, by the state and its government. What often appears today as a national community endowed with deep-felt collective emotions, pride of common history, and determination to experience a common future—elements of collective consciousness that seem almost independent of the present existence and performance of the national authority—frequently has had a synthetic beginning. Territorial authority in search of a nation and its rational as well as emotional supports may have come first. A conquest, an interdynastic agreement (that failed to consult the people concerned), a *coup d'état*, or the seizure of relinquished colonial power by native elites (without or with the consent of the former master) may create a unit of territorial government that is capable of protecting, coercing, servicing, and indoctrinating groups that initially had been artificially or forcibly brought together and that had nothing except the territorial authority in common. This in itself may induce a sense of group solidarity. Or, in other words, individuals often identify with one another and their territorial authority because they *must*. An important ingredient of internal cohesion and support of the authority is fear of the consequences that would result from disobedient behavior or active opposition. It is difficult to imagine a large national community endowed with such an angelic disposition that it would make any agency of legitimate coercion unnecessary; it is, unfortunately, much easier to visualize a territorial system that functions by coercion only, without any consensus, except in the negative sense, that is, a consensus based on ignorance, impotence, and fear. Two major types of group fear generate cooperative though quite unenthusiastic behavior.

First is simply fear of the unknown, the unfamiliar, the untried. Sometimes citizens support a government that is neither totalitarian nor responsive to their needs simply because they do not know any better. Ignorance, fear of experimentation, and traditional belief in the preordained and unchangeable nature of fate may effect a substantial degree of internal cohesion and tranquility. The traditional and familiar, however unsatisfactory, may seem preferable to a change that might not improve conditions but make them worse.

In fascist and communist states there is also the fear caused by the extreme risks involved in any attempt at internal opposition against a well-entrenched modern totalitarian system. Even without satisfying any major needs, a government may frighten people into submission and cooperation. A community of fear is, after all, also a community; it may produce an effective government. And a powerful government in turn produces internal cohesion and peace, because the people find it impossible or too risky to break the unity and order. The feeling of impotence may make people who in their hearts love freedom and hate tyranny accept and cooperate with a dictatorship. They may not see any rational alternative to their destiny. This is probably true of those artists and writers who under the conditions of totalitarian socialism or fascism have chosen to conform rather than be condemned to silence or jail. The majority of people, including the intellectuals, is evidently not composed of martyrs or heroes; Joans of Arc, Sakharovs, and Solzhenitsyns are the exceptions, not the rule. The majority chooses to live as best it can, recognizing its own powerlessness, especially under authoritarianism, and the regime's awesome capacity to coerce and determine and distribute education, culture, and jobs, in short, the power to distribute life itself.

No government, however, even the most totalitarian, seems to rely only on its capacity to enforce every single law or ordinance. In addition to police terror and the threat or actuality of economic punishment, all dictatorships engage in elaborate mass persuasion and indoctrination. The purpose is obvious: to elicit from the people some degree of cooperation based on motives other than fear. Ministries of propaganda in fascist states and the agitation and propaganda departments (Agitprops) of the communist parties glorify the system's alleged record in matters of material improvement and stress the advantages of conformism in contrast to the extreme risks of nonconformism.

The Westphalian Lesson

When in 1648 the Peace of Westphalia concluded the religious wars in Europe, it did not resolve the religious conflict but transferred it from the battlefields to the pulpits and, administratively speaking, to the domestic jurisdiction of respective Catholic or Protestant princes and kings; it was expressed by the formula *cuius regio, eius religio* (He who controls a realm determines its religion), which had been suggested for the first time at the Augsburg Peace Conference in 1555. After the Peace of Westphalia, the German Empire, previously a loose aggregate of over 900 states, was divided into 355 consolidated sovereign states—and the territorial state in the modern sense of the word appeared on the scene. As Carleton J. H. Hayes has noted in *The Historical Evolution of Modern Nationalism*, these states were not yet "nations" in the primitive tribal sense, and their "nationalism" had different foundations from present-day nationalism. The European nations of the sixteenth and seventeenth centuries were more akin to small empires than to large tribes. They were administrative creations of absolute monarchs in a period when loyalties were still dominantly religious, urban, manorial, regional, or universalistic (consonant with the concept of a universal Holy Roman Empire).

The emergence of territorial states marked the end of feudal localism and European universalism. The territorial states, with their centralized tax collection, internal pacification, common ideology (religion), and external defenses, were much larger than the former feudal fiefs and much smaller than the confines of the Holy Roman Empire. They also became more tightly organized than either the fiefs or the empire. People were not consulted about their preferences; with the exception of a few exiles, they were fenced in by the spatially delineated units imposed on them from above. There seemed to be no other choice for the people than to obey the territorial ruler. In doing so, however, they received from him what they had long desired—internal order and external protection, the two commodities that had been missing from the western European scene for the previous three decades of violent religious struggle. This, in turn, led the people to identify with the effective state organization.

When a territorial system is generally responsive to its people's most pressing demands for justice, order, social welfare, collective identity, external security, and national prestige, the result is satisfaction based on a rational evaluation and acknowledgment of past performance and an expectation, based on past experience, of more services and benefits to come. People find it useful to identify with and support their government if it is largely responsive to their basic needs; it is unnecessary to break peace and order. A responsive and effective government thus enhances internal cohesion, which in turn helps to produce an effective government.

From Kingdoms to Republics

In the eighteenth and nineteenth centuries the inhabitants of royal and princely states proved able to transfer their attachment from the physical person of the ruler, whom the democratic and republican revolutions had dethroned or decapitated, to the abstract concept of the nation and state and their new symbols. When in 1793 French revolutionary leaders beheaded Louis XVI, who was the personified expression of the French state, France (also suffering foreign intervention) remained a territorial state. Not only was Paris still the visible and effective source of all major domestic and foreign policies, but under the determined leadership of revolutionary nationalistic leaders it finally became the creator and administrator of national education, the national conscript armies, the national press, and a uniform national language. Having executed their king, the French endowed the abstraction of their nation with human features once more, in the guise of a young woman, singing the new anthem, *La Marseillaise*, and displaying the tricolor flag and the Phrygian cap of the Republic, the new symbols of the French state. This anthropomorphic expression of France appealed to citizens to take up arms and defend their national territory (*patrie*, that is, fatherland—a term derived from the word, "father," that is laden with emotion in French as well as in many other languages); the new symbol thus also advertised and justified another feature of the territorial state, national conscription. As so often happens, it was soon discovered in France—and elsewhere—that replacing an absolute sovereign with the abstract concept of a sovereign people can result in another type of personalized rule (in this case that of Robespierre, and later Napoleon) which, although governing in the name of the people, may become more cruel or more adventurous than the preceding regime. In Russia two centuries later it was discovered that replacing the Romanov dynasty with the concept of a victorious proletariat and its "vanguard," the Communist party, resulted in a much more effective oppression by one man than had existed under the Russian czars. Robespierre and Stalin, both revolutionary and national leaders of undeniable skill, are constant reminders that such great abstractions as France, revolution, republic, Russia, the people, socialism, and the proletariat may represent attractive and deceptive wrappings for the brutal fact of dictatorial rule. Robespierre and Stalin also symbolize the frailty of many a revolutionary hope for a better world when placed in the hands of unchecked ambition.

The Welfare State

In the twentieth century, the territorial state, partly under the impact of the Marxian critique of capitalism, became an agency of social welfare and economic planning and, in many parts of the world, owner of most means of production. As a result, the rational and emotional links between the masses and their state became even more intimate, underlining the fact that the dependence of the masses on the state for their welfare often has as its corollary the increased power of the modern welfare state over its citizens. This is the result of modern technology, automation, mass production, mass consumption, and mass communication—a way of life that requires a high degree of economic planning and discipline, not only in the totalitarian communist states but also in Western democracies. The state is now able to bestow on all its citizens important economic benefits or to inflict economic privations in an unprecedented way. The identification of the masses with their state and their dependence on it are currently more intensive than they could have been in preceding centuries. The economic needs of the working people have been brought to the forefront. As E. H. Carr has written,

> Their standard of living must be defended if necessary against the national trade (or political) policies of other states . . . [A]s custodians of the living standard, employment and amenities of their whole populations, modern nations are, in virtue of their nature and function, probably less capable than any other group in modern times of reaching agreement with one another. . . . The socialization of the nations has as its natural corollary the nationalization of socialism.[4]

These lines were written in 1945, long before the terms "national communism" and "socialist imperialism" became part of the political vocabulary.

Welfare and National Power as a Condition of Welfare The search for influence on the world scene has now become an accompanying feature of the welfare function of a modern state.

In developing countries the achievement of national power is often viewed not as a result of but as a precondition for the promotion of economic welfare. People are often asked to postpone the fulfillment of their rising expectations until the nation's power and independence are internationally more secure. "It would be a mistake to think that most of us [Indians] evaluate national achievement in terms of individual happiness and comfort," wrote M. R. Masani, one of the founders of the All India Congress Socialist party and a former member of the Indian Parliament. "Our main measuring rod is that of national strength and power. The sons of Asia who thrilled in response to the victory of Japan over Tsarist Russia in 1905 respond similarly to the military and diplomatic success of Communist China over the Americans in Korea and the French in Indochina."[5] These lines were written in 1955, in the period of India's extremely unrealistic appraisal of the People's Republic of China. In the 1960s, when India herself became a target for Chinese territorial claims, Masani would have cited different countries as examples. As a matter of fact, after 1964 many Indian political leaders advocated the need for India's own atomic deterrent in response to the Chinese atomic armament; India's first nuclear device was set off ten years later, on May 18, 1974. The device, using the implosion technique, was more sophisticated and more powerful than the first atomic bomb used by the United States against Japan in 1945. The Indian nuclear test did not violate the 1963 Test-Ban Treaty forbidding nuclear explosions on land, in the air, or under the seas; it was exploded about 330 feet under the ground. Some foreign critics of the Indian nuclear test pointed to the disparity between the Indian government's efforts in the field of atomic energy (about $40 million a year), on the one hand, and its efforts in the field of food production and population control, on the other.

The populations of most Asian and African countries are presented with the image of their nation's future power and welfare so that they will more readily accept additional years of privation. As a result, their emotional identification with a state that is expected to deliver welfare at some future date is, at least for some time, as intensive as the identification of a people with a state that has already delivered higher standards of living and security.

Thus, at the same time that modern technology and economic interdependence seem to be undermining some of the old foundations of states, a new vigor has been added to the state by a great increase in its role and power, by the people's dependence on and identification with its welfare system, and by fear that economic interdependence might result in dependence. National leaders necessarily protect the key levers of their national economies against any undesirable manipulation from within or without. Each state wants to decide for itself how much and what kind of cooperation with other nations is desirable in the framework of mutual interdependence. Thus the implication of economic interdependence has not decreased but has instead either maintained or increased insistence on national freedom of action. In his analysis of the challenges that powerful multinational megacorporations (see also Document 1.1) represent for nations and their states, Robert Gilpin concludes:

> Contrary to the argument that the multinational corporation will somehow supplant the nation-state, I think it is closer to the truth to argue that the role of the nation-state in economic as well as in political life is increasing and that the multinational corporation is actually a stimulant to the further extension of state power in the economic realm. One should not forget that

the multinational corporation is largely an economic phenomenon and that in response to this American challenge other governments are increasingly intervening in their domestic economies in order to counterbalance the power of American corporations and to create domestic rivals of equal size and competence.[6]

SHARING THE SAME CULTURE

People become attached to their territorial community and its institutions and values by a complex process that, in our context, we shall call nationalistic socialization. A more appropriate term might be "nationalization," but the term is today usually employed to describe expropriation and collectivization of either privately owned or foreign-owned assets and means of production.

Part of the process of nationalistic socialization is certainly the individual's need to belong, to be part of a community, not to be alone. But a much larger part of the process is learning. Obedience to public authorities is often the beginning; from a reluctant obedience a hesitant and later automatic *habit* of obeying, a tradition of cooperative behavior, may issue. The participants in the process of forming a customary habit of obeying and so supporting the authorities are usually unable to dissect the whole into a clear and chronological cause-and-effect pattern.

At first in the family, and then in school and peer groups as well as later by means of exposure to the mass media, everybody learns about the rewards and sanctions that the authorities have the power to apply in case of either supportive or deviant behavior; simultaneously one learns about community values and goals, the approved way of life, folk arts, and accepted forms of entertainment. Also largely through instruction rather than through detailed direct experience citizens learn about the configuration of national boundaries that separate one's own nation ("we") from the external alien world ("they"). (See Document 1.2 on the importance of schoolroom maps.)

Integral parts of the deliberate stream of nationalistic messages are the emotional appeals and the manipulation of symbols addressed to the citizens' feelings rather than their reason. Even absolute monarchs, who claimed to rule their subjects by divine right, did not disregard the usefulness of emotional links between themselves and their people: royal pageantry and an appropriate display of royal ceremonial symbols were used to enhance the prestige of the central authority and the people's loyalty to it. Similarly, modern dictators, fascist or communist, as well as elected leaders in democracies, rarely fail to stress nationalistic themes in their speeches, in public education, and in the mass media. All national leaders organize military parades, with their rousing marches and displays of national symbols, engage in emotional oratory on the occasion of national holidays (usually commemorating bloody battles for independence or revolutions), have the national anthem played to conclude important political events, require oaths of national allegiance (in some countries school children are required to repeat such oaths daily), and adorn their residences and public buildings with the national flag and emblem. It may also be noted that nations tend to adopt fierce rather than tame animals as symbols for their national emblems[7]: lions (which usually appear on the emblem with their fangs bared, holding spears, swords, or hatchets), eagles (some of which hold arrows or lightning or at least have two heads to be vigilant on two fronts), tigers, panthers, leopards, or rhinoceroses (Sudan, for example). Ferocious beasts depicted on the emblems seem to communicate to the world what nationalism is really about. No nation, understandably, has

FIGURE 2.1
NATIONAL EMBLEMS

USA

Albania

India

Kenya

USSR

Sudan

Iran

Czechoslovakia

Malaysia

chosen the chicken—or dove—as its national symbol. Only a few have other than zoological symbols. Switzerland has a white cross in a red field, a design that, with colors reversed, has become the symbol of the worldwide charitable organization of the Red Cross. Ireland has chosen a musical instrument, Japan the sun, Argentina the republican Phrygian cap, and Israel a menorah, a candelabrum used in Jewish worship. The Soviet Union features the communist hammer and sickle superimposed on the whole Eastern Hemisphere, including Africa; superimposition of a national-ideological symbol over territory other than one's own country could be interpreted as an example of "emblematic imperialism." Samples of national emblems are reproduced in Figure 2.1.

FIGURE 2.1 (Cont.)

Syria   Israel   Egypt

Ireland   Switzerland   Japan

Argentina   Australia   People's Republic) of China

History: A Tool and Source of Patriotism

Political leaders in all eras seem to have recognized the proper presentation of history as an important source of national enthusiasm. Glorification of past achievements may help a group overcome a distressing period or regain a lost sense of identity and self-confidence. An overwhelming stream of embellished memories, myths, and legends is produced in every nation by the government, the schools, the army, the media, patriotic organizations, historians, philosophers, poets, and artists. An aggregate of human beings is transformed into a collective person, endowed with feelings, memories, pride, sorrow, and hopes—in other words, with a "soul." This aspect of nationalism—emotional, intangible, related to the past and to the future—led the French historian Ernest Renan (1823-1892) to describe a nation as

> [a] soul, a spiritual principle . . . a great solid unit, formed by a realization of sacrifices in the past, as well as of those one is prepared to do in the future. . . . A nation implies a past; while, as regards the present, it is all contained in . . . the agreement and clearly expressed desire to continue the life in common. The existence of a nation is a daily plebiscite.

Renan went on to stress the spiritual over the concrete aspects, adding, "To have suffered, rejoiced, and hoped together, these are things of greater value than identity of custom houses and frontiers in accordance with strategic notions."[8]

A common past and present as well as a commitment to a common future make men conscious of being part of a unit that, with its collective will, is different and separate from the rest of humanity. The nation and its state are concrete, tangible, and understandable; the territorial state wields an impressive power to reward and punish—and it can be reformed. By contrast, to an average person and to those who represent him or her on the international scene, humanity and its interests still remain hazy, distant, amorphous, and unreal. This idea was succinctly expressed by the French writer Philippe de Saint-Robert: "As for the French, the fact is that the only cause around which they ever rallied was France." This was his comment on the futility of those of his compatriots who expressed European feelings rather than showing their true national feelings. When the *New York Times* reproduced de Saint-Robert's essay (February 25, 1974), it appropriately entitled it: "To Be French Is to Be French Is to Be French Is to Be French, etc." We may suggest that, on the whole, the term "French" can be replaced by the name of any other established nation today.

Family and Textbook Indoctrination In his best-selling novel *Portnoy's Complaint*, the Jewish-American writer Philip Roth describes what was probably his own personal experience with racial-religious indoctrination in his own family:

> The very first distinction I learned . . . was not night and day or hot and cold, but *goyische* and Jewish! But now it turns out, my dear parents, relatives and assembled friends who have gathered here to celebrate the occasion of my bar mitzvah . . . that there is just a little bit more to existence than what can be contained in these disgusting and useless categories! . . . Jew Jew Jew Jew Jew Jew Jew! It is coming out of my ears already, the saga of the suffering Jews! . . . *I happen also to be a human being!*
>
> But you *are* a Jew, my sister says. You are a Jewish boy, more than you know, and all you're doing is . . . hollering into the wind.[9]

Children in Indonesia and Malaysia are told a story in which God suffered two failures while creating man: first, when he overbaked his clay model, thus creating the black man; second, when he impatiently underbaked it, thus producing the white man. Only on his third attempt did the right, superior color emerge from the heavenly oven: that of the brown Malay race.

In the biethnic state of Cyprus, a scanning of the history textbooks used by Greek children and Turkish children shows indoctrination in interethnic intolerance. Throughout the Greek texts the Turks are depicted as "barbarians," "heathens," "ignorant," "avaricious," "mad," and "merciless." In a text for Greek sixth-graders, the description of the Turkish massacre of the Greeks on Easter Sunday in 1821 reads: "Turks with madness depicted on their faces seized, tortured and hanged the patriarch and left his remains hanging for three days." On the other hand, the Turkish textbooks extol the Ottoman Empire. A history book for Turkish sixth-graders concludes: "Our ancestors never attacked others unless they themselves had met with wrong or aggression. The sole reason why they won great wars was because they had right on their side." One can well imagine how grossly distorted will be the respective Turkish, Greek, and Cypriot descriptions of the Turkish invasion of Cyprus in 1974, following the Greek officers' *coup d'état* and the escape of the Greek Cypriot leader Archbishop Makarios abroad.

Following the Israeli-Arab six-day war in 1967, more than a million Arabs were subjected to Israeli military and administrative control. The number included about six hundred thousand Palestinian refugees who had fled their homes in the wake of the first Arab-Israeli conflict in 1949. An interesting problem developed in the refugee camps and schools under the United Nations Relief and Works Agency: 127 textbooks formerly used in the Palestinian refugee schools were found unacceptable by the Israeli authorities on account of their offensive anti-Jewish and anti-Zionist references. In a literature reader, for instance, pupils were given a passage from

Shakespeare's *The Merchant of Venice* and were asked, on this basis, to "describe in about twenty lines the vile character of a Jew." And in a geography book the refugee children were given the following definition of Israel: "The usurped portion of Palestine which, God willing, we shall soon fight to win back from criminal Jews."

Indoctrination by history textbooks is not, of course, a Greek, Turkish, Arab, or Israeli speciality. All national communities engage in it. At a time when Western Europe is attempting to create a higher supranational community, French and German history texts still condition children to the old Franco-German enmity. An agreement between the two countries has now enjoined the respective governments to promote a correct understanding of each other's countries by means of more objective textbooks.

Throughout the world, when the school takes over from the family, it only continues the nationalist indoctrination, usually at the cost of historical truth. From 1963 to 1966 a team of British and American historians engaged in a study of national bias in the secondary-school history textbooks of the two nations. National bias was found in *all* American and British history texts. Nearly all American textbooks depict the peace negotiations at Versailles in 1919 as a struggle between the Forces of Good (represented by the saintly Woodrow Wilson) and the Forces of Evil (represented by West European diplomats). Not a single junior-high-school textbook used in the United States fails to describe the burning of Washington, D.C., by British troops in 1812, but not one tells of the American burning of the Canadian city of York (Toronto) that led to England's retaliation. English textbooks describing the American War of Independence dwell with great affection on the triumphs of their generals, leaving the student bewildered that after such a series of victories they could have lost a war. American texts, on the other hand, recite the impressive record of George Washington's military victories, barely mentioning his defeats. It seems that the patriots (itself a biased word) lost only the Battle of Bunker Hill, and only because they ran out of powder. Ray Allen Billington, chairman of the investigating team, writes:

> If these discouraging results can be drawn from the reading of texts used in two countries that have been traditionally friendly and usually allied in world conflicts, what would be revealed by a study of German and American textbooks or of those used in the United States and Russia? . . . History is a dangerous subject, to be handled with caution. [Textbook] authors must learn that words are as dangerous as bullets and that each must be carefully weighed to detect the nuances of meaning that might prejudice the viewpoint of their readers. . . . Clearly national bias is a besetting sin of today's authors, and equally clearly it should be eliminated in the interest of world harmony.[10]

National monuments continue where high-school books leave off. In an article published in the *New York Times* (Travel and Resorts, December 15,

1968), an Englishman, Arthur Griffiths, finds the American war memorials of the Revolutionary War excessively biased in favor of the Americans:

> I lamented for the enemy—the bad guys, my ancestors, losers even when they were winners. Wherever they triumphed, I found no obelisks to their valor for King and Country, only memorials to the gallantry of the men they beat. . . . Of course, the Liberty Bell was originally cast in England. Not a lot of Americans know it. The English don't make a big fuss about it, possibly because of its metallurgical defect . . . the bell cracked in 1752. Even then, Britain was having trouble with its exports.

When nationalists point to the future, it is usually related to and colored by the past; the future is seen only as a better history telescoped into coming decades and centuries. Although nationalist propaganda seldom prefers to stress the future over the past, some nations did make their entry on the international scene by more or less denying their immediate past. This was true of the English colonies in America. The history of the American nation obviously did not start in England but in New England. The thirteen separate colonies "only gradually experienced the sense of community . . . which their war with the mother country made more solid."[11]

The past may be a burden rather than an asset when a newly free nation can look back only to slavery and, beyond that, to an unknown past. A recent study by Wendel Bell and Ivar Oxaal on nationalism in former British possessions in the Caribbean pointed out that

> no more than the state of Israel can construct its new national traditions solely on the basis of its experience with the practitioners of anti-Semitism and the pogrom can the West Indies hope to salvage a meaningful historical tradition solely from the colonial exploitation of the past three hundred years. This is so despite the salutary efforts to rewrite West Indian history—to exchange the degradation of slavery for the glory of the struggle for freedom. . . . Colonialism in many respects represents merely the harsh "pre-history" of the developing nations and may therefore be incapable of yielding a full and positive sense of solidarity.[12]

The authors of the study conclude that the emergence of the new solidarity will be helped not by romanticizing the past but by the creation and dissemination of images of a new future, consistent with nationalistic ideals and firmly grounded in a rational, scientific orientation toward action and common welfare.

Romanticizing the Past   Both long-established national states and revolutionary nationalist movements struggling for self-expression or territorial self-determination justify and propagandize their hopes and their programs for the future by combining them with emotional references to past achievements as well as to tragedies. Established nations usually have had enough time and resources to research and systematically describe their history; revolutionary movements tend to rely more on vague and emotion-laden concepts (Renan's definition of nationality as a soul is an example). Whether established or not, all national movements embellish or improve upon their histories: minor achievements are inflated, minor victories or tragedies grossly exaggerated, and outright falsification of history sometimes resorted to. In the nineteenth century two Czech scholars fabricated a document that was supposed to demonstrate that the Czechs had had their own culture long before the German conquests. This was done to combat defeatism in a period when the Czech nation seemed to be at the brink of national extinction and absorption by the German nation. Those who denounced the fraud and argued that the facts of ancient Czech political and cultural history were in no need of embellishment were denounced as traitors to the cause of Czech nationalism. In 1961 in Ghana, one could buy a series of twelve postcards packaged under the title "African History: Twelve Historical Views from the National Archives of Ghana." Colored pictures in the style of American Pop Art depict the contributions of African Negroes to world civilization. One card shows Negroes manipulating test tubes and bottles and asserts that "the science of chemistry was discovered by Africans in the old empire of Ghana." Other pictures show how stenography (as practiced by Cicero's African secretary Tyro), architecture, paper (Egyptian papyrus), and mathematics originated in Africa. On one card a black man is talking to white men; the caption reads: "Aesop expounds the wisdom of Africa to the Greeks." A German correspondent, writing for *Die Kultur*, reported in 1961 that the *Evening News*, the newspaper of Nkrumah's Convention People's party, claimed that both Beethoven and Haydn were black.[13]

Goethe, seeing the ill-effects of an excessive stress on a romantic concept of the past, warned nations against blurring the vision of present and future generations. He praised American nationalism for its alleged absence of the need to look to the past:

> America, thou art more fortunate than our old continent,
> Thou hast not ruined castles, and no ancient stones.
> No useless memories, no vain feuds of the past disturb thee from
> living in the present.
> And should thy children start to write poetry, may a kind Providence
> preserve them from stories of the romantic past.[14]

Whether it lacks one at its inception or not, every nation sooner or later acquires a meaningful history. Then, in due course, scholarly history books, textbooks, political speeches, monuments, national holidays, a national anthem, songs, poems, and children's stories will glorify and embellish the nation's past: how it started, built itself, fought, suffered, and endured. An emotional and powerful identification of the people with one another and with the nation's past achievements often will result. A nation does not spontaneously become an ultimate point of reference for loyalty and political action. This is a result of manifold pressures, manipulations and messages that stress common experience and a common future. A mixture of rational egoism and emotional elation in response to constant prodding underlies the nationalist feeling. All states make use of symbols that are intended solely to mobilize sentiments. Many a new nation today starts its life as an independent state by adopting a newly designed military uniform, a new emblem, a new stamp, a new flag or a newly composed national anthem.

In many cases one can say that the national stamp, anthem, or flag precedes the reality of the new nations. And yet, what is a national flag?

> A pathetically impermanent strip of dyed cloth, which withers to ribbons after a few days in a high wind. . . . It looks simple, but it is in fact extremely complex . . . it represents the continuity of a people, their common purpose, their traditions, their way of looking at the world, their defiance against their enemies. . . . The dead are present in it, as well as the living. We are made obscurely aware of the mystery when the flag is slowly lowered at dusk. . . . It is permanent and impermanent, sacred and profane, practical and impractical, rooted in ancient legend and in some of its applications wholly modern.[15]

For a great many people, though certainly not all, it seemed to matter, for instance, whose nation's flag would be the first to be planted on the moon. At the time of the launching of Apollo 11 at Cape Kennedy (July 16, 1969) Reverend Ralph Abernathy was leading 250 Poor People's Campaigners in a protest march to condemn incorrect national priorities. However, when the launch began, he said, "for those incredible two minutes I was so stunned and so proud of America that I forgot there was hunger."

In 1974 Liberia's President William R. Tolbert, Jr., announced his plan to change all the national symbols, originally designed by freed American slaves—Liberia's founding fathers. In order to stress Liberia's link with Africa rather than America the following were scheduled for "de-Americanization": the flag (based on the American flag but with only one star), the national anthem, the Constitution, and even the national slogan, "Love of Liberty Brought Us Here."

Past services and benefits as well as effective communication may create such an important storage of good will and emotional links between the citizens and the state that people forgive their state's lapses in political or social performance. In response to a serious danger to the national community—even in response to minor foreign pressures or competition—people tend to forget their grievances against the government. They postpone their rational evaluation of its record and close their ranks with various versions of the toast proposed in the nineteenth century

FIGURE 2.2
THE COUNTRY AND I

"What do you mean, 'My country, right or wrong'?
Just when has our country ever been wrong?"

Drawing by D. Fradon; © 1965 The New Yorker Magazine, Inc.

by the American naval officer Stephen Decatur: "Our country! In her intercourse with foreign nations, may she be always right, but our country, right or wrong."[16] (See Figure 2.2.)

National Language

In many parts of the world, particularly in Europe and Asia, language is one of the most important ingredients of the common cultural and historical heritage. It binds a group of people together, gives it a unified and manageable entity, and distinguishes it from other national communities. The history of many European conflicts contains elements of linguistic antagonism: the Poles sandwiched between the Russians and the Germans, the Dutch and Czech nations in the neighborhood of powerful

Germany, the Ukrainians under the shadow of the Russians, and the Irish next door to the English. The goal of national preservation has often been sought by means of cultivation, revival, and glorification of the national language as the most important instrument of national culture. "Nationalism feeds upon the desire and need of people to communicate with each other in their 'own' language,"[17] notes Carl J. Friedrich. He also deals with lingual nationalism's dominant concern with cultural self-identity and literary self-expression, in contrast to the other symbols of exclusive group loyalty.

Like any other ingredient of nationalism, the question of language has partly emotional and partly rational aspects. Language is an important part of one's national heritage. From the first lullaby, communication with one's environment and the learning of values and views usually occur in a single language; the identification with one's native language makes all other languages necessarily foreign and thus constitutes an important basis for national feeling. And there is also a purely practical aspect to the question of language: a linguistically homogeneous group can be molded into a manageable unit more easily and more effectively than a polyglot group. When citizens cannot properly communicate with one another and with their own government, new conflicts are added to those that are inevitable in any community.

If we choose to view a nation as primarily a social communication system (and a territorial state as a geographically delineated communication system), then its decisive boundary is represented by a "relative discontinuity in the frequency of communication."[18] Man, unlike other animals, learns complex patterns of social behavior by means of communication, and he does not communicate as frequently across a border as he does within his own territory. Thus a territorial or linguistic community becomes, in Karl W. Deutsch's words,

> a community of complementary habits and facilities of communication which permit a common history to be experienced in common. . . . The communicative facilities of a society include a socially standardized system of symbols which is a language, and any number of auxiliary codes, such as alphabets, systems of writing, painting, calculating, etc. They include information stored in living memories, associations, habits, and preferences of its members, and its material facilities for the storage of information, such as libraries, statues, signposts, and the like; and a good deal more. Taken all together, they include, therefore, in particular the elements of that which anthropologists call culture.[19]

In such a context the national language, the basic instrument of intranational communication, is a symbol and objective fact distinguishing one nation from another. The language barrier may raise to considerable heights the walls separating territorial nations.

The reality of territorial and national identity becomes obvious at the first word—one does not need to notice a signpost, flag, or passport officer to realize that he is no longer at home but among foreigners. But several important qualifications are necessary. In some areas lingual as well as cultural communications crisscross state boundaries; for political purposes the Germans coined a word, *Kulturnation*, to describe a nation in its lingual and cultural sense as distinguished from its political and territorial subdivisions. Lingual and cultural links between a nation and its migrant sons (ethnic minorities) may also create political connections, even though the migrant sons might have become citizens of foreign states. Good examples are the links between Germany and the German minorities in Eastern Europe, between China and the Chinese minorities in Southeast Asia, and between the "hyphenated" Americans and the lands of their origin.

On the other hand, many territorial nations with a common language feel themselves to be distinct and often inimical entities. The same language, understood and appreciated to the fullest, communicates different concepts, history, grief, pride, and hope to different territorial communities. In the United States, in all the disparate English-speaking member-nations of the Commonwealth, and in other countries where English has still remained the first or second language of officialdom, young people enjoy Shakespeare in the original and also labor through Chaucer in common. West Germans, East Germans, Austrians and German-speaking Swiss communicate contrasting political and cultural concepts, but all still read and appreciate Goethe and Schiller. Spain shares an admiration for Cervantes with lingual but not political brethren in Central and South America (including Cuba and Puerto Rico), but not with Brazil, which is the lingual brother of Portugal. With regard to France, an interesting development took place in February 1969, when a conference was held at Niamey, the capital of the West African republic of Niger, on cultural exchanges and cooperation between the thirty-three countries in which French is spoken by many inhabitants or by the ruling or cultural elites. Spread over four continents and containing over 200 million people, these countries include France, Belgium, Luxembourg, Switzerland, Canada, and fourteen former French and three former Belgian colonies in Africa, Madagascar and Mauritius in the Indian Ocean, Lebanon in the Middle East, and Laos, Cambodia, and North and South Vietnam in Asia. French is the official language or is among the official languages in all but four of these countries—Lebanon, Mauritius, North Vietnam, and South Vietnam, where it remains the language of only the cultural elite. In some of these countries French is scheduled to be phased out; Algeria and Morocco, for instance, are working toward complete Arabization.

English is the official language in the United States and is the official language or one of the official languages in the thirty-two independent countries that constitute the British Commonwealth (Britain, Canada, Australia, New Zealand, India, Bangladesh, Malaysia, Sri Lanka (formerly

Ceylon), Singapore, Nigeria, Tanzania, Mauritius, Zambia, Ghana, Sierra Leone, Lesotho, Kenya, Botswana, Swaziland, Uganda, Gambia, Malawi, Cyprus, Malta, Barbados, Bahamas, Jamaica, Trinidad and Tobago, Fiji, Tonga, Guyana, Western Samoa) and the more than forty dependencies of or states associated with India (Sikkim, for instance), Britain, Australia, and New Zealand (such as Hong Kong, the Pitcairn Islands, St. Helena, Nauru, and other minor territories). English also has a recognized status in South Africa and Cameroon.

The French and English languages, however globally useful, are idioms of former colonial masters and must face a growing competition from local vernaculars, however underdeveloped. The vernaculars are symbols of nationalism and important vehicles of mass communication. The history of nationalism shows that language may be elevated into the single most important ingredient in a people's awareness of its identity. Polylingual territorial states experience an awesome difficulty in effective communication within the national territory and so fail to socialize their various ethnic groups into an integrated whole. In combination with the possession of a compact territory, a separate lingual identity has frequently proved to be the most important immediate cause for a demand for secession and independent statehood.

Lingualism in India   A vehement emphasis on language as the basis of nationality is today noticeable in many parts of modern Asia where the previous strong bonds of religious unity (Hinduism or Buddhism) have been weakened by secularization and modernization. A potentially frightening example is India, where 845 languages and dialects are spoken, 14 of which (including English) are officially recognized by the Indian Constitution. The figure 845 is based on the 1927 Linguistic Survey of India, accepted also by the 1951 Indian census. The 1961 census, more carefully conducted, reported 1,652 "mother tongues" and 1,018 different "languages."

Ever since the proclamation of Indian independence, the ethnic and linguistic differences that had been submerged for centuries under the unifying lid of common Hindu religion and culture have been surfacing with the fervor and energy common to all nationalist movements. The Linguistic Provinces Commission, appointed by the Indian Constituent Assembly, reported in 1948 on the conflict between the national leaders' goal of building one indivisible nation and the "centuries-old narrow loyalties, petty jealousies and ignorant prejudices" of several sectors of India:

> We were simply horrified to see how thin was the ice upon which we were skating. Some of the ablest men in the country came before us and confidently and emphatically stated that language in this country stood for and represented culture, race, history, individuality, and finally a subnation.

India's subsequent struggle against illiteracy significantly increased the use of local vernaculars, because they had to be used in primary and secondary education. Local vernaculars have now become important instruments of political communication and participation on a local level and aids in the assertion in New Delhi of local and regional interests against the national Hindi-speaking center. Local politicians now usually have a secondary-school education in their local written language, and they find it irresistible not to utilize lingual territorialism in their strivings for power and status. The geographic boundaries of the twenty-one states that compose the Indian Union largely correspond to the major linguistic boundaries; thus, they strengthen the awareness of separate identity on the part of the major linguistic groups and encourage further demands for territorial subdivisions on the basis of language—a chain reaction that can culminate in an atomization of the Indian nation.

In India, in the rest of Asia, and in Africa, the problem is whether there is enough time left to socialize ethnic and territorial communities into accepting and supporting the concept of national unity. Optimists point to the self-evident demands of modern economy and technology, which are hampered by petty emotional parochialism; this is the age of ideological and economic ecumenism, they say. Pessimists point to the irrational and emotional aspects of nationalism, expressed by the explosive lingual, ethnic, and cultural tensions that now beset even long-established territorial states: Canada with its English-French frictions; the United States with its lingual, Puerto Rican, and Chicano tensions; Belgium with its two antagonistic lingual groups (the French-speaking Walloons and the Dutch-speaking Flemings); France, which in the 1970s, in the wake of semifederal regionalization, experienced violent agitation for autonomy in Brittany and in the Basque country and manifestations of discontent in Alsace, Corsica, French Catalonia, and Provence-Langued'oc (where there were attempts at a revival and modernization of the Occitan language)—in 1974 the French government felt compelled to ban separatist movements in Brittany, Corsica, and the Basque country; Great Britain, where Welsh and Scottish nationalism and even separatism have been steadily growing; Spain, where the old anti-Castilian forces in Catalonia and the Basque country have again reasserted themselves; Yugoslavia and Czechoslovakia, which had to give federal recognition to their component nationalities in order to maintain territorial unity; the Soviet Union, whose effective totalitarian controls allow us to suspect but not prove that the winds of nationalism and the desire for self-determination do not stop at the Soviet borders. More will be said about the centrifugal forces of ethnic and lingual nationalism in Chapter 3.

Religion

Religion has determined the concept of nationality among very few peoples. Israel is one of them. Israel's nationalism is strongly flavored by the Hebrew religion, from which such nationalist concepts as "the Chosen People" and "the Promised Land" have been derived and imitated by others. The tensions and bloodshed between Eire and Northern Ireland and within Northern Ireland in the 1970s have many causes but one of them certainly is the Catholic-Protestant antagonism and its social and economic consequences. Arab nationalism is partly religious and partly ethnic; the Arabs, unlike other Moslems (Indonesians, Pakistanis, Iranians, Turks, Afghans), can claim to be of the same ethnic origin as Allah's own prophet, Muhammad.

Pakistan before the secession of Bangladesh was the most recent example of a nation founded solely on religion. Following her liberation from England, India split into three parts: predominantly Hindu India, Moslem West Pakistan, and Moslem East Pakistan. The two segments of Pakistan, federated into one nation, were divided by a thousand-mile-long stretch of unfriendly Indian territory. Except for their religion and the fear of tyranny by a Hindu majority, East and West Pakistan had little in common. They could pray together with their heads turned toward Mecca, but they could not speak with each other, not even on the subject of their common enmity toward the Indians, for the Bengali language was spoken in the east, and Urdu, Punjabi, Sindi, Baluchi and Pushtoo were spoken in the west. Moreover, the West Pakistani way of life was predominantly Middle Eastern, while that of East Pakistan was shaped by the monsoon climate of Southeast Asia. Lingual nationalism in combination with the serious political and economic grievances of the East Pakistanis finally exploded in 1971. With India's military assistance the Bengali-speaking East Pakistanis seceded from the common state and established an independent Moslem nation, Bangladesh. In this case, common religion proved insufficient to create and maintain a nation.

While minimizing the contemporary strength of religion as a possible source of nationalism, some observers suggest that secular nationalism has, in fact, become a substitute for religion, a modern response to a widespread need for identity and mystique. According to Hans Kohn, the strength of nationalism simply reflects the important role that emotions and passions play in the affairs of men. "Most men are not guided primarily by aspirations of economic betterment or by enlightened self-interest but by collective passions and emotions which silence rational considerations and efforts to be objective."[20] Nationalism, it seems, still remains one of the most enduring collective passions of men.

SHARING THE SAME ENEMY: AN ANTI-FEELING

The nationalist emphasis on past glories, griefs, heroism, achievements, and survival in adversity is often underlined by a contemptuous and intolerant attitude toward other nations and races. Very often people think well of their own group because they think ill of the outsiders. It should be recognized that a common enemy may indeed create unity and collective spirit where in the absence of such an external danger discord would prevail; a feeling of being besieged may produce a high degree of internal cohesion. National leaders have often used the theme of national siege to enhance the unity of their people and the people's identification with their rulers. Many an African or Asian leader today emphasizes the danger of reemerging imperialism and the great powers' neocolonialism; the danger is sometimes real but, whatever the immediacy of that danger, the leader's alarm about external threats is also a convenient device to silence the opposition and keep his polyethnic or polytribal community united, mobilized, and ready, in the name of national security, for further sacrifices. After the 1917 October Revolution in Russia, the Bolshevik leaders continued to stress the dangers of capitalist encirclement and possible new intervention in order to discipline the Soviet people into a community dedicated to the consolidation and modernization of their Soviet fatherland in the name of defense against external threats. At the birth of many nations we find a common struggle against a common enemy. For example, the beginnings of American nationalism may be found in the assertion of a common continental destiny against a common external enemy, England. The leader of the Indian struggle for independence, Pandit Nehru, rightly referred to nationalism as "anti-feeling which feeds and fattens on hatred and anger against other national groups." Or, as the same idea is sometimes expressed in Central Europe: A nation is a group of persons collectively misinformed about their history and collectively suspicious of other nations.

Group Egoism

A nationalist tends to see humanity as basically an aggregate of more or less ill-intentioned foreigners. He concludes that aliens cannot be expected to understand or care about the needs and feelings of any national community as well as the elites that directly issue from, speak the same language as, and feel or can be made accountable to their national community. A cosmopolitan altruist may view everyone as his brother; a nationalist egoist sees everyone beyond the national boundaries as an egoist and therefore his adversary.

This assumption of egoism rather than altruism on the part of others is only a magnified reflection of man's intimate personal experience. However depressing such a conclusion may be, the assumption of the egoism of others mirrors one's own egoism. Notwithstanding all ethical and religious admonitions, people usually do not love their neighbors as well as themselves and their immediate family. During a sermon or a protest march, men elevate their minds to a sincere belief in brotherly love; yet rarely do they make selfless love the yardstick of their action in business or in a

FIGURE 2.3
THE PARADOX OF NONVIOLENCE

"I've got to be able to protect myself, don't I?"

Drawing by VIP. Reprinted from *Look*, June 28, 1966.

confrontation with a policeman, and rarely is it the basis for their expectations concerning the actions of others—for example, a participant in a peace rally who advocates nonviolence prepares himself for violent confrontation (see Figure 2.3).

Projected onto the international scene, the assumption of group egoism on the part of other nations reflects the self-interest of one's own nation. In international politics, charity or altruism seldom tempers the actions and goals of nations. The Protestant theologian Reinhold Niebuhr once noted that only "individual men . . . are able to consider interests other than their own in determining the problems of conduct, and are capable, *on occasion*, of preferring the advantages of others to their own."[21] In contrast, according to Niebuhr, societies and groups are less capable of self-transcendence. Relations among collectivities such as nations are therefore predominantly political rather than ethical: a group is a group and a nation is a nation because it feels that its members have some common interest to promote and to defend against the interests of other similar communities.

It should be admitted, of course, that often the general assumption of potential external enmity is well founded; this is why national leaders, both before and after achieving independent nationhood, do not take any chances. Even a friendly foreign nation may become an enemy following a revolution, *coup d'état*, or new elections. Nor can a former enemy suddenly be trusted when professing a change of heart. When many Western nations, for instance, attempted to convince their former African and Asian subjects that the end of imperial rule would result in local tyranny and a harsher type of government with fewer services than these communities had previously enjoyed, the Africans and Asians suspected that this sudden concern for their well-being had not been dictated by altruism but by an old egoism presented in the guise of new good intentions. The former colonial dependent peoples were largely justified in their conviction that no foreign government or foreign elite could be expected to identify fully with local pride, local priorities, and local prejudices. All other things being equal, domestic tyranny seemed preferable to foreign tyranny; even good foreign government was not viewed as a substitute for self-government. This was expressed in a more colloquial fashion by the Filipinos, who frankly and openly told the United States: "Better a government run like hell by Filipinos than one run like heaven by foreigners."

Nationalist Indoctrination and Stereotypes

A suspicious attitude toward foreigners is rarely a result of some spontaneous process. As noted previously, from his earliest years a citizen of a territorial state has been exposed not only to a systematic glorification of his nation's past, present, and future but also to a corollary debasement of the character and record of foreign nations. His mind has stored usually oversimplified and often deliberately distorted images and generalizations about his own country and foreign groups, both within and outside the national boundaries. Many of these stereotypes, which Walter Lippman called "pictures in our head,"[22] have been based on hearsay or outright lies. Yet if stored in our memory as truths, they will condition or color our perceptions of other nations in comparison with our own.

In his book on Englishmen, Frenchmen, and Spaniards, Salvador de Madariaga described the general tendency of most men to sum up the character of other nations in a pair of features, one of quality, the other of defect:

> Thus, to the pair hypocrisy-practical sense, which represents an Englishman, correspond the clearness-licentiousness for the Frenchman, the thoroughness-clumsiness for the German, dignity-cruelty for the Spaniard, vulgarity-vitality of the American.[23]

After World War II a study was conducted under UNESCO auspices in nine countries, in each of which a representative sample of about 1000 persons served as subjects. They were given a list of twelve adjectives from which they were asked to choose those that applied to themselves, to Americans, to Russians, and in some instances to two or three other national groups as well. The adjectives chosen most frequently by British persons to describe Americans were: progressive, conceited, generous, peace-loving, intelligent, and practical. Americans thought of the British as intelligent, industrious, courageous, peace-loving, conceited, and self-controlled. All of the groups studied were in agreement on one point: their own nation was the most peace-loving of all. Twenty years before that, in 1933, a study conducted by Katz and Braly at Princeton required the students to indicate three or four characteristics most commonly ascribed to several nationalities. The ascribed characteristics included, for the *Germans*: scientifically minded, industrious, stolid; for the *Italians*: artistic, impulsive, passionate; for the *Irish*: pugnacious, quick-tempered, witty; for the *English*: sportsmanlike, intelligent, conventional; for the *Americans*: industrious, intelligent, materialistic, ambitious; for the *Turks*: cruel, religious, treacherous; for the *Chinese*: superstitious, sly, conservative.[24] Other American stereotypes with an ethnic referent that are used colloquially are reproduced in Document 2.1. Document 2.2 reproduces French stereotypes about foreign nations, taken from a

---

DOCUMENT 2.1

AMERICAN STEREOTYPES

Where do national sterotypes come from? . . . One source may be the language we speak, which through the use of common expressions with an ethnic referent may contribute to the tendency to attribute specific characteristics to ethnic groups. . . . For example:

Dutch treat: when each person pays his own way.
Dutch courage: which is fortified by alcohol.
Dutch uncle: who gives advice or instruction strictly and severely.
His fine Italian hand; really subtle, devious, perhaps a bit Machiavellian.
A Chinese puzzle: very complicated.
To take French leave: to slip away quietly, when no one is watching. Interestingly enough, the French say *filer à l'anglaise* for exactly the same behavior. The Italians also do it "like the English" *(filarse a l'inglesa).*
To Jew him down: to bargain in order to get a lower price.

From Otto Klineberg, *The Human Dimension in International Relations.* New York: Holt, Rinehart and Winston, 1964, p.36.

DOCUMENT 2.2

FRENCH STEREOTYPES

Americans

They do not live in a country but on a continent. . . . In its origin, America is nevertheless only a reject of Europe. They all die of heart-attacks, ruined by their wives. There a woman is a queen. They are big babies and have more in common with the Russians than it is usually admitted.

British

No longer what they used to be but still a great nation. Less intelligent than we are but their morale is more robust. They love fresh air and the royal family. Since the war their women have dressed somewhat better, but still! . . . They often have beautiful skin, but their feet!

Chinese

Difficult to distinguish from the Japanese although they are really different and hate each other. . . . One never knows what these 600 million think. One never knows their age. With the Chinese you just never know.

France

(a) Everyone has two motherlands: his own and France; (b) we are the dump for the cosmopolitan scum [*salétranger*]. To note: The position of hereditary enemy of France, successively occupied by England and then Germany, is presently vacant. France always holds the torch of civilization. Without France, the most intellectual of nations, the world would not be the world, which implies that one could totally eliminate Albania, Bulgaria, New Zealand and a large portion of Oceania, Iceland and several Latin American republics without really altering the face of our universe.

Russians

Impossible to know what they have in their heads.[1] They do not reason as we do. Have a talent for foreign languages. They will always agree with the Germans at our expense [Peace of Brest-Litovsk]. Nobody could ever conquer them. Much more refined in diplomacy than the Americans. "And then there is this Slavic charm."

Yugoslavs, Bulgarians, Rumanians, Czechoslovaks, and Poles
All the same.

From Pierre Daninos, *Le Jacassin*. Paris: Hachette, 1962, pp. 213-222.

1. "I cannot forecast to you the action of Russia. It is a riddle wrapped in a mystery inside an enigma." Winston Churchill (Broadcast, October 1, 1939).

facetious French "encyclopedia" of the most current pictures in Frenchmen's heads.

Young men and women necessarily grow older, but they do not necessarily grow wiser; some of them may become presidents, prime ministers, foreign ministers, first secretaries of communist parties. Will they carry the stereotypes acquired in their youth about other nations with them to their highest political office? When the French president met with Lyndon Johnson or Richard Nixon did he interpret their behavior as representative of the American "vulgarity-vitality" category à la Madariaga or as "big babies who have more in common with the Russians than they like to admit" (see Document 2.2 on French stereotypes)? And did the American Presidents dealing with their French counterparts project onto them the French "clearness-licentiousness" characteristics? Certainly, during the 1973 war in the Middle East some foreign observers wondered whether the Arab leaders in dealing with Henry Kissinger would be guided by their stereotypes about the Jews and whether the first Jewish Secretary of State in American history would be unduly influenced by Israeli stereotypes about the Arabs (some Jews, on the other hand, expressed their fear lest Kissinger try to prove his position of detachment from his Jewishness by adopting excessively pro-Arab attitudes).

Our purpose here is not to renew the old controversy about whether there is such a thing as a racial or national character[25] and how quickly it may be subject to alteration through environmental changes (the reputation for aggressiveness of the Swedes under King Gustavus Adolphus in the seventeenth century and the French under Napoleon in the nineteenth century seems no longer valid today). The important fact is that if some people and, above all, some policy makers believe in such stereotypes, their belief will determine their perceptions and actions. An image with no basis in reality may mold or create reality and so trigger action.

Quakers and other groups have often suggested that the vicious circle of egoism, mistrust, and suspicion based on false images could and should be interrupted by a unilateral action of trust and charity. So far these sincere and well-intentioned appeals have gone unheeded, especially on the international scene. When nations occasionally decide on cooperative action with others, they are not guided primarily by a concept of some abstract common interest of humanity of which they are part but by the expectation that their particular interests might better be served by a common than by an isolated action. A cautious hope is often expressed that nations may learn to think in terms of the collective interests of humanity—not for altruistic reasons, but for the very selfish one of survival and order—in the same way that individuals learn that the peace, order, and well-being of their national communities are directly related to their own personal welfare.

But however we may lament the facts, the weakest of all supranational bonds so far has proved to be man's identification with the noble yet vague concept of mankind. A Nobel Peace Prize winner and former Canadian Prime Minister, Lester B. Pearson, has well expressed this deplorable truth of national and international life in a succinct statement: "The first reaction of millions of people today to any proposal for more effective international institutions, for international control of anything is: 'This means that foreigners will be taking charge of our affairs.' "[26] The masses have always listened more readily to the advocates of nationalism than to the preachers of internationalism. They keep on doing so.

Notes

1. Hans Kohn, *The Idea of Nationalism: A Study in Its Origins and Background*. New York: Macmillan, 1967, p. 16.

2. Arnold J. Toynbee, "Again Nationalism Threatens," *New York Times Magazine*, November 3, 1963, p. 23.

3. Leslie Lipson, *The Great Issues of Politics*. Englewood Cliffs, N.J.: Prentice-Hall, 1965, pp. 288-289.

4. Edward H. Carr, *Nationalism and After*. New York: St. Martin's, 1945, pp. 26-29.

5. M. R. Masani, "The Mind of Asia," *Foreign Affairs,* July 1955, p. 549.

6. Robert Gilpin, "The Politics of Transnational Economic Relations," in Robert E. Keohane and Joseph S. Nye, Jr. (eds.) *Transnational Relations and World Politics*. Cambridge, Mass.: Harvard University Press, 1972, p. 69.

7. For a more detailed treatment see Ivo D. Duchacek, *Power Maps: Comparative Politics of Constitutions*. Santa Barbara, Calif.: ABC-Clio, 1973, pp. 27-33.

8. Quoted in Alfred Zimmern, *Modern Political Doctrines*. New York: Oxford, 1939, pp. 202-205.

9. Philip Roth, *Portnoy's Complaint*. New York: Random House, 1969, pp. 75-76.

10. Ray Allen Billington, "History Is a Dangerous Subject," *Saturday Review*, January 15, 1966, pp. 59, 61, 81.

11. Reinhold Niebuhr and Alan Heimert, *A Nation So Conceived*. New York: Scribner, 1953, p. 15.

12. Wendel Bell and Ivar Oxaal, *Decisions of Nationhood: Political and Social Development in the British Caribbean*. Denver, Colo.: University of Denver, The Social Science Foundation Monograph Nos. 3 and 4, 1964, p. 89.

13. Wolfgang Bretholz, "No New Africa!" *Die Kultur,* February 1961; translated and published in *Atlas,* June 1961, pp. 15-26.

14. Quoted by Hans Kohn in *The Twentieth Century*. New York: Crowell-Collier-Macmillan, 1949, p. 225n. By permission.

15. Robert Payne, 'What's in a Flag? Everything," *New York Times Magazine*, August 30, 1964, p. 20.

16. Compare George Orwell's definition of nationalism ("England, Your England," 1941): "A family with the wrong members in control. . . . Good or evil, it is yours, you belong to it, and this side the grave you will never get away from the marks that it has given you." Compare also Albert Camus' often-quoted qualification of patriotism (*The Rebel*): "I should like to be able to love my country and still love justice."

17. Carl J. Friedrich, 'Federalism and Nationalism," *Orbis,* 10:4 (Winter 1967), 1009 (a special issue dedicated to the American historian of nationalism Hans Kohn).

18. Peter H. Merkl, "Federalism and Social Structure," paper presented at the Sixth Congress of the International Political Science Association, Geneva, 1964, p. 7. In his paper Merkl defines a territorial community as a unit aware of "common sharing of values, purposes, interests and fears" (p. 4.).

19. Karl W. Deutsch, *Nationalism and Social Communication: An Inquiry into the Foundations of Nationality.* Cambridge, Mass.: M.I.T. Press, 1966, pp. 96-97.

20. Hans Kohn, *Living in a World Revolution: My Encounters with History.* New York: Pocket Books, 1964, p. 30.

21. Quoted in Harry R. Davis and Robert C. Good, *Reinhold Niebuhr on Politics.* New York: Scribner, 1960, p. 84.

22. Walter Lippmann, *Public Opinion.* New York: Crowell-Collier-Macmillan, 1932, pp. 3-32.

23. Salvador de Madariaga, *Englishmen, Frenchmen and Spaniards.* New York: Oxford, 1928, pp. x, xi.

24. Otto Klineberg, *The Human Dimension in International Relations.* New York: Holt, Rinehart and Winston, 1964, pp. 35-36.

25. For further reference see the interesting March 1967 issue of *The Annals of the American Academy of Political and Social Sciences,* which contains essays on the national character of the Canadians, Brazilians, Mexicans, English, French, Swedes, Russians, Israelis, Indians, Japanese, Chinese, and Australasians. The essay on the "American National Character in the Twentieth Century," with a discussion on the effects of mass media, was written by David Riesman.

26. Lester B. Pearson, "Beyond the Nation-State," *Saturday Review,* February 15, 1969, p. 24.

Additional Readings

Additional readings on the subject of nationalism may be found in *Discord and Harmony: Readings in International Politics,* edited by Ivo D. Duchacek and published by Holt, Rinehart and Winston in 1972. Analyses of nationalism by Edward Hallett Carr, Mao Tse-tung, and Karl W. Deutsch constitute Chapter 2, "Nationalism," pp. 21-31.

3
External Consequences of Internal Tensions

Antagonistic fragmentation of the human race into over 140 national-territorial compartments is the usual—and also quite useful—way of describing and understanding contemporary international politics; evidently, in analyzing inter*national* politics we focus on *nations* and their interaction. In that context terms such as "France," "China," "Egypt," and "the United States" evoke an image of territorial units each of whose national governments speaks with one single legitimate voice on the international scene, recognizing the authority and ability of every other territorial unit to commit its national community to an international obligation or action. In the case of civil war or secession there are, of course, shorter or longer periods of international hesitancy as to which of the contending parties should be recognized as the legitimate government. Finally, a successful revolutionary or secessionist group succeeds in being recognized as the new legitimate spokesman of an old or new nation-state.

We find no reason to deny the basic accuracy of this description of the world of nation-states in which we live. But we should remind ourselves that the concepts and terms "state" and "nation" are only abstractions, useful for some analytical purposes but not for all. "Nation-state" is an oversimplified shorthand term for a very complex aggregate of individuals and groups. Externally, a nation-state is deemed one and indivisible; internally, however, every nation-state is divided by administrative or intrafederal boundaries (counties, regions, provinces), class antagonism, ideological clashes, political competition, and/or ethnic-racial conflict. One of the many issues that often split a nation into two or more rival camps is also the goals and methods of the nation's foreign policy. As a result nation-states speak with many conflicting voices, not only on matters of domestic concern but also on the subject of international relations. Instead of our previous compact image of a national actor endowed with one single legitimate voice on the international scene, there emerges another image, that of a *multivocal* actor, a nation-state whose internal cacophony is perfectly audible on the international scene. Its many discordant voices may affect or be affected by foreign governments or groups.

The abstraction of a nation-state as a single-voice actor is usually expressed in a diagram that depicts the state as a pyramid whose peak, the national government, speaks with one single voice to other nation-states (see Figure 3.1). The term "government" should be understood as a composite of the national executive (E on the diagram), legislature (L), and judiciary (J). In foreign policy and defense the executive has a dominant position, only partly affected by the legislature and the judiciary; international political relations occur mostly on the executive level. The authority of the government to act effectively on the international scene is based on its control of or support by party activists, voters, the mass media, interest groups, the military establishment, and the administrative bureaucracy, especially the diplomatic service.

INTERNATIONAL ROLES OF DOMESTIC OPPOSITION

There is no territorial state in the world without some form of internal dissent. Democracies are usually defined as systems in which legitimate opposition to the government and a free market of ideas are not only permitted but deemed essential to the functioning of the system; yet even in the most authoritarian socialist and fascist systems there are factions and individuals, within and outside the ruling group, that hope to capitalize upon the errors of the leaders. Like the government, the opposition is a complex composite of interacting groups and individuals. The existence of an opposition to a national government's domestic and foreign policies, whether legitimate, conspiratorial, or latent necessarily corrects and complicates the excessively neat image of a territorial state as a pyramid whose governmental peak has the sole right and ability to engage in cooperative or hostile contacts with other single-voice actors. Using for brevity's sake such terms as "France," "China," "Egypt," and "the United States," all governments know that within all nation-states there are groups that favor or advocate a foreign policy different from that espoused by the government. Governments sometimes hope and at other times dread that the barely audible or thunderous voices of legitimate or

FIGURE 3.1
THE ILLUSION: STATES AS MONOLITHS

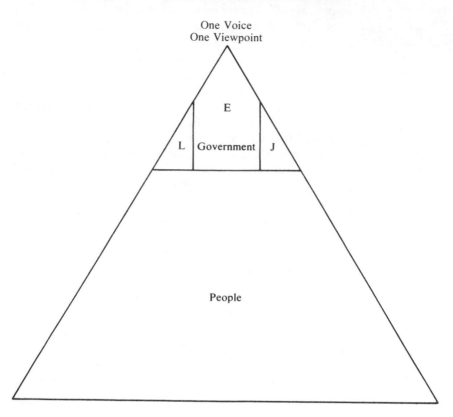

One Voice
One Viewpoint

E

L   Government   J

People

illegitimate dissent will become the official voice of a foreign nation tomorrow. Following the death of a statesman, a new election, a parliamentary vote of no confidence, impeachment in the presidential systems, or a *coup d' état,* the voice of dissent may be transformed into the official voice of a new government; in the case of a territorial secession, the leader of ethnic dissent may become the spokesman of a new nation and its first government.

For the purpose of a more refined analysis, therefore, the image of a nation as a neatly delineated Cheops pyramid should be altered; a more realistic symbol of a miltivocal actor may perhaps be the stepped pyramid of Saqqara (see Figure 3.2). In this scheme, the national government is still at the apex of the stepped pyramid because the government alone has the legal, political, and physical capacity to initiate and maintain its nation's commitments and actions on the international scene; it also has an awesome capability to control or suppress dissent, that is, to have the last coercive word. Under the apex, however, we find five horizontal layers, each protruding into the international environment; thus, each layer has its own point of actual or potential contact with foreign governments or related nongovernmental groups abroad.

The five major segments of a national system are: opposition groups in the usual political and competitive sense; ethnic-racial groups; functional interest groups, including multinational corporations; institutions and groups oriented toward the study, promotion, or critique of foreign policy; and the mass public. The five layers obviously represent an oversimplification of the reality, which, if depicted accurately, would have to be represented as a multilayered mosaic in which all elements are continually changing their positions. But however broad our five categories are, they deserve a further analysis.

Political Opposition

By political opposition we mean political and ideological groupings, open and clandestine, whether forming a legitimate political party, a faction within a single-party system, or an underground conspiracy. Whatever the form, an opposition group is potentially the government of tomorrow and this probability places it on the international scene before its accession to power. Within limits, dictated by prudence and courtesy to the existing government, foreign nations maintain discreet contacts with op-

FIGURE 3.2
THE REALITY: STATES SPEAKING
WITH MORE THAN ONE VOICE

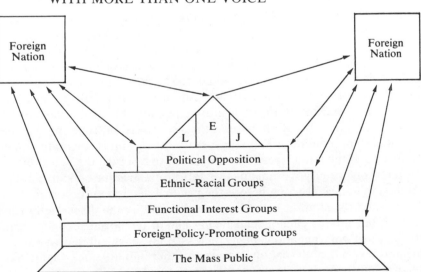

Solid lines with arrows at both ends indicate a two-way traffic from and to foreign nations; they illustrate messages and signals either initiated by foreign nations and addressed to receptive dissenting groups within the target nation or messages or signals initiated by dissenters from within the nation and addressed to receptive outsiders.

position leaders if they are deemed to be probable candidates for national leadership.

In the study of international politics analysts often use theatrical metaphors as shorthand expressions of a complex situation; thus we refer to nations as actors on the international scene, playing roles and occasionally withdrawing behind iron curtains. Elaborating somewhat facetiously on such theatrical metaphors, we may describe the government on our diagram as the principal star-actor, while the opposition groups appear to us as understudies who, like all understudies, hope for or actively contribute to the downfall of the star performer.

Ethnic-Racial Groups

The term "ethnic-racial groups" should be understood broadly as also including lingual and religious groups if they are aware of their separate identities and endow them with ethnic connotations. Three types of ethnic-racial groups with potentially significant roles on the international scene may be distinguished: (1) territorial ethnic groups, (2) dispersed groups, and (3) migrants. Another dimension to be considered is the presence or absence of "blood-relationship" to related ethnic-racial groups abroad constituted as sovereign territorial states, for example, the relationship of American blacks to African states, German minorities in East Central Europe to Germany, the French-speaking inhabitants of Canada, Belgium, or Switzerland to France, or the Turkish minority on Cyprus to Turkey. By contrast, Karens in Burma, Georgians in the Soviet Union, and Indian tribes in the United States cannot ethnically or racially relate to any particular foreign state.

A territorial ethnic community may be defined as an aggregate of individuals and groups that share common values, purposes, fears, and experiences within a more or less clearly delineated territory and are aware of the geographic confines of their common interest. Territorial ethnic communities may, and often do, seek an independent territorial destiny by means of national self-determination, that is, secession from the existing political system (empire or polyethnic state): their aim is to create a new nation-state. If their aim is realistic or deemed so by outsiders, it is often in the interest of foreign governments to establish clandestine or open contact with the ethnic leaders long before their actual accession to power.

Ethnic and racial groups that have settled and live in dispersion or as migrant labor groups cannot realistically aim at territorial secession and territorial self-determination; nevertheless, they have often played significant roles on the international scene as either initiators or recipients of foreign support. At times their domestic pressures on the national government have foreign inspiration, direction, and funds.

Foreign migrant labor became a major domestic and international problem in Western Europe in the 1970s. In 1973, for instance, there were over 4 million foreign workers in France among its 52 million inhabitants; the immigrants came mostly from the Mediterranean area. A similar situation existed in Germany, Belgium, Holland, and Switzerland. Thus a new interethnic tension developed in Europe on two levels: first, natives resented foreign workers and their different styles of life; second, foreign workers resented the low wages they were paid, discrimination in housing, and uncertain union protection. Necessarily, their grievances provoked an international echo, since the governments of Algeria, Spain, Portugal, Greece, Italy, and Turkey could not remain deaf to the complaints of their migrant citizens directed at the host countries. Chapter 11 will return to this issue in connection with foreign interference in domestic affairs. The explosion of ethnic intolerance in a Europe that, in principle, plans a supranational unification sounds a depressing note of irony.

The mass migration in Europe began in the early 1960s when the economic boom in the West European Community and Switzerland became an evident fact not only to the economists, statisticians, and tourists but also to the paupers in Spanish, Portuguese, Yugoslav, Greek, Turkish, South Italian, and North African villages. As an American journalist based in Brussels, the "capital" of the West European Community, put it,

> They come not so much because they see in the Community a chance for a better life but because the Community offers the *only chance* to make a living. Carrying their belongings in paper-and-string bundles or cheap cardboard suitcases, they depart for the North. . . . As in the United States, migrant workers have become indispensable. Without them, many industries would cease to function. Migrants willingly take on the low-paying, menial, but necessary jobs that no one else will do. By working for low wages, they give their employers a valuable competitive edge in world markets. After more than a decade of reaping these benefits, however, Europe now finds itself with an expanding and unassimilated group of foreign workers—increasingly costly to government and industry, newly militant in their demands for a share in the good life, and a growing threat to the social and political stability of their host countries.[1]

Strikes and violent clashes between foreign workers, on the one hand, and employers, authorities, and native workers, on the other, occur frequently. In 1973 about 400 striking foreigners idled 7,000 French workers at the Renault car factory near Paris. In the same year in the south of France, where a building boom had attracted great numbers of Algerian workers, hostility between local residents and "the too-foreign, too-numerous newcomers spilled over into physical release."[2]

Functional Interest Groups

Functional interest groups represent a very broad category of groups that often promote their special interests in competition or conflict with the national government. Some of these groups limit their activities to the domestic scene and try to influence the nation's foreign policy in their favor by pressure on the executive or legislative branches of government. Their international role is very indirect. Other special interest groups, such as those representing labor, business, agriculture, the professions, and the arts, have organizational links with related groups abroad.

Multinational Megacorporations These organizations, whose branches and assets are spread over the whole world, promote their special corporate interests and therefore find themselves in conflict not only with foreign (host) governments of developed or developing countries but also with their own (home) government. A good example of conflict with the home government, labeled a "flagrant case of corporate disloyalty" by Senator Henry M. Jackson, is the Exxon Corporation's obedience in 1973 to King Faisal of Saudi Arabia rather than to the United States Commander-in-Chief. When ordered by King Faisal to cut off supplies refined from Saudi Arabian crude oil to the United States armed forces in the middle of the fourth Arab-Israeli War in 1973, the Exxon Corporation complied. During a subsequent congressional hearing, held on January 24, 1974, J. K. Jamieson, chairman of the Exxon Corporation, explained this corporate behavior by the need to remain in business and added that the Saudi Arabian embargo on the export of crude oil and products derived from it to the United States "included deliveries to the United States military of products derived from Saudi Arabian crude. These developments and actions taken by Exxon were promptly reported to the Department of Defense." When an individual denies his cooperation to the military, he may invoke his right as a conscientious objector; are we perhaps entering an era of "corporate conscientious and financial objection"? A recent book on selective conscientious objection, entitled *A Conflict of Loyalties*, edited by James Finn (New York: Western Publishing, 1968), illustrated the main theme of the book by a cover design that featured a sword split in two: from the broken steel a peace dove rose to the skies. In the case of oil companies the conflict of loyalties could be illustrated by an oil well and tower emerging from a broken missile.

Several analysts and also a recent United Nations study (see Document 3.1) regard the mighty multinational megacorporations mostly American, but some British, Japanese, Dutch, French, or Swiss, as the single most serious challenge to the present division of humanity into sovereign nation-states; they see these corporations as actors on the international scene second only to and sometimes superior to a nation-state. One of the recent studies of multinational corporations, edited by Luiz Simmons and Abdul Said (New York: Praeger, 1974), is actually entitled *The New Sovereigns: Corporations as World Powers*.

An American banker expressed this thought in an address praising the

DOCUMENT 3.1

MULTINATIONAL CORPORATIONS AS ACTORS ON
THE INTERNATIONAL SCENE

One of the main actors in contemporary international relations is the multinational corporation. Although its interests and objectives usually transcend those of home and host countries, it can in turn be affected by intergovernmental relations and it may even be used by some governments as an instrument of foreign policy. Its power and spread allow it to influence, directly or indirectly, the policies and actions of home and host countries and at times to contribute to placing countries in interdependent or dependent positions.

Relationships between multinational corporations and nation-states can produce tensions and conflicts. . . . Traditionally, host countries, and recently some home countries also, have found that the global context in which corporations operate and the many options open to them can restrict the effectiveness of government policies. . . .

In spite of reservations, the majority of host countires have, on the whole, encouraged foreign direct investment. . . . To many host countries—especially developing—the location of decision-making centers outside their borders suggests that the multinational corporations may foster a pattern of international division of labour which perpetuates politico-economic *dependencia* [see p. 72 for a similar Chinese argument concerning the so-called socialist division of labor, which allows the Soviet Union to control and manipulate the economies of dependent people's democracies in Eastern Europe].

The impact of multinational corporations thus raises questions ranging from permanent sovereignty over resources to possible conflicts with national priorities and to distortion of consumption patterns and income distributions. . . . The economic impact is only one aspect of the effect of multinational corporations. . . . The perceived threat to the country's traditions and heritage often affronts the nationalistic or reformist forces of the host country.

Tensions have also arisen between multinational corporations and home countries. In the United States, the effect of multinational corporations on employment and the balance of payment is a matter of concern to organized labour. . . . The multinational corporation has also been singled out as affecting [the] monetary, fiscal, and trade policies [of the U.S. government].

From Department of Economic and Social Affairs, United Nations Secretariat, *Multinational Corporations in World Development,* New York: UN Publication ST/ECA/190, 1973, pp. 71-73.

role of the "new globalists" and "advance men," allegedly devoted to the idea of "economic one-worldism":

The political boundaries of nation-states are too narrow and constricted to define the scope and sweep of modern business. . . . Businessmen [who] often wear the robes of diplomats . . . are more influential than statesmen in many quarters of the globe.[3]

And another observer concluded that the multinational corporation is "a modern concept evolved to meet the requirements of the modern age [while the nation-state] is still rooted in archaic concepts unsympathetic to the needs of our complex world."[4]

Other observers hold a contrary view, denying the alleged impotence of nation-states. Their basic argument is that, confronted with the challenge of nonnational forces, nation-states will increase their control of natural resources, using them politically as the Arabs used oil in 1973-1974, supervise more closely all economic activities, using taxing powers as an instrument, and above all, tighten their control over any foreign entry into their national domains. The possibility of nationalization of multinational corporations will always be present (see Figure 3.3). In Samuel Huntington's words:

> These predictions [quoted above] of the death of the nation-state are premature. They overlook the ability of human beings and human institutions to respond to challenges and to adapt themselves to changed environments. They seem to be based on a zero-sum assumption about power and sovereignty: that a growth in the power of transnational organizations must be accompanied by a decrease in the power of nation-states. This, however, need not be the case. Indeed . . . an increase in the number, functions, and scope of transnational organizations will increase the demand for access to national territories and hence also increase the value of the one resource [access] almost exclusively under the control of national governments.[5]

Communist Multinational Enterprises   A similar competition between transnational economic imperatives and national interests has developed in the communist world, where all major enterprises have been socialized, that is, in our world of nation-states, *nationalized*. Industries, mines, and banks now belong to and are manipulated by communist governments that, despite their collective devotion to Marxism-Leninism, represent often competing or conflicting *national* economic and developmental interests. Therefore the collectivized world is not immune to national resentment directed against the power and direction of communist supranational "corporations." Whereas in the capitalist world multinational corporations are often resented because so many of them are based in the United States and therefore are deemed associated with the political and strategic interests of the United States, in the communist orbit multinational joint projects are resented because they have been planned or imposed by Moscow and are deemed intimately associated with the political and military might and interests of the Soviet Union.

FIGURE 3.3
MULTINATIONAL CORPORATIONS
OR NATIONALIZATION?

"Algún día, mi hijo, todo eso será nuestro."

Drawing by Stevenson; © The New Yorker Magazine, Inc. *The New Yorker Magazine*

In response to the challenge which the West European Community began to represent in the 1960s, the Soviet Union and its Eastern European allies developed various joint investment projects, including East German and Czech loans to the Polish coal-mining industry and the Polish-Hungarian joint enterprise "Haldex" to process coal slack. A joint electricity grid links the Soviet electrical system with those of Eastern Europe; "Friendship Oil Pipelines" feed oil from the Soviet Ural Mountains to Eastern Europe. There is also the communist International Bank for Economic Cooperation, set up in 1964, and the communist International Investment Bank, set up in 1971. The flow of technology, investment, and skills is supervised by the Council for Mutual Economic Assistance (Comecon), presided over and firmly controlled by the Soviet Union. In addition to the Soviet Union and its six East European allies (East Germany, Czechoslovakia, Hungary, Poland, Rumania, and Bulgaria), Mongolia and Cuba are also full members. Communist Yugoslavia attends some of Comecon's meetings, while pro-Chinese Communist Albania never attends. Comecon was set up in 1949 as a Soviet response to the Marshall Plan and now functions as a response to the West European Community.

The communist international system combines some features of the West European Community with several aspects of the multinational megacorporations of the Western world. And it contains, as mentioned previously, some of its ills and resentments. The Soviet Union coined the term "socialist division of labor" to describe, justify, and promote what, from a purely economic point of view, appears sound: that is, a principle according to which every people's democracy should specialize in accordance with its natural resources and skills, such as shipbuilding (Poland), heavy machinery and industry (Czechoslovakia), aluminum (Hungary), and oil and grain (Rumania). Understandably, the underdeveloped communist republics could not help seeing themselves cast in the permanent role of "specialists" producing raw materials for the more advanced communist republics, with the Soviet Union at their helm; in other words they were playing the role of subcolonies for industrial communism. Rumania refused to play such a role and has since 1963 vigorously insisted on its right to balanced modernization and industrialization. According to the Rumanian thesis, building communism on a world scale is incompatible with the notion of perpetuating the difference between advanced industrial and agrarian states; such a division would also perpetuate the dependence of the communist states producing wheat and raw materials on the industrially developed communist states. As early as 1949, John H. Herz correctly analyzed the problem of national-economic antagonism in the framework of a common creed:

> Such questions [as] "Who will be industrialized first?" or "Who will form the colonial raw material basis for exploitation by a more advanced comrade republic?"—questions which are the very basis of the Tito conflict—show that [the] security and power dilemma . . . has its impact on actual policies in a collectivized world as it has had in capitalistic and precapitalistic aeons.[6]

The issue of *simultaneous* growth in the communist world, a growth that would prevent the dominance of the industrial communist "north" over the underdeveloped communist "south," was already an issue in the first Soviet-Yugoslav dispute. It forms the background to both the Rumanian and Chinese objections to Soviet policies. Having freed itself from Western colonial encroachments, the People's Republic of China, in particular, was to experience a most brutal form of discriminatory practices and economic sanctions, applied by the "fraternal" party of the Soviet Union.

A bitter editorial, published in the ideological journal of the Chinese Communist party, *Hung Chi*, in 1964, accused the Soviet Union of a policy whose aim was "to force fraternal countries to abandon industrialization and become sources of raw materials and markets for Soviet surplus products." The editorial also equated the socialist division of labor with colonialism:

> In the name of the international division of labor the leaders of the Soviet Union oppose the adoption by fraternal countries of the policy of building Socialism by their own efforts and developing their economies on an independent basis. They attempt to turn them into economic appendages.[7]

As far as China was concerned, the Chinese journal illustrated the Soviet method of sanctions for nonconformity by recalling the

> unilateral decision to withdraw 1380 Soviet experts working in China, to tear up 343 contracts and supplementary contracts on the employment of experts and to cancel 257 projects of scientific and technical cooperation, and to pursue a restrictive and discriminatory policy against China.[8]

According to the program of the Communist party of the Soviet Union in 1961, the Warsaw Pact nations were to enter the era of coordination of national economic plans, combination of production within the world socialist system, and specialization. The program affirmed that

> it will be developed and perfected more and more. . . . the first country to advance communism [that is, Russia] facilitates and accelerates the advance of the entire world Socialist camp . . . it is a component of building of the Communist society by the people of the entire world Socialist system. . . . [the Soviet people are] destined by history to start on a new road, to blaze a new path of social development . . . breaking new roads for mankind.[9]

These assertions echoed the words of the Russian Bolshevik leader Zinoviev, who declared while addressing the Petrograd Soviet on September 17, 1920: "We cannot do without the petroleum of Azerbaijan or the cotton of Turkestan. We take these products which are necessary for us, not as the former exploiters, but as older brothers bearing the torch of civilization."[10]

As seen from the vantage point of Rumania, China, Cuba, Albania, Yugoslavia, Czechoslovakia, or Hungary, the slogans "breaking new roads for mankind" and "bearing the torch of civilization" are dangerously close to the old imperialist "white man's burden." The communist states suspect that the Soviet Union could conceivably promote its economic goals at the expense of lesser communist states, like any other imperial power. They may recall Lenin's words, uttered at the Eighth Party Congress in 1919: "Scratch many a Communist and you will find a Great Russian chauvinist."[11]

Only future developments can tell us whether the multinational megacorporations of the West and the socialist joint enterprises of the communist world represent new forms of truly transnational relations, challenging the old division of mankind into nation-states, or whether they represent new forms of great-power control, interference, and colonialism without actual political control of foreign territories. Chapter 7 will deal with imperialism and chapter 11 will deal with economic international relations more specifically.

Foreign-Policy-Promoting Groups

Foreign-policy-promoting groups and institutions include the mass media, activist segments of the scientific, academic, and student communities, opinion leaders, influential columnists, and private groups devoted to the study of foreign policy. By promoting particular policies (isolationist or interventionist, for instance) or protesting current government policies, these groups attempt to alter national policies rather than national leaders. In this sense they represent a less important subnational influence on the international scene than opposition groups or territorial-ethnic communities, whose chance of becoming a new government or a new nation-state places them squarely on the international scene long before they attain their goals. The promotional groups nevertheless often catch the attention of foreign powers since these groups may succeed in influencing government policies by means of mobilization of public opinion for or against a given policy or by direct influence on the lower echelons of the foreign-policy-making bureaucracy. Thus promotional groups, too, may become recipients of moral or financial support from abroad and so become secondary or tertiary actors on the international scene. Again using a theatrical metaphor, we may say that promotional groups play the modest role of "teleprompters."

The Mass Public

The mass public rarely plays any significant international role apart from its support or lack of it for the government or the forces that oppose it. The mass public is fairly uninformed about and usually uninterested in government policy; it begins to move only when aroused or organized by parties or interest groups or when panicked by a major crisis. A minor continuing role of the general public on the international scene is its increased mobility, which results in vastly increased foreign travel and unprecedented mass contacts between various nations and differing cultures. Like the applauding or hissing audience in a theater, the general public is invited to participate in the drama only by the most modern and daring producers.

An interesting recognition of the role of tourists on the international political scene was contained in a warning issued by the top ideological spokesman of the Soviet Communist party, Mikhail A. Suslov (*Kommunist*, Moscow, March 1962): "We evidently insufficiently take into account the fact that in contemporary conditions the influence of bourgeois propaganda is spread among us along many paths: through the press, radio, all kinds of delegations and *tourists*" (italics added). An American socialist magazine, *Monthly Review* (March, 1964), commented on the statistic that 1,300,000 foreign tourists spent 17,900,000 nights in socialist Yugoslavia and added: "These tourists bring with them not only their money but their prejudices, ideologies, and style of living. To say that they constitute a virulent source of capitalist infection in the Yugoslav body politic is an understatement."

Multilevel International Politics

The frequency, scope, and intensity of contacts between domestic nongovernmental groups, on the one hand, and foreign governments or nongovernmental groups, on the other, depend on two basic factors: the degree of *penetrability* of the walls of national sovereignty, which is evidently greater in open, free societies than in authoritarian states; and the degree of *receptiveness* of individuals and groups to transnational appeals. Both factors are obviously at variance with the traditional concepts of impermeable national sovereignty and undiluted national loyalty.

The contemporary relative penetrability of sovereign states is only partly due to modern technology. The revolutionary development of rapid mass communications and transportation has only accelerated and generalized what has been true since antiquity: Ideologies, concepts (good or bad), fashion, and solutions of technical problems seep through the walls or iron curtains of sovereignty, even if no one organizes such communications or exchanges. New communications techniques, from telecommunication satellites to tape recorders, and an unprecedented scope and tempo of travel have been added to what has always been the main cause for the circulation of ideas throughout the civilized world—the desire of the intellectual elite as well as the general public to be informed. No government can really erect around a nation an impenetrable wall of ideological sovereignty. Censorship can delay but cannot stop the circulation of ideas. Somehow people have always learned what is going on in the world and what might be worth emulating. Signals and symbols get through and thus affect the policy-making process. A neo-Westphalian peace, based on a peaceful division of the globe between two or more isolated ideological blocs, seems impossible in present times. Mass communications and transports mock the formula *cuius regio, eius ideologia* (He who controls a realm determines its ideology—a modern version of the earlier *cuius regio, eius religio*, a formula of the Westphalian Peace Treaty of 1648, discussed previously).

As for the actual or potential receptiveness of individuals and groups to foreign arguments or favors, it too is only partly a result of modern awareness of the growing interdependence of the nations of the world. Personal or group dissatisfaction with the existing conditions of life has always made individuals or groups more or less receptive to foreign promises, encouragement, or corruption. Foreign messages of sympathy and offers of cooperation for the purpose of causing damage to the national government are the more eagerly received the more intense is the dissatisfaction of individuals and groups with their government. Penetrability of the state and receptiveness of groups and individuals to foreign promises is the stuff of which foreign interference in the domestic affairs of another nation is made. Chapter 11, which deals with espionage, subversion, and propaganda, will return to this theme in more detail.[12]

From the preceding analysis two conclusions may be drawn: First, while national governments, acting on behalf of their states, definitely remain the decisive actors on the international scene, their interaction represents only one, though the primary, level of international politics. In addition, there are political relations that link national governments with foreign opposition parties or factions, and ethnic, functional, or foreign-policy study groups. Some of these links are established at the invitation of foreign nongovernmental groups; other links are initiated by governments; and still other transnational contacts among nongovernmental groups often occur without the knowledge or consent of any government. Transnational contacts among revolutionaries in various countries and transnational activities of multinational corporations belong to the last category. An effort is now being made to systematically differentiate between the traditional term "*inter*national relations" (meaning intergovernmental contacts) and the new term "*trans*national relations," meaning "contacts, coalitions, and interactions across state boundaries that are not controlled by the central foreign policy organs of governments."[13]

The fact of multilevel international relations may be illustrated by a diagram based on the concept of the multivocal actor. Figure 3.4 indicates three basic levels of international contacts:

The primary channel of interaction is marked *1*. It represents cooperative or hostile relations between national executives—international politics in the traditional sense of the word.

The dashed line marked *2* represents a two-way traffic of influences or pressures between the government of one nation and nongovernmental groups or individuals of another nation. These contacts are initiated by either the government or a nongovernmental group. Governmental interference in the domestic affairs of another nation belongs to this category.

The dashed line marked *3* illustrates transnational nongovernmental relations, including direct contacts between peoples. These relations usually affect national policies by passing through the national body politic. This is why the dashed line marked *3* turns upward to the governmental peak of the national pyramid. Multinational corporations and revolutionary organizations belong to this category.

Only three basic lines of contacts among nations are marked on the diagram. In fact, these contacts are innumerable; crisscrossing and over-

FIGURE 3.4
MULTILEVEL INTERNATIONAL
POLITICS

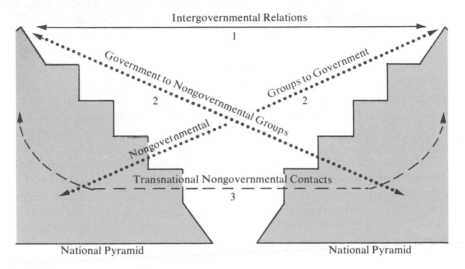

National Pyramid   National Pyramid

lapping one another, they are so intertwined that they form a very dense and complex web of interaction. It is never easy to disentangle this web and consequently it is never easy to determine who or what has primarily caused a particular international event. At this point our purpose is only to emphasize that internal dissent and tension—idcological, political, economic, social, class, ethnic, or racial—represent a necessary qualification of the excessively neat image of a nation-state as a monolith interacting with other seemingly monolithic units.[14]

ETHNONATIONALISM AND STATE-NATIONALISM

One internal challenge to the concept of the nation-state deserves a more detailed analysis. In the preceding discussion the terms "territorial state" and "nation-state" were often used interchangeably, as if the state and the nation were nearly synonymous, as in some cases they are. In many cases, however, they must be distinguished. The term "territorial state," or simply "state," as used in this study, should be understood in terms of the state's territory and boundaries, territorial government, claim to sovereignty, external recognition, and some degree of internal support for and cooperation with the territorial authorities. The term, "nation," if understood in terms of a cultural-ethnic community, may not coincide with the territorial state boundarics.

In the English language, and in American terminology in particular, two additional problems lead to confusing the terms "state" and "nation." In the United States "state" describes one of the fifty components of the federal union; the adjectives "federal" and "national" are frequently used interchangeably. On the other hand, the French, Swiss, Indian, or Soviet "State" (usually with a capital "S") refers to the French Republic, the Swiss Confederation, the Indian Federation, or the Soviet Union as a whole.[15] The second problem of the English language is its incapacity to form derivatives from the noun "state:" substitute adjectives are formed from the nouns "nation" and "city." Thus we are unable to refer to a government or territory as "statal" and use "national" instead. Politics among states are called international rather than interstatal. And when referring to legally recognized membership in a territorial state we call it either "nationality" (suggesting an ethnic, racial, or lingual content) or "citizenship" (suggestive of a legal connotation and in most languages derived from the noun "city"). Most Americans would reply "I am American" to a foreign passport officer's inquiry about their "citizenship" or "nationality."[16] None would probably think about his home city and only a few would consider it practical to stress their ethnic or racial alienation when presenting their "national" passport abroad.

Three State-Nation Relationships

Whatever difficulty our confusing terminology may present, three different relationships between "nation" in its ethnocultural sense and "state" in its politico-organizational sense can be listed:

1. The frame of the state is coextensive with that of the nation. A few nations have and administer such states. Only fourteen of the contemporary 140 states can be called truly national states or monoethnic units (composed of one nationality only). Seven of the 14 monoethnic states, however, have some of their ethnic brethren living beyond the state's boundaries.[17]
2. A nation may be temporarily divided by internal war or external force into two states. Two centuries ago an authority on international law, Emmerich de Vattel, wrote that civil war gives rise, within the state, to two independent parties that regard each other as enemies and acknowledge no common judge. These two parties may be viewed as forming, for a time at least, two different and hostile "states." If the division persists over a considerable span of time, the artificial split into two states may finally produce such an internal cohesion and identification of the population in each state with each other and with their territorial system that the two territorial systems may also become two nations in the ethnic-cultural sense. The same effect, as several observers have argued, can be produced by external force (sometimes in combination with internal war). If, for example, the present divisions of Germany, Korea, Vietnam, and China

(mainland China and Taiwan) are allowed to continue for a very long time, the communist and noncommunist halves of these nations may ultimately produce such contrasting traditions, histories, values, and institutions that nations in the ethnic and cultural sense will finally issue from what was initially an externally imposed division and an ideological conflict within a nation. One can also speculate whether today, in the area between Canada and Mexico, there would be two separate states *and* nations had the South, and not the North, won the civil war.

3. Most states in the world today are polyethnic or multinational, that is, they contain several ethnic groups (nationalities, minorities), some of which may view themselves as nations entitled to possess and administer their own territorial states. Living against its will in a polyethnic system (a multinational state or colonial empire), an ethnic group could be called a *stateless nation*. The principle according to which a nation should have a territorial state of its own, that is, should be able to transform its nation-hood into statehood, is usually called the right of *national self-determination*. As noted previously, one practical precondition for transforming nationhood into statehood is possession of and identification with a geographically delineated territory. A widely dispersed ethnic group can strive for dignity, respect, recognition, equal rights, or compensation for past injustices, but it can hardly claim statehood, except perhaps by inducing a mass exodus beyond the existing state boundaries in order to create a new territorial home somewhere else, as the Zionists have done.

THE EMERGENCE OF POLYETHNIC SYSTEMS

The origin of polyethnic empires and states is varied. Four of the most usual reasons for the emergence of polyethnic systems are conquest, migration and settlement, agreement, and alienation.

Conquest

Many polyethnic systems have resulted from military conquests or their variants or from consequences such as *interimperial* agreements on respective spheres of colonial expansion (England, France, Germany, Belgium, Spain, and Portugal in Africa), *intraimperial* imposition of convenient administrative delineation cutting across ethnic or tribal boundaries (France and England in Africa), or *interdynastic* agreements (England and Scotland, for instance), frequently in the form of marriage contracts exchanging people and territories as royal gifts. Step by step, invasion by invasion, or marriage by marriage, many an expansive nation has included in its "national" territory adjacent or distant areas and nationalities. Some conquests are less conspicuous than others. Expansion into contiguous areas inhabited by peoples of similar skin color, such as that of Russia into Siberia and central Asia, is less obvious than a maritime conquest of distant lands inhabited by peoples of a distinctly different race and color. The American conquest of a sparsely inhabited land in the west is somewhat similar to the Russian expansion into Siberia; the American conquest of the Philippines and other Pacific possessions is similar to the colonial conquests by western European nations.

Many Asians and Africans consider conquest over great distances and the difference in color the most essential element in the definition of imperialism. This is why they rarely view the Russian conquest of Moslem or Siberian nationalities as an imperialistic or colonial conquest. This is an obvious fallacy, sometimes referred to as a "salt-water fallacy"; it implies that imperialist conquest over rivers and mountains is less objectionable than conquest directed at territories over the seas. In this connection oppression of white men by white men is viewed by many Asians and Africans as different and perhaps less deplorable than the oppression of colored men by white men. Psychologically this is understandable. Politically it may lead to curious attitudes, such as the ambivalence of many Asians and Africans toward the "white" Soviet suppression of the "white" Hungarian revolt of 1956 or the Soviet invasion in 1968 of socialist Czechoslovakia when it tried to assert its own national brand of socialism. The Soviet "pacification" of both Hungary and Czechoslovakia, including the imposition of leaders acceptable to Moscow, did not essentially differ from the methods used by colonial imperialists in the past.

Because foreign colonial conquerors artificially grouped many different tribes or nationalities into centrally administered units, many a new state emerging from the former colonial framework must immediately deal with a legacy of unresolved interethnic tensions within its boundaries. Following a liberation achieved in the name of the principle of national self-determination, the successor governments are often plagued by the problem of a continuing demand for national self-determination on the part of groups comprising the nation.

With regard to Africa, many authors refer to the problem of "tribalism" rather than to terms such as "minorities" or "nationalities," which seem to be reserved for Europe and Asia. Tribalism is often quoted by the African leaders themselves as the reason for the instability within African states, whose boundaries, cutting across tribal lines, were imposed by colonial rulers. Sometimes the argument is heard that the democratic multiparty system, if adopted in African states, would only perpetuate tribal divisions instead of creating a party system in the Western sense that would cut across the tribal lines in a supratribal consensus. Western authors see in tribalism either an impediment to nationalism in African states or a reason for a different form of African nationalism. The fact that there are over seven hundred sub-Sahara African societies in an anthropological sense and almost fifty sub-Sahara nation-states in a political sense led an American scholar, Leonard W. Doob, to the following observation:

The majority of Africans, who as a matter of fact are not "detribalized," find the new nationalistic symbols quite meaningless or at least unrelated to the personal problems pressing down upon them. . . . The idea of the new nation, consequently, seldom throws them into ecstasy, and they continue to think of themselves primarily as tribesmen and not as nationals. . . . When the shift from tribalism to nationalism in Africa does occur, however, an intense patriotism regarding the new nation can be anticipated. . . . Traditional Africans are patriotic, which is perhaps only asserting that they are human beings.[18]

While the term "tribe" is appropriate in the anthropological and sociological respects, in the context of our present analysis there is practically no difference between the political implications of the existence of a tribe and the existence of a national minority.

S. O. Adebo, chief of the Yoruba tribe of the Nigerian federation (one portion of the tribe is also in the neighboring state of Dahomey), has pointed out that in the framework of the search for national unity African tribes are not different conceptually from European or Asian racial groups and national minorities. Chief Adebo also protested against the Western tendency to refer to African citizens as natives rather than nationals, and to African groups (which are often based on the identity of language or customs) as tribes rather than nationalities. In an article in the *New York Times Magazine* of March 1, 1964, Adebo added:

One of the tribal groups in Nigeria numbers as many as eight million people—more than the entire population of Austria, or Chile, or Sweden, or Israel. Any wish on their part, however, to retain their identity within the larger grouping of the Nigerian Federation would be called tribalistic. The continued reluctance of the Scots, on the other hand, to lose their identity in the British personality—or the movement in Quebec for greater recognition of the five million or so French-speaking Canadians—is called, not tribalistic, but nationalistic.

This is not to deny that these divisions could be an impediment to national unity, but my point is that they have the same effect, damaging or otherwise, whenever they occur in Nigeria, Great Britain, or Canada. Tribalism is tribalism everywhere.

Ten years later, Nigeria offered a good illustration of the close parallel between intolerant tribalism and intolerant ethnonationalism. There are more than 250 tribal-ethnic groups in Nigeria; the Hausas in the north, the Yorubas in the west, and the Ibos in the east are the three largest; until the census, held in 1973, each was thought to have accounted for about 15 percent of the total population. The preliminary results of the census indicated that, in population, the north had significantly surpassed both the west and the east. In July 1974, amidst growing tension, the leader of the Yorubas, Chief Obafemi Awolowo, openly challenged the honesty and accuracy of the census. The cause of the furor was not only emotion but also, as in all interethnic tensions, very practical economic considerations: The census was to be the basis for Nigeria's economic planning, including the sharing of more than $7.6 billion in oil revenues; for compulsory primary education; and for proportional representation of various ethnic-tribal regions, to be implemented when civilian rule and elections would replace the military rule, introduced in 1966.

Concern about the centrifugal tendencies in their polytribal or polyethnic states has led several African states to include in their constitutions prohibitions of racial or ethnic propaganda. The Constitution of Senegal (Article 51), for instance, prohibits "any regionalist propaganda which may threaten the integrity of the territory of the Republic." Similarly, the Constitution of Chad (Preamble) states that "all manifestation of propaganda of an ethnic nature will be punished by law." The Ivory Coast's Constitution (Article 6) interdicts "all particularist propaganda of racial or ethnic nature." Evidently, the possibility of secession is deemed a greater danger than possible threats to the freedom of speech and advocacy of unpopular ideas.

Migration and Settlement

Polyethnicity is often the result of migration and settlement that took place in eras in which linguistic and nationalistic intolerance was less developed than it is today. This is true of the Chinese and Indian minorities in southeastern Asia and the German and Hungarian minorities in south-eastern and central Europe. Unlike Switzerland, the multinational states of Europe and Asia have often been dominated by one ethnic group at the expense of the alien groups. These peoples, treated as aggregates of second- or third-class citizens, are called *dependent peoples* in imperial structures and *national minorities* in states. There are, for practical purposes, no differences between the two terms; both minorities and colonial dependent peoples are foreign-dominated nationalities whose interests, culture, and languages are inadequately represented—if represented at all—in the direction and administration of the polyethnic structure. National minority has been defined in a study undertaken by the secretary-general of the United Nations in 1950 as a "more or less distinct group living within a state which is dominated by another group."[19] The fact of domination rather than that of numerical superiority is the decisive point. Thus, paradoxically, according to the United Nations definition, the black (numerical) majorities oppressed by white (numerical) minorities in South Africa, Rhodesia, Angola, and Mozambique are "national minorities" in a political sense.

Agreement

Polyethnic states may have at their origin an agreement, buttressed by geography and external pressure, for defense against a common enemy. This is the case in Switzerland, which has grown into a solid federation of twenty-two cantons and three half-cantons around the original cluster of three German cantons, Uri, Schwyz, and Unterwalden. The Swiss state does not reflect the interest and culture of one nationality at the expense of another, and is largely neutral to the various nationalities under its jurisdiction. Thus, the four linguistic groups of Switzerland—German, French, Italian, and Romansh—have created, for all practical purposes, a "quasi-nation," a Swiss nationality that is deemed superior to its linguistic components. It took the Swiss over six hundred turbulent years to make their polyethnic state an example of interethnic cooperation and tolerance; only one hundred years ago Switzerland nearly split asunder in a civil war, caused by an antagonism between the Catholic minority and the Protestant majority. They are clearly aided by geography; the neighboring great powers, needing a buffer state between them, exercised adequate unifying pressure in that direction. Yet even today the model polyethnic state of Switzerland is not entirely free from some degree of inner tension. In the late 1960s, for instance, French-speaking Swiss in an area in the mountains of Jura contained in the German-speaking canton of Bern vehemently pressed their claim for territorial autonomy. With the exception of some extremists, they did not want secession from Switzerland or accession to France, but their own self-ruling canton or half-canton. In 1974 a plebiscite clearly decided in favor of a division of the biethnic canton into two half-cantons, one German and one French.

Alienation

Our analysis of multinational situations would not be complete if we were not also to consider possible divisions within a seemingly homogeneous nation endowed with a single language, religion, and culture. Alienation may occur as a result of unsatisfactory or oppressive rule by the government. If, for instance, as Karl W. Deutsch notes, a government fails to meet the increasing burdens put upon it by the population,

> a growing proportion of the population is likely to become alienated and disaffected from the state, even if the same language, culture and basic social institutions were shared originally throughout the entire territory by rulers and ruled alike. . . . The secession of the United States and of Ireland from the British empire, and of the Netherlands and of Switzerland from the German empire may serve in part as examples. . . . If [a government] proves persistently incapable or unresponsive, some or many of its subjects will cease to identify themselves with it psychologically.[20]

Decades or even centuries of seeming national harmony may be interrupted by an explosive disagreement over the present and future of the territorial state system. A group that becomes alienated, especially if it occupies a more or less well-defined area, may develop its own nationalist feelings, becoming antagonistic to the existing state and desiring a state of its own. As we have already noted in connection with internal wars and foreign-imposed divisions of homogeneous nations into hostile states, ideology too can become an incubator for ethnonationalism. An ideologically alienated portion of what has seemed a homogeneous national community may acquire a sense of separate destiny and a desire to form its own territorial state. It then may become necessary, as the American Declaration of Independence rousingly proclaims on behalf of totally alienated Englishmen, "for one people to dissolve the political bonds which have connected them with another, and assume among the powers of earth the separate and equal station to which the laws of nature and nature's God entitle them."

MINIMIZING INTERETHNIC TENSIONS

Systems composed of several ethnic groups experience all the difficulties in maintaining internal order that plague homogeneous nations, plus another; they must maintain harmony among mutually suspicious ethnic groups some of which may view themselves as potential national states. Interethnic tensions and mistrust within multinational systems are of interest to the student of international politics for two reasons: First, the behavior pattern of ethnic groups within a state closely resembles the behavior pattern among states; ethnic groups are therefore laboratories of sorts for the study of conflict and cooperation among established states. Second, interethnic tensions within multinational systems are an invitation to foreign meddling. Men treated as second-class citizens or as potentially disloyal elements tend to behave as such when an opportunity arises or when a helping hand from the outside is proffered; sometimes gaining external support is the only way to end domestic injustice. Outside nations will sometimes consider it their humanitarian or fraternal duty—or so they say—to protect the rights of some ethnic group against domestic oppression. Pursuing their own interests by fishing in ethnically troubled waters, they support or incite one group against another within the foreign state, thereby merging interethnic tension with international conflict. In just this way the Nazis promoted the claims voiced by the German minorities in eastern Europe before World War II; however justified or unjustified their recriminations against the Polish or Czechoslovak rules were, under the impact of Nazi power, manipulation, and propaganda, in the 1930s German ethnic groups became instruments of the Nazi expansion eastward. Similar fears of the minorities' identification with the outsiders, especially when the "outsiders" are ethnically, racially, or lingually related to the oppressed group, characterize the contemporary Indonesian, Malay, Thai, and Burmese attitudes toward the actual or potential links between the

People's Republic of China and the overseas Chinese. In this case too the new power and prestige of the People's Republic of China could conceivably transform the Chinese minorities in Southeast Asia into vanguards of a Chinese expansion southward. A large majority of these overseas Chinese have remained unassimilated for centuries. "They regard themselves as Chinese," notes A. Doak Barnett in his study of the People's Republic of China and its relationship to Asia.

> Their primary loyalties are toward China as their homeland. Throughout Southeast Asia they have great economic power. Southeast Asian governments, newly independent and nationalistic, fear possible political subversion by their Chinese minorities, and they also resent the concentration of economic power in the hands of unassimilated, alien groups.[21]

There are other examples of interethnic tensions that either cause or are influenced by tensions between states: the West occasionally promotes Ukrainian, Baltic, and other non-Russian nationalism within the Soviet Union; during his official visit to Canada Charles de Gaulle on behalf of France voiced support for the French separatists in Quebec; and the People's Republic of China, Cuba, and Algeria tend to support black militants in the United States.

In the preceding chapter nationalism was treated as a highly cohesive force, which, in many circumstances, it is. Nationalism has succeeded in the past in consolidating many different and even antagonistic groups into relatively homogeneous national communities, such as Germany, Japan, and to a lesser degree Italy and France.

In other situations nationalism has accentuated divisive trends within nation-states. While it is generally true that territorial-national unity tends to assert itself in the hour of common danger to all, the cementing effect of external enmity is not always so firm and so automatic as national leaders may wish. First, the exact meaning of a collective interest to be defended may be a matter of controversy. (Chapter 4 will deal with the concept of national interest in more detail.) Should a portion of the territory be sacrificed for the sake of human lives, or should human lives be sacrificed to preserve the state's territorial integrity? Second, individuals and groups may disagree on their estimates of the immediacy or gravity of common danger. There was little disagreement in the United States about common danger following the Japanese attack on Pearl Harbor in 1941; there was more disagreement following the German submarine warfare in World War I; and there was profound disagreement following the United States's escalated involvement in Vietnam. And, third, not all external threats are actually aimed at or perceived by the territorial community as a whole. In Lewis Coser's words:

> Outside conflict unites the group and heightens morale . . . [but] the

relation between outer conflict and inner cohesion does not hold true where internal cohesion before the outbreak of the conflict is so low that the group members have ceased to regard preservation of the group as worthwhile, or actually see the outside threat to concern "them" [the government, a ruling party, or a ruling ethnic group] rather than "us." In such cases disintegration of the group, rather than increase in cohesion, will be the result of outside conflict.[22]

The external threats are often quite selective, promising heaven to some groups (ethnic minorities, racial groups, workers, intellectuals, or ideological cousins) and threatening the ruling groups with hell. The aim of such selective threats, very frequent in the past quarter of a century, is to keep a nation from achieving or maintaining internal cohesion. This is a consequence of the simple fact that individuals as citizens of a given territorial state are also members of several communities other than the nation-state. Their identification with various communities they feel they belong to varies. Ethnic, racial, or ideological loyalty may be in conflict with the citizen's loyalty to the territorial state. Usually, but not always, people's loyalty to subnational groups is less intensive and less unconditional than their loyalty to the territorial state. In Chapter 1 we quoted Rupert Emerson's definition of a nation-state as the largest community which, "when the chips are down, effectively commands men's loyalty," overriding the claims of other groups. It is perhaps appropriate to qualify this definition and admit that at times, "when the chips are down," a nation-state may burst open at its ethnic, racial, or ideological seams. Oppression or neglect may endow localism or ethnic pride with the explosive ingredients of rebellious secession. Then a dissatisfied territorial-ethnic or territorial-ideological group, aiming at independent control of its own territorial destiny, may see itself as a future nation and state and may, like any other nation and state, seek foreign allies and support. The existing territorial national authority is bound to view such a revolutionary quest for national self-determination and secession with foreign support as high treason and collusion with the external enemies of the state. For the insurgents, however, it is simply the exercise of their sacrosanct right of national self-determination.

Interethnic tension represents a serious problem on both the domestic and international levels: internally, interethnic conflict threatens domestic peace, order, and progress; externally, interethnic conflict facilitates foreign meddling, which, in turn, may cause international tension and conflict. This has always been known, and history has therefore recorded various attempts to eliminate or minimize tensions between ethnic groups within multinational systems. Two basic approaches may be identified: (1) elimination of polyethnicity by such means as national self-determination resulting in territorial separation (secession), assimilation, expulsion or mass migration, genocide, and redrafting state boundaries; (2) acceptance and regulation of polyethnicity, which may include a grant of separate and unequal or separate and equal status, the imposition of a quota system, and the establishment of various forms of territorial autonomy.

National Self-Determination

The most radical solution of a tension between groups that feel they are potential nations is the exercise of the so-called right of national self-determination. It is closely related to yet different from the revolutionary right to make and unmake governments according to the will of the people. The right of democratic revolt seems to justify seizure of control of the state as a whole by dissatisfied citizens when and if procedures of peaceful adjustment fail. They do not secede from, but capture, the state. On the other hand, the right of revolutionary national self-determination presupposes that the political dissatisfaction is coextensive with a territorial sector of some broader administrative structure (empire or state). The dissatisfied citizens do not claim the right to change the government of the whole territory but only of that portion they claim as their own and desire to detach from the rest. If people have the right to determine their own government, logically they should also have the right to determine whether they desire to live as a part of some polyethnic structure or constitute their own territorial state. Since no contemporary group that is potentially a nation can live in a vacuum, in practice the right of national self-determination means the right to secede from the existing structure, be it an empire, a multinational state, or a territorial state in which the consensus has disappeared and the dissent is now expressed in territorial terms.

The right to constitute one's own national state may be claimed, as in fact it has been, by dependent conquered peoples, by foreign-dominated ethnic minorities, or by alienated groups that have developed a feeling of separate entity to the point of considering themselves a different nation. This claim can be a result of political, economic, or social discrimination. The reason for it may be a different concept and way of life from that of the larger group or a different program for the future. The French historian Ernest Renan, previously quoted, has defined a nation not only as a heritage of glory and grief in the past, but also in terms of an "agreement and a clearly expressed desire to continue life in common." If this desire disappears, nations may split asunder and become two or more nations. Abraham Lincoln, speaking in 1848 of the Mexican War, reemphasized the message of the American Declaration of Independence:

> Any people anywhere, being inclined so and *having the power*, have the right to rise up and shake off the existing government and form a new one which suits them better. . . . Nor is this right confined to cases in which the whole people of an existing government may choose to exercise it. *Any*

portion of it that can may revolutionize and make their own so much of the territory as they inhabit. [Italics added.]

Yet, a few years later Lincoln viewed the secession of the southern confederacy as inferior to the concept of the preservation of the Union. The right of the South to form a separate nation was dealt with on the battlefield. If military power had not determined the issue at that time, two American federations might now exist in the area between Mexico and Canada. The South and the North, after having shared the "glory" of 1776, discovered ninety years later that, so far as the South was concerned, they had no "agreement and desire to continue life in common," which Renan identified as the main fountain of national feeling and cohesion. As we have already seen, antagonism and mutual hatred do not need to be expressed in different languages to become an explosive charge in the foundations of a state. It was on December 4, 1860, that the spokesman of Georgia, Senator Alfred Iverson, proclaimed:

> Sir, disguise the fact as you will, there is an enmity between the northern and southern people that is deep and enduring, and you never can eradicate it—never! You sit upon your side, silent and gloomy; we sit upon ours with knit brows and portentous scowls. . . . We are enemies as much as if we were hostile States. I believe that the northern people hate the South worse than ever the English people hated France; and I can tell my brethren over there that there is no love lost upon the part of the South.[23]

Foreign observers of the American scene often note with marked sarcasm that the American nation, at least in the North, is strangely able to celebrate within a span of ten days in February both the symbol of successful secession and that of successful suppression of secession: On February 22 the secession from England is lauded on George Washington's birthday, while ten days before, on February 12, Abraham Lincoln is remembered for having saved the Union from southern secession.

The truth is that no nation, even when created in the name of national self-determination, likes to see the same principle applied internally against itself. This is one of the basic ambiguities of the concept of national self-determination and secession. In theory and from the point of view of those who have been denied statehood, the principle of national self-determination is a sacred right. From the standpoint of those who are at the helm of an empire or a territorial state, the revolutionary assertion of the right of secession must necessarily appear to be a major disturbance of peace and order that the state has every right to suppress. In spite of the profound difference in the merits of each case, this is substantially how George III must have viewed the revolutionary tactics of the American colonists, how Abraham Lincoln must have viewed those of the rebellious South, how France must have viewed those of the Algerian nationalists, and how Nigeria must have viewed the Biafran separatists.

Microstates   If we were to recognize without any qualification that every group that feels itself to be a nation has the right to establish its own state and determine its government, the question necessarily would arise, how can one reliably distinguish a potential nation from *any* dissatisfied group of citizens? In his brilliant study on nationalism, Rupert Emerson points out that "to accept the right of self-determination in blanket fashion is to endow social entities which cannot be identified in advance with a right of revolution against constitutional authority of the state, and even to obligate the state to yield to the demands of the revolutionaries.[24] Clearly, if self-determination were literally to be treated as a right, a corresponding duty would have to exist somewhere. It does not. Nor is there any consensus on the criteria by which one could determine which dissatisfied group has the right to break away from an established political unit. An international commission that examined the desire of a Swedish group inhabiting the islands of Aaland to separate from Finland and join Sweden (Finland used to be a province of Sweden) warned in its final report against excessive ethnic atomization of the existing states:

> To concede . . . to any fraction of a population, the right of withdrawing from the community to which they belong, because it is . . . their good pleasure, would be . . . to inaugurate anarchy in international life; it would be to uphold a theory incompatible with the very idea of the State as a territorial and political entity.[25]

Many yardsticks for potential states have been invoked on different occasions, all highly controversial: *defensibility* (does this apply in the atomic age?); political *maturity* of the people (how does one measure it?); economic *viability* (no nation is really self-sufficient); and adequate *size*.

By the 1960s, when many large colonies had become independent nations, one negative aspect of the demand for statehood had appeared on the scene with insistency, that is, that "some territories may not be able to stand alone by reasons of size and population if they become independent or attain self-government." That independence may degenerate into abject dependence seems to be the gist of several warnings that granting independence to very small (how small?) territories "leads inevitably to neocolonialism . . . states which are not viable run the risk of falling into the pernicious and selfish influence of larger states." The quotations are from a speech by Charles Pinochet, a United Nations representative of Chile (a former Spanish colony), delivered on November 30, 1963. Pinochet then suggested a special United Nations study, the purpose of which was to find some responsible limits to irresponsible exercise of the right of self-determination and secession. This was endorsed by E. R. S. R. Coomaraswamy, a United Nations representative of Ceylon, a former English colony, now renamed Sri Lanka. The irony of the situation in which two former colonies that had seceded from empires warned against the dangers of secession was underlined by the concluding words of the Chilean representative:

> I very much fear that when we come to what we might call the bottom of the barrel, we shall find that, for the major part, these colonies [to be granted independence and statehood] are very small, some with 1000 or less inhabitants living on five or six square miles, but which are nevertheless indicated as colonies with their own identities. To promote the independence of colonies and immediately thereafter to ignore the future of such people is easy to do but it is irresponsible. Liberty, yes; but not liberty to live in poverty and uncertainty in a world of super-powers where each day is fraught with peril.

The warning could, of course, be applied to a great many existing states and former colonies with more than a thousand inhabitants. Pinochet advised thinking in terms of larger federations—a recommendation that has not been followed by his own country. Eighteen sovereign Latin-American states now administer a territory that was once divided into only eight Spanish colonies. "In a world marching toward greater integration of sovereignties, economies and peoples, in the search of unity," concluded the Chilean spokesman, "it seems to be a backward step, a backward and illogical attitude, to put the emphasis on dismemberment and division, whether of political, economic, social or cultural nature."

This sounds like a very reasonable argument, which if it had been professed and adhered to in the last two hundred years, would not have led to the disintegration of the Spanish, Austro-Hungarian, English, or Dutch empires and the creation of Chile, Ceylon, India, Poland, Indonesia, and Algeria.

Of course, one can anticipate the argument that the comparison is entirely false, that this or that struggle for independence was right and therefore different. But, as often happens, the situation is usually viewed differently by those who maintain the *status quo* and those who have decided to oppose it actively.

In his annual report for 1967, the then secretary-general of the United Nations, U Thant, raised the question of the seventy-odd tiny islands or territories, all sparsely populated and poor, and their relationship to the United Nations when they become, as they all may, independent states. "While universality of membership is most desirable," noted Thant, "like all concepts it has its limitations and the line has to be drawn somewhere." Where should the line be drawn? Should a population of 300,000 or 500,000 be the minimum required? The Maldive Islands, with only 100,000 inhabitants, was admitted to full United Nations membership in 1965. But what should be done about a smaller entity, such as Anguilla with only 6,000 people? This Caribbean island refused a federal union with the neighboring islands of Saint Kitts and Nevis, and on February 7, 1969, by a vote of 1739 to 4, decided to eliminate all remaining ties with Britain. Such small entities should be allowed to join the specialized agencies of the United Nations when they need help with their economic, social, and health problems without becoming members of the political organs of the world organization. At the same time it might be useful to extend a United Nations collective guarantee of protection against aggression or occupation to these weak and vulnerable territorial entities. So far the trend in the United Nations General Assembly with its Afro-Asian-communist majority has been to press for full independence and United Nations membership even for microscopic islands. Freely chosen integration with the former master or territorial autonomy in a free association with the former ruling nation seem to have been ruled out as possible options in the exercise of the right of self-determination, although in 1960 (General Assembly Resolution 1541/XV) *free* integration or *free* association were listed as possible forms of self-government in addition to independence. A good illustration of a United Nations imposition of its own interpretation of what self-government and self-determination should mean was the case of a British mini-independency, the Seychelles Islands (54,000 inhabitants scattered over 85 islands in the Indian Ocean, northeast of Madagascar). The Seychelles leader, Prime Minister James Mencham, initially objected to the United Nations resolutions asking for full independence and argued for an economically and politically advantageous free association with Britain. Finally, Prime Minister Mencham had to yield to the combined pressures of the United Nations majority and the Organization of African Unity and accept the "challenge of independence" and United Nations membership for 1975.

In the 1970s the United States was confronted with the question of what to do with the Marshall, Mariana, and Caroline Islands in the Pacific, which were first a German colony, then a Japanese mandate, and now a strategic trust territory of the United States. The territory is an agglomerate of 2141 individual islands with a combined area of 687 square miles (about two thirds the size of Luxembourg). The majority of the people are Micronesians; the minority are Polynesians. A great insularity exists among the people in the Mariana Islands (Yap, Palau, Truk, Ponape, Kusaie, Nukuoro, and Kapingagamarangi; the last two are Polynesian). Each group speaks its own separate and distinct language. Each has its own customs and pattern of living. There is some cultural hostility. The United Nations received a complaint from the Marshall Islands, which resents the trade activities of the Ponapean tribe from the Marianas. Among other things, the petition said:

> We understand and appreciate the American ideal of "One People" but we are a separate country from Ponape with our own separate customs and culture and language and have no more desire to be classed or merged with the Ponapeans than France has desire to merge with Germany or China with Japan. We feel that it is unfair to us as a people to be lumped

together with other groups of Micronesian peoples as one people. We are proud of our race and our heritage.[26]

The point of absurdity has perhaps been reached, and yet one may ask, has it? In 1968 the tiny Pacific Island of Nauru became an independent state. Nauru has about 5263 acres and 3100 inhabitants. Half of them are Nauruans and the other half includes mostly Chinese and Gilbert and Ellice Islanders; there are also two hundred Europeans. The island, located 1300 miles northeast of Australia, had been administered by Australia under the League of Nations mandate system and later by Australia, New Zealand, and Great Britain under the United Nations Trusteeship system. Nauru has not yet applied for United Nations membership. Regular United Nations teams visited Nauru when it became independent and reported that the Nauruan people could not be regarded as a potential state and that all the Nauruans would have to be resettled in some other location in a few decades, when their phosphate deposits, the source of their present relatively high standard of living, are exhausted (see Document 3.2). On January 31, 1968, Nauru nevertheless became a state and celebrated its independence, displaying a new flag. The Nauruan police force dutifully presented arms and fired a twenty-one gun salute. There were almost as many visitors from the established nations and mass media as there were Nauruans. Economically and administratively sound arguments against independent statehood for many countries have often proved incapable of defeating emotional or absurd arguments. It is difficult to counteract the contagion of independent statehood in an era of emotional nationalism. The most reliable criterion for the achievement of statehood in the name of self-determination turns out to be the will and capacity of leaders to obtain a territorial state for their people despite the powerful arguments of peace, order, and economic viability invoked by the defendants of the status quo. In the final analysis, nothing less than the capacity of a national movement to obtain its own state—either by diplomatic means or by force— —determines the success or failure of the so-called right of national self-determination.

In another context some years before and during World War I, the Hapsburg imperial government tried in vain to convince its Czech, Polish, Croat, Slovak, and Slovene subjects that the otherwise admirable economic and administrative entity known as the Austro-Hungarian Empire was in need of reform and not dissolution. Prophecies were then heard that national independence of small successor states might result in misery and dependence on other big powers—as it finally did. But rational economic arguments are usually of no avail against an emotion-laden desire to become independent. The reactive nationalism of the Slavic peoples within the German and Hungarian-dominated empire could not think in terms of economics when it was dreaming of its own armies, flags, and coats of arms.

DOCUMENT 3.2

A UNITED NATIONS REPORT ON NAURU

The Mission noted that a change had also taken place in the outlook of the Nauruans who have progressively adapted themselves to a European way of life. In economic matters, the Nauruans are becoming accustomed to a higher standard of living which, it should be emphasized, is almost exclusively dependent upon the phosphate industry.

However, the phosphate deposits are a waning asset, which it is estimated will be exhausted in about sixty-five to seventy years at the present rate of extraction. With the closing down of the industry, the whole or most of the indigenous population will have no alternative but to look for a new livelihood. The Nauruans are beginning to be aware of this problem and are becoming concerned about their future on the island.

In regard to this and other related problems, the Mission feels it imperative to observe that the Nauruan people cannot be regarded as more than a small community, and in no case as a potential State; moreover, this community, isolated as it is on a small island in the Pacific, has services exceeding by far those of any other community of similar size.

The Mission is of the opinion that once the phosphate is exhausted the Nauruans cannot increase, or even maintain, their present standard of living. The Mission therefore believes that steps should be taken both by the Nauruans and the Administration to face this possibility realistically and in a manner which would enable Nauruans, as early as feasible, to make any necessary adjustment without further social complications. The Mission, without wanting to appear to be dogmatic, is of the opinion that resettlement in some other location, as expressed by the Nauruans themselves, may be the only permanent and definite solution.

From UN Trusteeship Council, *United Nations Visiting Mission Trust Territories, 1953: Report on Nauru.* New York: Publication T/1077, 1953.

Similarly, in the United States mistrust by blacks of the rule and interests of the white majority has led to black militant movements with clear and strident nationalist overtones. Scholars with field experience in European, Asian, or African nationalism were less surprised by the emergence of black nationalism and its forms of expression (from new poetry to a new flag and Afro-inspired hairdos and clothing) than were those who had accepted and believed in the liberal dream of the American melting pot. The search for black identity (''negritude'') and power, and the demands for equal but separate schools and for courses of study in black as well as Puerto-Rican or Chicano (American-Mexican) history and culture have all had their antecedents in other parts of the world. The only significant tragic difference between many European, Asian, and African ethnic quests for self-determination and self-expression and American black nationalism has been the relative absence in the United States of a noncontroversial territorial goal, except for the occasional glorification of ghettos and the somewhat vague demand for a separate black state in the South or North-west. Eldridge Cleaver, without being territorially specific, found a parallel between the outlook and goals of the ghetto Jews at the time of Theodore Herzl and the present territorial dimension of the black people in the United States (see Document 3.3).

A Right to Ethnic Homogeneity?

When a ruling group has the power to oppose secession and yet feels that interethnic tension has become internally or internationally un-bearable, elimination of polyethnicity by other means than secession may be envisioned. Several methods of eliminating undesirable ethnic groups from the national territory have been attempted and implemented; using these methods national governments have invoked a rather controversial "right" of ethnic or racial homogeneity. In such a context ethnic homogeneity has often been described as a protection against foreign

---

DOCUMENT 3.3

THE JEWS AND THE BLACKS:
A PARALLEL

The parallel between the situation of the Jews at the time of the coming of Theodore Herzl and the present situation of black people in America is fascinating. The Jews had no homeland and were dispersed around the world, cooped up in the ghettos of Europe. Functionally, a return to Israel seemed as impractical as obtaining a homeland for Afro-America now seems. Renowned Jewish leaders were seriously considering transporting the Jews to Argentina, en masse, and developing a homeland there. Others seriously considered obtaining from England the territory of Uganda in East Africa for the same purpose.

The gravitational center of the Jewish population at that time was in Eastern Europe. With the outbreak of massive pogroms in that area near the end of the 19th century, the Jewish people were prepared psychologically to take desperate and unprecedented action. They saw themselves faced with an immediate disastrous situation. Genocide was staring them in the face and this common threat galvanized them into common action. Psychologically, black people in America have precisely the same outlook as the Jews had then, and they are therefore prepared to take common action for the solution to a common problem.

From Eldridge Cleaver, *Post-Prison Writings, and Speeches by the Author of "Soul on Ice."* New York: Random House/Ramparts Books, 1967-1969, pp. 67-68.

---

interference as well as a guarantee of internal peace and progress. Here we shall discuss four of the usual methods of implementing the principle and ideal of ethnic homogeneity.

Assimilation Assimilation and integration of alien groups, whether voluntary or forced, may create national homogeneity instead of previous ethnic heterogeneity. Many nations that presently are relatively homogeneous have been formed by a long process of socialization of more or less dissimilar groups into one national integrated whole. Japan is a good example. Rarely, however, is assimilation totally successful. France, for instance, is today a relatively homogeneous composite of many Latin, Germanic, and Celtic groups. But even France experiences some ferment on the part of unassimilated groups in the Celtic portion of Brittany, in Provence (the Occitan movement), in Corsica, and among the Basques, an ethnic group that lives between France and Spain on both sides of the Spanish-French boundary and manifests discontent against both French Paris and Castilian Madrid.[27] Paradoxically, the plan for a united Western Europe has awakened some dormant separatist tendencies among groups that have been viewed as assimilated.

Redrafting State Boundaries Changing state boundaries so as to make them coincide with ethnic boundaries seems a possible method of achieving ethnic homogeneity between two neighboring states whose geographic boundaries are marred by minor ethnic overlaps. While seemingly simple, correction of state boundaries for the sake of ethnic homogeneity is rarely practiced: strategic, economic, historical, or political conditions usually militate against even a very minor shift of state boundaries.

Liquidation Extermination of undesirable ethnic or racial groups as a method of achieving national homogeneity is now prohibited by international law; the 1948 Genocide Convention (see Document 9.3) proclaims the destruction of an "ethnic, racial, or religious group as such" a crime which the nations "undertake to prevent and punish." Nazi Germany's commitment to the extermination of the Jewish race is one of the recent examples of mass murder for the purpose of attaining racial "purity."

Mass Migration Another method of achieving an ethnically acceptable way of life is mass migration. Some migrations have been initiated by a racial or ethnic group itself to escape discrimination, injustice, or death. The exodus of Jews from Egypt is one example. Another was the attempt of American freed slaves to migrate back to Africa in 1822. It finally led to proclamation of the Republic of Liberia on Africa's west coast. Its Declaration of Independence of 1847 (see Document 3.4) copied

DOCUMENT 3.4

LIBERIA'S DECLARATION OF INDEPENDENCE (1847)

We the people of the Republic of Liberia were originally the inhabitants of the United States of North America.

In some parts of that country, we were debarred by law from all the rights and privileges of men—in other parts, public sentiment, more powerful than law, frowned us down.

We were every where shut out from all civil office.

We were excluded from all participation in the government.

We were taxed without our consent.

We were compelled to contribute to the resources of a country, which gave us no protection.

We were made a separate and distinct class, and against us every avenue to improvement was effectually closed. Strangers from all lands of a color different from ours were preferred before us.

We uttered our complaints, but they were unattended to, or only met by alleging the peculiar institution of the country.

All hopes of a favorable change in our country was thus wholly extinguished in our bosoms, and we looked with anxiety abroad for some asylum from the deep degradation.

The Western coast of Africa was the place selected by American benevolence and philanthropy, for our future home. Removed beyond those influences which depressed us in our native land, it was hoped we would be enabled to enjoy those rights and privileges, and exercise and improve those faculties, which the God of nature has given us in common with the rest of mankind.

Under the auspices of the American Colonization Society, we established ourselves here, on land acquired by purchase from the Lords of the soil.

---

the format and structure of the American Declaration of 1776, but there are instructive differences, especially the list of grievances against racism. It does not read as an outdated document. After World War II, following the carving of Moslem Pakistan out of India, and in the wake of violent clashes between the Hindu and Moslem communities, about eight million Hindus and nine million Moslems began their unorganized migrations in both directions. Under the shadow of mass panic and communal murders, they left their ancestral homes and sought refuge within their respective religious communities, which had now become territorial states. In 1972, however, following the secession of East Pakistan, now Bangladesh, from West Pakistan, a new mass movement within the same religious community took place. This time the issue was ethnic-lingual hostility between the

Moslems of West Pakistan and Bihar living among the Bengali-speaking Moslems of Bangladesh.

Another form of migration on a mass scale is the expulsion of undesirable ethnic groups on the basis of a unilateral governmental decision or an agreement between the governments concerned. Following World War I, for example, Greece and Turkey (and also Bulgaria and Turkey) agreed on a forcible exchange of their respective minorities. The Turks were moved from Greece to Asia Minor, and Greek settlers there were correspondingly shipped back to Greece. The mass migration represented a considerable hardship for those involved. Families were uprooted from their homes and from occupations they had enjoyed for generations, without having adequate homes or jobs waiting for them on the opposite side of the migration line. This mass movement was undertaken with the clear aim of achieving national homogeneity and removing a cause of friction between the two neighbors. In favor of the exchange it can at least be said that Greece and Turkey, after having become more nationally homogeneous, were able to cooperate on the international scene more effectively than when their relations were constantly marred by accusations and counteraccusations of ill-treatment of their respective minorities. The new Greek-Turkish crisis over Cyprus at the end of 1963 and then again in 1974, however, revived much of the former antagonism and suspicion.

After World War II another mass migration took place in Eastern Europe. The summit meeting held at Potsdam between July 17 and August 1, 1945 (attended by Stalin, Truman, and Churchill, who was later replaced by Clement Attlee following the Labour Party's victory in the British parliamentary elections), authorized Poland, Czechoslovakia, and Hungary to expel their respective German minorities into Germany and thus become more or less nationally homogeneous states. For several reasons Hungary did not avail itself of the opportunity. Poland, on the other hand, expelled not only its former German-speaking citizens but also the Germans from the newly acquired territories in the west which were to compensate Poland at the expense of Germany for its territorial losses to Russia in the east. The Big Three authorized the expulsion of about eight million Germans from Poland and Czechoslovakia after both countries had begun to push their German-speaking populations into the Soviet and American zones of Germany. Only the later phases of the expulsion, the diplomatic term for which was "transfer," were properly organized and supervised by the American and Soviet authorities, who, as administrators of occupied Germany, were responsible for receiving and resettling six to eight million expellees in the midst of chaotic postwar conditions and food and housing shortages.[28]

In 1972 the black African state of Uganda expelled about 40,000 brown-skinned Asians who had migrated there and settled during the period of the British Empire and who, after Uganda's proclamation of independence in 1962, chose British citizenship rather than Ugandan. In one of his speeches

Uganda's President Idi Amin voiced his approval of Hitler's treatment of the Jews. Obviously, racism is not limited to the white race only.

In our nationalism-ridden world, the search for national or racial homogeneity as a corollary of the struggle for national self-determination represents a body-and-soul annihilating experience for the expellees; their opinion is rarely sought by the governments concerned. Nationalistic emotions, desire for revenge, and racial myths are, of course, not the only causes of the desire for national homogeneity. As noted previously, there are also pragmatic considerations of national security, immunity against foreign meddling, and concern for harmonious internal order and progress. No doubt, some ethnic groups commit treason and, in collusion with a foreign state, try to damage the state in which they live as citizens. This is particularly true of those ethnic minorities that are or consider themselves to be separated from their main ethnic body and tend to feel emotionally and politically bound to it; good examples are the German groups in Eastern Europe before World War II, the Chinese minorities in Southeast Asia, and the Palestinian Arabs in the state of Israel. It should be noted, however, that disloyalty and treason are not necessarily limited to ethnic groups but are also practiced by ideological groups and disgruntled individuals. Certainly, tensions and conflicts within nation-states are only partly caused by interethnic tensions. We may well ask whether ethnic homogeneity represents as great a gain for external security and internal harmony and progress as the advocates of drastic ethnic measures claim.

Recognition of Polyethnicity

Secession may often be prevented and the unity of a polyethnic state preserved by accepting the inalterable fact of polyethnicity and drawing appropriate constitutional and political conclusions therefrom. Four usual forms of acceptance and regulation of polyethnicity are discussed below.

Separate but Inferior Status The granting of separate but inferior status is one form of legal recognition of "nonexterminability" of an ethnic or racial group. Ethnic groups have often been reduced by law or practice to the level of second- or third-class citizens. They are separate, sometimes by choice and sometimes not by choice, and inferior despite their opposition to such a status. All colonial powers imposed this status on their colonies. South Africa and Rhodesia have incorporated this principle into their constitutions.

Separate and Equal Status Such a status, granted ethnic groups by law and practice, is possible only within a framework of practiced tolerance—a very rare occurrence in the world today. It basically guarantees that ethnic groups can, *if they wish so*, remain separate and develop their own identity, culture, institutions, and political as well as economic power while enjoying equality in all respects. If the separate-and-equal status does not include also the right of the group to change its aspirations and, for example, to abandon its separation in favor of assimilation, then such a status, in reality, implies inferiority because the separation has been imposed or is being maintained by the decisive will of the ruling group. It should be reemphasized that ethnic and racial groups vary in their resentments and goals. In some countries ethnic groups resent discrimination because their desire is assimilation and integration. Until the 1960s integration was generally the aim of the black community in the United States. In other countries, especially in Europe and Asia, many ethnic, racial, and religious groups resent being assimilated and integrated against their will and desire to remain distinct yet equal. Their claim is "Equal but Separate" which is now also the demand of various American black groups. As these ethnic or racial groups see it, they are in danger of being deethnicized ("denationalized") and of losing their identity. The dominated groups seek equality with dominant groups not only in the sense of nondiscrimination but also in the form of guarantees of special rights and the rendering of certain special services. Demands have been made for (1) separate but equal schools for the minority in its own language, culture, and history (a demand voiced by the Chinese minorities in Southeast Asia and by the German and Hungarian minorities in central Europe before World War II); (2) adequate facilities for the minority's use of its own language in the legislature, before the courts, and in the administration; (3) and respect for the family law and personal status of the minority and for its religious practices and interests.

Communal Proportional Representation Communal proportional representation, or the quota system, is another device that is supposed to guarantee equality to ethnic or racial minorities whose development depends on the will of a different ethnic or racial majority. It is self-evident that the democratic concept of deciding all issues by a majority vote cannot apply to a situation in which an ethnic minority represents a *permanent* minority, that is, a group that, unlike political or ideological groups, can never become the ruling majority. The application of communal proportional representation is a partial remedy and protection against tyranny by the permanent ethnic majority. Basically the quota system is a guarantee of participation in political processes, civil service, the police force, the army, universities (admissions and faculty), the mass media, cultural institutions, business firms, and banks. An ethnic or racial group may be granted by law a fixed proportional quota or more-than-proportional quota (for instance, to make amends for past injustice).

Of course, this does not eliminate altogether the danger of tyranny by a permanent majority over a permanent ethnic or racial minority; it only assures the minority of a presence and a voice in the decision-making processes. However ingenious a quota system may be, it cannot change a minority into a majority or replace the democratic principle of deciding issues by a majority vote with an even more controversial principle of deciding issues by the will of a numerical minority against the wishes of a numerical majority. If the minority is protected against the majority absolutely, by a *veto* (that is, all decisions must be unanimously agreed on by the voters or the leaders), such a veto power may paralyze the whole system. On Cyprus, for example, the numerically inferior Turks (about 18 percent) have always dreaded a permanent tyranny by the overwhelming Greek majority. And the Greeks, on the other hand, feared lest the central authority and economic planning be paralyzed by the constitutional veto that in principle was granted to the Turks. The communal system on Cyprus ended in failure and bloodshed; intercommunal violence had to be controlled by a prolonged stay of a United Nations internal peace-keeping force. While relatively successful in preserving intercommunal peaceful coexistence on the island, the United Nations peace-keeping force could not and did not prevent the escalation of the Greek-Turkish antagonism from the internal to the international level when on July 19, 1974, Turkey decided to invade the island in order to protect Cyprus against annexation by the Greek military regime in Athens.

Polyethnic Federalism   In cases in which ethnic or racial groups occupy more or less well-defined territories, polyethnic federalism is a possible way of easing interethnic tensions. A group may be granted self-rule within its own territorial domain as a component of a federal union of legally equal communities of unequal size and wealth. Federations based on the express recognition of the territorial autonomy of the major ethnic groups constituting the union attempt to recognize the inevitability of territorial ethnicity while promoting also loyalty to the concept of a supraethnic entity, a quasi-nation, to be called the Soviet, Swiss, Czechoslovak, Burmese, Yugoslav, or Indian "nation." The Soviet "federal nation" thus comprises fifteen major nationalities; the Swiss, four linguistic groups; the Burmese, five; the Yugoslav, four major peoples; and India, thirteen major lingual-ethnic groups. The federal Czechoslovak Constitution proclaims that the republic is a sovereign state, "composed of two Nations, the Czechs and the Slovaks." Some federal constitutions, at least on paper, recognize the separate status of national component units to the point that they are granted the right of secession. This is even stated in the Soviet Constitution. The Yugoslav Constitution of 1963 declares that "the peoples of Yugoslavia on the basis of the right of every people to self-determination, including the right of secession . . . , have united in a federal republic of free and equal peoples and nationalities." The first federal Constitution of the Union of Burma was unique in the sense that it prescribed in detail the procedure necessary for secession at any time in the future. The right of secession could not be exercised during the first ten years of independent existence (1947-1957).

In practice, a federal solution based on different nationalities does not work so well as the constitutional texts suggests. In the communist federations, the real power and dominance remain in the hands of a nonfederated communist party whose totalitarian organization and method of rule usually succeeds in preventing nationalistic and secessionist self-assertion from surfacing. But as soon as the communist system is somewhat liberalized, as in Yugoslavia and Czechoslovakia, the long-buried grievances of ethnic groups reappear and press more or less successfully for a change of the constitutional federal myth into a tangible reality of ethnic self-rule. In the 1960s, the minority ethnic groups in both Yugoslavia and Czechoslovakia were granted more real autonomy than has ever been enjoyed by any nationality in the Soviet Union.

All polyethnic structures, democratic as well as communist, suffer from two types of suspicion and distrust:

First, even if the constitutional promise of divided power and cooperation among equals was initially based on a sincere decision to grant generous concessions to a group's desire for territorial identity and autonomy, no group can entirely rule out the possibility that the federation will in the long run be dominated by its most energetic, populous, or developed component. Such fear obstructed both the Dutch and the French attempts (but not quite the British) to transform their former colonial empires into federal or confederal structures guaranteeing a new partnership of equals.

Second, those elites that have decided to grant generous rights to territorial and ethnic-racial groups often fear that territorial autonomy will become a stepping stone toward secession, as indeed it might.

INTERNATIONAL INSPECTION

There is justification for international concern and possible action in cases in which denial of human or group rights within a nation-state leads to an internal conflict so severe that it may directly or indirectly affect international peace and the security of other nations. Even in the absence of such a threat to international order, political, moral, and legal arguments have now developed to challenge the traditional view that treatment of individuals and ideological or ethnic-racial groups by their national government is a matter falling within the exclusive and sovereign domestic jurisdiction of a given state. The Nuremberg war crime trials, the Genocide Convention (see Document 9.3.), the Universal Declaration of Human Rights, and the related Covenant on Human, Social, Economic, and Cultural Rights (see Document 9.1.) point to a new concept of justified international "interference" in the domestic affairs of a sovereign nation-state; in their treatment of ethnic and ideological groups national governments cannot, so these covenants assert, justify the perpetration of inhumane acts by claiming that actions carried out within their sovereign territory are not the concern of any other nation. Thus the international community claims the right to examine and condemn certain domestic acts. Short of military and economic sanction in case of acts threatening international peace and security, neither the United Nations nor any other group of nations seems to have any effective means of preventing and punishing discriminatory practices or attempts at genocide or mass murder. In 1972, for example, the world witnessed but took no action to stop the mass slaughter that occurred in the spring and summer in the African state of Burundi, where the ruling Tutsi minority engaged in a mass killing of the Hutu tribe, each side accusing the other of genocide. The total number of Hutus killed between April and August of 1972 was estimated at 100,000 to 200,000—that is, more than twice the total number of people killed by the Hiroshima bomb. Similar horror coupled with international nonaction characterized the army coup in Indonesia in 1965, which was followed by a student-led outbreak of anticommunist violence; more than 300,000 people were killed.

Another example of international concern for the treatment of ethnic groups within polyethnic systems were attempts at some degree of international responsibility for and supervision of the treatment of ethnic minorities and dependent colonial peoples in selected areas. These attempts were connected with the conclusion of World Wars I and II and the new territorial order emerging from them.

Minority Treaties

Under the League of Nations all newly created states in East Central Europe (Poland, Czechoslovakia, Rumania, and Yugoslavia) were induced to sign the so-called Minorities Treaties. The purpose of these treaties was to protect national minorities against discrimination or forced assimilation. The existence of minorities in the new states represented an embarrassing deviation from the principle of national self-determination, in the name of which these new states had been created and which Woodrow Wilson, in his Fourteen Points, called "an imperative principle of action which statesmen will henceforth ignore at their peril." There were several reasons for the departure from the principle that ethnic and state boundaries should coincide. In some instances it was clearly impossible to draw boundaries in accordance with ethnic distribution: some territories were so hopelessly mixed that state boundaries would literally have had to pass through cities, houses, and even bedrooms. In other instances the state boundaries were drawn to correspond to strategic or economic considerations. A mountain ridge, a river, or a link between industries and a raw-material base or a railroad network was deemed a more important criterion than the ethnic line. And in all cases, state boundaries were drawn in such a way as not to permit the "imperative principle of national self-determination" to augment the national territories of the defeated states—Germany, Austria, Hungary, and Bulgaria. The goal was to diminish their territories, self-determination or not.

The case of Poland is particularly interesting. Following the October Revolution of 1917 and Lenin's ill-considered war against the Polish army, Poland was able to obtain a huge portion of former Russian territory that had a large Ukrainian and Byelorussian population. Anticommunist ally Poland was encouraged by the West to become as strong as possible at the expense of dangerous Russian bolshevism. It was perhaps inevitable that when Bolshevik Russia became an ally of the West in the war against Germany in 1941, Poland would lose to Russia all and more than she had gained in the 1920s. Then, in 1945, Poland was compensated at the expense of defeated Germany. These additions and reductions of the Polish national territory, once in the east, and at other times in the west, have made the Poles wryly refer to their state as a "nation on wheels."

The "founding fathers" at the Versailles Peace Conference following World War I were no doubt aware of the contradiction between the principle and the practice of national self-determination. This awareness led to the concept of international guarantees for the minorities who, in spite of the principle, found themselves on the territories of the newly created states. In theory, the Minorities Treaties should have led to the practice of international supervision of the behavior of the new sovereign states in the realm of human rights. In reality, the treaties guaranteeing the rights of national minorities within the framework of sovereign states remained largely paper pledges. Minorities' rights were respected or grossly violated regardless of such treaties.

There was another inconsistency concerning the principle of self-determination. Not only was the Wilsonian "imperative principle" limited in practice to the claims of those nationalities considered to be allies of the victorious great powers, but it was also limited to Europe. The principle was not applied to the dependent peoples within the English, French, Belgian, Dutch, and Portuguese colonial empires. It was a right of national self-determination "for whites only." Lenin and Stalin exploited this gross inconsistency on the part of the Allies, and since that time the Soviet Union has successfully claimed to be, and partly is still credited with being, a champion of the right of national self-determination of the colored peoples of the world. Only in the 1960s was this claim successfully challenged by the People's Republic of China.

The Mandate System

With regard to the Arab provinces of the Turkish Empire and the African and Asian colonies of Germany, after World War I the Allied powers agreed on an ingenious formula called the mandate system.

In view of the wartime pledge of the Allies not to seek annexation of foreign territories, there remained the problem of what exactly to do with the Arab provinces and the German colonies that were not to be left in the hands of defeated Turkey and Germany; in a word, the question was how to annex without saying so. The mandate formula gave the answer. It allowed the transfer of territories in the Middle East, Africa, and the Pacific to the administration of a few select members of the League. These administering nations did not become the owners of the territories. A commission of experts, the Permanent Mandates Commission, was to assist the colonial nations in administering the territories with due regard to the rights and well-being of their inhabitants, including their ultimate right of self-determination. The commission was also to receive and examine the annual reports of the mandatories and advise the Council of the League on all matters relating to the observance of the mandates. It is symptomatic that the administration of not a single German colony or Turkish territory was transferred to the League as a whole but only to those victorious Allies that already had their own colonies. The Arab territories were placed into the "Mandate A" category, that is, the most advanced category, not too far from the possible grant of self-rule. England obtained Palestine and Iraq, and France obtained Syria and Lebanon. "Mandate B" and "Mandate C" categories referred to the German territories in Africa and the Pacific. They were neatly divided between France (which obtained the German parts of Togo and the Cameroons), England (German Tanganyika and the remaining parts of Togo and the Cameroons), Belgium (Ruanda-Urundi, now the independent states Rwanda and Burundi), the South African Union (German Southwest Africa), Australia (the German colony of New Guinea), New Zealand (German Samoa), and Japan (the German colony of the Marshall, Mariana, and Caroline Islands).

The Trusteeship System

After World War II the former mandate system was transformed into the trusteeship system. Chapters XII and XIII of the United Nations Charter introduced an unprecedented degree of international supervision over the administration and progress of territories inhabited by dependent peoples. The administering countries were to submit an annual report on the political, economic, and social progress of trust territories; the report was based on a detailed thirty-five-page questionnaire covering every aspect of the political and economic life of a territory. United Nations inspection teams were to visit trust territories every two years with the right to receive petitions and complaints against the administrators on the spot. Furthermore, the trust territories were granted the right of direct petition and complaint to the United Nations. And a special organ of the General Assembly, the Trusteeship Council, was to deal with all questions concerning dependent peoples in trust territories.

Three types of territories were to be placed under this administration through international inspection: former mandates; territories detached from Germany, Italy, or Japan—the enemies of the United Nations during World War II; and colonies or protectorates that imperial powers might voluntarily place under the trusteeship system.

With the exception of Southwest Africa, which the Union of South Africa illegally kept, thus unilaterally terminating the mandate of the League (a procedure found illegal by the International Court of Justice), all mandates of the League were placed under the trusteeship system. One former enemy territory and colony, Somalia, was placed under the trust system for a period of ten years. Italy was granted the administration of its colony under the supervision of the United Nations with the provision that within ten years (in 1960) Somalia must become an independent nation, which it did.

No colony or protectorate has ever been voluntarily placed under the trusteeship system. Colonial empires agreed to only very limited United Nations supervision, provided for by Chapter XI of the Charter. Even the chapter's title, "Declaration Regarding Non-Self-Governing Territories," implies that it is a form of pledge that sovereign nations have assumed with regard to their territories, acquired and allegedly owned by them and immured against an effective international inspection by the principle of domestic jurisdiction. At the time the Charter was drafted, the non-self-governing territories included India, Indonesia, Burma, Pakistan, Indochina, all of Africa except Ethiopia and Liberia, as well as the United States-governed territories of the Philippines, the Virgin Islands, Guam, Samoa, Puerto Rico, Alaska, and Hawaii. By contrast, the former mandates, now trust territories, included eleven minute fragments of the non-self-governing world, such as Ruanda and Nauru. Signatories of the Charter accepted as a "sacred trust" the promotion of self-government in colonies (full independence, mentioned in the Trusteeship Articles, is not included here) but carefully avoided establishing any United Nations machinery that would supervise and control the European and American administration of their respective dependencies. Article 73e merely obligated the administering nations to "transmit to the Secretary General for information purposes [without instructing him what to do with such information except implicitly to file it], subject to such limitation as security and constitutional consideration may require, statistical and other information of a technical nature relating to economic, social, and educational conditions." Evidently information on *political* conditions and the development of self-government was not to be included. ("Self-government" in this context meant autonomy within a confederal or federal union with the former mother country.)

However farsighted in other respects the statesmen gathered at San Francisco in April 1945 might have been, they have proved shortsighted in their limited efforts to improve upon the existing forms of colonial rule over dependent peoples by subjecting them to effective international supervision and proclaiming the goal of ultimate independence or self-government.

Their expectations at the end of World War II have proved erroneous in two respects:

1. As we have said, none of the colonial empires has ever submitted any of its colonies to improved international supervision under the trusteeship system. The reason is obvious: The United Nations Charter provided for an unprecedented amount of international control of nationally administered trust territories. This in itself was enough to prevent any colonial possession from being voluntarily placed under the trusteeship system. Colonial empires limited themselves to submitting information on nonpolitical matters to the secretary general according to Article 73e of Chapter XI of the Charter.

2. Dependent peoples themselves did not desire an improved colonial administration but rather its total liquidation. The trusteeship system might have been a goal for dependent peoples in the 1920s; in the 1950s the goal was independence and equal and sovereign membership in the United Nations.

The sweeping tempo of anticolonial revolutions and the triumph of national self-determination in Asia and Africa transformed the colonial and trusteeship provisions of the United Nations Charter into documents of only historical interest without direct relevance to contemporary realities. What has remained of the former colonial world in Africa has become subject to resolutions, pressures, and actions outside the originally prescribed framework of the Charter (see Document 3.5).

One of the many intriguing "ifs" of world history is what the face of the world would be today if the polyethnic imperial or state systems had been internally tolerant and democratic instead of being oppressive and authoritarian. Yet, as the following chapters will indicate, even a world divided into several internally democratic and tolerant Switzerlands would not necessarily mean that these states would be similarly tolerant on the international scene. There is no proven direct link between internal tolerance and external peacefulness; nor is there, of course, a clear link between domestic intolerance and aggressive foreign policy.

Notes

1. John Nielsen, "A Dilemma: Migrant Workers Flood Europe," *European Community*, November 1973, p. 7. The whole issue of this information bulletin of the European Community is entitled "Immigrant Flow: Once a Solution, now a Problem."
2. Nielsen, "A Dilemma," p. 7.
3. William I. Spencer, "The New Globalists," an address delivered to the American Chamber of Commerce, Frankfurt, Germany, September 6, 1972. William I. Spencer is the president of the First National City Corporation.
4. George W. Ball, "Cosmocorp: The Importance of Being Stateless," *Atlantic Community Quarterly*, 6 (Summer 1968), 165.

DOCUMENT 3.5

UNITED NATIONS DECLARATION ON THE GRANTING OF INDEPENDENCE TO COLONIAL COUNTRIES AND PEOPLES, DECEMBER 14, 1960

The General Assembly, . . . Believing that the process of liberation is irresistible and irreversible, . . . solemnly proclaims the necessity of bringing to a speedy and unconditional end colonialism in all its forms and manifestations, and to this end declares that[1]

1. The subjection of peoples to alien subjugation, domination and exploitation constitutes a denial of fundamental human rights, is contrary to the Charter of the United Nations and is an impediment to the promotion of world peace and co-operation.

2. All peoples have the right to self-determination. . .

3. Inadequacy of political, economic, social and educational preparedness should never serve as a pretext for delaying independence. . . .

6. Any attempt aimed at partial or total disruption of the national unity and the territorial integrity of a country is incompatible with the purposes and principles of the Charter of the United Nations.

14. Everyone has the right to seek and to enjoy in other countries asylum from persecution.

This right may not be invoked in the case of prosecutions genuinely arising from non-political crimes or from acts contrary to the purposes and principles of the United Nations.

15. Everyone has the right to a nationality.

No one shall be arbitrarily deprived of his nationality nor denied the right to change his nationality. . . .

19. Everyone has the right to freedom of opinion and expression; this right includes freedom to hold opinions without interference and to seek, receive, and impart information and ideas through any media and regardless of frontiers.

28. Everyone is entitled to a social and international order in which the rights and freedoms set forth in this Declaration can be fully realized.[2]

1. The African, Asian, and communist states' delegations that sponsored and voted for this resolution were aiming at the continuation of the Portuguese colonies, South Africa, Rhodesia, and the remaining West European controls in Africa and Asia. They did not concern themselves with the Soviet domination in East Central Europe and the presence of Soviet armed forces in that area. This, in their opinion, is not colonialism.

2. The value of this article is debatable in the world in which we live.

Footnotes continued on next page.

5. Samuel P. Huntington, "Transnational Organizations in World Politics," *World Politics*, 25:3 (April 1973), 363.

6. John H. Herz, "Idealist Internationalism and the Security Dilemma," *World Politics*, January 1950, p. 127.

7. *Hung Chi (Red Flag)*, Peking, January 1964, p. 1.

8. *Hung Chi*, January 1964, p. 1.

9. "The New Program of the Communist Party of the Soviet Union," *The Current Digest of the Soviet Press*, December 13, 1961, p. 3.

10. Quoted by Merle Fainsod in *How Russia Is Ruled*, rev. ed. Cambridge, Mass.: Harvard University Press, 1963, p. 3.

11. Vladimir I. Lenin, *Works (Sochineniya)*, Vol. 24. Moscow: State Publishing House, 1941-1951, p. 155.

12. For a more detailed discussion of loyalty and dissent, see also Ivo D. Duchacek, *Power Maps: Comparative Politics of Constitutions*. Santa Barbara, Calif.: ABC-Clio, 1973, pp. 73-88.

13. Robert O. Keohane and Joseph S. Nye, Jr. (eds.), *Transnational Relations and World Politics*. Cambridge, Mass.: Harvard University Press, 1972, p. xi. The authors distinguish four major types of transnational interactions: (1) movement of information and ideas; (2) movement of physical objects, including weapons; (3) movement of money; and (4) travel, that is, movement of persons.

14. The author will discuss this subject in more detail in a book now in preparation, *International Roles of Dissident Groups*, to be published by ABC-Clio in 1976.

15. A good example of terminological confusion is the "Commonwealth of Puerto Rico," called "Commonwealth" in English but a "Free Associated State" in Spanish (*Estado Libre Asociado*).

16. Evidently, in the Spanish-speaking countries an American citizen would be well advised to qualify his nationality as "norteamericano" to avoid any confusion with the Latin Americans.

17. For a more detailed treatment see the excellent study by Walker Connor, "The Politics of Ethnonationalism" *Journal of International Affairs*, 27:1 (1973), 1-21. The fourteen states are Austria, Denmark, West and East Germany, Iceland, Ireland, Japan, North and South Korea, Luxembourg, the Netherlands, Norway, Portugal, and Swaziland. If we exclude the seven countries whose population, as it were, spills over into neighboring states (Austria, the Germanies, Ireland, the Koreas, and Swaziland), the total number of people living in a state closely corresponding to their ethnic group is small indeed: less than 4 percent of the world's population lives in a self-contained monoethnic state.

18. Leonard W. Doob, "From Tribalism to Nationalism in Africa," *Journal of International Affairs*, 16:2 (1962), 151-152. (The entire issue of the journal, entitled "Nation-Building: The Order of the Day," is recommended.)

19. UN Secretariat, *Definition and Classification of Minorities*. New York: UN Publication 50.XIV.3, 1950, p. 51.

20. Karl W. Deutsch, "Social Mobilization and Political Development," *American Political Science Review*, September 1961, p. 498.

21. A. Doak Barnett, *Communist China and Asia*. New York: Knopf, 1961, p. 172. See also Robert S. Elegant, *The Dragon's Seeds*. New York: St. Martin's, 1959, p. 319, a general book on the Chinese minorities in Asia.

22. Lewis A. Coser, *The Functions of Social Conflict*. New York: Free Press, 1956, pp. 87-89.

23. Quoted by Kenneth M. Stampp (ed.) in *The Causes of the Civil War*. Englewood Cliffs, N.J.: Prentice-Hall, 1959, p. 181.

24. Rupert Emerson, *From Empire to Nation*. Cambridge, Mass.: Harvard University Press, 1960, pp. 297-298.

25. Compare the recommendation of an American black leader, Roy Innis, that subnational ethnic and racial groups be internationally recognized as having a separate status. Is that statement a foretaste of the future? What would be the reaction of polytribal Africa and the polyethnic Soviet Union? Would the People's Republic of China accept an internationally recognized status for Tibet, Sinkiang, Inner Mongolia, and other non-Han groups and areas?

26. UN Trusteeship Council, *United Nations Visiting Mission to Trust Territories in the Pacific, 1953*. New York: UN Publication T/1077, 1953.

27. In 1973 a Basque militant organization, ETA—the initials of the Basque words for

"Basque Nation and Freedom"—assassinated, or so it claimed, the Spanish premier and designated successor to Franco, Admiral Luis Carrero Blanco. For the Basques Blanco represented a symbol of fascism and Spanish-Castilian domination of the Basque country.

28. The expulsion of the German minority from Czechoslovakia is analyzed and described by a Czech scholar, Radomír Luza, in his study *The Transfer of the Sudeten Germans: A Study of Czech-German Relations, 1933-1962*. New York: New York University Press, 1964. The German side of the story is presented in a multivolume collection of documents and analyses, Theodor Schieder *et al.* (eds.), *Documents on the Expulsion of the Germans from East Central Europe*. Bonn: Federal Ministry for Expellees, Refugees and War Victims, 1961 (English version).

Additional Readings

Additional readings on the subject of ethnonationalism may be found in *Discord and Harmony: Readings in International Politics,* edited by Ivo D. Duchacek and published by Holt, Rinehart and Winston in 1972. Analyses of national self-determination by Rupert Emerson, Ernest Renan, Chiang Kai-shek, Mao Tse-tung, Frantz Fanon, and Sekou Touré constitute Chapter 3, "Multinational States and Stateless Nations," pp. 32-44.

4

Why Nations and Their Leaders Act as They Do

Territorial states—the basic units of the international system —both result from and cause nationalism. As we have noted, people generally share with their political elites the belief that a national community can best protect itself against oppression and misery if it possesses and administers a territorial state of its own. Territorial communities that feel themselves to be nations struggle to establish their own sovereign states, daring all and sacrificing many lives, so that the independent existence of the nation may be assured. We have referred to this political drive as the principle of national self-determination.

SELF-PRESERVATION IN A SYSTEM OF STATES

Following the achievement of statehood, the principle of national self-determination, usually associated with the revolutionary struggle against foreign domination, transforms itself into the right of national self-preservation: the right of the national community to preserve and further develop its state by an independent determination of its domestic and foreign policies. It encompasses the right to make one's own estimates of dangers and opportunities on the international scene, to determine short-term and long-term priorities, and to select the most appropriate forms of action. In sum, the principle of national self-preservation represents the projection of the concept of national self-determination into the period of attained statehood.

Early nationalists believed that satisfaction of each nation's desire for statehood would eventually lead to a global community of equally satisfied nation-states. The world is now quite skeptical about the possibility of ensuring international harmony by universal satisfaction of national egoisms. No nationalist today assumes a world composed of equally satisfied, happy, and mutually tolerant nationalities, each possessing a state of its own. On the contrary, nationalism anticipates dissatisfied and ambitious nations against whose potential or actual threats it will be necessary to protect the security of the state and the well-being of its inhabitants. This leads to policies and actions that aim at improved strategic and economic boundaries; thus more territory, more people, and more resources have often been forcibly included within nationally controlled boundaries at the expense of the territory and national unity of other states. Some Caesars have argued that only the conquest of the whole world will ensure an absolute security and maximum well-being for their nations. In the concluding pages of his book on nationalism, Carlton J. H. Hayes illustrates this contrast between the idealistic and pragmatic aims of nationalism:

> Liberal nationalists of the first half of the nineteenth century were convinced that if every "oppressed" nationality was free and possessed its own national language, educational system, militia, and press, it would lie down lamb-like with others of the human flock in the broad green pastures of the world. They were optimists. A frightful series of wars of national unification quickly succeeded; and events soon proved that when "oppressed" nationalities actually became free, they transformed themselves from lambs into lions and roared at one another and in the twentieth century fought throughout the whole world the most destructive wars in human history.[1]

Not all nations pursue policies that can be classified as lions' roars; but assumed or actual hostility on the part of other nations has prevented any nation, big or small, from lying down like an innocent, unconcerned, and passive lamb. After having invoked the principle of national self-determination and succeeded in establishing their own states, national communities often dread, rightly or wrongly, that national independence, once won, may be lost again or at least impaired. Constant activity and vigilance are the corollaries of national self-determination and self-preservation. Nation-states are unequal in power, that is, in their capacity to impose their will on others or resist the will of others, and the very fact of this asymmetry induces small and medium nations to dread great powers' potential misuse of their superior might. The suspicion is there even if at present none of the great powers has any intention to misuse its economic or military superiority; but, as small and medium nations well know, great powers may develop such hostile intentions later. Although nations claim to be equally sovereign, they are not equally secure, equally ambitious, or equally vulnerable; consequently they are also not equally sensitive to and active in international politics. Generally speaking, a small nation is naturally more concerned with a potential threat to or even mere coolness to its existence on the part of its neighbors and great powers than is a mighty nation. But even a big nation is not an island—politically, economically, or culturally. A giant may fear another giant or a dangerous combination of dwarfs. Neutrality or isolationism is not a guarantee of immunity either. Even the most isolationist and neutralist nation must take into account the world around it, especially its own neighbors. During its period of glorified isolationism the United States had to pay close attention to the threats and opportunities emerging in Canada and Latin America and the changing power relations in then distant Europe and Asia. For several centuries neutralist and relatively inaccessible Switzerland has been constantly alert and sensitive to any changes in the power relations around her; Swiss neutrality has always been an *armed* neutrality, based on a conscripted citizens' army equipped today with sophisticated weaponry.

The Impact of the International System

Whatever its capabilities, no nation can afford to disregard the fundamental fact of its life and desire for survival in an environment in which very often might makes right; there is no central police establishment or life insurance company a nation can call upon in an emergency.

In the preceding three chapters the primary focus was on nations, states, and their internal tensions. The focus now shifts from single states to their pattern of interaction and to their composite, the international system. By their mutual interaction territorial states have shaped their system and endowed it with properties that the components singly do not possess; in turn, the states are shaped by their system—they are its captives as well as its mirrors. The behavior of the elements composing a system, in general, is obviously different when they act in awareness of being part of a whole and when they act as if they were in a vacuum.

We use the relatively neutral term "system" rather than the older terms "world community," which implies an optimistic value judgment, and "world jungle," which contains perhaps too large a dose of pessimism about the nature of men and nations. By "system" we mean a pattern of repeated interaction among components that shapes the behavior of these components and thus produces some degree of order and provides for occasional solutions of conflicts of interest.[2] The patterned political interaction of states develops within a broader nonpolitical environment shaped by nature and the impact of technology and new discoveries. This nonpolitical environment may be distinguished from both the system and its components even though the line dividing the environment from the system and the system from the states is quite blurred, one element extending into another in a complex interrelationship. Changes in the environment are produced by political as well as nonpolitical factors: "The number of nation states changes; the relative importance of such actors changes; war, conquest, revolution, peaceful change, population growth, and technological developments continually weave new threads in a complex woof of interrelationships."[3]

Our primary concern here is with the processes and structure of the international system that result from the political interaction among the component units, that is, from their efforts to influence the behavior of other states by argument, example, agreement, lure, threat, or violence.

National and International Systems

In structure and performance, national political systems, or territorial states, seem to differ so fundamentally from the international system (the global composite of states) that they are often placed in sharp contrast to each other.

A national political system has been defined by David Easton as "those patterns of interaction through which values are allocated for a society and these allocations are accepted as authoritative [binding] by most persons most of the time."[4] Using a different terminology, we have previously identified a government's monopoly of coercive force and a high degree of consensus and cohesion as the two most significant characteristics of a territorial state.

In contrast, the international system lacks authority and consensus, the two ingredients that make a territorial national system a relatively effective mechanism for solving conflicts by acceptable or enforceable rules and procedures. In the international system there is no overriding authority endowed with the right to make and enforce rules transcending the state boundaries. As we shall see in Chapters 12 and 13, the United Nations and the International Court of Justice are not such authorities. The law of nations, such as it exists, is narrow in scope and usually unenforceable, even though it is often observed in practice when vital issues of nations are not involved. There is no real international criminal code that defines international crimes with precision and provides for prosecution and punishment. In Chapter 13 we shall see how even the International Convention on Genocide, agreed on in the wake of the Nuremberg war crimes trials, becomes controversial as soon as we apply to it the strict standards that any criminal law must comply with to be considered valid or as soon as we try to apply the principles of the Nuremberg war crimes to any victor in any war. Having agreed on the definition of the crime of genocide, nations, symptomatically, failed to agree on the establishment of an international court with the right and duty to prosecute and punish criminals who practiced it.

In the international system the possibility of a threat or damage to a nation's life or vital interests is constant. However, a state has no recourse to a supranational court for an injunction or punishment of criminal behavior; it has no recourse to a central world authority for protection and enforcement of laws; and it cannot turn to a central legislative assembly for new and better laws. Such familiar and useful national institutions as courts, central executive and legislative authorities, and enforceable laws simply do not exist on the international scene.

Nor is there an international counterpart to the national cohesion that characterizes the territorial states, representing a mixture of rational consensus on goals and means and emotional identification of citizens with one another and with their state. Not only the power to make and apply rules but also concepts of what is right, just, and moral are highly fragmented in the international system. It is this absence of broadly shared common values that causes many an observer of the international scene to question the applicability of the term "community" to the contemporary composite of independent and competing states. A former member of the International Court of Justice, Charles de Visscher, notes that "to invoke the idea of an international community as the habit is, . . . is to postulate in men, shut in their national compartments, something they still largely lack, namely the community spirit, the deliberate adherence to supranational values."[5] Most of the time nations want to be and are very much on their own. Self-help or a cooperative coalition of one group of self-helping nations pitted against another group is the rule rather than the exception. The United Nations Charter sanctions nations' rights of individual and collective self-defense against aggression (Article 51). "It is the very lack of a supreme and generally accepted authority," writes Stanley Hoffmann, "which explains why the rules of the game of world politics differ so sharply from the rules of domestic politics: the overriding loyalty of each of the groups into which the world has been divided, belongs to the groups rather than to the world as a whole."[6]

Nevertheless, the sharp contrast between an orderly national system and a disorderly international system calls for qualification on two accounts.

First, the sharp contrast is somewhat artificial. On the one hand, we assumed a national system that largely satisfies the people's needs, proves responsive to change, demonstrates sensitivity to new demands, enjoys the people's rational and emotional support, and maintains a hierarchical order capable of making enforceable rules. On the other hand, we assumed an international system that consists of multiple sovereignties walled one from another by physical boundaries and mistrust and promoting their mutually exclusive interests by fraud and force. The contrast between the idyllic order and peacefulness of a national system and the near-jungle anarchy of an international system becomes much less sharp when we compare the international system in peacetime with a national system in the midst of a revolution or civil war. At such a time the profound split of the people into two hostile camps means not only the end of internal cohesion but also the end of the central authority's ability to make and enforce rules for the whole community. As a result, the participants in an internal conflict adopt patterns of behavior only too familiar on the international scene, where there is no central authority or consensus, namely impassioned and self-righteous rhetoric, deceit, blackmail, and mass violence. Sometimes, also, on the eve of elections internal order and consensus come close to breaking down. But even in times of order and normalcy, no national system is ever free from some internal violence or disorder resulting from acts committed by the criminal or pathological fringe of the society.

Second, the contrast between a peaceful national system and an anarchic international system may be qualified by pointing out that, even during wars that plunge a major part of the world into chaos and destruction, large segments of the world often carry on their business more or less as usual, adhering to some common standards and exercising some restraints. This was so in both world wars.

There are three admittedly rudimentary elements of consensus that somewhat mitigate what otherwise might be utter chaos or anarchy:

1. The single most widely shared value today seems to be the general agreement that the survival of all is better than mutual annihilation. This integrative element was obviously missing in the prenuclear age, when total destruction did not need to be dreaded. It is, however, only a mildly integrative element. Some nations still believe that a nuclear holocaust will eliminate only some while others will survive in a better world albeit amid heaps of radioactive dust. In the 1960s, for instance, Mao Tse-tung argued with a foreign statesman who had expressed the belief that the whole of mankind would be annihilated if an atomic war was fought: "I said that if worst came to worst and half of mankind died, the other half would remain while imperialism would be razed to the ground and the world would become socialist."[7] The Chinese concept, according to which only the nonsocialist half of the world would be the victim in a nuclear war, was attacked as unrealistic and dangerous by both anticommunist and communist media.

2. As to the general concept of what is moral, legal, humane, and just, we must distinguish between the frequent invocations of universal morality and the actual practice of men and groups who filter the universal principles, as it were, through the dyed cloth of national flags, distorting these principles in the process in order to make them fit parochial needs and goals. Nevertheless, even a fraudulent invocation of moral or legal concepts may be cited as proof of their subliminal existence. One of the leading authorities on international law, Professor L. F. L. Oppenheim, writes:

> The fact is that States, in breaking the Law of Nations, never deny its existence, but recognize its existence through the endeavor to interpret

the Law of Nations as justifying their conduct. And although the frequency of the violations of International Law may strain its legal force to the breaking point, the formal, though often cynical, affirmation of its binding existence is not without significance.[8]

Extreme caution is needed when evaluating the practical effectiveness of any supranational concept among nations; neither sincere self-deception nor utter cynicism can be ruled out.

3. The principle of the territorial *division*—that is, that the territorial state is and should remain the basic unit of the international system—is, paradoxically, the single most widely and effectively shared common value of mankind. Fortunately, there is an almost equally shared concept that the territorial states cannot, and in their own interest should not, avoid mutually regulated contacts. There does seem to be a general consensus that no nation can be totally isolated since none can be totally self-sufficient. The awareness of the general interdependence of nations is expressed by the establishment of an intricate web of diplomatic, economic, and cultural relations as well as by permanent international organizations ranging from common markets, military alliances, and regional or ideological blocs to the nearly universal United Nations and its specialized agencies that deal with the nonpolitical aspects of the worldwide interdependence of territorial states.

Contacts among nations, whether intentional or unintentional, lead to repeated interaction. This creates a pattern, an international system, that mirrors its interacting components, the territorial states. The states, in turn, individually reflect some of the pertinent characteristics of the whole; they are partial miniatures of the system. All reflect and interact in an intricate and complex manner. Many scholars (for example, Morton A. Kaplan, Andrew Scott, James N. Rosenau, and George Liska) have recommended or have themselves adopted a shift of emphasis in study and research from the classic concentration on nations to a focus on the comprehensive whole, the international system itself, or systemic analysis. Territorial states, embedded in the system, may be expected to adopt very similar patterns of behavior and perhaps predictable forms of interaction. "A repeatable or characteristic behavior"[9] is seen as resulting from or being intimately related to the system. Hans J. Morgenthau concluded that the main result of the contemporary system of politics among territorial states is that "statesmen think and act in terms of interest defined as power, and the evidence of history bears this assumption out. That assumption allows us to retrace and anticipate, as it were, the steps a statesman—past, present, or future—has taken or will take on the political scene."[10]

Macrolevel and Microlevel Analyses

Macrolevel analysis concentrates upon the composite rather than upon its parts, and the choice is itself a judgment of the relative utility of such a study. Microlevel analysis, on the contrary, focuses on the components rather than on the system. Looking at a ship, we may concentrate either on her beauty, shape, speed, maneuverability, resistance to storms and waves, and general efficiency (macrolevel) or on the captain, his crew, the stewards and cooks, the propellers, and the interior decoration of the staterooms (microlevel). And in international politics too, we may focus on the international system or on its components, the territorial nations and their leaders. We use macrolevel analysis to study

> . . . the patterns of interaction which the system reveals, and to generalize about such phenomena as the creation and dissolution of coalitions, the frequency and duration of specific power configurations, modification in its stability, its responsiveness to changes in formal political institutions, and the norms and folklore which it manifests as a societal system. In other words, the systemic level of analysis, and only this level, permits us to examine international relations as a whole, with a comprehensiveness that is of necessity lost when our focus is shifted to a lower, more partial level.[11]

In examining the system of states we may decide to inquire into (1) the existing technology, especially weapon and communication technology, (2) the prevailing ideological concepts, goals, and preferences, including the relative strength of parochial nationalism and awareness of transnational interdependence, or (3) the structural pattern: the number of states and their proportionate size,[12] and the number and size of organizations, formal and informal, that can act as regulators of conflict and discord among nations.

By "regulators of conflict and discord" we mean either institutional or informal forces in the system. International organizations such as the United Nations, the League of Nations, the Concert of Europe, and the Holy Alliance are examples of institutional regulators. A regulator of conflict may also be seen in the opposition of certain states in the system to the disturbing initiatives of other states. As Richard N. Rosencrance argues, "the national actors themselves are in this manner the sources of regulation in an alliance of balance of power system. The regulator then refers to the actions of institutions and states in the international system."[13]

The proportionate power of states in a system is one of the determinants of the behavior system. A system composed of a multitude of dwarfs changes its general behavior under the following circumstances: when there appears a closely knit alliance of dwarfs bent on subjugating the others, when a giant appears with the same intentions, when there emerge two competing giants (a bipolar system) whose enmity and competition may either reduce the dwarfs to satellite status or encourage them into successfully playing one giant off against the other, when there are more than two competing giants (a polycentric system), or when some of the giants and perhaps even some dwarfs have acquired the means to annihilate dwarfs and giants in a split second. The international system and its universal regulator, the United Nations, have undergone profound changes reflecting the revolutionary changes of weapon technology, although on the surface the principal actors and their common institutions have remained the same. The United Nations was one kind of institution when it was founded in the spring of 1945, still in the prenuclear age; it became a different kind of institution with the acquisition of the nuclear bomb by the United States (1945), the Soviet Union (1949), Great Britain (1952), France (1960), and the People's Republic of China (1964).

A macrolevel analysis has the undeniable advantage of comprehensiveness, but it also has some drawbacks: it tends to exaggerate the impact of the system upon the national actors, making their motives and goals appear more uniform than they actually are. This is one of the main criticisms addressed to Morgenthau's emphasis on power as the only goal and means in politics. Furthermore, if everything interacts with everything in a system, a meaningful analysis requires some dissection of the whole.

A microlevel analysis of international relations, on the other hand, may err in an excessive assumption of differentiation by its focus on the territorial states as the primary targets of examination. While its obvious drawback is the relative lack of comprehensiveness, the advantage lies in the depth and detail of the study; it permits a useful differentiation[14] in methods and goals as adopted by the basic components of the contemporary international system, that is, by the territorial states (individual national actors) or their coalitions (collective international actors).

THE CONTROVERSIAL CONCEPT OF NATIONAL INTEREST

The existence of some common interest causes and explains the existence of all groups. A nation may actually be viewed as the largest interest group, a national interest group. Individuals within a nation organize groups—parties or pressure groups—when they feel or rationally conclude that there is some common interest to protect or promote. Groups greatly differ from one another in their respective concepts of their collective interests and in their methods of promoting them. Yet groups constituting a national community feel that in addition to their subnational and often conflicting interests they also have one higher and general interest in common: the interest in remaining a state and in promoting its security and welfare. This collective interest represents a total of all individual and group interests, and something more. It usually stands above particular interests, and its emotional content is high. In the preceding analysis of nationalism we noted the importance of emotional identification of individuals and groups with each other notwithstanding their many conflicts in the field of politics and economics. In fact, the assumption of and the belief in the existence of a nation-state largely define and determine the reality of a nation-state, which, as its leadership sees it, lives and tries to survive in an anarchic, often hostile environment. Therefore the national leaders' major concern is—what else?—the promotion and defense of *national interest*, as perceived by them and their advisers. Hans J. Morgenthau expressed the link between interest and nation succinctly:

> The idea of interest is indeed of the essence of politics and, as such, unaffected by the circumstances of time and place. . . . Yet while the concern of politics with interest is perennial, the connection between interest and the national state is a product of history. The national state itself is obviously a product of history and as such is destined to yield in time to different modes of political organization. *As long as the world is politically organized into nations*, the national interest is indeed the last word in international politics.[15] [Italics added.]

It may often be the last word but a great many sharp controversies precede any agreement on its meaning, that is, what exactly a national interest is in a given situation, how serious and immediate are the external threats, and what are the best methods of promoting and defending that interest. Similarly, the "self" in the term "self-preservation" is much less clear than it may seem at first sight.

So far we have spoken of the national interest in the singular. But a nation usually has a number of interests that it considers vital or important, and its leaders promote more than one major national interest simultaneously. In addition to external security, a state aims also at greater productivity, improved standards of living, better social and medical services, fuller realization of moral and ideological values, and the preservation of internal order. All of these are national interests. In Morton Kaplan's words: "National systems of action, like other systems, are organized to satisfy system needs . . . and there are as many national interests as national needs."[16]

Given the nature of men and the groups they establish, total uniformity in goals and means of achieving them will never be possible. People, being men, can be expected to advance sentiments, ideological concepts, political goals, and material claims that are mutually incompatible. The task of politics, national and international, is not to eliminate conflicts and competition (clearly impossible) but rather to direct such inconsistencies and conflicts of opinion and interest into channels of nonviolent solutions and accommodation through negotiation and compromise.

Individuals as well as groups try to promote their interests or to deter what they deem a threat to their lives, their material possessions, or their beliefs. The threat may be real and immediate or it may be distant or only imagined; but it is never deemed to be totally absent. To protect their interests, individuals rely on civilized self-restraint, on a political authority and the law of their community, or on their own individual efforts, that is, individual or cooperative self-help, including insurance against unpredictable risks.

In order to protect their interests on the international scene, nations cannot rely on the superior authority, law, or civilized self-restraint of other nations. On the international scene there is no superior authority with the right and the power to make and enforce law and order. The law of nations is a weak law. As to civilized self-restraint, it is present in such modest amounts that nations have to assume constantly the possibility of serious external interference with their freedom to pursue those activities that they consider vital to their national welfare and security. "In interpersonal, inter-family or other inter-group relations, regardless of culture, normative restraints and superior third-party governors are sufficient to make murder, plunder, and mayhem the exception rather than the rule," notes J. David Singer in his study of reciprocal influences among nations. Singer continues:

> But in international relations the gross inadequacy of both the ethical and the political restraints make violence not only accepted but anticipated. As a consequence the scarcest commodity in the international system is security—the freedom to pursue those activities which are deemed essential to national welfare and to survival itself. . . . [On the international scene] each actor has the legal, traditional and physical capacity to severely damage or destroy many of the others.[17]

The assumption of possible interference or uncivilized behavior on the part of other nations induces states and their leaders to engage in activities and policies that aim at safeguarding or maximizing their freedom of action while minimizing and, if possible, eliminating any actual or potential threat to it. As noted above, the behavior of nations is conditioned by the nature of the present international system, which in turn mirrors the suspicions and ambitions of the states.

Simultaneity of Conflict and Cooperation

The fact that nations feel they have their own collective interests that differ from the interests of other nations does not mean that these interests are necessarily in direct and constant conflict with one another. For instance, some national interests are unrelated; also, a great physical distance between the states prevents their clash or even awareness of possible clash. Many other national interests are in harmony or may be brought into harmony by negotiation and compromise within regional, ideological, racial, religious, continental, or functional frameworks (for instance, coordination of several national interests in preventing epidemics or traffic in drugs).

But even when the interests of several nations seriously clash, it does not mean that these nations are in mutual opposition at all times and in all respects. Major antagonists, such as Soviet Russia and the United States, may have some explicit or implicit interests in common; they may prefer mutual coexistence to mutual annihilation, trade to boycott, and order to chaos. While preserving their atomic arsenals they may have a common interest in preventing further proliferation of atomic weapons. Likewise, despite its firm ideological hostility toward the capitalist West, Communist China had some degree of political understanding with France, lively trade with West Germany, and several wheat deals with Canada in the 1960s; and in the early 1970s the constant confidential contacts between the People's Republic of China and the United States were transformed into an open and well-publicized relationship that, in 1972, culminated in President Nixon's official state visit to China and his long interview with Mao Tse-tung in Peking.

The clash of various major national interests has never precluded conciliation or even cooperation among nations in other fields. Chapter 14, on diplomacy, will return in more detail to the art of compromising on one level while maintaining vigilance or even hostility on another level.

Five Components of National Interest

Whether we use the term "national interest" in the singular (and assume that it represents a sum total of many national needs) or in the plural, we should recognize that the components of national interest (or national needs) not only are interconnected but also compete with one another. The competition is particularly manifest between the five major components of national interest: (1) the physical substance of the nation, (2) the belief system, (3) the political system, (4) the economic system, and (5) territorial integrity. Ideally they should all be equally protected or promoted, but this does not hold true in practice.

The Physical Substance of the Nation   The first national interest, or its first value-ingredient, is the lives of the members of the national community—men, women, children, and the generations yet unborn. A nation without people is clearly inconceivable. Could anybody really argue that there are circumstances under which *all* citizens should die so that their nation can be preserved—as a monument, that is? If, on the other hand, the survival of every single member of a nation is deemed the irreducible minimum (as it may be so viewed by an integral pacifist), the discussion on the subject of national interest could usefully end right here. The British philosopher Bertrand Russell, for instance, seems to have given the physical survival of each and every individual an absolute priority over any other component of national interest. The slogan "Better Red than Dead" expresses Sir Bertrand's frequently voiced opinion that "a communist victory would not be so great a disaster as the extinction of human life." No counterpart to Sir Bertrand's slogan and statement could be quoted from communist sources that would, for instance, proclaim "Better Capitalist than Dead" or "Better Fascist than Dead."

There are two major arguments against the alleged choice between the extinction of human life and living in a communist (or capitalist) penal colony. First, the choice is falsely presented: Intelligent diplomacy and perhaps even the atomic deterrent make many other alternatives possible, including that of being alive and non-Red (or noncapitalist). The fierceness of the Sino-Soviet controversy in the 1960s, on the other hand, suggests that making the world safe for communism would not eliminate international violence; it would still be possible to be Red *and* dead.

Second, when the issue of life and death is considered, many people take into account not only physical survival but also the quality of life. In Sidney Hook's words:

> Paradoxical as it may sound, life itself is not a value. What gives life value is not mere existence but its quality. Whoever proclaims that life is worth living under any circumstances has already written for himself an epitaph of infamy. For there is no principle or human being he will not betray; there is no indignity he will not suffer or compound.[18]

Placing life without any qualification above any other consideration would expose individuals and nations to easy blackmail by those who dare to think in terms other than physical survival. The success of Palestinian terrorists is based on the assumption that governments or airline officials under extreme blackmail would consider any Palestinian demand more acceptable than the loss of lives of innocent hostages.

Bertrand Russell himself supported the war against nazism. Looking back at his life at the age of ninety-seven (*New York Times*, May 18,1969) he admitted his non-Gandhian inconsistency: "I set out with a belief that love, free and courageous, could conquer the world without fighting. I came to support a bitter and terrible war. In these respects there was failure."

If, however, efforts to attain or preserve the quality of life are deemed worthy of sacrifice of at least some human lives, the difficult question arises: How many lives—200 or 20 million—are worth sacrificing so that many times their number may preserve or attain a better life (better according to whose standards?)? Some people see a difference between an imposed sacrifice of drafted or conscripted individuals, on the one hand, and a voluntary sacrifice of professional soldiers or professional revolutionaries who have dedicated their lives to the profession and accepted the proposi-

FIGURE 4.1
NATIONAL PRIORITIES?

"Now let's be absolutely certain I have this all straight. Your taxes, regardless of circumstances, are not—I repeat *not*—to be used for waging war, manufacturing munitions, financing espionage, or for any other activity designed to subvert the legitimate democratic aspirations of peoples at home or abroad. Rather, these moneys will be spent to reduce poverty, advance education, fight pollution, and, in short, to do whatever is necessary to improve the human lot and make this planet a viable habitat for mankind once again."

Drawing by Mulligan; © 1973 The New Yorker Magazine, Inc.

tion that killing and dying are part of their career. Chapter 8 will return in more detail to the conflict of moral conviction in a life-or-death situation. At this point we will only note that in actual practice the defense of territorial integrity, an ideology, a way of life, or a political system has often been found worthy of the sacrifice of a very large portion of the physical substance of a nation. In World War I 9 million lives were sacrificed by both sides in the defense of what the national leaders viewed as their nations' interests. Mao Tse-tung once contemplated the possibility that following a third world war 300 million Chinese would perish, leaving the other 300 million to "rebuild swiftly, on the debris of a dead imperialism, a civilization thousands of times higher than the capitalist system and a truly beautiful future for themselves" (*Peking Review*, April 26, 1960).

The Belief System   The second interest or ingredient (closely connected with the first) is beliefs and principles shared by the nation and its leaders. A creed necessarily asserts itself in any process by which we try to determine the priority among national goals. If no principle such as socialism, democracy, freedom, or independence is considered worth dying for, could such principles also be sacrificed for other national purposes, such as territorial integrity? Are principles, ideals, and ideological programs the most or the least expendable components of national interest?

In the selection of means by which national values are to be preserved, the eternal question of the justification of the end by the means is always posed, if not by policy makers then by their critics. According to W. T. R. Fox, "moral principle enters into any valid formulation of national interest, which must itself reconcile the desirable and the possible."[19] Chapters 7 and 8 will deal in greater detail with the often disturbing but always fascinating conflict between ideology and survival and between morality and expediency.

The Political System   The political system includes the stakes that not only the people in general but their leaders, parties, and interest groups, in particular, have in the prevailing system. In connection with Sidney Hook's statement on the value of life many would argue that should a free country transform itself into a totalitarian but impregnable fortress in order to preserve the lives and the territory of its people, it would be physically alive but politically conquered. The question naturally arises how large a portion of democracy, socialism, fascism, or communism may be sacrificed, temporarily or permanently, in order to safeguard the other components of national interest. Some may argue that a nation would not be worth saving if its political system, culture, and national values were to be *permanently* sacrificed for purposes of defense.

The Economic System   What has been said about the political component of national preservation largely applies to the economic and social system and the nation's standards of living. Actually both the political and economic systems may be viewed, not as separate categories, but as results or outgrowths of the belief system. The conflict between the needs of security, on the one hand, and economic, social, and cultural needs, on the other, is so well known that it needs no elaboration. With particular reference to the consumers' need, Nazi Minister of Propaganda Joseph Goebbels once expressed (Berlin, January 17, 1936) the conflict between guns and butter in words that have since acquired a sinister fame: "We can do without butter, but, despite all our love of peace, not without arms. One cannot shoot with butter but with guns." All nations have to weigh the relative importance of their major national interests. Limited national means must be so distributed that a reasonable balance is maintained between the needs of national security and the goal of economic development and social progress. Nations and their leaders must determine what portion of their national resources and energies (10 percent? 50 percent? 75 percent?) should be allocated for nuclear-tipped missiles and what portion for hospitals, schools, antipoverty programs, hydroelectric dams, reforestation, and support of the arts.

Territorial Integrity   At first sight, the integrity and inviolability of the national territory would appear an irreducible minimum or a major component of national interest. If a nation is inconceivable without human life, can a territorial state exist without a territory? A nation that has permanently lost its entire territory ceases to be a state although it may still be a wandering nation. Evidently a territorial state and nation without a territory is impossible. However, as in the case of a nation that loses only some or all its members, the question may be asked whether a nation and its state needs the *whole* of the national territory to remain what they are. A substantial portion of the national territory may sometimes be sacrificed to preserve the remaining part or any or all of the other four ingredients of national interest. The spatial limits of many nations have been altered through centuries. In 1918 the Bolshevik leaders accepted a substantial diminution of their state territory at the peace-treaty negotiations with the German imperial staff at Brest-Litovsk. In 1938 Czechoslovakia accepted the loss of its German-inhabited strategic areas with the hope of preserving the Czech-inhabited remainder. In 1972 West Germany ratified formal treaties with the Soviet Union and Poland, renouncing force in their relations and acknowledging Poland's annexation of 40,000 square miles of former German territory; Germany also resumed normal relations with Czechoslovakia in a treaty that declared "null and void" the Munich pact that in 1938 gave Nazi Germany a portion of Czechoslovakia without the latter's voluntary consent.

In many cases when a portion of the national territory must be ceded in order to preserve other national interests, frequently under duress, the sacrifice is considered to be only temporary, and recovery is anticipated. Lenin, for instance, accepted the humiliating peace with Imperial Germany in 1918 in the hope that from the preserved base of communism—however small at that time—lost territories and more would be recovered in the future. He has proved to be right. In 1974 Israel was confronted with a most difficult dilemma: whether or not to exchange relatively defensible boundaries obtained during the third Israeli-Arab war in 1967 for Soviet, American, and Arab pledges to respect the existence of the Jewish state and its new territorial boundaries.

Competition Among Major Interests

The five components of national interest are more distinguishable on paper than in reality. Not only are they interconnected, but they also compete with one another. Since no nation is omnipotent, it cannot protect or promote each interest with equal vigor; nor can it protect or promote their sum total without rearranging priorities or sacrificing parts of some in order to reinforce others. The determination of national interest and the way to promote it always presents a difficult choice[20] between several alternatives, none of which, after a nation has discarded the clearly suicidal or unintelligent ones, is totally acceptable or totally unacceptable. In life, including international life, all situations are mixtures of necessity and choice. And in situations of danger, real or imaginary, necessities greatly outweigh freedom of choice. The goal of increased defense capability is usually asserted against the need for domestic progress, short-term expediency against long-term commitment, physical survival against moral principles, the imperative to keep secrets from the enemy against freedom of speech. In war, democracies accept strict censorship of the press and even that of the private mail of its soldiers on the eve of major military operations. In the spring of 1944 only a fool—or a Nazi—would have argued in England for unlimited freedom of information, including that concerning the date and place of the Allied invasion of Nazi Europe. In war, the free-enterprise system accepts wartime economic planning, centralized allocation of raw materials, price controls, and rationing. In the years from 1941 to 1945, its days of danger, Communist Russia promoted the temporary use of nationalistic, bourgeois, racial, and religious appeals instead of the Marxist-Leninist class slogans.

Not only do the five components of national interest conflict with one another, but they precondition one another. A well-satisfied population, an effective political and economic system, social progress and justice, and the realization of ideological and ethical values on the internal scene may be viewed as goals but also as preconditions for an improved defense posture with regard to an external enemy. A blooming economy and a satisfied and loyal population increase a nation's resistance to enemy threats, subversion, pressure, or lures. On the other hand, the achievement of a greater national security (felt and experienced by the population) through armament and alliances may help the nation to achieve an improved internal order, enjoyment of liberties, and economic and social progress. National security, often a goal, also may be viewed as an essential condition for attaining all other national—domestic, economic, and social—goals.

What to Preserve against What?

Lord Palmerston, a prime minister of England in the nineteenth century, once said: "We have no perpetual allies and we have no perpetual enemies. Our interests are perpetual." Perhaps this is so, but Palmerston failed to define exactly what they are. Hans J. Morgenthau noted that the concept of national interest exists in the minds and hearts of men, and men's minds and hearts are changeable. The exact content of a national interest may be revised. Thus, the guiding principle of a national action on the international scene is in reality a great ambiguity, not dissimilar to such other broad goals as "domestic tranquility," "promotion of happiness," "social justice," "welfare," "progress," and "peace." As nobody is really against peace, happiness, social justice, and welfare, nobody, or almost nobody, is really against a policy based on an enlightened national interest. The controversy begins when the noble goal is to be translated into concrete and immediate goals and actions.

Can we at least say that there is a minimum amount of controversy about the basic meaning of the national interest when the very existence of a nation—its preservation—is in jeopardy? In theory, yes; in practice, no. As we have seen, the different ingredients of national interest have different priorities and relative values. When a nation is about to be defeated, the controversy is about the wisdom of a continuing resistance, an immediate surrender, or a conditional surrender. Even after the second atomic bomb was dropped on Nagasaki and the Russians had invaded Japanese-held Manchuria, there was a controversy in Tokyo between the peace and war parties about what the Japanese national interest commanded the empire to do. And when a nation is confronted with less than an immediate danger to its territory, the life of its people, its political system, or its sovereignty, the controversy is about the intensity or immediacy of danger. "Clear and present danger" is a controversial yardstick not only in the matter of civil rights but also in the matter of national liberty.

Controversy on Vietnam

In the late 1960s the United States found itself profoundly split by the dramatic controversy concerning the war in Vietnam. The central issue was the question, What vital American interest, if any, was really at stake on the 18th parallel of Asia's mainland?

Those who favored the war often did so for opposing reasons. The six main arguments on the hawkish side were:

1. War in Vietnam was a question of American security, a protection of one particularly sensitive segment of the American defense perimeter in Asia. In the light of the Chinese guerrilla doctrine that takes into account the unwillingness of the atomic powers to use their major weapons (the

paper-tiger theory), the communist challenge had to be met right there and then. Why wait until the threat manifested itself elsewhere? When Hawaii or California is threatened, it may be too late.

2. It was a crusade—a part of democracy's worldwide struggle against totalitarian communism.

3. It was a fulfillment of an allied obligation to a small country; the image of the United States as a faithful and reliable ally was at stake. If Vietnam were allowed to fall, other nations in Asia would either succumb to China's blackmail or seek accommodation with China (the domino theory and its many variants).

4. If war in Vietnam were to lead to a duel with China, it would be better to engage in it while the Sino-Soviet conflict was taking place and while China had not yet developed an effective delivery system for its nuclear weapons. This was the superhawk argument of a relative few. (In April 1970 China successfully launched its first satellite into earth orbit; it was twice the size of the very first Russian Sputnik in 1957. It confirmed the general estimate that by 1980 China may have missiles capable of delivering nuclear warheads to United States and European targets.)

5. It was simply a frontier war in the American "imperium," a necessary sideshow that the nation can and must afford even though the war, like all frontier wars, was bound to be long, frustrating, and cruel.

6. Whatever the original reasons for mass involvement—and they could have been wrong—it was now in the national interest of the United States to conclude the war with victory or a favorable negotiated settlement. Several variants of this basic line of reasoning could be identified: Some simply argued that America had never been defeated in war and must not be defeated now. Others maintained that in the atmosphere of turbulence and distrust that would inevitably follow an American defeat in Vietnam, the risk of another major or perhaps world war would actually increase, not decrease. Another argument against any form of nonvictory pointed to the probability of a slaughter of thousands following a communist takeover in the South. An anticipation of a rightist backlash in the wake of a defeat or humiliating withdrawal characterized a liberal variant of the fear of nonvictory in Vietnam. The point was sometimes made that after France's defeat in Algeria de Gaulle came to power and not the socialist, liberal, and communist critics of the war.

The opposing side was equally heterogeneous. Besides the arguments of integral pacifists who opposed any war at any time in any place, and the communists who opposed negotiated settlement because they wished for communist victory and capitalist America's defeat, the following six major arguments may be identified:

1. The war in Vietnam was a wrong war at a wrong place at a wrong time. No national interest was involved in that distant small country about which

Americans knew nothing and cared even less—as Chamberlain said about Czechoslovakia in 1938. But where the fall of Czechoslovakia opened the way to the conquest of Europe, the fall of Saigon could not possibly open the way for Mao or Brezhnev to Japan or California.

2. This was not and could not be a crusade for democracy since the system in South Vietnam was as dictatorial as and more corrupt than that in North Vietnam. The choice was between two dictatorships—a choice of no interest to the United States.

3. It was a war waged by the United States military-industrial complex at the expense of American social progress. A less biased variant of this argument was simply the opposition to the cost of an unsuccessful war in terms of domestic priorities, racial issues, and order.

4. The American intervention in Vietnam was illegal from the standpoint of international law. This was the general thesis of the well-documented symposium and book sponsored by the American Society of International Law and edited by Richard A. Falk in 1968.[21]

5. War may escalate beyond control to the atomic plateau. On the other hand, if an atomic dimension of the war in Vietnam is ruled out, the war cannot be won by conventional forces. It should therefore be concluded as speedily as possible by any means, including unilateral withdrawal.

6. If the national interest was ever at stake in Vietnam, the mass involvement of the United States armed forces should have been better explained and the war conducted like a major national commitment, including full mobilization of human and economic resources for a clear-cut victory. If it is a sideshow, it should end as a sideshow. The war was not only a wrong war, but also a bungled one.

Some of the dovish and hawkish arguments became intertwined as the war dragged on and on, patently unsuccessful and excessively cruel. The domino theorists had to consider the domino effect of the American failure to win speedily and America's responsibility for causing so much destruction and suffering in the process. The war in Vietnam was the first to receive daily television coverage, thus bringing the war casualties and the sufferings of the Vietnamese peasants right into the American home. The evening news broadcasts gave the American family dinner an unusually bitter taste, especially following the revelations concerning the Mylai massacre in 1968 and the extension of the war into neutral Cambodia in 1970. (More about Mylai will be said in Chapter 8.)

The national controversy about the war, which to a large extent was a debate about the concept and content of national interest, reached a peak of intensity in 1968 when President Johnson coupled his announcement of resignation with his plans for negotiations with North Vietnam, thus accepting, to say the least, a nonvictorious conclusion to the war.

During the closing months of President Nixon's first term his principal foreign policy adviser, Henry A. Kissinger, made a successful effort to place the inconclusive Vietnam conflict into the broader framework of possible détente between Washington and Moscow and Washington and Peking. Whatever other motives and goals Kissinger might have had, one of the purposes of his attempts at détente was the conclusion of the conflict in Vietnam without victory for any side. The first breakthrough and compromise was reached in October 1972 by means of secret negotiations between Kissinger and Le Duc Tho, his North Vietnamese counterpart, in Paris. It took an additional three months and severe new United States bombing of North Vietnam before the final agreement on a cease-fire was reached by Kissinger and Tho in January 1973. After President Nixon had halted the bombing, mining, and shelling of North Vietnam, Kissinger and Tho held one more session and completed a detailed agreement with numerous clauses concerning a cease-fire, repatriation of all prisoners, and the recognition by the United States and North Vietnam of the existence of three parties to the Vietnam conflict, namely the Saigon government, the Vietcong, and the Hanoi government; they also reached a vague agreement that the three parties should try conciliation, cooperation, and possibly coalition. The formal agreement was signed on January 27, 1973, in Paris by the then United States Secretary of State, William P. Rogers, and the foreign ministers of South Vietnam, the Provisional Revolutionary Government of the Vietcong, and North Vietnam.

The long, cruel (see Document 4.1.) and controversial war ended in nonvictory, basically within the framework of the Geneva accords of 1954, which then had ended the French colonial and military involvement in Indochina but which, at that time, were not signed by the United States and its principal foreign policy maker under President Eisenhower, Secretary of State John Foster Dulles. Nineteen years and over three million military and civilian casualties later another cease-fire with an uncertain future was signed; in the fall of 1973 the Nobel Prize for Peace was bestowed upon Henry A. Kissinger and Le Duc Tho; the latter refused to accept it.

Leaders' or Nations' Interests?

We can generally assume that national leaders never pursue national policies that are in the interest of any nation other than their own. Different national interests may overlap or may be in harmony with one another, but no president, prime minister, or foreign secretary in full possession of his faculties—especially his sense of his own political and personal survival—would openly and knowingly initiate or implement policies that would favor another nation and damage his own. Only a traitor or a corrupt or blackmailed politician might do so. But even in the case of some national leaders who are generally viewed as corrupt or of traitors who have abjectly collaborated with the nation's enemy, we may sometimes hear the argument that their crime was not betrayal but either a commitment to an insane concept of national interest or simply political

---

DOCUMENT 4.1

TWELVE YEARS OF WAR IN VIETNAM: CASUALTIES

Result of War: nonvictory, January 27, 1973

Military Casualties
United States: 45,933 killed
                       303,616 wounded
South Vietnam: 183,528 killed
                       499,026 wounded

North Vietnam
and Vietcong: 924,048 (estimate by Saigon, probably inflated)

Civilian Casualties
South Vietnam: 415,000 killed
                       935,000 wounded
                       31,463 killed by Vietcong actions against civilians
Vietcong: 20,587 killed by Saigon actions against civilian Vietcong
North Vietnam: casualties by U.S. intensive bombing and shelling are not
                       known
Total of officially claimed or admitted killed and wounded: 3,358,406[1]
The damage to the social, human, and political fabric of the United States cannot be
measured or expressed in figures.

1. Total United States casualties in World Wars I and II, killed and wounded, were 1,396,763.

---

shortsightedness. The pro-Nazi premier of Norway, Vidkun Quisling, whose name has become a symbol of the betrayal of national interest, pursued, after all, his concept of Norway's national interest in what he had conceived would be a victorious community of Nordic peoples. He invited

> all people of Nordic race and outlook in every country—Norwegians, Swedes, Danes, Icelanders, Britons, Germans and Dutch and all others of Nordic blood and spirit—to unite in a Nordic World Movement to create peace and cooperation between all Nordic peoples throughout the world and to carry on the struggle for the salvation and progress of our civilization.[22]

No previous commitment to the Nazi Aryan doctrine motivated the French ''quisling,'' Marshal Philippe Pétain, and other leaders of France such as Pierre Laval and Admiral Darlan. Following the collapse of France in the fateful six weeks of the late spring of 1940, they pragmatically concluded that collaboration with the Nazis and not further principled resistance was in the interest of France and the survival of its people. They most probably believed that everything had been lost to victorious Germany for at least one generation. It was a gloomy period indeed: The whole of western and central Europe had been conquered by Hitler, while England alone stood awaiting the Nazi invasion. The United States was still neutral and the Soviet Union had a treaty of friendship and cooperation with Nazi Germany. Marshal Pétain, the hero of the anti-German resistance around Verdun in World War I, proclaimed that further resistance and opposition would make Frenchmen suffer in vain, and therefore, "sacrificing his own person," he was personally to ensure a smooth collaboration with the Nazis and thus at least somewhat reduce (as he did) the harshness of the Nazi occupation in the southern half of France. In London, in the meantime, under the protective wing of Winston Churchill, a young French general and former subordinate of Pétain, Charles de Gaulle, declared that France had lost only a battle, not the war; he became the symbol and the leader of the French resistance against the Nazis. His interpretation of the national interest of France was directly opposite to that of Marshal Pétain. The Allied victory proved de Gaulle right and Pétain wrong. What would have been the verdict of France and history had Germany won the war? Many other such historical "ifs" may be posed; they would point to personal opportunism, lack of courage, or the frailty of human judgment, especially in the realm of decisions made under extreme duress.

Many a national leader who tries to determine the concrete meaning of the vague and ambiguous concept of national interest might agree with Abraham Lincoln, who once somewhat bitterly pondered the use of success as the most frequent yardstick of policy: "I do the very best I know. If the end brings me out all right, what is said against me won't amount to much. If the end brings me out wrong, the angels swearing I was right would make no difference."

Assumption of personal responsibility for national action involving use of violence has always been an awesome task and is even more so in our era of atomic missiles. Former President Lyndon Johnson described the feeling of relief experienced after January 26, 1969, when he was no longer in charge of American foreign and defense policy. In a CBS interview with Walter Cronkite eleven months later (December 26, 1969) Johnson said:

> I no longer had the fear that I was the man that could make the mistake of involving the world in war, that I was no longer the man that would have to carry the terrifying responsibility of protecting the lives of this country and maybe the entire world, unleashing the horrors of some of our great power if I felt that that was required.

Uncertain about what exactly must be done now and what later and how to do it, statesmen are keenly aware of the necessity that something must be done and of the crucial consequences of whatever they do or do not do. Nonaction may sometimes be a deliberate and wise policy; at other times nonaction is simply a result of the policy maker's inability to make up his mind. Whatever its cause, nonaction holds the policy maker responsible for consequences over which, having surrendered initiative to others, he has no control.

SIX TASKS OF FOREIGN POLICY: A SUMMARY

In conducting his nation's foreign and defense policies, a statesman must understand and evaluate as accurately as possible the following:

1. The nature of the international environment in which he is to act in behalf of his nation. This includes estimates of the prevailing technology, ideological conflicts and commitments, and structural features of the system of states: the number and ratio of super, major, minor, and small powers, the number and solidity of alliances and coalitions, the number and importance of nonaligned nations, and the importance or nonimportance of restraints imposed by international organizations and law.
2. His nations' vital and less vital interests. This includes the determination of both short-term and long-term national goals.
3. Foreign nation's vital or nonvital interests. This includes estimates of their probable intentions and goals which, as we see them, may or may not be in the foreign nations' "real" interest.
4. The compatibility or incompatibility of his and foreign nations' interests *and* actual goals. Here, again, we must bear in mind that nations often pursue goals that are not in their own best interest.
5. His and foreign nations' capabilities to pursue their respective objectives—that is, can they afford to want what they want? Not all that is desirable is possible.
6. Foreign nations' perception of his own nation's interest, actual goals, and capabilities as well as their estimate of his own perception of *their* goals and capabilities. A policy maker, as Charles Burton Marshall expressed it, "embraces in his quest an understanding of his own government's understanding of them, and assumes that the process is reciprocated."[23]

Stated in this manner, the six main tasks of any nation's foreign policy point to the central *human* factor. The process of determining what is nationally desirable and internationally feasible is in the hands of policy makers and their staffs who, being only men and women, are not immune to human error. They may be misled by a false report, a wrong estimate of their own or a foreign nation's power, inaccurate perception and interpretation of an international event, their own or their aides' passions, ideological blindness, shortsightedness, inexperience, stupidity, or lack of skill.

At this point, our focus necessarily shifts from social entities and concepts such as states, nations, interest groups, and the international system to that capricious, erring, and ever so often prejudiced variable, the individual human being.

Notes

1. Carlton J. H. Hayes, *The Historical Evolution of Modern Nationalism*. New York: Crowell-Collier-Macmillan, 1931, pp. 304-305.

2. Compare two other definitions of "system": (1) "A set of components with identifiable attributes, among which patterned relationships persist over a period of time" (Andrew Scott, *The Functioning of the International Political System*. New York: Crowell-Collier-Macmillan, 1967, p. 27); and (2) "A system of action is a set of variables so related that describable behavioral regularities characterize the internal relationships of the variables to each other" (Morton A. Kaplan, *System and Process in International Politics*. New York: Wiley, 1964, p. 4).

3. Kaplan, *System and Process*, p. 4.

4. David Easton, *A Framework for Political Analysis*. Englewood Cliffs, N.J.: Prentice-Hall, 1965, p. 96.

5. Charles de Visscher, *Theory and Reality in Public International Law*. Princeton, N.J.: Princeton University Press, 1957, p. 98.

6. Stanley Hoffmann (ed.), *Contemporary Theory in International Relations*. Englewood Cliffs, N.J.: Prentice-Hall, 1960, p. 2.

7. Mao Tse-tung, *Peoples of the World Unite for the Complete, Thorough, Total, and Resolute Prohibition and Destruction of Nuclear Weapons*. Peking: Foreign Language Press, 1964, pp. 41-42.

8. L. F. L. Oppenheim and H. Lauterpacht, *International Law*, Vol. 1. New York: Longmans, 1955, p. 14.

9. Morton A. Kaplan, "Balance of Power, Bipolarity and Other Models of International Systems," *American Political Science Review*, September 1957, p. 684. The article is based on Kaplan's *System and Process in International Politics*. See also Scott, *The Functioning of the International Political System*; Klaus Knorr and Sidney Verba (eds.), *The International System: Theoretical Essays*. Princeton, N.J.: Princeton University Press, 1961; and J. David Singer, *Human Behavior and International Politics*. Chicago: Rand McNally, 1965.

10. Hans J. Morgenthau, *Politics among Nations*, 4th ed. New York: Knopf, 1967, p. 5.

11. J. David Singer, "The Level-of-Analysis Problem in International Relations," in Knorr and Verba, *The International System*, pp. 81-82.

12. Singer, "The Level-of-Analysis Problem." p. 83.

13. Richard N. Rosencrance, *Action and Reaction in World Politics*. Boston: Little, Brown, 1963, pp. 229-230.

14. Singer, *Human Behavior and International Politics*, p. 37. It may be noted that Singer differentiates between systemic analysts who build their concepts around *action, behavior, interaction relationship,* or *role* (Gabriel A. Almond, James S. Coleman, Kenneth Boulding, Karl W. Deutsch, David Easton, Morton Kaplan, and Talcott Parsons) and general systems theorists who pay equal attention to those who participate in action and interaction, that is, individuals, groups, or associations. Here the major unit of analysis is a social entity. Among those who usually employ the entity-oriented concepts are Ludwig Von Bertalanffy, Donald T. Campbell, Alfred Kuhn, James G. Miller, Bruce Russett, and Singer himself. For details see J. David Singer "A General Systems Taxonomy for Political Science" (a 22-page module). New York: General Learning Press, 1971.

15. Hans J. Morgenthau, *Dilemmas of Politics*. Chicago: University of Chicago Press, 1958, pp. 67-68.

16. Kaplan, *System and Process in International Politics*, p. 151.

17. J. David Singer, "Inter-Nation Influence: A Formal Model," *American Political Science Review*, 57:2 (June 1963), 422.

18. Sidney Hook, "Foreign Policy for Survival," *New Leader*, April 7, 1958, p. 10.

19. William T. R. Fox, "The Reconciliation of the Desirable and the Possible," *American Scholar*, Spring 1949, p. 215.

20. Charles Burton Marshall, "Understanding the Unaligned," in Laurence W. Martin (ed.), *Neutralism and Nonalignment*. New York: Praeger, 1962, p. 16.

21. Richard A. Falk (ed.), *The Vietnam War and International Law*. Princeton, N.J.: Princeton University Press, 1968, p. 633.

22. Vidkun Quisling, "A Nordic World Federation," *British Union Quarterly*, 1:1 (1937), 101.

23. Marshall, "On Understanding the Unaligned," p. 17.

Additional Readings

Additional readings on the subject of national interest may be found in *Discord and Harmony: Readings in International Politics*, edited by Ivo D. Duchacek and published by Holt, Rinehart and Winston in 1972. Hans J. Morgenthau's key concept of interest in terms of power and a critique by Stanley Hoffmann are in the chapter "National Interest and Power," pp. 99-123.

Part II
LEADERS
Their Perceptions
and Beliefs

5
Foreign-Policy Making: The Certainty of Uncertainty

Scanning the international horizon, national leaders have the responsibility to ponder how much *security* against what kind of *threats* to what *values* should be attained by what *means* and at what *cost* to other values. National leaders always know that something must be done and that they will bear responsibility for whatever is done or not done; rarely, however, if ever, do they know all that they need to know. In the process of foreign-policy making, beset by many uncertainties, there is often, ironically, only one certainty—the certainty of uncertainty. Two uncertainties are basic: first, the comparative capacity of nations to achieve their objectives, and, second, the question of what nations intend to do with the power they have.

NATIONAL CAPABILITIES

The need to influence or control others is always present in domestic and international politics. This is what politics is about: the pursuit, exercise, and control of power.

By power, we mean the ability to move others, to produce intended effects, to realize one's own will. The definition may be elaborated in many ways with different emphases. Hans J. Morgenthau defined power as control over the minds and actions of men; his definition concentrates on

139

the problem of affecting the minds of men so as to provoke the desired action on their part: cooperation, submission, restraint, or enthusiasm, as the case may be.

Louis J. Halle defined power as an "ability to get what one wants by whatever means—by eloquence, reasoned argument, bluff, trade, threat, or coercion; but also by arousing pity, annoying others, or making them uneasy." His definition reminds us that power in politics should not be equated with physical coercion or the threat of it. Certain uses of naked force alienate consent. But, Halle noted, "certain uses of naked force may attract consent. Enough force to make up for the loss of consent may, in fact, keep the consent from being lost."[1] The use of naked force for the purpose of attack, seizure, extermination, or defense against an invading army should therefore be distinguished from the use or threat of violence to produce compliance or another change of behavior on the part of the victim. If violence is credible yet *avoidable* by compliance, a victim may change his behavior in order to avoid or shorten the inflicted pain. In his study *Arms and Influence* (1966) Thomas C. Schelling analytically distinguished the power to repel or expel, penetrate or occupy, and disable or destroy from the *power to hurt* for the purpose of coercion. Terrorism, seizing hostages, atomic deterrence, and blackmail are good examples of Schelling's concept of the power to hurt, that is, coercive violence. In its function as a bargaining power (which takes into account the victim's interests and fears) the power to hurt is an instrument of diplomacy rather than military strategy in the narrow sense of the word.

Arnold Wolfers distinguished between influence and power. Influence is defined as the "capacity to move others through promises and grants of benefits," while power means the ability to move others by "the threat of infliction of more or less serious deprivations."[2] But as Halle noted, the threat may be implicit. Behind the proffered hand a menacing sword may flash. Although in theory it is better to achieve consent by persuasion than compel acquiescence by threat of violence, in practice the line between the two may be quite unclear. If a superpower endowed with the capacity to inflict considerable economic damage (for instance, by its manipulation of tariffs or credits or by the imposition of a blockade) offers a small country a new form of close economic cooperation, can the target country dissociate the lure of possible benefits from the implicit threat of economic sanctions? The expectation of benefits merges with that of anticipated damage into one powerful stream of influence that may bend the will of a nation exposed to it. The implicit threat accompanying many a diplomatic negotiation will be further analyzed in Chapter 14.

The interplay between those whose aim is to influence or control others and those who are exposed to power is extremely complex. It is, first of all, a two-way flow: The stream of influence that emanates from one power source is penetrated in the opposite direction by either resistance or counterinfluence. The exercise of political influence is affected from both ends, just as the nature of war is determined not only by the method of aggression but also by the method of defense.

In so complex a framework it seems almost impossible to try to isolate and yet comparatively evaluate the power of any nation. However, it is being done and must be done. Those who endeavor to influence or control others by persuasion or threats need to know the resistance of their target to power as well as their own capacity to counterinfluence others.

In estimating one's own and other nations' power a serious error could be committed if one were to take into consideration only the obvious and physical elements of national power, such as the size of the armed forces, and neglect the elusive and nonphysical ingredients of power, such as reputation.

Elements of National Power

Physical Elements   Some of the elements of national power are quite evident and to a great extent measurable. Four broad categories of tangible resources may be identified:

1.   *Military strength, actual and potential*—the size of the armed forces; the effectiveness of its weapons; the quality of its officer corps; the training, skill, and morale of the rank and file; the quality of its strategic concepts and tactical plans; and the reliability of the intelligence and counterintelligence services.
2.   *The advantages or drawbacks of the nation's geography*—its size, topography, climate, the defensibility of its approaches, its location in relation to sources of danger or support.
3.   *The favorable and unfavorable aspects of the nation's demography*—the size, age, health, and decline and growth of its population, especially in relation to food and industrial production.
4.   *The overall performance of the nation's economy*—the correct estimate of the nation's gross national product, actual and potential raw material resources, food and industrial productivity, trade and payment balances, capital available for investment; the state of the nation's technology, research, technical skills, and other kinds of education; the degree and ratio of skills in the nation's labor force; the degree of modernity and efficiency of the nation's industrial plants, research laboratories, and transportation system, including the number and sophistication of the nation's computer systems; the quality of industrial and financial management; and the extent of the nation's dependence on imports of fuel, food, fodder, and essential minerals and metals.

It is difficult to estimate a foreign nation's capabilities in these categories, especially in the case of an enemy nation interested in concealing its weaknesses and emphasizing its strengths. Secrets often have to be pierced by cloak-and-dagger espionage activities. Information of military significance is now being increasingly obtained by regular surveillance by satellites. Relatively accessible data concerning the power of nations are obtained by constant research and field observation by diplomatic and consular officers and by military attachés who have been assigned to foreign countries with the task, among others, of obtaining reliable information concerning their power and intentions.

Nonphysical Elements The nonphysical elements of national power, which elude exact measurement, may sometimes be more important than the estimates of a nation's geography, demography, economy, and military power. In domestic politics, when we refer to the effective power of an individual—a party secretary or a chairman of a congressional committee—we rarely refer to his muscular structure or his power to coerce. Rather, the quantity and quality of his power depends on such elusive ingredients as prestige, reputation based on past achievements, character, brilliance of mind, oratorical talent, and skill in tactics of persuasion. To a great extent, this observation applies also to the power of nations on the international scene. The effectiveness of the physical might of nations depends on the quality of the nonphysical aspects of national power. These may be described in the following four categories:

1. *National character* It is important to know whether an ally or enemy, on the basis of its national character (whether shaped by previous history or inherited), tends to face an adverse situation boldly, prefers to compromise, or just muddles through. National character may or may not be reflected in the personalities of national leaders. Sometimes national leaders represent the very opposite of what is considered the national character and therefore stand out in history as truly exceptional. At other times it may be said that national leaders personify the best or the worst characteristics of their national communities. The concept of national character may be quite unscientific but, as noted in Chapter 2, it may represent an important factor in actual decision making if policy makers believe a particular national stereotype is true.

2. *Internal cohesion* The degree and quality of internal cohesion may be a more decisive factor in a given situation than any of the four physical components of national power listed earlier. By internal cohesion we mean the identification of the people with one another and with the policies and ideology of their government. Divisions in an ethnically heterogeneous state, a disgruntled opposition to the government's policies, or the realization on the part of the population that the government has been lying to it may decrease considerably the military and economic power of a nation, however formidable its size and quality may appear statistically. A half-hearted support of national policies may reduce by more than half the

nation's economic and military effort. The international consequences of internal dissent were examined in Chapter 3.

3. *Reputation* A nation's image and the corresponding admiration and trust, or hatred and suspicion, on the part of other nations may considerably increase or decrease the nation's effectiveness on the international scene. Reputation is closely connected with all the other elements of national power, including military and economic might. Sir Harold Nicolson, the famous British authority on the subject of foreign policy, once posed the question whether it was possible "for power based upon reputation to maintain itself against reputation based on power." His answer to the question was, "It is not possible."[3] Yet in connection with its physical power, the attractive or repulsive features of a nation's image abroad represent an important asset or drawback in the nation's efforts to influence or persuade others. A nation's reputation should be viewed as a composite of many ingredients. These include its present wealth and physical might, past and present achievements on the international and domestic scene (such as economic progress, social welfare, technical innovations, performance in outer space, and national contributions to the arts, literature, medicine, and sciences), and the nation's known stand on major world issues of the day: colonialism, the United Nations, foreign aid, and war and peace. Part of the nation's reputation is also its skill in projecting a favorable image abroad through information activities and cultural exchanges. The failures of a nation in one field may outweigh some of its achievements in others. Despite its high standard of living, its military and economic might, its record in democracy, technology, and space exploration, the image of freedom and generosity projected by the United States in humanitarian aid programs is damaged by some aspects of its record in the matter of food and fuel waste. In an age where the mass media bring wars, the suffering of civilian populations, and the maimed bodies of women and children right into our living rooms the war in Vietnam in particular marred the image of the United States, which is now seen as a callous yet unsuccessful military power. To the Vietnam war should be added the violent death of three national leaders within a decade—John F. Kennedy, Martin Luther King, Jr., and Robert F. Kennedy—crime statistics, and the worldwide focus on racism and other aspects of the black-white tension as damaging the image of the United States. (See Fig. 5.1.)

The image of the Soviet Union similarly suffers from the obvious disparity between the often proclaimed superiority of communism over capitalism and from the purges, the succession crises, and the people's dissatisfaction, especially in the areas of food, housing, art, literature, and freedom of opinion and travel. Also, nobody can disregard the fact that some of the glorified major projects of the various Soviet Five-Year Plans were in part based on forced labor, the cruelest form of labor exploitation. Under Stalin the GULAG (Penal Camps Adminis-

FIGURE 5.1

AN ENGLISH VIEW OF THE UNITED STATES

—"Always there is a black spot in our sunshine—It is the shadow of ourselves"—Carlyle

Drawing by Franklin in the *Daily Mirror*, London.

tration) became the single largest employer in the Soviet Union, then often labeled a "workers' paradise." Some of the most depressing documentary evidence of the Stalin era of building socialism is contained in Alexander I. Solzhenitsyn's book *The Gulag Archipelago, 1918-1956*. In the book the Russian writer (expelled in 1974 from the Soviet Union) quotes a plea, uttered by the former head of the Soviet secret police, Yagoda, during his trial in 1936 and addressed to Stalin: "I appeal to you! *For you* I built two great canals."

Many of the ingredients of a nation's image abroad are true, some are distorted, and some have no basis in reality at all. But in international politics as in love affairs, as Hans J. Morgenthau pointed out, what others think of us is as important as what we actually are.

4. *Leadership* One of the most important components of the power of a nation is its leadership, which includes the intelligence, alertness, and expertness of the leaders as well as the nature of the political system, which may be either modern or obsolete and whose constitutional and organizational setup may either significantly enlarge or restrain the

leaders' policy-making process. In evaluating another nation's leadership we therefore include the interaction between a given political system and the personal qualities of its top policy makers and their staffs, the quality and completeness of their information, and the performance of diplomatic officers, intelligence agents, and military and scientific personnel and planners. An inept foreign minister may squander a nation's assets and transform its political, economic, and military potential into sterile elements. On the other hand, an expert and alert political leadership, endowed with imagination as well as common sense, may multiply the nation's capabilities, its international influence as well as its internal cohesion, to the nth degree. Under good leadership, changes on the international scene are quickly perceived, foreign nations' goals and planned actions are properly evaluated, opportunities are wisely exploited, and challenges are flexibly and efficiently met.

Weighing all the ingredients of foreign national power is a tremendous task never fully accomplished, because a great amount of data is unobtainable even by the best of spies. Furthermore, one must not only evaluate but also compare one's own and one's adversaries' tangible and intangible factors. The intangible factors defy precise measurement and therefore meaningful comparison. In addition, one should be able to project the comparison into the future, that is, anticipate changes in one or all components of national power. The untimely death of a statesman, a scientific breakthrough in a military laboratory, an economic crisis, or social unrest may profoundly alter the original estimate of a nation's potential.

EVALUATING FOREIGN GOALS AND INTENTIONS

However approximate all estimates of other nations' capabilities in comparison with one's own may be, such estimating is still an easier task than trying to estimate what a nation *intends* to do with the power it has or may mobilize. A mighty nation may have modest aims; a medium-sized nation may have excessive ambitions. Two mathematically equal powers would represent quite different problems on the international scene if one were led by a Hitler and the other by a Gandhi. Comparative analysis of national capabilities is therefore intimately entwined with evaluation of foreign goals and intentions, all the way from the estimate of measurable tangible factors to the estimate of intangible elements such as national morale and the quality of foreign leadership. In other words, the foreign-policy maker tries to find out whether what another nation deems desirable is also feasible or whether what seems feasible may become desirable because attainable.

A nation's power both opens and sets limits to opportunities for new goals. The nation knows it, and its neighbors and other nations know it too—all, of course, very roughly. Geographic location, transportation, and resources to some extent determine attainable national goals. In Morton Kaplan's words: "Logistic considerations predispose nations to some objective rather than others which—apart from logistic considerations—may be equally desirable."[4] A small nation often fears a mighty nation because the latter may conceivably abuse its power sometime in the future, however unambitious its intentions are in the present. Many small nations feel that where there is power, there may be ambition, especially those whose fate it has been to live very close to a superpower, such as Poland and Czechoslovakia uncomfortably squeezed between Russia and Germany, Mongolia between Russia and China, and Mexico and Canada living along the borders of the United States. "Living next to you is in some ways like sleeping with an elephant," said Canada's Prime Minister Pierre Elliott Trudeau at the National Press Club in Washington (March 26, 1969). "No matter how friendly and even-tempered is the beast, if I can call it that, one is affected by every twitch and grunt."

If power without hostile intentions may frighten, hostile intentions without power usually do not. If, for instance, the Grand Duchy of Luxembourg (a NATO ally with a population of 400,000 and an area of 999 sq. mi.) were to announce its intention to conquer the United States next year, no real crisis would develop in Washington unless such a public threat were a grossly exaggerated way of announcing that Luxembourg was severing its relations with the Atlantic Alliance and joining the People's Republic of China in a military alliance. On the other hand, a more modest intention announced by China—for instance, a plan to conquer only Hawaii—would have quite a different effect.

The relationship between power and intentions has been illustrated artificially by the use of two extreme examples: a superpower with or without superambitions and a minipower whose ambition has no effect. In reality such extreme contrasts are relatively rare. There exist only two superpowers in the world today; their capabilities, however, are certainly not unlimited and their use not uninhibited. The rest are small, medium, more-than-medium powers and three potential great powers—China, Japan, and Western Europe. History has also taught us that national leaders are only partly restrained by available capabilities, for they can mobilize or improvise untapped resources for the purpose of promoting an ambitious goal.[5] Even a nation endowed with modest power may have unmodest regional intentions; and in a situation of danger, a small power may also hope to repeat a feat similar to David's against Goliath. Even an accurate "perception of one's own inferior capability, if anxiety, fear, or perceptions of threat or injury are intense enough, will fail to deter a nation going to war."[6]

A word of caution should be added about military power as a codeterminant of policy goals. In 1938 Mao Tse-tung, commenting on Chiang Kai-shek, made this frequently quoted statement:

> Whoever has an army has power, for war settles everything; [Chiang Kai-shek] has firmly grasped this crucial point. In this respect we ought to learn from him. And in this respect both Sun Yat-sen and Chiang Kai-shek are our teachers. . . . *Political power grows out of the barrel of a gun.* [Italics added.][7]

In international politics of the nuclear age, it would be inaccurate to rewrite Mao's thought as "Political power grows out of the MIRV (Multiple Independently-Targeted Reentry Vehicle)." That political power growing out of the barrel of a gun or the nose of a missile may be ineffective is indicated by the survival of Cuba as a communist outpost off the American shores, by the challenge to the American superpower demonstrated by North Vietnam and by North Korea's downing of an American intelligence plane and capture of the intelligence ship *Pueblo*, by the increased loss of timidity on the part of Latin-American nations (Peru's seizure of American oil companies and fishing vessels in 1968 and 1969), and by the demonstrated vulnerability of the United States and Western Europe to Arab oil blackmail (1973-1974). In particular, a superpower's capability to destroy coupled with a fear of escalation and possible self-annihilation has actually decreased its political power, that is, its capacity to influence and control others. A succinct and characteristic comment on this point was made by Carlos P. Romulo, foreign secretary of the Philippine Islands and formerly its representative at the United Nations. Stressing that the United States had been unable to use its superstrength in Cuba and in Vietnam, he expressed the belief that the United States was no longer dependable as an ally: "Giants cannot use the strength of giants. . . . After Vietnam I do not think the American people will ever consent to involving their troops in Asia. Thus an American defense of the Philippines in the future is highly dubious."[8]

Foreign Policy: Is It Conservative or Radical?

Both laymen and statesmen tend to reduce complex situations and events to simplified concepts and categories, often expressed in two neat opposites, one with a favorable and the other with an unfavorable connotation. Thus, goals of national leaders, political parties, ideological movements, and nation-states are often classified as either conservative or radical. In international politics a national conservative policy is usually referred to as *status quo* policy, that is, one that aims at preventing a radical change of the existing situation but does not object to minor, gradual changes. There is no convenient all-encompassing term for the opposite policies, which aim at preventing the continuation of the situation as is, the *status quo*. For lack of a better word, we shall use the terms "radicalism" or "radical foreign policy" to describe policies that aim at a drastic change, for instance, a dissolution of an empire or, conversely, expansionism and imperialism, that is, an attempt to establish an empire. We should bear in mind that policy aimed at preserving an empire which has already been established belongs to the category of conservative, *status quo* policies. The issue here is not to condemn or praise antiimperialism or imperialism (which can be a policy of radical change or a *status quo* policy) but to examine the appropriateness of a nation's response when confronted with either a policy of radical change or a *status quo* policy.

The proper answer to a policy of radical expansion, when detected, is, as a minimum, a policy of containment. Its goal is to raise a barrier to further advances. On the other hand, a *status quo* policy that aims at some minor adjustment in a given situation should not be answered by military containment but by a willingness to negotiate. The question, however, is how to distinguish a conservative foreign policy from a radical one.

This question, so difficult to answer in a particular situation with any degree of certainty, lies behind many contemporary controversies concerning the choice of an appropriate policy with regard to the communist powers: should it be détente or military vigilance, cooperation in the economic and scientific fields but ideological competition, peaceful coexistence combined with mutual interpenetration (convergence), or neo-Westphalian division of the world into two ideologically isolated camps? Quoting communist statements, many analysts suggest that a policy of compromise and détente is useless if Moscow and Peking, each in its own way, aim at an aggressive conquest of the whole world. Their programmatic declarations sometimes imply that this is their goal, but do they really mean it? Are they really ready to disregard realities and push forward? If the West were confronted with a *clear* case of reckless radicalism, then peacemaking could become "appeasement," a highly emotional concept borrowed from the preatomic era. At the time of Western concessions to Hitler in Munich, appeasement was usually defined as an offer of substantial (what is the exact meaning of "substantial"?) concessions in return for a mere hope of a decrease in the threat of pressure, usually coupled with a readiness to bow to an accomplished fact. Does this definition, taken out of the 1938 context, fully apply to the 1970s? Not at all, says one American scholar, John H. Herz, and offers his new definition of appeasement for the present era of nuclear balancing and adjustments.

> Charges of appeasement levelled against a policy that aims at avoiding war are no longer relevant in an age when major war, because of its nature,

has ceased to be an instrument of policy even on the part of expansionist regimes. Stigmatizing as appeasement policies of balancing and adjustment misses the point in a world where such policies are the only means to assure peaceful coexistence of, or peaceful competition among, antagonistic blocs and systems.[9]

According to the dictionary, "appeasement" means pacification or conciliation, and there should be nothing wrong with this meaning in our era. In the 1930s, however, the term "appeasement" was used to describe a basic error in foreign-policy evaluation, namely responding to a radical foreign policy that aimed at the conquest of the world as if it were a conservative policy that aimed only at minor changes within the framework of the *status quo*.

Theoretically, it may be assumed that nations satisfied with the existing situation pursue a policy of *status quo*; like all conservatives, they can only profit from preserving a given order of things. Often such a policy is praised for its opposition to war, an extreme disturbance of the *status quo*. But automatically endowing a *status quo* policy with a blanket approval of its opposition to war might be wrong. A conservative policy, while peaceable, may be objectionable when it aims at keeping conquered nations enslaved. Typically, Churchill once proclaimed that he would not preside over the dissolution of the British Empire. India at that time was against the *status quo* and was a revisionist power. Similarly, Communist Russia is a *status quo* and conservative nation with regard to the order of things in East Central Europe. Speaking at Minsk in January 1958, Soviet Premier Nikita Khrushchev proclaimed himself a *status quo* politician; on other occasions he continued to advocate the total elimination of capitalism from the surface of the earth:

> What then do Messrs. Eisenhower and Dulles want? . . . They evidently want us to give up socialist construction and to restore the capitalist order [in East Central Europe]. Some people go so far as to suggest a public opinion poll in the Socialist countries as to whether they are for socialism or capitalism. . . . If the *status quo* is not recognized . . . and if the domestic affairs [of the Socialist states] are interfered in, then it is, of course, absolutely impossible to come to terms.[10]

This was a criticism of the United States's policy on the liberation of Soviet satellites, proclaimed in 1952, which had placed it in the category of radical nations with regard to that particular area. As the attitudes of both the Soviets and the Americans demonstrate, a nation may simultaneously be *status quo* and radical with respect to different geographic areas. In other words, nations try to keep what they have but try to take or alter what others have. The Soviet view that the Russian sphere of exclusive influence in East Central Europe is a nonnegotiable issue was reconfirmed by the so-called Brezhnev Doctrine on the Soviet Union's right to impose its own brand of socialism on other communist countries (see Document 11.7).

A policy of radicalism is usually adopted by nations that are highly dissatisfied with the *status quo* and trying to upset it; for this reason, it is often associated with war and condemned. Here again one should exercise caution before either condemning or praising radicalism as such. The merit of such a policy depends on whether it opposes an order of things that one views as just or unjust. One man's well-being may be another man's injustice.

Policy Changes

Statesmen and newspapers use the terms *status quo*, anti-imperialism, and expansionism in order to praise or condemn one or the other policy, depending on their point of view. In practice, however, the distinction between these policies is less clear than their frequent praise or condemnation would suggest. This is so for several reasons.

First, no nation is ever fully satisfied or dissatisfied with an existing situation. As soon as we add that we mean a *highly* satisfied or *highly* dissatisfied nation, our question becomes one of degree rather than of kind. Dissatisfaction with a given situation is often tempered by the notion that an attempt at change might create a worse situation than the present one. Thus, temporarily, an unsatisfactory situation is accepted. The "temporary," however, may become permanent.

Second, the dynamics of economic and social progress impose constant changes; even the most conservative nation cannot freeze the present into perpetuity. But in this case, the question arises, Which are the changes that remain within the *status quo*, and which are those that fundamentally (how fundamentally?) alter it?

Third, a nation's policy changes under the impact of other nations' countermeasures and counterpolicies. This represents a very complex problem in the never-ending process of evaluating other nations' real intentions. A nation may pursue a highly desirable and apparently attainable objective until it discovers that what is still highly desirable has become unattainable as a result of a change of policy or the adoption of effective countermeasures on the part of the adversary. Goals and means are constantly modified in the light of changing opportunities or dangers.

Successful containment of an expansionist power may transform the power's radical goals into a reluctant acceptance of the *status quo*. On the other hand, a *status quo* nation may become a radical power when it discovers that its modest demands for minor changes in the *status quo* framework are met with what seems an unjustified resistance; a *status quo* nation may thus be prodded into risky adventures. Radical-ism on the part of a *status quo* power may also result from the fact that the first concessions have been obtained with an ease that encourages the nation to press for more.

Although change of policy as a result of the appearance of an in-superable obstacle or a tempting opportunity is probable, we cannot be certain that an obstacle or opportunity is correctly perceived and evalu-ated by other nations. History is replete with examples of policies and commitments that failed to be recognized by the other side: Germany under the Kaiser underestimated the reality of the British commitment to the defense of France, and Germany in 1914 was genuinely sur-prised by the immediate British reaction to the invasion of Belgium. Similarly, Hitler in 1939 unrealistically hoped that his treaty with Stalin (which also had relieved him of any worry about a Soviet counterattack in the event of a European war) would frighten England and France into another Munich at the expense of Poland. Both England and France were still ruled by the same appeasers who had surrendered their ally, Czechoslovakia, to Germany. Speaking of Neville Chamber-lain and Edouard Daladier to his generals, Adolf Hitler boasted: "The men I got to know in Munich are not the kind that start a new world war."[11] Hitler's plan at that time was to limit his military opera-tions to Poland; world war was planned for a later date.

The problem of making a commitment clear to the opposite side was interestingly raised in 1963 by French Minister of Information Alain Peyrefitte when he argued for an independent French atomic deterrent. He expressed the opinion that, so far as France was concerned, it con-fidently relied on the promise of the President of the United States not to hesitate to use its atomic arsenal in defense of Paris. But, according to Peyrefitte, the problem was not that of French doubts but of Soviet hopes that the United States would not dare to risk its cities for Paris. In view of these Soviet doubts, the United States's atomic arsenal, he argued, was not an effective deterrent to Soviet aggression against Western Europe. France needed better security in the form of her own *force de frappe*.

Miscalculations in Korea, Israel, and Finland

It is sometimes argued that the beginning and then the climax of the Korean conflict were due to the Soviet-North Korean and Amer-ican failure to evaluate properly each other's real intentions. It is alleged that the North Korean Communists felt justified in the expecta-tion that their conquest of South Korea would not be opposed by the United States in view of the latter's withdrawal of armed forces from Korea during the preceding year and in view of Dean Acheson's speech on United States policy in the Far East, delivered on January

12, 1950, in which Korea was not included in the defense perimeter in the Pacific. Acheson said:

> What is the situation in regard to military security of the Pacific area and what is our policy in regard to it? . . .
> The defensive perimeter runs along the Aleutians to Japan and then goes to the Ryukyu Islands [Okinawa] . . . and those we will continue to hold. . . . The defense perimeter runs from the Ryukyus to the Philippine Islands. . . .An attack on the Philippines could not and would not be tolerated by the United States. . . .
> Should an attack occur [in other areas in the Pacific] . . . the initial reliance must be on the people attacked to resist it and then upon the commitments of the entire civilized world under the Charter of the United Nations.[12]

The references to the "civilized world" and the "United Nations" instead of a clear promise of United States military aid were probably read by Moscow as a suggestion that American military power would not be made available for the purpose of repelling an attack on South Korea. It is possible that President Truman's decision to act immediately and with vigor came as a complete surprise.

Five months later, the United States, on the other hand, seems to have grossly miscalculated the effect on Peking of its crossing the 38th parallel in pursuit of the defeated North Korean army. On October 7, 1950, the Indian representative at the United Nations warned against the possible extension of the Korean conflict if the American armies approached the sensitive area of Chinese Manchuria: "My government fears that the result [of crossing the Yalu River] may be to prolong North Korean resistance, and even to extend the area of conflict. Our fears may turn out to be wrong, but each government has to judge the situation upon the best information at its disposal and to act accordingly."[13]

A month before (September 5), Secretary of State Acheson had declared, "I should think it would be sheer madness on the part of the Chinese Communists to do that [enter the Korean conflict] and I see no advantage to them in doing so." With the benefit of our present knowledge of the Chinese concern with Soviet imperialism and "great power chauvinism," it is interesting to note that Dean Acheson then tried to present the military action of the United States in Korea as being directed solely against "imperialism coming down from the Soviet Union"; therefore, as he alleged, the military action of the United States actually protected the Chinese national interests that, in Acheson's words, were threatened by "a great cloud from the North, where Russian penetration is operating."[14]

These words also reflected the American government's conviction, as John W. Spanier noted in his study on the Truman-MacArthur controversy,

. . . that the Sino-Soviet conflict would absorb all the energies of the Chinese Communist leaders in the coming months. Consequently, Red China's intervention came as a complete surprise. When one Senator later commented, "They really fooled us when it comes right down to it; didn't they?" the Secretary could only reply: "Yes, Sir."[15]

It was also in the early phase of the Korean conflict that the Pentagon became a victim of a false alarm that Soviet bombers were on their way to attack the United States (geese on a radar screen?). All aircraft in the United States were placed on an immediate alert and the American fighter planes in Canada were sent aloft. This was revealed nine years later by Dean Acheson, who had been Truman's secretary of state at the time. In a speech delivered at a strategy seminar for a group of reserve officers (July 21, 1959) he said that the then Secretary of Defense, Robert A. Lovett, had telephoned him the alarm just a few moments before British Prime Minister Clement R. Attlee was to confer wtih President Truman at the White House. Acheson, in turn, telephoned the alarm to the British ambassador, Sir Oliver Franks, whose unperturbed reply was, "You don't say so." He was right.

Another example of a fateful miscalculation was that of Israel in 1973 when she did not anticipate and prepare for a well-prepared Arab attack aimed at the reconquest of territories lost in 1967 and before. In a dispatch from Beirut the *New York Times* (October 10, 1973) summarized the Western diplomats' observations as follows:

> Western diplomats here are convinced that the Arabs, by keeping their plans confined to a few top leaders, and through a rare miscalculation in Israeli intelligence, were able to achieve surprise in their attacks last Saturday. . . . "Regardless of the outcome of the battles, a number of myths are being destroyed," a Westerner said in an interview. "One is the myth that the Arabs can't fight. Another is that the Arabs can't keep a military secret. And a third is that Israeli intelligence is perfect."

A subsequent study of Israeli intelligence errors, undertaken by the Israelis themselves as well as by United States, neutral, and Arab intelligence experts, revealed that the Israeli intelligence service was committed to the idea that Egypt would attack only if she had enough air power to knock out the Israeli Air Force and its bases. Blinded by their belief in this idea, the Israelis discounted the significance of the Russian evacuation of Soviet families from Egypt and did not properly evaluate various warnings, communicated by junior Israeli officers, that the deployment of the Egyptian ground forces in September was not maneuvers but camouflage for a general offensive. When finally the offensive began, it was not preceded by air-strikes because it was based on the Soviet-Egyptian "meat-grinder" strategy. That strategy rejected the aerial preparation concept and concentrated on the extensive use of tanks, Soviet ground-to-ground and ground-to-air missiles, and artillery.

An investigating commission, headed by Israel's chief justice, found that the Israeli chief of staff, Lieutenant General David Elazar, as well as the commander on the Egyptian front and the director of military intelligence, was responsible for the wrong assessments and therefore for the lack of preparedness. The commission recommended the replacement of all these and other officers, adding that it was "painful to criticize General Elazar because he had eventually led the armed forces to victory."

Well-organized dictatorial regimes do not appear any more immune to human errors or wishful thinking than democratic systems. The German High Command was in possession of various correct pieces of information concerning the date and place of the Allied storming of Hitler's "Fortress Europe" and yet the Allied landings on specific beaches in Normandy came as a costly surprise. In another authoritarian context, that of the Soviet Union, former premier Nikita Khrushchev described in his memoirs how costly Moscow's underestimation of the Finnish determination and skill in defending their land had proved to be:

> Finland represented a real threat to us because its territory could be used by more powerful governments. We wanted the Finns to give up a certain amount of territory and so move the border farther away from Leningrad. The Finns refused, so we were left with no choice but to decide the question by war. . . . This was Stalin's idea. . . . In this case I agreed that it was the right thing to do. All we had to do was to raise our voice a little bit, and the Finns would obey. If that didn't work, we could fire one shot and the Finns would put up their hands and surrender. So we thought. . . . Of course we didn't have any legal right. As far as morality is concerned, our desire to protect ourselves justified ourselves in our own eyes. . . . I'd say we lost as many as a million lives. Timoshenko [a Soviet marshal] told me that faulty intelligence hadn't been to blame; our intelligence services had known about the Finnish defenses all along. The trouble was that no intelligence officers had been consulted when our first strike was planned. I can't imagine how this kind of stupidity was permitted.[16]

The international scene abounds with more wrong or belated responses to true warnings and false alarms than even the domestic scene. This is so for many reasons. First, there is the sheer amount of information to be recorded, sorted out, digested, and evaluated according to reliability, importance, and relevance. Inaccuracy and incompleteness are frequent. This problem of communication gaps in international politics will be examined in more detail later. Second, there is the general international practice of bluff and deceit. Facts and data are deliberately concealed or distorted, especially those that are concerned with national survival, secret weapons and strategic plans. In the case of the Egyptian preparation for attack against Israel in October 1973, for instance, the Egyptian army staged its usual autumn exercises in the Suez canal area; the brigades involved in the exercise, as observed by the Israelis, appeared to withdraw from the canal area each evening. In fact, the Egyptians were withdrawing only one battalion of the brigades each evening and leaving two-thirds of the units in assault positions close to the canal. Third, a national government usually finds it technically easier to penetrate the secrets of its domestic opposition with spies or electronic bugs[17] than to plant a spy or a bug in the Kremlin, Mao's chambers, or Castro's bedroom—all places where such efforts are anticipated and therefore guarded against by counter-intelligence and counterbugging. Fourth, even if the national leaders believe the intelligence estimates to be true, they may disregard them because acting according to them could have unpleasant consequences for the leaders' political investment in a particular policy, their public commitment, and therefore their position on the domestic scene. Allegedly, one of the reasons why Daniel Ellsberg decided to publish confidential documents concerning the decision-making processes in the conduct of the war in Vietnam (the *Pentagon Papers*, 1971) was his realization that no amount of documentary evidence and rational argument seemed to have produced any effect on the President's commitment to continue the war in Vietnam as he saw fit.

INTERNATIONAL POLITICS AS A COMMUNICATION GRID

The system of territorial states in which all constantly influence all may be imagined as a global communication grid, a rather haphazardly woven web of constantly interacting messages and signals that in part deliberately, in part unintentionally, cross national boundaries. National leaders (and their advisers) as well as subnational groups such as the political opposition, ethnic-racial groups, special interest groups, and foreign-policy-promoting associations, including the mass media (the transnational roles of these groups were discussed in Chapter 3) initiate, transmit, process, evaluate, interpret, and react to political information. "The communication process pervades politics as an activity," Richard Fagen pointed out. "Almost all political behavior involves communication activity of some sort."[18] This fully applies to the subject of our study, international politics. Some messages and signals with potential or actual political consequence remain within national boundaries, others cross them to be processed, studied, and reacted to by foreign foe or friend.

"Messages and signals" include the following three general types of transnational communication:

1. *Public statements* made by national leaders or their opponents and

intended to be read and reacted to by domestic or foreign audiences or both. A public speech or declaration may be read, evaluated, and acted upon also by those for whom it was not initially intended. For instance, a public address intended for home consumption that justifies new tax burdens imposed on the citizens by social needs may be internationally read and understood as an indication of that nation's decision to engage in an armament race—an interpretation which may or may not be correct.

2. *Coded secret information* contained in intelligence and diplomatic reports sent from foreign posts all over the world to the national headquarters. Such reports often transmit information the foreign governments tried but failed to conceal. Former United States Secretary of State Dean Rusk described the continuous stream of diplomatic messages into the State Department Operations Center

> Day and night information pours into this center from all over the world, including up to 1000 telegraphic dispatches every 24 hours. Responsible officers are on duty around the clock and others meet here continuously to be briefed and to work out plans. . . . All this intensive activity is directed essentially to our main business: the advancement of American interests in our foreign relations. . . . Daily, sometimes hourly, we ask ourselves: What does this particular development mean to the United States and the rest of the free world? Does it endanger our interests? If so, are we taking the right action to protect them? What more can be done?[19]

The physical appearance of the Operations Center is a "mixture between Walter Cronkite's TV newsroom millions of Americans see on television every night and a Dr. Strangelove's office," reported the *New York Times* (January 26, 1968). There are teletype machines that encode and decode the top-secret messages transmitted through them, wall clocks giving the times around the world, a white telephone that rings at the White House Situation Room, a gold telephone connected with the Pentagon, and a powder-blue telephone for the Operations Center at the Central Intelligence Agency. And there is a small soundproof "Telecon Room," where the secretary of state may "talk" to American outposts by means of wall screens that instantly flash incoming and outgoing questions and answers.

Halfway between public declarations and secret messages are formal diplomatic notes that are transmitted from one national capital to another and whose contents usually remain confidential until both parties agree to their publication. Another form of confidential message whose contents often find their way into public statements is the direct exchange of views and arguments that takes place between diplomats or national leaders at summit conferences (see Document 5.1). To permit such direct and confidential exchange of views at the summit in nuclear

DOCUMENT 5.1

JFK ON SOVIET GOALS

Mr. Khrushchev and I had a very full and frank exchange of views on the major issues that now divide our two countires. . . .

I had read his speeches of his policies. I had been advised on his views. I had been told by other leaders of the West—General de Gaulle, Chancellor Adenauer, Prime Minister Macmillan—what manner of man he was. But I bear the responsibility of the Presidency of the United States and it is my duty to make decisions that no advisor and no ally can make for me. It is my obligation and responsibility to see that these decisions are as informed as possible; that they are based upon as much direct, first-hand knowledge as possible. I therefore thought it was of immense importance that I know Mr. Khrushchev, that I gain as much insight and understanding as I could on his present and future policies. At the same time I wanted to make certain Mr. Khrushchev knew this country and its policies; that he understood our strength and our determination, and that ke knew that we desired peace with all nations of every kind. . . .

Our views contrasted sharply, but at least we knew better at the end where we both stood. . . . The gap between us was not, in such a short period, materially reduced but at least the channels of communication were opened more fully. At least the chances of a dangerous misjudgment on either side should now be less, and, at least, the men on whose decisions the peace, in part, depends have agreed to remain in contact.

Generally, Mr. Khrushchev did not talk in terms of war. He believes the world will move his way without resort to force. He spoke of his nation's achievement in space. He stressed his intention to outdo us in industrial production, to out-trade us, to prove to the world the superiority of his system over ours.

Most of all, he predicted the triumph of communism in the new and less-developed countries. He was certain that the tide was moving his way, that the revolution of rising peoples would eventually be a Communist revolution, and that the so-called wars of liberation supported by the Kremlin would replace the old methods of direct aggression and invasion.

From John F. Kennedy's Address to the Nation on his meeting with Khrushchev in Vienna, June 6, 1961.

emergencies, the United States and the Soviet Union introduced the so-called hot line between the White House and the Kremlin (see Document 5.2). This was negotiated and agreed on two years after Kennedy's meeting with Khrushchev in Vienna and eight months after the Cuban missile crisis, which, among other things, may have proved that Kennedy learned more from their direct contact than Khrushchev, who in the middle of the Cuban missile crisis complained that he could not understand Kennedy and added: "How can I deal with a man who is younger than my son?" This was reported by William Knox, an

DOCUMENT 5.2

WHITE HOUSE–KREMLIN DIRECT LINK

For use in time of emergency the Government of the United States of America and the Government of the Union of Soviet Socialist Republics have agreed to establish as soon as technically feasible a direct communications link between the two Governments.

Each Government shall be responsible for the arrangements for the link on its own territory. Each Government shall take the necessary steps to ensure continuous functioning of the link and prompt delivery to its head of government of any communications received by means of the link from the head of government of the other party. . . .

Done in duplicate in the English and Russian languages at Geneva, Switzerland, this 20th day of June, 1963. . . .

The direct communications link between Washington and Moscow established in accordance with the Memorandum, and the operation of such link, shall be governed by the following provisions:

1. The direct communications link shall consist of:
   a. Two terminal points with telegraph-teleprinter equipment between which communications shall be directly exchanged;
   b. One full-time duplex wire telegraph circuit, routed Washington-London-Copenhagen-Stockholm-Helsinki-Moscow, which shall be used for the transmission of messages;
   c. One full-time duplex radio telegraph circuit, routed Washington-Tangier-Moscow, which shall be used for service communications and for coordination of operations between the two terminal points. . . .
2. In case of interruption of the wire circuit, transmission of messages shall be effected via the radio circuit, and for this purpose provision shall be made at the terminal points for the capability of prompt switching of all necessary equipment from one circuit to another.

From U.S. Department of State, *Treaties and Other International Acts*, Series 5362. Washington, D.C.: Government Printing Office, 1963.

A Postscript Ten Years Later

In 1973 the Washington-Moscow hot line was transferred to a network of Soviet and American communication satellites. The new system was chosen in part to place the hot line beyond the reach of human interference. During the ten years of its existence, parts of the hot line cable have been blacked out by fire, stolen, and, in one case, plowed up by a farmer in Finland. The radio route has also been subject to atmospheric interference. However, there is no indication that the new hot line will be used any more than the old one, which reportedly was used once during the third Israeli-Arab war in 1967 but not during the fourth war in 1973.

American businessman then in Moscow who was summoned by Khrushchev to the Kremlin to hear and report on the Soviet thunder.[20]

3. *Mass media reports* on (*a*) political *events*, such as elections, revolutions, monetary crises, unemployment, or the death of a statesman; (*b*) political *acts*, such as the appointment of a new foreign minister, a leader's resignation, a new budget, new laws, or mobilization, and (*c*) industrial and technological *developments* with potential or actual political consequences, such as an increase or decline in the gross national product, a landing on Mars, a new laboratory invention, or a new weapon. Thus the stream of official public or confidential messages is daily increased many times its volume. (Political messages and acts as deliberate signaling techniques are also discussed in Chapter 13.)

On the international scene even more than on the domestic political scene we are permanently concerned with what Harold Lasswell so succinctly expressed as "Who Says What, In Which Channel, To Whom, and With What Effect."[21] We might well add, "With What Intention."

The political consequences of any signal or message that has crossed national boundaries will depend on the way in which the leading personalities and their staffs perceive and evaluate it. When a policy maker's evaluation of a message is translated into a verbal reaction (for instance, a protest or a promise of support) or an act (cooperation, war, or surrender), the event becomes a new message or signal to be fed back into the international communication system, where it is again received, evaluated, and possibly acted upon by all, or almost all, in a never-ending communicative interaction.

In international politics some of what is said may occasionally fail to reach those for whose benefit it has been said. In other instances the message reaches the policy maker but may be dismissed as unimportant, unreliable, irrelevant, or only fit to be filed for possible future reference. Still other messages are carefully studied, evaluated, and acted upon although some of them may be false. Time and again false information triggers a fateful action while correct information is disregarded.

In his *Memoirs*, the American diplomat and scholar George F. Kennan notes with some bitterness that his memoranda, papers, and suggestions usually ended up in wastepaper baskets or filing cabinets; he expresses a doubt that they were ever read, much less appreciated. Kennan served his country at different European posts—Prague, Belgrade, and twice in Moscow—as a subordinate to Ambassador Averell Harriman during World War II and after the war as an ambassador himself. Kennan reports Ambassador Harriman's belief that he could learn more from one interview with Stalin than Kennan or any other diplomatic aides could learn from months of pedestrian study of Soviet publications.[22]

Quality of Information

The usual sources of our information about foreign nations and their immediate or long-term objectives and contemplated actions are basically two: (1) the communications that the foreign nations themselves supply by public statements and actual behavior on the national and international scenes, and (2) the reports sent by our diplomatic and intelligence agents that try to penetrate other nations' nonpublic and often secret political, economic, and military activities.

Public Declarations Public declarations or foreign-policy statements give us some indication of the general line of policy, as both dictators and democratic leaders need to inform their public and to orient its efforts in a desired direction. Yet there are limits to our capacity to read between the lines. Some public statements intentionally have a double meaning. Although stressing foreign policy, they are really intended solely for domestic consumption. Other statements are outright lies intended to deceive the nation's adversaries. Policy objectives that are damaging to other nations would certainly be carefully concealed until the last moment, so that the element of surprise could be fully exploited. In the late 1930s Nazi leaders used to emphasize peaceful coexistence on the eve of their most brazen aggressive acts. Sometimes national leaders publicly present exaggerated claims in order to obtain at least some minor concession. And then there are times when national leaders mean every word of what they say but their words appear so preposterous that they are considered a mere bluff. In the early 1930s this was a common error on the part of too many West European statesmen, who tended to treat Hitler's blueprint for the conquest of Europe, *Mein Kampf*, as the work of an Austrian crackpot. This estimate had to be belatedly revised in the late 1930s, when Hitler's extraordinary ambitions were in the process of being successfully implemented.

Most public political declarations, even those made by aggressors, tend to deceive the audience by their overemphasis on the theme of defense. Everybody seems to desire to make the world safe for something he considers worthy of defending. It may be his nation, a monarchy, ideology, or a race. In the name of such a defense, many invasions were started; in the name of defense, conceivably, the whole world may be conquered.

Our knowledge of another nation's code of ethics or political ideology, as we shall see in Chapters 7 and 8, is only of limited help. A thorough study of such seemingly detailed plans for political action as communism and nazism would still not permit us accurately and reliably to forecast what

FIGURE 5.2
COUNTERESPIONAGE FAILURE

"I've checked and double checked but I'm damned if I know how the information is getting out."

Drawing by Mahood; © *Punch* 1966.

concrete steps the leaders may take when confronted with a new challenge or an opportunity to enhance what they consider their nation's or their ideology's interests. Knowledge of democratic philosophy would yield even less information about what an English Labourite or Conservative, an American Republican or Democrat, or a French Socialist or Catholic may adopt as policy in response to danger or relaxation on the international scene.

Diplomatic and Intelligence Reports The diplomatic and intelligence service is sometimes referred to as the nation's eyes and ears abroad (see Fig. 5.2). But they are only human eyes and ears, as noted previously, even if greatly helped by electronics and miniature bugging devices. The intelligence penetration into another nation's political and military secrets is never adequate. The gaps are enormous. Even in a democracy, which prides itself on its openness, not only foreign spies but even some top political leaders usually find blank spots on the national map. Vice-President Harry S. Truman, for instance, learned only twenty-four hours after President Roosevelt's death (April 12, 1945) that the United States was close to the first atomic test in history. However, the secret Truman did not know was relatively well-known to Stalin, thanks to the communist atomic spies at El Alamogordo, notably Klaus Fuchs. On that same day President Truman learned that the Joint Chiefs of Staff secretly estimated that the war in Europe would be over in six months (it was over in twenty-five days), and the war in Asia in eighteen months (it took four months).

The journey of a piece of information from actual acquisition by a diplomat or a spy to its destination on the desk of a policy maker is long and full of the dangers of possible distortion or delay. An intelligence agent located in some distant land can initiate or stop a major action by his report, provided, of course, the report reaches the leadership at all and in time and is not stopped halfway by the wrong estimate of a subordinate or by neglect or sinister design. Even when such a report reaches the top policy makers, the question remains whether they are believing and acting upon inaccurate information or whether accurate information is being discarded as a false alarm or simply as unbelievable.

During World War II, one Nazi agent working in neutral Turkey was able to obtain accurate information concerning the exact date and spot of the Allied invasion of Europe in 1944. The information was passed on to his superiors, who, unable to double-check the agent's source, discarded the information and never sent it to the top.

In 1964, on the twenty-fifth anniversary of the beginning of World War II, the Soviet Union publicly acknowledged the accuracy of intelligence information obtained by Richard Sorge, a former press officer at the German Embassy in Tokyo and head of a very successful Soviet spy ring. According to *Pravda* (September 3, 1964) Sorge was able to inform Soviet intelligence two months before Pearl Harbor that the Japanese were ready for a war against the United States in the Pacific. This vital information (which was not communicated to the United States by Moscow) enabled the Red Army to shift urgently needed reinforcements from the Far East to help stem the tide of the Nazi advance against Moscow in the late fall of 1941. Sorge further supplied information in 1941 about the impending Nazi attack on the Soviet Union, including the extent of troop concentration and the exact date. The Soviet spy was finally discovered by the Japanese counterespionage agency and was executed in Tokyo in 1944. Echoing the general 1964 line of condemnation of Joseph Stalin's war record, *Pravda* added that Stalin ignored Sorge's and similar reports that accurately predicted the Nazi onslaught and its date.

Hierarchy Corrupts Communication

One final point should be made concerning quality of information: Many people report what their superiors expect or like to hear. The reason is sometimes simply a fear of reporting the disagreeable, the unpopular, or the unorthodox. In the United States in the McCarthy period some foreign-service officers must have felt the impact of the "witchhunt," for one of its focuses was on those officers who reported on developments in communist countries in less than a totally negative way. One can guess that a Soviet diplomat or spy will think twice before reporting on events favorable to the United States, which would be an implicit questioning of some of the Marxist-Leninist theses about the moribund American capitalism. "Hierarchy always corrupts communication," argues Kenneth E. Boulding:

> An information-gathering apparatus always tends to confirm the existing image of the top decision-makers, no matter what it is. This organizational "mental illness" . . . akin to paranoia in individuals . . . is nowhere better illustrated than in the international system, which is composed of numerous foreign-office and military establishment hierarchies that thrive on self-justifying images.[23]

During the Cuban missile crisis President Kennedy deliberately refrained from participating in the discussions of the fifteen-member *ad hoc* executive committee of the National Security Council in order not to impede their deliberations and recommendations. Theodore Sorensen noted:

> The absence of the President encouraged everyone to speak his mind. . . . And when [Kennedy] did preside, recognizing that lower-ranking advisers such as Thompson would not voluntarily contradict their superior in front of the President, and that persuasive advisers such as McNamara unintentionally silenced less articulate men, he took pains to seek everyone's individual views.[24]

The Quantity of Messages

Among the major sources of possible errors in international policy making we must include the sheer amount of international problems and communications about them that call for evaluation and either immediate decision or at least planning for future action. A former head of the research and analysis division in the U.S. Department of State frankly admitted that one of the reasons why it was difficult to find the facts was that there were so many facts:

> There is simply no end of facts. Yet at the summit of government, there are only one President, one Secretary of State and one Secretary of Defense, who, no matter how great their appetite for facts, cannot digest them all. Facts have to be gathered, reported, selected, arranged, varnished, packaged, and presented. Facts have to be added together to make patterns of facts.
> The policy-maker gets his facts where he finds them—at the end of this process, or anywhere along the way. So he may properly ask the questions: Which facts? Whose facts? Whose selection? Whose varnish?

Who is selecting the selectors of facts? And the variables implicit in these
questions are complemented by the consumer's own personal variables of
time, context, toleration, and receptivity for facts.[25]

Evidently, no national leader can possibly follow all the national and
international developments with the same intensity: Images of the national
and international system are always perceived, evaluated, and acted upon
selectively; a national leader must rely on aides for the observation and
estimate of less critical issues. But which issues are really less critical than
others in terms of their future impact?

In 1968 a good illustration of the problem of the impact of the quantity of
information on the quality of analysis and interpretation was given by a
study undertaken by the House Subcommittee on Defense Appropriations.
It revealed that in the Defense Intelligence Agency it takes an average of
eight workdays from the time of receipt for a document to reach the
analysts. At that time the unprocessed reports on Southeast Asia alone
filled 517 linear feet of file-drawer space at the Defense Intelligence
headquarters. In a word, the American spy output was so large and grew so
fast that the intelligence chiefs did not have time to read it. The backlog
allegedly contributed to several intelligence failures such as the capture of
the intelligence ship *Pueblo* off North Korea. Decisions on the
international scene will continue to be based on less than adequate
information and therefore will be replete with the hazards of gross
miscalculation. The process by which decision makers derive their images
of the international scene was described by a perceptive scholar, Kenneth
Boulding, as

> . . . a melange of narrative history, memories of past events, stories and
> conversations, etc., plus an enormous amount of usually ill-digested and
> carelessly collected current information. When we add to this the fact that
> the system produces strong hates, loves, loyalties and disloyalties, and so
> on, it would be surprising if any images were formed that even remotely
> resembled the most loosely defined realities of the case.[26]

Eloquence of Acts

Words are often intentionally deceptive, and statesmen frequently
insist that nations must prove their good faith or a change in their policy
orientation by acts, not words. This has very often been the content of
messages from the United States to the Kremlin. Yet, if words can have a
double meaning, so can actions. An observable retreat from an advanced
position may be a prologue to attack. When in 1955 the Austrian Neutrality
Treaty was signed and the Soviet army left the country, optimists viewed
the act as a proof of Soviet good will. Pessimists, on the other hand, argued

that, for the Soviets, Austria's neutrality was merely a "Danubian sprat to catch a fatter German mackerel." Not only words, but also acts may be differently interpreted by different observers. The English scholar Joseph Frankel noted that previous experience has often prevented national leaders from viewing new statements and acts as departures from past patterns. "Once a statesman has formed an image of an issue," he writes, "this image acts as an organizing device for further information and as a filter through which this information must pass. Images, not detailed information, govern political behavior." Frankel illustrated the point by suggesting that ingrained images dominantly govern Soviet-American relations much more than do the details of the actual behavior of the two nations:

> Where this behavior does not correspond with the image, it is simply ignored—the Russians took no notice of the elementary fact that the allegedly aggressive Americans did not destroy them when they had the monopoly of nuclear weapons nor did the Americans acknowledge the conciliatory nature of some Soviet moves after Stalin's death.[27]

It is, of course, also conceivable that the American distrust of the conciliatory nature of some Soviet gestures was wise and right; if so, Frankel's condemnation of the American interpretation of Soviet behavior and probable intentions is wrong. It is difficult to be sure about such matters. How does one separate illusion from reality in a world of images? "How could I have been so far off base?" asked President Kennedy after the disaster at the Bay of Pigs. "All my life I've known better than to depend on the experts. How could I have been so stupid, to let them go ahead?" His adviser and friend Theodore C. Sorensen added: "That so great a gap between concept and actuality could exist at so high a level on so dangerous a matter reflected a shocking number of errors in the whole decision-making process, errors that permitted bureaucratic momentum to govern instead of policy leadership."[28] (Decision making as bureaucratic bargaining will be examined in Chapter 6.)

PLANNING FOR FUTURE CONTINGENCIES

Our analysis has so far been concerned with the past and the present: How good is the information received, how well is it interpreted, and what can one do to deter a present threat or exploit a present opportunity? But whatever the past and whatever the present, tomorrow will be different. If we are uncertain about the interpretation of the past and the meaning of the present, how much more uncertain we all are with reference to the future—especially since our present perception and action may alter it! As James A. Robinson noted:

> The past is knowable, within limits to be sure, but in principle recordable, testable, and verifiable. The future is not knowable, because man can affect it in alternative ways. . . . It is within our powers to anticipate "what may happen," not "what will happen."[28]

This is another major difficulty in the foreign-policy-making process: planning for future contingencies. Policy makers must look ahead and be ready for new crises or opportunities. As we have seen, some factors of other nations' power and intentions can only be roughly estimated. Errors are always possible. This is why, in planning for the future, policy makers tend to double-insure themselves against miscalculation by producing more weapons and signing more alliances than may be necessary. The leadership of an allied, or enemy, or neutral nation may be replaced by elections, a *coup d' état*, or an assassination. Will the new leadership adhere to old commitments and old policies? Provisions must be made for a future rainy day.

We mentioned previously the French official who in 1963 expressed his confidence in President Kennedy's commitment to France. But what was the guarantee, asked many Frenchmen, that in 1968, 1972, 1976, and forever after the American people would keep sending to the White House men whose commitment to the nuclear defense of France would be as firm as that of Kennedy? Writing on the atomic dimension of international politics ten years before he became President Nixon's Secretary of State, Henry A. Kissinger noted:

> Since the chief impetus for the European nuclear programs derives from intangibles of political and psychological influence, it is immature to turn the issue into a personal debate about the integrity of a particular President. For the Europeans to forgo national nuclear programs would be to resign forever from a realm of technology on which their future security and indeed their economic welfare would depend to a greater or lesser extent. It would mean entrusting their fate not to this president but to all future presidents, and not only on clear-cut issues of war and peace but with respect to every nuance of policy. In effect, this would transform Europe from a partner into a satellite.[30]

Uncertain about many features of the present situation, all nations nevertheless must and do plan for contingencies in the still more uncertain future. Military and diplomatic plans for the future abound. Under the United States Joint Chiefs of Staff, three agencies work on separate strategy plans. One, the Joint Strategic Capability plan, looks forward only one year. It deals with immediate procurement problems. The second, the Joint Strategic Operating plan, tries to estimate the military needs of the United States and their nature, quality, and cost for the next ten years. And, finally, a long-range strategic group contemplates a fourteen-year period.[31] In such a long-term projection, military considerations and evaluations necessarily merge with, or rather result from, political and economic ones. The planning soldier must be joined by scientists, economists, and political analysts.

Similarly, at the Department of State, a policy-planning staff tries to think ahead for one year, five years, and ten years.

Some observers doubt that real planning for a distant future is possible when we are so uncertain even about tomorrow. "The nature of concrete policy issues and the character of government action," noted a Senate subcommittee headed by Henry M. Jackson of Washington in 1964, "push for a pragmatic one-thing-at-a-time-on-its-own-terms approach." This was quoted by Max Frankel, writing in the *New York Times* (June 28, 1964). Frankel added:

> Preparation of "contingency" policies is useful to prepare a government or an alliance for the subtleties and possible consequences of future events, and to train military intelligence and diplomatic officers to think in each other's terms. But the way in which a particular convoy to Berlin is stopped and the state of the world at that moment will determine the response much more than any plan. . . . No responsible official will ever write a blank check on his future decisions and concerns. Even when the expected happens, officials all over town, from their separate perspectives, will weigh American power and interests against reaction near and far. They may act on predetermined aspirations, but they will be guided by a momentary set of priorities, pressures and preferences.

The Deputy Assistant Secretary of State for policy planning, George Allen Morgan, describing the inevitable frustrations of policy planners, seemed to agree with Frankel's observations:

> To work honestly at planning in foreign affairs is to learn many lessons in humility, and to admit again and again how many requirements exceed capabilities. It is also to see some events mock prudence and reward folly, and to wonder whether it would have been better not to plan. . . . Given the uncontrollability of the foreign environment and the stormy character of our age, no conceivable amount of excellence of planning can hope to avoid rough times in the years ahead.[32]

The American policy planner then suggested three types of long-range planning that may usefully be pursued:

1. Analyzing future sociopolitical consequences of nonpolitical changes. Some hard data from the fields of economics, engineering, and military technology may permit projections of policy for the next five or ten years.
2. Studying in depth and analyzing present forces and trends likely to determine some aspects of the future.

3. Developing a comprehensive philosophy and strategic concept for the national effort as a whole. Here, clearly, the policy planner must coordinate his efforts with those of social, economic, and military planners.

Even a perfunctory examination of those very general proposals indicates the definite limits of long-range planning in foreign policies. Our preceding analysis of the great uncertainties that accompany any honest evaluation of national power and intentions has already warned us against optimism with regard to the possibility of blueprints in foreign policy. Only broad lines of diplomatic strategy and very general policy goals can be established in advance; details that in the final analysis will matter the most will have to be filled in later, usually in the period of crisis. Commenting on the Cuban missile confrontation with the Soviet Union in 1962, Secretary of State Dean Rusk said: "When something like this happens, and you haven't read your basic papers, it's too late. You just have to deal with things as they happen."

In 1973 both West Europe and the United States were taken by what appeared to be a complete surprise when the Arab countries, former have-nots, proved capable of coordinating their oil policies and so demonstrating the vulnerability of the developed North to blackmail by the underdeveloped South. Futuristic studies and scenarios of alternative futures[33] did not prepare political leaders for the eventuality and efficacy of the Arab oil embargo and its various consequences, including the West European Community's cooperative agreements with the Middle East at the expense of the United States and its ally, the state of Israel.[34]

While planning in foreign policy—that is, thinking ahead with a view to action on the international scene—has its definite limits, it can and does deepen the policy makers' knowledge of developing trends; it sharpens their focus and thus prepares the top personnel for future crises, however unexpected or unorthodox they may be. If for no other reason, every foreign-policy or military establishment should contain an enclave that is more or less cloistered from the daily routine and operational hubbub. Such an enclave should be inhabited by the kind of thinking men whom George Allen Morgan called the "apostles of the future," because they speak for the changes that are coming and the problems we must one day confront and should now be getting ready for. These "apostles" should have not only all available information at their disposal and scholarly trained minds, but also, as Morgan realistically suggested, "intuitive flair, a sixth sense for relevance and timing"[35]—a quality not easily come by. But the stress on instinct and flair does remind us that the policy maker's vision and educated hunches often replace what a cautious scholar would consider a missing link in the logical chain of policy making. The result is that leaders finally make decisions and act more swiftly and confidently than our analysis of the difficulties in the evaluation and policy-making processes would suggest. In the opinion of many a scholar, political leaders often improvise with breathtaking audacity, while political leaders and policy makers perhaps suspect that scholars with their search for absolute certainties would never dare to make decisions that are vital for the existence and welfare of the state.

Notes

1. Louis J. Halle, *The Nature of Power*. London: Rupert Hart-Davis, 1954, pp. 68, 76.
2. Arnold Wolfers, *Discord and Collaboration*. Baltimore, Md.: The Johns Hopkins Press, 1962, p. 103.
3. Harold Nicolson, *The Meaning of Prestige*. New York: Cambridge, 1937, p. 9.
4. Morton A. Kaplan, *System and Process in International Politics*. New York: Wiley, 1957, p. 15.
5. Stephen D. Jones, "The Power Inventory and National Strategy," *World Politics*, 5:3 (1954), 421.
6. Robert C. North, "Perception and Action in the 1914 Crisis," in John C. Farrell and Asa P. Smith (eds.), *Image and Reality in World Politics*. New York: Columbia University Press, 1967, p. 117.
7. Mao Tse-tung, *Selected Works*, Vol. 2 (1937-1938). New York: International Publishers, 1956, p. 271. A similar thought, grafted onto Stokely Carmichael's famous statement that violence is as American as apple pie, was expressed by the chairman of the New York Black Panther party, David Brothers. Addressing worshipers at a Methodist Church he said, "Violence is as American as cherry pie. You put a .38 on your hip and you get respect." *New York Times*, May 26, 1969.
8. From an interview with *New York Times* correspondent Tillman Durdin, January 5, 1969.
9. John H. Herz, "The Relevancy and Irrelevancy of Appeasement," *Social Research*, 31:3 (Autumn 1964), 320.
10. *Radio Moscow*, January 14, 1958.
11. Statement made by Hitler on August 14, 1939, at a secret conference at Obersalzberg; recorded in "The Last Days of Peace, August 9-September 3, 1939," *Documents on German Foreign Policy, 1918-1945*, Series D. London: H.M. Stationery Office, 1956, p. 7.
12. Dean Acheson, "Crisis in Asia—An Examination of United States Policy," *Department of State Bulletin*, 22 (1950), 111-118.
13. *UN General Assembly Records*, 294th Meeting (October 7, 1950), p. 230.
14. Dean Acheson, "United States Policy in the Korean Crisis," *Department of State Bulletin*, 23 (1950), 463.
15. John W. Spanier, *The Truman-MacArthur Controversy and the Korean War*. New York: Norton, 1965, pp. 99-100.
16. Nikita S. Khrushchev, *Khrushchev Remembers*. Boston: Little, Brown, 1970, pp. 151-155.
17. In 1973 two governmental attempts to bug domestic opposition made the front pages of the world press. One was the Watergate affair in the United States and the other was the French government's attempt at electronic bugging of the Paris satirical weekly *Le Canard enchaîné*.
18. Richard N. Fagen, *Politics and Communication*. Boston: Little, Brown, 1966, pp. 8, 17.
19. Dean Rusk, *Red China and the USSR* (Department of State Publication No. 7497). Washington, D.C.: Government Printing Office, February 1963, p. 34.
20. Reported by Elie Abel in his *Missile Crisis*. New York: Bantam, 1966, p. 322.
21. Harold D. Lasswell, *The Future of Political Science*. New York: Atherton, 1963, pp. 15-16.
22. George F. Kennan, *Memoirs: 1925-1950*. Boston: Little, Brown, 1967, p. 233.
23. Kenneth E. Boulding, "The Learning and Reality-Testing Process in the International System," in Farrell and Smith (eds.), *Image and Reality*, p. 10.
24. Theodore C. Sorensen, *Kennedy*. New York: Harper & Row, 1965, p. 679.
25. Thomas L. Hughes, "Policy-Making in a World Turned Upside Down," *Foreign Affairs*, January 1967, p. 204.
26. Boulding, "Learning and Reality-Testing Process," p. 9.

27. Joseph Frankel, *International Relations*. New York: Oxford, 1964, p. 54.

28. Sorensen, *Kennedy*, pp. 301-302.

29. James A. Robinson in his critique of Bertrand de Jouvenel, *The Art of Conjecture* (New York: Basic Books, 1967) in the *American Political Science Review*, 62:1 (March 1968), 236.

30. Henry A. Kissinger, "NATO's Nuclear Dilemma," *Reporter*, March 28, 1963, p. 27.

31. This information was contained in a feature article on the Joint Chiefs of Staff in *Time*, February 5, 1965, p. 23.

32. George Allen Morgan, "Planning in Foreign Affairs: The State of Art," *Foreign Affairs*, 39 (January 1961), 275.

33. See, for instance, Herman Kahn, "The Alternative World Futures Approach," in Morton A. Kaplan (ed.), *New Approaches to International Relations*. New York: St. Martin's, 1968, pp. 83-136. See also Jouvenel, *The Art of Conjecture*, and O. K. Flechtheim, *History and Futurology*. Meisenheim am Glan, Ger.: K. G. Hain, 1968.

34. The negotiating position of the European Economic Community, prepared on the eve of the Washington Conference of oil-consuming countries (February 11 and 12, 1974) stated, for instance: "The Community should reserve its *total* freedom to decide the form it will give to its Community energy policy and *to its relations with producer* [that is, Arab] *countries*" italics added.

35. Morgan, "Planning in Foreign Affairs," p. 275.

Additional Readings

Additional readings on the subject of foreign-policy decision making may be found in *Discord and Harmony: Readings in International Politics*, edited by Ivo D. Duchacek and published by Holt, Rinehart and Winston in 1972. A case study of the United States attempt to overturn the Castro regime by an invasion, as described and analyzed by Arthur M. Schlesinger, Jr., is part of Chapter 7, pp. 124-141, entitled "Certainty of Uncertainty."

6
Perceptions: Springs of Action

In their daily reporting on international events, the mass media cannot avoid using shorthand expressions that, especially in the form of headlines, try to reduce a complex problem of conflict and cooperation among nations into a few words. At any given moment we may hear or read, for instance "Hitler and Stalin Sign Friendship Pact," "South Africa Blasts the UN," "Paris and Bonn Agree," "U.S. Angered by Indonesia." A student of international politics who goes beyond such headlines and analyzes the issue in some depth is bound to discover that such shorthand expressions, while in many ways useful and inevitable, are often misleading if not downright false.

The last headline, "U.S. Angered by Indonesia," suggests an angry tension between 200 million Americans and 100 million Indonesians, but neither nation can be viewed as a monolithic entity having only one viewpoint and speaking with only one single voice on the world scene. Both Indonesia and the United States are complex composites of a great number of groups and subgroups, many of which have conflicting material interests and sharply differing opinions and views of the world.

The terms "Indonesia" and "the United States" include the present national leaders and the national administrations of these countries, as well as their public or latent opponents, their informed and interested elites, their news media, their career military personnel, and their usually uninterested and uninformed general public, including the average reader of newspapers. Like his Indonesian counterpart, the American reader may actually have experienced a feeling of surprise when reading about the anger of the United States at Indonesia. Personally he had had no specific feeling of bitterness toward Indonesia before he began to read his morning paper. While the national anger was being communicated through diplomatic channels to Jakarta, presumably on his behalf, he was actually enjoying a musical comedy and was not thinking about Indonesia or any other foreign country. He certainly did not feel that he was taking part in the action.

Who, then, was angered by whom? Clearly, a tension developed primarily between the policy makers in Washington and Jakarta, who have the right and responsibility to speak and act on behalf of their respective states on the international scene. This is why so many writers and speakers on the subject of international politics prefer to focus on policy makers rather than on the abstract concept of nation. They refer to leading personalities by name, as in "Hitler and Stalin Sign Friendship Pact," or to capital cities where policy-making processes take place, as in "Bonn and Paris Agree."

THREE STAGES OF THE FOREIGN-POLICY-MAKING PROCESS

Foreign-policy decision making represents a sequence of several interlocked processes. Three major stages may be identified: formulation, decision, and execution.[1]

Formulation

Thousands of international issues compete for the attention, time, energy, and skill of the top leadership. The first necessary step in policy making is to establish some crude, tentative priorities among those problems that require closer identification and evaluation with reference to possible action. The way in which a problem is formulated and related to attainable national objectives is often of decisive importance. The recognition that there is a problem may lead to the irritating but frequently unavoidable conclusion that there is a present dilemma with no solution in the foreseeable future. Sometimes a problem fades away without actually having been solved; at other times the solution proves possible much later, when the international situation has substantially changed though the main features of the problem have not. In international politics one has to get accustomed to the idea that nations often have to live with a problem for decades (for instance, divided Germany, China and Taiwan, the Indian-Pakistani dispute over Kashmir, the Middle East). "Americans live in an environment uniquely suited to an engineering approach to policy-making," Henry A. Kissinger warned in 1964, five years before he became President Nixon's principal adviser in matters of foreign policy. "As a result, our society has been characterized by a conviction that any problem will yield if subjected to a sufficient dose of expertise." Kissinger contrasted the American scene with the European one, where the margin of survival has always been more precarious, and he added: "Europeans live on a continent covered with ruins testifying to the fallibility of human foresight. In European history the recognition of a problem has often defined a dilemma rather than pointed to an answer."[2]

Decision

The second phase of policy making means primarily the *final policy* decision. We have seen that the formulation phase has already included a number of important *preliminary* decisions on such matters as the credibility of the information received, its significance and possible consequences, and the channeling of information from the bottom of the diplomatic and intelligence establishment to the very top of the political system.

When an international problem is formulated as a policy-decision proposal, it usually means not only a selection of a particular definition of the situation but also a specific plan of response to be chosen from among several hypothetical alternative solutions (wait-and-see, surrender, war, deterrence, or compromise). This means, therefore, that the immediate objective must be determined, the possibility of its attainment estimated, and appropriate technique selected—all in relation to and, one hopes, in harmony with long-term national objectives. Thus, inevitably, the final decision reflects also a choice between conflicting values, some of which must be sacrificed so that the preferred ones may be maximized. These are the notoriously painful dilemmas that beset policy makers since, among other things, they have to determine whether social welfare is to be sacrificed for the sake of some uncertain increment of external security (for instance, the 1969-1970 controversy in the United States concerning the ABM system) or economic progress on earth sacrificed for the sake of exploratory progress in outer space.

The second, core stage of foreign-policy making may then be defined as

> a process which results in the selection from a socially defined, limited number of problematical alternative projects . . . objectives and techniques . . . of one project intended to bring about the particular future state of affairs envisaged by the decision makers.[3]

This phase, in which the nation is committed to a particular course of action, includes the process of marshaling resources and support for the execution of policy. Even a dictator must convince his generals, departmental chiefs, diplomats, and allies, and solve some interservice or interfactional rivalries, before he can embark on action. In democracies the process is quite complex. It usually includes the effort on the part of policy makers to enlist the support of legislators (whose criticism and power over appropriations is often of decisive importance), the mass communications media, major economic and professional interests (whose cooperation or lack of opposition might be quite important in the case of punitive trade or tariff policies), and the voting public at large. Policy is often modified in this phase, and in relation to this, many observers and critics of foreign policy make a distinction between policy initiatives and policy responses. The advantage of initiating a policy and the drawback of having to react —usually belatedly—to the initiatives of others are obvious. But the line between an initiative and a response in international politics is often difficult to draw. No initiative, however bold, is ever taken in the abstract; an initiative is a response to a threat or an opportunity, actual or anticipated.

Execution

A policy decision must ultimately be translated into a specific course of action. Sometimes doing nothing, waiting and observing what others do, may be the best policy available; at other times, as noted previously, it is only a manifestation of indecision that pretends to be a decision. Like the two preceding phases, the execution phase is marked by great uncertainties since no policy maker can ever be quite confident that the adopted technique will be effective. The chosen means may prove wrong because the original estimate of the situation was based on misperception; or the estimate may have been correct but an inappropriate method of action was adopted. There is a gap not only between the desirable and possible but also between the possible and the actually executed. Whether that which is feasible is also implemented depends on the degree of skill of the many persons who are in charge of the execution of policy: diplomats, military personnel, propagandists, economists, and scientists. The execution phase is necessarily related to the first two phases, for it includes the problems, in the words of Paul H. Nitze, "of meeting unforeseen obstacles and capitalizing on unforeseen possibilities. This final phase of execution often takes on continuing elements of the formulation and decision phases. Objectives and methods are modified in the light of actual practice."[4] It has often been said that execution represents more than half of a policy.

To sum up: While a foreign-policy decision may be basically defined as a choice of one course of action from two or more alternatives, the choice in fact represents the conclusion of a complex process by which statesmen have chosen between alternative interpretations of available facts as well as between values (ideological, moral, external security, and domestic-social, and domestic-economic) to be maximized or sacrificed. Martin Landau therefore defines a policy decision as "a conclusion drawn from a set of factual and valuational premises."[5] Four possible types of decisions, depending on the presence or absence of agreement among national policy makers concerning facts and values and goals and values may be distinguished:

1. There is, first, the relatively rare case where ends are agreed upon and there is full knowledge of the value-maximizing means to achieve them.
2. A more frequent case is that where there is agreement as to preferred outcomes (ends), but lack of knowledge or agreement as to the appropriate means.
3. An equally frequent case is that where there is consensus about what the problem or conflict is about, but disagreement as to the desirable outcome. During the war in Vietnam, for instance, the Nixon administration and the Communist Party of the United States might have been in complete agreement as to the facts of the situation (the prestige and power of the United States being directly linked up with the survival of the Saigon regime) but both sides wished and worked for opposite outcomes.
4. A fourth possibility is disagreement as to both facts and value-maximizing action.

Uncertainty, including unforeseeable accidents, remains a constant in all four types of decision making. The result is that decisions in international politics rarely stem from a careful consideration and comparison of clear alternatives; more frequently, the decisions represent sporadic, peripheral, and sometimes panicky adjustments to the constantly changing challenges and opportunities on the international scene. Some analysts define the most characteristic feature of foreign-policy making as "playing it by ear"; a scholarly analysis used the term "disjointed incrementalism" to describe policy making, guided by a relatively low level of understanding of both facts and consequences:

> It is a decision-making through small or incremental moves on particular problems rather than through a comprehensive reform program. It is also endless, it takes the form of an indefinite sequence of policy moves. Moreover, it is exploratory in that the goals of policy-making continue to change as new experience with policy throws new light on what is possible and desirable.[6]

WHO EVALUATES AND WHO DECIDES

When we analyze the various phases of the decision-making process, we should avoid the frequent error of totally identifying leaders with the national communities in whose name and behalf they make decisions. Experience shows that, particularly in the field of foreign policy, not only dictators but also democratic presidents, prime ministers, foreign secretaries, ministers of defense, chiefs of staff, intelligence agencies, and top executive officers very often make—and sometimes *must* make —decisions without informing or consulting the people. Only later is the nation asked to applaud, approve, sacrifice, suffer, or die for a decision made without its participation or knowledge.

One reason for the dominant position of the leaders in foreign-policy making is their access to relevant, often secret information. An international event or communication is necessarily interpreted by the informed leader in one way, by the semiinformed elite in another, and by the uninformed general public in a third way. Another reason for leaders' domination of policy-making processes is their political and constitutional responsibility, their assigned task, to act in behalf of the nation abroad. A better access to information and constitutional responsibility to act do not, of course, guarantee a correct decision. The preceding chapter illustrated the fact that, while political leaders are better informed about international politics than the general public, they are rarely, if ever, in possession of all the pertinent information they should have in order to make a rational and wise decision on a given problem. Only some international data can be reliably obtained or double-checked; other data are doubtful; still other data can at best be guessed at; and there are always a few data that are unknown and unforeseeable. Instinctual responses and more or less educated guesses are, for better or worse, integral parts of any foreign-policy making despite frequent protestations to the contrary. When during the fourth Arab-Israeli war in 1973 the Israelis began to push the Egyptian armies back to Cairo and Moscow *appeared* ready to airlift its "marines" to the Suez area and so save the Egyptians from a major setback, were President Nixon and Secretary Kissinger right, adventurous, or foolish when on October 24 they ordered an unprecedented worldwide atomic alert? According to President Nixon (*New York Times*, October 26, 1973), the United States leadership "obtained information which led us to believe that the Soviet Union was planning to send a very substantial force into the Mideast—a military force." Had Senators Jackson, Kennedy, Percy, Proxmire, or McGovern—or the reader of this book—been president in 1973, would their interpretation and reaction to the same piece of information on probable Soviet intentions have been the same or different?

The destinies of many nations have often been determined primarily by their leaders' will power, wisdom, sense of history, diplomatic skill, common sense, and individual courage, as well as by their leaders' emotions, anxieties, foolishness, fickleness, manias, psychoneuroses, or "extrasensory" capacity to make guesses. The capacity for prophetic anticipation often differentiates a successful leader from a failure. Commenting on General Douglas MacArthur's memoirs, the military editor of the *New York Times,* Hanson Baldwin, noted that MacArthur had "uncanny intuition. In international politics he possessed a stronger vision than some of the eight presidents he served." And yet General MacArthur was proved entirely wrong in his anticipation that the Chinese armies, only ten months after the conclusion of their protracted civil war, would not dare to engage the armed forces of the greatest nuclear power in the world, the United States, north of the 38th parallel in Korea. The British statesman Winston Churchill, who had proved so right in his early warnings against Nazi Germany and Fascist Italy and his critique of appeasement policies in 1938, was entirely wrong in his underestimation of the power of the Indian nationalist movement and its leader Mahatma Gandhi—in the 1930s he called Gandhi a "half-naked dervish" who should not have been received with any respect in London by the Labourite Prime Minister Ramsay Macdonald.

Whatever the national leaders' foresight or blindness may be, terms such as "Hitler's Germany," "the Stalin era," "Mao's China," "the Kennedy Years," and "Kissinger's era" express the widely held opinion that individual leaders have shaped their environment and times at least as much as they were themselves marked by them. Their biographers, and many historians and political writers as well, analyze international politics mostly in terms of the talents or shortcomings of leading personalities on the world scene; they note that the death or decline of the physical health or mental capacity of a national leader may alter the course of national and international events. National leaders themselves tend to view the period of their power as being decisively molded by their own vision and energy as well as by the personal characteristics of their rivals or partners. In the wake of the fourth Arab-Israeli war in 1973 President Anwar el-Sadat of Egypt had this to say about United States Secretary of State Henry Kissinger (*New York Times,* March 25, 1974):

> Kissinger is a man of his word. I trust him completely. He is the first United States Secretary who has dealt with our problems, who has proved himself to be a man of integrity—direct, frank, and far-sighted. We have suffered a lot with American officials in the last two decades, beginning with Dulles and ending with Rogers . . . What Nixon and Kissinger did with China and the U.S.S.R. was unthinkable a few years back. They are now doing the unthinkable in the Middle East."

Foreign Minister Abba Eban of Israel came to a similar conclusion in his talk with the *New York Times* representative:

> I believe that the association of the American prestige with Secretary Kissinger's skills [has] been crucial in creating a new climate. I think that Secretary Kissinger's personal role refutes the view that history is the product of impersonal forces and objective conditions in which the personal human factor does not matter.

Some policy makers may even prefer a foreign counterpart whom they dislike, but at least know, to a successor who might act in unpredictable ways. In 1973 several analysts maintained that the Soviet and Chinese leaders were quite disturbed by the Watergate affair and the repercussions it would have on the Nixon administration; they were not, of course, morally concerned with the issue of bugging a political opponent, a practice they themselves had perfected to a fine art, but worried that two men, Nixon and Kissinger, whom they had begun to know and even have some trust in, might suddenly be replaced with an unknown entity. There was even some evidence indicating that both Brezhnev and Mao had given a marked preference to Nixon over McGovern in the election year of 1972 on the assumption that a man with a known record of dynamic anticommunism might be better equipped to rally the American people's support for détente between communism and capitalism than a left-oriented McGovern, whose policies, even if identical with those of Nixon, might provoke a right-wing backlash. Some of the Soviet and Chinese decisions in foreign policy could be presented as discreet steps destined to help President Nixon be reelected.[7]

LEADERS AND THEIR ENVIRONMENT

The role of leaders and policy makers is conditioned by their national environment, which in turn is embedded in and influenced by the broader world environment. A national leader's own nation is not an amorphous entity that he can manipulate at will according to his preferences or prejudices. Even a powerful dictator cannot completely disregard his nation's geographic location, the limitations of its resources, its history, and its people's physical endurance, traditions, biases, and preferences. Although often a caricature of his nation, a dictator is nevertheless to a great extent the product of the national environment, and he remains bound to it; in the case of democratic leaders, the fact of their accountability to an organized opposition and, periodically, to the voters, makes the link between the environment and the policy makers even more meaningful than in the case of totalitarian rulers. All leaders issue from given conditions, which they in turn are anxious to affect.

If it is easy to overstress the decisive importance of personalities, it is equally tempting to overemphasize the impact of the national and international environment upon policy makers. Early Marxism in particular was guilty of degrading leading individuals to the position of mere pawns of economic forces. Friedrich Engels proclaimed that economic relations are those whose action is *ultimately decisive,* forming a red thread which runs through all the other relations and enables us to understand them. In 1898 the Russian Marxist George Plekhanov wrote in his book *The Role of the Individual in History* about the role of Robespierre in the French Revolution:

Let us assume that [Robespierre] was an absolutely indispensable force in the party; but even so, he was not the only force. If the accidental fall of a brick had killed him, say, in January 1793, his place would, of course, have been taken by somebody else, and although this person might have been inferior to him in every respect, nevertheless, events would have taken the *same course* as they did when Robespierre was alive. . . . Talented people can, as we have said, change only individual features of events, but not their general trend; *they are themselves the product of this trend.* [Italics added.][8]

In the third of his *Theses on Feurbach,* however, Karl Marx warned against economic determinism: "The materialistic teaching that human beings are the products of circumstances and education, and changed human beings the products of changed circumstances and education, leaves out of count the fact that circumstances themselves are changed by human beings."

At the time of the funeral of Karl Marx in 1883, his intimate associate and friend Friedrich Engels, delivering a speech over Marx's coffin, concluded by wondering what the world would have been like had Karl Marx not been born. This still somewhat hesitant stress on the importance of one man in the shaping of human history did not anticipate the truly fantastic scope of the glorification of individual leaders of communism in the twentieth century. It is indeed one of the major ironies of history that socialism and Marxism, which started with deemphasis of the role of the individual and overstress on material determinism and the concept of class consciousness, has become a "cult of personality" from Lenin, Stalin, and Mao (see Documents 6.1 and 6.2) to the leaders of smaller Communist nations such as Tito, Castro, and Ho Chi Minh. The Nazi principle of the führer's undisputable leadership was the closest parallel to the communist placing of leading individuals high above the masses. Symptomatically, the idealization of one leader has often been accompanied by extreme vilification of his defeated or dead opponents: Khrushchev defamed Stalin, and Mao did the same to Khrushchev. In the Chinese context the adjective "Khrushchovite" is still the quintessence of evil. The implied consequence of such propagandized denigration is a thesis that inhumanity and other malfunctions of the socialist system are to be ascribed to the criminal or pathological traits in the character of a given leader rather than to the system itself.

Does the era create its own tools or is the era a product of its leading men? "I claim not to have controlled events," wrote Lincoln to A. G. Hodges (April 4, 1864), "but confess plainly that events have controlled me." On his eightieth birthday Winston Churchill described his role in relation to the British people when confronted with the direct threat of a triumphant nazism as both superior and subordinate. Recalling the year 1940, when France collapsed militarily in six weeks under the Nazi onslaught and when Britain stood alone (America and Russia were not yet in

DOCUMENT 6.1

STALIN'S DEIFICATION

In connection with Comrade Stalin's 70th birthday, the State Music Publishing House has issued A. Alexandrov's "Cantata about Stalin," and M. Blantner's and Khachaturian's "Songs about Stalin," as well as instrumental music and Russian, Ukrainian, Byelorussian, Georgian and other folk songs about Comrade J. V. Stalin.

From *Izvestia*, December 21, 1949.

The highest Soviet peak—Stalin Peak—rises 7495 meters above sea level. Members of an alpine expedition placed a bronze bust of Stalin on its summit in 1937. . . . Busts of Comrade Stalin have been set up on more than 30 of the highest mountain summits of Soviet Central Asia.

From *Pravda*, December 20, 1949

. . . thanks to Comrade Stalin the peoples of Hungary, Rumania, Poland, Czechoslovakia, Bulgaria and Albania stand on the path of construction of socialism.

From Khrushchev, *Pravda*, December 21, 1949.

The shoots of everything new, beautiful, progressive and elevated in our life are attracted to Stalin as to the sun. . . . What an inexhaustible treasure of philosophy and art theory is contained in Stalin's numerous utterances on literature and the arts.[1]

From M. Chiaureli, *Pravda*, December 20, 1949.

One had to be present in order to see and feel the love of Stalin for children and the delight of the children as they approached him. Their faces beamed with happiness, their voices rang with joy: "We thank you for our happy childhood. There's no brighter, no happier youth in the world."

From Polevoy and Ryabov, *USSR Embassy Information Bulletin*, January 13, 1950.

1. Stalin's daughter, Svetlana Alliluyeva, described her impressions of an exhibition honoring her father in her book *Only One Year* (New York: Harper & Row, 1968, p. 391): "There had never been such a prostitution of art as the exhibition in 1949, arranged in honor of my father's seventieth birthday. The immense exhibition in the halls of the Tretyakov Gallery featured one subject only: Stalin. From every canvas the same face looked at you, sometimes in the garb of a Georgian lad, his eyes raised to heaven, or as a gray-haired general in a Russian Imperial uniform with epaulets. Armenian artists gave the face an Armenian look, the Uzbeks made it look Uzbek; in one picture there was even a certain resemblance to Mao Tse-tung—they were represented sitting together in identical semimilitary tunics and with an identical expression on their faces."

DOCUMENT 6.2

MAO'S DEIFICATION

Wuhan was overjoyed as the news [of a nine-mile swim in the Yangtze River by Chairman Mao] passed from one person to another. Everybody was saying: "Our respected and beloved leader Chairman Mao is in such wonderful health. This is the greatest happiness for the entire Chinese people and for revolutionary people throughout the world." . . . Chairman Mao stretched out his arms and swam with steady strokes. On a broad expanse of water Chairman Mao at times swam sidestroke, advancing as he cleaved through the waves, and at other times he floated and had a view of the azure sky above. . . . When he boarded the boat he was vigorous and showed no sign of fatigue. . . . Cheers "Long live Chairman Mao!" on both banks lasted well over four hours.

From a report on Mao's swim at the age of 72 as distributed by the offical agency Hsinhua, July 25, 1966.

Cheng Huan-chang, a 50-year-old worker who became deaf and dumb after an attack of measles when he was a baby came for treatment [by army medical workers]. In the autumn of 1957, Chairman Mao inspected the factory where Cheng Huan-chang worked. When he saw our respected and beloved great leader Chairman Mao, Cheng was overwhelmed with joy and wanted to shout: "Long live Chairman Mao!" at the top of his voice. But he could not utter a word. [The medical worker in charge of Cheng's case] used the method of acupuncture[1] to make the old worker who had been deaf and dumb for half a century regain his hearing to a large extent. Tears came to the old worker's eyes when, for the first time in his life, he joined others in cheering: "Long live Chairman Mao!" . . . Many patients and their relatives . . . said: "Your close concern for us poor and lower-middle peasants shows the truth of the saying, dear as are father and mother, Chairman Mao is dearer."

From "A Hospital for Deaf-Mutes Serves the Peoples' Heart and Soul," *Peking Review,* April 1, 1969.

We have to come to understand deeply that Chairman Mao's every sentence is the truth and that each of his sentences carries more weight than 10,000 ordinary sentences.

From People's Liberation Army unit 8341 at the Peking General Knitwear Mill, *Peking Review,* April 11, 1969.

1. Acupuncture is a surgical procedure devised in China several centuries before Christ. The practice consists of the insertion of needles of various metals in various shapes and sizes into one or several of 365 designated spots over the entire human body, including the head. It is supposed to relieve internal congestion and to restore the balance of the bodily functions. In the current anti-Western and nationalistic atmosphere of China the merits of acupuncture as a native and therefore superior form of medicine are extolled and combined with Mao's thought.

the war), Churchill said: "It was the British that had the lion's heart; I had the luck to be called to give the roar."[9] Yet the same British people had not roared but uttered a plaintive whimper two years before, when another of their leaders, Neville Chamberlain, appeased Hitler by the Munich agreement of 1938 at the expense of Czechoslovakia's territorial integrity. Was it the difference in the leaders or in the circumstances? Thomas Carlyle noted in 1833,

> Man makes the Circumstances, and spiritually as well as economically is the artificer of his own fortune. But there is another side of the same truth, that the man's circumstances are the element he is appointed to live and work in; that he by necessity takes his complexion, vesture, embodiment from these, and is in all practical manifestations modified by them almost without limit; so that in another no less genuine sense, it can be said that Circumstances make the Man.[10]

It is extremely difficult to determine in each political act or decision how large a proportion of it is to be ascribed to the impact of circumstances or social forces and how much to the personality structure of individual actors. Sometimes one might facetiously suggest that the proportion may very well be 100 percent personality and 100 percent circumstances. Generally speaking, the study of the relationship between personality and politics is relatively underdeveloped. There are several reasons for this neglect besides the elusiveness of the subject. First, many analysts of the behavior of men in politics consider personality characteristics much less important than social characteristics. Second, some observers point to the fact that many decisions are made collectively by groups or committees in which personality characteristics are randomly distributed and so intertwined that it is nearly impossible, and also not useful, to focus on personality traits. There is also the argument that different personalities tend to behave similarly when confronted with similar situations and that individual actors are usually quite limited in the impact they can have on events. A thoughtful study by Fred I. Greenstein challenges these and other objections to the study of personality in politics and demonstrates how significantly the impact of an individual actor's personality will vary with (1) his position in the system (leader or subordinate), (2) his particular skill or weakness, and (3) the nature of the system, which may or may not restrain its leading actors and which may be confronted with routine or unusual challenges.[19] A particular personality may be expected to assert itself, for instance, in ambiguous situations, that is, in situations in which there are no familiar clues or, on the contrary, in which there are a great number of options.[12] Evidently, this applies to the international scene, an environment that abounds in options and the novelty of cues. The constant interaction between policy makers and their environment represents, not a two-way, but actually a triangular multilevel traffic of mutual influences and pressures, for in addition to the impact of the national environment on the leaders and vice versa there is the combined and extremely intricate influence of all the other leaders and their national environments:

> All are influencing all, directly or indirectly, merely by sharing the same spatial, temporal, and sociological environment. The international system is neither a dyad (duopoly) nor a multitude of dyads . . . the system is characterized not only by reciprocity but by multiple reciprocity.[13]

A proper reaction to changes, dangers, and opportunities on the international scene basically depends on two factors: (1) accuracy and timeliness of information (the preceding chapter focused on this problem) and (2) the policy maker's capacity and skill to interpret, evaluate, and react to events and information, differentiating the relevant from the irrelevant, the reliable from the unreliable, the more urgent from the less urgent, the manageable from the best ignored (the subject of this chapter).

"Factors external to the actor," Arnold Wolfers writes, "become determinants of foreign policy only as they affect the mind, heart, and will of the decision maker."[14] In the course of history these external factors —events and communications—have often been misperceived, misinterpreted, and therefore "misacted" upon by national leaders and their staffs. This is the fundamental problem not only of false information but, even more important, of false interpretation of a true report.

IMAGES AND PERSONALITIES

Bearing in mind our previous emphasis on the constant interaction between the environment and the leaders, we may think of the policy maker's process of evaluating and reacting to information and events as a constant scanning of the political horizon, looking for opportunities and early warnings of danger. The leader's skill at making valid judgments appears then as his capacity to use an imaginary mental telescope or sonar or radar device, selectively focusing on different sectors of the international scene. The image the leaders obtain and accept as real is more important than any other image, including the correct one. Only a tremendous pressure from below or an unanticipated direct confrontation with a reality at variance with the accepted image can cause a readjustment of focus and policy. Kenneth Boulding calls such elimination of false images by means of confrontation with reality "disappointment feedback." Unless this happens, the policy maker's image of the situation, however distorted or totally incorrect it may be, will have momentous consequences. A blurred vision or sheer delusion may become a cause of war if the leader has power to translate his image into national policy and action. Objective factors on the international political scene (if there are such things as objective factors) are perceived by the very subjective eyes of individual policy makers. This is why, in Quincy Wright's words, international relations is so frequently concerned less with relations between nations than with relations between false images of nations. Stanley Hoffmann suggested that

> international politics today should be defined less as a struggle for power than as a contest for shaping of perceptions. When force loses some of its prominence, power—my exercise of control over you—becomes the art of making you see the world the way I see it, and of making you behave in accordance with that vision. International politics in the past was often an arena of coercion without persuasion; it is tending to become an arena of persuasion, more or less coercive.[15]

The way we use ordinary binoculars depends on our vision, our skill in focusing, our previous experience, our alertness or fatigue, the amount of available light, the position from which we observe the scene, and the reason for which we observe. Much depends on what we are looking for and expecting to find. Similar variables are present when a national leader views the international scene by manipulating, as it were, an imaginary political telescope. How he sees will be affected by (1) his personality structure, (2) his background and education, (3) the impact on him of experience and previous decisions, (4) his bewitchment by history and ideology, (5) his concept of role, (6) his physical and mental health, and (7) chance and accident.

Personality Structure

The better we know the personality structure and character of foreign leaders and their aides, the more reliably we can anticipate their reaction to information and events that we are also reacting to and trying to evaluate. Whether we consider the personality structure dominantly formed by heredity, by experiences in childhood, or by environment, it is clear that psychology and psychiatry may usefully contribute to the study as well as the conduct of international politics. Interpretations of an international situation or event are bound to be colored by both our own and foreign leaders' rationality, passion, idealism, cynicism, pragmatism, dogmatism, pedestrian attitude, stupidity, intelligence, imagination, flexibility, stubbornness, cautiousness, or tendency to risk and gamble—and, of course, mental disorders such as mania, depression, anxiety, schizophrenia, paranoia, hysteria, and the obsessional state (these are mentioned again below in a different context).

It would be inaccurate to say that only since Freud or the growth of the modern psychologist's interest in "psychohistory" and international politics have diplomats been exhorted to combine diplomacy with psychology. For many centuries kings and their philosophers have advised diplomats to "freelance" in applied psychology. A scholarly study by Pierre Renouvin and Jean-Baptiste Duroselle traces the instructions given by kings and governments to French diplomats from 1561 to the present. For example, a French nobleman, de la Sarray du Franquesnay, admonished the French envoys in 1731 as follows:

> The personality traits of men are almost as different as their faces. . . . It is necessary to know their difficulties or their faculties; their generosity or their avarice; their presumption or their modesty; their candor or their obliquity; their vitality or the slowness of their spirit; their intelligence or their stupidity; their boldness or their moderation; their capacity or their ignorance; their tendency to, or their abstention from, pleasures; and, above all, their interest or lack of it in the affairs that we have with them. . . . Diplomats would negotiate with statesmen at a great disadvantage if they had not a considerable insight into the principles and motives that shape the conduct of these men.[16]

Several documents show that French ambassadors generally had the duty to prepare personality analyses of monarchs, princes, and prime ministers and to verify those made by the previous envoy. Diplomatic memoirs, dispatches, and autobiographies indicate the most frequent and useful types of questions concerning the personalities of foreign statesmen that ambassadors and statesmen attempt to answer. On this purely empirical basis Renouvin and Duroselle described and analyzed prominent statesmen of the nineteenth and twentieth centuries in terms of pairs of contrasts such as dogmatic-opportunist, fighter-conciliator, idealist-cynic, inflexible-imaginative, gambler-cautious. In most cases personalities had to be described as falling between two opposite poles; every statesman had also to be analyzed according to more than one pair of contrasts. Thus to these French analysts Woodrow Wilson appears as idealist and fighter, Bismarck as fighter and cynic, and Roosevelt as imaginative and opportunist. These broad and relatively simple categories become more intricate as soon as we relate imaginative, inflexible, idealistic, or cynical leaders to their rivals of either identical or opposite qualities. Thus, the extremely prudent Neville Chamberlain may appear as having acted with extreme imprudence when he had to deal with the audacious gambler Hitler in Munich. The usefulness of these categories seems rather limited, but they illustrate well the need to study the personalities of leaders with the aim of predicting their policies, an imperative yet admittedly hazardous task.[17]

In his study of Napoleon, the Italian historian Guglielmo Ferrero showed how Napoleon's feeling of having illegitimate power and his fear of challenges were translated into constantly aggressive moves even when his power was reasonably secure.

> With Germany and Italy subdued, with Russia as an ally, he had become the master of the continent. He should have felt secure: what could

England do, alone and without allies? But, instead, he became more uneasy than ever. . . . Napoleon was the aggressor in so many wars for only one reason, and always the same one: that he might avert the danger of a future attack, a danger which was either completely imaginary or very exaggerated. But, if all the courts of Europe trembled before him and if the coalitions that interfered with his sleep were difficult to establish, it was he himself in the end who brought on the coalition that defeated him, by his frightful panic and by the insane blows that this panic caused him to rain upon Europe in every direction.[18]

Mao Tse-tung admonishes the party members always to remember the words of Sun Wu-tzu: "Know the enemy, know yourself; one hundred battles, one hundred victories" (*Chih Pi, Chih Chi; Pai Chan, Pai Sheng*). It is useful advice, but difficult to follow. It is most difficult to know the personality and mode of thought of one's enemy and to avoid projecting one's own logic or personality onto him. How often we say or hear, "If I were Nixon (Ho Chi Minh, Mao, Brezhnev, Dubček), I would. . . . " The problem is precisely that I am *not* he, and he is *not* I. In the battle of the Ardennes in Belgium ("The Battle of the Bulge"), the last big European battle of World War II, military intelligence warned repeatedly that the enemy could be mounting a main offensive that might hit the U.S. 8th Corps front any day. The evidence was convincing—German armor was massed within six hours of the Ardennes sector—yet the warning was disregarded. General Harold E. Bull explained why:

Because we reckoned we were dealing with the German General Staff mind. It would not be in character for them to take such a gamble. Here they were comfortably fitted into winter quarters, in some respects better off than our own forces. It was in their interest to prolong the war, hoping for a more favorable settlement.[19]

What had been missing in this evaluation was the fact that Hitler's grip on the German High Command had tightened like a vise, and Hitler's mind, not the General Staff mind, should have been evaluated.

Whatever the national or military leaders' training in applied psychology may be, consciously or not they all make psychological assumptions about their adversaries whenever they take actions with a view to eliciting response and reaction from their counterparts. As Greenstein shows, this was clearly so in the Cuban missile crisis (see Fig. 6.1) when,

with the nuclear war in the balance, decisions had to be made by American decision-makers about which stimuli would produce which Soviet responses. The decisions necessarily entailed assumptions about the psychology of the Soviet leadership—the ways in which alternative stimuli were likely to be processed with what behavioral consequences. The option of not presenting the Soviet leadership with a stimulus was

FIGURE 6.1
THE CUBAN MISSILE CRISIS

"Test of nerves."

Cartoon by David Low by permission of the trustees and *The London Evening Standard.*

nonexistent, since even inaction is a stimulus; and, in a sense, the option of making no assumptions about the psychology of the Soviet leadership, "since our knowledge of these matters is so uncertain," did not exist. Whenever actions are taken with a view of producing reactions from one's counterparts, psychological assumptions are being made, whether or not self-consciously.[20]

In conclusion, it should be noted that seeming polarities such as fear and aggressiveness, cautiousness and tendency to gamble, rationality and passion are often intimately interlaced in political action. A political decision inspired by passion may be implemented with detached, near-scientific coolness.

Background and Education

Childhood and teen-age experiences, family and social background, and education combine to determine what we are and how we interpret and react to other men and events. Looking at the international scene, we can certainly note the obvious widespread differences that distinguish well-educated millionaire Kennedy from shrewd peasant Khrushchev and former theology student Stalin from military careermen de Gaulle and Franco, Brezhnev's bureaucratic background from Castro's guerrilla background, Woodrow Wilson's academic and religious background from the militaristic and aristocratic background of the Kaiser, or aristocratic Churchill from proletarian Hitler. Then there are the less obvious and probably more decisive differences that only a psychologist or psychiatrist can detect and that explain why much of what these men wanted to build or destroy may be traced back to their childhood and adolescence. A study[21] of Hitler's childhood noted that one could discover in the youth a seemingly harmless romantic escapism from the world of hard realities into a world of romance colored by majestic architecture and sonorous music. This was later transformed into a quest for world empire and a demand for extreme solutions. The controversial book on Woodrow Wilson by Sigmund Freud and William C. Bullitt maintains that Wilson's intense childhood relationship to his father stood at the center of his emotional life and dictated all his later action, including his messianic zeal and masterly use of language for denying reality and whitewashing facts:

> His reason, in the service of his fear of a masculine fight and his unconscious desire to be Christ, invented the comforting theory that he could obtain all that he wished without a fight, that he could hand all his weapons to his enemies and convert them by that noble gesture into saints.[22]

Other studies point to Wilson's need to react with an unperceptive and ineffective blend of self-justification and defiance against sarcastic older critics such as his father (a Presbyterian minister), Dean West of Princeton University, and Senator Henry Cabot Lodge.[23]

In the case of Stalin, not only his Georgian family background but also his ethnic minority origin has been presented by several authors as the fundamental reason for his fear of the nation he ruled and for his suspicious attitude and sternly repressive policies toward the non-Russian half of the Soviet Union. Lenin, the Great Russian, may have had an illusion about the existence of a proletarian brotherhood between the Russians and the ethnic minorities, but Stalin, as well as the first head of the secret police, Felix Dzherzhinsky (who was of Polish origin), thought he knew better than Lenin how the minorities really felt; "both were convinced that concessions to the wishes [for self-government] of the Ukrainians, Georgians, and many more constituted a mortal peril to the Moscow dictatorship."[24]

Widely different backgrounds may at least partly explain why national leaders are often truly incapable of viewing the same event or of interpreting the same information in the same way. Some neurophysiologists suggest that there may also be a firm physiological basis for the common occurrence of two persons witnessing the same event and giving different accounts of it; this may be traced back to the cultural and family surroundings, which are embedded in the memory and serve as a filter for interpreting any new information.

The Impact of Experience and Previous Decisions

A leader's vision may be significantly sharpened by his experience in manipulating the imaginary political telescope through which he views the world scene. He may thus acquire a considerable skill in selective focusing. But experience may also prove an impediment to a leader's flexible reaction to the novel and unexplored. Experience in the form of rigid preconception, predisposition, or prejudice may act as a distorting filter that endows the new and disturbing information with a familiar hue.

A good example of the impact of a previous experience on the perception of new events is given by President Truman in his memoirs. Writing with frankness, Truman confessed to his error of supporting the Neutrality Act of 1937, although Hitler's accession to power, the Spanish civil war, and Mussolini's adventures in Africa should have counseled a change of policy.

> It was a mistake for me to support the Neutrality Act (which I thought would keep us out of involvement in the civil war then going on in Spain). I was misled by the report of the munitions investigation, which was headed by Gerald Nye, a demagogue senator from North Dakota. . . . The Nye Committee, which was backed by isolationists and "America Firsters," was pure demagoguery in the guise of a congressional investigating committee. . . . I did not know it at the time. . . . However, I saw the need for its revision in 1939 and again in 1941 as global war made the original measure unworkable.[25]

As may be recalled, the Nye Committee tried to prove (and evidently succeeded in convincing a substantial portion of the American public, including Harry Truman, who was then a senator) that American participation in World War I was only the result of the pressure that the profit-seeking munitions manufacturers (today the term would be "the military-industrial complex") had exercised on Woodrow Wilson.

In their study of the effect of events on national and international images, Karl Deutsch and Richard Merritt confirm the findings of other scholars attesting to the resistance of human thinking to sudden pressures and changes:

> Men conform, admire, and obey largely within the limits of the images and habits they have learned earlier and that they have made into a part of their inner lives. . . . They distort many of their perceptions and deny much of reality in order to call their prejudiced souls their own.[26]

In a paper presented to the American Political Association in 1963, the psychologist Urie Bronfenbrenner described the strong tendency of human beings to maintain consistency in their perceptions, particularly when these perceptions are shared by their fellows. "New events are apprehended in such a way," said Bronfenbrenner, "as to be compatible with previous experience and expectation. The tendency is so powerful that facts which, on objective grounds, seem capable of any but contradictory interpretation are reorganized so as to maintain consistency." He demonstrated his theory by showing the cumulative effect of the Soviet people's previous experiences with the West, starting with Napoleon's invasion, through the two German invasions, up to and including the U-2 intelligence plane incident over the USSR in the 1960s.

Closely related to the impact of previous experience, stored in one's mind for future reference, is the policy maker's commitment to an initial decision to pursue a specific limited goal by specific means. In such a context a limited goal may blur the vision of the whole, and the means may become an end unto itself. The defeat of the limited goal and abandonment of the chosen means may become emotionally unacceptable.

A good example is the French disregard of the German plan to attack France by passing through neutral Belgium. One of the reasons for the French disbelief was Marshal Joffre's reluctance to abandon the carefully prepared original plan of defense. Jerome D. Frank writes in his thought-provoking study:

> Nothing could convince Marshal Joffre that the Germans were following the Schlieffen Plan . . . since to believe this would require that the French General Staff abandon their "Plan 17." . . . Military leaders show extraordinary ability to reject information that would necessitate a change of their plans.[27]

An example of the tragic result of inertia deriving from reluctance to change an initial decision was the bloody battle of Verdun in World War I, which continued for ten months and resulted in 800,000 to 1 million casualties (the French admitted to 377,231 and the Germans to 337,000 dead, ten times as many as at Hiroshima). Because both sides had militarily and emotionally committed themselves to the battle for the forts and the city of Verdun, it went on and on after its "strategic significance had long since passed out of sight; . . . yet the battle had somehow achieved a demonic existence of its own, far beyond the control of generals of either nation. Honor had become involved to an extent which made disengagement impossible."[28] A similar concept of honor, based on a previous decision and commitment, may explain some of President Johnson's and President Nixon's decisions in Vietnam, Cambodia, and Laos.

Bewitchment by History and Ideology

Any reader of political memoirs is bound to discover that most political leaders have found the study of their nation's and other nations' history the single best preparation for their future leadership role. Time and again we find entries in statesmen's diaries asserting that their guesses about future events were based on their own interpretation of the past. The leaders' speeches and declarations are usually full of historical allusions, thus making past history an active partner in the creation of the present. Yet a historian may ask, "Is the history [explicitly] invoked really the source of policies, or is it the source of arguments designed to vindicate policies adopted for antecedent reasons?"[29] This question will be posed again with reference to ideology and morality, which, like history, are often invoked only to vindicate a decision adopted for nonideological or non-moral reasons. As with ideology and morality, the lessons of history

> are generally so ambiguous that the antecedent reasons often determine the choice between alternative historical interpretations. . . . Historical models acquire a life of their own. Once a statesman begins to identify the present with the past, he may in time be carried further than he intends by the bewitchment of analogy.[30]

Not only generals but political leaders as well have the tendency to reenact old conflicts and fight old campaigns all over again although new circumstances would recommend new strategy and tactics. In his memoirs George F. Kennan sarcastically notes that President Roosevelt could not easily distinguish World War II from World War I. In President Johnson's mind the war in Vietnam might have appeared as a carbon copy of the relatively successful war in Korea. And the Soviet political leaders most probably viewed their armed invasion of Czechoslovakia in 1968 as a mere repetition of their armed intervention in the Hungarian revolution of 1956, an invasion that had the approval of all the communist leaders, including Tito. Moscow was therefore genuinely surprised when so many foreign communist parties publicly condemned their invasion of Czechoslovakia, including the parties of France, Italy, Rumania, Yugoslavia, Albania, and the People's Republic of China.

The impact of the leaders' commitment to ideology, a code of ethics, religion, or some other belief system is similar to that of historical analogy: It may significantly affect their ability to interpret and react to information and events. Just as a paranoiac rejects offers of friendship, a statesman, prisoner of his own creed, may reject information that challenges his preconditioned view of the world; he reinterprets contradictory information or events so that it will confirm and conform with his dogmas.

Commitment to a belief system, a political ideology, or a code of ethics will be the subject of more detailed analysis in Chapters 7 and 8.

Concept of Role

The political aphorism "Where you stand depends on where you sit" needs two additional qualifications. A leader's interpretation of an event and his reaction to it will depend in part on his view of the security of his seat and on what he believes is expected of him in the position he presently occupies.

A leader's feeling of permanence (tenure), authority, and responsibility within a given political system will influence his use of authority. There are no available data, but we may assume that the decision-making process of a national leader is bound to be affected, in the case of a democratic leader, by his periodic accountability to legislators and voters and, in the case of a dictator, by either a total lack of accountability or an informal responsibility to some factions within an authoritarian structure. It is possible that a democratic President's interpretation and reaction to international events will significantly differ depending on whether an event occurs in the period either closely preceding or closely following his reelection for a final term.

When engaged in pursuing what they consider the promotion or protection of their nation's interests, not only do political leaders base their actions on different values than they use in their private lives, but "they are able to act as they do because of the power and influence generated by their nations organized as corporate bodies."[31]

Depending on their personality structure, national leaders demonstrate different attitudes toward the institutional or informal checks and balances that may limit their freedom of action in foreign policy. American presidents, for instance, present an interesting gamut of contrasting concepts as to what a President should or should not do in a situation that he deems a clear and present danger to the national interest. In his autobiography, Theodore Roosevelt writes:

> My view was that . . . every executive officer in high position was a steward of the people bound actively and affirmatively to do all he could for the people, and not content himself with the negative merit of keeping his talents undamaged in a napkin. I declined to adopt the view that what was imperatively necessary for the Nation could not be done by the President unless he could find some specific authorization to do it. My belief was that it was not only his right but his duty to do anything that the needs of the Nation demanded unless such action was forbidden by the Constitution or by the laws.[32]

President Truman ordering United States troops to Korea, President Kennedy authorizing the ill-fated invasion of Cuba and then, a year later, successfully engaging in atomic brinkmanship over the Russian missiles in Cuba, and President Johnson escalating war in Vietnam all had concepts of their authority and responsibility that were broadly similar to Theodore Roosevelt's. In May 1970 President Nixon invoked the duty and right of the commander-in-chief of the armed forces to protect American lives after he had ordered a major offensive thrust into communist staging areas in neutral Cambodia: "We will not allow American men by the thousands to be killed by an enemy from privileged sanctuaries." His concept of his role and authority subsequently became a major constitutional issue; in connection with the Watergate affair, the proven corruption of his Vice-President, Spiro Agnew, and other controversial practices in and around the White House, serious efforts were made to impeach and convict the President who was finally forced to resign on August 9, 1974.

Another important aspect of a leader's concept of his role is his estimate of what people or history expect of him—however conceited or inaccurate this estimate may be. It may range from the world-reforming role of a messiah to a parochially limited orientation in which international problems are viewed as an occasional and quite disturbing interruption of his concern with the economic progress and social welfare of his people. Presidents with the personal characteristics of a messianic crusader, a practical businessmen, or a social reformer are bound to differ in their respective reactions to the same international event.

Physical and Mental Health

A sleepless night, fatigue, problems of digestion, headache, and serious illness all have important effects on our reaction to news. This naturally applies to the policy maker's ability to interpret and react to events. He is human too. While not underestimating the effects of minor ailments, we are concerned in the following observations with more serious illnesses and their impact on international politics.

Of the Russian leaders, it is known that Lenin experienced several strokes prior to his death in 1924, that Stalin was afflicted with hypertension, and that Khrushchev in the presence of journalists often referred to his high blood pressure and the necessity of maintaining a fat-free and alcohol-free diet.

During Hitler's rise to power, three British prime ministers suffered marked physical or mental declines.[33] During the last years of Ramsay MacDonald's premiership (which ended in 1935), his speeches became increasingly incoherent. Stanley Baldwin's diaries during the period in which Hitler reoccupied the Rhineland (March 1939) make reference to his being more tired than usual; he was also having trouble making decisions. Neville Chamberlain's letters while he was prime minister mention gout and "minor ailments." On June 16, 1940 (the fall of France), Chamberlain's diary refers to "considerable pain," presumably in the lower abdomen. In July he was operated on; he died after a second operation in November 1940, by which time he had been replaced by Churchill. Arnold Rogow writes:

It would be absurd, of course, to explain the appeasement era in terms of the illness of three British prime ministers. But it is equally absurd to dismiss the possibility that these illnesses, including the treatment of them, affected certain decisions, made or not made.[34]

Mussolini's son-in-law and foreign minister, Count Galleazzo Ciano, noted in his diary that the recurrence of an old venereal disease made the Italian leader restless after the outbreak of World War II. Bocchini, the head of the Italian secret police, went so far as to suggest to Ciano that Mussolini should undertake an intensive syphilitic cure. Ciano added: "It surprised and annoyed me very much that Bocchini should have said this, although I myself recognize the fact that Mussolini's contradictory behavior is truly upsetting to anyone who works with him."[35]

Franklin Delano Roosevelt's impaired health at the summit meeting at Yalta in February 1945, and his death soon after (April 12, 1945), profoundly affected the shape of events on the eve of V-E and V-J days. Roosevelt's death occurred at the most important moment of any war—the moment when the political structure of the postwar world is about to be determined. It is often alleged that shortly before his death he had already reached the conclusion that in view of the brutal Soviet behavior in eastern Europe, American hopes about a postwar collaboration with Stalin's Russia were unrealistic. The course of American foreign and military policy, as well as the tone of American public opinion with respect to Soviet Russia, was to be changed. President Roosevelt, so it seems, had neither the energy nor the time left to initiate and lead the necessary adjustment to the reality of Soviet postwar ambitions. His successor, Harry S. Truman, handicapped by less experience and prestige, at least in the early period of his presidency, could implement the necessary change in American outlook and policy only step by step. Truman's changes culminated in 1947 when, in response to perceived Soviet pressure, President Truman promised aid to Greece, Turkey, and other nations resisting Soviet and communist expansion (the Truman Doctrine, contained in a message to Congress on March 12, 1947) and then promised aid to western Europe (the Marshall Plan, announced on June 6, 1947). This interpretation of the beginning of the Cold War was challenged by several historians who ascribe the sole responsibility for the Cold War to President Truman and his assumption that the use of the atomic bomb against Japan, which was militarily unnecessary, should give the United States a decisive upper hand in its postwar dealings with Russia.[36]

When political leaders fall ill, it is now common practice to issue official bulletins that inform the nation and the world at large of the exact state of their health. The nation may feel sorry, the world less so, but both may be equally worried lest the physical disability of the leader unfavorably affect policy making at the top. Even when in good health, American presidents now go for a physical checkup every year at Walter Reed Hospital, an event that has become more than just a national affair: The result of the checkup is announced as important news of the day to the nation and the world.

When confirmed, a serious illness or the death of a statesman adds a new element of uncertainty to the international scene—an unexpected illness or death upsets many prophecies and anticipations. By contrast, an illness that affects the mental capacity of a major policy maker but remains unknown to all but a very few of his intimate associates represents an element that may belie any estimate of that leader's policy. The problem of mental illness striking a top policy maker is even more serious, especially in our era of potential nuclear destruction, since destructiveness directed either inward against oneself or outward against others, and often in both directions, is an intrinsic component of all mental illnesses. However frightening such a prospect may be, the incidence of mental illness is high enough to assume the possibility that a key decision maker or one with the power to start a nuclear war may become insane while in office or may suffer from serious mental disorder. The fate of the world may lie in the hands of a paranoiac, schizophrenic, or maniac, or a person with a high degree of hysteria, depression, anxiety, or obsession.

During the American presidential campaign in 1964, a new magazine, *Fact*, tried to increase its appeal and circulation by a publicity gimmick that seemed to suggest that one of the candidates for the highest office in the land was not mentally balanced. A full-page advertisement in the daily newspapers posed the problem in the form of a question: "Is Barry Goldwater psychologically fit to be the President of the United States?" According to the advertisement, 1846 psychiatrists had examined Goldwater's "fitness to keep his finger on the atomic trigger . . . his tendency to view issues from extremes, either all good or all bad . . . his veneration of the military, his aversion to compromise, his mistrust of strangers, and the impulsive statements he later modifies or denies."[37]

Although the magazine's poll of the prevailing opinion among psychologists and psychiatrists (none of whom had ever actually examined Goldwater) could not be taken seriously from a scientific point of view, the existence and probable appeal of such an advertisement was a good indication of the general concern with the mental health of those who might be called upon to make vital decisions in behalf of their nation and mankind. In 1972 Senator George McGovern, candidate for the United States presidency, agreed with the leaders of the Democratic party that Senator Thomas F. Eagleton of Missouri was politically unfit to become Vice-President (and so potential successor to the President) because, some years before, Senator Eagleton had undergone psychiatric treatment to overcome strain and fatigue.

In another context, the psychologist Otto Klineberg, noting that psychological tests have been required for potential police officers and for employees of such governmental organizations as the U.S. Information Agency, concluded: "We have already reached the point, in many countries, of requesting a physician's report on the candidate for public office; we are not yet prepared to ask for a similar report on his psychological condition."[38]

If we require that candidates for minor jobs submit to psychological tests, how illogical or absurd is it to require tests for candidates for much more important jobs, such as President of the United States or premier of Soviet Russia or China? Some of the proposals in this respect, however, strike us as facetious: One proposal suggested that world leaders should submit to psychological tests administered by the World Health Organization, the World Federation of Mental Health, or a panel of world-famous psychiatrists and psychoanalysts, who would apparently probe in depth into the leaders' memories and dreams and into other obscure corners of their souls, including their real attitude of love and hatred for their mothers. It may be, as some writers have suggested, that exceptional leaders of the past, including Caesar, Napoleon, and Lincoln, would have had problems in passing such tests.

The problem is also complex from a psychiatrist's professional standpoint. While an obviously insane person is perhaps not likely to be elected president or appointed prime minister or party secretary, a man who is not psychotic when appointed or elected may become so while in office. The psychiatrist Mortimer Ostow expands on this point:

> Our criteria for the diagnosis of psychosis are fairly clear and reliable. But no responsible psychiatrist would offer a definite prediction that a given person will or will not become ill during a specific interval. . . . On the other hand, the destructive character disorder in a megalomaniacal demagogue, while dangerous, is not a clear-cut psychiatric diagnosis. Hitler and Stalin . . . are probably better categorized in these terms rather than as psychotics. The kind of irrational devotion and subservience which such destructive leaders command is likely to defy . . . sober and cautious medical opinion.[39]

If the words of former Soviet Premier Nikita S. Khruschev can be believed—granting that he is neither a psychologist nor a psychoanalyst and was speaking from political motivations—Soviet Russia was ruled and directed between 1927 and 1953 by a man who was "hysterical," a "persecution maniac," "capricious," "sickly suspicious," "irritable," and "brutal." In addition, according to Khrushchev, Stalin was also "unaware of reality" both inside and outside Russia (see Document 6.3).

But was Stalin really so insane and so ignorant of reality as his successor maintained? Testimony of noncommunists who knew and negotiated with Stalin seems to deny in particular the accusation that Stalin was uninformed and unaware of realities. On the contrary, Churchill's memoirs, especially his descriptions of his meetings with Stalin at Moscow in 1942, at Teheran in 1943, and at Yalta in 1945, depict Stalin as a man unusually well

---

DOCUMENT 6.3

KHRUSHCHEV'S ANALYSIS OF STALIN'S PERSONALITY

After the war began, the *nervousness* and *hysteria* which Stalin demonstrated, interfering with actual military operations, caused our Army serious damage. . . .

After the war began, Stalin became more *capricious, irritable,* and *brutal;* in particular, his *suspicion* grew. His *persecution mania* reached unbelievable dimensions. . . .

Stalin was a very *distrustful* man, sickly *suspicious;* we knew this from our work with him. He could look at a man and say: "Why are your eyes so shifty today?" Or, "Why are you turning so much today and avoiding looking at me directly in the eyes?" This *sickly suspicion* created in him a *general distrust* toward eminent party workers whom he had known for years. Everywhere and in everything he saw "enemies," "two-facers," and "spies." . . .

Stalin had completely lost *consciousness* of reality; he demonstrated his suspicion not only in relation to individuals in the USSR, but in relation to whole Communist parties and nations. . . .

Stalin *never traveled* anywhere. He knew the country and the agriculture from films. . . . The last time he visited a village was in January 1928. . . .

Stalin *never visited* any sector of the front or any liberated city, except one. . . . Stalin planned military operations on a globe. Yes, comrades, he used to take the globe and trace the front on it. . . .

From a speech made at the Twentieth Soviet Communist Party's Congress, February 25, 1956. Washington, D.C.:, Public Affairs Press, 1956. Italics added.

---

informed and interested in every aspect of the military and political situation.

President Truman recorded his first impression of Stalin in his *Memoirs*; it was a favorable one:

> The next day I met Stalin for the first time. . . . I was impressed by him and talked to him straight from the shoulder. He looked at me in the eye when he spoke, and I felt hopeful that we could reach an agreement that would be satisfactory to the world and ourselves.[40]

Those who prefer to believe Khrushchev's analysis of Stalin's imbalance and ignorance can point to the obvious fact that Khrushchev must have known Stalin better and more intimately than Churchill, Roosevelt, and Truman, none of whom seems to have underestimated Stalin's cleverness and knowledge. Those who doubt Khrushchev's image of Stalin may point to the obvious effort on the part of Stalin's successor to enhance his own image by denigrating that of his predecessor. Our purpose here is not to take a definitive stand on this issue, but rather to point to the possibility of completely irrational behavior on the part of top policy makers whose rationality otherwise should be assumed.

The Role of Chance

Historians and philosophers sometimes play at "contrafactual conditionals," a parlor game of sorts, sometimes called "If." "If Cleopatra's nose had been shorter," said the French philosopher Pascal in reference to the history of the Roman Empire, "the whole aspect of the world would have been changed." The historian Arnold Toynbee once asked whether the Turks, had they won Vienna and Gibraltar, would have explored and colonized the New World rather than the Spaniards. We might also speculate as follows: If Wolfe and the British had lost at Quebec, might North America have become French and George Washington a Loyalist refugee in England? Or, to continue, if Lenin had fallen off the train that was bringing him back to Russia from his Swiss exile to produce a revolution, would Kerensky have remained in power and the Bolshevik revolution not occurred?

Many historians, adherents of the "confusion theory" of history, assign an important role to chance and the sheer intricacy of the situation. This is the view of Arthur M. Schlesinger, Jr., who writes about his experience at the White House:

> Nothing in my present experience has been more chastening than the attempt to penetrate into the process of decision. I shudder a little when I think how confidently I have analyzed decisions in the ages of Jackson [the book *The Age of Jackson* earned the Pulitzer prize for the author at the age of 28] and Roosevelt, traced influence, assigned motives, evaluated roles, allocated responsibilities and, in short, transformed a disheveled and murky evolution into a tidy and ordered transaction.[41]

Other historians—and many policy makers—adhere to what James MacGregor Burns called the "conspiracy theory" (if something happened, somebody planned it) and consider that the terms "chance" and "bad luck" refer to situations beyond the main actor's direct control or so unexpected that even a brilliant mind could not imagine their occurrence. "This is one of those cases in which the imagination is baffled by the facts," said Winston S. Churchill after the most intimate top aide of Adolf Hitler, Rudolf Hess, parachuted into Scotland (May 13, 1941), allegedly on his own initiative, to negotiate peace with England prior to the German attack on Russia, which was to come six weeks later.

Many aspects of international politics are indeed beyond the control of main actors. Their decisions set in motion collectivities of men and women: citizens, soldiers, and a multitude of subordinate officers who have the responsibility to implement decisions in detail. By their intelligence or stupidity, their resourcefulness or lack of imagination, their perseverance or negligence, an intelligent decision can be transformed into an error, an erroneous estimate into a success. The decision makers are both masters and captives of the momentum they have created. Especially in military conflicts, when millions are on the move under the command of thousands, the protagonists often fail to assess correctly the consequences of war because the fighting usually produces unexpected results beyond their control. The leaders have often been proved wrong or right *despite* their original estimates. Commenting on Nixon's decision to extend the war in Vietnam into Cambodia in 1970, one of his loyal supporters, Senator Robert Dole, pointed to the element of gamble present in so many major decisions made by national leaders: "If it works, it's a stroke of genius. If it doesn't, he strikes out" (*Time*, May 11, 1970, p. 10).

At other times, the terms "luck" and "chance" describe favorable results that cannot be traced back to a major cause and therefore appear to be due to chance or accident. Former Secretary of State Dean Acheson, for instance, considered President Kennedy's handling of the Cuban missile crisis in October 1962 "a gamble to the point of recklessness but skillfully executed," in which the President had been "phenomenally lucky." The luck, however, seemed to have consisted mainly of Premier Khrushchev's "befuddlement and loss of nerve."[42]

Analyzing the United States failure in invading Cuba in 1961, President Kennedy's special assistant, Arthur M. Schlesinger, Jr., explained the decision partly by the President's lack of experience ("He had been in office only 77 days") and partly by his enormous confidence in his own luck ("Even this dispassionate and skeptical man may have been affected by the soaring euphoria of the new day").[43] Another Kennedy assistant, Theodore C. Sorensen, ascribed the Bay of Pigs disaster to "the newness of the President and his administration," to the momentum of the plan and action, which had been set into motion by Eisenhower and "seemed to move mysteriously and inexorably toward execution without either the President's being able to obtain a firm grip on it or reverse it," and, finally, to Kennedy's fear of "wrong interpretation of his real reasons for cancelling an action against Communist Cuba, prepared and planned by the previous Republican administration."[44] Had the invasion been a success because, by coincidence, Castro had died of a stroke that day, what would have been the comments of Kennedy's critics, friends or enemies? As we have noted previously, success or failure endows a decision with a dimension that is not, cannot be, present at the time. As President Kennedy aptly reminded reporters at the press conference following the disaster at the

Bay of Pigs: "There's an old saying that victory has a hundred fathers and defeat is an orphan."

Here and elsewhere, the terms "luck" and "accident" describe seemingly minor and unexpected incidents with major consequences, such as an adversary's loss of nerve or logic or a decisive influence that originated outside the policy-making inner circle, for instance, with the leader's wife, mistress, or friend. One example of a major result accruing from a friendly visit is given in Truman's *Memoirs* in connection with the 1947-1948 Palestine crisis. When pressure mounted, President Truman decided not to see any spokesman of the Zionist cause at the White House. He even put off seeing Dr. Chaim Weizmann, subsequently the first president of Israel, who had returned to the United States and was asking for an interview. Initially, the request met with refusal. Truman finally granted the interview, and the single reason given in his *Memoirs* for changing his previous political decision to stand above the Arab-Zionist dispute was pressure applied during a visit by an old friend from his days in the haberdashery business, Eddie Jacobson. Speaking about Chaim Weizmann, Jacobson told President Truman in emotional terms: "He is the greatest Jew alive, perhaps the greatest Jew who ever lived. . . . He is an old man and a very sick man. He has traveled thousands of miles to see you, and now you are putting off seeing him. That isn't like you." And Truman concludes: "When Eddie left I gave the instruction to have Dr. Weizmann come to the White House as soon as it could be arranged."[45]

Another illustration of an American President's change of mind caused by the extragovernmental influence of an intimate relationship was given by Lyndon Johnson in his interview with Walter Cronkite (CBS, December 26, 1969). He referred to his 1964 decision not to run for the presidency. His prepared statement to this effect read partly as follows:

> The time requires leadership about which there is no doubt and a voice that men of all parties and men of all color can and will follow. I have learned after trying very hard that I am not that voice or that leader.

His wife read the statement and disagreed. In a note she then wrote

> To step out now would be wrong for your country and I can see nothing but a lonely wasteland for your future. Your friends will be frozen in embarrassed silence and your enemies will be jeering. I am not afraid of time or lies or defeat. In the final analysis I can't carry any of the burdens that you have talked of so I know it's only your choice but I know you're as brave as any of the 35 Presidents. I love you always. Bird.[46]

Five years later, Johnson admitted, "As I often have, I took her judgment instead of mine." Bird changed Johnson's mind and so influenced the course of history. How much?

To document the importance of the human factor, this chapter has utilized some of the better-known memoirs of national leaders and some daily press reports that focus on the interpretive skill of a principal actor on the scene. The list of such sources could be profitably extended much further to include ancient history, diaries, autobiographies, and biographies of top leaders written by their intimate associates. In all these books and press reports many unpredictable, irrational, or accidental aspects of interpretation and action come to light. One has constantly to bear in mind, however, that in their books decision makers and their aides have a tendency to rationalize or justify their decisions with the benefit of hindsight. Not everything that now appears as an accident or wild guess was considered such at the time. And much of what seems logical and premeditated now was in reality a sheer gamble or an intuitive hunch.

DIFFERENT PERSONALITIES, SIMILAR REACTIONS

The personality structures of key policy makers, their backgrounds and education, intelligence and skill, physical and mental health, experience and commitment to a creed present an extraordinary variety. One might expect that their interpretation of a reaction to international events would also differ so dramatically that no generalizations or predictions would be possible. In a sense this is so: The choice between such extremes as war and peace, resistance and surrender, or truth and falsehood necessarily reflects the personal preferences of the leaders in the framework of their perception and evaluation of events. Yet in another sense, although the personality of an outstanding leader shines through all national decisions, one can detect some similarity in the behavior and decisions of leaders in general. Even though details are of course unpredictable, broad generalizations and general predictions of the key policy makers' probable actions are possible; despite contrasting personalities, world leaders often act with less contrast than our preceding analysis has implied.

Three factors seem to mold the great variety of national approaches and individual behavior into a common pattern:

1. All policy makers, whatever their personality differences, are, after all, *politicians*.
2. In one way or another, leaders, however towering their personalities may be, *share* their decision-making processes and the execution of their policies with an aggregate of advisers, administrators, and critics.
3. All national leaders have the same *basic task*, to protect and enhance the security and well-being of their particular nations in the international system.

Politics as a Vocation

All leaders have reached their top positions in a keen power competition in which they successfully defeated the ambitions and intrigues of the opposite party or the opposite faction in the same party. They have reached the apex of national power seasoned by the struggle for political influence. They all understand that this power, that is, the capacity to influence and control the behavior of men, may produce security, order, and peace. They know that these are not self-engendering, and they work toward them as desirable goals; for organized power underlies any order, in contrast to anarchy. Political leaders are neither too naive nor too optimistic about people; they do not believe that man's conduct can be shaped solely by reasoned argument or by his good qualities. Coercion and the threat of coercion are inevitable ingredients of all exercise of power. But political leaders are not pessimists either: They believe and trust that a combination of reason and coercion can produce order and progress as they conceive them and as they deem them desirable. "Only he has the calling for politics," noted the German sociologist Max Weber, "who is sure that he shall not crumble when the world from his point of view is too stupid or too base for what he wants to offer. Only he who in the face of all this can say 'In spite of all!' has the calling for politics."[47] Leaders on the international scene obviously have such a calling; without it they would not have reached the top.

In the minds and hearts of national leaders their personal interests easily merge with the interests of their nations as they see and conceive them, that is, with the preservation, progress, and security of their states. Policy makers rise and fall with the political and economic success of their states. There was some logic, however sinister, in the final decision of Adolf Hitler to commit suicide simultaneously with the destruction of his own creation, the Nazi Reich. However insane, stupid, or erroneous their original concept or program of action was, even those national leaders who finally cause the utter destruction of their state and themselves initially intended to do some good for both. No man would be elected chief of state or even succeed as a usurper if his publicly avowed goal were to cause the decline of the external security, domestic tranquility, and welfare of his nation, however his nation defines these goals. The decline or destruction of the leader's state could lead only to his own political or physical destruction, a prospect no sane man is willing to contemplate.

Those who rely on divinity rather than on politics for the improvement of human society do not as a rule become prime ministers or foreign secretaries; they tend to stay in the woods to pray and meditate. When, exceptionally, such holy men become prime ministers, it is necessarily at the cost of their holiness. They have to learn quickly the basic rules of the political struggle for or against power under the impact of international realities and under the influence of their advisers and assistants.

Public and Private Spheres

The similarity of means and goals on the part of dissimilar personalities is sometimes also explained by what is referred to as the duality of man's personality. The same man may have two different personality structures, which, while intimately interconnected, are concerned with two different responsibilities: a private one to his conscience as a man, and a public one as the leader of a national community. Men who in their private lives are gentle and tender may act in a radically different manner when confronted with an extreme danger to their own survival or that of their nations. The acceptability and desirability of many cruel acts is often measured by the concept of a collective good to be achieved by them. It is not unusual for personal values to be sacrificed in the name of the interest of the whole and for inhuman acts to be perpetrated in the name of humanity.

The conflict between the private and public side of a single personality was admirably expressed by Abraham Lincoln in his much quoted statement about the Civil War: "If I could save the Union without freeing any slave, I would do it. I have stated my purpose according to my view of my official duty and I intend no modification of my often expressed personal wish that all men everywhere should be free."

Lincoln's concept of his official duty happened to coincide with his personal preference. But had it been otherwise, as in many other cases in the history of politics, the private "sector" of his personality would have had to yield to the public one.

However seasoned a national leader might be in terms of domestic politics, upon accession to the position of ultimate responsibility he always seems to need some training period to adjust his former concepts to the new, much harsher, and more complex facts of the international scene. Some leaders learn quickly, some slowly; but all are bound, sooner or later, to discover that punishment for wishful thinking or an error on the international scene is usually more severe than on the domestic one.

A good example of such change from revolutionary, idealistic, prepower concepts to those of responsibility is offered by the transformation of the leaders of independent India; a series of severe shocks made them adjust many of their preindependence political concepts, partly Gandhian, to the inescapable realities of a hostile international situation. First, the Moslems, their partners and brothers-in-arms in the national struggle against British colonialism, became an independent and hostile nation, Pakistan. In the subsequent dispute over Kashmir, Nehru, who had so often preached conciliation and negotiation, finally declared that the question of Kashmir was too vital to India for it to be decided by an allegedly objective verdict of the World Court. In another instance, when negotiations over the Portuguese colony of Goa proved of no avail, the Indian leaders did not hesitate to use military force to occupy and annex Goa. Thus while honoring Gandhi and his nonviolent teaching that ends never justify immoral means, the political leadership of India learned rather quickly the age-old lesson that the application of force may bring results when negotiations prove unfruitful, provided that the opponent is weak or far away. During the Chinese invasion of Ladakh and Assam, the Indian leadership rationalized its principle of nonalignment into a new "interpretation," according to which neutralism is not altered by the acceptance of military aid from two sides (Soviet Russia and the United States) against a third (the People's Republic of China). Later, following China's acquisition of nuclear capability, the political leadership had to give serious thought to the development of India's own nuclear deterrent; India's first successful test of a powerful nuclear device took place on May 18, 1974.

A similar reaction to a similar problem on the part of otherwise dissimilar leaders results principally from responses to situations that are deemed to be matters of life or death for the respective nations. All men bow their heads in order to dodge a stone aimed at their foreheads; under the guidance of their leaders all nations assume with similar automatism a defense posture when confronted with a threat, be it an ultimatum, a stone, an arrow, or an ICBM (intercontinental ballistic missile) with a thermonuclear warhead.

But the similarity ends here. The defense posture adopted in response to a clear and present danger can cover a very broad range of actions indeed; it may include such radically different concrete methods as elimination of the threat by war, raising sufficient intimidatory power against it, compromise by negotiations, or capitulation. The choice of concrete means and ways of reacting to a threat may reflect personal rather than collective preferences.

In addition, in international relations, situations that may be qualified as clear and present dangers or as unadulterated good opportunities are relatively rare. There are opportunities that are coupled with considerable risks. There are dangers that are distant and unclear. In situations short of immediate danger or riskless opportunity, the whole gamut of ideological, pragmatic, moral, and personal considerations will affect the final course of action.

Policies as Group Decisions

In the study of international politics we tend to personify national decisions by referring to Brezhnev's, Stalin's, Mao's, Churchill's, or Nixon's policies; as mentioned previously, this personification of national actors is facilitated by the mass media, which focus on a single leader as he personally announces and justifies a momentous decision: He identifies with the decision and we identify the decision with him. In this context the decision appears highly personal and, through his justification, also rational; an important decision is deemed to have an important cause; a large action has been undertaken for a large reason. This is often correct. But is it always so? Is it the whole story? Major foreign-policy decisions frequently issue from group deliberations over which the national leader may or may not preside; his ultimate responsibility for the consequences of the decision does not exclude the possibility of his nonparticipation in the process of making it.

The decision-making group may be viewed as a composite of relatively loosely connected organizations, specializing in various aspects of international contacts—diplomacy, intelligence, the armed forces, trade and economic aid, propaganda; each of them has a life of its own and its routinized forms of operations, as well as its own collective interests, prestige, physical facilities, and view of the world. All foreign offices in the world, for example, are expected both to initiate policy and to execute the policies initiated by the national leader. The intertwining of initiatives from below and from above is complex.

One of the studies of problem solving in the U.S. Department of State examined in detail the operation of a single regional office responsible for United States relations with a specific geographic area (that is, two or three countries). The study was based on twenty-eight short case studies of low-level problem solving in that office, called for the purpose of anonymity the XYZ Office. Its author, Dean G. Pruitt, obtained his material mostly from interviews with personnel of the XYZ Office. Although Pruitt's conclusions apply only to low-level policy making, they are a very worthwhile illustration of both the complexity of the decision-making process and the influence of experts on leaders:

> It is clear that important decisions receive their final validation at a high level of government and are sometimes implemented at this level in audiences with foreign dignitaries. Yet it is also clear that policy recommendations often originate at a much lower level and that high level validation is seldom denied. Hence, one can agree with Acheson that "while great decisions are, for the most part, made at the top . . . the springs of policy bubble up; they do not trickle down."
>
> The main basis for the power of lower echelons probably lies in their expertise. At the bottom of the organization are the real authorities, the men who know the most about France, or foreign exchange, or nuclear energy. The generalists at the top must be able to weigh and reconcile diverging interests and sometimes to devise novel solutions to nontechnical problems. But when it comes to specialized knowledge and theory, as it often does, they must bow to the opinion of their subordinates.
>
> Of course, higher officers are usually responsible for setting the broad lines of policy, the basic values and goals toward which individual decisions will strive. Yet even here one suspects that the authority of higher echelons is somewhat limited. . . . [Lower echelons] would continue arguing for the validity of the [basic] goals. . . . As one respondent said, in summarizing his reasons for persisting in proposing to higher management a policy to which they did not initially seem favorable, "We know what we believe."[48]

The argument has been made that decisions in a particular field of international contacts (diplomatic, military, or economic) may not result from a rational examination of possible alternatives, made by the national leadership, but from *outputs* of large organizations functioning according to a routinized pattern of operation. "Large acts result from innumerable and often conflicting smaller actions by individuals at various levels of bureaucratic organizations in the service of a variety of only partially compatible conceptions of national goals, organizational goals, and political objectives."[49] Governmental actions in *inter*national politics issue from *intra*national mechanisms. In this sense a foreign-policy decision often represents a sum total of decisions reached by different governmental organizations as arbitrated or coordinated by the top leadership. "Governments perceive problems through organizational sensors,"[50] and they solve them through organizational instrumentalities that determine the scope of, and set the limits to, the political solution.

Many a national decision may be also viewed as an outcome of *bargaining* among different personalities either on the approximately identical level of authority and responsibility (a group of presidential assistants or heads of departments) or hierarchically positioned, from the top leader and his immediate aides down to generals or ambassadors in the field. The national decision may then result from "compromise, coalition, competition, and confusion among government officials who see different faces of an issue." While sometimes a national decision reflects the triumph of one group over the others, more often, "different groups pulling in different directions yield a resultant distinct from what anyone intended."[51] A compromise or an outcome of various overlapping bargaining games within the governmental apparatus evidently differs from, and is perhaps less predictable than, a decision that we assume is based on the best available information and rationally oriented toward maximizing national goals and objectives.

When in 1968 President Johnson decided not to seek reelection, he also announced that he had ordered the United States Air Force and Navy to halt air and naval bombardment over most of North Vietnam. Deescalation as a prelude to peace talks in Paris then began. The almost accidental and yet clearly group process of decision making was described one year later in the *New York Times* (March 6, 1969):

> On that day at the end of February, President Johnson and his closest aides assembled for breakfast around the Chippendale table in the elegant family dining room on the second floor of the Executive Mansion. Before rising from the table, they had set in motion the most intensive policy review of the Johnson Presidency—and one of the most agonizing of any Presidency.
>
> The wrenching debate began almost by accident and then gained a momentum all its own. One dramatic record of its progress appeared in the 12 versions of a Presidential speech that evolved during the month—the

last draft pointing in the opposite direction from the first.

The entire episode also provided a remarkable demonstration of how foreign policy is battled out, inch by inch, by negotiation rather than decision. The turnabout emerged through sharp confrontations and subtle, even conspiratorial, maneuvering—with compromises struck for bureaucratic purposes and with opponents in agreement for contrary reasons.

However personal Johnson's decision not to seek reelection (in combination with the question of the war in Vietnam) may appear, the decision-making process bore the undeniable marks of intragroup negotiations. How much more marked by the group process are other foreign-policy decisions! Many of them can therefore be studied as *compromises* between various bargaining actors, such as the minister of foreign affairs, the principal party secretary, the minister of defense, the director of the central intelligence agency, the minister of finance, the national leader's top personal advisers, and, of course, the national leader himself. In analyzing these negotiations and compromises, one has to take into account the complex interaction between the participants' different perceptions of international events and positions and of various nations' power, motivations, and maneuvering skills, that is, in Graham Allison's words, one has to discover "who did what to whom that yielded the action in questions."[52] If we choose to view policy decisions as results of intragroup compromises rather than personal choices of national leaders, the study of small-group dynamics may perhaps shed some additional light on the frequency of errors in foreign-policy making. In one such study Irving L. Janis analyzed the tendency of individuals in all groups to conform; according to Janis, some of the United States's major fiascoes in foreign and military policies (the Bay of Pigs invasion, the intervention in Korea, the failure to anticipate the attack on Pearl Harbor, and the involvement in and escalation of the war in Vietnam) can, in part, be explained by what he calls "groupthink."

> When we are trying to understand how certain avoidable policy errors happen to be made, we should look into the behavior of the small group of decision makers . . . . The members of policy-making groups, no matter how mindful of their exalted national status and of their heavy responsibilities, are subjected to the pressures widely observed in groups of ordinary citizens. . . . Members [of the group] tend to evolve informal objectives to preserve intragroup friendly relations and this becomes part of their hidden agenda at their meetings. . . . I use the term "groupthink" as a quick and easy way to refer to a mode of thinking that people engage in when they are deeply involved in a cohesive in-group, when the members' strivings for unanimity override their motivation to realistically appraise alternative courses of action. . . . Groupthink refers to a deterioration of mental efficiency, reality testing, and moral judgment that results from in-group pressures.[53]

The group decision-making process seems to be typical of democracies but, of course, even dictators, who often seem to decide on major issues of war and peace by consulting only their "inner voices," have some advisers; a politburo, a group of generals, and always their personal aides. Furthermore they too, however absolute their rule may appear to be, must rely on others in the execution of their decisions; dictators' reliance on them brings the soldiers and diplomats into a group decision-making process to some extent.

In democratic countries leaders act and decide not only under the group influence of their advisers, experts, and backers but also under the influence of a critical press and the opposition parties, which at the next election may sway the majority of the voters away from the present leadership and its policies toward the course of action advocated by the critics. The *anticipated* critique and its effect on a key policy maker is institutionalized in a democracy; but it also plays some restraining or prodding role in fascist or communist regimes. Totalitarian leaders do not need to fear a critical press or an open opposition, but they must take into account possible plots by a potential successor or by a faction of their own party. Khrushchev's policies in the 1960s were influenced not only by his backers and admirers but implicitly also by his enemies, including a potentially pro-Chinese faction within the party. His fall in late 1964 indicated that he had underestimated the power of those who could capitalize upon some of his failures in the foreign and economic spheres.

The direct or indirect involvement of so many elements in a decision-making process dominated by the leading personality may explain why, especially in democratic countries, changes in the orientation of the nation's foreign policy are rather slow and gradual despite some dramatic personnel changes at the helm of the nation. Morton Kaplan noted that the replacement of a Conservative government by a Labour government in Great Britain resulted in changes in the speed and willingness with which given policies were carried out rather than in the sweeping replacement of previous goals and methods of foreign policy:

> The Labour Government probably gave India and Burma their freedom faster than a Conservative government would have, but a Conservative government almost surely would have granted independence eventually. Nevertheless, these differences in priority are not lacking in importance. . . . France finally accorded independence to Vietnam. But it might have been much better for France if Mendès-France had come to office a year earlier.[54]

Foreign-policy changes have often been abrupt and sweeping after a revolution or in a dictatorship, although perhaps not as abrupt and sweeping as the revolutionaries or dictators hoped. The brake on the scope of change is applied by the limits of national power and the impact of the international system. As we shall see in Chapter 7, a profound revolutionary change has not fundamentally altered the worry that the czars had and that the Bolsheviks continued to have about their western boundaries, nor has it altered the czarist dreams about Constantinople and the eastern Mediterranean.

Lonely Leaders?

The importance of the group dimension of national decisions should now be qualified by a return to our previous emphasis on the importance of the personalities of the top national leaders, with whom the final word and the ultimate responsibility for action or nonaction so often lie. There are numerous cases in which national leaders are correctly described or describe themselves as being quite alone in their final decisions despite the complex apparatus of advisers and experts they have at their disposal. When looking at the world in ferment and deciding on appropriate actions at the very summit of national power, national leaders seem to experience a real feeling of loneliness. The preparatory work of the advisers has been done; now comes the moment of truth.

A statesman familiar with General de Gaulle's working methods for over twenty years offered this description of how French foreign policy was formulated in the 1960s:

> When he deals with foreign policy, the General goes into seclusion and plunges into prolonged meditation. He seldom consults experts or advisers, even those very close to him. For a long time he mulls over the questions that need to be resolved. Then, suddenly, often without even informing his ministers, he announces his decision. The Minister of Foreign Affairs, and certainly the Council of Ministers, are called upon only to execute and apply the decisions which the General made entirely by himself.[55]

Yet while secluded and alone in the physical sense, General de Gaulle (or any other lonely political leader) was really not alone in the political sense. First, he had brought with him into his seclusion policy papers, dispatches, or estimates that the ministry of foreign affairs, embassies abroad, and intelligence experts had previously prepared; second, even without any papers, he carried in his mind the impressions or information obtained through previous reading of policy papers, and of books about his nation's history and newspaper reports of attacks by the opposition as well as previous discussions with other politicians, national and foreign.

The need for isolation as well as a link with events, information, and counsel is, of course, typical of all decision-makers. In an interview with the historian Henry A. Graff (*New York Times Magazine*, July 6, 1965), President Johnson described his method of reaching a major decision to broaden the war in Vietnam. Down at the ranch, the President said, he wanted to think, "to smell some blue-bonnets, watch the deer and the antelope, and get some sand between my toes . . . to roam by the river with nobody but a dog for company." He was also going to visit the graves of his parents and grandmother and do some "hard praying." Yet as in de Gaulle's case, one may argue that during his "hard praying" President Johnson was not entirely alone; he too had other silent company than the dog, the deer, and the antelope. In his mind the nation's history, current position papers (including, perhaps, some written by Daniel Ellsberg), yesterday's cables, and critiques read and heard had been stored and were selectively retrieved while the lonely President was "getting some sand between his toes."

Captives of the International System

Whatever their background, skill, or commitment to an ideology, national leaders discharge an identical, fundamental duty: protecting and enhancing the security and welfare of their nation in the framework of a system of states. Chapter 4, which dealt with some aspects of systemic analysis, outlined the characteristic features of a basically anarchic and constantly changing system of states, in which threats to national interests are frequent, self-help is the rule, and misperception of power and intentions is a daily occurrence. When the international system undergoes important changes, these changes, whatever they are, affect *all* the members of the system. And this is another reason for the anticipation that dissimilar personalities and national systems may have generally similar reactions to perceived or misperceived threats or opportunities.

PERCEPTION AND MISPERCEPTION

In conclusion, it should be reemphasized that in international relations individuals acting in behalf of their nations react frequently to appearances rather than to reality—and each fiction is productive of another fiction. As previously noted, an image with no basis in reality may mold or create reality. This is particularly so when policy makers assume foreign enmity. Such an assumption translated into corresponding behavior will provoke a counterimage, counterbehavior, and counteraction such that enmity will indeed ensue, thus confirming what initially might have been a totally false stereotype.[56] "Enemies are those who are defined as such, and if one acts upon that interpretation, it is more likely that the original definition will be confirmed,"[57] writes Ole R. Holsti. In support of his observation, Holsti quotes George F. Kennan, who has partly explained the Soviet-American enmity by the communist insistence on viewing the United States as its implacable enemy:

> It is an undeniable privilege of every man to prove himself right in the
> thesis that the world is his enemy; for if he reiterates it frequently enough
> and makes it the background of his conduct he is bound eventually to be
> right.[58]

The perpetual circle of images producing counterimages can conceivably result in a situation in which policy makers deal with problems whose reality, if it ever existed, has already, so to speak, evaporated into thin air, a fact perceived by no one. A recent study on image and reality in international politics[59] appropriately uses a statement by Epictetus as its leading motto: "Appearances to the mind are of four kinds. Things either are what they appear to be; or they neither are, nor appear to be; or they are and do not appear to be; or they are not, and yet appear to be. Rightly to aim in all these is the wise man's task."

Political leaders rarely accomplish the wise man's task with full success; often they react to things that "are not and yet appear to be" or do not react to things that "are and do not appear to be." (See Document 6.4.)

The fundamental reason for the frequency of misperception among both nations and individuals is simple enough. The process of initiating, evaluating, and reacting to messages or events is in the hands of men—and men are fallible. They respond to situations as they perceive them, that is, by the use of their senses and reason, and the result can be common sense, nonsense, passion, irreducible prejudice, or irresponsible fickleness. The capacity of men to apprehend facts as they are is limited. Facts that have not been apprehended exist perhaps in reality (and philosophers have often argued whether there is such a thing as reality beyond man's senses), but they do not exist politically. They cannot be triggers of political action. On the other hand, a mirage, a dream, or a nightmare is a "fact" insofar as it may be a springboard of action. "If men define situations as real, they are real in their consequences," is the famous theorem of William Isaac Thomas (1863-1947),[60] accepted as valid in the social sciences. Or as Walter Lippmann once put it in his *Public Opinion* (1921):

> What each man does is based not on direct and certain knowledge but on
> pictures made by himself or given to him. If his atlas tells him that the
> world is flat he will not sail near what he believes to be the edge of our
> planet for fear of falling off. . . . For the most part we do not first see, and
> then define, we define first and then see. . . . We imagine most things
> before we experience them.[61]

Distinguishing between the relation of environmental factors to policy decisions, on the one hand, and to the operational *results* of decisions, on the other, Harold and Margaret Sprout correctly concluded:

> With respect to policy-making and the content of policy decisions, our

DOCUMENT 6.4

SOVIET AND AMERICAN IMAGES

A Soviet Scholar's View of the United States
At present, the traditional black hat which symbolizes the diplomatic profession has been discarded by the United States political leadership. American foreign policy now wears a heavy military steel helmet upon its complacent head. . . . The influence of the military-industrial complex has reached an unprecedented level. . . . Note that the Democratic and Republican Parties which represent the interests of American monopoly capital, have made strenuous efforts during the past decades to eliminate from the American political scene other parties, bourgeois as well as truly progressive ones, and primarily the American Communist party, which voices the interests of the American labor. . . . The monopolies are the main force in the United States which, aided by the military clique and the central political apparatus, determine the country's domestic and foreign policies. . . . The President of the United States, the venerable senators, the smartest members of the House of Representatives, and the entire bureaucratic apparatus are, in fact, in the service of the monopolists. . . . In his actions President Kennedy was, above all, the executor of the will imposed upon the United States of America by the monopolistic bourgeoisie.

From Anatolii A. Gromyko, *Through Russian Eyes: President Kennedy's 1036 Days.* Washington, D.C. International Library, 1973, pp. 82-83, 224-227.

An American View of a Soviet Scholar's View of America
I have just read, and written an epilogue for, a book on the Kennedy years by Anatolii Gromyko. . . . Gromyko is not just another Party hack mouthing the official propaganda line. He is the son of the Foreign Minister of the Soviet Union and head of the Foreign Policy Section of the Soviet Academy of Sciences' America Institute. . . . Reading his book is a frightening experience. For it is a compendium of every nonsense every uttered by Soviet propaganda about the United States. The nonsense permeates not only factual reporting and political interpretation but also moral judgment: The Soviet Union appears as the champion of all that is good in the world, especially peace, while the United States, bent on war, is the incarnation of evil. If the leaders of the Soviet Union believe the fictions Gromyko presents as facts—and there is no reason to assume that they do not, since the America Institute is their main source of information about the United States—détente can be no more than a breathing spell in an ongoing struggle for total stakes.

From Hans J. Morgenthau, "Missing: A Moral Consensus—The Danger of Détente," *The New Leader*, October 1, 1973, p. 6.

position is that what matters is how the policy-maker imagines [the international scene] to be. With respect to the operational results of decisions, what matters is how things are, not how the policy-maker imagines them to be.[62]

In his famous speech on the crimes of the Stalin era (February 25, 1956), Nikita Khrushchev described vividly, although with a visible personal bias, a situation in which vital and accurate information was available and yet failed to influence the policy maker's mind, heart, and will to act. According to Khrushchev, although Stalin was in possession of numerous warnings about the impending Nazi attack on Russia,

> Soviet borders were insufficiently prepared to repel the enemy. When the fascist armies had actually invaded Soviet territory and military operations began, Moscow issued the order that the German fire was not to be returned. Why? It was because Stalin, despite evident facts, thought that the war had not yet started, and this was only a provocative action on the part of several undisciplined sections of the German Army, and that our reaction might serve as a reason for the Germans to begin the war. As you see, everything was ignored: warnings of certain Army commanders, declarations of deserters of the enemy army, and *even the open hostility of the enemy*. Is this an example of the alertness of the chief of the party and of the state at this particularly significant historical moment? [Italics added.][63]

Thirteen years later, however, this was at least partly challenged by Marshal Zhukov, known in Russia as the "Soviet Union's Greatest Soldier." In his memoirs he defends Stalin's military and political record during World War II:

> Since his death it has been said that Stalin never listened to anyone and made military and political decisions by himself. If arguments were presented to him in convincing fashion, he listened. And I know of cases where he gave up his own views and decisions.[64]

Ten years before World War I, French leaders learned about the German plan (Schlieffen Plan) for a main thrust through neutral Belgium in the event of war with France. The plan required the Germans to use reserves as active troops, which the French General Staff deemed preposterous. The Schlieffen Plan was dismissed as "a feint designed to draw the French army away from the real attack."[65] When the war finally came and the German armies did follow the Schlieffen Plan, using reserves as active troops, the French still refused to abandon their "Plan 17," which called for leaving two thirds of the neutral Belgian frontier undefended. As late as the ninth day of war, when Germans were beginning to cross into Belgium, the French General Staff felt "confirmed in the impression that the principal German maneuver would not take place in Belgium."[66] In another context (Chapter 5) we noted the Israeli rejection of early (September) warnings of the Syrian-Egyptian assault planned for early October 1973.

AND THE PEOPLE?

Admittedly, our discussion of foreign-policy making neglected the role of the general public in favor of the top national leadership and groups of advisers, experts, and managers of military, intelligence, diplomatic, and economic establishments. The reason is obvious: as a rule, the general public plays a minor role in the conduct of international politics. One reason for this is inherent in the nature of international politics. Information on which the ultimate decision is made is often secret and cannot be revealed to a wide circle, as leakage could jeopardize either the contemplated action or the source of information. This is why the actual daily conduct of foreign policy is limited to an aggregate of specialists, the inner core of the executive branch of the government. Another reason for the low degree of influence of the general public on foreign policy is its basic lack of interest in the world scene except in periods of crisis that affect it directly. And even at these moments the reactions are more emotional than rational, for the public lacks adequate information about international developments as well as the necessary sophistication and skill to evaluate such information even if it were available. There is a considerable danger of distortion when one tries to oversimplify foreign-policy issues in order to bring them down to the level of the average voter, usually in the form of a slogan or headline.

Yet the general public, however indirectly and imperceptibly, does share in the policy-making process to the extent to which its leaders' efforts to provide for external security affect the internal life of the state. International politics extends into the internal fabric of a territorial state in the form of taxes, military conscription, industrial mobilization, competition in outer space, problems of internal security and foreign espionage, and the mass media that inform or misinform the public on what is going on internationally. Thus the public is part of the process since its support for the execution of a given policy is necessary. Key policy makers do not serve in the armed forces, industry, or agriculture. Without the support of these three areas of national power, leadership may so decline in effectiveness that adopted policies simply could not be executed. Even in a totalitarian system, the leader cannot exclude from his calculations of what is desirable and what is possible the problem of his people's physical endurance. His ambitious foreign aims may require that the nation neither sleep nor eat until the goal is achieved. The need of people to eat and sleep therefore represents a limitation on what otherwise may appear to be his omnipotence. It has been said that all governments are based on their ability to either respect or manipulate public opinion. Democratic and totalitarian leaders alike recognize the importance of the public —especially the potentiality of its restraint upon foreign policy by civil disobedience or noncooperation. This is why we can observe their constant efforts to inform, educate, or *deceive* the public on the subject of priorities in the nation's foreign policy.

The lack of participation in and direct influence on policy making on the part of the general public is often deplored not only as a violation of democratic principles but also as a loss for the cause of peace among nations. The common sense and alleged peacefulness of average men and women are often contrasted with the aggressiveness and prejudices of leaders. But is this contrast correct? In the early days of the American republic Alexander Hamilton challenged those who maintained that popular majorities are by definition more peaceful than aristocratic leaders:

> Are there no aversions, predilections, and desires of unjust acquisitions, that affect nations as well as kings? Have republics in practice been less addicted to war than monarchies? Are not the former administered by men as well as the latter? Are not popular assemblies frequently subject to impulses of rage, resentment, jealousy, avarice, and other irregular propensities?[67]

Hamilton's questions indicate that opportunities for or dangers to peace and order should be sought in the nature of all human beings rather than in whether they act singly or collectively. We must leave the question as to whether the nature of individuals and collectivities can be altered unanswered. We can only note that so far there have been very few indications that human nature can be changed for the better in the foreseeable future.

Notes

1. The terminology used is that of Paul H. Nitze in his article "National Policy-Making Techniques," *The Johns Hopkins School of Advanced International Studies Review*, 3:3 (1958), 3-5.

2. Henry A. Kissinger, "Coalition Diplomacy in a Nuclear Age," *Foreign Affairs*, July 1964, p. 536.

3. Richard C. Snyder, H. W. Brucks, and Burton Sapin, *Decision-Making as an Approach to the Study of International Politics* (Monograph No. 3 of the Foreign Policy Analysis Project Series). Princeton, N. J.: Princeton University, 1954, p. 60.

4. Nitze, "National Policy-Making Techniques," p. 3.

5. Martin Landau, "The Concept of Decision," in James B. Christoph and Bernard E. Brown, *Cases in Comparative Politics*, 2d ed. Boston: Little, Brown, 1969, p. 20. Our four types of foreign-policy decisions vary slightly from Landau's four models: Programmed Decisions ("computational decision-making" in the Thompson-Tuden terminology), Pragmatic Decisions, Bargaining, and Inspiration.

6. David Baybrooke and Charles E. Lindblom, *A Strategy of Decision: Policy Evaluation as a Social Process*. New York: Free Press, 1963, p. 73.

7. Paul E. Zinner wrote "The Soviets, in particular, had a unique opportunity to compound the President's problems by calling off their summit meeting with him because of the bombing raids he ordered against North Vietnam on the very eve of his departure for Moscow. The blame for the collapse of the talks would have rested squarely on him. Surely, their decision not to take advantage of the near-perfect excuse provided by Nixon reflected their own policy priorities and not their concern for his welfare: they considered it in their self-interest to make common cause with *this* President instead of hastening his retirement from office." *The New Leader*, October 1, 1973, pp. 12-13.

8. George Plekhanov, *The Role of the Individual in History*. New York: International Publishers, 1940, p. 46.

9. In his book *The People's War: Britain, 1939-1945* (New York: Pantheon, 1969) Angus Calder partly destroys the traditional image of wartime England as a tight little island, patient, courageous, and solidly united under the brilliant leadership of Churchill. If it had been so, it would be difficult to understand why after V-E Day but before V-J Day the patient British people so impatiently turned Churchill out of office and voted in the Labour party by a large margin.

10. Thomas Carlyle, "Diderot," *Critical and Miscellaneous Essays,* Vol. 5. London: Chapman and Hall, n.d., p. 47.

11. Fred I. Greenstein, *Personality and Politics*. Chicago: Markham, 1969, p. 34.

12. Stanley Budner, "Intolerance of Ambiguity as a Personality Variable," *Journal of Personality*, 30 (1962), 30.

13. J. David Singer, "Inter-Nation Influence: A Formal Model," *American Political Science Review,* 57:2 (June 1963), 421.

14. Arnold Wolfers, *Discord and Collaboration*. Baltimore, Md.: The Johns Hopkins Press, 1962, p. 42.

15. Stanley Hoffmann, "Perception, Reality, and the Franco-American Conflict," in John C. Farrell and Asa P. Smith (eds.), *Image and Reality in World Politics*. New York: Columbia University Press, 1968, pp. 58-59 (paperback.) The book is a reprint of *Journal of International Affairs*, 21 (1967), which focused on "Image and Reality in World Politics."

16. Pierre Renouvin and Jean-Baptiste Duroselle, *L'Introduction a l'histoire des relations internationales*. Paris: Librairie Armand Colin, 1964, pp. 284-313 (published in English by Frederick A. Praeger in New York and Pall Mall Press in London, in 1966, under the title *Introduction to the History of International Relations*).

17. Facetiously it may be suggested that we should beware of world leaders who are below 5 feet 5 inches tall since this was the average height of Napoleon, Hitler, Lenin, Stalin, and Franco. Alexander the Great was even smaller than that.

18. Guglielmo Ferrero, *Principles of Power*. New York: Putnam, 1942, p. 110.

19. Quoted by General S. L. A. Marshall in his review of Hanson Baldwin's *Battles Lost and Won: Great Campaigns of World War II* (New York: Harper & Row, 1966), in the *New York Times Book Review*, October 9, 1966, p. 62.

20. Greenstein, *Personality and Politics*, p. 153.

21. Bradley F. Smith, *Adolf Hitler: His Family, Childhood and Youth* (Hoover Institution Publication No. 62). Stanford, Calif.: Stanford University Press, 1969, p. 181.

22. Sigmund Freud and William C. Bullitt, *Thomas Woodrow Wilson: A Psychological Study*. Boston: Houghton Mifflin, 1967, p. 307.

23. Karl W. Deutsch and Richard L. Merritt, "Effects of Events on National and International Images," in Herbert C. Kelman (ed.), *International Behavior: A Social-Psychological Analysis*. New York: Holt, Rinehart and Winston, 1965, p. 168.

24. Louis Fischer, "Lenin's Legacy," *Columbia University Forum* 7:4 (Fall 1964), 6. In his *Stalin as Revolutionary 1879-1929* (Norton, 1973) Robert C. Tucker also contrasted Stalin's harsh treatment of non-Russian ethnic groups in the Soviet Union (including his own Georgians, whom he despised) with Lenin's more Marxist critique of "Great Russian chauvinism."

25. Harry S. Truman, *Year of Decisions* (Memoirs, Vol. 1). New York: Doubleday, 1956, pp. 153, 189-190.

26. Deutsch and Merritt, "Effects of Events on National and International Images," pp. 182-183.

27. Jerome D. Frank, *Sanity and Survival*. New York: Random House, 1967, p. 188. (Vintage Book, 1968.)

28. Alistair Horne, "Verdun: The Reason Why," *New York Times Magazine*, February 20, 1966, p. 42.

29. Arthur M. Schlesinger, Jr., *The Bitter Heritage: Vietnam and American Democracy, 1941-1966*. Boston: Houghton Mifflin, 1967, p. 81.

30. Schlesinger, *The Bitter Heritage*, p. 81.

31. Wolfers, *Discord and Collaboration*, pp. 8-9.

32. Theodore Roosevelt, *An Autobiography*. New York: Crowell-Collier-Macmillan, 1913, p. 389.

33. H. J. C. J. L'Etang, "The Health of Statesmen and the Affairs of Nations," *The Practitioner*, January 1958, pp. 113-118.

34. Arnold A. Rogow, "Psychiatry as a Political Science," *Psychiatric Quarterly*, 40:2 (April 1966), 328.

35. Count Galleazzo Ciano, *The Ciano Diaries, 1939-1943*. New York: Doubleday, 1946, p. 184.

36. This thesis is presented in Gar Alperowitz, *Atomic Diplomacy: Hiroshima and Potsdam*. New York: Knopf, 1965.

37. *New York Times*, September 20, 1964 (section E), p. 5.

38. Otto Klineberg, *The Human Dimension in International Relations*. New York: Holt, Rinehart and Winston, 1964, p. 66.

39. Mortimer Ostow, "Mental Health in Office," *New York Times*, October 2, 1964.

40. Truman, *Year of Decisions*, p. 341.

41. Arthur M. Schlesinger, Jr., "The Historian and History," *Foreign Affairs*, 41:3 (April 1963), 493.

42. Dean Acheson, "Dean Acheson's Version of Robert Kennedy's Version of the Cuban Missile Affair," *Esquire*, February 1969, p. 46.

43. Arthur M. Schlesinger, *A Thousand Days: John F. Kennedy in the White House*. Boston: Houghton Mifflin, 1965, pp. 250-277. (Also a Fawcett Crest paperback.)

44. Theodore C. Sorensen, *Kennedy*. New York: Harper & Row, 1965, pp. 326-347. (Also a Bantam paperback.)

45. Harry S. Truman, *Years of Trial and Hope* (*Memoirs*, Vol. 2). New York: Doubleday, 1956, p. 166.

46. The full text of the CBS interview was reproduced in the *New York Times* on December 27, 1969.

47. H. H. Gerth and C. Wright Mills, *From Max Weber: Essays in Sociology*. New York: Oxford, 1958, p. 128.

48. Dean G. Pruitt, *Problem Solving in the Department of State*. Denver, Colo.: University of Denver Monograph, 1964-1965, pp. 50-51.

49. Graham T. Allison, *Essence of Decision: Explaining the Cuban Missile Crisis*. Boston: Houghton Mifflin, 1971, p. 6.

50. Graham T. Allison, "Conceptual Models and the Cuban Missile Crisis," *American Political Science Review*, 63:3 (September 1969), 698. In his analysis Allison distinguishes three conceptual models we may employ in analyzing national decisions: the Rational Policy Model, the Organizational Process Model, and the Bureaucratic Politics Model.

51. Allison, "Conceptual Models and the Cuban Missile Crisis," pp. 707-708.

52. Allison, *Essence of Decision*, p. 7.

53. Irving L. Janis, *Victims of Groupthink: A Psychological Study of Foreign-Policy Decisions and Fiascoes*. Boston: Houghton Mifflin, 1972, pp. 8-9.

54. Morton A. Kaplan, *System and Process in International Politics*. New York: Wiley, 1957, p. 155.

55. Michel Gorday, "The French People and de Gaulle," *Foreign Affairs*, July 1964, p. 546.

56. For further reference see David J. Finlay, Ole R. Holsti, and Richard R. Fagen, *Enemies in Politics*. Chicago: Rand McNally, 1967, p. 257.

57. Ole R. Holsti, "Cognitive Dynamics and Images of the Enemy," in Farrell and Smith (eds.), *Image and Reality in World Politics*, p. 17.

58. "X" (George F. Kennan), "The Sources of the Soviet Conduct," *Foreign Affairs*, July 1947, p. 569. Compare Nathan Leites, *A Study of Bolshevism*. New York: Free Press, 1953, p. 28: "It is a central Bolshevik belief that enemies strive not merely to contain the Party or roll it back, but rather to annihilate it. . . . If the Party acts on the belief that its enemies are annihilative, it is apt to render that belief less unrealistic by the very reactions which its conduct evokes. If imaginary enemies are treated as enemies, they are apt finally to become real enemies."

59. Farrell and Smith (eds.), *Image and Reality in World Politics*, p. 140.

60. See *International Encyclopedia of Social Science*, Vol. 16. New York: Crowell-Collier-Macmillan, 1968, pp. 1-6. Compare Epictetus' theorem: "Men are tormented by the opinion they have of things, not by the things themselves."

61. Walter Lippmann, *Public Opinion*. New York: Crowell-Collier-Macmillan, 1932, pp. 25, 81, and 90.

62. Harold and Margaret Sprout, "Environmental Factors in the Study of International Politics," *The Journal of Conflict Resolution*, 1 (1957), 328.

63. Khrushchev's speech, although never officially published in the Soviet Union, was reproduced in full in most countries of the world. Its text was translated and released by the U.S. Department of State on June 4, 1956, and subsequently published in pamphlet form by Public Affairs Press, Washington, D.C., under the title *The Anatomy of Terror: Khrushchev's Revelations about Stalin's Regime*. The quotation above may be found there on pp. 46-47.

64. Georgi K. Zhukov, *Marshal Zhukov's Greatest Battles*. New York: Harper & Row, 1969, p. 304.

65. Barbara Tuchman, *The Guns of August*. New York: Dell, 1964, p. 60. (Paperback.)

66. Tuchman, *The Guns of August*, p. 217.

67. Alexander Hamilton, James Madison, and John Jay, *The Federalist*, No. 6 (Henry Cabot Lodge, ed.). New York: Putnam, 1888, p. 27.

Additional Readings

Additional readings related to this chapter may be found in *Discord and Harmony: Readings in International Politics*, edited by Ivo D. Duchacek and published by Holt, Rinehart and Winston in 1972. Chapter 8, "Perceptions: Springs of Action" (pp. 142-80), contains a study of the Cuban missile crisis of 1962 as seen by Theodore C. Sorensen, Nikita S. Khrushchev, Charles Burton Marshall, the *Peking Review*, and Robert F. Kennedy. See also Ole R. Holsti, "Enemies Are Those Whom We Define as Such," pp. 184-194.

7

Ideology as a Guide for Action

If a national leader proclaims his commitment to a specific ideology whose contents and goals we know, how much do we really know about the leader's future actions and reaction to our actions? We should actually know a great deal, because ideologies, by definition, are supposed to be guides for interpreting the world and reacting to it, usually by attempts at improving and transforming it. Some ideologies claim to be based on scientifically accurate analyses of historical evolution that provide leaders with a reliable insight into the future. Marxism-Leninism, for instance, is often described by communists as the "science of sciences."

According to the *International Encyclopedia of the Social Sciences,* which focuses on selected internationally relevant ideologies in three areas—religious, democratic, and undemocratic—ideology is defined as

> the more or less coherent and consistent sum total of ideas and views on life and the world (belief system, doctrine, *Weltanschauung*) that guides the attitudes of actual or would-be power holders: leaders of political units, such as nation-states or city-states, or of major organizations or movements, such as churches or political parties.[1]

In the context of our study "ideology" refers to what has been called "mobilized belief systems," that is, those integrated systems of assertions, beliefs, and goals that are meant to imbue the masses with a sense of direction and so become a spring for collective action. For the purpose of our analysis we will relate ideology to the spread of literacy and the modern mass media, both of which facilitate the mobilization of the masses by their leaders for the support of political programs and action.

Four functions of ideology will be of particular concern to us in this chapter:

1. Ideology as a perceptional filter or lens for the leaders of movements or states. It may be imagined as composed of two basic layers: one represents a *diagnosis* of what is wrong with the world and the other represents the main elements of a recommended *cure* of the existing political, economic, and social ills. Such a filter, especially when used with a passionate belief in its accuracy, can both sharpen and blur the leader's vision of reality.

2. Ideology as a guide for action by the leaders. To paraphrase Karl Mannheim: ideology is a "wish image which takes on a political and international function."[2]

3. Ideology as a social agent: in its simplified version ideology serves as a tool for mobilizing national as well as foreign support. In this chapter we are particularly concerned with transnational ideological links.

4. Ideology as a message to the enemy. As such ideology may have more effect on the adversary than on its advocates; thus it may paralyze him or, on the contrary, provide the impetus for counteraction. Some analysts have argued, for instance, that communist ideology had a greater effect on the makers of *American* foreign policy, notably John Foster Dulles, than on the Kremlin. According to one study,[3] Secretary of State Dulles, who had studied communist writings with scholarly thoroughness, concluded that "one could understand both the character of Soviet leaders and the blueprint of Soviet policy" by carefully reading Stalin's *Problems of Communism* (which Dulles equated with Hitler's *Mein Kampf*). During a Senate Foreign Relations Committee hearing, the following dialogue took place:

> Senator Jackson: Would you not agree on this: that international communism has been used as an instrument of Russian foreign policy since 1918?
>
> Secretary Dulles: I would put it the other way around. Russian foreign policy is an instrument of international communism.[4]

Chinese propaganda concerning China's aim of encircling the industrial North by revolutionary guerrilla warfare (the so-called Lin Piao doctrine) was perhaps at the base of American perception of the adversary in the 1960s. Some analysts have argued that the Chinese ideological commitment to constant Vietnam-type revolutionary warfare formed the background for President Johnson's order in 1964 to bomb the North

Vietnamese PT-boat bases as a response to the allegedly unprovoked North Vietnamese attack on United States warships in the Gulf of Tonkin; President Johnson's dramatic escalation of American involvement was subsequently approved by Congress in a broadly stated resolution, the so-called Tonkin Gulf Resolution of 1964.

THREE CAUTIONS

Our preceding analysis of the role of personalities, the force of nationalism, and the impact of the international system suggests the following three general cautions with reference to ideologies as perceptional filters and guides for foreign policy: (1) Do the political leaders believe in the ideology they preach? (2) Is the ideology a precise blueprint for future contingencies or is it only a set of general ideas whose ambiguity permits personal interpretations by various practitioners? (3) Can the leader's commitment to a particular supranational ideology such as Christianity, Islam, communism, socialism, or liberal democracy be separated from its territorial-national base and the promotion of national interests? And if an ideology becomes territory- and nation-bound, can it avoid the imperatives of the international system?

True Believers?

Many national leaders invoke their commitment to a particular ideology. But there is no proof that they really believe in their invocations. We can never be sure. Ideology that inspires the masses has often been cynically invoked in a personal or national search for political or economic advantage. In such a context ideology may become a collective hallucinogen that may take the leader's nation or its adversaries on a trip from which there is no return. (Utopia, derived from the Greek *ou topos*, literally means "no place.") History is also full of examples of deliberate distortions of a creed for the purpose of eliminating opponents and critics within the movement on the basis of false accusations of heresy, betrayal, or deviation. Many a struggle for personal dominance within an ideological movement tends to be falsely presented as a principled crusade against heretics. In reality, the control of the movement or the church is the end and the dogmatic incantation only a means.

And then there is the possibility of an initially perhaps unintentional but finally inevitable corruption of ideology stemming from the need to acquire and keep political power. To achieve the ideology's goals here on earth, it is usually necessary to strive for control over the mass media, the national economy, and the instruments of coercion (police, the armed forces, frontier guards), in order to transform the masses into supporters and to punish or eliminate enemies of the ideology as well as heretics. But the means may become the end. The original lofty ideals may be left so far behind that the ideology becomes only a glittering wrapping around a cynical quest for power for the sake of power. It is said that Sicilian bandits recite the "Hail Mary" before committing an un-Christian act and make the sign of the cross before murdering their victims. During a communist purge the political victors may be imagined as invoking Lenin and making a "hammer-and-sickle" sign over their hearts while sending their comrades to the gallows.

In this connection a further question imposes itself: Are there bound to be differences between the leader's attitudes to ideology in various phases of his political career? Experience indicates that there is often a shocking contrast between a leader's orthodoxy before he attains power and his unorthodoxy after he has attained power. A leader's adherence to his ideology is the purest when, instead of any exercise of power, he can only engage in exciting rhetorics and pamphleteering in a free society or in ideological daydreaming while sitting in jail, in a guerrilla hideout, or as an exile in a café. The same leader's ideological orthodoxy begins to ebb as soon as he is in power and confronts the facts of life and unanticipated events.

Personal Interpretation

Even the most elaborate ideologies or doctrines—such as fascism, communism, and socialism—are bodies of broad assertions and general aims, not detailed blueprints for specific action in every future contingency. Zbigniew Brzezinski writes:

> A reformist social doctrine ceases to be an intellectual abstraction and becomes an active social agent, or an ideology, when it is applied to concrete situations and becomes a guide for action. . . . No doctrine, however elaborate or sophisticated, can provide answers and guidelines to fit all aspects of historical development.[5]

Even when an ideology is reasonably detailed, its guidelines cannot be expected to be as precise as norms in a legal system. After all, even laws written to eliminate ambiguity are not immune to conflicting interpretation; this is what lawyers thrive on. Ideological guidelines are sometimes unwittingly but often deliberately ambiguous. A guide that gives a general direction and suggests a hope for a better future but omits details necessary for its step-by-step execution lends itself to contradictory interpretations by true believers. Sincere and honest disagreement on the ideology's true meaning is possible. Because of the differences in men's character, temperament, ambition, fear, experience, mental or physical health, or simply age, facts that either confirm or deny the general ideological assumptions will be differently perceived and may lead to diametrically opposed conclusions. Nazism as a guide for action meant one thing to

Hitler, another thing to Rudolf Hess, and quite a different thing to the opponent of both, the left-oriented Nazi Gregor Strasser. Conflicts within religious organizations (such as that between Martin Luther and the Pope) and within political ideological movements may be explained on many different levels, but one of them is certainly the conflict of personalities. The character and background of Khrushchev, Brezhnev, or Suslov as opposed to that of Mao, Castro, or Ceausescu contribute to their conflicting interpretations of their common creed.

National Distortion

No political ideology, however universal it claims to be, has ever achieved success otherwise than nationally; by its success it becomes wedded to a nation-state in whose territorial framework it is implemented, promoted, and—distorted. A former ideological leader now in charge of a triumphant yet territory-bound creed must take into account his nation's geopolitical position, history, traditions, political culture, resources, military capabilities, and industrial development. Ideological utopia must prove its worth in the real world.

As we shall see later, the common ideology of Marxism-Leninism lends itself to different and conflicting interpretations depending on whether the interpreter presides over a well-developed, Europe-oriented Russia or over the destinies of developing, overpopulated, relatively poor, and Southeast-Asia-oriented China. And there is obviously a difference in interpretation of the common creed between a mighty nation and the small nations living under its shadow, such as land-locked Czechoslovakia and Hungary on the Soviet borders or North Korea and North Vietnam on the Chinese borders. When the survival and well-being of the state point in one direction and ideological purity in another, which should prevail? If a threat to the life of a nation seems often to justify almost any means of defense, it certainly justifies some occasional deviations from official ideology such as (in communist history) the cooperative agreements between Hitler and Stalin or between Nixon and Mao. National interest, not ideology, becomes the last word in a state's foreign policy when the leader concludes that it would be suicidal to sacrifice the national interest on the altar of ideological purity.

Whatever its ideology, a territorial state, as shown previously, cannot avoid having as its primary goal its own survival in the anarchic system of nation-states. Islam, for instance, may ideologically preach a holy war against *all* infidels in general and Israel in particular, but there may be situations in which an Islamic state may accept peaceful coexistence with many infidels, including the state of Israel. The Jewish creed may require that on Yom Kippur all be quiet on the western front, but an Arab offensive may impose a nonobservance of the holy day, as it did in 1973. In 1926 Stalin quite realistically reminded the Executive Committee of the

Communist International (Comintern—the general staff of the world communist movement) that "in order to build socialism, we must first of all exist,"—that is, as a Soviet national state. He added: "And to assure the existence [of the Soviet state], compromise [with ideological enemies], humiliation, and retreat may become necessary."[6] Speaking to the Seventh Party Congress, Lenin admonished the party idealists and ideological sentimentalists: "If you are not inclined to crawl in the mud on your belly, you are not a revolutionary but a chatter box."[7]

The history of communist national states illuminates the problem of the mutual interpenetration of a supranational creed and nationalism quite sharply, but it should be recalled that, long before the first national success of socialism, clashes and compromises between socialist supranationalism and nationalist emotions marked the whole life span of the Second International (founded in 1889; divided in 1919 by the conflict between the democratic socialists and the totalitarian communists). In World War I the European socialists supported the war effort of their various national states with considerable enthusiasm and dedication despite their previous pledge to pacifism and proletarian internationalism. In the case of the German and French working classes, for instance, proletarian loyalty would have required the sabotaging of their respective countries' war efforts by general strikes and other actions. The German-French socialist brotherhood yielded to nationalism and jingoism. This was in part so for emotional reasons; it was nearly impossible to resist the nationalist contagion of the first days and months of the war. But there were also practical reasons: The French workers and their socialist leaders could not be certain that their general strike and nationwide sabotage of the French war effort would be paralleled by an equally successful paralysis of the German war effort by the German socialists and workers, and neither socialism nor peace would have been enhanced if the successful sabotage of the French war effort by its working masses resulted in a quick victory over France by Kaiser Wilhelm and his allies, the German industrialists.

CONFLICT BETWEEN IDEALS AND REALITY

Some of the distortions of a creed may be ascribed to cynicism, loss of faith, or the sinister purposes of its adherents. More often, however, as noted earlier, an ideology is bent, twisted, and sometimes abandoned under the impact of hard facts that it did not anticipate, cannot control, and must rationalize itself into yielding to.

All ideologies pay a heavy tribute to reality in the period of their successful attainment and exercise of power. While opposing or subverting an existing order ideologies usually reflect a high degree of idealism and utopianism, including excessive idealization of men's reaction to a new order of things. But success and power induce a great intimacy with reality, and this has a devastating effect on both the optimism and the theoretical premises of the original theory. Conceived in the period of revolutionary daydreaming, much of reality could be overlooked so as not to impede a bold vision of things to come. Exile, jail, and libraries afford time and opportunity for only one type of revolutionary "activity," ideological theorizing. When leaders of ideologies attain power, it is the primary and imperative need to preserve it and use it rather than the inherent hypocrisy of the leaders that makes them relegate some of their erstwhile ideals to the role of decorative although useful accessories. A few principles have to be quietly discarded as the embarrassing burden of a dreamy past. Some concepts have to be rationalized into their near-opposites. The movement's enemies as well as its zealots label such compromises of theory with reality "betrayals." In this sense, a "revolution betrayed," to use Trotsky's label for Stalin's successful consolidation of the Soviet state, is often, quite paradoxically, the twin brother to a successful maintenance of power. Napoleon, too, both betrayed *and* consolidated some of the gains of the French Revolution. Some may argue that the conservative founding fathers at Philadelphia in 1787 also betrayed *and* consolidated the revolutionary thought of the signers of the Declaration of Independence.

A similar process of adaptation to the hard facts of internal and international politics may be seen in democracies when the parliamentary opposition emerges from its position of relative "irresponsibility," that is, from the position of aggressive critics whose only aim is to attack and displace the "ins" and assume a position of power and the responsibility for the consequences of its actions. Victory at the polls is usually followed by disappointment on the part of militant supporters of the former opposition, now the government. This is particularly true in the field of international politics, in which the former leaders of the principled opposition are forced to make some "unprincipled" compromises with stubborn realities. As a prisoner of national geography, past history, limited resources, and the acts of previous governments, the new regime can rarely pursue a foreign policy that radically differs from that of the former "ins," now transformed into "outs." And in democracies, after all, the government and its opposition operate within the framework of consensus about essentials—and these essentials include the broad outlines of foreign policy.

In a postrevolutionary situation, the contrast between the high expectations of ideological daydreaming and the harsh realities of the days following the triumph is more drastic. Revolutionary leaders, when finally in power, are bound to make more conspicuous compromises with international reality than their democratic counterparts (who, in any case, proclaim compromise to be a virtue rather than a heresy). It is particularly embarrassing for leaders of messianic movements to enter into unholy alliances with principal enemies or into open conflict with ideological cousins.

In conclusion we should add that no ideology is immune against time; an ideology may simply become outdated. New discoveries and technological breakthroughs may be of such import that even a very ambiguous and flexible ideology cannot withstand the weight of contrary evidence. Yet the personal stakes that its adherents have in the system built upon the ideology will prevent its abandonment; instead, a tortuous and confusing reinterpretation will take place. The Soviet reinterpretation of the original dogma concerning the inevitability of wars—a reinterpretation so energetically contested by China—is a good example. Clearly, neither Marx nor Lenin could possibly have taken into account the thermonuclear dimension of present-day international politics. The strenuous efforts of the leaders of ideological movements to make a doctrine fit the unexpected and the practical by the so-called *creative* interpretation of the original doctrine should not prevent us from realizing that the doctrine has either been altered or abandoned while lip service is still being paid to it.

THE IMPORTANCE OF IDEOLOGY

The preceding three caveats on the subject of ideology as a guide for political action should not be interpreted to mean that ideology is an unimportant factor in politics. It is one of the possible codeterminants of foreign policy; the controversy is usually about its importance relative to other factors.

Four points about the possible role of ideology in policy making should be borne in mind:

1. A leader may be a "true believer" and may be inclined to place his commitment to an ideology above any other. The first caveat of ideology merely suggested that nobody can be really certain about the intensity of a leader's ideological commitment. He may lie about his dedication to a creed but he may also be telling the truth. A fanatical true believer in international politics is a great danger to peace and order because his principled devotion cannot conceive of any possible compromise between, as he sees them, irreconcilable fighting faiths.

> The mere existence of another group professing a different ideology is threatening to the true believers because it suggests that their own may be wrong—an atheistic society that survives and prospers is, by this very fact, a threat to a theistic one, and vice versa. . . . Thus, wars initiated wholly or in part by ideological conflicts are usually especially bitter and prolonged, sometimes terminated only when the holders of one belief system are exterminated.[8]

2. Incantations of ideology are not only tools to influence recipients. As Karl W. Deutsch noted:

What we tell others also tends to be fed back into our own memories and to shape the premises of our own decisions tomorrow. Those who use communications to manipulate other people often end up having manipulated themselves, for today's manipulative message is often tomorrow's decision premise of the actor who first uttered it. Causation in the communication process moves not in straight lines but in feedback loops.[9]

In an ideology-impregnated political system (fascist or communist) the creed, promoted and propagated from cradle to grave by schools and the mass media, may finally act as a screen through which people sift and interpret information about the external world. The binoculars through which a leader perceives the world are thus equipped with a permanent filter, which gives a uniform hue to the observed scene, thus improving the observation of some details while impeding the view of others.

When ideologies become guides to selective perception and recall of information, not only individuals, as Deutsch argues, but also

groups of people, . . . societies, and nations try to reduce their particular cognitive dissonances [imbalances between preconceived expectations and perceived reality that are psychologically uncomfortable] by repressing or denying inconvenient bits of information—even if these happen to be true and vital to their prosperity or their survival.[10]

3. Even if the leaders treat ideology as "grass for the mass," it acquires some reality since the leaders tend to make their acts consistent—or make them appear consistent—with ideological precepts. Regardless of belief, adherence to ideology may sometimes be a good policy since it assures the leader of the continuing support of party zealots and the masses both at home and abroad.

The *inspirational* aspect of revolutionary doctrine cannot be underestimated. Focusing on the adversary, with whom a real compromise and understanding is ruled out by the doctrine, keeps all the members of the ideological movement, so to speak, on their toes, an undeniable asset in the world in which we live. Those in the movement who believe in the doctrine feel they have a sense of direction and, what is more important, the future on their side. Marxism-Leninism was described by Isaiah Berlin as an ideology with a prescribed happy end. As is illustrated in Crane Brinton's comparative study of the American, English, French, and Russian revolutions, an essential ingredient in major revolutionary ideologies is the presence of some abstract, all-powerful force, a perfect ally: *God* for the English puritans, *nature* and *reason* for the French revolutionaries, and *dialectical materialism* for the socialists and communists. In Brinton's words

Not only does God, nature, or dialectic materialism make the victory of the present underdog certain. The present upperdog can be shown—perhaps for propaganda purposes *must* be shown—to have acquired this preponderance by an accident, or a particularly dirty trick, while God or nature was temporarily off duty.[11]

As far as communism is concerned, two inspirational aspects of the ideology deserve mention:

First, the alleged communist *shortcut to modernization* and industrialization has some favorable echo in developing countries, especially because it represents an alternative to the kind of industrial development practiced by the West, the former imperial colonizer. Rarely do the communist leaders fail to stress the rapidity of communist economic planning as opposed to the leisurely tempo of Western development in the past. The appeal of communism as particularly fitting modernizing countries should neither be underestimated nor overestimated. The chronic food crises in the communist countries, the Soviet and Chinese mass purchases of grain from capitalist countries, and the inferior quality of Soviet, Czechoslovak, and Chinese manufactured goods in contrast to those from the United States or Western Europe have already caused many a sophisticated African and Asian nationalist to wonder about the relevance of communist models.

Second, and closely related to our study of international politics, there exists an *international network of communist parties*, linked together by their commitment to Marxism-Leninism. This network has provided the Soviet Union, and to a lesser degree the People's Republic of China, with a worldwide organization; it serves as a source of important intelligence data (Soviet intelligence has often relied on the cooperation of local communists for collecting and transmitting material), subversion, and fifth-column activities. Even if Soviet or Chinese leaders were utterly cynical about their ideology, they might consider it useful to feign following dogma in their every step so that others might believe. By equating the Soviet national interest with that of world communism, the Soviet Union has often been able to secure intelligence data without any cost. Some atomic scientists, for instance, have served as spies without payment in the belief that they had thus served the cause of communism and of peace.

4. Commitment to an ideology can usually be detected more easily in the way in which a policy maker handles a domestic problem than in the way in which he reacts to international events. The reason is simple enough: When a true believer is territorially in power he possesses the coercive means to make reality yield to his ideology. Police, monopoly-power over job distribution in a socialized economy (therefore power over the life and death of all citizens), and propaganda can, at least temporarily, deny facts and enthrone ideological dreams.

On the international scene, however, facts do not and cannot yield so easily to ideological plans and hopes. Unlike the domestic scene, international realities resist being subject to control by one center or one person.

What, then, is the role of ideology in foreign policy? Nobody has as yet given a satisfactory answer that would apply to all situations at all times. It is evident that ideology acting as a particularly colored lens may sometimes sharpen and at other times blur one's vision. In this sense ideology is one of very many codeterminants of foreign policy, but rarely, if ever, the decisive one.

In the following case study, the interrelationship between ideology and foreign-policy decisions will be explored in more depth. The focus will be on the communist ideology, the major political phenomenon of our times. It is the most detailed and elaborated doctrine, viewed by its adherents and leaders as a reliable guide for political and social action. It is also the doctrine that allegedly determines the goals and workings of the political systems of two great powers, Russia and China, and of eleven medium and small states with a total population of more than one billion, and is an article of faith and a guide for action for about eighty political parties active within noncommunist states. Our case study will be limited to the examination of the relationship between ideology and foreign policy.

COMMUNIST THEORY AND FOREIGN POLICY—A CASE STUDY

"Facts are stubborn things, as the English proverb says," wrote Lenin in 1916 in *Imperialism, the Highest Stage of Capitalism*. He was to repeat this statement later in many forms. Addressing the Eighth Party Congress on March 19, 1919, in the midst of serious difficulties that the new Bolshevik regime was having, Lenin again warned against wishful denial of adverse realities: "We cannot refuse to recognize what actually exists; it will itself compel us to recognize it."[12]

Commenting on the Bolshevik adjustments to realities, Merle Fainsod has described the transmutation of means into ends as follows:

> Like many revolutionaries before them, [the Bolsheviks] found themselves involved in a complex struggle to master the recalcitrant realities of their environment. They pressed forward where they could, and they gave way where they had to. The tragedy of unintended consequences overtook them. As they sought to come to terms with the pressures which impinged on them, vision of the future had to be modified or abandoned. Instruments became ends; their retention and consolidation of power dwarfed all other objectives. The party of revolution was transformed into the party of order.[13]

In the context of our study, we may add: The party of revolution also had to learn the art of great-power politics and diplomacy. This does not mean that communist theory has not played or will not still play an important part in shaping the Soviet citizen's image of the outside world and the Soviet national scene. The national scene in particular may be molded by the mass media and by censorship in accordance with the official ideology. The history of communist foreign policies in the past half-century, however, confirms the compelling effect of the "stubborn things" of which the international system is composed—namely the territorial states, their power, and their national policies. Communist theory and practice have been more profoundly altered by the international system of states than the working of the system has been affected by communism.

The evolution and changes in communist theory and practice in the field of international politics may be conveniently divided into three major phases: the period of ideological daydreaming up to the October Revolution, the adjustment of theory to the system of sovereign states and nationalism, and the present phase of further adjustment to the realities of our atomic age.

Ideological Daydreaming

The original concepts of communist theory were not formulated in its period of success and geographic extension but, on the contrary, in its period of weakness, uncertainty, and persecution. The founding fathers of communism often had to fight for sheer physical survival. With the czarist police on their heels, isolated from the masses and other immediacies of life, and often languishing in prisons or idly waiting in exile, the communist leaders were bound to focus their main attention on overturning the existing system. In the abundant communist writings of that period very little is found on the subject of future communist foreign policies beyond the hope that one worldwide communist commonwealth could emerge from intercapitalist world wars transformed into socialist revolutions. Old methods of diplomacy and alliances were to disappear with capitalism. World communism was to provide a federative world of permanent peace based on the concept of comradely cooperation and proletarian internationalism.

The inevitability of imperialist and intercapitalist wars was the main premise of Lenin's theory on the downfall of capitalism and his hope for a worldwide communist revolution. According to Lenin, imperialism represents the monopoly stage of capitalism, in which the bank capital of a few big controlling banks has merged with the capitalist combines of manufacturers into what Lenin called "finance capital." The result is that, following the colonial expansion of capitalist states, the territorial division of the whole world is complete. In such a context, capitalist states would inevitably clash with one another over colonies and over further opportunities for the export not only of goods but of capital itself.

In his polemics with the German Social Democrat and Marxist Karl

Kautsky, one of the leaders of the Second International between 1889 and 1919, Lenin attacked Kautsky's concept that imperialism and the annexation of one nation by another was only a *preferred*, not an inevitable policy of capitalism: "Kautsky detaches the politics from its economics, speaks of annexations as being a policy 'preferred' by finance capital, and opposes to it another bourgeois policy [of nonimperialism and peace] which he alleges is possible on this very basis of finance capital."[14] Lenin labeled as ultranonsense Kautsky's concept of ultraimperialism, that is, a phase under capitalism when wars may cease and joint exploitation of the world by internationally combined finance capital may begin.

Lenin excluded the possibility of any permanent peace while capitalism existed. He labeled peaceful alliances between capitalist countries mere preparations for the inevitable intercapitalist wars of the future. It is impossible to prove or disprove whether Lenin fully believed in his own theory. But from the standpoint of revolutionary tactics Lenin rightly insisted on depicting capitalism as the unreformable prisoner of its economics and therefore as an undiluted evil and an incurable warmonger. The concept that capitalism may rationally change and become peaceful and socially responsible rather than blind in its profit-seeking drive could not fit the needs of an all-out revolutionary struggle; one does not start building barricades against an enemy who can reform himself. The insistence on the total evil of capitalism could, therefore, have been less a result of economic theorizing than of the practical revolutionary need to keep the masses in an uncompromising mood. Lenin wrote:

> Kautsky called ultra-imperialism and super-imperialism what Hobson, thirteen years earlier, described as inter-imperialism. Except for coining a new and clever word, replacing one Latin prefix by another, the only progress Kautsky had made in the sphere of "scientific" thought is that he has labeled as Marxism what Hobson, in effect, described as the cant of English parsons. . . . No matter what the good intentions of the English parsons, or of sentimental Kautsky, may have been, the only objective, i.e. real, social significance Kautsky's "theory" can have is that of a most reactionary method of *consoling* the masses with hopes of permanent peace being possible under capitalism, distracting their attention from the sharp antagonism and acute problems of the present era, and directing it toward illusory prospects of an imaginary "ultra-imperialism" of the future. Deception of the masses—there is nothing but this in Kautsky's "Marxian" theory. [Italics added.][15]

This primarily political argument was revived fifty years later by the Chinese Communists in their violent polemics against the Soviet thesis of peaceful coexistence with capitalism. The Chinese Communists attacked the thesis as having the effect of a tranquilizer on the revolutionary zeal of anticolonial masses. The Chinese ideological journal *Hung Chi* (January 1964) condemned the Soviet thesis of peaceful coexistence as serving "to paralyze the revolutionary will and to obstruct the revolutionary struggle of the people of the world."

In sum, prior to the communist seizure of power in Russia, Leninism provided the leaders and the movement with arguments against capitalism and imperialism, with a program for revolutionary thoroughness and action, especially with the hope and the plan for transforming intercapitalist wars into socialist revolutions on a world scale, and with a utopian hope for permanent peace in the framework of a worldwide communist society. There was really no plan for or concept of communist diplomacy or foreign policy in a world only a portion of which would become communist while the rest would remain noncommunist or hostile to communism. This was not expected to happen, but it actually did happen.

Adjustment to the International System

The story of the communist movement—which is a success story when measured in square miles of geographic expansion—began with a triumphant denial of theory: communism, a creed based on the concept of anational class struggle, first captured just a national territory, not a class. It established itself actually only in European Russia, which then served as a territorial-national basis for forcible reannexation of the non-Russian ethnic groups and territories by the Red Army. Ukrainians, Tatars, Caucasians, and Moslems were incorporated against their will into a Russian-dominated Soviet Union. Thus, under the doctored blessing of Karl Marx, communism was married to Russia and Russia to communism. When, in 1948, Tito of Yugoslavia grafted proud nationalism onto communism, he only did what the Russians had already accomplished in the 1920's. Mao Tse-tung produced the same fusion of communism and nationalism in China.

Another concomitant denial of previous theory was the fact that, at the same time, despite all prophecies and expectations, the advanced capitalist countries of Western Europe did not follow the path prescribed by Marx and his theory. With the exception of Russia, the communist attempts to seize and maintain power—in Hungary, Bavaria, and Berlin—were defeated despite the optimistic prediction made at the time by the Bolshevik leader Zinoviev, eagerly awaiting the fulfillment of the dream of an international revolution: "When these lines will be published six or an even greater number of Soviet republics will exist. With dizzying speed Old Europe rushes toward the proletarian revolution." But there was no rush. Not even defeated Germany, in which chaos, frustration, and misery proved to be such valuable allies of communism, conformed to the theoretical anticipations; the defeat of Germany in World War I finally produced a Hitler, not a Lenin. By the time Zinoviev's lines were published (printing was not too efficient in revolutionary Russia), the number of communist republics was reduced to one. Lenin's prediction of one "All-World Federative Soviet Republic" seemed very far away indeed.

On their way to power the Bolshevik leaders perhaps sincerely believed that they were a part, or at best the vanguard, of a proletarian international revolution. In April 1917 Lenin referred to the Russian proletariat as "the skirmishers of the world revolution." The Russian leaders were internationalists, partly as a matter of principle, partly for pragmatic reasons: They feared that without a revolution in at least industrial Germany, the Russian revolution and Russian development would be in peril.

By the early 1920s, a self-evident fact denied the validity of the earlier communist expectations: The world revolution was not on the agenda of the day. With the exception of Russia, the world remained capitalist and hostile to communism. Yet the capitalist countries, however powerful and despite their implacable hatred of Russian communism, were either unwilling or unable to dislodge the movement from its national base. The failure of the international revolution to materialize might have been a source of disappointment for such communist internationalists and theoreticians as Trotsky. On the other hand, the survival of Communist Russia despite capitalist enmity—and, we may add, despite the failings of the communist theory—must have been a source of considerable satisfaction and pride to such pragmatic political leaders as Lenin and Stalin. Certainly the sheer size of Russia, coupled with the general fatigue of the West after four years of a cruel war, was a help. "Russia is boundless, an enormous country, on whose territory it is possible to hold out for a long time by retreating into the hinterland in case of reverses," Stalin realistically noted in 1920. "Had Russia been a small country like Hungary, where it is difficult to maneuver, where there is no room to retreat—had Russia been a small country like it, it would scarcely have lasted all this time as a socialist country."[16]

Living in a potentially or actually hostile world, Communist Russia has had to adapt itself, like any other state, to the imperatives of the international system and its balancing processes. Although the rest of the world was Soviet Russia's enemy (partly because, in its capitalist form, it was marked by communist theory and practice for total extinction), some of her enemies were more dangerous than others. While theory had taught the Russian leaders that capitalism was an undiluted evil, the communist state had to adopt the usual policy of treating some capitalist countries as a lesser evil. After World War I, the USSR, as an international outcast, understandably viewed the dissatisfied and defeated countries such as Germany and Turkey as lesser evils than the self-confident victorious Entente. When Hitler came to power, the USSR found France and England preferable to the Nazi Reich. But after Munich, which Moscow interpreted as tacit Franco-British approval of German expansion eastward, the situation was reversed. A partnership with Nazi Germany in 1939 appeared to be a good opportunity for Soviet Russia to remain neutral in World War II, which Moscow hoped would result in a weakening of both Germany and the western European democracies on the western front. However, when in 1941 Nazi Germany, unable to conquer England, decided to attack Russia, the former enemies of Communist Russia and Nazi Germany, the western democracies, were welcomed as the main suppliers of food and weapons for Russia's difficult struggle against the Nazi Reich.

All these changes, some undertaken with considerable foresight, others with incredible shortsightedness, can be understood in terms of pragmatic power considerations. There is nothing to indicate that communist theory has played any significant role in Soviet decisions to oppose or align the USSR with any particular combination of foreign nations. These reversals of alliances can be explained, rather, on the ground of the pragmatic considerations that any state has in the process of maximizing its national interests. Nor is there any indication that communist ideology has endowed communist leaders with any better insight than noncommunist leaders into the potential developments of the international situation. The Soviet leaders, however committed to communist ideology, seem to play it—no less and no more than other statesmen—by ear.

The adjustment of the Soviet state to the "stubborn facts" of the international system has also had consequences for the structure of the communist state: While the expected "All-World Federative Soviet Republic" would not have required any ministry of foreign affairs, the Soviet state soon needed one for the purpose of maintaining diplomatic contacts with its potential or actual partners or enemies. Soviet embassies and missions appeared in all corners of the world, first feigning proletarianism, later imitating the former czarist diplomatic missions to the point of adopting colorful diplomatic uniforms and engaging in lavish entertainment with the proverbial heaps of Russian caviar and gallons of vodka (thus they easily overtook the more modest forms of Anglo-Saxon entertainment, which have always been kept under the watchful eyes of the pennywise legislatures, too prone to view all diplomats as glorified cookie pushers). Simultaneously, however, the world communist headquarters, the Comintern, with its network of nonofficial and conspiratorial international party contacts, was maintained in Moscow.

Soviet Communist theory and practice did contribute something to one particular form of international relations, *bilevel diplomacy*. On one level the Soviet government maintains civilized or even friendly relations with foreign governments through the intermediary of embassies and consulates. As a government, the Communist party of the USSR is also a member of the United Nations. On a second level, the party maintains conspiratorial contacts with the communist parties of other nations, which either run their government or plot the overthrow of the existing government with which the Soviet state maintains cordial official relations. Thus it is conceivable that before a dinner the Soviet ambassador may propose a toast to the good health of the prime minister whose overthrow he may plot with the leaders of the local communist party after dinner.

Communist ambassadors were not the first to develop contacts with the enemies of the government to which they are accredited. Such tactics are used for the purpose of being in touch with those who might be the government of tomorrow or for the purpose of helping them to reach their objective. The Soviet state has, however, greatly refined, perfected, and organized bilevel diplomacy, which combines traditional international relations with conspiracy or subversion.

In some cases the conspiratorial revolutionary level of Soviet foreign policy may run counter to the Soviet state's need to maintain cordial relations with the given noncommunist government. Here again, as in the case of possible conflict between communist ideology and reality, the possible conflict between the interests of Soviet diplomacy and of the communist conspiracy has usually been resolved in favor of the former and at the cost of the latter. Egypt's and India's harsh policies toward local communists did not prevent the Soviet Union from maintaining cordial relations with both countries. Similarly, when in 1973 Communist East Germany became the first communist state to establish diplomatic relations with Franco's Spain, the party and its main organ, *Neues Deutschland* (January 27, 1973), explained to the protesting readers that "foreign policy cannot be based on emotions" and that the government of East Germany was ready to establish diplomatic relations with "capitalist countries, monarchies, and even dictatorships." Speaking to the officers of the Chinese diplomatic service in December 1967, Premier Chou En-lai noted that "in international relations, there are certain norms which we must respect: a majority of countries we deal with are imperialist, revisionist [the USSR] or reactionary, not leftist." And Chou En-lai criticized the "ultra-leftists" in China's Ministry of Foreign Affairs who had ignored these norms, thus becoming guilty of "Great Power Chauvinism."

Adjustment to Nationalism

Closely related to the communist need to adjust to the international system is the search for an appropriate answer to nationalism, whose robust assertion the communist ideology did not anticipate, especially not within the communist system of states. Here again theory had to yield to reality, however reluctantly. But then a new problem arose: a conflict between the communism grafted onto Russian nationalism and the communism of non-Russian nationalities both inside and outside the Soviet Union. Here militant international dreamers within the original communist movement may have been right in their contention that such a fundamental compromise with reality as playing with nationalist fire could boomerang and hit the movement at its most vulnerable spot, that is, at its internationalist base.

The unholy Russian proletarian alliance with nationalism may well be communism's "original sin." This sin—or in Lenin's words, "exception" from the principle of centralism and class unity—was to visit "the iniquity of the fathers upon the children unto the third and fourth generation." With Mao, Dubcek, Castro, Hoxha, Ceausescu, and Longo we have not even moved fully to the level of the second generation.

Initially, the conflict between bourgeois nationalism and the Marxist concept of the class struggle—the fundamental idea of communism—was deemed irreconcilable. Karl Marx's concept of the decisive importance of a struggle between the exploiting capitalist and the exploited proletarian classes had led to the conclusion that, in a classless world, proletarian international harmony would prevail and make the national antagonisms of the capitalist era things of the past. If it were true that man's membership in a given socioeconomic class determined his fundamental loyalties, then it would follow that, as the Communist Manifesto had put it in 1848, "the workingman had no fatherland" under capitalism. The state, which, according to Lenin's definition, was only an instrument of class domination and exploitation, could not elicit love or loyalty on the part of the exploited class; instead, the workers' loyalty was deemed necessarily to transcend national boundaries and to "unite proletarians of all countries" into one supranational anticapitalist front, the International. The capitalists, on the other hand, according to the same analysis, felt national loyalty to the state that was their own creation, an instrument of domination and exploitation and therefore the cause of their wealth and power.

Mistaken Premises The concept of supranational or anational class unity seems logical provided it can be proved that the three premises on which it is based are correct. They are not. The first and fundamental error is the premise according to which nationalism can be explained as a class phenomenon belonging to the capitalist era. The socialist President of Senegal, Léopold Sédar Senghor, has described Marx's mistaken attitude toward the virulence of nationalism in the following terms:

> Marx underestimated political and national idealism, which, born in France upon the ruins of provincial fatherlands with the Revolution of 1789, won over the world. "Justice," Marx writes, "humanity, liberty, equality, fraternity, independence . . . these relatively moral categories . . . sound so nice, but . . . in historical and political questions, prove absolutely nothing." I repeat: *independence*. If [Karl Marx] the creator of scientific socialism returned to this earth, he would perceive with amazement that these "chimeras" as he called them, and above all the concept of *Nation*, are living realities in the twentieth century.[17]

The second mistaken premise, derived from the first, is the Marxist belief that loyalty to a class is or may become the strongest of human bonds, stronger than man's identification with his nation's history, welfare, and future. Marx not only underestimated nationalism but overestimated the international solidarity of the working class irrespective of national boundaries, especially in the case of imperialist nations and their colonies. As Senghor put it, Marx demonstrated a "blind confidence in proletarian generosity and conscience." As an African nationalist and socialist, Senghor could not help noting how limited was the feeling of solidarity on the part of the French working class, while its well-being was partly the result of the French exploitation of the riches of Africa and Asia. "In a word," wrote Senghor, "the European proletariat has profited from the colonial system; therefore, it has never really –I mean, effectively —opposed it."[18]

Furthermore, the technological revolution of the twentieth century—the economic growth, the strength of the labor unions, social legislation, and progressive taxation—in combination with the welfare functions of the modern state, denied the original Marxist expectation that nonsocialist society would split into two opposite poles: that of wealth shared and controlled by a very few, and that of misery shared and experienced by the ever-increasing numbers of proletarians. Instead, the class structure of developed nations has become extremely complex; the dividing line between different social strata or classes is quite unclear. How is one to feel any significant identification with something so amorphous as a social class when the nation is so clearly identifiable and recognizable? The nineteenth-century Victorian flavor of the Marxist concept of class finally became an issue even within the communist movement itself, especially in the advanced Western countries. Before his disgrace, Roger Garaudy, a member of the French Politburo, was permitted publicly to argue in the party daily *L'Humanité* (January 2, 1970) that contrary to Marx's prophecy the proletariat was shrinking in advanced countries and that technicians and other "workers of the brain" should be treated as members of the working class and not of the middle class. Garaudy, who was inspired by and approved of Czechoslovak humanist socialism, specifically condemned the Soviet socialist theory and practice: "The socialism that our party wants to install in France is not that which is imposed militarily today upon Czechoslovakia."

The third premise of proletarian internationalism was the communist expectation that capitalism, in the process of its race to inevitable doom, would create everywhere, irrespective of national circumstances and traditions, identical conditions of oppression and exploitation. Common international misery was to lead to a common struggle against capitalism. "Modern industrial labor, modern subjugation to capital," proclaimed the Communist Manifesto of 1848, "the same in England as in France, in America as in Germany, has stripped the proletariat of every trace of national character . . . National differences and antagonism between people are daily more and more vanishing."

Instead, the working-class movements have developed differently because their nations followed different patterns of economic development. "For many years it could be said," noted an American study of socialism in

Western Europe, "that the only thing the socialists had nationalized was socialism."[19]

We assume but are never sure that the propagators of a faith really believe in what they are saying. Thus we assume but cannot be sure that the early advocates of proletarian internationalism really believed in it. In the midst of the intolerant nineteenth-century nationalistic atmosphere, and then again during World War I, the emphasis on internationalism was a natural reaction to the excesses and conflicts that nationalism had brought about.

Whatever their respective commitments to proletarian internationalism, Lenin and Stalin were soon to be confronted with some hard facts in their struggle for power in the midst of a revolutionary ferment in Russia. One of the dominant elements on the Russian scene prior to the October Revolution was the weakness of the Communist party and the absence of a class-conscious proletariat. With the exception of the dissatisfaction of the workers in Petrograd and Moscow, the dominant feature of general discontent was the desire of the peasants for *land*—basically a desire for private property and enterprise, a petty-bourgeois ideal. Another important source of discontent was the desire for *peace* on the part of exhausted soldiers whatever their class origins, although naturally the peasant element among them did predominate. And finally there was the *nationalistic* ferment on the part of the non-Russian nationalities of the czarist "prison of many nations." Only the industrial workers of Petrograd and Moscow, and the Social Democrat party of Russia with its Bolshevik and Menshevik wings, fitted the ideological premises of a socialist revolution. Lenin, however, proved able to combine a weak socialist movement and a powerful nonclass revolutionary discontent into one mighty torrent that swept away the czarist system.

Support of National Self-Determination   On December 17, 1917, Stalin and Lenin issued an appeal to the Russian Moslems that implied the right of secession on the basis of the principle of national self-determination. The usual emphasis on class and proletarian internationalism was missing. Instead, the appeal (published by *Izvestia* on December 5, 1917) abounded in respectful references to national culture and religion:

> The rule of the robbers, who have enslaved the peoples of the world, is falling. Under the blows of the Russian Revolution the old edifice of servitude and slavery is shaking. . . . A new world is being born, a world of workers and of freed people. . . . We appeal to you, working and penniless Moslems of Russia. . . . Tartars of the Volga and the Crimea, Kirghiz and Sarts of Siberia and Turkestan, Turks and Tartars of the Trans-Caucasus, Chechens and Gortsi of the Caucasus, all those whose mosques and prayer-houses were destroyed, whose beliefs and customs

were trampled on by the Czars and oppressors of Russia! From now on your faiths and customs, your national and cultural institutions are declared free and untouchable. Build your national life freely and unhindered. You yourselves must arrange your lives as you choose. You have the right to do so, because your fate is in your own hands.[20]

In January 1918 the Third Congress of Soviets adopted a Declaration of Rights of the Peoples of Russia, which stated specifically:

The First Congress of Soviets, in June 1917, proclaimed the right of the peoples of Russia to free self-determination. The Second Congress of Soviets, in October 1917, reaffirmed this right inalienable of the peoples of Russia more decisively and definitively. The united will of these congresses, the Council of People's Commissars, resolved to base its activity upon the question of the nationalities of Russia as expressed in the following principles:

1. The equality and sovereignty of the peoples of Russia.
2. The right of the peoples of Russia to free self-determination, even to the point of separation and the formation of an independent state.[21]

Before 1917 Lenin, Trotsky, and Stalin were primarily concerned with the problem of seizing and preserving power. After the October Revolution the preservation of the multinational empire against the hostile world became the dominant task of the new regime. While the mobilization of the anti-Russian ferment was useful in the process of achieving power, it was found quite harmful in the process of consolidating power. According to the theory, nations were, first, to liberate themselves from capitalist oppression, and second, to amalgamate into a higher proletarian supranational union. In the critical period of the first five years of communism, the non-Russian nationalities, inhabiting the border regions of what was to become the USSR, were to exercise their right of national liberation from czarist oppression, so to speak, simultaneously with their proletarian duty of amalgamation.

Suppression of National Self-Determination   Secession from Russia was equated with accession to the enemies of the Soviet government. As Stalin noted,

The recognition of the right to secede must not be confused with the expedience of secession in any given circumstances. . . . Thus we are at liberty to agitate for or against secession, according to the interests of the proletariat, of the proletarian revolution. . . . We are *for* the separation of India, Arabia, Egypt, Morocco and other colonies from the Entente, for the separation in this case means the freeing of these oppressed countries from imperialism, the weakening of imperialist positions, the strengthening of revolutionary positions. We are *against* the separation of the border-territories from Russia, because separation in this case means imperialist slavery for the border-territory, the weakening of the revolutionary capabilities of Russia, the strengthening of the imperialist positions. . . . When a life-and-death struggle is being waged, and is spreading, between Proletarian Russia and the imperialist Entente, only two alternatives confront the border regions: either they join forces with Russia, and the toiling masses of the border regions will be emancipated from imperialist oppression; or they join forces with the Entente, and the yoke of imperialism is inevitable. There is no third solution. So-called independence of so-called independent Georgia, Armenia, Poland, Finland, and so forth, is only an illusion.[22]

By its effective suppression of the right of national self-determination, combined with and somewhat tempered by the constitutional recognition of the linguistic and cultural autonomy of its thirty to forty national groups, the Soviet Union has become a potential target of criticism and agitation. The period of dynamic nationalism in the world, as we have seen, is far from over. It would, indeed, be astonishing if the storm of nonclass nationalism that so irresistibly swept through Africa and Asia and has affected such old, established multiethnic states as Belgium and Canada were to stop conveniently at the gates of Soviet Russia.

Nationalism outside Russia Since the 1920s the Soviet Union has assumed the self-appointed role of champion of the right of national self-determination in Asia and Africa. This too has required some adjustment of the ideology, since nationalism in colonial areas, like nationalism anywhere else, is basically a nonclass or supraclass phenomenon. The communist leaders have tried to overcome the contradiction between communism and nationalism by comparing the struggle of an exploited nation against its colonial and imperial exploiters to the struggle of an exploited class against its exploiters within a nation. The concept of one nation-class fighting another nation-class erases the class differences and contradictions *within* such national units. But then a nation appears as an entity standing above the classes that struggle primarily not among themselves, but against the outsiders—which sounds like a bourgeois nonclass definition of nationalism.

It may prove increasingly difficult for the Soviet Union to continue to play the role of the nationalist devil's advocate while circumscribing national self-determination of the non-Russian ethnic groups in the Soviet Union (half of its total population) as well as that of 100 million eastern Europeans, the inhabitants of the eight "people's democracies." The Brezhnev Doctrine (a portion of which may be found in Document 11.6) authorizes Soviet interference in the domestic affairs of other communist states whenever their leaders' concept of the national interest is deemed by Moscow to threaten the broader interests of "world communism" as led by the Soviet Communist party. This doctrine of limited sovereignty of medium and small communist states was invoked in the wake of the Soviet armed intervention in Czechoslovakia (August 1968), whose Communist leaders, Alexander Dubček and Ludvík Svoboda, in accord with their nation's humanist traditions and with the support of the majority of the people, had decided to follow their own path to socialism ("socialism with a human face"). In protest against the Russian occupation of their country the Czechoslovak leaders invoked the authority of Lenin, who had condemned the denial of the right of national self-determination. Moscow replied by quoting Lenin on the merits of proletarian internationalism. The Soviet tanks determined whose quotation from Lenin would prevail. (See the cartoon in Figure 7.1, which appeared in Prague two weeks before the Soviet invasion.)

The Soviet formula on the subject of nationalism may be expressed as "That which weakens my enemy I support; that which weakens me, I oppose." But such a double standard is not peculiar to the communist world. Earlier we observed that at the Versailles Peace Conference the Western powers interpreted the right of national self-determination as one to be limited to Europeans. African and Asian nationalism was not to be allowed to weaken Western colonial empires. Eastern European nationalism, on the other hand, was to be supported, as it could weaken and destroy the Allies' main enemies, Germany and the multiethnic Austrian empire. Similarly, nowadays the Western democracies use propaganda and economic lures to promote nationalist opposition to Soviet dominance in the communist bloc of nations while curbing similar centrifugal tendencies in the Atlantic and other free-world communities. The Soviet leaders, on the other hand, stress the benefits of unity in their part of the world but try to exploit any divisive tendencies within the Western bloc of nations.

Asymmetry and Nationalism   The assertion of the Soviet state's national interest against and above the national interests of non-Russian communist states or parties has marked and marred the history of proletarian internationalism since the creation of the world headquarters of international communism, the Comintern, in 1919. The Brezhnev Doctrine represents only another version of the old formula that conveniently places an equal sign between the collective interests of communist parties in the world and the national interest of the Soviet state as a base or level of international revolution. In Stalin's words:

> . . . the very development of world revolution . . . will be more rapid and more thorough, the more thoroughly Socialism fortifies itself in the first victorious country, the faster this country is transformed into a base for further unfolding of world revolution, into a lever for the further disintegration of imperialism. While it is true that the *final* victory of Socialism in the first country to emancipate itself is impossible without the combined efforts of the proletarians of several countries [a necessary complimentary

FIGURE 7.1
RUSSIAN COMMUNISM VERSUS CZECH COMMUNISM

"I quote Lenin, you quote Lenin—whose Lenin shall prevail?"

Drawing by Jelinek in *Dikobraz*, Prague, August 6, 1968 (sixteen days before the
Soviet invasion).

bow in the direction of proletarian internationalism], it is equally true that
the development of world revolution will be the more rapid and thorough,
the more effective the aid rendered by the first Socialist country to the
workers . . . of all other countries.

In what should this aid be expressed?

It should be expressed, first, in the victorious country carrying out the
maximum realizable in one country *for* the development, support,
awakening of revolution in all countries. . . .

> It should be expressed, second, in that the "victorious proletariat" of
> the one country . . . "after organizing its own Socialist production should
> stand up . . . *against* the remaining capitalists attracting to itself the op-
> pressed classes of other countries, raising revolts in those countries
> against the capitalists, and in the event of necessity coming out even with
> armed force against the exploiting classes and their governments. . . ."[23]

The identification of the power and interest of the Soviet national state
with the world communist movement had several initial advantages. Having captured the vast territory, population, and resources of a great power,
the communist movement could now add the might of a modern state to its
conspiratorial and subversive underground techniques and to above-the-
ground agitation. Those branches of the national government that the
communist leaders in the underground, in jail, or in exile had had to fear,
dodge, or fight from a position of weakness could now be turned not only
against their domestic enemies but also against their foreign enemies. It
was indeed "common sense," as pointed out by Historicus in his excellent
analysis of Stalin's concept of communist revolutions, "to use the foothold
won in the Soviet Union as a base of world revolution."[24]

Ironically, the drawbacks of the automatic identification of the world
communist movement with the national interests of the Soviet state were to
catch up with the initial advantages of such an association and finally
overtake them in proportion to the territorial expansion of communism; the
seeds of the nationalist erosion of world communism were the inevitable
corollaries of its geographic spread and success. When, after World War II,
established states, conscious and proud of their separate national histories
and traditions, were included in the world communist movement, this
process necessarily raised questions concerning the selflessness of the
leading member of the international community of communist states.

While Russia was the only communist state in existence, most of the
doubts concerning the automatic equation between the interests of world
communism and those of the Soviet state could easily be silenced by
Moscow: Any foreign communist who was critical of the possible selfishness of the Soviet "base" could be reminded of the simple fact that his own
party had first to show what it could do nationally before it could talk back
to the Russian leaders. All the other communist parties had been dismally
unsuccessful in their efforts to duplicate the October Revolution in their
own nations. Some communist parties had to remain underground to avoid
persecution, others were in an uneasy alliance with nationalists (an example was the political alliance between the Chinese Communists and Chiang
Kai-shek's Nationalists until 1927), and still others were engaged in parliamentary opposition, which, however noisy, clever, or radical, was still
very far from achieving communist objectives. On the other hand, the
Russian Bolshevik party stood as a symbol of success: It was in possession
of all the military, economic, intelligence, and propaganda means of a

major modern state. Although hated and discriminated against by the rest of the world, Russia remained undefeated. Its obvious triumph and power thus ended many an argument or doubt concerning the equation between communism and Russia and the resulting Russian right to inspire, criticize, purge, and direct the rest of the world communist movement.

In all asymmetric alliances or coalitions (that is, associations of nations that are highly unequal in power), sooner or later, three types of friction and suspicion develop:

1. There is, first of all, the suspicion, so often fully justified, that the leading power will misuse its dominant position for the promotion of its own national interest at the expense of the other members; in its hands internationalism and the common interest of all participants may become a convenient garb to cloak the leading power's egoism. This suspicion has plagued all modern alliances.
2. There is, second, a resentment against the tendency of the leading power to dictate the line of common policy or action to other member nations instead of consulting with them and treating them as coequals.
3. And finally there often is the feeling that the leadership exercised in behalf of all by the leading power is in the hands of inept and unskillful individuals or at least that the leading power is negligent or ignorant of problems that are of immediate and pressing concern to some member nations but are deemed secondary by the power at the helm. Sometimes the neglect of local problems is indeed the result of ignorance; at other times it may be the result of the leading power's concern with a balanced approach to all local and general problems.

All three of these suspicions necessarily appeared as a consequence of the Russian bungling of the Chinese national revolution in the 1920s, from the period of the Communist party alliance with Chiang Kai-shek to the period of the Russian-ordered armed uprisings in the Chinese cities to be supported by peasant armies from the outside. (The uprisings all ended in defeat.) Following the failure of the Chinese Communists to storm the city of Changsha, the demoted secretary-general of the Chinese Communist party, Li Li-san, had to defend his previous policies and tactics, for although they were initially ordered by the Comintern, they resulted in failures on Chinese soil. Contrasting his loyalty to the Comintern with his loyalty to the Chinese Communist revolution, Li Li-san proclaimed: "Russian Communists take care of their own racial interests to the neglect of the Chinese situation which they do not understand."[25]

Li Li-san's statement accused the Russian leadership of nationalism, neglect, and ignorance—the familiar accusations that thirty-five years later formed much of the background of the Chinese, Rumanian, Albanian, and Yugoslav objections to Russia and her alleged "great-power chauvinism," as well as of haughtiness in the manner in which it imposed its shifting policies on the others. While all the communist parties agree on the necessity of leadership in their own ranks and countries, the matter is quite different when it is transferred to the world scene, where they have to contend with national susceptibilities. One of the Chinese objections during the Cuban crisis of 1962 was that the Soviet Union did not consult the comrade parties about its decision to place aggressive atomic weapons in Cuba; nor did it consult with anybody—except with Kennedy—when it decided to dismantle them. Even Cuba, the party directly concerned, was apparently not consulted, nor was its view on the matter sought.

Theoretically, of course, it can be argued that the interest of world communism—as interpreted by Soviet Russia—may require some national communist parties to sacrifice their appeal to the masses, their electoral successes, and their control over their own labor unions or membership. Viewed from the standpoint of the ultimate victory of international communism on a world scale, a temporary sacrifice of a national communist party might actually facilitate the common march toward the final triumph. But is it certain? Is the Soviet Union's perception of the situation correct and its reaction appropriate? Is it as farsighted as it claims to be? And is the Soviet Union, as a nation, as selfless and dedicated to the interests of world communism as it says it is?

Such questions were occasionally raised by foreign communists before World War II. They surfaced with vigor during the period of Soviet-Nazi cooperation (1939-1941), which many French, Belgian, Czech, Jewish, and, of course, German Communists found rather difficult to stomach. Chapter 8 will deal with the Nazi-Soviet pact in more detail.

Imperatives of the Great Patriotic War The situation changed when in 1941 the Nazis attacked the Soviet state and thus the world base of communism. Practical considerations and the need for a successful defense of the Soviet Union against the Nazis soon pushed proletarian internationalism to a secondary position: World communism went nationalistic and has never recovered from this wartime affliction.

The Soviet leaders soon discovered that they could not rely on internationalism and proletarian solidarity to win the war. The German proletariat, now dressed in the uniforms of advancing Nazi armies, did not show any inclination to desert to Russia as soon as their feet touched the holy grounds of the fatherland of socialism. Relatively soon after the outbreak of World War II, the Soviet leaders realistically reached the conclusion that dynamic nationalism and hatred of the Germans, not proletarian solidarity, were the forces that would help them win the war and chase the Germans out of Russia, thus saving the Soviet state as well as the Russian basis of world communism. The war became a "Great Patriotic War." The German nation was no longer divided into the exploiting and the exploited classes; the Soviet writer Ilya Ehrenburg was publicly allowed to differentiate between good Germans who were dead and bad Germans who were still alive.

A new Soviet anthem replaced the old battle song of proletarian internationalism, the "Internationale," which had promised that "the International Party shall be the human race." The new anthem spoke of "an unbreakable union of free republics—forged forever by Great Rus" (the term "Rus" refers to the early Slavic kingdom from which the Russian nation and state finally emerged to become the leading nation in the polyethnic Soviet Union). The old slogan "Proletarians of all countries, unite" was suddenly dropped from the top righthand corner of all communist publications: Clearly, little could be expected from transnational class solidarity. On the other hand, a great deal could be expected from the reemphasis on traditional national values. The names of the czarist military heroes Suvorov (1730-1800, a field marshal who had helped to suppress the Polish uprisings and the revolutionary forces of France in northern Italy) and Kutuzov (1745-1813, a field marshal who had successfully defeated Napoleon in Russia) were associated with the highest military decorations to be bestowed on the new heroes and marshals of the Great Patriotic War. The traditional Russian Orthodox Church was somewhat artificially revived and was requested, so to speak, to join the Soviet war effort against pagan nazism. The nineteenth-century racial slogans of Pan-Slavism were introduced into the communist propaganda output with the aim of prodding all Slavic nations east of Germany into supporting the Soviet defense against the German onslaught.

Dissolution of the Comintern The process of "chauvinizing" proletarian internationalism reached its climax on May 15, 1943, when Stalin ordered the symbol and the instrument of proletarian internationalism, the Comintern, disbanded.

The decision "to dissolve the Communist International as a guiding center of the international labor movement, releasing the sections [that is, the "national" communist parties] of the Communist International from obligations ensuing from the constitutions and decisions of the congresses of the Communist International" was signed by twelve leading members of the Comintern. As at any other funeral, good words were uttered on the subject of the now defunct Comintern. The Presidium of the Executive Committee of the Comintern, now transformed into an aggregate of the leaders of *national* communist parties, had this to say: "[The Comintern] helped . . . the workers' parties to mobilize the mass of toilers . . . for the support of the Soviet Union as the main bulwark against fascism." But, as the announcement significantly admitted, "long before the war it had already become increasingly clear that to the extent that the internal as well as the international situation of individual countries became more complicated, the solution of the problems of the labor movement in each individual country through the medium of some international center would meet with insuperable obstacles." The Communist International, as was pointed out in the announcement, "more and more outlived itself in proportion to the growth of this movement and to the increasing complexity of problems in each country; . . . [the Comintern] even became a hindrance to the further strengthening of the national workers' parties."

The public and publicized dissolution of the Comintern had a profound impact on both the leaders and the rank and file of communist parties outside the Soviet Union, especially those who had participated since 1941 in their own local patriotic wars against Germany. Owing to the constant shifts of the eastern front and to the fighting, the contacts between Moscow and the local communist parties participating in the resistance movements had noticeably decreased. In Moscow there was perhaps not much time or energy left for promoting organizational links between the widely scattered communist groups engaged in underground or partisan warfare, especially during the periods when the Red Army was either in full retreat or in full advance toward the west.

The Merger of Communism and Chauvinism   This, then, was the framework in which the merging of communism and nationalism was not only permitted but actually ordered by Moscow under the conditions of war against Germany.

Following the Russian example, all the other communist parties abandoned the previous stress on class loyalty and proletarian internationalism and adopted the concept of the struggle of oppressed nationalities against the oppressing Nazi Reich. The combination of jingoism and communism that until then only the Russian Communists had enjoyed was now to be emulated by all other communist parties.

This was indeed a period of chauvinistic frenzy within the proletarian movement. The French Communists, symbolically and literally, placed the French tricolor over the Red flag. The French national anthem, the "Marseillaise," with its appeal to the "children of the Fatherland" ("Allons, enfants de la Patrie!"), preceded the proletarian song of the "Internationale" ("L'Internationale sera le genre humain"). The conspiratorial organization of the European communist parties, initially established for the purpose of subverting democracies from within, proved during the war also quite effective in the underground activities of the European resistance; but there the interpenetration of communism and nationalism worked, of course, in both directions: Not only were the nationalist groups contaminated by their contacts with the communists, their doctrine, and their tactics, but also the communist leaders and rank and file were influenced and seduced by the fervor of the nationalists. However superficial or temporary the communist espousal of nationalism originally was intended to be, it sank deeper into the consciousness of the members of the communist movement than Moscow had anticipated.

Following the defeat of the Axis powers, European communists emerged from the underground or from concentration camps endowed with an aura of patriotic respectability, heroism, or martyrdom. Because human memory is very short, their ambivalent attitude during the period of the Soviet-Nazi pact was either forgotten or generally ignored. The European communists also profited from their identification with the Soviet Union, whose armies had impressed Europe by their victories over Nazi Germany. While in Western Europe the communists were able to secure for themselves only minor cabinet portfolios, in Eastern Europe the presence of the Soviet armies catapulted the communists to the leading positions in the national-front governments. Former agents of the Comintern thus became national prime ministers or ministers of foreign affairs; guerrilla leaders were promoted to positions as ministers of national defense or chiefs of staff; and former communist saboteurs obtained the portfolios of ministers of public works and national reconstruction.

As either leaders of or partners in postwar coalition cabinets in Europe, the communists, willy-nilly, became involved in the promotion or defense of their own country's national interests vis-à-vis the interests of other communist-led nations. The former links between the communist parties were thus further weakened, and within national communities the mutual interpenetration of communism and nationalism was accelerated. National communism became, in the words of the Yugoslav Milovan Djilas, "a general phenomenon." In the opinion of Djilas, "in order to maintain itself, communism must become national."[26] Apparently uninhibited by their former internationalism, the communists often tried to outdo right-wing parties in intolerance of other nations and jingoism.

The Soviet-Yugoslav Clash over Trieste   One explosive territorial issue is worth noting at this point: the city of Trieste. The Yugoslav-Italian dispute over its final destiny is an important portion of the background of the first open clash in the history of communism.

At the end of the war, Communist Yugoslavia in unmistakably nationalistic terms began to claim from Italy the city of Trieste on the Adriatic Sea without showing the least proletarian concern for the possible consequences that the loss of Trieste might have for the electoral appeal of the Italian Communist party. Unlike the Yugoslav party, the Italian party was not in power and had to compete for popular support in free elections in an environment where feelings about the Trieste issue ran very high. Yugoslavia failed to obtain Trieste from Italy and blamed the Soviet Union. The Yugoslav Communists felt that they had become a victim of a horse-trading deal between the Western powers and the Soviet Union. The Trieste question figured prominently in the subsequent dispute between Belgrade and Moscow. For the Yugoslavs, the failure was an illustration of the Soviet neglect of Yugoslav national objectives; for the Russians, the Yugoslav anger was an indication of Yugoslav chauvinism (see Document 7.1).

DOCUMENT 7.1

SOVIET CONDEMNATION OF YUGOSLAV CRITICISM

The Yugoslav leaders . . . put the foreign policy of the USSR on a par with the foreign policy of the English and Americans. . . . In this respect, the speech by Comrade Tito in Ljubljana in May 1945 is very characteristic. He said: "We demand that every one shall be master in his own house; we do not want to pay for others; we do not want to be used as a bribe in international bargaining; we do not want to get involved in any policy of spheres of interest."

This was said in connection with the question of Trieste. As is well known, after a series of territorial concessions for the benefit of Yugoslavia, which the Soviet Union extracted from the Anglo-Americans, the latter, together with the French, rejected the Soviet proposal to hand Trieste over to Yugoslavia, and occupied Trieste with their own forces, which were then in Italy. Since all other means were exhausted, the Soviet Union had only one other method for gaining Trieste for Yugoslavia—to start war with the Anglo-Americans over Trieste and take it by force. The Yugoslav comrades could not fail to realize that after such a hard war the USSR could not enter another. However, this fact caused dissatisfaction among the Yugoslav leaders. . . .

Excerpted from a letter sent by the Central Committee of the Soviet Communist party to that of the Yugoslav Communist party on May 4, 1948. The full text of the letter is contained in *The Soviet-Yugoslav Dispute*. London: Royal Institute of International Affairs, 1948, pp. 35-36.

The Soviet-Yugoslav clash over Trieste is one of the very few conflicts over objectives and methods of foreign policy between two communist states that have been documented. Impatient, frustrated, and daredevil young Yugoslavia opposed the cautious and more responsible policy of an experienced great power. We have not seen and may perhaps never see the confidential letters exchanged between the Chinese and Soviet Communist parties between the 1950s and 1970s in which a similarly impatient, frustrated, and daredevil Communist China criticized the more sedate and conservative Soviet Union, which was conscious of all the consequences of a direct confrontation with the United States and therefore unwilling to take unnecessary risks. If and when such documentation is published, it would be astonishing if we were not to find there a similar tone and similar criticism. Instead of the city of Trieste, the island of Taiwan, the Indian frontiers, Laos, Vietnam, Korea, sharing the A-Bomb, economic assistance, the Khrushchev-Kennedy deal over Cuba, and the off-shore islands of Quemoy and Matsu represent major chapters in the continuing story of the Sino-Soviet conflict. Like Yugoslavia in 1945, Communist China must view the Soviet pragmatic approach to international politics as a sign of revolutionary flabbiness, an expedient policy whose purpose is to preserve for Russia a relatively comfortable *status quo*.

The Cominform　It should be recalled that, as seen from Moscow's vantage point, the period of 1947-1948 was a difficult one for the Soviet Union and communism and needed careful coordination and discipline rather than hazardous improvisations on the part of foreign communist parties. It was the peak of the Cold War, full of opportunities as well as extreme dangers. The Soviet Union did not yet have the atomic bomb but it was preparing for its first atomic test. In the Far East, the civil war in China, albeit favorable to the communists, was still inconclusive. The Greek civil war was far from being successful in spite of the substantial help rendered the Greek communist partisans by neighboring communist states—Yugoslavia, Bulgaria, and Albania. On March 12, 1947, President Truman offered a multimillion-dollar military and economic aid program to Greece and Turkey, both of which were exposed to direct Soviet and communist pressures. The United States decided to replace weakened Britain as the guardian of the eastern Mediterranean against traditional Russian encroachments. Then, on June 5, 1948, the Marshall Plan of aid to Western Europe was announced. Both the Truman Doctrine and the Marshall Plan signaled the political, economic, and possibly military reentry of the United States into western and southeastern Europe.

In order to reassert its dominant and coordinating role within the communist movement and, in particular, to prevent pragmatic national leaders of communist states from falling prey to the economic lures of the United States, the Soviet Union decided to call a halt to creeping nationalism and reimpose the rigid discipline of the prewar Comintern. This was done on October 5, 1947, at a meeting of the European communist parties in Poland; the parties were compelled to agree to establish a new world center of communism, the Cominform (The Information Bureau of the Communist and Workers' Parties). In view of the forthcoming showdown between Tito and Stalin, Belgrade was chosen as the Cominform's seat. Although the main purpose of the Cominform was to reestablish the old Comintern disciplined unity around its base, Russia, its birth bore many marks of the new era of national communism: 1947 was simply not 1919. Unlike the headquarters of the Comintern, the seat of the Cominform was not to be Moscow; Russian dominance of the movement could not be that blatantly publicized. Furthermore, the Cominform was composed only of the Soviet, French, Italian, and East European Communist parties; none of the Asian or African parties was included. Nor were the Communist parties of West and East Germany included. Apparently, the war against Germany and the resulting anti-German feelings prevented the association of the German Communists with the new center of proletarian "internationalism."

In Poland, Czechoslovakia, Hungary, Rumania, Bulgaria, and Albania the reimposition of rigid Soviet discipline did not encounter major difficulties. All these regimes resulted from the sweep of the Red Army over East Central Europe. In none of the above countries did the communists succeed in seizing power on their own. Directly or indirectly they were helped by the presence or proximity of Soviet military might. The Eastern European nations were frightened into communism rather than seduced by it. Following the Soviet tanks at a safe distance, former Comintern agents became national leaders in Warsaw, Prague, and Bucharest. Their feeling of dependence on the Soviet Union and its protection was not a matter of sentimentality or faith; it was a matter of pragmatic politics. Furthermore, even their national interests seemed to point to the Soviet Union as the main protector against any renewal of German aggression, which, according to Stalin, was to result from the Marshall Plan and its by-product, a mighty West German state.[27] Yugoslavia, however, was a different story.

National Interests of Communist States   The Cominform, although perhaps primarily directed at Yugoslavia, came to Belgrade too late. The virus of nationalism had already contaminated the upper echelons of both the party and the government. Yugoslavia differed from all the other communist countries in several respects. Temperamentally, the Yugoslavs had been conditioned by national history to face political issues bravely rather than by means of political compromise. There is also a difference in geographic position. Unlike Hungary or Czechoslovakia, Yugoslavia is not the Soviet Union's next-door neighbor. It faces the sea and can look far beyond its horizon for other alternatives, an outlook that is denied to land-locked countries encircled by the Soviet armies. Above all, the Yugoslav Communists had marched to power from their own guerrilla bases, largely unaided by the Soviet armies except in the concluding chapter of World War II.

In 1948 the clash between Soviet and Yugoslav nationalist communism came into the open: Long-accumulated tensions and irritations were dogmatized into new ideological positions.

The Yugoslav revolt against Soviet leadership and policy was followed by Stalin's incapacity to initiate a purge of Tito and his associates from within the ranks of the Communist party of Yugoslavia, a procedure that under the Comintern had never failed to produce desired results.

Inevitably, in a system of communist states, the question would have to arise sooner or later as to which national communist interest would prevail in a clash with the Soviet Union. Nothing in previous communist theory or practice indicated exactly how international relations among the sovereign communist states would develop. The communist concept of vanguard leadership, elitism, and monolithic power does not allow for a give-and-take procedure among equals—a procedure proper to a democratic framework but alien to a totalitarian framework. The

Cominform solution of this problem was as straightforward as that of the Comintern: the interest of the Soviet Union as the base of world communism is under all circumstances primary; all other interests are secondary. To this clearly imperial concept Communist Yugoslavia had the courage to reply to the Russians a resounding *Nyet!* The Soviet Union, on the other hand, had to insist that the central issue in the relations of communist states and parties was their subordinate attitude to Soviet leadership; in such a framework suspicion of Soviet selfishness, opposition to the Soviet line, insistence on the promotion of national interests, and manifestation of national Communist pride became major crimes. The Soviet party and the final communiqué of the Cominform expelling Tito's party from the communist commonwealth said this with vigor and with seeming finality (see Document 7.2).

The Soviet-Yugoslav dispute, like the later Sino-Soviet, Soviet-Albanian, and Soviet-Rumanian ones, demonstrated that the national and economic interests of communist states not only are dissimilar but often may be in direct conflict with each other. Furthermore, the Titoist revolt proved that a communist state can oppose Soviet dictatorship and get away with it. There has proved to be an alternative to the position of inferiority in a Soviet-dominated bloc of states: A state could be communist and independent of Russia at the same time, while improving its economy by trading successfully with both the West and the East. This lesson in pragmatic, businesslike, national communism was to be learned by other communist leaders. Since Tito's successful revolt, world communism has not been the same, nor could it be. The Yugoslav challenge to Soviet imperial authority and Cominform discipline brought to the surface what had been inherent in international communism since it spread beyond the confines of the Soviet state: the inevitability of the assertion of national interests by communist territorial states. By his revolt against foreign domination, Tito had actually strengthened the basis of communist power. However anticommunist the majority of the Yugoslavs were, they did identify themselves with Tito's assertion of the Yugoslav national interest against the Soviet Union. This lesson was not lost on other communist leaders. It was only a matter of time (and of Stalin's death) until the image of communism in crisis, with major parties in open rebellion, would replace the old monolothic and Russian-centered image.

Following the open rift with Tito, the violence and intensity of the Cominform propaganda on the theme of Soviet superiority was a good indication of Soviet efforts to coordinate the communist states into a disciplined and coordinated bloc. Everything was mobilized: The prestige of the Soviet Union as the country of the first communist revolution was stressed. The Soviet military might and the victories of the Red Army were presented as the main reason for Communist successes in the area between Germany and Russia. But this was not enough, and Moscow's efforts to bolster Russian prestige reached ridiculous proportions: In addition to its

DOCUMENT 7.2

COMINFORM: "YUGOSLAVIA HAS TAKEN
THE ROAD OF NATIONALISM"

The Yugoslav leaders . . . do not suffer from undue modesty . . . are still intoxicated with their successes, which are not so very great. . . . Their heads were turned by the successes achieved. They became arrogant and now feel that the depth of the sea reaches only up to their knees. Not only have they become arrogant, but they even preach arrogance, not understanding that arrogance can be their own ruin. . . .

There are anti-Soviet rumors circulating among the leading comrades in Yugoslavia, for instance that the "CPSU is degenerate," "great-power chauvinism is rampant in the USSR," the "USSR is trying to dominate Yugoslavia economically," and "the Cominform is a means of controlling the other Parties by the CPSU."

The Communist Information Bureau (Cominform) denounces the anti-Soviet attitude of the leaders of the Communist Party of Yugoslavia, as being incompatible with Marxism-Leninism, and only appropriate to nationalists. . . . Nationalist elements, which previously existed in a disguised form, managed in the course of the past five or six months to reach a dominant position in the leadership of the Communist Party of Yugoslavia, . . . consequently the leadership of the Yugoslav Communist Party has broken with the international traditions of the Communist Party of Yugoslavia and has taken the road of nationalism. Considerably overestimating the internal, national forces of Yugoslavia and their influence, the Yugoslav leaders think that they can maintain Yugoslavia's independence and build socialism without the support of the Communist Parties of other countries, without the support of people's democracies, without the support of the Soviet Union. . . .

The first two paragraphs are excerpted from the letters sent by the Central Committee of the Soviet Communist party (CPSU) to the Central Committee of the Yugoslav party on March 27 and May 4, 1948, respectively. The third paragraph is from the Resolution of the Cominform expelling Yugoslavia from its ranks, published on June 28, 1948. The full text of these documents is contained in *The Soviet-Yugoslav Dispute*. London: Royal Institute of International Affairs, 1948, pp. 14, 50, 62, 69.

claims to be first in communism and first in the victory over nazism, Moscow also claimed to be first in the history of all human inventions, from the steam engine and the lightning rod to the X-ray and the telephone. At one point a Soviet magazine even claimed that the Greeks had won the Trojan War on account of the weapons and armor forged by the superior craftsmen living on the now-Russian shores of the Black Sea.

Stalin's death in 1953 accelerated the erosion of world communism. The succession crisis in Russia, especially with the execution of Beria and the demotion of Malenkov, emphasized the purely personal factors in what used to be presented as the scientific doctrine and international practice of communism. If Moscow were to manifest doubt and uncertainty as to who should eventually lead and authoritatively interpret communism, how could it claim an indisputable leadership over the other communist states and parties? When the succession crisis in Moscow was finally resolved in favor of Khrushchev and his "thaw" program, the communist nations had to absorb a new shock. In a speech delivered at the Twentieth Congress of the Soviet Communist party, Khrushchev denounced Stalin as the source of all evil in communism (February 24-25, 1956). This was done for several reasons: to inspire the masses, and in particular the younger generations, to initiative and renewed efforts; to revamp the economic structure; to place Soviet relations with both communist and noncommunist states on a new basis; and to enhance Khrushchev's image in contrast to that of the tyrannical Stalin.

Two months after the speech, the logical step followed: The Cominform, Stalin's creation, was disbanded (April 17, 1956). A communiqué explained that the reason for the liquidation of the second world center of communism was a changed international situation. Three key arguments are worth noting:

1. "The emergence of socialism from the confines of a single country. . . . " This phrase might be interpreted as a sign of confidence in the strength and further growth of the world communist system; it also implied the belated recognition of the problems that the existence of communist nations had created.
2. "The formation of a vast 'peace-zone' that includes European and Asian states, socialist and nonsocialist friends of peace. . . ." Evidently, the Russian leaders recognized that in their efforts to capitalize upon anti-American nationalism in Asia and Latin America (and later in Africa), the Cominform had become a burden rather than an asset, being in composition purely European, that is, a white man's affair. The Cominform, as a symbol of proletarian internationalism with emphasis on the working-class character of the revolutionary parties, did not quite fit the era of multiclass explosive nationalism. As seen by Moscow, anti-Western nationalism, regardless of the role which the local communists were to play in it, seemed in the 1950s to be a more promising aspect of the international situation than proletarian parties in Western countries, where no communist takeover could be expected in the foreseeable future. The disadvantage that would result from disbanding the Cominform and loosening interparty ties seemed more than balanced by the advantages derived from the convergence of communism and nationalism in developing countries.
3. "The task of overcoming the splits in the working-class movement. . . ." This third key phrase in the final communiqué of the Cominform referred to the Soviet desire for reconciliation with Yugoslav

communism so that the latter would not veer even further toward real neutralism, a trend that Moscow was determined to halt.

Further Erosion of Communist Unity The period following the disbanding of the Cominform proved that further erosion of communist unity was inevitable, with or without the Cominform. Had the Cominform been maintained and perhaps enlarged by Asian and African parties, others besides the Yugoslav Communists would have eventually found its Soviet-centered iron discipline intolerable.

The implication of the disbanding was that communist parties and nations should now follow their own communist way of doing things. The USSR kept hoping that the communist nations' common enemies, the Western democracies, and common problems of socialist modernization and industrialization would create unity out of national diversity. Instead of using a permanent and central organ, the Soviet leaders transferred their efforts at coordination of policies to occasional gatherings of communist dignitaries, usually held on the occasion of the Soviet celebration of the October Revolution in Moscow. The moribund Council for Mutual Economic Assistance (CEMA, or Comecon) was revived to promote closer economic links between communist states in response to the challenge of the West European Community.

The process of erosion could not be stopped. Like the sorcerer's apprentice, Khrushchev tried in vain to keep it within bounds, but failed. When, on October 14, 1964, Khrushchev was finally deposed, he seemed to be blamed for everything: "immature conclusions," "hasty decisions," "bragging and phrase-mongering," "harebrained schemes," "commandism," "unwillingness to take into account the achievements of science and practical experience" (from the editorial in *Pravda*, October 17, 1964). But was the nationalist erosion of communism really Khrushchev's fault? Nationalist communism had lain dormant since 1917; it had only waited for the opportune moment to surface.

The opportune moment came in the 1950s and 1960s; many elements contributed to this growth of nationalist communism, of which three were of major importance.

1. The first was the nuclear stalemate, which activated a self-confident nationalism on the part of all the smaller nations, including the communist ones, caught between the mutually paralyzed atomic superpowers. Thus the eroding force of nationalism and parochialism not only affected but significantly infected international communism, an ideology dominant in more than a third of the world and still, in principle, committed to the idea of a supranational proletarian monolith. Having successfully spread west from Moscow to Berlin, Prague, and Belgrade, east and south to Peking, Hanoi, and Pyongyang, and across the Atlantic to Havana, communism both triumphed and was atomized by its merger with nationalism.

2. The second element that injected doubts and a bacillus of heresy into the communist creed was the relatively successful postwar performance of Western economies, earmarked by Marx and Lenin for an early doom. In particular, the prosperity of Western Europe, coupled with a relatively peaceful decolonization, has upset many a Marxian prophecy. The crisis of communism as a tool of political analysis is therefore at least partly due to the refusal of the West to conform to the gloomy prophecies of Marxist Cassandras. First some of the Eastern European communist states and then the Soviet Union and the People's Republic of China established trade relations and technological cooperation with the most advanced Western nations, especially the United States. These contacts were in part motivated by economic and technological considerations; in part they also reflected the new dimension of international relations: the awareness of the nuclear paralysis among the ideologically irreconcilable powers.

3. The third element—and another cause for the loss of communist faith and zeal—may be generally referred to as the normally unsatisfactory performance of the communist system wherever it was established. While the inefficiency of communist economies when compared with Western economies, especially in the field of consumer goods and services, housing, and agriculture, is the single most important aspect of the disappointing record of communist practice, there are other issues that have shaken communism's foundations: the various succession crises and their aftermaths, often bloody, in Moscow; the generally antiintellectual bias of party bureaucrats and managers; the documented revelations of the extent of terror and inhumanity under communism, especially in the era of Stalin; the Soviet-Yugoslav, Sino-Soviet, Soviet-Albanian, Soviet-Hungarian, and Soviet-Czech crises, with their proofs of Soviet chauvinism or its great-power callousness. Thus another previously attractive appeal of communism has faded away: its promise of peace among proletarian states. There is now ample evidence that a single socialist ideology and identical political and economic systems based upon it do not guarantee concord among socialist states. A world made safe for communism does not promise to be any more peaceful than a world made safe for monarchy, capitalism, fascism, or democracy.

Because of the observable discrepancy between communism's original promise and the present reality, today there are very few true believers in communism as a doctrine, a hope, and a dream. Originally communism appealed mostly to idealists and downtrodden people who were aroused by the injustice and cruelty of early industrialism, which Marxism had analyzed and had promised to replace by a happy life in a free and classless society. Communism, however, has made headway and maintained itself by coercion, not by persuasion. As a consequence, it has been deserted by intellectuals and humanitarian idealists, who are now forming an amorphous New Left in search of a program and an ideal. Today pragmatism, cynicism, and disillusionment characterize those who operate the national and international communist establishments and their military-industrial complexes. Communism now appears as a technique that teaches its users how to maximize territorial state power, that is, how to make the opposition, not the state, wither away.

Adjustment to the Atomic Age

According to Lenin, writing in the prenuclear age, intercapitalist wars were inevitable, and in a sense, desirable. His hope was that intercapitalist wars could and would be transformed into communist revolutions. When, following World War I, communism was established in Russia, his prophecy seemed partly confirmed and partly negated: While Russia became communist in the wake of an intercapitalist war, the rest of the world remained capitalist. The theory of the inevitability of war had to be adjusted to the new reality, that is, to the existence of a communist state within a system of sovereign capitalist states.

The adjustment to the new reality was expressed in the analysis Lenin made on November 26, 1920 (subsequently quoted by Stalin on several occasions):

> As long as capitalism and socialism exist, we cannot live in peace. . . . We live not only in a state, but *in a system of states*, and the existence of the Soviet Republic side by side with a number of imperialist states for a long time is unthinkable. In the end either the one or the other will triumph. And until that end comes, a series of the most terrible collisions between the Soviet Republic and the bourgeois states is inevitable.[28]

"Clear, one would think" was Stalin's comment on Lenin's forecast of several world wars before the end of capitalism. Yet, already under Stalin and long before Khrushchev, the inevitability of war, despite its definitive meaning, was qualified by Stalin's expectation (expressed in a speech to the Eighteenth Congress of the Communist party in 1939) that perhaps in the distant future

> if the proletariat wins in the most important capitalist countries and if the present capitalist encirclement is replaced by a Socialist encirclement, a "peaceful" path of development is fully possible for some capitalist countries, whose capitalists, in view of the "unfavorable" international situation, will consider it expedient to make serious concessions to the proletariat "voluntarily."[29]

This statement does not depict capitalist statesmen as pawns of their own economic system; a rational political estimate of the international situation was expected to make them behave in a different fashion despite the theory that capitalism leads inevitably to war. "If what was inevitable," wrote

Louis J. Halle (*New York Times Magazine*, November 15, 1959), "gets over being inevitable, then it could not have been inevitable to begin with."

In 1956, Stalin's successor, Khrushchev, made Stalin's expectation of possible "voluntary" surrender of capitalism to communism the core of his thesis that peaceful coexistence would lead to a peaceful burial of capitalism. In his speech to the Twentieth Party Congress (February 14, 1956) Khrushchev declared:

> The Leninist thesis remains valid: as long as imperialism exists, the economic base giving rise to wars will also remain. Reactionary forces, representing the interests of capitalist monopolies, will continue their drive toward military gambles and aggression and may try to unleash war. *But war is not a fatalistic inevitability.*[30.]

In this speech and subsequent statements, Khrushchev identified two major reasons why capitalism, in spite of the imperatives of its incurable economic ills, was capable of a rational evaluation of the new shift in the world balance of powers:

> . . . the principal feature of our epoch is the emergence of socialism from the confines of one country and its transformation into a world system. Capitalism has proved impotent to hinder this world historic process. . . . A world camp of socialism [has] not only moral but also . . . the material . . . formidable means to prevent the imperialists from unleashing war.

Translated into concrete terms the two major reasons are:

1. The existence and the combined power of the Communist system of states, particularly its military alliance, the Warsaw Pact, directed and equippped by the Soviet Union.
2. The existence and might of the Soviet thermonuclear deterrent and Soviet advancement in missile technology, which, at the time of Khrushchev's speech, was evidenced by the superiority of Soviet outer-space achievements (the first Sputnik) over American achievements.

On this basis, the Soviet thesis of the need and possibility of peaceful coexistence with the United States was built and propagandized, but in time it was challenged by the People's Republic of China, Cuba, and others who saw in the Soviet thesis a misperception and misinterpretation of the situation. According to the critics of the Soviet thesis, the world balance of power either tilted in favor of the communist commonwealth or created a mutual atomic paralysis between the two superpowers; either case would facilitate further advancement of communism by guerrilla wars and national liberation movements. In this context China depicted the United States as a paper tiger, that is, a superpower that possesses a superweapon of such a destructive capacity that it cannot be used either because it is ineffective against guerrilla warfare or because the superpower dreads the possibility of atomic retaliation by its atomic enemies. China also concluded that the more countries that have the atomic deterrent, the more paralyzed the United States would be (see Document 7.3). In China's view, therefore, the existence of atomic weapons did not justify the overcautious Soviet attitude; as China's Foreign Minister Chen Yi said in 1963, "it is imperative to wage a serious struggle and to take risks. Only this way will we be able to win."[31]

The communist ideology did adjust itself to the atomic age, but in the 1960s the Soviet Communists and their allies, and the Chinese Communists and their allies, reached diametrically opposed conclusions. Four variants of the communist attitudes toward the thesis of peaceful coexistence may be identified:

1. Peaceful coexistence is the best and most clever policy to "bury" capitalism, whose economic doom and political fragmentation are inevitable and may be speeded up by the absence of major wars, which force capitalists into planned mobilization of their national economies and so, in a sense, represent an invigorating injection into the ailing body of capitalism.

2. Peaceful coexistence, however, as preached by the Soviet Union, may also be a Chamberlain-like appeasement policy for the purpose of safeguarding the present-day conservative and sedate generation of Soviet bureaucrats at the expense of the revolutionary programs of other communist parties. In 1962 Communist China and Albania denounced the Soviet Union for its alleged Munich-like solution of the Cuban crisis at the expense of Castro's interests and prestige. In 1969 the *Peking Review* (May 16, p. 23), continuing the "Munich" theme in a long article entitled "U.S. Imperialism and Soviet Revisionism Step Up 'Middle East Munich' Plot," denounced Soviet and American joint efforts to deescalate the tension between Israel and her Arab neighbors.

3. Peaceful coexistence is viewed by many communists as a pragmatic adaptation of Leninism to the realities of the atomic age in which, for the communists, it is preferable to keep their half of the world than to risk conquering a global waste of atomic dust. This view is quite popular in Eastern Europe.

4. Peaceful coexistence may also be a silent alliance between conservative communist Russia and conservative capitalist America to divide the world between the two while restraining Communist China. In such a context the atomic test-ban and antiproliferation agreement, as perceived from Peking, may appear as a thinly veiled Soviet-American plot to deprive China of its right to a national atomic deterrent. Furthermore, peaceful coexistence, which implies reasonableness on the part of capitalism, acts as a damper to the revolutionary *élan* of the anticolonial masses in Asia, Africa, and Latin

DOCUMENT 7.3

WAR AND PEACE: THE RUSSIAN
AND THE CHINESE VERSION

Let us not approach the matter commercially and figure out the losses this or the other side would sustain. War would be a calamity for all the peoples of the world. . . . Imagine what will happen when bombs begin to explode over cities. These bombs will not distinguish between communists and noncommunists. . . . No, everything alive can be wiped out in the conflagration of nuclear explosions.

From a speech by Khrushchev to the members of the French Peace Council, *Pravda*, February 12, 1960.

The present Peking leadership's fight against the Marxist-Leninist parties for hegemony in the Communist movement is linked closely with its great power aspirations, with its claims to territory of other countries. The idea that China has a messianic role to play is drummed into the heads of the Chinese workers and peasants.

Possibly, many of the comrades here remember Mao Tse-tung's speech in this hall during the 1957 meeting. With appalling airiness and cynicism he spoke of the possible destruction of half of mankind in the event of an atomic war. The facts indicate that Maoism is not calling for a struggle against war, but, on the contrary, for war, which it regards as a positive phenomenon in historical development.

From a speech by Brezhnev, *Pravda*, June 6, 1969.

If the imperialists insist on unleashing another war, we should not be afraid of it. . . . World War I was followed by the birth of the Soviet Union with a population of 200 million. World War II was followed by the emergence of the socialist camp with a combined population of 900 million. If the imperialists should insist on launching a third world war, it is certain that several hundred million will turn to socialism. Then there will not be much room left in the world for the imperialists while it is quite likely that the whole structure of imperialism will utterly collapse.

From *Hung Chi (Red Flag)*, March 30, 1960.

China hopes that Afro-Asian countries will be able to make atom bombs themselves, and it would be better for a greater number of countries to come into possession of atom bombs.

From a speech by Chen Yi at a press conference, *Peking Review*, September 29, 1965.

America, which China has set out to lead. It may be noted that the division of the world into Soviet and American spheres of influence is resented and objected to by both noncommunist and communist states, including Cuba. While Castro's stomach is predominantly in Russia and Eastern Europe, his heart frequently has a Chinese beat.

The Sino-Soviet Conflict It would be wrong to interpret the enmity between Moscow and Peking solely in terms of their conflicting reinterpretations of a common ideology to fit the age of nuclear missiles. Their conflict includes many more issues than just the Soviet thesis of peaceful coexistence in the nuclear era—an issue that the Western European and Eastern European communists almost never challenge (with the exception of pro-Chinese Albania and pro-Peking factions within the European communist parties). China fully shares the implicit or explicit objections of the European communist states to Soviet intracommunist policies, namely: (1) Soviet economic stakes and the manner in which they are imposed on others ("Socialist division of labor"—see Chapter 1) and (2) the self-appointed role of the Soviets as guardian and protector of the common faith, including the right of intervention (the Brezhnev Doctrine—see Document 11.6).

It may be noted, at this point, that several Eastern European communist parties (for example, the Rumanian party), otherwise unsympathetic to Chinese revolutionary theses, have discovered that the continuation of the Sino-Soviet dispute, short of war, has several beneficial side effects: Medium and small communist states and parties have acquired an increased bargaining power vis-à-vis Moscow through the possibility of playing one communist superpower against the other. When in June 1969 the representatives of seventy-five communist parties of the world met in Moscow, the Soviet Union proved unable to obtain a unanimous endorsement of its policies, an endorsement that used to be a regular feature in preceding conferences and in the days of the Comintern and Cominform. Five parties did not sign the final communiqué: those of Britain, Norway, Sweden, Cuba, and the Dominican Republic. Four parties signed a portion of it: those of Italy, San Marino, Australia, and Réunion. Five signed after expressing serious reservations: those of Rumania, Spain, Switzerland, Morocco, and Sudan. The Yugoslav, Albanian, and Japanese parties did not attend. Nor did the Chinese party, of course. The final communiqué recorded the lack of unanimous support—a public admission that is indeed a milestone in the history of the communist movement.

> The communist and workers' parties, regardless of some difference of opinion, reaffirm their determination to present a united front in the struggle against imperialism. Some of the divergences that have arisen are eliminated through the exchange of opinion and disappear as the development clarifies the essence of the outstanding issues. Other divergences may last long.[32]

In such a situation, common ideology notwithstanding, it was in the interest of China to inspire, instigate, support, and propagandize all grievances, however debatable from the strict ideological point of view, that any communist party, especially those in power, could have against Moscow. "Divide and rule" applies to all disputes among great powers, not only those among imperialist powers. Thus in the 1960s there was almost no issue on which China, invoking the purity of the original dogma, did not take a position opposite to that of the Soviet "revisionist." Everything could be rationalized in ideological terms: the Chinese condemnation of the Soviet condemnation of the excesses of the Stalin era, the Soviet occupation of Czechoslovakia, Moscow's restrained attitude toward the racial strife in the United States, the Soviet-American atomic test-ban and nonproliferation agreement, Soviet economic planning, and Soviet political and economic management of the socialist camp, which, as Peking asserted, Moscow transformed from splendor into a mess (see Document 7.4). Any détente between Moscow and Washington elicited extremely hostile reaction on the part of Peking; on the other hand, any rapprochement between Peking and Washington provoked nervousness in Moscow. The Moscow-Washington-Peking circle became a highly jittery triangle—however preposterous this metaphor may appear from the standpoint of geometry. In the continuous circular movement of suspicions and countersuspicions Washington, of course, could not help dreading that Peking and Moscow might sooner or later rediscover the advantages of their formidable geomilitary position: If in the event of a renewed harmony the rear of Russia and China were made again secure, both nuclear powers would face outward from the opposite ends of Eurasia and so cause maximum dissipation of the military might of the United States, the only power capable of frustrating their separate or common designs.

Enough has already been said about the different images of the external world that are being perceived by different national communist leaders for us to realize that even some obvious common interest, common ideology, and geomilitary advantage may not suffice to eliminate conflict of views, estimates, and conclusions or to overcome mutual suspicions.

Using the previous parallel of a telescope through which national leaders look at the world, we may say that both the Soviet and the Chinese political telescopes have been provided with identical Marxist-Leninist lenses. Yet all the craftsmanship and material that went into their production was national; and in the final analysis, their manipulation was individually that of Mao Tse-tung and Stalin, Liu Shao-ch'i and Khrushchev, Chou En-lai and Brezhnev. They were bound to focus on different areas and perceive different images when looking from their respective vantage points at Taiwan or Berlin, Cuba or India, the Sino-Soviet boundaries or the United States.

Different National Histories The Soviet Union has its center of gravity in Europe; it is traditionally preoccupied with invasions from the west—from Sweden, Poland, France, and, most recently, Germany. In the final analysis, unlike China, which has been carved up like a melon among

DOCUMENT 7.4

CHINA TO RUSSIA: "YOU HAVE MADE A MESS OF THE SPLENDID SOCIALIST CAMP"

The leaders of the Communist Party of the Soviet Union . . . pursued a policy of great power chauvinism and national egoism toward fraternal Socialist countries and thus disrupted the unity of the Socialist camp. . . . They have made a mess of the splendid Socialist camp. They have arbitrarily infringed the sovereignty of fraternal countries, interfered in their internal affairs, carried on subversive activities and striven in every way to control fraternal countries. The leaders of the CPSU consider themselves the natural leaders who can lord it over all the fraternal parties. . . . All the fraternal parties must submissively listen and obey and are absolutely forbidden to criticize or oppose them. This is outright tyranny. It is the ideology of feudal autocrats, pure and simple. . . . Khrushchev has more than once described a fraternal party as a "silly boy" and called himself its "mother." With this feudal psychology of self-exaltation he has absolutely no sense of shame. . . .

The leaders of the CPSU regard fraternal parties as pawns on their diplomatic chessboard. . . . They endeavor to sacrifice fraternal parties and countries on the altar of their political dealing with the United States imperialism. . . . It is absolutely impermissible for them to treat enemies as friends and friends as enemies and to ally themselves with the U.S. imperialists, the reactionaries of various countries and the renegade Tito clique . . . in the vain pursuit of world domination through U.S. Soviet collaboration.

From *Hung Chi (Red Flag)*, January 1964.

the Western powers, including Russia, the Russian Empire has proved unconquerable. It has now recovered all the former czarist territories and more, and since 1945 it has been protected by a belt of East European communist nations. The Soviet Union is a highly developed industrial superpower with a tremendous atomic weapon and delivery system, and it is sophisticated about the system's uses and potential destructiveness. Unlike China, it is also a very rich country without any population problem.

China, with its center of gravity in Asia, has a tradition of greatness followed by extreme humiliation at the hands of the Western powers. It is a developing country, with an almost unmanageable population problem. For twenty-three years it remained unrecognized by a great many nations; it was admitted into the United Nations only in 1972, and it was unable to conclude its civil war: its enemy on Taiwan remained protected against final defeat by the might of the United States. For too long China was indeed, as Doak Barnett suggests, the most frustrated great power in the world.

There are other differences between China and the Soviet Union resulting from their different experiences in their respective marches to power. The Russian seizure of power in 1917 was a rapid, breathtaking affair. Trotsky, Lenin's friend and associate, described Lenin's first reaction to the Bolshevik success as follows:

> Lenin has not yet had time to change his collar, even though his face looks so tired. He looks softly at me, with that sort of awkward shyness that with him indicates intimacy. "You know," he says hesitatingly, "from persecution and life underground, to come suddenly into power. . . . " He pauses for the right word. *"Es schwindelt"* [My head spins], he concludes, changing suddenly to German, and circling his hand around his head. We look at each other and laugh a little.[33]

There was no dizziness of speed in the case of the Chinese Communists: their protracted civil war started in 1927, included the Long March in 1934 and the wartime experience at Yenan, and culminated only in 1949. The Chinese Communist party, although in power only since 1949, has been engaged in military actions all its life. One year after its victory over Chiang Kai-shek, a victory that took twenty-two years to accomplish, the Communist Chinese army was engaged in battle with the United States north of the 38th parallel in Korea. The Chinese armies then pursued military actions in Tibet, against India, and indirectly in Vietnam. Continuous war has been a much more integral part of Chinese thinking and experience than of the Russians'.

The Soviet leaders in 1917-1920 experienced a great fear of backsliding because of the absence of the anticipated world proletarian revolution; the Chinese Communists initially had a greater feeling of security. When they came to power, communism had been a going concern in Russia for more than twenty years and in Eastern Europe for three or four years. The selfless assistance of the more advanced communist countries of Europe in the name of proletarian solidarity could be expected. But it did not materialize for many reasons, one of them being the inefficiency of the communist economies in general. The Chinese disappointment and anger at the lack of Soviet generosity or actual capacity to help while noncommunists such as Nehru, Nasser, and Nkrumah were recipients of relatively large amounts of Soviet and East European assistance forms much of the background for the abuses and ideological arguments hurled at Moscow by Peking. Instead of there being simultaneous development and modernization, as the Chinese bitterly note, the gap between communist industrial and underdeveloped nations, as in the capitalist world, has become bigger, not smaller.

Another large source of friction between China and Russia is the problem of the unsettled borders, a problem reaching back into their respective imperial pasts. In the period of its imperial expansion, czarist Russia annexed considerable chunks of Chinese territory taken from the Manchu Empire at its period of decline. Communist Russia has so far kept all these territories and denied them not only to Chiang Kai-shek but also to its fraternal ally. According to *Pravda* (September 2, 1964), Mao Tse-tung spoke of these claims in an interview he granted a group of visiting Japanese Socialists. *Pravda* complained about the following Mao statement in particular:

> There are too many places occupied by the Soviet Union. In keeping with the Yalta agreement the Soviet Union, under the pretext of insuring Mongolia's independence, actually placed this country under its domination. . . . About a hundred years ago the area east of Lake Baikal became the territory of Russia, and from then on Vladivostok, Khabarovsk, Kamchatka, and other points were the territory of the Soviet Union. . . . We have not yet called for an account. . . .

The 1969 border clashes between the Soviet Union and China may have constituted the first Chinese call for an account (see Document 1.3).

"Social Imperialism" The direct Chinese experience with the Soviet Union (including the border disputes, the lack of Soviet economic aid, and the frequency of Soviet interference) must be added to Peking's reactions to the Soviet political and economic control of East Europe (including the Soviet military invasion and occupation of Hungary in 1956 and Czechoslovakia in 1968) and the détente with the United States, which, Peking alleges, has led to American-Soviet collusion in the Middle East at the expense of the Arab cause—small wonder that Peking tends to view the pattern of the Soviet policies as basically expansionist and imperialistic. Labeled by the Chinese "social imperialism," the Soviet policy may indeed appear to Peking as more immediately dangerous than United States policy: the United States is far away but Russia is China's immediate neighbor in the north; moreover, Russia's power and influence have now, by means of diplomacy and military aid, been projected—in a pincer movement of sorts—into India, Bangladesh, North Vietnam, and North Korea. What Lenin called imperialism as the monopoly stage of capitalism has become, in the eyes of Peking in the 1970s, "imperialism as a monopoly stage of the Soviet Party development" (see Document 7.5).

"MARXOLOGY" AND INTERNATIONAL POLITICS: A CONCLUDING NOTE

A fascinating political and ideological controversy between Moscow and Peking (and to a lesser extent between Moscow and Albania, Rumania, Czechoslovakia, Cuba, and other communist states) has sprung from a background composed of the contrasts among leading communist personalities and their equally contrasting national histories, capabilities,

DOCUMENT 7.5

WHO IS THE GREATER IMPERIALIST?
THE PEKING REVIEW VERSUS THE MOSCOW PRESS

The Soviet revisionist renegade clique talks about world hegemony, works for world hegemony, and even dreams of world hegemony. But it has a guilty conscience . . . It claims that whoever puts the "Soviet Union, a socialist country, on a par with the world capitalist powers" has "ill intentioned lucubrations."[1] Soviet revisionist gentlemen! It is not that others are indiscriminately pinning labels on you but that your hegemonic words and deeds have shown you up for what you are. If you do not want to dominate the world, why have you invaded and occupied Czechoslovakia, massed troops along China's border, sent troops into the People's Republic of Mongolia, intervened in Egypt, dismembered Pakistan. . . . ? What is this if not naked hegemonism? What is it if not outright imperialism?. . . . Since the Soviet revisionists have taken the old road of imperialism, they will, of course, be subjected to the laws governing imperialism and the logic of hegemonists' history and will end up being transformed into their opposite. *"Revolution is the main trend in the world today."* [A quotation from Mao.] Great disorder in the world shows that the world situation is excellent.

Peking Review, November 30, 1973.

Replies from the Moscow Press

[China is] posing as a champion of developing countries to secure a power base in the Third World [and engages in] rude provocations against Soviet-Arab friendship. . . . The adventurism, unscrupulousness and hegemonistic ambitions of Peking leadership pose a threat to all nations and to universal peace. . . . China is pursuing an openly expansionist policy toward almost all her neighbors and is using every means from secret subversive activities to armed border conflicts.

Za Rubezhom, December 7, 1973.

[Chinese expansionism is most frankly manifested in Southeast Asia . . . [by] encroachments by Chinese detachments into northern Burma to assist local rebels, tireless propaganda broadcasts to Burma, Malaysia and Taiwan[!] from Chinese territory" [and attempts] to hinder the consolidation of the young state of Bangladesh.

International Life, December 1973.

[China has] a kinship of souls with the military junta in Chile [that overthrew Allende.]

Pravda, December 8, 1973.

political styles, goals, and needs. The dispute centers around the question as to what might be the most appropriate strategy and tactics in an era of atomic missiles, dynamic evolution of Western technology, and global unrest. In spite of the Chinese ideological emphasis on the need for bold offensive actions against moribund capitalism, Communist China exercised extreme caution with regard to the United States in regard to conflicts in or over Korea, the Taiwan straits, the Quemoy and Matsu islands, and Vietnam. On the other hand, in spite of the Russian ideological stress on the need for and possibility of peaceful coexistence, it was Moscow that in 1962 had nuclear-tipped long-range missiles installed in Cuba, thus bringing the world to the brink of a thermonuclear war. Ideological statements may have quite different implications in practice.

The problem of communist strategy is connected with the question of leadership, that is, the superior right to determine both short-term and long-term priorities. The Soviet Union claims it in the name of superior experience and power. China tends to claim it in terms of an orthodox ideology and occasionally also in the name of the nonwhite races and the underdeveloped portion of the world.

The fragmentation of the communist world is self-evident. The purpose of this chapter has been to demonstrate its inevitability: Nationalism, the system of territorial states, and differences in the personality structure, temperament, background, experiences, and intelligence of the communist leaders diversified and "nationalized" as well as "personified" what used to be considered a globally valid doctrine and a reliable guide for political action.

More than half a century of communist practice in international politics seems to indicate that the communist ideology has not forced upon the Soviet Union or other communist states any policy that they could not have adopted on grounds of nonideological estimates of threats against and opportunities for their states in any given situation. Experience points to the conclusion that communist ideology has often been the basis for major decisions in *internal* politics, where realities can be forced to yield to theory. But in *international* politics, realities usually prove stronger than ideology, whether or not they are properly perceived. In some cases ideology as one of the many ingredients of foreign policy has significantly colored the decision. For instance, the ideological filter affixed to their political telescope prevented the leaders of Communist Russia from properly evaluating nazism when it appeared on the scene in the early 1930s. The Communist party of Germany was then ordered to view the Social Democrats as the primary target of attack, while the National Socialist party was viewed by the German Communists as either a secondary target or a temporary ally for the purpose of the destruction of the bourgeois Weimar Republic. Subsequently, the German Communists and the Social Democrats met in the Nazi concentration camps.

This often-quoted example of the impact of ideology on Soviet decisions should not be overstressed; early nazism was underestimated not only by the communists but also by British, American, French, and other statesmen, whose vision was said not only to be unimpaired by any ideological blinders but also to be sharpened by the free exchange of ideas.

The evidence shows that ideologies, communist ones included, do not provide the leaders with any specific guidance under a given set of circumstances. Nor do they provide their opponents with insights into the future actions of ideological systems. If instead of trying to interpret communist ideology we take the position of communists trying to interpret Western ideology and imagine, as one writer did, that Moscow has established

> an institute of Christology, manned by renegade divines and dialectical students of comparative religions, to deduce logically what President Johnson, Prime Minister Wilson, and General de Gaulle will do because they are, after all, Christians, even though they may be bad Christians, it would be little more fanciful than some of the efforts in Marxology.[34]

Returning once more to the communist doctrine, we may note that it informs its opponents and instructs its practitioners that aggressive revolutionary tactics should be timed in accord with a rising tide, and tactics of defense and even retreat timed in accord with an ebbing tide. But how can one be certain that the tide is actually rising or ebbing? In 1929, for instance, Stalin criticized another communist leader, Bukharin, who maintained that at the time the tide of international capitalism was not yet ebbing: "This question, comrades, is of decisive importance for the sections of the Comintern. Is the capitalist stabilization going to pieces or is it becoming more secure? On this the whole line of the Communist parties depends."[35] Stalin argued that it was a period of revolutionary upswing. His opponent, basing his arguments on the same doctrine, held the opposite view. Bukharin lost his argument, and subsequently, during the purges, also his head.

Looking back at Bolshevik forecasts and early hopes for world revolution, without which he could not imagine the survival of communism in Russia, Lenin, perhaps more humbly than Stalin, admitted in his address to the Ninth Soviet Congress (December 23, 1921): "Nobody, surely, foresaw or could foresee then that the situation which results, would result." Writing in *Pravda* two years later (May 23, 1923), he added:

> Napoleon, one recalls, wrote: *On s'engage, et puis on voit*. Rendered freely that means: One must first start a serious engagement and then see what happens. Well, we first started a serious engagement in November 1917 [October Revolution], and we saw such details of development . . . as the Brest-Litovsk peace, the New Economic Policy, and so on.

Communist ideology[36] does not free its leaders from the permanent task of all who are engaged in international politics—a constant evaluation, as objective as possible, of threats and opportunities, without the rigid preconceptions of a political ideology.

Notes

1. John H. Herz, "Ideological Aspects —International Relations," *International Encyclopedia of Social Sciences*. New York: Crowell-Collier-Macmillan, 1968, p. 69.
2. Karl Mannheim, *Ideology and Utopia: An Introduction to the Sociology of Knowledge*. New York: Harcourt Brace Jovanovich, 1936, pp. 192-193. Mannheim writes: "Wish images which take on a revolutionary function will become utopia . . . [that is,] that type of orientation which transcends reality and which at the same time breaks the bonds of the existing order." See also M. Rejai (ed.), *Decline of Ideology?* (Chicago: Aldine-Atherton, 1971), in particular the essays by Daniel Bell and Seymour Martin Lipset.
3. David J. Finlay, Ole R. Holsti, and Richard R. Fagen, *Enemies in Politics*. Chicago: Rand McNally, 1967, p. 48. The book also quotes John Foster Dulles telling Assistant Secretary Andrew Berding "I've done a great deal of reading on communist ideology . . . including *The Problems of Leninism* and the *Short History of the Communist Party*. This resulted in my understanding of the aim of international communism and produced a steadfast American policy in meeting that threat" (p. 45).
4. U.S. Senate, Committees on Foreign Relations and Armed Services, *Hearings*, January 15, 1957, pp. 176-77.
5. Zbigniew Brzezinski, *Ideology and Power in Soviet Politics*. New York: Praeger, 1962, p. 97.
6. Joseph V. Stalin, *Works (Sochineniya)*, Vol. 9. Moscow: State Publishing House, 1946, p. 25.
7. Vladimir I. Lenin, *Works (Sochineniya)*, Vol. 7. Moscow: State Publishing House, 1941-1951, p. 297.
8. Jerome D. Frank, *Sanity and Survival: Psychological Aspects of War and Peace*. New York: Random House, 1967, p. 131.
9. Karl W. Deutsch in his critique of W. Phillips Davison's *International Political Communication* (New York: Praeger, 1965) in the *American Political Science Review*, 62:2 (June 1968), 970.
10. Karl W. Deutsch, *Politics and Government: How People Decide Their Fate*. Boston: Houghton Mifflin, 1970, p. 9.
11. Crane Brinton, *The Anatomy of Revolution*. New York: Random House/Vintage Books, 1965, p. 48.
12. V. I. Lenin, *Selected Works*, Vol. 8. New York: International Publishers, 1943, p. 344.
13. Merle Fainsod, *How Russia Is Ruled*. Cambridge, Mass.: Harvard University Press, 1953, p. 87.
14. V. I. Lenin, *Imperialism, the Highest Stage of Capitalism*. New York: International Publishers, 1939, pp. 92-93.
15. Lenin, *Imperialism, the Highest Stage of Capitalism*, pp. 117-118.
16. Stalin, *Works*, Vol. 4, pp. 375-376.
17. Léopold Sédar Senghor, *African Socialism*. New York: Praeger, 1964, p. 47.
18. Senghor, *African Socialism*, p. 33.
19. Val R. Lorwin, "Working Class Politics and Economic Development in Western Europe," *American Historical Review*, 53:2 (January 1958), 338-351.
20. The full text may be found in William Henry Chamberlin, *The Russian Revolution*. New York: Grosset and Dunlap (Universal Library), 1965, p. 485.
21. *Russian Documents*. New York: American Association for International Conciliation, 1919, pp. 418-419.
22. Stalin, *Works*, Vol. 4, pp. 353-354. Originally published as an article in *Pravda*, October 20, 1920. In his book *Marxism and the National and Colonial Question* (London: Lawrence and Wishart, 1936, pp. 191-198) Stalin also stresses that antiimperialist revolutionary and national-liberation movements do not need a proletarian, republican, or democratic leadership and program. Thus, according to Stalin, "the struggle which the Emir of Afghanistan is waging for the independence of his country is objectively a *revolutionary* struggle, for it weakens, disintegrates and undermines imperialism, whereas the struggle waged by 'desperate democrats,' 'Socialists,' 'revolutionaries' and 'republicans' . . . during the imperialist war, was a reactionary struggle, for it resulted in the embellishment, the

reinforcement, and the victory of imperialism. For the same reason, the struggle which the Egyptian merchants and bourgeois intellectuals are waging for the independence of their country is objectively revolutionary despite the bourgeois origin and bourgeois calling of the Egyptian national movement and despite the fact that they are opposed to socialism."

23. J. V. Stalin, *Problems of Leninism* (*Voprosy Leninizma*). Moscow: State Publishing House, 1932, p. 132. The latter portion of the passage, including the reference to using armed force, is actually a quote from Lenin's analysis (August 23, 1915) of the Social Democratic slogan of the United States of Europe. The passage was newly translated by Historicus (George Allen Morgan) in "Stalin on Revolution," *Foreign Affairs*, 27:2 (January 1949), 199.

24. Historicus, "Stalin on Revolution," p. 199.

25. As quoted in Claude Buss, *The Far East*. New York: Crowell-Collier-Macmillan, 1955, p. 321.

26. Milovan Djilas, *The New Class*. New York: Praeger, 1957, p. 174.

27. See Dana Adams Schmidt, *Anatomy of a Satellite*. Boston: Little, Brown, 1952, p. 101, which contains the contents of a secret report prepared by a Czechoslovak diplomat, Arnost Heidrich, who recorded Stalin's words as follows: "The Marshall Plan will lead to a situation in which Germany would be used either as a military or an industrial base against the Soviet Union."

28. Lenin, *Works*, Vol. 24, p. 122. Also J. V. Stalin, *Problems of Leninism*, 11th ed. Moscow: State Publishing House, 1945, p. 140, and "A Reply to Ivanov," *Pravda*, February 14, 1938, p. 3. See also Historicus, "Stalin on Revolution," p. 204.

29. Stalin, *Problems of Leninism*, p. 32.

30. *New York Times*, February 15, 1956, p. 10.

31. Chen Yi, "We Must Take Risks in Anti-U.S. Fight," Peking Overseas Service Broadcast, October 15, 1965.

32. *New York Times*, June 19, 1969, p. 6.

33. Leon Trotsky, *My Life*. New York: Scribner, 1930, p. 337.

34. Norton E. Long, "Open and Closed Systems," in R. Barry Farrel (ed.), *Approaches to Comparative and International Politics*. Evanston, Ill.: Northwestern University Press, 1966, p. 165.

35. J. V. Stalin, "On the Right-Wing Deviation in CPSU (b)," *Bolshevik* (Moscow), December 1929, p. 20.

36. Compare Nathan Leites, *A Study of Bolshevism*. New York: Free Press, 1953. It is the best available and most accessible analysis of the Bolshevik doctrine as a possible *operational code* of the communist policy makers. Functionally divided, the book contains pertinent quotes from major communist books and pronouncements juxtaposed with quotes from the Russian classics (Gogol, Dostoevsky, and others) to indicate continuity or contrast. For the student of international politics the chapters on "The Range and Limits of Prediction," "Ends and Means," "Enemies," and "Retreat" are particularly useful.

Additional Readings

Additional readings on the role of ideologies in international politics may be found in *Discord and Harmony: Readings in International Politics*, edited by Ivo D. Duchacek and published by Holt, Rinehart and Winston in 1972. Chapter 9, entitled "The Role of Ideology" (pp. 181-215), contains Ole R. Holsti's case study on communist ideology as a guide for American counterpolicies under John Foster Dulles, Lenin's theory on imperialism, the Chinese condemnation of Soviet "social imperialism," and Richard J. Barnet's "The Third World: Why Do We Interfere?" See also pp. 264-286, "How World War II Came: Nazi-Soviet Cooperation, 1939-1941," as documented by the original secret dispatches exchanged between the German Embassy in Moscow and the German Ministry of Foreign Affairs in Berlin.

PART III

RESTRAINTS
Moral, Legal,
and Social
Limitations

8
Politics and Morality

Do moral considerations restrain national leaders when they determine political goals and the most effective means of achieving them? Is the presence of moral constraints constant, frequent, rare, or nonexistent? Or are the imperatives of national survival in a menacing environment so overwhelming that the survival itself becomes the highest moral value, thus making all other considerations—moral, legal, or social—secondary?

Many polemics have been written on the subject of ends and means in politics in general and in international relations in particular. Ever since men have developed their capacity to think and evaluate acts and events in abstract and relative terms, the question of the priority of individual or collective survival over other considerations has been constantly posed and debated, but so far no answer acceptable to all has emerged. It would, therefore, be more than brazenly presumptuous on our part to do more in this chapter than describe some of the major controversies about the relationship between morality and international politics.

ON ENDS AND MEANS

In any discussion on the subject of international politics and morality the central question is: Does the end, national self-preservation, justify some means that under a different set of circumstances, when survival is not the issue, would be reprehensible? Many of us have a natural inclination to answer this question with an emphatic negative. But what should our answer be if all the other nations answer with an emphatic positive?

Moral perfectionists would still maintain that, whatever the cost, ignoble means can never be justified by noble ends.

The opposite argument is that in politics desirable collective ends justify all means necessary to attain them: deception, blackmail, or violence. Those who argue this way are usually called moral cynics, callous realists, or Machiavellians.

In between the moral perfectionists and the cynics we find the allegedly most numerous group of political leaders, those who make the best compromise they can between ethical considerations and the exigencies of the situation. Arnold Wolfers calls this category "moral imperfectionists"; they make "the best moral choice the circumstances permit."[1]

Moral Perfectionists

The idealistic approach maintains that the code of universal ethics is absolute and should apply to all human actions in both the private and public realms regardless of circumstances. What is morally wrong in peace is deemed equally wrong in defense against an attack. What is reprehensible among individuals, such as lying, bullying, stealing, or killing, is equally reprehensible when practiced among nations. According to Wolfers, such moral perfectionists

> will always deny that any action that would be evil under one set of conditions could be morally justified under another. If men are held morally bound to act in accordance with an absolute ethic of love such as the Sermon on the Mount, obviously no set of circumstances in which the survival of a nation were at stake could justify acts such as a resort to violence, untruthfulness, or treaty violation.[2]

The admonitions of the Sermon on the Mount *seem* to be clear: "Resist not evil: but whosoever shall smite thee on thy right cheek, turn to him the other also. . . . And whosoever shall compel thee to go a mile, go with him twain." (Matthew 5:39-4l).

Nonresistance to evil is, then, the logical conclusion of those who have decided to follow what the famous German sociologist Max Weber called "the ethic of ultimate ends" in contradistinction to the ethic of responsibility for foreseeable consequences. In Weber's words, a man who is guided by the ethic of ultimate ends "does rightly and leaves the result with the Lord." If his action of good intent leads to bad results, "then, in the actor's eye, not he but the world, or the stupidity of other men, or God's will who made them thus, is responsible for the evil. The believer in an ethic of ultimate ends feels responsible only for seeing to it that the flame of pure intentions is not quelched.''[3] Pacifism, which leads to defenselessness and may invite aggression, does not result in guilt feelings. The fault is with the aggressor's evil mind and strength and not with the victim's vulnerability.

Moral perfectionists are not to be found where responsibility for foreseeable consequences of action or nonaction have to be shouldered; rather than in prime ministers' offices, we occasionally find moral perfectionists on the opposition benches, a position that often gives men the right to criticize in the name of lofty ideals without the responsibility for action and its consequences. Even more frequently, moral perfectionists withdraw from the world of politics altogether, seeking refuge in contemplation. Like hermits in a forest, they pray, contemplate, and hope for the best. Their hands will not be soiled by compromises with reality.

Moral Cynics

The opposite of moral absolutists are utter cynics who do not even feel pangs of conscience when determining the most effective means in relation to desirable goals—whether their goal is making the world safe for democracy, for communism, for the Aryan race, or for themselves. They often argue that a noble goal so transmutes the means that the latter become intrinsically noble themselves and not merely necessary for achieving a given end.

Perhaps the oldest known statement on the justification of any means by the need of defense against evil is contained in the ancient Indian book on the science of policy, *Arthasastra (300-200* B.C.*).* Its author, Kautilya, critically examined and then summarized several Indian political precepts thousands of years old on the subject of politics. Kautilya was not only a political thinker but a practicing administrator, politician, and diplomat. In this sense there is a close parallel between him and the sixteenth-century Florentine writer and politician Machiavelli. Kautilya was the chancellor (prime minister) of the founder of the Great Indian (Mauryan) Empire. His advice to a weak king who was threatened by a powerful aggressor teaches us how little has changed in the basic political attitudes over the past three millennia. The summary of his advice, as presented by a modern Indian scholar, is as follows:

> The weak king should adjust his policy of purchasing safety accordingly as the aggressor belongs to one or other of the three types of conquerors, namely, the righteous, the greedy, and the demoniac . . . he should meet the danger in one or the other of three ways, namely, by treaty, or by a battle of intrigue, or by an unrighteous fight. . . . Beginning with the first, Kautilya tells us how the king should as a preliminary to suing for peace cause harm to the aggressor.
> Describing the second line of policy, namely, the battle of intrigue,

Kautilya shows by concrete examples how the king should behave when his overtures for peace have failed. These refer to various methods of seducing the enemy's chief civil and military officers, assassinating the enemy-king and his officers, instigating the neighboring kings against him and destroying his stores. . . .

The third and the last line of policy, namely, treacherous fighting, comprises the king's use of fire, sword and poison against the enemy's kingdom through his secret agents. Spies in the guise of vintners or of dealers in cooked food and meat are to poison the enemy's military officers and men at camp; other spies are to poison the fodder for the enemy's elephants and horses . . . others are to destroy the enemy at his fortified refuge by fire and poisonous fumes. Other methods of treacherous fighting include burning down the wood and the grass, poisoning the water and letting out the same, digging false pits or underground tunnels in the enemy's land and attacking him at his disadvantage. . . . Kautilya devotes a whole section of his work to the employment of secret weapons. . . . He gives a long and curious list of vegetable, mineral as well as organic preparations causing instantaneous or widespread death, blindness, deafness and dumbness, madness and other diseases as well as those causing the poisoning of fodder, fuel and water.[4]

As we see, well over two thousand years ago chemical warfare was already under consideration as a morally justifiable means of defense against aggression.

In the early sixteenth century, Niccolò Machiavelli expressed his thoughts on politics in the following familiar passage:

In the actions of men, and especially princes, the end justifies the means. . . . A prudent ruler ought not to keep faith when by doing so it would be against his interest, and when the reasons which made him bind himself no longer exist. If men were all good, this precept would not be a good one; but as they are bad, and would not observe their faith with you, so you are not bound to keep faith with them. . . . A prince . . . cannot observe all those things which are considered good in men, being often obliged, in order to maintain the state, to act against faith, against charity, against humanity, and against religion. And, therefore, he must have a mind disposed to adapt itself according to the wind, and as the variations of fortune dictate, and, as I said before, not deviate from what is good, if possible, but be able to do evil if constrained. . . . Some things which seem virtues would, if followed, lead to one's ruin, and some others which appear vices result in one's greater security and well being.[5]

Terrorism In the twentieth century, another political theoretician and practitioner, the most intellectual of the Communist leaders, Leon Trotsky, justified the use of terror against the enemies of the Bolshevik revolution:

Intimidation is a powerful weapon of policy, both internationally and internally. . . . The revolution works the same way: It kills individuals, and intimidates thousands. . . . "But, in that case, in what do your tactics differ from the tactics of Czarism?" we are asked by the high priests of Liberalism. . . . You do not understand this, holy men? We shall explain it to you. The terror of Czarism was directed against the proletariat. . . . Our Extraordinary Commissions [the secret police] shoot landlords, capitalists, and generals who are striving to restore capitalism and the capitalist order. Do you grasp this—distinction? Yes? For us Communists it is quite sufficient.[6]

In 1972 the United Nations gave consideration to international terrorism, especially as practiced by Palestinian highjackers and terrorists. The Arab countries and those closely aligned with them opposed this study and suggested that the United Nations should focus not on terrorism itself, but on the underlying causes of terrorism; the implication was that the cause was the existence of the state of Israel and the extension of her controls over Palestinian Arabs. The chairman of the Legal Committee of the General Assembly, Eric Suy of Belgium, reported the results of the extensive consultation he had held with member nations on the subject of international terrorism and his report reflected the perennial problem of whether the end justifies the means. One of the basic questions presented by Suy (*New York Times*, November 10, 1972) was: "Should activities undertaken in the context of the rights of peoples to self-determination be regarded as international terrorism?" What seemed to be implied here is that terrorism on an airfield whose aim is oppression of the right of national self-determination is an evil act, but that if the aim is self-determination the character of the act has somehow changed so that the Assembly cannot deal with it as an international crime. The Arab-led majority in the General Assembly simply shelved the issue in 1973 and then again in 1974.

Relation of Means to Goals and Results Those who disagree with Kautilya, Machiavelli, and Trotsky that the end justifies any means in politics (provided that the end itself is justified) should be reminded of the fact that not only political or revolutionary leaders but also average citizens tend to relate the means to the desirable goals. If we look closely, we may discover that terms such as "good" and "evil" are frequently related more to desirable or undesirable goals than to the absolute moral quality of the action itself. Killing in individual self-defense or execution of a vicious murderer is usually not considered a crime. Intentional killing for private reasons is viewed as murder by both the jury and the public prosecutor; a head of state who had caused the death of one single man for his personal or private reasons would be treated as a common criminal. Yet the same head of state would be viewed quite differently if he had intentionally caused the death of many thousands of men by ordering them to lay down their lives in defense of the country. History might rank him among the great leaders who had saved the life of the nation by sacrificing the life of many of its sons. "Thou shalt not kill" may thus transform itself in war into "Thou shalt kill as many aggressors as possible and get a medal for it."

In this context not only an actual but also an anticipated danger may hallow any suitable defensive means. If one finds a government morally justified in opposing a treacherous attack by war, does it not follow that a government is equally if not more justified in preventing or minimizing expected aggression, actual attacks, or blackmail by less evil means than mass killing in war (such as subversion of the aggressor's political, economic, or military system, breaking solemn pledges, bluffing, counterblackmail, spying, or lying).[2] In his memoirs, Dag Hammarskjöld, the former secretary-general of the United Nations and a deeply religious man, posed the question of lying for the sake of truth: 'The most dangerous of all moral dilemmas: when we are obliged to conceal the truth to help the truth to be victorious. If this should at any time become our duty in the role assigned us by fate, how strait must be our path at all times, if we are not to perish.'[7]

In addition to the goal also the result—success or failure—often determines our attitudes toward dubious means. A government that has intentionally deceived its citizens and so caused them harm may be toppled by an indignant population at the next election or revolution. The real issue is not the lie but the harm done. If, on the other hand, a government has intentionally lied to the national enemy, a course of action that necessitated lying to its own people about the intended measures, and if by doing so aggression has been deterred, citizens will praise their government for its wise statesmanship. Similarly, praise is usually in order when a government lies to its people in order to prevent stock-market speculation on the eve of a necessary currency reform. However much we may deplore the fact, in the eyes of the general public success tends to hallow many a debatable means, while failure, on the contrary, sharply illuminates all the ingredients of an erroneous decision, including the decision maker's misperception or stupidity, but not his immorality. The question has been often posed, How many people would have referred to the American involvement in Vietnam as "immoral," had the war been much shorter, less costly, and, above all, successful.

The above observations on the actual behavior of governments and the value judgments of citizens represent a very sharp contrast to the admonitions of the Sermon on the Mount. The gap between the idealistic concept of absolute commands of ethics, regardless of circumstances, and the cynical concept of the relativity of all values appears unbridgeable.

Indian Philosophers

The impasse between idealism and cynicism led some ancient Indian philosophers and many of their successors to the conclusion that politics and ethics are, and should be viewed as, completely separate domains. Politics cannot be moralized. He who attempts it either fails, becomes a hypocrite, or goes mad. The nature of existence—and of politics—is struggle, and what is natural, some Indian philosophers argued, cannot be censored. Commenting on the Hindu epic *Mahabharata* (1500-1000 B.C.), which is some 24,000 verses long, the modern Indian philosopher K. Satchidananda Murty notes that "no Hindue thinker regarded it possible to moralize statecraft. Either one should choose to be in it and ignore ethics. Or if one wholly wants to be ethical, he must remain aloof from statecraft."[8] This is reminiscent of Hans Morgenthau's controversial statement that the very fact of acting in politics destroys one's moral integrity. The Hindu epic does raise the question, Why practice politics if one has to ignore ethics? And how does politics really differ from other immoral activities such as robbery? One type of answer suggests that politics must be based on empirical knowledge and the logic of facts, about which the scriptures have nothing to say. Another type of answer, also to be found in *Mahabharata,* suggests that the king and the state are above morality: "There must be no hesitation to kill anybody, whether a relative or friend, for achieving one's ends. Without cruelty kings cannot attain felicity."[9]

One Indian solution to the problem of the conflict between ethics and politics is the separation of the two by a neat division of specialized roles in society. This is part of the Hindu caste system, which divides all the Aryans into four occupational "guilds": the caste of the rulers (Kshatriyas), the caste of priests (Brahmins), the caste of the merchants (Vaisyas), and the caste of the manual workers (Sudras). The caste of rulers was given by birth and the scriptures the duty of engaging in domestic and international politics. The rulers' duty to fight, defend, or conquer was inescapable and preordained. They were thus placed above morality. It could not be immoral for them to justify their means by political ends.

This type of solution by specialization seems, at first sight, so typically Hindu and so closely connected with the caste system that one can hardly imagine its transplantation into other cultures. Yet, on second thought, the Western double standard with regard to a given act, undertaken by some individuals for private gain and by others for public interest, approximates the convenient Hindu division of roles in society.

The division of labor, however, did not absolve the ancient Hindu "political scientists" from their duty of advising the ethically pure priests what to do when even they were confronted with a wicked world. Some Indian writers forbade the Brahmin priests to take up a weapon even for the purpose of examining it; other authors authorized the Brahmins to use weapons for the specific purposes of self-defense, preventing the intermixture of castes, and protecting the sacred cow and wedded wives. The end could hallow the means, as it were.

Moral Imperfectionists

While we have placed idealists and cynics on opposite poles of the political spectrum, we have now clearly reached the point in our analysis at which they are no longer so far apart. A realist with some pangs of conscience and an idealist ready sometimes to compromise represent intermediate positions where one concept imperceptibly slips into another. The number of positions between moral perfectionists and cynics seems to be infinite. Even Machiavelli, whose name is now connected with utter moral cynicism, admonished leaders to be moral when they can, and commit evil only when they must. Thus, even a most pressing necessity to resist evil (which cannot be eliminated altogether from our wicked world) does not push the selection of means beyond the pale of moral judgment. Kautilya, while recommending quite horrible methods of resistance to evil, could not help describing the means as "unrighteous" or "treacherous," thus clearly slipping into the domain of moral judgments.

Is "moral perfectionism" less frequent among statesmen than among individuals, who in their private behavior and action, tend to be more ethical? Are there then *two* moral codes, one for the statesmen, and another one for the citizens, as Machiavelli seemed to argue? Not at all, answers Wolfers, and suggests that

> politics conducted in a multistate system is not necessarily any more immoral than average private behavior . . . the chief difference pertains . . . to the circumstances under which men are required to act. Much of what strikes people as the immoral practices of governments may prove to be morally justified by the peculiar and unhappy circumstances that the statesman has to face and, as a rule, cannot hope to change.[10]

A political leader, according to the German philosopher Fichte, does not even have the right to presuppose the goodness and perfection of men. He is and must feel responsible for foreseeable results of his individual action. One of the most frequently quoted passages from Max Weber's *Politics as a Vocation* warns all of those who engage in politics (and we may add those who engage in the study of international politics):

> No ethic in the world can dodge the fact that in numerous instances the attainment of good is bound to the fact that one must be willing to pay the price of using morally dubious means or at least dangerous ones—and facing the possibility or even the probability of evil ramification. From no ethics in the world can it be concluded when and to what extent the ethically good purpose "justifies" the ethically dangerous means and ramifications. . . . The proponent of an ethic of absolute ends cannot stand up under the ethical irrationality of the world. . . .
>
> He who seeks the salvation of the soul, of his and others, should not seek it along the avenue of politics, for the quite different tasks of politics

can only be solved by violence. The genius or demon of politics lives in inner tension with the god of love, as well as with the Christian God as expressed by the church. This tension can at any time lead to an irreconcilable conflict. . . . Machiavelli . . . has one of his heroes praise the citizens who deemed the greatness of their native city higher than the salvation of their souls.[11]

CHOOSING AN ETHICAL CODE

References to Hindu ethics and the Christian Bible should remind us of the obvious facts that more than one code of ethics exists. Our previous analysis of the strength of nationalism suggested the absence of universally accepted standards of behavior. Is there, then, such a thing as a universal code of ethics that could be applied to foreign policies and to the actions of different nations?

While men and nations label their decisions and acts either moral or immoral, the value system on which they base their judgments is an extremely varied one.

In the second half of the nineteenth century the French statesman Walewski (a natural son of Napoleon I and adviser to Napoleon III) allegedly told the Prussian leader Otto von Bismarck: "It is a business of a diplomat to cloak the interests of his country in the language of universal justice." Hypocrisy apart, Walewski probably had the Judeo-Christian concept of justice in mind. But there are other concepts of universal justice. Some statesmen are inspired by Islam, which, in the Koran, still teaches constant warfare on the infidel; in 1974 some observers might have argued that Islamic morality did not represent a restraint but a source of justification for aggressive policies as recommended by the religiously motivated leader of Libya, Colonel Muammar el-Qaddafi. We have already noted the ambivalent message contained in Hinduism. One of the Indian leaders, Gandhi, read into Hinduism the inspiring message of passive resistance (see Document 8.1); his successors placed the security interests of the Indian nation above everything else and initiated military actions in order to obtain the colonial enclave of Goa from Portugal in 1961 and facilitate the separation of Bangladesh from Pakistan in 1972. Despite the similarity of their names, a great political abyss evidently separates Mahatma Gandhi from Prime Minister Indira Gandhi, who in 1974 transformed India into the sixth nuclear power.

Morality and Ideology

If a statesman's concept of his nation's vital interests, his commitment to a political ideology such as communism, socialism, democracy, or fascism, and his code of ethics point in the same direction, there is no problem as to what to do; a statesman then can do what is required by his nation's needs, his ideological commitment, and his

DOCUMENT 8.1

GANDHI'S PASSIVE RESISTANCE
AND INDIA'S DEFENSE

Kings will always use their kingly weapons. To use force is bred in them. They want to command; but those who have to obey commands do not want guns, and these are in a majority throughout the world. They have to learn either body-force or soul-force. . . .

When I refuse to do a thing that is repugnant to my conscience, I use soul-force. . . . If by using violence, I force the government to repeal a law, I am employing what may be termed body-force. If I do not obey the law, and accept the penalty for its breach, I use soul-force. It involves sacrifice of self.

Passive resistance is a method of securing rights by personal suffering. It is the reverse of resistance by arms. . . . Wherein is courage required—in blowing others to pieces from behind the cannon, or with a smiling face to approach a cannon and be blown to pieces?

From Gandhi's pamphlet on Indian Home Rule, written in 1909.

Even after Gandhi completely abjured violence he was honest enough to see that in war it is usually necessary to take sides. He did not—indeed, since his whole political life centered round the struggle for national independence, he could not—take the sterile and dishonest line of pretending that in every war both sides are exactly the same and it makes no difference who wins. Nor did he, like most Western pacifists, specialize in avoiding awkward questions. In relation to the late war, one question every pacifist had a clear obligation to answer was: "What about the Jews? Are you prepared to see them exterminated? If not, how do you propose to save them without resorting to war?"

From George Orwell, "Reflections on Gandhi," 1949.

The explosion of a nuclear device by China has shocked peace-loving people all over the world. . . . To strengthen India's defenses a five-year defense plan, covering the years 1964-1968, is being implemented. New divisions are being raised and equipped according to schedule. . . .

From a speech by Dr. Radhakrishnan, president of India, famous philosopher, and Gandhi's associate, at the budget session of the Indian Parliament, February 17, 1965, *India News.*

conscience. But what should one do when national survival points in one direction, ideology in another, and the moral code in still a different one? Our previous discussion has indicated that more often than not the leader's concept of his nation's interest tends to prevail over both ideological and moral considerations.

The distinction between morality, on the one hand, and ideology or nationalism, on the other, is, however, quite arbitrary. In the context of this chapter we have focused on those creeds that their adherents deem generally separate from or even opposite to political ideologies or nationalism. Such "nonpolitical" codes of ethics are primarily concerned with the "inner man," man's conscience, or, in terms of otherworldly religions like Christianity, Judaism, Hinduism, Islam, and Buddhism, with man's good behavior here on earth as a preparation for another life. Moral codes address their messages to the *conscience* of an individual rather than providing guidance for collectivities of men and their internal and foreign policies.

In discussing the role of morality in international politics three problems should therefore be emphasized:

1. Many an ideology, as a program for political and social action, is viewed by its adherents as *the* code of ethics. Lenin, for instance, described communism as the "highest form of morality," placed above and superseding such a bourgeois code of ethics as religion, which, according to Lenin, is a reflection and a tool of class society.

2. The same process that has placed an ideology on the highest rung of the ladder of moral values applies also to nationalism with its concomitant concept of national interest and its defense: Many people consider national self-preservation the highest moral value, to which all the other values are subordinated. What other values can be expected to survive, they ask, if the leaders, the trustees of the national destiny, allow the nation and its state to be enslaved or erased? Raymond Aron writes: "No prince is entitled to make his nation the Christ among nations. A nation which seeks to live, hence which asserts a will to power among nations, is not thereby immoral."[12]

Furthermore, in our world, divided as it is into nations, men are reared in different national traditions and ethical concepts; they live different lives, think different thoughts, and, as a consequence, tend to make different value judgments. Men living in misery and illiteracy and searching for new political and ethical codes of action are bound to have a different hierarchy of values than men who, for instance, share the same Judeo-Christian ethos and live in relative prosperity and stability in northwestern Europe and North America. Kenneth Thompson has noted that

> for men and for nations, the universal practice is to justify every evil measure by claiming it serves an ethical goal. . . . For Stalin the gross brutality of liquidating the kulaks found justification as an inevitable step in the history-fulfilling Communist design; for Hitler the cremation of so-called inferior races was excused as a necessary hygienic measure if Teutonic superiority were to continue unimpaired. Since nations in the present anarchic world society tend to be repositories of their own morality, the end-means formula has prevailed as an answer to the moral dilemma, for undeniably it is a concealed but essential truth that nations tend to create their own morality.[13]

3. Various *personal* interpretations of what a particular moral code permits and what it prohibits further complicate our task when we try to

estimate the restraining influence of morality on policy making. The problem of personal interpretation of an ideology has already been discussed in Chapter 7; there it was noted that an interpretation of a political belief system often depends on the leader's personality structure, background, experience, position of responsibility, age, health, and intelligence. These variables should also be borne in mind when it comes to a leader's interpretation of a moral code; here, too, the ambiguity of ethical codes contributes to the frequency of contradictory interpretations. Even the Sermon on the Mount, as we shall see, has been interpreted in diametrically opposite ways by various Christian statesmen as well as theologians.

Moreover, the basic Christian concept of love and peace has been conceptually combined with that of a just war (*bellum justum*) to defend against inflicted or threatened injury. Even the great medieval pacifist, Erasmus (1469-1536), approved "just, defensive wars"; nevertheless, he advised the clergy not to grant burial in consecrated ground to those who died in battle and insisted that wars not be initiated by leaders unless the whole people had fully and unanimously consented to it. A similar stress on the justification of defense has been noted in connection with Hinduism. If some circumstances justify a *defensive* use of violence, then the controversy, often imperceptibly, shifts from the contents of a moral code to the political question of who determines, and how accurately he determines, the nature of the *absolute necessity* that justifies inflicting injury on another collectivity of men. In controversies following an action that failed, men often label as "immoral" what, in fact, could be viewed as "misperceived" or "unwise" since it proved patently unsuccessful.

The Bible: A Political Guide?

In Christianity, the many interpretations of the message of the Bible and its relation to politics form a broad spectrum ranging from Tolstoian nonresisters to interventionists, from integral pacifists, Quakers, and Jehovah's Witnesses to high-church Protestants and Roman Catholics, who occasionally feel authorized by the same scripture to bless the instruments of war.

Three major sources of disagreement concerning the Bible are particularly relevant:

1. Does the Bible address itself to individuals or to the collectivities and their leaders? Some theologians argue that the precepts on the subject of ethics contained in the Bible are addressed to individuals and not collectivities. The Protestant theologian Reinhold Niebuhr differentiates

> . . . between the moral and social behavior of individuals and of social groups, national, racial, and economic; and this distinction justifies and necessitates political policies which a purely individualistic ethic must

always find embarrassing. . . . There is an increasing tendency among modern men to imagine themselves ethical because they delegated their vices to larger and larger groups. . . . All men are naturally inclined to obscure the morally ambiguous elements in their political cause by investing it with religious sanctity. This is why religion is more frequently a source of confusion than of light in the political realm.[14]

Similarly, a Jesuit political scientist, Joseph C. McKenna, concludes that the Sermon on the Mount, often cited as categorically condemning all resort to violence,

... in all literalness was addressed to individual persons in their individual capacities, not social collectivities or social leaders as such. Its admonitions . . . do not necessarily imply, therefore, that the statesman and his nation are morally obliged to sacrifice every other consideration and advantage for the sake of peace. The Sermon's advices must, in fact, be harmonized with the quite different indications which appear elsewhere in Scripture. Among these is the minatory dictum of St. Paul: "But if thou dost what is evil, fear, for not without reason does [the public power] carry the sword. For it is God's minister, an avenger to execute wrath on him who does evil" (Rom. 13:4). While this is directly relevant only to social order, it does bestow a position of moral quality upon coercive power in official hands. The interpreter of Scripture must confront, then, with caution even the incisive prohibition in the decalogue: "Thou shalt not kill."[15]

2. Does the Bible prohibit the use of coercion? Here, again, as already implied in the previous quotation, the answer is negative. According to Niebuhr, when collective power such as imperialism or class domination exploits weakness, it can never be dislodged unless power is raised against it. Similarly, McKenna, the Roman Catholic priest, stresses:

Horrifying though the vision be, inhumane and unchristian though war seem, some segments of mankind still find a promise of gain in the use of threat or force. As long as this is so, the other segments of mankind must deal with a temptation of their own—to cancel out coercion's promise with a menace of counter coercion. It is this which raises the moral question: Are war and threat of war legitimate, and under what circumstances?[16]

McKenna's answer is that war, even initiation of a war against an anticipated threat, can be morally justified. The right of defense is clearly recognized although it is not absolute: "it may be exercised only if action is urgently needed and no other remedy is at hand; only so much violence is allowed as will repel the unjust aggressor."[17]

The evaluation of the urgent need, the unavailability of other remedies, and the amount of necessary violence are in themselves controversial issues. (See the discussion on Hiroshima at the end of this chapter.) In practice they may not be related to the moral issue itself but to the accuracy and wisdom of the leader's estimate of circumstances and to his choice of the most effective and the least value-destructive measures.

As to the moral issues, both the Protestant minister and the Catholic priest reject the integral pacifism of the Christian groups that invoke the same scripture in defense of their program. Specifically, Reinhold Niebuhr condemns pacifism as Christian heresy:

> If we cannot accept the simple hopes of the pacifists, it is not because we have eliminated Christ from our convictions or decisions. It is because we interpret life, man, history, and even God and Christ in different terms than some of our brethren. We believe that evil in man is more stubborn, that life and history are more tragic, and that the God who is revealed in Christ is more terrible in His judgments than is envisaged in sentimentalized versions of the Christian faith. The pacifists do not know human nature well enough to be concerned about the contradictions between the law of love and the sin of man, until sin has conceived and brought forth death. They do not see that sin introduces an element of conflict into the world and that even the most loving relations are not free from it. . . . It is because men are sinners that justice can be achieved only by a certain degree of coercion on the one hand, and by resistance to coercion and tyranny, on the other.[18]

3. Is the use of force always a sin? On this issue, McKenna opposes the Protestant concept of the inevitability of sin. It is not a lesser evil but an actual good to oppose evil, if need be, by force, says the Jesuit priest. He concludes in a direct polemic with Niebuhr:

> Reinhold Niebuhr, adapting classic Lutheran theology, finds man necessitated to sin, not only by the intrinsic corruption of human nature but also by the extrinsic dilemmas of the social milieu. For the Scholastic [Catholic], by contrast, sin is never inevitable; an act of self-defense or an act of vindictive justice [which may lead to offensive war], although imposed by circumstances which are regrettable, is morally good. This conclusion may be censured as leading to an easy identification of selfish national interest with high moral purpose. Yet the doctrine may actually be more humanizing than the other, bleaker, views. It holds conscience to account, first for the reason, then for the measure, of violence—instead of giving over the moral agent to the uninhibited hopelessness which often follows from seeing sin as unavoidable. . . . For the Catholic thinker war is not the lesser of two evils, but the lesser of two goods (one of which appears, at the moment of choice, unattainable). . . . Catholic thinkers believe that war can be morally justified in the light of both reason and revelation. Given the contemporary international setting, this judgment is to all intents and purposes valid only for defensive action.[19]

MORAL VALUES AND NATIONAL INTEREST

Should we now completely discard moral values as possible restraints on foreign policy? We do not believe we should. While it is impossible to measure the magnitude of the commitment of both the leaders and the masses to a moral code whose unavoidable ambiguity has been noted, the perceived morality or immorality of a state's action represents at least one component that policy makers take into account when determining the meaning of national interest and the means of maximizing it. Moral values are part of the foreign-policy decision-making process for two reasons:

First, some leaders are more committed to their personal, national, or transnational code of ethics than others. Even if they are "moral imperfectionists," they may prefer to act in accordance with this code if they can. And the evaluation of "if they can" may expand or shrink the range of what they consider they must do.

Second, concern for a given code of ethics may color the contents and influence the methods of policy because it is sometimes *expedient* to make political decisions conform to moral standards. Objecting to the realists and their preoccupation with the search for power (Morgenthau), and recommending that idealism in foreign policy be maintained, Robert Endicott Osgood included the argument of "expediency of morality," stressing that

> . . . ideals are as much an instrument of national power as the weapons of war. . . . The strength of America's moral reputation and the persuasiveness of the American mission are as vital a factor in power equation as planes, ships, and tanks. . . . Ideals and self-interest are so closely interdependent that even on grounds of national expediency, there are cogent arguments for maintaining the vitality of American idealism. . . . The effectiveness of the American foreign policy depends heavily upon winning the moral and intellectual allegiance of vast numbers of people in the throes of social and nationalistic revolution.[20]

Cynical leaders sometimes pretend they act morally so as not to antagonize the moral standard of those whose support, domestically and internationally, they deem necessary for the pursuit of their policies. It should be recalled that policy makers can effectively act on the international scene only if a sufficient number of people—both the elites and the masses—in their own as well as other national communities feel able to identify with their policies or at least do not feel obligated to oppose actively their choices of goals and means. This is why in our era of worldwide contacts and mass communications "moral" postures in international politics may often be publicly adopted for utterly cynical reasons.

Some observers tend to translate this phenomenon into the comforting thought that at least in this subtle and quite indirect way ethical standards influence international behavior. In his polemic against Morgenthau's concept of national interest and opposition to policy based on moral abstractions, Robert W. Tucker noted that there was, unseen by the realists with Professor Morgenthau at their helm, an

> empirical proof that awareness of the existence of universal moral principles having a definite content existed. It can be seen in the almost daily protestations of foreign offices that their conduct, but not that of their opponents, is in conformity with recognized principles of international morality.

Tucker, however, had to add the following caution: "That these principles are not very effective in regulating the conduct of states is still another question."[21]

It should also be noted that moral arguments may often be only an expression of self-deception. The capacity of men to rationalize their behavior, that is, to interpret in such a manner as to make it seem just and reasonable, is frighteningly great. Man incessantly seeks to compromise with his conscience or with his innate humanitarianism by rationalizing his predatory behavior. He must convince himself that the act of grabbing is somehow noble and beautiful, that he can rape in righteousness and murder in magnanimity. He insists upon playing the game, not only with an ace up his sleeve, but with the smug conviction that God has put it there.[22]

Otto Klineberg views this description of the mechanism of rationalizing bad into good as perhaps extreme; nevertheless, he cannot resist adding a slightly cynical definition of his own: Rationalization, he writes, is "giving good reasons instead of true ones, since the true reasons are never good, and the good reasons are never true."[23]

Although the adoption or rejection of many policies is often justified by the use of moral arguments, a close examination of the real motives for a particular course of action will reveal that the decision had been reached on other than moral grounds. Moral justification was added simultaneously or later. Often, as policy makers may discover with a sigh of relief, what is practical may also be viewed as ethical. The great powers abstained from using gas in World War II because they had found a better way to destroy each other rather than because of their concern for ethics or international law.

SEVEN CONTROVERSIES OF WORLD WAR II

How difficult it is to avoid rationalization and to evaluate properly a political action on either moral or ideological grounds may be demonstrated by the following seven case studies. They represent the major controversies that characterized the preparation, conduct, and conclusion of World War II and they were all marked by life-or-death situations. They are typical of the realities to be faced on the international scene because they represent, singly and collectively, a labyrinth of intertwined and conflicting values as well as perceptions and misperceptions of the situation and available options. The actual decisions were debated not only on moral and ideological grounds but also on practical, nonideological, and amoral grounds. In his *Discourses* Machiavelli would perhaps advise on all of them:

> Where the very safety of the country depends upon the resolution to be taken, no considerations of justice or injustice, humanity or cruelty, nor of glory or of shame, should be allowed to prevail. But putting all other considerations aside, the only question should be: What course will save the life and liberty of the country?[24]

Exactly five hundred years later, a Catholic priest, the Most Reverend Pierre Boillon, Bishop of Verdun, declared at a conference of 120 bishops held at Lourdes in 1968:

> Personally, I have killed. I killed four Germans. I try to justify myself before God but I did not accuse myself at confession of a sin. I had a conflict of duty of defending my country [Boillon was a Resistance commander during the German occupation of France] and that of respecting human life. Killing those Germans was evil but not a sin. . . . If somebody came to me in confession and told me he had killed Hitler, I would tell him to go out and commit a sin so as to have something to confess.[25]

Whether one rejects or agrees with Machiavelli and Boillon one may find it instructive—and quite disturbing—to imagine oneself in the position of a wartime decision maker in the seven cases described here and to try to decide each issue in one's own mind, not with the benefit of hindsight but in the context of the limited knowledge then available about the consequences of the decisions and the final turn of international events.

Case I: The Munich Settlement

In September 1938, England and France decided to sacrifice the territorial integrity and security of their ally Czechoslovakia by approving the surrender of its strategic territories, inhabited by the Sudeten Germans, to Nazi Germany. The British prime minister, Neville Chamberlain, believed that in this way peace could be saved for a generation. It was not. War started one year later, in September 1939; Munich was therefore condemned as a folly of appeasement. The lack of wisdom of the Munich decision seemed clear, at least to many. Yet, twenty-four years later, reminiscing on the subject of Munich in the London *Observer* (September 16, 1962), Sir Alec Douglas-Home, Britian's foreign secretary in 1962 (and again after the Conservative victory in June 1970), said:

> I was in favor of the Munich settlement. At the time I still thought Hitler might not be a madman, might be diverted from war, and I thought time must be gained to bring him to reason. I thought it was the best settlement

possible given the state of public opinion and popular feeling in this country at the time. You couldn't have got this country to fight in 1939 if they hadn't felt that they'd gone the limit and beyond in 1938. British public opinion is like that. I think we have learned our lesson, though. I don't think we would feel it necessary now to let another potential aggressor go half so far before we felt justified in telling him to back-pedal.

What about the moral issue, if any? Munich was condemned by many not only as unwise but also as immoral, because twelve million Czechs and Slovaks were sacrificed so that West Europe could live in peace. What would have been the judgment of history had the slavery of twelve million Czechs and Slovaks ensured the life and prosperity of many times their numbers in the world? What if Hitler had been murdered soon after Munich? What if the West had so increased its power that Hitler would never have dared another conquest after Czechoslovakia?

Case II: The Soviet-Nazi Pact

On the night of August 23, 1939, Stalin and Hitler's foreign minister, Ribbentrop, concluded the famous Soviet-Nazi Pact. It was publicly announced as a treaty on nonaggression; in reality it was an agreement on annexations. Poland was to be completely erased from the map of Europe by the German annexation of its western half and by the Russian annexation of its eastern half. In addition, the Soviet Union was later to annex the three Baltic states, Estonia, Latvia, and Lithuania, as well as two Rumanian provinces, Bessarabia and northern Bukovina. Implicitly, the Soviet Union was also to recognize the Munich agreement and its consequences, that is, the liquidation of the Czechoslovak state. When, on March 15, 1939, the Nazi Reich annexed Bohemia, Moravia, and the western half of Czechoslovakia, Slovakia was transformed into a pro-Nazi puppet state and Ruthenia was annexed by Hungary. In the fall of 1939 the Soviet Union recognized the Nazi Slovak state, thus confirming the dismemberment and disappearance of Czechoslovakia from the Soviet-Nazi version of the map of Europe.

Communist propaganda tried first to justify the Soviet-Nazi agreement as a service to European peace. The organ of the French Communist party, *L'Humanité*, explained to its readers that the pact was a "major contribution to the cause of peace among nations." The shock was most severe for European and American Communists. The literary editor of the American communist magazine *The New Masses*, Granville Hicks, pinpointed the date of his leaving the party as August 23, 1939, when he heard the radio announce the Soviet-Nazi accord. "Jesus Christ, that knocks the bottom out of everything," he said to his wife. (His remark is recorded in his autobiography, *Part of the Truth*, published in 1965.) On the part of many Russian Communists the reaction was similar; in his memoirs Nikita Khrushchev wrote

> I think the vast majority of the Party considered the signing of the treaty
> tactically wise, even though nobody could say so publicly. We couldn't
> even discuss the treaty at Party meetings. It was very hard for us—as
> Communists, as antifascists—to accept the idea of joining forces with
> Germany. It would have been impossible to explain it to the man in the
> street.[26]

One can only speculate what might have been the feelings toward the
Soviet-Nazi Pact of German and German-Jewish communists who by the
time the pact was negotiated had already spent five years in Nazi
concentration camps. The Nazi archives, captured by the English and
American armies at the end of the war, described the cordiality prevailing
between the Nazis and the communists at the Kremlin in their jokes and
toasts. "In the course of the conversation," one secret Nazi memorandum
reports, "Herr Stalin spontaneously proposed a toast to the Fuehrer, as
follows: 'I know how much the German nation loves its Fuehrer; I should
therefore like to drink to his health.' "[27] The German and Jewish
communists, however, were to remain in the concentration, labor, or
extermination camps.

When the war started nine days after the conclusion of the pact, the
September issue of *Comintern* justified the Soviet need for improved
relations with the Nazi Reich by pointing out that the pact simply meant
"additional years of construction and peace for the Soviet Union." It
concluded that "the touchstone in determining the faithfulness and
frankness of the labor organizations was their attitude towards the Soviet
Union." The implication was that there would be little hope for
communism in France, England, or Germany if the only communist power
in existence, the Soviet Union, were to be dragged prematurely into war
and thus weakened. The Soviet decision to sit back quietly until Nazi
Germany and the Western powers would mutually exhaust each other on
the western front was implicitly presented as a master stroke for world
communism.

No doubt some communists were able to rationalize the pact, the
cordiality that accompanied it, and the subsequent European war as
necessary ingredients of a policy aimed at "making the world safe for
communism." Perhaps some German, Jewish, French, and Polish
communists were even able to rationalize their sufferings and deaths at the
hands of the Nazis as inevitable sacrifices in the interest of the broader
goals of world communism. In the same way some communists found it
possible in the 1930s to regard their confessions to crimes they had never
committed and the resulting death sentences during the Moscow purge
trials as their last services to the cause of communism.

Many doubts and apprehensions among the communists caused by the
Soviet-Nazi cooperation of 1939 were abruptly ended on June 21, 1941,
when the Nazi armies attacked the Soviet Union. Everything seemed to be
clear again: One could be communist, nationalist, and pro-Soviet all at the

same time—a rare occurrence in the world communist movement in its first two decades.

Was there any *moral* issue involved when the Nazis and the Soviet Communists first agreed on erasing Poland from the map of Europe? Was one side more justified than the other? What role, if any, did ideology play in the matter? On May 30, for instance, the German ambassador in Moscow, Schulenburg, was informed by the permanent secretary in the German Foreign Office, Weizäcker, of the contents of his conversation with Astakhov, the Soviet chargé d'affaires in Berlin, as follows:

> I asked the Chargé, Astakhov, to see me today. The Soviet request for further continuance of their trade mission at Prague as a branch of the trade mission [in Berlin] provided the starting point of our conversation. . . . I recalled to the Chargé certain conversations . . . about the possibility of . . . further improvement of Russo-German political relations. . . . I said that in my personal opinion Germany was not narrow-minded as respects Soviet Russia but also not importunate. Communism would continue to be rejected by us, while we, on the other hand, expected no affection for National Socialism from Moscow. The Chargé emphasized strongly in that connection the possibility of a very clear separation between principles governing internal policy on the one hand and the attitude adopted in foreign policy on the other.[28]

This interesting proposal for separating ideologies (as the only valid and guiding principles for domestic purposes) from the realities on the international scene, where, by mutual agreement, they should not be allowed to play any disturbing role was, of course, not novel in the history of international relations. A similar separation of internal concepts from foreign-policy considerations has characterized many international compacts between conflicting ideological systems in the past, just as it now underlies the current concept and practice of peaceful coexistence. The United States, for instance, has combined with Imperial Japan in World War I, with Communist Russia in World War II, with Latin-American dictators, with Communist Yugoslavia and authoritarian Spain, Portugal, and Greece, in the 1950s and 1960s, and with the USSR and Communist China in the 1970s. Soviet Russia, on the other hand, has combined with the German Weimar Republic (1919-1933), capitalist England, France, and Czechoslovakia (1935-1938), America (1941-1945), and Egypt and other authoritarian Arab countries whose treatment of native communists was far from tender.

The ideological truce (see Figure 8.1 for Low's famous cartoon on this subject) formed the basis of the Soviet-Nazi cooperation until June 21, 1941, when Germany invaded Russia. Then—a typical case—the ideological conflict was suddenly invoked again and formed the opening paragraph in the German formal declaration of war, which was handed by the German

FIGURE 8.1
THE NAZI-SOVIET PACT

"Rendezvous."

Drawing by David Low, 1941. By permission of the Trustees and The London
Evening Standard.

foreign minister, Ribbentrop, to the Soviet ambassador in Berlin and
simultaneously by the German ambassador in Moscow to the Soviet
foreign minister, Molotov. A portion of the German coded cable, marked
"For the Ambassador personally—VERY URGENT—STATE SECRET," reads
as follows:

> The Soviet Ambassador in Berlin is receiving at this hour from the Reich
> Minister for Foreign Affairs a memorandum giving in detail the facts
> which are briefly summarized as follows:
> In 1939 the Government of the Reich, putting aside grave objections
> arising out of the contradiction between National Socialism and
> Bolshevism, undertook to arrive at an understanding with Soviet Russia.
> Under the treaties of August 23 and September 28, 1939, the Government
> of the Reich effected a general reorientation of its policy toward the USSR
> and thenceforth adopted a cordial attitude toward the Soviet Union. . . .
> The Government of the Reich therefore felt entitled to assume that
> thenceforth both nations, while respecting each other's regime and not
> interfering in the internal affairs of the other partner, would arrive at good,
> lasting, neighborly relations. Unfortunately it soon became evident that
> the Government of the Reich had been entirely mistaken in this
> assumption.[29]

Early the next morning the Nazi attack on Russia began, and in a few days the German armies penetrated deep into the Soviet Union, which was evidently taken by surprise and was ill-prepared for the onslaught.

As to the Soviet-Nazi Pact of 1939, now a scrap of paper, there still remains the question, Even if deemed ideologically or morally doubtful, was it, from the Russian point of view, wise? The Soviet leadership has never condemned the short-lived collaboration with the Nazis, even though it did criticize Stalin on almost all other accounts. The argument in favor of the pact usually is that it obtained two years of peace for Russia and therefore increased its readiness for the allegedly anticipated defense against Germany. A different conclusion may be deduced from the German confidential documents that the British and American forces captured. When analyzed the secret decision-making processes of Russia and Germany reveal three basic misperceptions on the part of the Soviet leadership in 1939:

1. Stalin and his associates counted on the war in the west to be long and costly. "As long as the world carnage continues over there in the West," said Lenin on June 21, 1918 (a strange coincidence of dates), "we are secure."[30] No doubt, the Russian Communist leader was basically right in his calculation, according to which the new revolutionary regime in Russia would be safe as long as the mutual bloodletting between the capitalist powers on the western front lasted. Thinking in historical analogy, Stalin might have hoped in 1939 that a "world carnage over there in the West"would again give his country four or more additional years of peace and military buildup. His hopes for a long protracted war on the western front collapsed ten months later when France was defeated by Germany in a six-week campaign. The anti-French pique manifested by Stalin during and immediately after the war may be partly explained by the fact that he had never quite forgiven France for her inconsiderate upsetting of his 1939 calculations.

2. Stalin overestimated the possibility of harmonizing through diplomacy his own and German territorial ambitions in Eastern Europe—Rumania, Bulgaria, the Balkans, and Finland—and in the Middle East.

3. Finally, Stalin, like everybody else, underestimated Hitler's political cunning and military insatiability.

These are some of the reasons the Nazi attack came as a complete surprise to Stalin and why it took some time before he could bring himself to believe it had actually occurred.

According to his daughter, Svetlana Alliluyeva, Stalin's "immense miscalculation" was responsible for both his deep depression at the start of the war and his extreme revengefulness toward the Germans during and after the war:

"We'll show them how to gut people!" he would say malevolently of the Germans—those same Germans with whom he had wanted so to be in a long, solid alliance. He had not guessed or foreseen that the pact of 1939, which he had considered the outcome of his own great cunning, would be broken by an enemy more cunning than himself. This was the real reason for his deep depression at the start of the war. It was his immense miscalculation. Even after the war was over he was in the habit of repeating: "Ech, together with the Germans we would have been invincible."[31]

Case III: The British Alliance with Communist Russia

After June 21, 1941, the first day of the Nazi attack against the USSR, England had to decide quickly whether it should view the Soviet dictator as an ally against Nazi Germany. There was not a moment of hesitation or embarrassment on the part of the former crusader against bolshevism, Winston Churchill.[32] Whatever Churchill's feelings might have been in 1917, he now warmly welcomed the communist totalitarian state as a partner in a war to save democracy from the Nazi totalitarian state. "If Hitler invaded Hell," said Churchill, "I would make at least a favorable reference to the Devil in the House of Commons." If one is tempted to question this attitude as correct, one has to consider the alternative for the Western democracies: letting Hitler win the war rather than permitting the ideal of democracy to be soiled by an alliance with the communist dictatorship.

Case IV: Eisenhower and Darlan

In 1943 the United States decided on a major diversionary operation prior to the decisive invasion of Europe planned for 1944. The target was French northern Africa, administered by Vichy France, then collaborating with Nazi Germany. The hope was that the important bridgehead in Africa could be won with a minimum of bloodshed. Contrary to all intelligence estimates and plans based on them, the Allied invasion was met by a considerable resistance on the part of the French troops. However, the purely accidental presence in Algiers of the most prominent collaborator with the Nazis, the French Admiral Darlan, made it unexpectedly possible to reverse this trend and to eliminate the loss of all those human lives by accepting Darlan as an ally. During the fall of France, in June 1940, Admiral Darlan had broken his promise to the British to bring the French fleet over to the British ports. In England he was more hated than any other Nazi puppet in Europe. But now, by a second turncoat maneuver, Darlan could help the Allies achieve their objectives in Africa by issuing a fake order in the name of Marshal Pétain to the effect that the

American invasion should not be resisted but should be welcomed as a liberation. Following an agreement between Darlan and Eisenhower, the order was issued. All resistance stopped. Thousands of American lives were saved by the sacrifice of a wartime principle that collaborators should be hanged, not promoted. "Passion ran high in England about the Darlan deal," wrote Churchill in his memoirs. "It affected poignantly some of my friends who had been most affronted by Munich. . . . 'Is this then what we are fighting for?' they asked."[33] In his speech to the House of Commons, Churchill had to do a great deal of explaining. "Many Americans," he said, among other things, "think more of the lives of their own soldiers than they do about the past records of French political figures."[34]

What then was the issue? Were human lives—and the French fleet—more important than principles, or was it the other way around?

Case V: The Lives-for-Trucks Plan

In the spring of 1944 Adolf Eichmann sent Joel Brand, then a Budapest resident, now an Israeli citizen, to Istanbul as a go-between to offer Jewish agencies a trade of one million Jewish lives for ten thousand trucks from neutral countries and the United States, the arsenal of democracy. The trucks, as the Nazis assured the negotiators, would be used on the Russian front only. Although in the $2 million deal a down payment of $200,000 worth of valuables was made, the ransom plan was never carried through. The political aspect of the deal prevailed over the humanitarian one, on which the Nazis had counted in their last-minute desperate effort. The United States and other truck-producing countries refused to strengthen the Nazi war machine in the period of its doom on the eastern front and so close to the time of the Allied invasion of Europe. Furthermore, German use of the trucks on the eastern front would have provoked a serious rift in the Soviet-American-English coalition, which, at that time, was still considered a necessity for victory both in Europe and in the Pacific. In Germany 1944 was the year of hopes for a Nazi-Western coalition against Moscow as the way out of a lost war. At the trial in Frankfurt of two of Eichmann's closest collaborators, Joel Brand as a witness admitted (*New York Times*, May 21, 1964) that he, personally, made "a terrible mistake in passing on the Nazi offer to the British." Here, again, one may find it useful to place oneself in the position of either Brand or the Western political and military leaders in the context of 1944, when victory was near but not yet assured. Can one say that ten thousand trucks traded for one million Jewish lives would not have tipped the balance in favor of Hitler? If it did, the ensuing continuation of the war might have meant more than one million additional casualties on both the western and eastern fronts. Perhaps, on the other hand, the political aspect of the Nazi proposal—to transform Nazi Germany into a silent ally against Soviet

Russia— was the decisive factor that, in this case, did not allow the Allies seriously to consider either the practical or the moral aspects of the proposal.

Case VI: The Dresden Raid

In the fourteen-hour period bridging the night of February 13 and the morning of February 14, 1945, when Nazi Germany was practically defeated, thousands of British and United States bombers destroyed the city of Dresden, now in East Germany. In the bombing and fires that followed, an estimated total of 135,000 people died, almost twice as many as were killed by one atomic bomb at Hiroshima six months later. It is unclear why the raid was ordered at such a late stage of the war. Air Marshal Sir Robert Saundby, deputy chief of the wartime bomber command, wrote the Foreword for David Irving's book on the Dresden raid, in which he states:

> I am still not satisfied that I fully understand why it happened. . . . That the bombing of Dresden was a great tragedy none can deny. That it was really a military necessity few, after reading this book, will believe. It was one of those terrible things that sometimes happen in wartime, brought about by an unfortunte combination of circumstances. Those who approved it were neither wicked nor cruel, though it may well be that they were too remote from the harsh realities of war to understand fully the appalling destructive power of air bombardment in the spring of 1945. . . . It is not so much this or the other means of making war that is immoral or inhumane. What is immoral is war itself. Once full-scale war has broken out it can never be humanized or civilized, and if one side attempted to do so it would be most likely to be defeated.[35]

The Introduction to the book, written by the commander of the United States Eighth Air Force in England from 1942 to 1944, Lieutenant General Ira C. Eaker, concluded: "I deeply regret that British and U.S. bombers killed 135,000 people in the attack on Dresden, but I remember who started the last war and I regret even more the loss of more than 5,000,000 Allied lives in the necessary effort to completely defeat and utterly destroy nazism."[36] Lord Boothby, in a letter to the London *Sunday Times* (May 17, 1964), commented: "This was just about the worst crime Britain has ever perpetrated. It puts us—at long last—on a par with the Nazis." The *New York Times* (May 19, 1964) reported the following apparently typical comment made by a Londoner: "There are too many bleeding hearts. The Germans pasted us and got it back. They didn't get enough back, that's the only trouble."

On the other hand, a Jewish pilot of a British Lancaster, Group No. 3, looking down on the Nazi city of Dresden, reported his feeling in a different vein: "The fantastic glow from two hundred miles away grew even brighter as we moved into the target. At 20,000 feet we could see details in the unearthly blaze that had never been visible before; for the first time in many operations I felt sorry for the population below."[37] And a flight engineer of No. 1 Group wrote: "I witnessed the shocking sight of a city on fire from end to end. . . . My immediate reaction was a stunned reflection on the comparison between the holocaust below and the warnings of the evangelists in Gospel meetings before the war."[38]

What is the correct judgment here? Do we accept or reject the idea that the purpose of any war is to win and that in a modern war the destruction of industrial centers, mostly cities, and the lowering of their inhabitants' morale may be considered an essential prerequisite for victory? Or are we now ready, when pondering about the six preceding cases, to agree with Robert Scholes, who in his review of the brilliant book on Dresden by Kurt Vonnegut, Jr., *Slaughterhouse-Five* (New York: Delacorte Press, 1969), concluded:

> Violence is not only (as Stokely Carmichael put it) "as American as apple pie." It is as human as man. We like to hurt folks, and we especially like to hurt them in a good cause. . . . The thing that offends me equally in our recent Secretary of State [Dean Rusk] and his most vicious critics is their unshakable certainty that they are right. A man *that* certain of his cause will readily send a bunch of kids off to rescue his Holy Land. His rectitude will justify any crimes. Revolution, wars, crusades—these are all ways of justifying human cruelty.[39]

This is perhaps the appropriate tone for introducing the last case, the first use of the atomic bomb.

Case VII: The Hiroshima Raid

The controversy about the raid in which the use of nuclear weapons began will probably last forever, although fewer people (71,379) actually perished in Hiroshima than in the previous conventional raids on Tokyo (March 9-10, 1945: 83,793 killed) or on Dresden (135,000 killed). (See Document 8.2)

However, the fact remains that on August 6, 1945, an atomic bomb was used for the first time. According to Truman and his top advisers, the purpose was immediate peace through terror. According to Truman's critics, the real reason was to demonstate the superiority of the United States vis-à-vis the Soviet Union and thus influence its postwar behavior. Because the atomic bomb was used for the first time against a nonwhite race, the Chinese and Japanese communists as well as the leaders of those political movements that emphasize the racial dimension of domestic and

DOCUMENT 8.2

WAR CASUALTIES

War	Deaths of Military Personnel and Civilians	
Civil War: Union	140,414	
Civil War: Confederacy (plus an estimated 26,000 to 31,000 Confederate personnel who died in Union prisons)	74,524	
World War I	8,538,315	
World War II (approximate; includes casualties in the Japanese war against China, 1937-1945, and those sustained in partisan warfare)	16,774,000	
Battle of Verdun in World War I	760,000	
Battle of Stalingrad in World War II	1,000,000	
Nazi siege of Leningrad (900 days)	1,300,000	
Dresden air raid, February 13, 1945	135,000	
Tokyo air raid, March 9, 1945	83,793	
Hiroshima atomic air raid, August 6, 1945	71,379	
Korean War, June 25, 1950-July 27, 1953 (American casualties)	33,629	
Vietnam War, 1961-1973 (American battle deaths)	46,063	
Intertribal war in Burundi, 1972	200,000	(est.)
Purges and terror in Uganda, 1971-1975	90,000	(est.)
Hitler's race war against the Jews	6,000,000	Jews (est.)
Stalin's class war against the peasants	6,000,000	peasants (est.)

international politics ascribe the atomic decision to American racism. For instance, in his autobiography Malcolm X writes:

> The white man—give him his due—has an extraordinary intelligence, and extraordinary cleverness. . . . You can hardly name a scientific problem he can't solve. . . . But in the area of dealing with human beings, the white man's working intelligence is hobbled. His intelligence will fail him altogether if the humans happen to be non-white. The white man's emotions superseded his intelligence.
> Where was the A-bomb dropped . . . "to save American lives"? Can the white man be so naive as to think the clear import of this *ever* will be lost upon the non-white two-thirds of the earth's population?"[40]

But the atomic bomb was not ready before Germany surrendered. If any racial issue was present in the American decision to develop the bomb, it was the revulsion against Nazi racism. The atomic bomb's production in the United States was started at the suggestion of two Jewish exiles from Europe, Leo Szilard and Albert Einstein, who had known about similar efforts on the part of Nazi scientists; Germany rather than Japan was the original cause for the nuclear research and expenditure (see Document 8.3).

On May 5, 1964, former President Truman welcomed several Japanese who had survived the atomic explosions at Hiroshima and Nagasaki (the second bomb was exploded on August 9, 1945) and succinctly explained the reason for his decisions as being "to end the war in such a way that not a half million more people would be killed on each side and that many injured." This allegedly was the main rationale for the atomic bomb, based on the military estimate according to which the full-fledged invasion of Japan, planned for 1945 and 1946, would result in approximately one million casualties, half of them killed, half maimed for life. On the basis of simple mathematics there can hardly be an argument that the loss of 100,000 enemy lives is preferable to the loss of one million Japanese and American lives.

The spokesman of the Japanese group, Takuo Matsumuto, told Truman simply: "Your decision was a very heavy responsibility on your part. It was wartime."[41]

President Truman's secretary of war, Henry L. Stimson, emphasized the need to shock the Japanese leaders into unconditional surrender. As recorded in the book *On Active Service in Peace and War* by Stimson and McGeorge Bundy, Stimson felt

> that to extract a genuine surrender from the Emperor and his military advisers, there must be administered a tremendous shock which would carry convincing proof of our power to destroy the Empire. Such an effective shock would save many times the number of lives, both American and Japanese, that it would cost.[42]

Much of the subsequent criticism of the use of the first atomic bomb has not really been directed against Truman's equation of one million lives, most probably saved, against less than one-tenth of that figure actually killed. The main line of criticism has been that the choice between one million and 100,000 casualties was not the real choice. This is possible. The fundamental question posed here, however, is, If the policy makers *honestly* believed at that time that the atomic bomb was the only alternative to a long and costly war, what should have been their decision? President Truman, so far as his memoirs indicate, had hardly any hesitation about the issue. He believed and subsequently confirmed that this had been the choice as he had seen it. Some scientists had proposed as late as the summer of 1945—and the American government knew this—that the

DOCUMENT 8.3

EINSTEIN AND THE ATOMIC BOMB

F. D. Roosevelt
President of the United States
White House
Washington, D.C. August 2, 1939

Sir:

Some recent work by E. Fermi and L. Szilard, which has been communicated to me in manuscript, leads me to expect that the element uranium may be turned into a new and important source of energy in the immediate future. Certain aspects of the situation which has arisen seem to call for watchfulness and, if necessary, quick action on the part of the Administration. . . .

In the course of the last four months it has been made probable through the work of Joliot in France as well as Fermi and Szilard in America that it may become possible to set up a *nuclear chain reaction* in a large mass of uranium, by which vast amounts of power and large quantities of new radium-like elements would be generated. Now it appears almost certain that this could be achieved in the immediate future. . . . It is conceivable –though much less certain—that extremely powerful bombs of a new type may thus be constructed. . . .

Yours very truly,
A. EINSTEIN

From Otto Nathan and Heinz Norden (eds.), *Einstein on Peace*. New York: Schocken Books, 1968, pp. 294-296. By permission of Estate of Albert Einstein.

After Hiroshima, Einstein wrote:
I do not believe that civilization will be wiped out in a war fought with the atomic bomb. Perhaps two thirds of the people of the earth might be killed, but enough men capable of thinking, and enough books, would be left to start again, and civilization could be restored. . . . Since I do not foresee that atomic energy is to be a great boon for a long time, I have to say that for the present it is a menace. Perhaps it is well that it should be. It may intimidate the human race into bringing order into its international affairs, which, without the pressure of fear, it would not do.

From *Atlantic Monthly*, November, 1945.

atomic bomb should be kept secret and perhaps never used. Some had hoped that the atomic age could be delayed forever. This was naive. From Einstein, Presidents Roosevelt and Truman knew that other nations had been feverishly working on the secret of the atom. It was only a matter of time before somebody, somewhere, for some purpose developed the first device. There is no evidence that the thought of possible future impeachment because he would not use the bomb ever entered the President's mind. One cannot completely exclude the possible negative verdict of history and of the American people had it been discovered after a long and costly invasion of Japan that the atomic bomb had been available but not used for some false "humane" reasons with the result that 500,000 American soldiers were killed or maimed for life.

Scientists were not the only ones who opposed the use of the atomic bomb in 1945. In his White House memoirs President Eisenhower disclosed that in 1945 he believed that dropping[43] the atomic bomb on Japan was no longer mandatory to save American lives because Japan was already defeated. Furthermore, Eisenhower thought that "our country should avoid shocking world opinion" by the use of a nuclear bomb; he apparently informed the secretary of war, Stimson, of his misgivings. If "shocking world opinion" was an issue, Eisenhower's memoirs do not explain why world opinion would have been less shocked if atomic bombs had been used in the Korean war. For in 1953 Eisenhower, no longer a subordinate general but a top policy maker, actually considered using the atomic bomb in Korea, not against frontline positions but against strategic targets in North Korea, Manchuria, and on the Chinese coast. As in the case of Japan, peace through terror was the goal. Furthermore, President Eisenhower concluded that the United States could not maintain its military commitments around the world "did we not possess atomic weapons and the will to use them when necessary." It would seem that the issue in the Stimson-Eisenhower disagreement of 1945 was not one of concern for world public opinion but of different military estimates of the necessity of bringing Japan to surrender by the use of atomic bombs. Perhaps the difference between Eisenhower's attitude toward the bomb in 1945 and in 1953 also lies in the difference in view that a man has as a general who executes orders and as a head of state with the final and irrevocable responsibility for action and its consequences.

Some critics of the atomic decision tend to blame the inflexible Allied policy of unconditional surrender for the unnecessary prolongation of both the Nazi and the Japanese resistance. They say more people were killed and maimed for life by the "unconditional surrender" than by the two atomic bombs. In the case of Japan, finally, her surrender was not unconditional: The Japanese condition that the person and the institution of the Japanese emperor be preserved was met.

Another line of argument was the suggestion that the first atomic bomb should have been exploded on Japan with previous warning, so that Japan might evacuate the target area. Those opposed to this expressed the fear that the Japanese military would evacuate the Japanese civilians and replace them by American prisoners of war.

A more convincing argument against the Hiroshima explosion was the proposal to explode the bomb on a deserted atoll somewhere in the Pacific to allow Japan and other nations to witness the destructive effect of the new weapon without any loss of human lives whatsoever. This proposal took into account that Japan's leaders had already known for some time they had lost the war but were not ready to accept the terms of unconditional surrender. The argument against the proposal was that the atomic bomb might fail to explode at the time of its demonstration. Another argument was that a laboratory experiment might not shock the Japanese leaders into surrender, whereas public pressure in the wake of atomic destruction of a city would. It may be noted that those Japanese leaders who had advocated resistance to the bitter end were not substantially shaken even by the Hiroshima raid and the people's reaction, since it did not seem to them dramatically different from the other forms of American indiscriminate bombing of Japanese cities. When, after the second bomb on Nagasaki, the Emperor and the "peace party" in Tokyo won over the "war party" and the fanatics, the final decision to surrender was a combination of several factors, which, while dominated by the mushroom cloud, also included some power conflicts in internal Japanese politics as well as the impact of the Soviet declaration of war and the announcement of the Soviet invasion of Japanese-held Manchuria. The situation was indeed desperate for Japan, which was totally isolated and exposed to atomic annihilation, invasion, or both.

If the main purpose of the atomic bomb in 1945 was to produce such terror that the Japanese people would force their government into surrender, it was finally this political and psychological goal that, twenty years later, came under renewed attacks. The immediate cause was the presentation of modest claims for compensation (from $550 to $825 plus 5 percent interest from May 1955, when the suit began) on the part of five survivors of the Hiroshima and Nagasaki raids, suffering from serious aftereffects. The case was adjudicated by the District Court of Tokyo (*Shimada et al.* v. *Japan*). The Japanese court refused the claim, having concluded that the claimants had no remedy since international law did not yet allow individuals to pursue claims on their own behalf against their own or a foreign government and that, at any rate, the Japanese government had no responsibility to compensate individual victims of atomic damage. After careful examination, the court also ruled on the broader question of the legality or illegality of the use of atomic bombs in war. Its general conclusion was that international law did not prohibit the use of the atomic weapon *if it had great military efficiency*. This, admittedly, is not an easy yardstick to apply. A lack of military efficiency would also condemn any conventional bombardment, like that of many German cities where bombing was indiscriminate. The Japanese court did, however, express its opinion that an atomic attack, in general, cannot discriminate between military and nonmilitary targets (if it could, would it be more acceptable?)

and, further, that "the cruelty of the bomb was contrary to the fundamental principles of law of war that unnecessary pain must not be given." Here, again, we find a very controversial yardstick of more or less necessary suffering in war. Is death, for instance, a more unnecessary suffering than the lifelong consequences of radiation, gas, or simple napalm bombs? Commenting on the finding of the Japanese court in the case of the five plaintiffs from Hiroshima and Nagasaki, the American author Richard E. A. Falk condemned the atomic bomb in terms that dismiss what had been, according to Truman, the main reason for its use:

> The full and direct charge against the United States [based on the finding of the Japanese Court] is: We used these cruel weapons for doubtful military purposes, in an unusually inhumane way [military targets were not particularly concentrated in Hiroshima and Nagasaki] that has permanently seared the imagination of men, and has left an unextinguished legacy of actual suffering among civilians selected arbitrarily as victims of terror practices on a gigantic scale.[44]

A closely related moral question concerns the responsibility of the scientists; clearly, without them the political and military leaders could not make use of nuclear mass terror. The realization of this responsibility dawned on Kenneth Bainbridge, J. Robert Oppenheimer's principal assistant at Los Alamos. A few seconds after the first atomic test near Alamogordo, July 16, 1945, he exclaimed: "Now we are all sons-of-bitches." This was reported by William L. Laurence, science editor of the *New York Times*, the only journalist permitted to witness the first test.

On the other hand, even with the benefit of hindsight, other scientists had a different view of their moral duty when their nation was confronted with aggressive and totalitarian evil. Twenty years after Hiroshima, for instance, Eugene P. Wigner, a Nobel prize winner, and one of the group that lit the first atomic fire at the University of Chicago on December 2, 1942, made the following statement to the *New York Times* (August 1, 1965):

> I had no sense of guilt, since I did not make the decision. The scientist in a democracy has the right to refuse to do anything distasteful to him. But as long as scientists in totalitarian countries have no such choice (the German scientists were ahead of us in the development of a nuclear weapon. I shudder to think what would have happened if Germany had been first to acquire the weapon), it would not be right to exercise such legal rights for, if one did, there soon would not be any democracy. The scientists, like any other civilian, should not act in such a way as to make democracy impossible.

The head of the Los Alamos scientific team, J. Robert Oppenheimer, who subsequently opposed the development of a hydrogen bomb, kept on supporting the morality of the initial plan to develop the atomic bomb for use against Nazi Germany. Speaking to the *New York Times* (August 1, 1965) on the twentieth anniversary of Hiroshima, he said:

> It was a damn good thing that the bomb was developed. . . . In that world [of 1945], in that war, it was the only thing to do. I only regret that it was not done two years earlier. It would have saved a million or more lives. . . . I never regretted, and do not regret now, having done my part of the job. I have a deep, continuing, haunting sense of the damage done to European culture by the two world wars. The existence of the bomb has reduced the chance of World War III.

NONNUCLEAR INHUMANITY

The absence of nuclear violence on the international scene since August 1945 has not reduced the scope and degree of violence and inhumanity by nonnuclear means. The last decades have been as violent as, if not more violent than, other comparable periods of history. As the experience of Carthage at the hands of the Romans shows, men do not need an advanced weapon technology to inflict inhuman horror upon their fellow men on a mass scale in both international and civil wars. In Chapter 3 we mentioned the cruel intertribal war in the tiny East African state of Burundi in 1972 in which about 200,000 members of the Hutu tribe and about 50,000 of the ruling Tutsi minority perished. In 1965, in the wake of a military coup in Indonesia, there was mass killing of an "ideological" minority, that is, members of the Communist party; about 300,000 people were murdered—about twice as many as the combined casualties of the two atomic bombs dropped on Hiroshima and Nagasaki in 1945.

A report by the International Commission of Jurists, issued in 1974, described the constant violations of human rights by the government of General Idi Amin in Uganda as a "reign of terror." At that time most diplomatic observers estimated that more than 90,000 (that is, approximately as many as in Hiroshima) had been killed since General Amin took power in 1971. One writer (Hal Sheets in the *New York Times*, August 3, 1974) bitterly noted:

> Nearly thirty years after the horrors of Dachau, Buchenwald, Auschwitz, and Treblinka, the Uganda case and others, such as genocide in neighboring Burundi, demonstrate that human rights continues to be a minor issue in international politics.

In the 1960s and 1970s the United States bombing of North Vietnamese cities and harbors continued up to and even during negotiations aiming at a cease-fire. Presidents Johnson and Nixon believed that devastating raids would force the North Vietnamese leaders into a more accommodating mood at the negotiating table. Public opinion in the United States and abroad condemned the bombings as immoral and/or pointless because they were ineffective: More bombs were dropped on Vietnam than the total of all bombs dropped in all wars since the invention of aircraft. Some bomb experts, however, argued that the final readiness of North Vietnam to conclude a cease-fire agreement resulted from the United States's development of highly accurate, so-called smart bombs, which, unlike all previous bombs, were not "gravity" bombs but "glide" bombs—that is, bombs equipped with a terminal guidance system, using either a television camera or a laser beam to direct the bomb to its target, even one that is moving. The accuracy of the new glide bomb was demonstrated in September 1972 (four months before the cease-fire was agreed upon) by the successful attack on the vital Longbien bridge in central Hanoi. Over the preceding five years United States Air Force and Navy planes had aimed thousands (!) of conventional bombs at the bridge without scoring direct hits; what had happened to the surrounding area is left to the imagination of the reader. Finally, the bridge was destroyed by four planes equipped with "smart bombs." It may be added that soon afterward the ruined bridge was replaced by a quite efficient pontoon bridge. Besides the moral issue involved the United States conventional bombing of North Vietnam seems also to confirm the lesson of World War II which both the Nazis and the Allies had learned: conventional air bombardment of urban and industrial targets, however painful and accurate, can rarely be decisive either militarily or politically; there seems to be no clear case in which the industrial spine and political will of an opponent had ever been broken by TNT alone.

In addition, in the 1960s both sides in Vietnam persisted in terrorizing the civilian population with weapons more typical of the nineteenth century than of the nuclear age. In 1967 a Viet Cong assault on a Montagnard tribe's new settlement at Dak Son, 75 miles northeast of Saigon, resulted in the bayoneting and gunning down of 252 unarmed persons, nearly all of them women and children. In the 1968 *Tet* offensive in and around the old imperial capital of Hué the communist slaughter of the civilian population reached grisly proportions: Following the communist withdrawal, nineteen mass graves were discovered, yielding, according to the Saigon government, around 5,800 bodies, almost all of whom were civilians, their hands tied behind their backs. Most of them were shot or bludgeoned to death; some were buried alive.

In 1969 world public opinion in general and the American people in particular were profoundly shocked by the discovery that at least in one case, and perhaps in more, American soldiers in Vietnam were guilty of similar atrocities. This was the story of My Lai 4, one of the four hamlets composing the village complex of Songmy (Truongan on the French maps) in the province of Quangnai. The evidence indicated that on March 1, 1968,

Company C, First Battalion, 20th Infantry, 101 Light Brigade, was ordered to search the village complex of Songmy. On March 16, at My Lai, it ran into some sniper fire that left several men wounded, increasing the bitterness of the American unit, which had previously been decimated by Viet Cong snipers and mines. In retaliation the population of the hamlet, assumed to be helping the Viet Cong, was gunned down. Between 100 and 300 Vietnamese peasants, mostly old men, women, and children, were killed. An Army photographer took color pictures of the massacre, which eighteen months later were published in *Life* Magazine (December 5, 1969). The cruelty and senselessness of the action at My Lai led to self-examination on the part of many Americans. Two aspects of the massacre seemed particularly disturbing: In its senselessness My Lai was more reminiscent of the Dresden raid than of Hiroshima, which seemed to have at least one justification, however controversial, that of ending the war more rapidly by the use of nuclear mass terror. Not even that sort of rationalization seemed to apply to the My Lai massacre. The other disturbing factor was that the massacre was committed by men who for the most part seemed normal. *Time* (December 5, 1969, p. 26) commented on this point:

> To argue that the enemy has done worse (as he has), is to beg a graver issue. The fact remains that this particular atrocity—a clear violation of the civilized values America claims to uphold—was apparently ordered by officers of the U.S. military and carried out by sons of honorable, God-fearing people. . . . They were Everymen, decent in their daily lives, who at home in Ohio or Vermont would regard it as unthinkable to maliciously strike a child, much less kill one. Yet men in American uniforms slaughtered the civilians of My Lai, and in so doing humiliated the U.S. and called in questions the U.S. mission in Viet Nam in a way that all the anti-war protesters could never have done.

In the ensuing national debate two additional disturbing questions were raised. First, what is the difference, if any, between slaughtering at close range the civilians whose faces one can see and the massacre of civilians one cannot see, as in the case of either an aerial bombardment or a siege that kills civilians by starvation (1,300,000 civilian casualties in besieged Leningrad or thousands of women and children in Biafra.)[45]

The second question was who should be held responsible for any atrocity committed in the course of a war—soldiers, low-ranking officers, commanding officers, political leaders, or the war itself, which holds all of them entrapped in inhumanity?

Both questions, that of killing at close or long range and that of personal accountability, were raised poignantly by Norman Cousins (*Saturday Review*, December 20, 1969):

> What well-springs of sense and humaneness are to be found in the orders

DOCUMENT 8.4

WHAT SHOULD ONE DO?
A CONTINUING DEBATE

What should an airman do when asked to drop an atomic bomb? Should he obey the order or refuse on the ground that using this weapon violates the international law of war? He may end up between the Charybdis of being shot for insubordination in wartime and the Scylla of being hanged, if a military tribunal organized by the victor decided that his act shocked the conscience of civilized peoples. . . . Today, given the potency of the new weapons, the refusal to obey on the part of a single important individual could spell a nation's defeat, though it might save the world from ruin, and so would make his decision all the more fateful.

From Guenter Lewy, *American Political Science Review*, March 1, 1961.

The person I cannot get out of my mind these days is the young man who dropped the first atomic bomb. I suppose he is a nice young man, characteristic of American manhood, yet the odd thing is that, if he had been ordered to go and drop it on Milwaukee, he almost certainly would have refused. He might have been well enough trained by the Army to obey instructions even in that case, but I suspect he might have refused. Because he was asked to drop it on Hiroshima, he not only consented but he became something of a hero for it. I imagine he was quite handsomely rewarded. Of course, I don't quite see the distinction between dropping it on Milwaukee and dropping it on Hiroshima. The difference is a "we" difference. The people in Milwaukee, though we don't know any of them, are "we," and the people in Hiroshima are "they," and the great psychological problem is how to make everybody "we," at least in some small degree.

From Kenneth E. Boulding, "Discussion of World Economic Contacts," *The World Community*, edited by Quincy Wright. Chicago: Chicago University Press, 1948, pp. 101-103.

It was the only time I ever felt sorry for the Germans. But my sorrow lasted only for a few seconds; the job was to hit the enemy and to hit him very hard.

From a statement by a bomb-aimer of a Lancaster, R.A.F. Squadron 635, commenting on the Dresden raid, 1945. Quoted by David Irving, *The Destruction of Dresden*. New York: Holt, Rinehart and Winston, p. 142.

I don't like to hit a village. You know you're hitting women and children, too. But you've got to decide that your cause is noble and that the work has to be done.

From a statement by an American pilot in Vietnam, *New York Times*, July 7, 1965.

The fantastic glow from two hundred miles away grew ever brighter as we moved into the target. At 20,000 feet we could see details in the unearthly blaze that had never been visible before; for the first time in many operations I felt sorry for the population below.

From a statement by a Jewish pilot of R.A.F. Lancaster Group No. 3, commenting on the Dresden raid, February 1945. Quoted by Irving, *The Destruction of Dresden,* pp. 142-143.

. . . The fires stormed. At the station entrances were mounds of dead children, and others were being piled up, as they were brought out of the station. There must have been a children's train at the station. More and more dead were stacked up, in layers, on top of each other . . .

From Irving, *The Destruction of Dresden,* p. 175.

The Army has honored a helicopter pilot, Chief Warrant Officer High C. Thompson, Jr., 27, of Decatur, Ga., with a Silver Star Medal. The citation said he twice landed his helicopter at My Lai that day—once to extricate 15 children trying to hide in a bunker and then to rescue a wounded child in disregard of his own safety.

From *New York Times,* November 30, 1969.

Imagine that you are creating a fabric of human destiny with the object of making men happy in the end, giving them peace and rest at last, but that it was essential and inevitable to torture to death only one tiny creature—that baby beating its breast with its fist, for instance—and to found that edifice on its unavenged tears, would you consent to be the architect on those conditions? . . . It's not God that I don't accept, Alyosha, only I must respectfully return Him the entrance ticket.

From Fyodor Dostoevsky, *The Brothers Karamazov.*

to destroy *whole* villages from the air? Is a man in a plane exempt from wrongdoing solely because he does not see the faces of the women and children whose bodies will be shattered by the explosives he rains on them from the sky? How does one define a legitimate victim of war? What of a frightened mother and her baby who take refuge in a tunnel and are cremated alive by a soldier with a flamethrower? Does the darkness of the tunnel make them proper candidates for death?

CONFLICTING ORDERS AND VALUES

At My Lai and in the seven major controversies of World War II described in this chapter, and in many other similar dilemmas in the past and in the future, both the policy makers and those who executed their decisions had to find their own human way in a labyrinth of conflicting norms, values, necessities, orders, and possible sanctions. Policy makers are confronted with extremely difficult and, in the atomic era, truly apocalyptic dilemmas: Should war be shortened and therefore made more humane by an inhumane terror concentrated in a few nuclear seconds? Or should principles or victory be sacrificed so that human lives may be saved? As to the individual executors of policy decisions—soldiers, generals, and pilots—ever since the Nuremberg war crimes trial and Hiroshima a debate has been going as to what an individual should do if he believes he will be violating international law or morality by executing an order that, if disobeyed, may lead to his being shot for insubordination. It is a continuing debate (see Document 8.4), and there is no reason to believe that it will soon be ended.

In conclusion, the fundamental issue confronting both the leaders and their subordinates is the decision to use or not to use violence to resist evil, real or imaginary. An absolute pacifist naturally argues that in a struggle with evil one should die by offering the other cheek rather than try to survive by violence. Most men, however, seem to have assumed, in theory and in practice, that it is moral to resist evil by violent means *if there is no other way*. In order to prevent might from making right, they maintain, it has to be opposed at the right time and by the right method. Once the decision to use violence has been made, the controversy about the right time and the right method shifts to two problems of perception and strategy:

1. Is the survival of a man or a community really at stake? A mortal danger to oneself or to one's nation may often be a pretext or a figment of one's imagination. Here, again, the persistent problem comes to the foreground: the problem of correct or false perception of other nations' intentions and power. Very often a controversy about moral issues in the conduct of violent international politics is in reality a debate concerning conflicting estimates of the severity of danger and the best means of coping with it. What is considered moral from one position of knowledge and foresight may appear reprehensible from another.
2. Is the issue at stake worth the contemplated method of action or is another alternative not available—a limited rather than general war, conventional rather than nuclear violence, timely armament that may deter a war rather than unilateral disarmament that may make war inevitable, negotiations rather than deterrence? Practical rather than ethical considerations often color the debate as to whether the same result could have been obtained by means less costly, but not costless, in terms of national or personal moral or other preferences.

My Lai and the Nazi bombardments of Rotterdam, Coventry, and London, the Japanese attacks on Chinese cities, the Anglo-American devastation of Berlin, Dresden, Tokyo, Hiroshima, and Nagasaki point to the near-inevitability of dehumanization of all the participants once the dividing line between violent and nonviolent means of conflict solution has been crossed. This is particularly so in modern total wars, in which the civilian population—their cities, work, and morale—are viewed as justifiable targets for attack.

The preceding controversies of World War II, My Lai, and the record of all modern wars, including the revolutionary and guerrilla type, seem to confirm what Gandhi once succinctly expressed in five words: "Morality is contraband in war."[46]

Notes

1. Arnold Wolfers, *Discord and Collaboration: Essays on International Politics.* Baltimore, Md.: The Johns Hopkins Press, 1962, p. 50.
2. Wolfers, *Discord and Collaboration*, pp. 49-50.
3. H. H. Gerth and C. Wright Mills, *From Max Weber: Essays in Sociology.* New York: Oxford, 1958, pp. 120-121.
4. Upendra Nath Goshal, *A History of Indian Political Ideas.* New York: Oxford, 1959, pp. 144-153 and *passim.*
5. Niccolò Machiavelli, *The Prince and the Discourses.* New York: Random House, 1950, pp. 64-66.
6. Leon Trotsky, *Dictatorship vs. Democracy: A Reply to Karl Kautsky.* New York: Workers' Party of America, 1922, pp. 54, 57-59.
7. Dag Hammarskjöld, *Markings.* New York: Knopf, 1964, p. 147.
8. K. Satchidananda Murty, "Ethics and Politics in Hindu Culture," in Harold D. Lasswell and Harlan Cleveland (eds.), *The Ethic of Power: The Interplay of Religion, Philosophy and Politics.* New York: Harper & Row, 1962, p. 85.
9. Murty, "Ethics and Politics in Hindu Culture," p. 85.
10. Wolfers, *Discord and Harmony*, p. 49.
11. Gerth and Mills, *From Max Weber*, pp. 126-127.
12. Raymond Aron, *Peace and War: A Theory of International Relations.* New York: Praeger, 1966, p. 781.
13. Kenneth W. Thompson, *Christian Ethics and Dilemmas of Foreign Policy.* Durham, N.C.: Duke University Press, 1961, p. 46.
14. Harry R. Davis and Robert C. Good, *Reinhold Niebuhr on Politics.* New York: Scribner, 1960, pp. 84, 193. By permission.
15. Joseph C. McKenna, S.J., "Ethics and War: A Catholic View," *American Political Science Review*, September 1960, p. 648. By permission.
16. McKenna, "Ethics and War," p. 650.
17. McKenna, "Ethics and War," p. 650.
18. Davis and Good, *Reinhold Niebuhr on Politics*, pp. 147-148.
19. McKenna, "Ethics and War," pp. 650, 658.
20. Robert Endicott Osgood, *Ideals and Self-Interest in America's Foreign Relations.* Chicago: University of Chicago Press, 1953, pp. 446-451.
21. Robert W. Tucker, "Professor Morgenthau's Theory of Political Realism," *American Political Science Review*, 46 (1952), 222.
22. E. A. Hooton, *Apes, Men and Morons.* New York: Putnam, 1937, p. 151.
23. Otto Klineberg, *The Human Dimension in International Relations.* New York: Holt, Rinehart and Winston, 1964, p. 83.
24. Machiavelli, *The Prince and the Discourses*, p. 528.
25. *Le Monde* (Paris), November 8, 1968.
26. Nikita Khrushchev, *Khrushchev Remembers.* Boston: Little, Brown, 1970, p. 129.
27. "Memorandum of a Conversation Held on the Night of August 23 to 24 between the Reich Foreign Minister, on the One Hand, and Herr Stalin and the Chairman of the Council of People's Commissars, Molotov, on the Other," in *Nazi-Soviet Relations, 1939-1941* (U.S. Department of State Publication No. 3023), Point 8, entitled "Toasts."
28. *Nazi-Soviet Relations, 1939-1941*, pp. 15-16.

29. *Nazi-Soviet Relations, 1939-1941*, p. 356.

30. V. I. Lenin, *Collected Works*, Vol. 23. New York: International Publishers, 1945, p. 83. Compare with Khrushchev's memoirs in which the former secretary of the party wrote: "We were all together in the Kremlin when we heard over the radio that the French army had capitulated and that the Germans were in Paris. Stalin's nerves cracked when he learned about the fall of France. He cursed the governments of England and France. 'Couldn't they put up any resistance at all?' he asked despairingly." *Khrushchev Remembers*, p. 134.

31. Svetlana Alliluyeva, *Only One Year*. New York: Harper & Row, 1968, p. 329.

32. After World War II, *Pravda*, on March 13, 1946, described Churchill as follows: "He did not like the appearance of the Soviet regime in Russia after World War I. Then [Churchill] organized an armed expedition of fourteen states against Russia with the aim of turning back the wheel of history. But history turned out to be stronger . . . and the quixotic antics of Churchill resulted in his complete defeat."

33. Winston S. Churchill, *The Hinge of Fate*. Boston: Houghton Mifflin, 1950, p. 638. The deal with Darlan is fully described by Dwight D. Eisenhower in his book of wartime memoirs *Crusade in Europe* (New York: Doubleday, 1948). The interplay of the term "crusade" and the actuality of the deal with a collaborator is interesting.

34. Churchill, *The Hinge of Fate*, p. 640.

35. David Irving, *The Destruction of Dresden*. New York: Holt, Rinehart and Winston, 1964, pp. 9-10.

36. Irving, *The Destruction of Dresden*, p. 8.

37. Irving, *The Destruction of Dresden*, p. 163.

38. Irving, *The Destruction of Dresden*, p. 163.

39. Robert Scholes, "Like Lot's Wife, He Looked Back—At the Destruction of Dresden and 135,000 Dead," *New York Times Book Review*, April 6, 1969.

40. Malcolm X, *The Autobiography of Malcolm X*. New York: Grove, 1966 (paperback), p. 268.

41. *New York Times*, May 6, 1964.

42. Henry L. Stimson and McGeorge Bundy, *On Active Service in Peace and War*. New York: Harper & Row, 1947, p. 698.

43. Dwight D. Eisenhower, *The White House Years: Mandate for Change, 1953-1956*. New York: Doubleday, 1963.

44. Richard A. Falk, "Claimants of Hiroshima," *The Nation*, February 15, 1965.

45. Anthony Enahoro, the Nigerian minister of information, explained in 1968 that "hunger was a legitimate weapon in the effort to reduce the Biafran uprising." *New York Times Magazine*, September 7, 1969, p. 149.

46. Mahatma Gandhi, *Non-Violence in Peace and War*, Vol. 1. Ahmedabad, India: Navajivan Publishing House, 1948, p. 268.

Additional Readings

Additional readings on morality in politics may be found in *Discord and Harmony: Readings in International Politics,* edited by Ivo D. Duchacek and published by Holt, Rinehart and Winston in 1972. Chapter 10, "On Noble Ends and Ignoble Means" (pp. 216-254), contains brief excerpts from Max Weber, Kautilya, Machiavelli, and Trotsky. "The Politics of Nonviolence" as explained by the Quakers is contrasted with a description of the first atomic explosion in New Mexico by Thomas F. Farrell and Louis Morton's analysis of the "Decision to Use the Atomic Bomb" on Hiroshima. See also Philip Green, "Nuclear Deterrence and Moral Considerations," pp. 316-321.

9
International
Law

Contacts among men may be friendly or hostile, cooperative or competitive, deliberate or unintentional, systematic or haphazard, desired or dreaded, but whatever their form, frequency, intensity, or purpose they are inevitable; even hermits and gurus have some difficulty in maintaining their isolation. People's awareness of the inevitability of their contacts is the starting point of legal rules for human conduct. Practical need, not abstract speculation, is the parent source of national legal systems; their purpose is to define and regulate contacts among individuals and groups within a national community and provide some mechanisms, such as courts, that may help to solve conflicts arising from these contacts. When a national community translates its shared assumptions, expectations, and moral preferences into laws, it adds to the moral sanctions or pangs of conscience that follow violation of a moral rule the threat of coercion by a public authority in case of violation of the law.

Among nations, hostile, competitive, and cooperative contacts are today as inescapable as they are among members of a national community. Many centuries ago, perhaps, when there were still many thinly inhabited areas in the world, it was conceivable that a territorial unit—a tribal territory, a city-state, or even an empire—could organize itself without coming into direct contact with other similarly organized units. This is now inconceivable. We all are neighbors.

313

In contrast to man's acceptance of a territorial legal system as a consequence of social interdependence, the territorial nations have been relatively slow and hesitant to subject their intercourse to legal restraints and regulation. Yet, here too, practical need rather than some legal theory has initiated a process in which the increase in contacts among territorial states—economic, cultural, and political—has been accompanied by the growth of various rules, defining rights, duties, and acceptable behavior for those who interact on the international scene. This body of rules for national conduct has come to be known as international law or the law of nations.

CONTACTS AND COMPACTS AMONG NATIONS

In the absence of any central law-making authority, how did the legal rights and duties of nations come into being? Some interests of the interacting territorial states were so patently common to several or most of them that their mutual observance did not require a precise formulation and a formal written agreement on the rules to follow. A mutually acceptable conduct hardened in time into custom and acquired the validity of legal rule, recognized as precedent and observed by nearly all. This was the origin of the international custom law, a law based on *implied* consent, or consent manifested by conduct.

Other contacts and interests required a precise definition in a formal document or a compromise solution reached by means of negotiation, much as individuals negotiate and conclude contracts among themselves. Definition or compromise as reached among nations was incorporated into a formal treaty binding upon those—and only those—who had consented to it. This was the beginning of law among nations, based on *explicit* consent. Having generally agreed on their respective right to go it alone, that is, sovereign territoriality, the states could not stop there. The inevitable intercourse among sovereign states necessarily led to additional agreements and regulatory rules concerning the international movement of goods, currencies, and persons (merchants, tourists, diplomatic envoys and consuls), the traffic of mail, trains, ships, aircraft, and orbiting spacecraft, and the circulation of books, patents, and radio and television programs. Constant and intensive contacts among nations—such as navigation on a river forming a boundary between two soverign states—required not only agreements on mutual rights and duties but also permanent agencies with the authority to implement the common agreements on a day-to-day basis. This was the beginning of international organizations. International organization is always based on a formal international treaty that determines the purpose and techniques of the organization. Both the international treaty and the international organization are therefore products of preceding successful negotiatiations among sovereign states. At the same time they both represent a basis for creating additional rules and establishing additional organs and institutions (Chapter 10 will deal with international organization in more detail). By defining their mutual rights and obligations, nations are able to eliminate at least those conflicts that could result from uncertainty or misunderstanding as to what these rights and obligations are. As an authority on international law rightly noted: "International law is a means of enabling the day-to-day business of state to be conducted in normal times along orderly and predictable lines, and that is no small service."[1] Nations, like individuals, often behave within the law and without enforcement simply because a general respect for law is usually preferable to uncertainty, chaos, or even the short-term advantage that could be obtained by violating a law.

In analyzing the effectiveness and completeness of any legal system, national or international, it is useful to inquire into the following five fundamentals:

1. Does a given legal system express a more or less general consensus of the community, and is there a community?
2. How and by whom are legal rules created and changed? That is, what is the nature of the legislative process?
3. Are the rules clear and accessible to all members of the community? Can codification help?
4. How and by whom are legal rules interpreted and conflicts resolved? That is, what is the nature of the judicial process?
5. How and by whom are the rules enforced in the case of noncompliance? That is, what is the nature and effectiveness of the machinery of enforcement?

INTERNATIONAL COMMUNITY

If law is defined as a body of rules for human conduct, set and enforced by a sovereign political authority, international law cannot be called law. There is no supranational political authority that can give and enforce law to be observed by all nations. There is no central judicial authority that has compulsory jurisdiction and that hands down final and enforceable interpretations of legal obligations among nations. There is no permanent international penal court nor is there any central "police" mechanism that can apprehend and punish lawbreakers. The absence of central lawmaking, law-adjudicating, and law-enforcing authority causes many authors to view the law of nations as a set of moral preferences and assumptions that some but not all nations wish were enforceable rules; thus international law appears as something that should be but is not.

If, on the other hand, law is defined as a body of rules for human conduct within a community that by common consent of this community shall be enforced by a power other than that residing within an individual (such as conscience), then international law may be defined as law, provided that the existence of a global community and its general consent can be proved. This is debatable. Does a universal world community exist from which a universal international law can issue? The preceding chapters dealing with territorial states, nationalism, and ideologies have already indicated that an answer to this question must be extremely cautious. Some nations have established relatively close-knit regional or ideological communities, and in their case there is evidence of the existence of law, a body of rules developed by political accommodation of competing interests and views that expresses consensus. The West European Community is a good example. The problem we deal with here, however, is whether there is a *universal* community on which a *universal* international law can be based and made effective.

The existence of a universal world community is usually denied on two counts: first, the division of the world into three antagonistic ideological sectors, broadly defined as Western, Communist, and Third World; and second, the division of the world into 140-odd territorial states, all claiming sovereign equality. The two kinds of division, according to this pessimistic analysis, result in an international system in which all territorial states interact, but the matters on which they agree are much less in number and importance than those on which they disagree. This is deemed a direct opposite, and not an analogy, to national territorial communites that are based on a high degree of internal cohesion and are effectively controlled by a central authority. The nonexistence of an international community is, however, viewed as analogous to the loss of the sense of community and the erosion of its legal system that characterize a territorial state in the midst of a serious civil strife.

The ideological and territorial divisions of the world and their effect on the existence and effectiveness of international law will now be examined.

Ideological Blocs

International law as a system of restraints and coercive rules for international conduct has been developed in Western Europe, reflecting its sense of community and serving its interests. It was not a universal law; the hope was that it might become so. In the past, the law of the "civilized" Western Christian nations actually excluded a major part of the world on the basis that it was still uncivilized, mostly because it was not Christian or was ignorant of the merits of Roman or Anglo-Saxon common law. When more intimate contacts with the non-Christian portions of the world became inevitable (Moslem Turkey and Persia, and later China, Japan, and India), the Western concept of international law was extended, usually by forceful imposition rather than by agreement. The unequal treaties in China are a classic example.

The Third World   The Third World, including its oil-rich segment, the "Fourth World," is often reluctant to accept as binding those portions of international law that have been developed by the Western European states for the purpose of protecting Western conquest and ensuing interests such as exploitation of colonial resources and guarantees against nationalization, both of which violate what Africa and Asia tend to consider the most basic political and economic right, that of national self-determination, which includes the right freely to dispose of one's national natural resources. The 1966 International Covenant on Economic, Social, and Cultural Rights seems to authorize a denial of economic rights to *nonnationals*, which in the postcolonial context usually means citizens of the former master-nation (see Document 9.1, in particular Article 2, paragraph 3). The critical attitude toward the Western orientation of international law was succinctly expressed by Justice Radhabinod Pal, the Indian member of the United Nations International Law Commission:

> It was questioned to what extent the new states ought to be bound by rules of international law which they had not helped to create and which very often ran counter to their interests. The formal answer, it was suggested, was very simple: when a state acceded to the international community it automatically was understood to conform to its rules and institutions. The substance of the problem was, however, declared much more complex and difficult. If numerous rules of international law did not have the active support of a large sector of the international community, the entire machinery for the peaceful solution of disputes would, it was felt, be without foundation.[2]

The disinclination of many African and Asian states to feel bound by international law as created and nurtured in the entirely different culture of the West was explained by Oliver J. Lissitzyn not only as a matter of a cultural gap but also as a result of "resentment of past foreign domination and attitudes of superiority, and of a low level of economic development with resulting economic and technological dependence on the more advanced countries."[3] None of the developing nations, however, denies the existence of international law; all have invoked its norms in disputes with other states and in debates in international organizations. Several have submitted their disputes to the International Court of Justice, created at the time when they were still colonies. Their discontent generally leads to a demand to reform the existing international law so as to include the concepts and needs of the newly independent nations. The problem, however, seems to be that the reform of international law to accommodate the Asian and African needs proceeds, according to Julius Stone, at the cost of a "continuous dilution of its content, as it is reinterpreted for the benefit of the newcomers."[4] Another problem is the overwhelming majority which the Third and Fourth Worlds represent in the United Nations General Assembly and various conferences and law study groups. If the developing nations used their numerical strength to stampede the

DOCUMENT 9.1

INTERNATIONAL COVENANT ON ECONOMIC, SOCIAL, AND CULTURAL RIGHTS, 1966[1]

Article 1

1. All peoples have the right of self-determination. By virtue of that right they freely determine their political status and freely pursue their economic, social and cultural development.

2. All peoples may, for their own ends, freely dispose of their natural wealth and resources without prejudice to any obligation arising out of international economic co-operation, based upon the principle of mutual benefit, and international law. In no case may a people be deprived of its own means of subsistence. . . .[2]

Article 2

1. Each State Party to the present Covenant undertakes to take steps, individually and through international assistance and co-operation, especially economic and technical, to the maximum of its available resources, with a view to achieving progressively the full realization of the rights recognized in the present Covenant by all appropriate means, including particularly the adoption of legislative measures.

2. The States Parties to the present Covenant undertake to guarantee that the rights enunciated in the present Covenant [such as the right to work, including vocational guidance and training programs, the right to equal job opportunities, the right to rest and leisure, the right to form trade unions, the right to an adequate standard of living, the right to the highest attainable standard of physical and mental health, and the right to education] will be exercised without discrimination of any kind as to race, color, sex, language, religion, political or other opinion, national or social origin, property, birth or other status.

3. Developing countries, with due regard to human rights and their national economy, may determine to what extent they would guarantee the economic rights recognized in the present Covenant to non-nationals.

1. Adopted at the 1496th plenary meeting, December 16, 1966, 21st Session of the United Nations General Assembly.

2. Article 1 of this Covenant is identical with Article 1 of the Covenant on Civil and Political Rights, indicating, among other things, how thin is the line that separates civil and political rights from economic and social ones.

minority, consisting of great and medium powers, into resolutions and recommendations without a general consensus, the result would be a great deal of paper and a minimal if any amount of enforceable law. More about this problem will be said in connection with the new law of the sea.

Communist Nations The attitude of the communst nations toward international law represents a complex mixture of opposition in principle and invocation of the legal rules when they clearly benefit the national interests of communist nations.

The opposition in principle is based on the doctrine of Marxism-Leninism, the dominant creed of fourteen territorial states[5] extending from Berlin to Peking and Havana; their governments rule more than a billion people. According to Lenin, law and government express and implement the interests of the ruling class, those of the capitalist exploiters in the West and those of the proletariat in the communist world. Lenin said that the territorial state and its law are the organs of "class domination, the organ of oppression of one class by another." Lenin's definition excludes the possibility of a common legal ground between opposing classes within a territorial state and among territorial states dominated by antagonistic classes. How can a state dominated by the proletariat and a state dominated by its class enemies, the capitalists, conceivably form a community of shared values, goals, and legal concepts? In the 1930s Nazi writers similarly excluded the possibility of a community among different races. Some Nazi writers stressed the concept of intercorporative international law, built on the principle of racial consanguinity.

The Marxist-Leninist emphasis on the class character of any legal system has not, however, prevented the Soviet Union from invoking international law quite frequently and signing legal documents and treaties with noncommunist nations, whether they were led by an Adolf Hitler, a Franklin Delano Roosevelt, a Charles de Gaulle, or a Richard Nixon. The formula was bluntly expressed by a Soviet writer in the late Stalin era: "Those institutions in international law which can facilitate the execution of the stated tasks of the USSR are recognized and applied by the USSR, and those institutions which conflict in any manner with these purposes are rejected by the USSR."[6]

As to the actual record of the Soviet accession to international treaties, a recent study[7] shows that the Soviet Union found it advantageous to enter into 2516 international treaties during the first forty years of its existence. However, these treaties predominantly dealt with nonpolitical subjects such as trade, communications, natural resources, health, and consular relations. The ratio of nonpolitical treaties is approximately the same for all nations—capitalist, fascist, and socialist.

National Sovereignty

Sovereignty and equality were previously discussed as two of the characteristic features of nation-states. They deserve additional consideration in the context of international law.

Sovereignty has been defined as the supreme legal authority of the territorial state to give and enforce the law within a geographically delineated space. Its concomitant meaning seems to be that sovereign and independent nations do not recognize any authority above them except the one they have consented to create and submit to on the basis of their sovereign and independent will.

The English term "sovereignty" has been adapted from the French word "souverain," which at the end of the Middle Ages described the authority of a king who did not have any superior authority above himself. It was introduced into political and legal science by Jean Bodin in *De Republica*, which appeared in 1577. Bodin tried to justify the centralization of royal power initiated by Louis XI (1461-1483) against the opposition of former feudal lords and barons (former souverains) and continued under Henry III (1551-1589). To Bodin "the essence of statehood, the quality that makes an association of human beings a state, is the unity of its government; a state without a *summa potestas* [supreme sovereign power] would be like a ship without a keel." For the purpose of maintaining internal order, Bodin was convinced, there must be only one source from which decisive legal rules proceed. Does this principle of an *internal* order based on centralized and unchallengeable lawmaking make the sovereign lawmaker (an absolute monarch in Bodin's time and a nation-state in our time) supreme without any restriction whatsoever? One school of thought concludes that if a legislative authority is indeed supreme it cannot be bound by the laws it makes since it can change them at will. Yet, as J. L. Brierly argues, even Bodin in the sixteenth century considered some laws binding on the absolute monarch:

> the divine law, the law of nature or reason, that law that is common to all nations, and also certain laws which he calls the *leges imperii*, the laws of government [or as we would say today, the laws of the constitution]. . . . Sovereignty for [Bodin] was an essential principle of internal political order, and he would certainly have been surprised if he could have foreseen that later writers would distort it into a principle of international disorder, and use it to prove that by their very nature states are above the law.[8]

Many political analysts and legal experts view international law as an intersovereign law, that is, a law *between* and not above nations, a law of coordination and not of subordination. Nations are deemed subject to international law to the extent that they freely decide to place themselves under their own legal creations; nations may sovereignly decide to be less sovereign. The question naturally arises as to whether a consent of subordination, once given, can later be withdrawn, as a nation's membership in an international organization may be ended at the nation's will.

Whatever the legal theory may be, as a rule, national leaders tend to view international law as a law of coordination rather than subordination. The solemn process of signing international treaties, convenants, conventions, and charters is followed by a complex process of ratification (formal approval and sanction by national lawmakers). The text of international legal documents usually contains a list of principles and standards, internationally agreed on, but left to nations nationally to implement. A good example is the 1965 International Convention on the Elimination of All Forms of Racial Discrimination in which the signatories

> condemn racial discrimination and undertake to pursue by all appropriate means and without delay a policy of eliminating racial discrimination in all its forms; . . . each State Party shall take effective measures to review governmental, national and local policies, and to amend, rescind or nullify any laws and regulations which have the effect of creating or perpetuating racial discrimination wherever it exists; . . . States Parties particularly condemn racial segregation and *apartheid* and undertake to prevent, prohibit and eradicate all practices of this nature in territories under their jurisdiction [that is, within their own boundaries].

Two more aspects of the concept of national sovereignty as a supreme and therefore independent authority to give and enforce laws within the national territory should be mentioned:

1. If people and its state are deemed sovereign, can there be such a thing as a discrepancy between *popular* and *state* sovereignty? Soviet leaders and lawyers answer this question in the affirmative. Their argument, directed against the West, is that in capitalist societies the state, being an instrument of capitalist exploitation, represents a separation between "state sovereignty" and "popular sovereignty." As we shall see in Chapter 11, dealing with the general practice of foreign interference in the domestic affairs of nations, the Soviet Union feels entitled to interfere in support of "popular sovereignty"; the Soviet Union considers that such interference is an act not against the real sovereignty but against the false sovereignty. As the Brezhnev doctrine (see Document 11.7) expresses it:

> Formally juridical reasoning must not overshadow a class approach to the matter. . . . One who does it . . . begins to measure events with a yardstick of bourgeois law. Such an approach to the question of sovereignty means that, for example, the progressive forces of the World [meaning the Soviet Union] would not be able to come out against the revival of neo-Nazism in the Federal Republic of Germany, against the actions of butchers Franco and Salazar, against reactionary arbitrary actions of "black colonels" in Greece, because this is "the internal affair" of sovereign states.[9]

With reference to the Soviet Union itself, it is, of course, asserted that there the sovereignty of the people and the sovereignty of the state are one and inseparable.

2. If states claim to be sovereign, is their legal right to claim supreme authority in accord or in conflict with the practical possibility of asserting

this claim under concrete political and economic conditions? This is obviously not the case. Quite realistically, although with an obvious anti-Western bias, a Soviet textbook on international law states that "not all formally sovereign states are actually independent. Many sovereign states direct their foreign policy completely in accord with the counsel of other powers. . . . The sovereignty of a bourgeois state may in actuality be only a paper sovereignty and cover over a very real dependence of the given state."[10] Although the Soviet text focuses only on capitalist states, the Soviet distinction between *formal* and *real* sovereignty fully applies to the formal sovereignty but complete dependence of East European communist states on the Soviet Union.

The contrast between the national claim to sovereignty and the stark reality of dependence has induced many observers to conclude that the term "sovereignty," though constantly invoked, has become so meaningless that it should be eliminated from our vocabulary altogether. "We propose to waste no time in chasing shadows and will therefore discard the word entirely,"[11] warns an American text on international law.

Unequal Equals

Equality may mean absolute equality in power, wealth, and intellectual capacities. Obviously such equality exists nowhere in the world. Within a nation, individuals are rich or poor, clever or stupid, privileged or underprivileged. Some have influence, others have none. The same is true of nations. Terms such as "great powers," "medium powers," "small powers," and "microstates" refer to the different capacities of nations to act or resist the actions of others.

Equality may also mean equality before the law. Law may impose identical duties or confer identical rights upon individuals or groups of unequal capacities and thus make them equal before the law. It should be noted, however, that equality before the law does not necessarily mean equality of rights and duties.

Individuals within a nation are deprived of some rights in spite of the recognized principle of equality before the law: minors, feebleminded persons, and criminals have lesser rights than others. Women, as a general rule, have no duty to engage in fighting in wars.

In international law we also notice a disparity between legal rights and legal duties among sovereign, equal states. Coastal states have rights and duties different from those of inland states. In peace treaties victors usually impose heavy burdens on the vanquished nations (reparations or acceptence of military and political controls), and so the law sanctions very unequal rights and duties. There is also a difference between the manner in which international obligations are underwritten by unitary states in which lawmaking is centralized and by federal unions, whose component territorial units usually preserve the right to accept or reject obligations in matters within their police powers (education, health, social welfare, labor standards).

Hans Kelsen defines the concept of equality in the law and before the law as follows:

> Legal inequality of states is not incompatible with a legal regulation of interstate relations. As a matter of fact, there are treaties by which privileges are conferred upon some of the contracting states, and are not conferred upon the others, which do not lose their quality as states by such treatment. The charter of the United Nations confers upon five great powers the privilege of the so-called veto right, without violating the principle of equality allegedly established by general international law. And in spite of the legal inequality of the states under the Charter, the latter proclaims in its Article 2, paragraph 1: "The Organization is based on the principle of the sovereign equality of all its Members." It is evidently not equality in the law, but equality before the law, by which is meant the right of equality attributed by jurisprudence to individuals as well as to states, in spite of the fact that men as well as states are actually not equal. But there are differences which the law does and differences which the law does not recognize as relevant. Equality before the law means that the law-applying organs, in applying the law, must not make a difference which is not recognized by the law, that the law shall be applied as the law intends to be applied. Equality before the law means application of the law in conformity with the law, lawfulness, legality. It is a postulate directed at the law-applying organs, not a "right" of the subjects.[12]

Has the principle of equality been seriously impaired by the veto arrangement of the United Nations Charter? Kelsen, as we have seen, believes that inequality of rights and duties is compatible with the principle of equality before the law. L. F. L. Oppenheim, on the other hand, writes as follows:

> While in the General Assembly the principle of equality of representation and of voting power is, in general, the guiding rule . . . the principle of equality of voting power in the Security Council is substantially impaired as the result of the requirement, as a rule, of the concurrence of all the permanent members of the Security Council in decisions other than those relating to matters of procedure. One of the consequences of that inequality of voting power is that the ascertainment and enforcement, by an overriding decision of the Council, of obligations of pacific settlement and of International Law generally is legally possible only as against those members of the United Nations which are not permanent members of the Security Council. To that extent the relevant provisions of the Charter must be deemed to be contrary to the principle, which is of fundamental character, that, regardless of any other aspect of equality, all members of a political community ought to be equal before the law.[13]

Community of Interest or Balance of Power?

Profound differences in ideology, development, and national aims, coupled with extreme discrepancies in national power, have raised some doubts as to the existence of a universal community from which universal international law could issue. Certainly, on a global scene we do not see any meaningful approximation of the consensus and awareness of community that characterize most nation-states. And yet, here and there, and increasingly now, nations seem to form a community of sorts, a community in some areas of common concern, while they leave other areas in chaos. Where there is clear evidence of mutual benefits resulting from agreement on and observance of some legal rules, they are subsequently scrupulously adhered to and do not need enforcement. This is so, for instance, in the case of many international treaties dealing with nonpolitical matters such as trade, finance, tariffs, communications, diplomatic immunity, and some customs that are not even incorporated into treaties. There may emerge, at least regionally, a supranational community, consensus, and a set of rules that may function as well as any national legal system; that is, many legal rules will be obeyed by a lot of people, while some rules will occasionally be violated by a few people. In this connection we may admonish ourselves not to ask from an emerging international community a total consensus and a total adherence to all rules, which we do not expect in our own national community.

If there is no community of interests, can the balance of power provide a secondary basis for international law? "Where there is neither community of interest nor balance of power," states Hans J. Morgenthau, "there is no international law." In support of his statement Morgenthau quotes Oppenheim, the foremost modern teacher of international law, who in his original version of his major work (1912 edition) called the balance of power "an indispensable condition of the very existence of international law." Oppenheim then added:

> . . . a Law of Nations can exist only if there be an equilibrium, a balance of power, between the members of the Family of Nations. If the Powers cannot keep one another in check, no rules of law will have any force, since an overpowerful State will naturally try to act according to discretion and disobey the law. As there is not and never can be a central political authority above the Sovereign States that could enforce the rules of the Law of Nations, a balance of power must prevent any member of the Family of Nations from becoming omnipotent.[14]

HOW LAW IS CREATED AND CHANGED

Legal rights and duties may flow from two major sources. The first is a central lawmaking agency that enacts laws binding upon all members of the community without asking them specifically and individually for their consent. In democracies a general consent for this legislative activity is assumed and periodically confirmed by parliamentary elections. In dictatorships delegation is imagined or legislative authority simply usurped. The result of such a creation of legal rules is a legal system that is uniformly and automatically binding upon all. This does not mean, of course, that there are no violations of the law. The law tries to deter deviant behavior and provides for punishment of the violators. We do not know of any legal system in the world that can rightly claim *total* success in preventing or punishing any infraction of law.

In some societies, particularly in federations, there may be more than one legislative authority. In such a case either the constitution, the people's vote, or a supreme court has the power to delimit each legislature's domain and determine the hierarchy of norms in the case of local legislation clashing with federal law. But there is no central legislative authority on the world scene; neither is there a supreme court endowed with authority to solve legal conflicts on the basis of compulsory jurisdiction.

The second source of legal rights and obligations is a specific consent to them by all parties concerned. Rights and duties are defined and created for those, and only those, who have indicated their agreement. As already noted, such an agreement may be implied (*implicit* or *tacit* consent is the basis of customary law) and expressed by observance; in other words, the lack of objection to a situation or behavior may be construed as consent. The consent may also be formally recorded in a document. Such an *explicit* consent of territorial states is today the principal source of international law.[15] It resembles the law of contracts among individuals; it expresses an agreement obtained by preceding negotiation in which conflicting interests and views were brought into harmony. Individuals and nations thus limit or expand their rights by contracts beyond what these rights might be in the absence of a treaty. A great majority of such treaties based on mutual consent are usually observed. A minor portion of them are violated and require enforcement, if that is possible.

If international law is viewed as a system of coercive norms controlling the actions of states but based on their consent, can peace treaties imposed by victors on the vanquished be viewed as legal, or are they exceptions to the general principle of implied or expressed consent? Lawyers often disagree on this point. Some lawyers point to the observable practice of the vanquished nations, which in due time object to imposed inequality and other burdens and invoke their right to equality by arguing that their consent to the treaty was obtained illegally, under duress. Other lawyers construe the state's surrender in war as implying a general consent to anything the victor might request. When some lawyers argued that the 1945 International War Crimes Tribunal required that the German government consent to its jurisdiction and proceedings, the answer was given that the unconditional surrender of Nazi Germany included consent to everything—military occupation, reparations, and the Nuremberg trials.

Contracts

Like individuals, territorial states conclude written agreements in which they limit their freedom of action in order to obtain some benefit that they consider outweighs their self-imposed restraints, contributions, or sacrifices. This exchange and calculation characterizes all contracts. In a lease, a landlord limits the exercise of his sovereign power over his house by permitting the tenant to occupy and use part of the house within set limits (no dogs, for instance), while the tenant limits his sovereign power over his income by reserving a portion of it every month as the rent for his apartment. An international treaty on the subject of a lease of a tracking station for orbiting satellites or a lease of a naval base may contain identical elements of a contract—provided, of course, that the lease was freely negotiated and not imposed by a superior on an inferior power by force or blackmail.

Contracts among nations are usually called treaties, compacts, pacts, conventions ("convention" usually describes a multilateral treaty, not the meeting which has led to it), covenants, or charters. The United Nations Charter is a multilateral treaty to which nearly all territorial states have acceded.

At this point three differences between contracts familiar on the national scene and international treaties may be noted. First, on the national scene, the term "contract" usually evokes an image of two or more but not too many contracting parties. An international treaty, on the other hand, often bears the signatures of a great many nations. Second, a contract between individuals is usually concerned with very specific and limited issues. In contrast, some international treaties embody general principles or norms that on a national scene would never be found in a contract but only in the text of a law or a constitution. Such an international treaty, usually called "a lawmaking convention," may indeed become a part of nearly universal law if all or practically all the states have subsequently acceded to it or made their conduct conform to it. Conceivably, even extremely fragmented lawmaking by express or tacit international consent may in the long run result in a universal and codified law (the problem of codification is discussed later), if the consent includes "such an overwhelming majority of the members that those who dissent are of no importance whatever, and disappear totally from the view of one who looks for the will of the community as an entity in contradistinction to the wills of its single members."[16]

A third difference is that the validity of private contracts is rarely exposed to the extreme test of life-and-death situations, that is, the choice between adherence to a contract, which might result in death, and its violation, which might result in survival. Territorial states, however, often feel that their adherence to a particular international norm—ideological, moral, or legal—may result in national suicide while its violation may guarantee victory and survival. This point was noted in our analyses of the role of ideologies (Chapter 7) and morality in politics (Chapter 8).

The subject of contracts among individuals is extremely varied, ranging from personal matters, such as marriage, divorce, gifts, and wills to complicated business and corporation contracts. Similarly, contracts among sovereign nations cover a great variety of problems regulated or defined by their mutual consent: leasing of military bases; modes of acquiring state territory by cession, occupation, or subjugation; commerce, agriculture, finance, transport, communication, and copyright; registration and interpretation of treaties; extradition of criminals; regulation of fisheries and whaling and navigation on the open sea and on international rivers, territorial waters, gulfs, and bays, tariffs; exploration of outer space; diplomatic and consular immunities; foreign aid and technical assistance; political and military cooperation; and cooperation among nations on a universal basis.

The preceding subjects are considered to be part of that branch of international law called the *law of peace*. It regulates the rights and obligations of nations in the periods of peace.

The Law of War The second branch of international law is called the *law of war*. It regulates the rights and obligations of belligerents and nonbelligerents in war. Traditionally it includes legal arrangements concerning the following partial list of subjects: distinction between regular and irregular armed forces; declaration of war; rupture of diplomatic intercourse and consular activity; treatment of the wounded, of prisoners of war, and of the shipwrecked; punishment of war crimes by international organs; rights and duties of nonbelligerents; blockade; contraband; visitation, capture, and trial of neutral vessels.

The difference between the law of war and the law of peace was originally formulated by Hugo Grotius (1583-1654), whose book, *On the Law of War and Peace*, represents the first attempt to study, interpret, and codify existing customs in the intercourse among nations. These customs had gradually hardened into a set of legal obligations and duties. The present-day standard book on international law, by Oppenheim, is similarly divided into two volumes, the first entitled *Peace*, the second *Disputes, War and Neutrality*.

However controversial it may appear to be in our atomic age, war is not an illegal intercourse among nations. War is not considered an international crime even though war does consist of acts that, in times of peace, would be considered criminal, such as destroying human lives or property. In their supreme laws of the land—the constitutions—nearly all nations actually proclaim war in defense of one's country to be their citizens' legal and moral duty.

War Crimes Military operations whose evident purpose is to destroy the enemy's capacity and will to act are not, however, without some international legal limits; although committed in the course of a legal war, some acts may be treated as "war crimes." The Hague Convention of 1907 (Article 22), for instance, records the international agreement that "the right of belligerents to adopt means of injuring the enemy is not unlimited." The Convention specifically prohibits killing of soldiers who have surrendered, bombing of undefended places, pillage of captured cities, and use of poisoned arms calculated to cause "unnecessary" or disproportionate suffering. The line between necessary and unnecessary suffering in war is, of course, unclear. After World War I nations outlawed gas warfare; the skeptics argued that an agreement on gas warfare was possible because poisonous gas had proved a rather ineffective weapon, especially when the direction of the wind changed; others argued that nerve gas might actually prove to be a less pain-inflicting and nonlethal method of incapacitating the enemy than machine-gun bullets. On the other hand, nations have so far not agreed on banning napalm bombs, certainly inhuman weapons

After World War II the Nazi leaders were tried and condemned for war crimes. An executive agreement, negotiated by the United States, the Soviet Union, England, and France (and subsequently adhered to by the wartime coalition of the nineteen "United Nations"), was signed on August 8, 1945, in London (three months after the war in Europe ended and two days after the atomic bomb was dropped on Hiroshima). Four substantive offenses were defined:

1. *Crimes against peace,* namely, planning, preparation, initiation or waging of a war of aggression or a war in violation of international treaties.
2. *War crimes,* namely, violations of the laws or customs of war, such as murder or ill-treatment of the civilian population or prisoners of war, wanton destruction of cities, killing of hostages, or devastation not justified by military necessity.
3. *Crimes against humanity*, namely, murder or persecution of civilian population on political, racial, or religious grounds.
4. *Conspiracy* to commit any or all of the three categories of crimes.

While there seems to be a general agreement that politically and morally justice was done at the Nuremberg war crimes trials when out of twenty-two top Nazi leaders nineteen were found guilty and ten condemned to hanging, a serious legal controversy arose. Four of the major controversies deserve to be briefly stated:

1. Was the executive agreement of August 8, 1945, an explicit formulation of what had been implicit in international law or was it an *ex post facto* law, that is, a retroactive criminal law that transforms an act that was not a crime at the time of its commission into a punishable offense?

2. In our world of sovereign states, has an individual a moral, legal, or practical alternative to obeying a national or other enforceable legal order? Do international obligations (usually unenforceable before one's own nation's defeat) really transcend citizens' and soldiers' duties to their own nation-states? The general principle of the Nuremberg trials was that international crimes are committed by men and not nations or states as abstract entities. This principle was directed at the top Nazi leaders; their personal responsibility seemed clear. Less clear was the responsibility of those obeying orders from superiors, such as privates, noncommissioned officers, and officers. How much more responsible is a colonel than a major or a captain?

3. Who has the right to determine what is "wanton" destruction, not justified by "military necessity" and resulting in "needless" suffering? Both the Allies and the Nazis engaged in mass bombings of cities and indiscriminate submarine warfare; neither type of warfare was considered in the Nuremberg trials.

4. Is it realistic to assume that, based on the Nuremberg precedent, a victor in a future war would be tried for identical or similar acts?

Both sets of major war crimes trials, those held at Nuremberg and those held in Tokyo for the Japanese war criminals, were presided over by victorious Allied powers; not even one single neutral judge was added for decoration. Some skeptics sadly conclude that, instead of creating a precedent, the Nuremberg and Tokyo trials merely confirmed that defeat in war is an international "crime" to be punished by the victors.

The controversy on the strategic, that is, indiscriminate, mass bombing of large cities, practiced on a large scale during World War II, emerged once more with dramatic emphasis during the war in Vietnam. Was such bombing a clear case of international crime or only an inhuman and ineffective form of warfare? The former chief U.S. prosecutor at the Nuremberg war crimes trials and a professor of law at Columbia University, Telford Taylor, was in Hanoi during the massive United States attacks in 1972. Subsequently he wrote an article on this subject in which he concluded that the American bombings, however cruel and senseless, were not an international crime (see Document 9.2).

To sum up: Legal rules among territorial states are based on either explicit or implicit consent, that is, on treaties or custom. When there is no such explicit or tacit agreement, there is no law; there is only a chaos of unilateral claims as to what the rights and obligations are or ought to be. We speak of so-called gaps of law (*lacunae legis*), most frequent on the

DOCUMENT 9.2

WAS THE BOMBING OF HANOI A WAR CRIME?

The results of our bombing undeniably are horrible. . . . Immoral and senseless this bombing may well be, but where is the law under which to call it criminal?

When I put this question to the North Vietnamese lawyers, they gave two answers. The first was that our bombing is part of an aggressive war launched by the United States against their country. Even assuming the truth of the premise, this is not a satisfactory analysis, for if aggression alone is the test of criminality, every military operation carried out by the aggressor would be a war crime—a view put forward and rejected, I believe rightly, at Nuremberg. It would also follow that the North Vietnamese, who on their assumption are not aggressors, would be legally justified in bombing Saigon into bloody ruins.

Their second and more substantial response is that the laws of war cannot remain frozen at the Nuremberg level, but must respond to the march of events and that by now the futility and inhumanity of "strategic" bombing has been so clearly demonstrated that it must be outlawed, much as poison gas was after the First World War. To this I can only say amen, but objectivity obliges the response, that efforts to formulate such a law have failed over half a century . . .

But surely the bombing of Hanoi does raise serious legal questions under the principle of "proportionality"—the rule that there must be a reasonable relation between the military objective and the damage and suffering which its attainment will entail. A single enemy soldier is a legitimate target whether he is in the front line or on home leave, but to level a city block to kill him at home is beyond the bounds of proportionality.

From an article by Telford Taylor, former chief U. S. prosecutor at the Nuremberg war crimes-trials, in the *New York Times*, January 11, 1973.

international scene, where law is created in such a fragmented manner, from issue to issue and from nation to nation. It is symptomatic that, for instance, a criminal code that looms so large in any organized territorial system is practically nonexistent on the international scene. Essential features of any criminal law are (1) a precise definition of an act that constitutes a crime (for instance murder equals *deliberate* killing as opposed to manslaughter) and (2) provision for punishment. With the exception of a few international conventions that define the international crimes of piracy or genocide but that usually fail to provide for an international criminal court and international prosecution (see Document 9.3), nations have not agreed on the definition of the most frequent international crimes or, of course, on procedures for their prosecution and punishment.

The most common international "crime," that of unprovoked armed aggression, eludes clear definition. For twenty years international lawyers

DOCUMENT 9.3

GENOCIDE CONVENTION (ADOPTED BY THE UN ON DECEMBER 9, 1948)

Article 1

The Contracting Parties confirm that genocide, whether committed in time of peace or in time of war, is a crime under international law which they undertake to prevent and punish.

Article 2

In the present Convention, genocide means any of the following acts committed with intent to destroy, in whole or in part, a national, ethnical, racial or religious group as such: (a) killing members of the group, (b) causing serious bodily or mental harm to members of the group, (c) deliberately inflicting on the group conditions of life calculated to bring about physical destruction in whole or in part, (d) imposing measures intended to prevent births within the group, (e) forcibly transferring children of the group to another group.

Article 3

The following acts shall be punishable: (a) genocide, (b) conspiracy to commit genocide, (c) direct and public incitement to commit genocide, (d) attempt to commit genocide, (e) complicity in genocide.

Article 4

Persons committing genocide or any of the other acts enumerated in Article 3 shall be punished, whether they are constitutionally responsible rulers, public officials, or private individuals.

Article 5

The Contracting Parties undertake to enact, in accordance with their respective Constitutions, the necessary legislation to give effect to the provisions of the present Convention and, in particular, to provide effective penalties for persons guilty of genocide or any of the other acts enumerated in Article 3.

Article 6

Persons charged with genocide or any of the other acts enumerated in Article 3 shall be tried by a competent tribunal of the State in the territory of which the act was committed, or by such international penal tribunal as may have jurisdiction with respect to those Contracting Parties which shall have accepted its jurisdiction. [No such tribunal has been established.]

Article 7

Genocide and the other acts enumerated in Article 3 shall not be considered as political crimes for the purpose of extradition.

The Contracting Parties pledge themselves in such cases to grant extradition in accordance with their laws and treaties in force. . . .

at the League of Nations tried to define it, but no agreement proved possible. Then for another thirty years, the United Nations Special Committee on the Question of Defining Aggression and a special working group of experts met (throughout the late 1940s, the 1950s, and the 1960s) and repeatedly failed to reach agreement on the distinctions between the illegitimate and the legitimate use of force (as a means of defending against aggression), between the initiation of armed action in the exercise of the right of national self-determination and the use of force for purposes other than self-determination, between aggressive and nonaggressive intent; and they also failed to agree on various acts to be included in the definition of aggression, such as clandestine infiltration of armed bands into the territory of another state or smuggling of an atomic bomb across the border by a terrorist. On April 12, 1974, the United Nations Special Committee finally reached an agreement on the definition of aggression. The definition is three full pages long. The first article in the eight-article text states that aggression is

> the use of armed force by a State against the sovereignty, territorial integrity, or political independence of another State or in any other manner inconsistent with the Charter of the United Nations.

Subsequent articles list acts qualifying as acts of aggression, such as invasion, military occupation, bombardment, blockade, the dispatch by or on behalf of one state of armed bands, groups, irregulars, or mercenaries into another state, where they carry out acts of armed force of such gravity as to amount to aggression. Nothing in the definition of aggression, the United Nations definition states, can prejudice the right to self-determination, freedom, and independence of peoples forcibly (who can prove that?) deprived of that right, "particularly peoples under colonial and racist regimes or other forms of alien domination" (Soviet domination of Mongolia and Eastern Europe?). Nor, the text adds, would the right of those people "to struggle to that end and to seek and receive support" be prejudiced by the definition. It means therefore that an armed initiative, and support thereof, directed against a government deemed alien or colonial by the insurgents and their external supporters is not an aggression. Pondering the future application of the United Nations 1974 yardstick one concludes that the definition seems to contain so many loopholes that an army could march through. Furthermore, several delegations, while approving the text in a spirit of compromise, voiced their reservations. Syria, for instance, objected to Article 2, which states that "the *first* use of armed force by a State constitutes *prima facie* [legally self-evident] evidence of an act of aggression," and noted that part of the Syrian territory was at that time still under foreign occupation as a result of Israeli aggression. The Syrian delegate also suggested that the right of colonial people to use *all means at their disposal* to achieve independence should have been included;[17] he probably meant an approval of Palestinian terrorism as an appropriate defensive measure against foreign rule.

The Law of the Sea

A serious gap in international law is the unresolved issues in the law of the sea, especially the present-day conflicts concerning the extension of the authority of coastal states into the sea. The major issues include: absolute national control of offshore waters (the territorial sea), the right to control, protect, and exploit living resources (fish and whales) and mineral resources (oil, gas, and minerals) found in the so-called continental margins (continental shelf, slope, and rise), and international ownership and exploitation of deep seabeds under the authority of a world agency that would issue and receive payments for licenses to nations or corporations to mine the oceans. The oceans are known to contain vast stores of manganese nodules from which nickel and copper can be derived. Some nations already can drill and cap oil wells at a depth of 700 feet. Western mining companies know how to extract minerals from an oceanic depth of 20,000 feet. In addition there is the problem of the military uses of the seabed for the emplacement of nuclear-missile launching pads and electronic devices. The various attempts at a radical extension of sovereign national controls far into the sea naturally conflict with the tradition and continued desirability of free navigation for the purpose of international trade and national defense.

There is little agreement on these matters except for the general principle that "the high seas being open to all nations, no State may validly purport to subject any part of them to its sovereignty." This is a quotation from Article 2 of the Geneva Convention on the High Seas of April 27, 1958, passed at the first Law of the Sea Conference.

The principle was expressed for the first time by Hugo Grotius in his *Mare Liberum* (*Freedom of the Seas*), published in 1609. Grotius defended the right of the Dutch and everybody else to navigate around the Cape of Good Hope and to trade with the Indies against the Portuguese claim to exclusive rights of navigation and commerce on the sea.

Since the freedom of navigation for ships of all nations is in harmony with the interests of all nations, this principle has not been seriously contested since the seventeenth century. Thus, when in 1958 a conference on the law of the sea was held in Geneva, the principle was reaffirmed in a new convention.

The problem, however, is that nations do not agree on the point—3, 6, 9, 10, 12, 100, or 200 miles from the coastline—where the open sea, free for all to use, starts. The contemporary tendency is to push the national-territorial line further from the coastline: Eighty-six nations attending the 1958 Law of the Sea Conference in Geneva failed again to agree on the point where the high seas begin and the territorial waters end. Problems touching upon the extension of territorial sovereignty into the sea exemplify the difficulty of creating a valid legal system when national interests and concepts are in sharp conflict. The great maritime nations (Japan, England, France, and the United States) had the greatest interest in free global navigation; their fear was that the extension of the three-mile limit to nine, twelve, or more miles would close many sea lanes and straits to commercial traffic. Thus, while more and more nations tended to claim a twelve-mile limit (all communist states, practically all developing nations, and France as of 1971), several nations continued to adhere to the traditional three-mile limit, and a few temporarily adopted a six-mile (Greece and Italy) or ten-mile (Yugoslavia as of 1965) limit.

The second Law of the Sea Conference, held in Geneva in 1960, marked little progress in this matter, so a third Law of the Sea Conference was held in Caracas in 1974. Altogether 148 governments were listed as participants. It should be noted that following the first two Law of the Sea Conferences (1958 and 1960), out of 113 coastal states who were members of the United Nations on May 1, 1972, only 51 proclaimed themselves to be bound by the Geneva Conventions on the High Seas and Continental Shelf, 33 by the Convention on Fishing and Conservation, and 43 by the Convention on the Territorial Sea. At the time of writing, there were no strong indications that the 1974 Conference whose main task was to prepare an agreement to be refined and signed in Vienna in 1975, would result in a much more impressive general acceptance of international sea accords.

Even though by 1974 most nations proved ready to agree on a general twelve-mile limit to their territorial waters, over which their sovereignty, in its fullest sense of the term, could be exercised, new technological advances as well as a dramatic increase in the industrial pollution of oceans gave rise to new political and legal problems that were to prove much more explosive than the old problem of the territorial sea and the *contiguous zone* (a belt of high seas contiguous to a state's territorial sea, not extending beyond twelve miles from the base line from which the breadth of the territorial sea is measured, in which the state can exercise control for the purposes of prevention and punishment of infringements of its customs, fiscal, immigration, or sanitary regulations). The most difficult of the new problems is that of outer limits of national control over sea resources, including fishing, oil, and minerals.

Conservation and Allocation of Fisheries Until 1974 international law permitted the establishment of an exclusive twelve-mile *fishing zone*. The area beyond was deemed high seas open to all fishermen on an equal basis. Possible overfishing by fishermen from great industrial nations, (Japan, the Soviet Union, the United States, and England), employing modern and highly efficient equipment in floating fish factories, was bound to be challenged by ecologists and, of more importance, by underdeveloped nations. Even when there was no immediate danger of depletion of resources, developing nations wanted more territorial control of the sea because they feared competition with better-equipped fishermen. In the 1960s this fear repeatedly led Peru, Ecuador, Uruguay and Chile, for instance, to assert control over a 200-mile fishing zone (see Figure 9.1); within that area apparently all tuna and whales were considered Chilean, Ecuadorian, Uruguayan, or Peruvian, and foreign ships catching them were subject to seizure and confiscation of the catch. In the period between 1961 and 1971 at least 109 American trawlers were seized; several American boats were raked by machine-gun fire off the Peruvian coast and a Soviet trawler was shelled off Argentina. American tuna men paid more than $790,000 in fines and license fees in 1970 alone. On the other hand, great industrial and fishing nations accused several coastal nations of neglect and lack of utilization of their coastal fish resources in a period of global food crisis. The advanced countries therefore proposed international arbitration procedures which would permit foreign nations to fish in the underutilized 200-mile fishing zones.

This proposal was denounced by various developing countries and the People's Republic of China, whose official view was given in the *Peking Review* (July 26,1974):

> The representative of Soviet revisionism. . . . put forward a proposal which is seemingly sympathetic to a 200-mile economic zone but in essence obstinately persists in maritime hegemonism. . . . The U.S. representative put forward a similar proposal later. The Soviet representative's hoax, however, was exposed then and there by representatives from Third World countries. The Peruvian representative nailed down the trick of the Soviet representative as a "Trojan horse." The Ecuadorian representative declared categorically that "Ecuador will not accept a convention which impairs in any manner the integrity of its rights over the renewable and non-renewable resources in the 200-mile sea area." The strong opposition evoked by the speeches of the representatives of Soviet revisionism and the other super-power is a clear indication that the two hegemonic powers are in a predicament. As the verse goes: "Flowers fall off, do what one may."

Continental Margins   The development of floating derricks and of techniques for drilling on the seabed led the 1958 Law of the Sea Conference to consider and define the rights of coastal states to exploit not only the seabed below the territorial limits (from three to twelve miles). The seabed under shallow coastal waters is called the *continental shelf*. The Fourth Geneva Convention (1958), which dealt with the continental shelf, defined it in its Article 1 as follows (note the last sentence allowing an extraordinarily flexible interpretation, changing with any new invention in seabed exploitation):

> The sea-bed and subsoil of the submarine areas adjacent to the coast but

FIGURE 9.1
THE UNITED STATES AND PERU:
COMPETITION OVER FISHING RIGHTS

"No wonder the Peruvians don't want us fishing in their waters."

Drawing by Henry R. Martin; Copyright 1969 Saturday Review, Inc.

outside the area of the territorial sea to a depth of 200 meters or, beyond that limit, to where the depth of the superjacent waters admits the exploitation of the natural resources of these said areas.

The coastal states were thus authorized to exercise sovereign rights over the continental shelf, but at that time only for the purpose of exploring the seabed and subsoil and of exploiting its natural resources. This was particularly aimed at the exploitation of offshore oil deposits, but, as subsequent events demonstrated, the right to one's continental shelf could include also the right to exclusive control of those species of animal that live under water and are not fish, since their habitat is the continental shelf rather than the water above it. This was an important issue in the

Soviet-Japanese negotiations in 1969, when both sides failed to agree on the question, Do king crabs swim or crawl? The issue was crucial because if the crabs only crawl they are considered part of the Soviet continental shelf and thus the property of the Soviet Union; if they also swim, then they are not part of the continental shelf, and Japanese fishermen can take them. The export of king crabs is a major item in Japan's balance of payments. According to the Japanese press, the Soviet diplomats argued that "king crabs crawl, their feet rest on the surface of the sea bottom and hence, [they are] sedentary denizens of the continental shelf."

The Japanese argued against the Soviet nationality of crabs by claiming that they both crawl and swim:

> Would the king crab fall straight down to the sea bottom like a piece of metal when it is thrown into the sea from a ship? No, sir. The crab sinks slowly, slowly, flapping to and fro like a Japanese paper fan hurled in the air. . . . Also the king crab uses a kicking motion to jump to great heights—just like an Olympic pole-vault ace does with his glass fiber pole.[18]

A temporary compromise was reached on April 12, 1969, when the Soviet Union agreed to further Japanese fishing but on a reduced scale. The Japanese crab haul was reduced by 20 percent, and the *New York Times* noted that this left the Japanese unhappy, even crabby.

Since modern technology now permits exploitation of the seabed to much greater depths than the 100 fathoms (200 meters) used to define the continental shelf, a new concept has emerged, that of the *exclusive economic zone*, or Patrimonial Sea; as these terms indicate, they represent various claims of coastal states to control and exploit all living and mineral resources on the continental *shelf*, continental *slope*, and continental *rise*—leaving the question open as to the limits of national control and exploitation of the ocean abyss.

The problem of the economic zone is further complicated by the fact that some nations, such as the Soviet Union and the United States, have a very extensive continental shelf, slope, and rise (the Arctic shelf of Russia extends over 700 miles), while many coastal states are, so to speak, "flat-chested": their coast abruptly descends to the abyssal depth of the ocean. If a universal 200-mile exclusive economic zone were agreed on, 35 percent of the entire ocean surface would be brought within national control; slightly more than half of it would go to six developed states and four developing nations.

If the so-called continental margins (see Figure 9.2) were to be handed in their entirety over to the coastal states, as the United Nations Association Magazine *Vista* alarmingly put it,

> this would constitute a collective land grab of 20 percent of the entire ocean-bed area, or one seventh of the planet's surface. If the "coasties"

FIGURE 9.2
THE CONTINENTAL SHELF, SLOPE, AND RISE

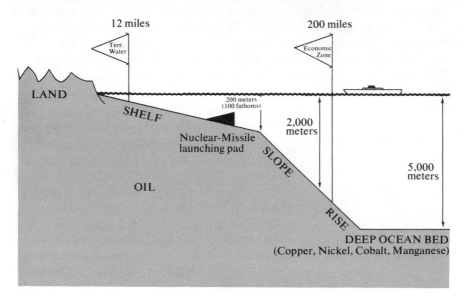

got the continental shelf plus slope (but not the rise), this would still give them 15.3 percent of the ocean floor. In fact, even if they got only out as far as the 200-meter isobath, they would still have 7.7 percent of the total seabed.[19]

The general tendency to bite off large chunks of high seas either by extending controls over the seabed or by pushing territorial waters and fishing zones farther into the open sea represents a new threat to the global movement of goods and persons in a period in which the world's nations claim to be more interdependent than ever before. Extension of territorial waters to the twelve-mile limit would change more than a hundred formerly international straits (including Dover, Gibraltar, Malucca, and the entrance to the Red Sea) into territorial zones, possibly clogging international oil and other traffic, as well as some of the traditional sea routes between islands composing various archipelagic nations (Indonesia, Malaysia, the Philippines)—nations that have already presented their claim that all water between their islands be considered their "national territory," inaccessible to foreign navigation.

Since 1973 both the Soviet Union and the United States have pressed for a new international guarantee of the freedom of transit through and over international straits. Under the prevailing doctrine of international law, the "right of innocent passage," that is, the right to transit through territorial waters connecting two bodies of water that are designated high seas, seemed already guaranteed. There were, however, two problems: First, under the doctrine of "innocent passage," the coastal states have kept the right to oblige foreign submarines to surface in transit and to prohibit overflights—which, as the two superpowers saw it, could impede movement of their nuclear submarines and planes. Second, under the doctrine of "innocent passage," each coastal state could determine for itself whether a passage was "innocent," "hostile," or "not so innocent" as it might appear. A politically biased interpretation of "innocence" could bring international traffic through some straits to a standstill, as in the case of the Arab closure of the Strait of Tiran (connecting the Red Sea and the Gulf of Aqaba) before the third Arab-Israeli war in 1967. The United States' position on the territorial sea and traffic through international straits was presented by the Department of State in 1973:

> The U.S. straits position is based on the fact that global communications require movement through and over straits and that an extension of the territorial sea from 3 to 12 miles would cause a large number of important international straits to become overlapped by territorial waters. . . . The doctrine of innocent passage is inadequate for it has been interpreted subjectively [!] by some coastal states as to what is prejudicial to their "peace, order, and security."[20]

Nuclear and Electronic Uses of Oceans The Antarctic Treaty of 1959, agreed to by both the Soviet Union and the United States, prohibits the use of Antarctica for other than peaceful purposes; it also guarantees to all nations the "freedom of scientific investigation in Antarctica." In 1969 the Soviet Union and the United States agreed to make the ocean floor a nuclear-free area, since new technology made it possible to use the seabed for emplacement of nuclear missiles. Concealed in submerged barges, invisible from the air, and controllable from a distance, such missiles could be fired not only against nuclear submarines but also against land and air targets. Article 1 of the Soviet-American proposal contains the following pledge:

> The states [who are] parties to this treaty undertake not to emplant or emplace on the seabed and the ocean floor and in the subsoil thereof beyond the maximum contiguous zone [twelve miles] provided for in the 1958 Geneva Convention on the Territorial Sea and on the Contiguous Zone any objects with nuclear weapons or any other types of weapons of mass destruction, as well as structures, launching installations or any other facilities specifically designed for storing, testing or using such weapons.

As may be noted, the treaty does not prohibit emplacement of nuclear weapons within twelve miles of the coast. Furthermore, each party is to determine for itself whether a bay (such as the Soviet Sea of Okhotsk) or an estuary (such as the United States Hudson Bay) is or is not part of the open sea. Evidently, new technology creates new problems of territorial delineation even in those uninhabited places where there had been none before.

The problem of electronic violation and penetration of sovereign territory and coastal waters was demonstrated by the North Korean seizure of the American electronic spy ship *Pueblo* in January 1968 and the downing of an American EC-121 spy plane in April 1969. At the 1969 meeting of the American Society of International Law it was argued that the established law of the seas has been outmoded by the advent of electronic intelligence, since today modern monitoring devices can penetrate to the heart of a country's inland defenses; coastal states therefore cannot be blamed if they view offshore electronics intelligence operations as a substantially new phenomenon in international life. Furthermore, it seems that the great powers, with their wealth and technological capabilities, are taking unfair advantage of smaller, poorer countries that cannot afford their own reconnaissance systems. The great powers all engage in espionage while claiming an immunity of the high seas intended originally to protect navigation.

The argument on the other side should be heard too: First, since a state cannot prohibit a passing vessel from looking at the shore through field glasses, why should it prohibit modern electronic "looking glasses"?

Second, intelligence collection serves peace rather than war because a nation is less likely to strike out blindly at some country if it is getting reasonably accurate intelligence (an argument proffered by Clark M. Clifford, former secretary of defense under Lyndon Johnson).

Third, if electronics espionage is objectionable beyond the twelve-mile limit, what is the real limit, and should the objection apply also to monitoring from orbiting satellites?

In 1972 Libya declared a hundred-mile radius from Tripoli as a "restricted air zone" that foreign planes could not enter without permission. A United States C130 transport that was on an electronic reconnaissance mission eighty-three miles off the Libyan coast over the Mediterranean was subsequently fired on by two Libyan fighters. Libya ignored the United States protest about the incident.

So it seems that modern technology, which has so greatly shrunk distances among nations, has also shrunk the extent of the nonnational high seas and the air above them.

A New Era of Ocean Politics   Opening a preliminary meeting of the Third Law of the Sea Conference in New York in 1973, the secretary-general of the United Nations, Kurt Waldheim, warned:

> Time is not on our side and delay would be perilous. . . . We face the very real probability of increasing the causes of disputes between nations unless agreement [on the law of the Sea] is reached.[21]

A scholarly study of the problems connected with the new era of ocean politics suggests that the effort to fashion a new international order for the oceans, reflecting modern technological, economic and political development, would occupy national leaders for most of the remainder of the twentieth century. The reason for this forecast is that ocean politics has become entangled with the perennial problems of politics among nations, that is,

> reconciling national security with the need to contain the arms race; finding rational, just and peaceful ways of allocating the world's supply of energy, food, and industrial raw materials; searching for syntheses between the competing demands of economic development and ecological care; narrowing the economic and political gap between the poor and the affluent peoples; and, in general, managing the growing ability of nations to affect one another for ill or for good.[22]

CODIFICATION OF LAW

Clarity and precision add to the effectiveness of law. They also help eliminate some conflicts based on misunderstanding of the law. If nations agree on the principles of a given law, subsequent codification by legal experts may contribute to a greater clarity of the law provided that any vagueness and ambiguity in the law was not intentional in the first place.

Article 15 of the Statute of the International Law Commission defines codification as "the more precise formulation and systematization of international law in fields where there has been extensive State practice, precedent, and doctrine." This may mean one of two distinct processes: (1) Custom law and the decisions of tribunals may be translated into formal treaties or codes with little or no alteration of law, or (2) custom or existing treaties may be modified so as to reconcile different practices and concepts.

The difference between making a completely new law and substantially modifying an old one may disappear in actual practice. The United Nations Charter (Article 13) states: "The General Assembly shall initiate studies and make recommendations for the purpose . . . of encouraging the progressive development of international law and its codification." The preceding discussion on the law of the sea has shown that one and the same conference can be engaged in both codifying existing rules and customs and developing new ones. Such a conference tries to reconcile conflicting views and practices, modifies them, and thus creates new rules.

The process of codification reduces the confusing multitude of conflicting claims and practices. But in order to secure ratification of a new international treaty by as many nations as possible, international lawmakers often sacrifice the demand for precision and clarity for the sake of uniformity. Resulting rules are then easily accepted because they are vague and ambiguous and lend themselves to different national interpretations. The danger of this process has already been noted in connection with the Third World nations acceding to preexisting international norms.

The codification of international law must, therefore, avoid two dangers: imprecision and rigidity. Rules that are too specific would either prevent ratification by national governments or result in ratifications that would be essentially meaningless because the ratifiers would be reluctant to comply with such new rules.

Under the auspices of the League of Nations, a conference was held at The Hague in 1930 for the purpose of trying to codify important branches of international law. It proved to be an overambitious conference for many reasons. To begin with, it tried to complete its work in one month, but the hurried atmosphere of an international conference was hardly suitable for such work. Most important, however, the conference, bound by the rule of unanimity in all important questions, demonstrated the difficulty of agreeing on a uniform code for a community that did not exist. The diversity of interests and conditions in different regions and nations of the world rendered uniformity either undesirable or impossible. And what was true in the 1930s is certainly no less true in the 1970s.

If through codification international law becomes more precise, more uniform, and more generally known, this justifies all the efforts that codification necessitates. It should be borne in mind, however, that a greater compliance with legal rules may not necessarily ensue. Nations that are resolved and have the necessary strength to break the law will do so whether it is codified or not.

In order to facilitate development of international law and codification of existing rules, practice, doctrine, and precedent, the United Nations General Assembly established (on November 21, 1947) an International Law Commission. In November 1948 it elected its first fifteen members, experts who were to serve in their private capacity rather than under instruction from their governments. The quality of this expert body's work has been high. Its recommendations have formed the basis of many international treaties. The 1958 Geneva Conference, which succeeded in codifying large portions of the law of the sea, "could never have accomplished its task without the International Law Commission's carefully prepared draft," notes Max Sorensen. "Whatever happens, the International Law Commission has proved its worth."[23]

Unfortunately, it is not the quality of the International Law Commission's work that will determine the acceptability of its recommendations by national governments. "Experts might agree upon principles which would contribute to the well-being of the international community," said a standard text on international organization, "but governments would weigh these principles in terms of national interest."[24]

ARBITRATION AND JUDICIAL SETTLEMENT

Within nations the difference between arbitration and judicial settlement is a major one.

Arbitration denotes the process by which two parties to a dispute agree on an umpire and further agree that they will abide by his decision. This "third-party" technique was known to ancient civilizations and to Europe in the Middle Ages. Individuals have used it instead of duels; and groups have used it instead of violence.

Judicial settlement means a process by which parties to a dispute or an individual violating a public law may be compelled to appear before a court. The judge then hands down an enforceable decision.

Among nations the difference between arbitration and judicial settlement is a relatively minor one; it refers mostly to the structure, principles, and permanency of the court in contrast to arbitrators. International arbitration and international judicial settlement resemble each other in two important aspects: (1) No state can, as a general rule, summon another to appear before either an arbitrator or a judge for the purpose of settling a dispute; but (2) states can establish the jurisdiction of a court or an arbitrator either by a general agreement with regard to all or some of their future disputes or by a special agreement with reference to one particular dispute. The blurred line between international arbitration and international judicial procedure suggests again that the similarity between some domestic and international institutions is more in the name and external forms than in the content.

The development of arbitration among nations has extended over many centuries. But real progress was made in the development of its techniques at the first Peace Conference at The Hague in 1899 and at the second Peace Conference at The Hague in 1907.

The second Hague conference agreed on the convention for the pacific settlement of international disputes. Out of its ninety-seven articles more than half deal with arbitration. Under Article 55 of that convention (1907), either states may select one or more arbitrators as they please, or they may use the Permanent Court of Arbitration, which had been organized on the basis of a previous convention agreed to in the first Hague conference. The term "Court of Arbitration" is to some extent a misnomer, for the Court of Arbitration does not decide the cases as a body. A panel is established for each special case by selecting a number of arbitrators from the list of the members of the Court. Those lists are established by nation-states that are supposed to choose and then appoint not more than four individuals "of recognized competence in questions of international law, enjoying the highest moral reputation" (Article 44). The Permanent Court of Arbitration is therefore not a permanent agency but only a permanent list of names out of which the parties in each case select one or more individuals and thus establish the arbitration panel.

A new step forward was made after World War I, when in addition to the Permanent Court of Arbitration, but not quite superseding it, a Permanent Court of International Justice was established under the Covenant of the League of Nations. This court, again created at The Hague, was supposed to resemble a domestic court of justice by its permanency and constant availability to the parties in a dispute. Its jurisdiction could be established only on the basis of agreement of parties to a dispute.

The World Court

After World War II the Permanent Court of International Justice was dissolved (April 1946), and in its place the International Court of Justice, often referred to as the World Court, was established (see Document 9.4). According to the United Nations Charter, the International Court of Justice at The Hague is among the six principal organs of the United Nations. Article 93 declares that all members of the United Nations are *ipso facto* parties to the statute of the International Court of Justice. The Court has a new name, but in reality it is a continuation of the old world court. The statute of the International Court of Justice is practically identical with that of the Permanent Court of the League of Nations.

The public at times thinks or speaks of the World Court as if it were a parallel to a domestic court of law or even to a supreme court. This is not so. The International Court of Justice is not a superior court; there is no network of inferior international courts from which parties could appeal to the World Court. Furthermore, no nation can be compelled to accept its jurisdiction—no nation can be served a subpoena to appear at The Hague: The jurisdiction of the Court can be established only on the basis of prior negotiations that also determine the exact frame of reference for the Court. When this is done, the Court's decisions, based on a majority of voters, are binding. This is not a departure from the sovereign right of consent to any international obligation because the jurisdiction of the Court can be established only by consent. A nation voluntarily accepting the jurisdiction of the World Court has already sovereignly decided, if need be, to accept an unfavorable decision. Rather than violate an unacceptable decision, nations have ample opportunity to avoid the Court's jurisdiction altogether. As the Permanent Court of International Justice stated in one of its advisory opinions,

> It is well established in international law that no state can, without its consent, be compelled to submit its disputes with other states either to mediation or arbitration, or to any other kind of pacific settlement. Such

DOCUMENT 9.4

THE INTERNATIONAL COURT OF JUSTICE

Location
The Hague, Netherlands.

Composition
Fifteen judges elected for nine years by an absolute majority of votes in both the General Assembly and the Security Council. The veto power does not apply.

Qualification
Persons who possess the qualifications required in their respective countries for appointment to the highest judicial offices.

Selection
No two of the fifteen judges may be nationals of the same state. The Court as a whole should represent the main forms of civilization and the principal legal systems of the world.

Jurisdiction
Only states may be parties in cases before the Court. The jurisdiction may be established by special agreement in a particular dispute or on the basis of a general agreement (optional clause) to submit narrowly defined legal disputes to compulsory adjudications. The Court may give advisory opinions.

Applicable Law
Treaties, customs, and general principles of law. The decision of the Court has no binding force except between the parties and in respect of that particular case. The doctrine of *stare decisis* (adhering to precedents in applying the same principle in similar situations) does not apply. Judicial decisions and the teachings of the most highly qualified publicists are only auxiliary, not primary means for the determination of rules of law.

Decisions
By majority (quorum equals nine).

consent can be given once and for all in the form of an obligation freely undertaken, but it can, on the contrary, also be given in a special case apart from any existing obligation.[25]

The jurisdiction of the Court can be established on the basis of the express consent of the parties concerned and with regard either to the specific (*ad hoc*) dispute or to all their future legal disputes.

The statute of the International Court of Justice contains the so-called *optional clause* (Article 36), which creates the possibility (hence the term "optional") of establishing compulsory jurisdiction of the court, *ipso facto* and without special agreement, in relation to any other member-state accepting the same obligation—the jurisdiction of the Court in all legal disputes.

This would appear to open the way for sovereign nations to transfer their deadly disputes from the battlefield to the Court. In this manner nations could establish an international judiciary system if they really wished to do so. They do not. About one third, including the Western powers, have adhered to the optional clause; no communist nation has ever signed it. No dispute between communist and Western nations can be submitted to the Court on the sole basis of the optional clause because it is operative only on the basis of reciprocity. A specific agreement is necessary, as in the case of the dispute between Communist Albania and Great Britain after World War II concerning the mining and the destruction of British destroyers in the Corfu Channel in 1946.[26]

Can one infer that the optional clause makes the jurisdiction of the Court automatic and compulsory at least in all disputes among Western nations? Not at all. Here, again, the jealous protection of national interests and sovereignty makes the compulsory jurisdiction of the Court much less automatic than a superficial reading of the optional clause might suggest.

First, most nations that have signed the optional clause have done so with important reservations. In particular, they have excluded from international jurisdiction those disputes that are "essentially within the domestic jurisdiction." The exact meaning of the term "essentially" is debatable. It is possible to say only that it is broader than that of the term "exclusively." Furthermore, it appears that the nation itself would interpret in each case whether a dispute with another nation is, in its view, more or less, essentially or partially within the domestic jurisdiction. This indeed is quite an "escape clause." The British declaration of acceptance (September 1929) excluded from international jurisdiction "disputes with regard to questions which by international law fall exclusively within the jurisdiction of the United Kingdom." The United States, which in 1946 for the first time found it possible to accept the optional clause, went even further in limiting the acceptance of the clause. The United States excluded "disputes with regard to matters which are essentially within the domestic jurisdiction of the United States, as determined by the United States." There are other reservations by the United States, especially with regard to disputes arising under multilateral treaties, but the exception just quoted means that the United States is practically free from any obligation to submit even a legal dispute if it chooses to claim that the matter is essentially within the domestic jurisdiction as determined by either the President or Congress.

Second, the optional clause speaks of a compulsory jurisdiction in all *legal* disputes. There is a fundamental difference between legal and political, or "justiciable" and "nonjusticiable" disputes. As in domestic law, no court would accept, for instance, the role of a final arbitrator in a controversy concerning a claim that an existing law is bad and should be replaced by a new one. This a court cannot do; it is the function of legislators. A court that, like the United States Supreme Court, has the power of judicial review may only annul an unconstitutional law; it cannot proclaim a new law and it cannot annul a bad though constitutional law.

POLITICAL OR LEGAL CONFLICTS

The International Court of Justice is not endowed with the power of judicial review. It cannot annul; it can only interpret a law that the plaintiff and the defendant accept as their common ground. And certainly the International Court of Justice, like a domestic court, cannot make a new law. We know that no society is static; circumstances change, new problems arise, old laws become outdated or impractical—new laws become necessary. If a citizen wants a law changed, he does not go to a judge but sees or writes to his congressman, exercises pressure through his interest group, influences the lawmakers by means of voting at the elections, or uses revolutionary violence from which a new legal system may emerge.

When a change of international law is desired, nations cannot and do not go to the World Court for a new law; they also cannot write to international lawmakers since they themselves are the legislators. They have to negotiate a new treaty or convention, because only consent, now usually embodied in a negotiated legal document, is the source of international law. Or they can fight it out on a battlefield whose smoke and ruins become foundations for a new legal order. New international law is the end product and not the beginning or cause of a political compromise or settlement. Major conflicts among nations are basically about what a new law should be and therefore, legally speaking, they are not justiciable; they are political although some of their aspects may appear to be legal.

The determination of what is legal and what is political has traditionally been left to the discretion of sovereign nations. A nation may prevent the submission of its dispute to an objective nonpartial judicial body by claiming that a dispute which appears to the opposing party as legal is really political in nature. At one time an attempt was made by the United States and England and France to permit a third party to decide whether a dispute was legal or political. This sensational departure from the traditional principle that sovereign nations sovereignly decide whether their conflicts are to be submitted to international adjudication was embodied in the arbitration treaties signed on August 3, 1911, between these nations. Article 3 provided that in cases where the parties disagreed on whether or not a dispute was subject to arbitration the question should be submitted to a third party (the Joint High Commission of Inquiry), and that if all (or all but one) of the members of that commission decided the question in the affirmative, the case should be settled by arbitration. Such a departure from the principle of sovereignty was possible only among these three Western democracies, which in 1911 represented a very close association, very similar to a real community. Yet, this article was struck by the American Senate and the treaties were never ratified.

The most serious disputes that divide one nation from another are precisely of this kind. Their subject is not an interpretation of the existing law but a desire to change a situation that is based on a treaty, custom, or past political event. In the war between the Algerian nationalists and France, the French government could invoke the law, as would any party that tries to maintain a *status quo* anchored in some legal document. The document in this case was the French Constitution, which proclaimed northern Algeria a part of metropolitan France. The Algerian nationalists were challenging the legal order and wanted to create a new legal situation, the result of which would be the separation of Algeria and France, and peace between the two. The Court could not help to solve the issue; fighting and negotiations finally did.

When, in 1958, the Soviet premier presented the Western powers with an ultimatum to abandon their positions in West Berlin, he did not even challenge their original legal right to be in Berlin. He demanded a change, using a very simple and blunt argument: It was impossible, he said, "to prolong the situation any longer."

When, in 1935, Hitler challenged the post-Versailles legal order in Europe (especially the demilitarization of the Rhineland, the disarmament clauses, the independence of Austria, the inclusion of the German minority in Czechoslovakia, and the existence of the Polish state), his aim was to change the *status quo*. No interpretation of the existing legal order by a court could satisfy his demand for a complete change.

These three examples of political conflict, in which one side invokes the existing law and the opposite side claims the revolutionary or political right to change it, sufficiently demonstrate that courts cannot help in disputes of a nonlegal nature. Conflicting parties have no common legal ground. The demand for change and the opposition to it constitute a conflict that can be solved only by negotiation or violence. Then a new order would result, one either agreed to or imposed.

The nations' willingness to submit to adjudication or arbitration only those disputes they choose to view as *legal* rules out any consideration by the World Court of such major problems as the Berlin issue, the unification of Germany, the Sino-Soviet dispute, tensions between the Soviet Union and the United States, wars in Korea, Vietnam, the Congo, the Middle East or elsewhere, and other issues in which the contending nations' "vital interests, their independence, their honor, or the interests of third states" are involved. The quotation is the actual wording of the French-British Treaty of 1903, in which the two states agreed to settle by arbitration all their legal differences *except* those which could "affect" (a very broad term indeed) any of the four interests mentioned above. This has been every nation's reservation to the present day. This is why sovereign nations present only rather marginal and unimportant issues for adjudication by the World Court. The record of the Permanent Court of International Justice under the League of Nations (1920-1945) shows sixty-five cases and twenty-seven advisory opinions. The overwhelming majority of these cases concerned claims for payment or minor territorial matters.

The record of the International Court of Justice so far has remained as unimpressive as that of its predecessor. Technical and marginal issues are the rule; a mildly explosive one is an exception. India's Prime Minister Nehru once noted that the dispute with Pakistan over Kashmir was too serious a business to be determined by a handful of judges. In 1973 France ignored the World Court's attempted injunction in connection with her new nuclear test series at Mururoa Atoll in the South Pacific. In May of that year Australia and New Zealand requested the Court to ask France to suspend her tests since the preceding ones in the period of 1966-1972 allegedly infringed on those two countries' rights under international law; the specific complaint was that nuclear fallout had reached the Australia-New Zealand area within three weeks after each test. France denied that the Court had any jurisdiction in the matter and boycotted all its proceedings. The vote of the Court in favor of an interim injunction was eight to six; among the six who voted in favor of the French argument were Justice André Gros of France, Justice Louis Ignacio-Pinto of Dahomey (a former French colony), and Justice Isaac Forster of Senegal (also a former French colony).

The simple truth is that sovereign nations are reluctant to submit their vital problems to a group of judges because they fear either that the Court might be impartial—and who wants impartiality when vital national issues are at stake?—or that it might be partial in a way that is against their interests, for the judges under their international robes remain nationals and therefore biased. It is significant that Article 31 of the statute of the International Court of Justice provides that the "judges of the nationality of each of the parties shall retain their right in the case before the Court." Furthermore, the same article provides that a party may add an additional judge to the bench if the Court includes upon the bench a judge of the nationality of the opposing party. In domestic law, if a judge were a brother of an accused person, he would be disqualified. In the law among sovereign nations, if party has no brother on the court, he can name one. This was done in the case involving the determination of guilt and duty of compensation between Albania and Great Britain in their dispute about the mining of British destroyers. As Albania had no judge on the Court, and Britain did, she named a cousin, a Czechoslovak communist judge, to sit on the bench.

To sum up: Eight major differences between a court system as we know it nationally and the rudimentary international judiciary system may be noted:

1. The International Court of Justice is for nation-states only; it cannot deal with complaints or conflicts among individuals or subnational groups (Article 34).
2. It has no compulsory jurisdiction; no nation can be forced to appear against its will (Article 36).
3. In interpreting the existing law the Court is handicapped by important gaps in the international legal system (Article 38). While in domestic law very few areas of human conduct remain legally unregulated, in international law it is the other way around. We have already noted the near-absence of international criminal law and the disagreements concerning the law of the sea.
4. A precedent is not allowed to play the same role in the Court as in the Anglo-Saxon legal systems. Article 59 of the Statute of the Court specifies: "The decision of the Court has no binding force except between the parties and in respect of that particular case."
5. There is no hierarchy of international courts; there are no inferior courts from which to appeal to the World Court and there is no appeal from the World Court.
6. A national judge is not disqualified if his nation is a party in a case before the Court; on the contrary, Article 31 stipulates that a nation may choose an additional judge "if the Court includes upon the Bench a judge of one of the parties."
7. The Court may give an advisory opinion (Article 65), in contrast to the United States Supreme Court, which cannot give advisory opinions. The Court can decide legal issues only on the basis of a real and substantive controversy.
8. There is no central coercive machinery to be mobilized against a party that refuses to abide by the judgment of the Court. There are no international police or jails to keep nations from violating the law.

HOW LAW IS ENFORCED

In domestic law self-help is an exception to the rule: Generally speaking, citizens rely on centralized law enforcement for the protection of their legal rights. Only in exceptional cases, such as self-defense against assault, do individuals resort to legitimate self-help. Domestic law, as Richard A. Falk rightly noted, deters an unauthorized use of violence by monopolizing its legitimate use. By contrast, among nations means of effective coercion are not concentrated in any world police agency but in the hands of individual nations; there is "a virtual monopoly by nations of the instruments of violence."[27] An analogy with the international scene on the domestic scene would be a situation in which all citizens had machine guns except the police.

In international law, enforcement in any way other than through self-help is exceptional and difficult to set in motion, as we shall see in the following chapter, which examines collective enforcement. The use of collective enforcement, however, is limited to the most serious threats to international peace and security, such as unprovoked aggression. Thus, when an international obligation is violated and the violation cannot be construed as a major threat to peace, the general practice is that nations take the defense of their threatened interest into their own hands.

Two qualifications should be added: First, self-help does not necessarily mean the use of international violence. In response to a violation of some international obligation, nations have often merely threatened a remedial action and thus obtained compliance. Compliance or damages have sometimes been obtained by seizure of other nations' assets, vessels, goods, or citizens as hostages. Second, as has already been noted, many international rules and obligations do not need any enforcement to be complied with because it is in the interest of the parties concerned to abide by the rules. This is so, for instance, in the case of commercial treaties or agreements concerned with the immunities of diplomatic personnel.

As for the World Court and its decisions, there is no central authority to execute a decision against a state that refuses to comply with it although the state had originally accepted the Court's jurisdiction and the binding character of its award; there are no World Court marshals. There are practically no cases, however, of simple refusal to abide by the decision: States that think the Court's decision might go against them simply do not submit their cases to the Court. Occasionally, however, the losing party has claimed that the Court has exceeded its jurisdiction. When on December 15, 1949, the International Court of Justice ruled in the dispute between Britain and Albania concerning the naval incidents in the Corfu Channel that Albania was to pay damages to Britain for the British ships Albania had destroyed, Albania refused to pay. She argued that she had accepted the jurisdiction of the Court only on the question of whether the duty to pay damages existed but that she had never consented to the jurisdiction of the Court to fix the amount to be paid.

We should add that violation of any law—for instance, the law against murder—certainly cannot be construed as proof of the law's nonexistence. Even the most centralized lawmaking, law-enforcement, and law-adjudication in territorial states do not prevent frequent deviant or criminal behavior. When men on the national scene—like nations on the international scene—behave illegally and use violence, their acts do not prove the absence of law; paradoxically, they confirm it by its violation. The problem of whether a law exists arises when violations of the law are constant and general, while its observance occurs rarely, if at all. And this, some argue, is the case of international law, which is manifest by its violation more than by its observance. But this, perhaps, is too sweeping a judgment.

In sum, the fragmented nature of international lawmaking and law enforcement rather faithfully mirrors the national fragmentation of our world. If and when international law is centrally created, interpreted, and enforced, it will cease to be a law of nations and will become a "global national" law, that is, the law of a worldwide federal or unitary territorial state. Such a situation, however, seems to be separated from our era of divisive nationalism by distance that it would be unwise to measure by decades or even perhaps by centuries.

Notes

1. J. L. Brierly, *The Law of Nations.* New York: Oxford, 1954, p. 5.
2. Radhabinod Pal, "Future Role of International Law Commission in the Changing World," *United Nations Review*, 9:9 (1962), 31.
3. Oliver J. Lissitzyn, "International Law in a Divided World," *International Conciliation*, 542 (March 1963), 37-38.
4. Julius Stone, *Quest for Survival: The Role of Law and Foreign Policy.* Cambridge, Mass.: Harvard University Press, 1961, p. 88.
5. East Germany, Poland, Czechoslovakia, Hungary, Yugoslavia, Albania, Rumania, Bulgaria, the Soviet Union, Mongolia, the People's Republic of China, North Vietnam, North Korea, and Cuba.
6. F. I. Kozhevnikov, *Sovetskoie Gosudarstvo i Mezhdunarodnoie Pravo.* Moscow: Yuridicheskoie Izdatel'stvo, 1948, p. 25; translated by John H. Hazard in his *Law and Social Change in the USSR.* Toronto: Carswell, 1953, p. 275.
7. J. F. Triska and R. M. Slessor, *The Theory, Law, and Policy of Soviet Treaties.* Stanford, Calif.: Stanford University Press, 1962, p. 4.
8. Brierly, *Law of Nations*, pp. 8-10, *passim.*
9. *Pravda*, September 26, 1968, as translated by the Novosti Press Agency and reproduced in the *New York Times*, September 27, 1968.
10. *Mezhdunarodnoye Pravo (International Law)*, edited by V. N. Durdeneveskii and S. B. Krylov. Moscow, 1947, p. 117.
11. Roland R. Foulke, *A Treatise on International Law.* New York: Holt, Rinehart and Winston, 1920, p. 69.
12. Hans Kelsen, *Principles of International Law.* New York: Holt, Rinehart and Winston, 1952, p. 155.
13. L. F. L. Oppenheim and H. Lauterpacht, *International Law,* Vol. 1. New York: Longmans, 1955, pp. 279-280.
14. L. H. L. Oppenheim, *International Law,* Vol. 1, 2d. ed. London: Longmans, 1912, p. 193. In his *Politics among Nations* (New York: Knopf, 1967), p. 266, Hans J. Morgenthau notes that Lauterpacht, the editor of subsequent editions of Oppenheim's standard work, has eliminated the statement concerning the balance of power. Morgenthau agrees with Oppenheim's original statement.
15. See also Lissitzyn, *International Law in a Divided World*, p. 6: "Treaties have become the principal means of creating new norms which are regarded as binding on the states that accept them and of entrusting rule-making powers to international organs."
16. Oppenheim and Lauterpacht, *International Law*, Vol. 1, p. 10.
17. UN Document L/2092, April 12, 1974, Special Committee's 112th meeting.
18. *New York Times*, April 12, 1969.
19. Brian Johnson, "Will the Law be for—or against—the Sea?" *Vista*, June 1973, p. 52.
20. Charles N. Brower, legal adviser, U.S. Department of State, in a statement made at a hearing before the Subcommittee on Oceans and International Environment of the Committee on Foreign Relations, U.S. Senate, June 19, 1973. *U.S. Oceans Policy.* Washington, D.C.: Government Printing Office, 1973, p. 4.
21. *New York Times*, December 4, 1973.

22. Seyom Brown and Larry L. Fabian, "Diplomats at Sea," *Foreign Affairs*, 52.2 (January 1974), 301. See also Robert G. Wirsing, *International Relations and the Future of Ocean Space*. Columbia, S.C.: University of South Carolina Press, 1974.

23. Max Sorensen, "Law of the Sea," *International Conciliation*, 520 (November 1958), 255.

24. L. Larry Leonard, *Internatinal Organization*. New York: McGraw-Hill, 1951, p. 273.

25. Permanent Court of International Justice, "Eastern Carelia Advisory Opinion," *Series B*, No. 5. The Hague: July 23, 1923, p. 27.

26. Urban G. Whitaker, Jr., *Politics and Power*. New York: Harper & Row, 1964, p. 523. The book is a combination of text and cases and represents a useful source for additional readings in the field of international law.

27. Richard A. Falk, "World Law and Human Conflict," in Elton B. McNeil (ed.), *The Nature of Human Conflict*. Englewood Cliffs, N.J.: Prentice-Hall, 1965, p. 229.

Additional Readings

Additional readings on international law may be found in *Discord and Harmony: Readings in International Politics,* edited by Ivo D. Duchacek and published by Holt, Rinehart and Winston in 1972. Chapter 5, "International Law and World Community" (pp. 70-95), contains the conflicting opinions of L. F. L. Oppenheim, J. L. Brierly, Oliver J. Lissitzyn, Stanley Hoffman, and Charles de Visscher on the subject of law and community and excerpts from articles by John H. E. Fried, Hans J. Morgenthau, and Richard A. Falk.

10

International Organizations

The international organizations analyzed in this chapter are associations of nation-states whose governments have translated their awareness of some common interests into a formal compact (treaty, covenant, charter) and established some machinery in common (regular meetings, a secretariat, common institutions). The United Nations and its specialized agencies, and such predecessors as the League of Nations, the Universal Postal Union, the Rhine River Commission, and the Permanent Court of Arbitration, are good examples; others are those modern alliances that are endowed with some permanent machinery, such as the North Atlantic Treaty Organization, the Warsaw Pact, or the Organization of American States.

Other international organizations are nongovernmental or partly nongovernmental. Among the nongovernmental international organizations are churches and multinational corporations, the World Federation of Trade Unions, and numerous other professional, special-interest, or ideological organizations; in the category of partly intergovernmental and partly nongovernmental international organizations were the Communist International (Comintern, 1919-1943) and the Communist Information Bureau (Cominform, 1947-1956), which linked the Soviet and other communist governments with communist parties in open or underground opposition to their respective national governments. While worthy of analysis, the nongovernmental and mixed intergovernmental and nongovernmental international organizations are beyond the scope of this chapter.

So long as any international organization lasts, its function, performance, and continuation are determined by the assumptions, expectations, and actual behavior of its members; their behavior, in turn, is influenced by the frequency, intensity, and scope of intraorganizational contacts: the composite and its components condition each other. When in 1972 the People's Republic of China joined the United Nations some observers expressed the hope that Communist China might be more significantly and beneficially affected by its permanent exposure to the United Nations milieu than the other way around. The pessimists pointed to the absence of any visible effect of the United Nations milieu upon the behavior of Stalin's Russia.

And yet it may be argued that interaction among members of any organization, especially if sufficiently frequent, is bound ultimately to produce some effect on the members' views and actions; it is an observable fact that, after having joined a group, a man behaves somewhat less individualistically and somewhat more as a member of the group. A similar evolution may perhaps be anticipated when a nation joins and remains in an international organization (provided that that nation's goal is not to destroy the organization from within). However strong a given nation's original intention to disregard the interests of others and misuse the organization for its own interests, its national behavior may undergo certain changes in the light of its perception of what is possible. The United Nations lobby, for instance, can quickly teach a newcomer about the feasibility or preposterousness of a proposal, goal, or deal. By walking through the main delegates' lounge, a national representative can sample and evaluate the reaction of almost the whole world and reach a new conclusion or adopt a modified stand before his dry martini is stirred and served. In this limited sense we can therefore speak of social and organizational influences as restraints on national behavior.

International organizations represent a special category of corporate actors on the international scene—multinational subsystems embedded within the universal system of states and therefore influenced by and influencing that system. Like any other system, an international organization is not static; it undergoes constant changes. Two extreme changes are possible: (1) An international organization may dissolve when its components decide to resume their full freedom of independent or antagonistic action. (2) Or, on the contrary, the components may so merge with one another as to form a new supranational unit, a new territorial state endowed with a single authoritative voice on the international scene (qualifications of this image are discussed in Chapter 3); thus a new corporate personality, collective will, and common institutions might emerge and overshadow those of the components, especially in matters of foreign policy, defense, and international trade—issues that have international significance. History records a few cases of transformation of alliances or loose organizations into a new supranational unit, usually a federal territorial state; Switzerland, the United States, and Germany are examples—but they should not lead one to think that such amalgamation is likely; very few, if any, of the contemporary international organizations seem to be heading toward a supranational destiny. Perhaps only the European Economic Community may, in time, develop into a West European federal nation-state. The nine member nations (France, Germany, Belgium, Holland, Luxembourg, Italy, England, Denmark, and Ireland) have some chance of achieving such an objective because they have for centuries shared the same culture and forms of civilization that made them, to a certain extent, distinct from England and America in the west and from eastern and Balkanic Europe and Russia in the east. Their labor pains suggest, however, that even in this relatively hopeful case nationalist parochialism is proving a stubborn stumbling block to regional ecumenism. Many more years will have to pass before a final judgment on West European supranationalism can be made.

INTERNATIONALISM AND SUPRANATIONALISM

At this point it is useful to distinguish between two different meanings of the word "internationalism" as it is currently used: One meaning of the term negates nationalism and replaces loyalty to one's nation with an identification with a broader (regional or global) community; the other meaning of "internationalism" does not negate but instead complements nationalism and its cause and effect, the nation-state—it combines devotion to one's own nation with understanding of, practical cooperation with, and even respect for other national communities.

In its first, antinational meaning "internationalism" actually means *supranationalism*, the term usually employed with reference to national collectivities, or *cosmopolitanism*, a term describing an individual's feeling of belonging to all the world rather than to any national compartment of it. The classic expression of cosmopolitanism was uttered by Socrates: "I am not an Athenian or a Greek, but a citizen of the world." In France, two hundred years before the French Revolution helped shape the modern concept of nationalism, Michel de Montaigne (1533-1592) expressed his cosmopolitanism: "Not because Socrates said so but because it is in truth my own disposition—and perchance to some excess—I look upon all men as my compatriots, and embrace a Pole as a Frenchman, making less account of the national than of the universal and common bond."

In the age of atomic weapons, speeches and articles often stress the need for supranational loyalty to mankind. In 1965, in connection with the proclamation of International Cooperation Year, Dr. Radhakrishnan, the President of India, expressed this need as follows:

> We have no choice now but to live together as members of a single world community. The twentieth century man who is already probing the mysteries of the universe cannot restrict his very existence to a narrow corner of the world in which he happens to dwell. Our true nationality is the human race; our home, the world.

These noble hopes, printed on the first page of *India News* (March 12, 1965), have to be contrasted with the hard facts of Indian politics, equally well described on the first page of the same issue: the "Arrest of Left Communists in Kerala," the Indian defense minister's announcement that India "was fully prepared to meet any military adventure Pakistan might care to embark upon," and India's protest to the United Nations Security Council against Pakistan's activities in her part of Kashmir. The protest also stated that "Pakistan's agreement with China under which Pakistan has given away to the Chinese over 2000 square miles of territory in the State of Jammu and Kashmir [India also claims the Pakistani part for herself] amounted to further aggression against India." The President's words about world brotherhood were a dream; nationalist and ideological antagonism were the reality.

In the category of supranational loyalties, we sometimes find the sense of belonging to a universal community determined by professional, class, or age interests: For instance, students usually feel more akin to foreign students and their goals than to their own national establishments, their own fathers, or, generally, to all adults over forty; Karl Marx hoped for the transnational solidarity of workers against their national employers and exploiters; in the past, religion often pitted groups against one another on a transnational basis—Catholics versus Protestants or Moslems versus Christians or Jews; and scientists, as members of an international community, often oppose their national political leaders on the basis of their common humane standards. In like manner, artists, poets, writers, and musicians frequently feel they have much more in common with similar groups abroad than with the politicians or "lowbrows" in their own nations. "We poets, American or Russian," noted the Soviet poet Andrei Voznesensky, "we do understand one another. Wouldn't it be marvelous if we had our own capital on wheels, a train in which we could wander about the world like gypsies?"[1] The call for an international brotherhood of poets and other similarly hopeful calls for cosmopolitan understanding, supranationalism, humanism, universal fraternity, and love have a long history, but so far they have had few, if any, direct political consequences.

Another form of supranational loyalty, highly selective, is oriented not toward the whole world but toward a particular nation that seems to offer an alternative to the traditional forms and goals of national and international society. The identification of the communists in Western countries with either Russia or China and what they respectively stand for and the affinity felt with the United States and its way of life by many anticommunists in Eastern Europe and Russia belong to this form of loyalty that transcends national boundaries, a "selective supranationalism" of sorts. The atomic spies for the Soviet Union in the West and their counterparts in the communist countries were not all primarily motivated by sordid material interests or by some pathological urge but by their dedication to an ideology that a particular foreign government symbolized and promoted and that their own government opposed. Governments everywhere tend to treat such manifestations of selective supranational loyalty as subversion, collusion with the enemy, or high treason.

COOPERATION AMONG NATIONS

As it is now most generally used, internationalism basically means pursuing one's own national interests by means of cooperation with other nations that are assumed to be doing the same thing. Internationalism of this sort is based on the expectation that each nation will promote and defend its own interests, some of which will necessarily conflict with other nations' interests, but many of which either are in harmony or can be brought into harmony with other nations' interests. When sovereign nations reach the conclusion that they have one or more interests in common and their common promotion requires a common framework or agency, they translate their conclusion into a formal document that describes the accord and provides for some mechanism for coordinating efforts, planning, and further harmonizing national interests. Thus, great and small powers that are members of an international organization contribute, as it were, an equal portion of their freedom of action (sovereignty) for the sake of coordination of efforts, that is, their future freedom of action is mutually limited by the acceptance of some contractual and organizational restraints. Thus they hope to achieve a higher benefit, individually and collectively, than they could by going it alone. Enlightened self-interest is the foundation of contemporary internationalism.

In 1970, for example, the United States belonged to over fifty different international organizations, including the United Nations, the World Bank, the International Labor Organization, and the World Meteorological Organization; it also contributed to nearly thirty international operating programs, mostly sponsored by these organizations. Every year, the United States attends between five and six hundred intergovernmental conferences, mostly dealing with technical, ecological, and scientific subjects. In the words of the assistant secretary of state for international organization affairs, "these international organizations exist simply because they are needed. We belong to them because it serves our national interest."[2] Well and honestly put. The primacy of self-interest could hardly be expressed more succinctly and realistically. The growth of international organizations, agencies, and operating programs has been impressive. Their number and scope reflect the widely felt need for them; their work represents an eloquent denial of the nations' claims to self-sufficiency and complete independence.

However, the increased number of international organizations does not mean a rise in supranationalism. These associations remain rather loosely structured. Nations join international organizations for national motives, in order to enhance their individual interests. In cooperative internationalism, the goals and fears of nationalism are not replaced by supranational idealism or cosmopolitan utopianism. Instead, nationalism assumes new forms of expression and promotion that may or may not lead to a more orderly and cooperative world order. A hope has often been expressed that, step by step, nations may discover that in the present age of nuclear weapons and global interdependence the interests they have in common are more numerous and more important for their survival and progress than the interests that seem to pit them against one another. For the time being, however, existing international organizations enjoy only limited support from their members, since the members' confidence in the compatibility of their various national interests remains limited. Nations that join international organizations insist on imposing significant limitations upon their duration, scope, and authority. These limitations are not unlike the checks and balances which are familiar in democratic or federal settings and which demonstrate that men both need and dread authority. "In framing a government which is to be administered by men over men," James Madison noted in *Federalist* No. 51, "the great difficulty lies in this: you must first enable the government to control the governed; and in the next place oblige it to control itself." Similarly, in framing international intergovernmental organizations, national leaders impose on their common international structure more severe limitations than their individual counterparts do on the national scene. This in part reflects their belief that they actually do not need any strong international authority; it also demonstrates their dread of its potential power.

Limiting International Authority

The following four limitations are the most usual in international organizations:

1. Many international organizations are limited in *time*. In particular, alliances usually contain a time limit, although this is usually coupled with a provision for a renewal.

2. Accepting membership in more or less permanent organizations, states usually insist on including a clause that permits *withdrawal of membership* (secession) in case of a profound disagreement. This is so in the United Nations Charter; no nation can be forced to join or to remain in the world organization.

3. Member-nations usually insist on the voting formula *one nation, one vote*. The principle of sovereign equality is thus translated into equal votes. The vote cast by India, with 550 million inhabitants, is equal to the vote of the Maldive Islands, with 110,000 inhabitants.

4. The principle of *unanimity* is the most characteristic feature of international organizations. Every major issue is to be determined by unanimous consent. The concept of sovereign equality, politically speaking, mirrors the fundamental distrust of other communities; this distrust explains the known reluctance of territorial states to accept the democratic method of deciding issues by majority vote. To submit to a numerical majority presupposes that both the majority and the minority form integral parts of a community, bound together by an agreement that issues can and should be decided in so mechanical a fashion. Nations rarely agree on this, as they do not consider themselves to be part of a single world community. As Charles de Visscher noted:

> Experience shows that the rule of unanimity must hold, wherever there is not a high enough degree of solidarity in an area of vital or major interests to permit exceptions without arousing in States particularly liable to find themselves in the minority a spirit of mistrust that sets them a priori against any concession to general interest.[3]

Objections to Deciding by Majority

The reluctance of nations to submit their vital interests to a judgment by other sovereign states (even if their collective judgment represented a majority of all less one) reflects some of the following doubts about the majority-vote technique of solving conflicts of interest:

1. The majority, as we all know, is not always right; often it is wrong. It would be a fallacy to equate the majority with wisdom or justice. While in domestic societies injustice and lack of wisdom may be repaired at the next election, on the world scene an error on the part of an international majority can be fatal. Furthermore, an international majority, especially when manipulated in some great power's interest, may be of a permanent rather than a transient nature. "Great decisions that men regard as vital," Walter Lippmann once noted, "shall not be taken by the vote of the majority until the consent of the minority has been obtained." Lippmann referred here to the American internal situation and the role of the filibuster, which,

according to him, is to prevent a transient majority from acting in a tyrannical way. The fear of tyranny by a majority over a minority is much greater on the international scene because nations do not feel they constitute a community; they tend to place almost all decisions concerning their interests into Lippmann's category of "great decisions."

Alexis de Tocqueville, the French statesman and critic, wrote these wise words on the subject of majority rule more than a century ago:

> A majority taken collectively may be regarded as a being whose opinions, and most frequently whose interests, are opposed to those of another being, which is styled a minority. If it be admitted that a man, possessing absolute power, may misuse that power by wronging his adversaries, why should a majority not be liable to the same reproach? Men are not apt to change their characters by agglomeration. . . . The power to do everything, which I should refuse to one of my equals, I will never grant to any number of them.[4]

Nations, it seems, are even more reluctant than individuals to grant any significant power to another nation or to any number of them.

2. Of a national majority composed of more or less equal citizens it may be said that at least it is superior in numbers if not always in wisdom. On the world scene, however, even such an assumption of the numerical superiority of a majority is debatable.

If in any parliament a vote of 400 to 16 were announced, the conclusion might safely be drawn that only an insignificant minority had opposed a legislative measure desired by almost all. No such deduction could be made from the same proportion of votes in the United Nations General Assembly. If a headline were to announce that a measure was adopted by 100 votes against four dissenters, it would be a dangerous illusion to interpret such a vote as a verdict of mankind. If the four defeated nations were, let us assume, Communist China (800 million people), India (550 million), the Soviet Union (250 million), and the United States (215 million), their combined population would represent the majority of mankind (well over 1.8 billion). Yet the majority of mankind would have only 4 votes, that is, as many as Panama, Luxembourg, Laos, and Gambia, with a total population of under 5 million. Sir Harold Nicolson wrote in 1961:

> It was not foreseen by those who drafted the Charter at San Francisco that the principle of one-state—one-vote might in the end prove irrational. Today the votes of the 99 sovereign states in the Assembly bear no relation to the amount of power they can exercise or the degree of responsibility they can assume. . . . The major decisions in this world are taken by those who possess power and are prepared to exercise it. The substitution of votes for force has given the United Nations a certain unreality which hampers its authority.[5]

Karl Lowenstein made the following proposal in a letter to the *New York Times* (March 3, 1957) with reference to the extreme inequality of nations and their equal votes in the General Assembly: Five votes should be assigned to a great power, three votes to a middle power, and one vote to a small power. This proposal has a poor chance of being adopted. Because there is no reasonable yardstick of national power—population, per-capita income, productive capacity, literacy, and others proved inadequate or inacceptable—Professor Lowenstein added:

> To escape this dilemma it is suggested . . . that each nation determine for itself to which category it wishes to belong. . . . There is no danger that every small nation will aspire to the rank of a great power. . . . No stampede for the front row in the UN is likely to occur . . . because great powers—and this is the core of the proposal— . . . will have to bear the sacrifices in manpower and money for the effective enforcement of justice and peace.

There is no chance whatsoever that Lowenstein's proposal will be accepted by the majority of nations—which are small and poor and therefore the more insistent on their status and illusion of equality. Furthermore the proposal, although stressing the sacrifice in manpower and money, cannot quite exclude the possibility that an oil-rich sheikdom would pay for an additional two or four votes and thus achieve, so to speak, a crude great-power status.

3. In international organizations governments, not their people, cast the votes. In many cases governments do not express the will of the people; on the contrary, the people's opposition to the government is widespread but is kept in bounds by authoritarian measures.Thus even a unanimous vote by the United Nations General Assembly should not be equated with world public opinion, because many of the voting delegates—national representatives—are quite unrepresentative of their people.

4. Although a majority decision on important matters is not accepted as legally binding and may be quite unrepresentative of the will of the people, the publicity surrounding it represents a form of social pressure that is not without effect on governments. No state likes to have the majority of national governments voting against it; headlines reporting the vote may tarnish the image of the dissenting nation and thus decrease its influence on the international scene. A democratic nation, in particular, may feel restrained by actual or anticipated international censure; its opposition at home, especially on the eve of general elections, may seize upon international criticism of its national government and identify itself with the criticism. Governments that yield to the pressures of domestic public opinion can be expected also to be sensitive to international public opinion. Noting the lack of responsiveness to United Nations' votes by totalitarian

states, Sir Winston Churchill, addressing American and English lawyers in London's Guildhall (*Time,* August 12, 1957) said: "We cannot be content with an arrangement where our new system of international law [?] applies only to those who show themselves willing to keep it." This was said in reference to the United Nations General Assembly's condemnation of the 1956 French-English-Israeli operation against Egypt, which had some effect, and the simultaneous condemnation of the Soviet military invasion of Hungary, which had no effect whatsoever. Totalitarian socialist and fascist regimes, which are fairly immune to any internal public pressure, are even more immune to international pressure, which they can so easily censor out of their press and communications media. The average Soviet citizen did not even know in 1956 that the General Assembly had passed judgment on his government's suppression of the Hungarian revolution. Yet even in this case the Soviet Union tried its very best to prevent the United Nations' condemnation of its action. In like manner, dictatorships that have no regard for domestic public opinion have of necessity some concern for the opinions of their allies or of neutrals on the international scene. Failure to prevent international censure may be interpreted as lack of diplomatic skill. Following the Soviet invasion of Czechoslovakia in 1968, for instance, Soviet diplomats at the United Nations and all the world's capitals spent a great deal of time and energy convincing their friends and enemies as well as neutrals that it was not only the Russian right but the Russian duty to intervene in the internal crises of the socialist states.

While national leaders may have no respect for world morality, world public opinion, and international law, they attempt to avoid a manifestation of any callous disregard. No nation, small or large, likes to see the world ganging up against it. The fear of an adverse publicity that the unenforceable recommendations of the General Assembly may generate, induced the United States (a speech by John A. Scali, December 6, 1974) to condemn the pursuit of mathematical majorities as a "particularly sterile form of international activities," since the outraged minority "may in fact be a practical majority in terms of its capacity to support the organization and implement its decisions;" moreover, "when the rule of the majority becomes the tyranny of the majority, the minority will cease to respect and obey it." Ambassador Scali recommended negotiation and compromise instead of voting confrontations—a wise advice which, however, the United States did not follow in the 1950s when it was in control of the Assembly's majorities.

Exceptions to the Principle of Unanimity

Notwithstanding the justified objections to "majoritarian" solutions of international problems, there have been several departures from the principle of unanimity. A closer examination of these departures seems to confirm rather than to deny that major powers and small powers insist on the right of international filibuster when it comes to their vital interests.

When nations agree to majority decisions, it is usually under one of the following four sets of circumstances:

1. When matters to be determined by a vote are unimportant, nations often agree to a majority-rule or a weighted-vote system. This plan is accepted in some international administrative agencies, such as the Universal Postal Union. Its decisions are not expected to affect the vital national interests of member-states. In the United Nations Security Council a majority determines procedural matters only.

2. Nations depart from the principle of unanimity and agree to majority votes when these result not in binding orders but merely in recommendations to adopt some measures. Such international recommendations are not decisions in the real sense of the word. They are usually described as resolutions, authorizations, or permissions; they leave it to the sovereign decision of the addressees to determine whether to follow the recommendation, which may carry with it a considerable moral or psychological weight. Yet, recommendations are not legally binding upon those who have not voted for them. They are not even binding upon those who did vote for them. This is why nations accepted the principle of majority votes in the United Nations General Assembly, in its Economic and Social Council, and in its Trusteeship Council. Although they often seem to submit their cases to them, in actuality they do not submit anything at all, because the decisions of these organs are not binding nor do they imply or propose enforcement.

The only instance of a majority decision that is legally binding is that of the International Court of Justice. However, this does not mean very much because the jurisdiction of the court itself has first to be established by the consent of the parties involved. If a nation feels that in a given dispute it would be difficult for it to comply with an objective finding of the court, it chooses not to accept its jurisdiction. This is deemed preferable to a situation in which a nation voluntarily accepts the jurisdiction of the court and then does not comply with its verdict if it turns out to be contrary to that nation's vital interests. Anticipated adverse publicity at home and abroad usually proves the decisive factor in a nation's decision to go or not to go to World Court.

3. In some instances nations feel obliged to agree to the principle of decisions based on the amount of financial contribution to some common pool, such as the International Monetary Fund. If recipient and poor nations were to insist on the equality of all votes, the result would be an empty safe. The alternative is to accept the principle that those nations will have most voting power who contribute most. Rich nations would not let

themselves be taxed without proportional representation. The principle of "one nation, one vote" is easily abandoned when it comes to the question of credits and grants. In the International Monetary Fund and the International Bank for Development and Reconstruction, the United States has more than a hundred times as many votes as the member-state with the lowest contribution. In the International Institute of Agriculture, England has twenty-two votes, the United States twenty-one, France nineteen, and other nations lesser numbers.

4. Nations depart from the rule of unanimity when they feel that *politically* they have no other choice. The "sovereign" and "equal" nations that gathered in San Francisco in 1945 agreed to be treated as not quite equal and not quite sovereign. By their voluntary assent, all founding member-states delegated their most decisive power—to determine the identity of an aggressor and decide on economic and military sanctions—to the five Great Powers—the United States, the Soviet Union, the United Kingdom, France, and the Republic of China—plus any two —later four— nonpermanent members of the Security Council (Articles 39-51, forming Chapter VII of the United Nations Charter). The acceptance of the five Great Powers' dominant position is expressed in Article 25 of the Charter, which says: "The Members of the United Nations agree to accept and carry out the decisions of the Security Council in accordance with the present Charter." Theoretically, if the Great Powers were unanimous, they could, with the help of four nations, rule the world and make decisions that would be legally binding upon all and enforceable; thus nine nations could impose their will upon the other 130. Every nation that has decided to join the world organization and remain in it has accepted the potentiality of such control by the Great Powers.

The reason for the acceptance of such potentiality was in part a general though reluctant recognition by the small and medium-sized nations that on the international scene little if anything can be achieved, especially in the matter of peace, unless the mighty nations first agree among themselves. On the other hand, if they so agree, their unanimity may constitute such an awesome concentration of power that little could be done against it. The small and medium-sized nations at San Francisco also realized that, in fact, they had little choice in the matter: Either the United Nations would be without great powers and therefore meaningless, or it would include them, but on their terms—that is, their participation was dependent on the guarantee that in major matters they could never be outvoted by any combination of member-nations. The Soviet Union under Stalin, the United States under Roosevelt and Truman, England under Churchill, and France under de Gaulle would not have joined any organization in which a superpower would have to accept as legally binding any decision to which it did not give its consent. This principle has come to be known as a Great-Powers veto in the United Nations Security Council, an international filibuster of sorts, for no enforcement action could ever be directed against one of the Great Powers. The United Nations was clearly inconceivable without the Great Powers, and potentially quite uncomfortable with them.

Finally, many small and medium-sized nations also anticipated that a directory by the unanimous Big Five was improbable. They were right. The constant disharmony among the five Great Powers has had two results. The United Nations is inefficient as an instrument of international enforcement, but smaller nations play a more significant role in the arena between the four or five centers of real power than they would if the United Nations were efficient, because they would then be dominated by the five Great Powers acting in harmony. Thus the member-nations' voluntary limitation of sovereignty (Article 25), which has the appearance of a delegation of decisive powers to the Security Council, did not result in any drastic transformation of the system of states as we have known it from the Peace of Westphalia to the peace in Vietnam.

The Inevitability of Leadership and Resentment

The effectiveness and quality of any international organization that reflects the existence of some common interests is determined, first, by the continuity and intensity of such common interests and, second, by the extent to which the organization develops concrete measures for protecting or promoting these interests. When and if the intensity or the importance of common interests decreases, an international organization tends to become an aggregate of empty rituals; but it is equally true that when and if the organization fails to deliver expected results through faulty structure or inept leadership, it may find itself in a serious crisis even though its initial community of interests has not disappeared. This is not dissimilar to a situation in territorial states, where the effectiveness and quality of the national system also depend on cohesiveness at the base and successful performance by the common authority at the top.

The problem of leadership in international organizations is, however, a much more delicate problem than that in national organizations, for the latter are characterized by a relatively high degree of consensus and equality among their individual members. In contrast, international organizations are marked by a relatively low degree of consensus and a gross inequality in power and status among the nations. Such inequality usually has two corollaries: a suspicion or fear of power and a dominance of the mighty nations over the weaker ones.

It should be noted that even in national institutions the fear of domination of the many by the few is constant. In his famous study of political parties, Robert Michels described how democratic socialist parties dedicated to the idea of democracy and egalitarianism had developed into oligarchic institutions in the course of their honest struggle against financial oligarchies. According to Michels, the principal cause of the general tendency toward oligarchy in all organizations is the technical indispensability of specialization, division of roles, and coordination. "Leadership," says Michels, "is a necessary phenomenon in every form of social life." But organization and the need for leadership imply a tendency toward oligarchy. Leaders who have sincerely and honestly conceived of their roles as servants of common interests tend to organize themselves and consolidate their leading positions to the point at which they would have enough power to detach themselves from the common base and develop their own interests, including that of self-perpetuation. "It is Organization," wrote Michels in 1915, "which gives the dominion of the elected over the electors, of the mandatories over the mandators, of the delegates over the delegators. Who says Organization, say Oligarchy."[6]

Centuries-old experience on the international scene has made it quite unnecessary for nations and their leaders to read Michels' study and apply some of its conclusions to international organizations. Nations have known all along about the tendency of leading powers to dominate international organizations and to transform them into agencies that finally serve their interests primarily at the expense of the interests of other members. Who says international organization, to paraphrase Michels, often seems to say domination by great powers. As seen from the point of view of small or medium-sized nations, the leading role in international organizations usually goes to those nations that have already played a dominant role on account of their awesome potential, irrespective of their wisdom or capacity for leadership; the cost of efficiency must be paid by the smaller nations' acceptance of the leading role of great powers.

In all international organizations, alliances (tensions within alliances will be discussed in Chapter 13), and international ideological movements, all marked by asymmetry of power, the minor members inevitably suspect or dread the self-interested motivation, ineptness, ignorance, and the tendency toward dictatorial behavior of the leading group, all of which lead to the neglect or sacrifice of the minor members' vital interests. These four sources of suspicion and erosion within multinational groupings have already been examined in Chapter 7 in the discussion of the erosion of international communism. Our stress on the consequences of power asymmetry in international organizations does not mean that the problem would be solved if all nations were truly equal, not ony legally but in every other way: even this hypothetical egalitarian international community would not be quite free of fear that the majority of equals might gang up against the minority and so transform the latter into an oppressed or at least neglected group.

FUNCTIONALISM

Functionalism is a set of theories and practices that attempts to shift international attention away from the preoccupation with national security and politics toward those problems that horizontally cut across the vertical national boundaries that divide our world into sovereign states. Functional activities therefore refer primarily to nonpolitical problems, such as economic cooperation and development; technological advancement; the fight against illiteracy, epidemics, or slavery; the protection of human rights; and the prevention of traffic in drugs. The functional approach to peace, sometimes referred to as "peace by pieces," is expressed and practiced in the United Nations by the following institutions:

1. *The Economic and Social Council* and its commissions. Some of its commissions concentrate on various functional issues within a geographically delineated area, such as the Regional Economic Commissions for Europe, Asia, Africa, Latin America, and the Middle East. Other commissions deal with specific problems such as human rights, the status of women, and narcotics on a global basis, without any particular geographic focus.

2. *The Specialized Agencies*. These agencies, whose membership slightly differ from that of the United Nations General Assembly, have their own separate budgets, agendas, and personnel, and are located in other cities than New York. They are loosely connected with the Economic and Social Council. Major specialized agencies are listed here according to their broad areas of concern:

Development International Labor Organization (ILO), with central offices in Geneva; World Health Organization (WHO), in Geneva; Food and Agriculture Organization (FAO), in Rome; International Atomic Energy Agency (IAEA), in Vienna; and United Nations Educational, Scientific, and Cultural Organization (UNESCO), based in Paris.

Communication Universal Postal Union (UPU), in Berne; International Telecommunications Union (ITU), in Geneva; International Civil Aviation Organization (ICAO), in Montreal; and World Meteorological Organization (WMO), in Geneva.

Finances International Monetary Fund (IMF) and the International Bank for Reconstruction and Development (World Bank), in Washington, D.C.

There are also several special organizations based on voluntary contributions, such as the United Nations Children's Emergency Fund (UNICEF), the United Nations Agency dealing with the Palestinian refugees, and many others.

Functionalism[7] is an attractive theory for two reasons: Functional activities in the social, humanitarian, cultural, and economic spheres produce some good on their own merits even if they do not (or perhaps cannot) influence political conflict or cooperation among nations. Functional activities are, however, also undertaken with the hope that their spirit of cooperation may usefully permeate and influence the political sphere. In *Can Peace Be Won?* Paul G. Hoffman wrote: "When you cultivate habits of unity in the economic sphere, they naturally spread over to the political sphere and even to the military sphere when the need arises."[8] Other advocates of functionalism have also expressed the hope that from international cooperation in the economic and humanitarian spheres nations will proceed step by step toward a closer unity in the political sphere. Functionalism was referred to as "federation by installments" by its most prominent spokesman, David Mitrany. "The problem of our time is not how to keep the nations peacefully apart but how to bring them actively together," Mitrany wrote in 1946, advising a shift from efforts to solve concrete political conflict to the search for an organization of those interests "which are common, where they are common, and to the extent to which they are common." In his opinion, international cooperation is

> more likely to grow through doing things together in workshop and market place than signing pacts in chancelleries. . . . [Functional activities] overlay political divisions with a spreading web of international activities and agencies, in which and through which the interests and life of all nations would be gradually integrated.[9]

The question to be examined is not whether functional activities are useful per se when they succeed in promoting economic cooperation, a better standard of living, social justice, and the protection of human rights, for they obviously are. Rather, the question is whether functional activities are capable of reducing or eliminating political conflicts or whether they will be curtailed or eliminated by such conflicts. In the short run, at least, the prospect seems to be that the development of truly international cooperation in nonpolitical fields extends or contracts in direct relation to the political situation. Politics determines the scope and intensity of functional activities, and not the other way around.

In his critical analysis of functionalism, Inis L. Claude expressed the following points that are useful to ponder:

> [Functionalism asserts that] the separability of economic and social problems from political problems is only provisional, and they are ultimately inseparable. International action at one level affects the other level, and leads to comparable action at the other level. This assumption of a connecting link lies at the heart of functional theory. . . . Functionalism assumes that political unity must be built, pearl-wise, around a central

> irritant; it offers a new type of common enemy—such as poverty, pestilence, or ignorance—to serve as the focal point around which men may unite.[10]

Claude then shows, in the light of the United Nations experience, that political and economic issues cannot be separated and that the connecting link that functionalism assumes may not operate in the direction desired by functionalists (from the functional level to the political) but in the opposite direction. Functional activities that were supposed to bring an end to political conflict are often interrupted or terminated because the political conflict does not permit their financing or their continuation.

> The record to date indicates that functional activity is, at least in the short run, more dependent upon the political weather than determinative of the political weather. . . . Is it in fact possible to segregate a group of problems and subject them to treatment in an international workshop where the nations shed their conflicts at the door and busy themselves only with the cooperative use of the tools of mutual interest? Does not this assumption fly in the face of the evidence that a trend toward the politicization of all issues is operative in the twentieth century?. . .We may ask whether states can in fact be induced to join hands in functional endeavor before they have settled the outstanding political and security issues which divide them. Functionalism's insistence upon putting first things first does not settle the matter of what things are first. . . .[11]

A similar caution concerning the decisive importance of the political weather was voiced in 1969 when during the flight of Apollo 11 to the moon the Soviet Union showed a spirit of cooperation and supplied information about the orbit of Soviet Luna 15, assuring the Americans that the Soviet Luna would not interfere with Apollo 11. The information was given in response to a telephone call by Colonel Borman from Houston to Moscow. One specialist on the Soviet space program was quoted by the *New York Times* (July 19, 1969): "Cooperation and space exploration between the United States and the Soviet Union will turn on the political atmosphere between the two nations, not vice versa." The political détente in the 1970s, as a matter of fact, permitted a cooperative plan for orbital docking of Soviet and American spacecraft.

THE UNITED NATIONS

The United Nations is the most universal and multipurpose international organization that has ever existed. According to its Charter it is supposed to deal cooperatively with all the general problems of peace, order, welfare, and progress. No approach to peace is neglected in the text of the Charter: peaceful solution of international conflicts by *diplomacy* and third-party techniques such as conciliation, arbitration, and judicial settlement (Chapter VI); solution of conflicts through *regional* organizations (Chapter VIII); development of *legal* rules (Chapter XIV); the *functional* approach to peace (Chapters IX and X); and solutions of *colonial* problems that cause international conflicts and injustice (Chapters XI, XII, and XIII). The most fundamental concept, that of enforceable security against aggression, is contained in the core of the Charter, Chapter VII (see below).

Membership

The purposes, membership, and organization of the United Nations are described in the first five chapters of the Charter. Almost all territorial states recognized by others as such have become members of the United Nations. In 1965 Indonesia became the first nation to announce its withdrawal from the United Nations because of its dispute with another member-nation, Malaysia. Following a military *coup d'état* in the wake of which well over 100,000 pro-Chinese communists were murdered, Indonesia adopted a new foreign policy and rejoined the United Nations in 1967.

Nonmembers

For nearly three decades three territorial states had been prevented from becoming members of the United Nations Organization by the political tensions between the United States and the Soviet Union. Recognition of one portion of divided Vietnam, Korea, and Germany by the United States and of the other by the Soviet Union had precluded the acceptance of either sector by the General Assembly and the Security Council, in which one superpower would simply veto the application of the other superpower's ally or puppet. In that period, however, West Germany and South Korea were allowed to participate in many nonpolitical specialized agencies of the United Nations. In 1973, the Soviet-American détente and the positive policy of West Germany toward Eastern Europe led to the membership of both Germanies, thus paving the way for North and South Korea and, eventually, perhaps even for North and South Vietnam if the two sectors do not unite by agreement or by force.

The controversial case of the People's Republic of China differs from the preceding cases of divided countries in the important fact that, until 1971, the Republic of China had always been a member and was actually one of the founders endowed with Great-Power status: It was one of the five permanent members of the Security Council. It had the veto power. The controversy concerned which government had the right to represent China in the United Nations. For twenty-seven years China was represented by Chiang Kai-shek's Nationalist government, although since 1949 the Chinese mainland has been under the effective control of the communist regime in Peking. The control and authority of the Chinese Nationalists has remained limited to Taiwan, Penghu (the Pescadores), and the offshore islands of Matsu and Quemoy. In 1971 Communist China replaced Nationalist China as one of the five Great Powers; on August 25, 1972, after a bitter attack on the Soviet Union and India, the People's Republic of China cast its first veto to bar Bangladesh from membership. Taiwan left the United Nations rather than face expulsion; nevertheless, Taiwan retained diplomatic relations not only with the United States, but with a number of other countries as well.

Switzerland is by its own free choice not a member of the United Nations, although it is recognized as a sovereign and independent state by all. Switzerland considers some of the obligations imposed by the United Nations Charter incompatible with its traditional concept of strict neutrality, that is, nonpartisanship in any conflict among nations. Under an exceptional set of circumstances (unanimity of the five Great Powers), members of the United Nations could be obligated by the Security Council to discriminate against an aggressor and favor his victim. Such action, however improbable it may be in practice, could include both economic and military sanctions. Neutral Switzerland has so far felt that this kind of theoretical possibility precludes its membership in the political organs of the United Nations; it participates, however, in the nonpolitical (economic, social, and humanitarian) activities of the world organization.

Some countries appear on the international scene as recognizable and recognized units in some but not all respects. Vatican City is the spiritual and administrative center of the Roman Catholic Church, but it is recognized by many nations as a sovereign territorial state—the Papal State. As such, the Vatican maintains diplomatic relations with many West European and Latin-American countries. Heads of the Vatican missions abroad have the title of *nuncio* and the rank of ambassador. In many countries nuncios serve as deans of the diplomatic corps. The Vatican is a member of the Universal Postal Union and the International Telecommunication Union, both specialized agencies of the United Nations.

The problem of microstates and their relationship to the United Nations has been discussed in another context in Chapter 3. The hope is that some formula may be found so that they can be associated with the humanitarian, social, and economic activities of the world organization without contributing to or suffering from the political disputes and tensions. There is a saying that the first thing a newly independent country does is to join the United Nations, the second to join the Red Cross. The state of West Samoa in the Pacific (a former colony and trust territory that obtained its independence from New Zealand in 1962) decided not to apply for membership because, apparently, West Samoan leaders feared the impact of the Great Powers' dispute on the development of their own country. However, it sought and obtained United Nations assistance in the economic and technical fields. West Samoa's position resembles that of other long-established countries that have many attributes of territorial states, including a very long history, a marked individuality, and a large measure of internal autonomy, but that have no right or wish to conduct their own foreign and military policies and participate in the political organs of the United Nations. This is true of the principality of Monaco on the French Riviera, which is a participating and contributing member of the Educational, Health, Postal, Telecommunication and Atomic Energy agencies of the United Nations.

The Soviet Republics

Finally, there is the very unusual case of the Ukraine and Byelorussia, two Soviet provinces. These are integral parts of the Soviet federation and yet individually both are members of the United Nations as if they were really sovereign and independent nations in the same category as Spain or Ghana. The Soviet Union is composed of fifteen Union republics (see Document 10.1), including the Ukraine and Byelorussia, which according to the Soviet Constitution of 1935 (amended in 1944) have the right of secession, the authority to conduct their own foreign policies, and the privilege of having their own republican military formations. At Yalta, in February 1945, Stalin asked and obtained from President Roosevelt and Prime Minister Churchill three votes for the Soviet Union in the United Nations General Assembly. He claimed separate membership for the two Soviet provinces in addition to membership of the Soviet Union as a whole. His argument was more emotional than legal. By giving two votes to the Soviet Ukraine and Byelorussia, according to Stalin, the free world would manifest its debt of gratitude for the heroic resistance and sufferings of the people of these regions during the Nazi onslaught of 1941-1945. There is no doubt that these two republics were indeed brutally devastated by the Nazi armies. But under other than these sentimental considerations the Yalta arrangement granting the USSR three votes does not seem to make any sense. Either the Soviet Union as a federal state should have been given one vote like any other federation (the United States, Canada, Nigeria, India, Australia, West Germany, Argentina, or Brazil) or if the constitutional grant of the right of secession and independent foreign policy were to be taken at its face value, the Soviet Union as a "confederation" or "commonwealth" should have been given fifteen or sixteen votes, for according to the Constitution all fifteen republics (sixteen in existence in 1944) had the same rights and privileges as the Ukraine and Byelorussia[12]

The case of recognition of the Ukraine and Byelorussia as full-fledged members of the United Nations is strange in another respect: Neither of these Soviet republics has diplomatic relations with any other member of the United Nations. The embassies of the USSR everywhere collectively

DOCUMENT 10.1

THE FIFTEEN SOVIET SOCIALIST REPUBLICS

Republics and Nationalities	Racial or Religious Background	Number (in Millions)
Russians (Great Russians)	Slavic	115
Ukrainians	Slavic	37
Byelorussians	Slavic	7.8
Uzbeks	Turkic, Moslem	6.3
Kazakhs	Turkic, Moslem	4.9
Azerbaidzhanis	Iranian, Moslem	2.7
Georgians	Caucasian	2.6
Lithuanians	Baltic	
Moldavians	a former, racially mixed, Rumanian province of Bessarabia	
Latvians	Baltic	2-2.2 each
Kirghiz	Turkic, Moslem	
Tadjik	Iranian, Moslem	
Armenians	Thraco-Phrygian	
Turkmen	Turkic, Moslem	
Estonians	Ugro-Finnish	1.0

represent all fifteen republics and their Union. The Soviet Ukraine and Soviet Byelorussia have not even established diplomatic and consular relations with neighboring communist states such as Poland or Czechoslovakia, although quite a strong case could be made in favor of direct relations between these countries for the sake of regional common interests. Thus, in the United Nations Ukrainian and Byelorussian "foreign ministers" discuss, agree, vehemently disagree, and enthusiastically vote as if they were representatives of sovereign nations, while on the rest of the international scene as well as within the Soviet Union proper these republics are endowed with less autonomy than states in the United States, provinces in federal Canada, departments in unitary France, prefectures in Japan, and counties in England. Although they are members of the world organization, the Soviet republics are in actuality less autonomous in their internal politics and external contacts than such miniature states as Monaco and West Samoa.

Organization and Functions

The United Nations is composed of six principal organs. They are:

1. The Security Council, which, in principle, functions continuously.
2. The General Assembly, which meets once every year in regular session, although special and emergency sessions may be called.
3. The Economic and Social Council, which holds two sessions a year and is composed of twenty-seven members, elected by the General Assembly. Its main concern is international cooperation in economic, social, health, cultural, educational, and related matters. It also tries to coordinate the activities of the specialized agencies.
4. The Trusteeship Council, which has now become one of the least important organs, as there are practically no trust territories left to fall under its jurisdiction; it meets twice a year. The problem of trust territories was discussed in Chapter 3.
5. The International Court of Justice, composed of fifteen judges elected concurrently by the General Assembly and the Security Council. It is, in principle, permanently in session at The Hague. (Chapter 9 dealt with the International Court in more detail.)
6. The Secretariat, which consists of a secretary-general and his international staff. The secretary-general is appointed by the General Assembly on the recommendation of the Security Council for a period of three years. Being the chief administrative officer of the organization, the secretary-general is expected to execute the will and the decisions of the main organs. Article 99, however, gives the secretary-general the right to "bring to the attention of the Security Council any matter which in his opinion may threaten the maintenance of international peace and security." In a limited way, therefore, the secretary-general can exercise some political initiative; its final effect, however, depends on the Security Council.

Politically, the two most important organs are the Security Council and the General Assembly. The Council is composed of five permanent members—the five powers that mutually recognized each other as "great" in 1945 (America, Britain, China—until 1971 represented by Nationalist China, after that, by Communist China—France, and Russia)—and ten members elected by a two-thirds majority of the General Assembly, to serve for a term of two years. The Security Council is an organ clearly superior to the General Assembly because (1) the Charter assigns it *primary* though not exclusive responsibility for the maintenance of peace and security (Article 24); (2) the General Assembly cannot make any recommendation with regard to any dispute in respect of which the Security Council is exercising its appropriate functions (Article 12) unless the Council so requests it to; and (3) it is the only organ of the United Nations that can make decisions binding upon its members. (In Article 25 the member-nations agree to carry out its decisions.)

On *procedural* matters, Security Council decisions are passed by any nine affirmative votes. The difference between the permanent and the elected members of the Council plays no role.

On *substantive* matters, such decisions as the determination of the fact of aggression and any preventive or punitive measures to be taken require nine votes, including the concurrent votes of the five Great Powers. This is the famous veto power, which makes it impossible for the Council to impose any measure against the will of any Great Power. A negative vote of one Great Power nullifies the decision of the other fourteen members. Abstention is not interpreted as a veto, although the Charter speaks of five *concurring* affirmative votes. The effect of a Great Power's deliberate absence is controversial. Some view it as similar to abstention from voting and therefore not a veto; others argue that a deliberate absence, for instance as a protest against an unconstitutional procedure or the composition of the Council, represents an even stronger act than veto itself.

In a controversy regarding the substantive or procedural nature of an item, a vote of one Great Power may transform any procedural matter into a substantive one and thus veto it (the double veto). According to the Charter no collective enforcement can ever be directed against any of the Great Powers. This provision simply records and confirms what has always been true even without the Charter. Great Powers expect, and are expected, to play the dominant role in international politics. The veto provision also permits the small and medium-size member-states to assume, in Arnold Wolfers' words, "that they never would be expected to participate in police action which would seriously antagonize one or more of the major powers."[13]

According to the Charter, the General Assembly is composed of all member-nations of the United Nations, each irrespective of its power having one vote, and each having the authority to make recommendations, passed by a two-thirds majority when the issue is important and by a simple majority in other cases. The Assembly also has the authority to regulate United Nations budgetary matters.

The recommendations of the General Assembly, unlike the decisions of the Security Council, have no legally binding force. Assembly resolutions can authorize action by willing member-nations, but they can never order it. If nations are not willing, a resolution of the Assembly becomes a scrap of paper.

Since the developing nations have become a dominant majority in the United Nations General Assembly, some of their representatives, supported by a few wishful thinkers in the Western world, tend to present the General Assembly's resolutions as having the force of law. A number of Asian and African delegates have even suggested that majority opinions of the General Assembly might come to represent the "general principles of law recognized by civilized nations"; this terminology may be found in Article 38 of the Statute of the International Court of Justice (see Document 9.4). As may be recalled, the World Court recognizes three main sources of international law: conventions, customary law, and the general principles of law which traditionally were to be found in judicial decisions. Evidently, claiming today that the General Assembly's recommendations represent the general principles of law is one thing, and having such a view accepted and followed in practice by great and medium powers is another. In the Western world there is no lack of caustic comments on the Afro-Asian support of the democratic majoritarian technique of counting the "nays" and the "ayes" in order to decide an issue with finality since the Afro-Asian majority in the United Nations consists of military and one-party dictatorships that at home would never submit a major issue to a competitive vote. On the other hand, the Western powers, which employ the majoritarian technique to conduct their business at home, appear quite reluctant to use the same method on the international scene.

There is no constitutional provision for making the Security Council and the General Assembly come together in their views. Theoretically, the organization could speak with two dissonant voices; if, for example, in the Security Council the five Great Powers plus four of the nonpermanent members agreed to say *yes,* the General Assembly by a vote of 100 to 9 might say *no.* In theory, there is no link between the two bodies that would correspond to that between a cabinet and a parliament. When cast in the Security Council, the nine votes, including those of the five Great Powers, are decisive. When cast in the General Assembly, constitutionally they represent an insignificant minority. In practice, of course, the nine votes in the Security Council would count more than the hundred votes in the General Assembly. This was particularly manifest during the twenty-fourth session of the General Assembly in 1969, which was nicknamed the "Small-Powers Session." Their majority succeeded in ramming through the Assembly a large number of resolutions that were opposed by one or both superpowers, the Soviet Union and the United States. Some of these resolutions had no chance of being carried out, including the resolution declaring illegal the use of tear gas and defoliants. The more the small powers try to impose their views on the Assembly rather than convincing the superpowers by means of quiet diplomacy, the more the superpowers are tempted to make the really important decisions outside the United Nations. One disenchanted delegate expressed this possibility (*New York Times,* December 20, 1969) by saying, "The little ones run the beautiful building on the East River, the two big ones run the rest of the world."

PEACEFUL SETTLEMENT OF DISPUTES

The United Nations Charter distinguishes between two possible forms of pacific settlements of disputes among nations: diplomatic negotiations—that is, direct communication between parties to a dispute with a view to finding and agreeing on a compromise solution—and procedures involving a third party. The Charter considers diplomacy the most promising method and prefers it to all other possible methods which add a third party—a mediator, arbitrator, or a court—to the parties to a dispute.

In the words of Chapter VI, Article 33, of the Charter:

> Parties to a dispute the continuance of which is likely to endanger the maintenance of international peace and security, shall, first of all, seek a solution by negotiation, enquiry, mediation, conciliation, arbitration, judicial settlement, resort to regional agencies or arrangements, or other peaceful methods of their choice.

Working definitions of third-party techniques follow. It should be noted that the third party cannot be imposed or impose itself on sovereign nations; for a third party to enter a dispute it is necessary that the two parties in conflict agree tacitly in the case of inquiry and mediation and explicitly in the case of conciliation, arbitration, and judicial settlement.

Inquiry

The technique of inquiry consists in the service that a third party or a commission may offer by ascertaining the precise facts that have given rise to a dispute. Since the excitement and emotional involvement often obscure the facts that have caused the dispute, inquiry may be helpful.

Mediation

Mediation and good offices refer to the offer of a third party to help bring about negotiations between two nations in conflict. Good offices are usually described as various kinds of action to bring about a new contact between the conflicting states. Mediation consists in offering a direct channel for negotiations. In practice, good offices, mediation and concilition often merge.

Conciliation

Conciliation represents an effort to settle a dispute by referring it to a conciliator or a commission of persons who, following an inquiry, suggest a settlement of the dispute. It is this proposal of a settlement that differentiates conciliation from mediation. In the press the terms "mediator" and "conciliator" are used interchangeably.

Arbitration

Arbitration represents a settlement of a dispute among nations through a binding decision rendered by either an umpire or a commission on the basis of a previous agreement of the conflicting parties to abide by it. The difference between conciliation and arbitration lies in the fact that the proposal of settlement offered by a conciliator is not considered binding. Parties to a dispute can take it or leave it. The arbitral award, however, is binding. (See the discussion of the Hague Permanent Court of Arbitration in Chapter 9.)

Judicial Settlement

Judicial settlement refers to an actual arbitration award issued by the International Court of Justice. In international law, the difference between arbitration and judicial settlement is not fundamental. Both awards are based on law. Both are legally binding on the parties to a dispute only on the basis of previous agreement to abide by the award. The main difference is in the character of the adjudicating body. The possibilities and limits of the International Court of Justice were described and analyzed in Chapter 9.

If nations decide to settle their disputes without resort to violence, diplomatic negotiations or the third-party techniques offer them a reasonable choice. Nevertheless, as the Charter realistically acknowledges, aggressive or defensive use of violence can never be excluded among men and nations. The Charter therefore proposes to prevent international violence or punish it by an overwhelming threat or use of collective violence, that is, collective security under the provisions of Chapter VII.

COLLECTIVE SECURITY AND ENFORCEMENT

The concept of collective security and enforcement, as first embodied in the Covenant of the League of Nations under Article 16 (see Document 10.2) and then in the United Nations Charter in Chapter VII

DOCUMENT 10.2

COVENANT OF THE LEAGUE OF NATIONS, ARTICLE 16

1. Should any Member of the League resort to war in disregard of its covenants under Articles 12, 13 or 15, it shall, *ipso facto*, be deemed to have committed an act of war against all other Members of the League, which hereby undertake immediately to subject it to the severance of all trade or financial relations, the prohibition of all intercourse between their nationals and the nationals of the Covenant-breaking State, and the prevention of all financial, commercial or personal intercourse between the nationals of the Covenant-breaking State and the nationals of any other State, whether a Member of the League or not.

2. It shall be the duty of the Council in such case to recommend to the several Governments concerned what effective military, naval or air force the Members of the League shall severally contribute to the armed forces to be used to protect the covenants of the League.

3. The Members of the League agree, further, that they will mutually support one another in the financial and economic measures which are taken under this article, in order to minimize the loss and inconvenience resulting from the above measures. . . .

4. Any Member of the League which has violated any covenant of the League may be declared to be no longer a Member of the League by a vote of the Council concurred in by the Representatives of all the other members of the League represented thereon.

(Articles 39-51), was supposed to make peace secure and alliances unnecessary.

The underlying principle of collective security is that peace is indivisible: An attack against any nation is supposed to be treated as an attack against all. If this were so, a potential aggressor would be deterred from action by the image of all nations automatically coming to the aid of a nation threatened or attacked. In contrast to the traditional concept of securing peace or preventing domination by a rough approximation of the balance of power, collective security aims at creating an overwhelming imbalance of power, an intimidatory machinery of such scope and dimension that an aggressor would not dare to start a war or would be annihilated if foolishly he did. Neither the League nor the United Nations to date has proved able to translate the concept of collective security into a reality that would deter the aggressor by a credible imbalance of power and thus provide member-nations with the feeling and the actuality of a collective intimidatory power.

Nations would create an overwhelming concentration of deterrent power only if the following two conditions were met:

1. Nations endowed with the power to coerce[14] would have to be able to

agree who in an actual conflict is the aggressor and who is the victim. According to the United Nations Charter, the determining of an act of aggression, a breach of the peace, or a threat to the peace was placed in the hands of the five Great Powers plus four nonpermanent members of the Security Council. Thus nine members of the United Nations could, on behalf of the world organization, decide on the all-important preliminary question concerning the identities of the aggressor and the victim. But history teaches us that some situations of international conflict are so confused and unclear that an honest disagreement may arise as to who has attacked whom and who has provoked whom.

Furthermore, collective security presupposes that nations would collectively act as a phalanx of avenging angels against an aggressor regardless of whether he was their friend or foe. This is, evidently, quite unrealistic: damaging a friend or helping an enemy within the contemporary framework could result in one's own ruin. Also, sometimes a nation has to determine whether losing an old friend is worth gaining a new friend. In the 1956 Suez crisis there were many reasons why the United States and the Soviet Union opposed the French-English-Israeli adventure, but one of the most important was the courting of Arab friendship (and control over the oil deposits).

2. Even if nations should reach an identical conclusion as to the perpetrator and victim of a breach of the peace, they would still have to be willing and ready to act. In theory, peace is indivisible; in practice, war has always meant war and destruction for some and peace and even prosperity for others. In wartime, neutrals are particularly criticized for the profits they make and the comforts they enjoy while others die. Nations also find it difficult to interrupt their period of peace and development for the purpose of some punitive and costly action in a distant place about which they know nothing, as Neville Chamberlain described Czechoslovakia at the period of the Munich crisis in 1938. It is a question not only of willingness but also of feasibility: When a nation is required to act according to the principle of collective security, its hands may be more than full with domestic problems[15] (an economic crisis, social tension, political ferment) or its own international responsibilities. In the 1960s, the French war in Algeria sucked away from Europe many French troops needed in the NATO structure; in 1964, in the midst of the mounting tension between Sukarno's Indonesia and Malaysia, Britain had to send some paratroop units away from their regular duty, protecting West Germany against Russia, to a new duty, deterring Indonesia from attacking Malaysia. What a nation can do with the power it has is quite limited. And the demands of collective security might be in excess of the available power.

Collective Security, UN Style

Chapter VII of the United Nations Charter has quite realistically made the working of collective security dependent on the unanimity of the five Great Powers (see Document 10.3). If the USSR, the U.S., China, Great Britain, and France were in harmony, they conceivably could police the world through a pool of their respective conventional and atomic powers. The Charter even contains a provision (Article 43) for the establishment of a permanent international police force, to be built around the nucleus of the armed forces of the five powers. A military staff committee under the Security Council (Article 47) was to act as a high command of the permanent United Nations army under the political directive of the Security Council. The military staff committee, composed of the representatives of the chiefs of staff of the five Great Powers, was established, but not a single regiment, not a single plane, and, as a matter of fact, not a single soldier has ever been assigned to it. The collective security provisions of the United Nations Charter have remained a dead letter. The first decades of the world organization have been marked by conflict, not cooperation, among the Great Powers. Since collective security was originally supposed to be the result of the harmony among the Great Powers, their disharmony has necessarily produced collective insecurity,[16] which could only be mitigated and kept within bounds by the primary balancing process between the Great Powers and their allies, satellites, or customers, and by the secondary balancing process within their blocs as well as between the committed and nonaligned nations. The often-quoted and praised collective action in Korea, recommended, *but not ordered*, by the Security Council in 1950, was due not to the collective security mechanism as it was originally envisioned by the United Nations Charter, but to an unusual set of circumstances, the most significant being the absence of the Soviet Union at the decisive meeting of the Security Council, which on June 27, 1950,

> having determined that the armed attack upon the Republic of Korea by forces from North Korea constituted a breach of peace, . . .recommended that the Members of the United Nations furnish such assistance to the Republic of Korea as may be necessary to repel the armed attack and to restore international peace and security in the area.[17]

"Uniting for Peace"

Subsequently, several attempts were made to increase the role and the power of the General Assembly in matters of collective security beyond the authority given to it by the Charter. The most notable of such attempts was the "Uniting for Peace" Resolution passed at the fifth session of the General Assembly, on November 3, 1950. The resolution tried to circumvent the fact that, as a consequence of the Cold War, collective security had failed to materialize: During the first five years of the world

DOCUMENT 10.3

COLLECTIVE SECURITY—CHAPTER VII
OF THE UNITED NATIONS CHARTER

Article 39

The Security Council shall determine the existence of any threat to the peace, breach of the peace, or act of aggression and shall make recommendations, or decide what measures shall be taken in accordance with Articles 41 and 42, to maintain or restore international peace and security.

Article 41

The Security Council may decide what measures not involving the use of armed force are to be employed to give effect to its decisions, and it may call upon the Members of the United Nations to apply such measures. These may include complete or partial interruption of economic relations and of rail, sea, air, postal, telegraphic, radio, and other means of communication, and the severance of diplomatic relations.

Article 42

Should the Security Council consider that measures provided for in Article 41 would be inadequate or have proved to be inadequate, it may take such action by air, sea, or land forces as may be necessary to maintain or restore international peace and security. Such action may include demonstrations, blockade, and other operations by air, sea, or land forces of Members of the United Nations.

Article 43

All Members of the United Nations, in order to contribute to the maintenance of international peace and security, undertake to make available to the Security Council, on its call and in accordance with a special agreement or agreements, armed forces, assistance, and facilities, including rights of passage, necessary for the purpose of maintaining international peace and security. . . .

Article 51

Nothing in the present Charter shall impair the inherent right of individual or collective self-defense if an armed attack occurs against a Member of the United Nations, until the Security Council has taken the measures necessary to maintain international peace and security. Measures taken by Members in the exercise of this right of self-defense shall be immediately reported to the Security Council and shall not in any way affect the authority and responsibility of the Security Council under the present Charter to take at any time such action as it deems necessary in order to maintain or restore international peace and security.

organization the Soviet Union used the veto nearly fifty times, thus successfully blocking the decision-making process of the Security Council.

The Charter clearly placed the General Assembly in a secondary position. The General Assembly can never make any binding decision. It can only recommend an action and hope that nations will be willing and ready to execute it. This is, of course, a far cry from the original concept of collective security and automatic deterrence. It may be argued that a collective action authorized by the General Assembly is not an action *by* the United Nations, but only an action *permitted* by the majority of the United Nations. This may seem a subtle difference, but, in reality, it is an important one. Furthermore, the permissive authority of the General Assembly is severely limited by Article 12, which authorizes the General Assembly to make recommendations only if the Security Council permits; no recommendations may be made "while the Security Council is exercising in respect to any dispute or situation the functions assigned to it . . . unless the Security Council so requests."

The Uniting for Peace Resolution attempted to remedy both the constitutional weakness of the General Assembly and the political incapacity of the Security Council to make any decision whatsoever. Under its general heading, three resolutions were adopted, two of which (Resolutions B and C) represented a new appeal to the Security Council to take the necessary steps to implement the collective security provisions of the Charter and discuss problems "likely to threaten international peace." These resolutions represented only a bow in the direction of the Security Council, which, according to the Charter, has the *primary* responsibility in matters of war and peace. The key provision was contained in Resolution A, by which the General Assembly authorized itself to meet in an emergency special session on twenty-four hours' notice on the vote of any seven (now nine) members of the Security Council or on the vote of a majority of the General Assembly if the Security Council, because of the lack of unanimity among the permanent members, fails to act in any case where there appears to be a threat to the peace, breach of the peace, or act of aggression. A great controversy developed on the subject of the constitutionality of the provision, especially in two respects: First, it was viewed as a violation of Article 12, which does not permit the General Assembly to make recommendations with regard to peace and security unless the Security Council so requests; second, the Resolution's ruling that the Security Council's decision to call a special session of the General Assembly was procedural and therefore did not require the unanimity of the five Great Powers was seen as arbitrary. The majority of the member-nations argued, however, that the inability of the Security Council to discharge its primary responsibility for maintaining international peace and security (demonstrated by the Soviet use of the veto nearly fifty times) made it imperative for the General Assembly to use its residual rights to make recommendations on matters of war and peace.

The minority, led by the Soviet Union, insisted that a decision of the Security Council not to act, whether this was a result of a vote or a veto, could not be construed as authorizing the General Assembly to take over from the Security Council. The communist nations argued that the resolution was tantamount to an amendment of the Charter (all amendments require the unanimity of the five Great Powers) and viewed the whole procedure as a thinly disguised attempt by the American-led majority in the General Assembly to usurp the rights of the Security Council and thus eliminate the principle of unanimity of the Great Powers on which the world organization had originally been built. On this point the Soviet arguments had some merit in view of the history and the text of the Charter.

In practice, however, the Soviet Union itself has taken the opportunity to transfer issues from a deadlocked Security Council to the General Assembly when it was profitable to do so from the Soviet point of view. When in 1956 the English and French vetoes in the Security Council killed a Council resolution calling for a cease-fire in the Suez area, the Soviet Union worked with gusto for a General Assembly condemnation of the French-English-Israeli actions there. In 1967 the Soviet Union tried to get the General Assembly to condemn Israel again and to exert pressure on her to withdraw her forces from the Arab territories she occupied in the six-day war. The Soviet request for an Assembly meeting invoked "Resolution 377A of the fifth session of the General Assembly"—which is no other than the American-sponsored Uniting for Peace Resolution of November 3, 1950. Whether called Resolution 377A or the Uniting for Peace Resolution, this legally controversial interpretation of the Charter has now become an operative device in the hands of those who can mobilize majority support for it in the Assembly.

The principle of collective security was based on the assumption of the willingness and readiness of *all* nations under the League, and of the five Great Powers under the United Nations Charter, to put aside their national interests and deal with any threat to the peace as if their own vital interests were threatened. If such a revolution in the minds of the nations and their leaders were to occur—and it would indeed be nothing less than a revolutionary transmutation of nations—the result of such a universal consensus would be collective security. To incorporate the collective security mechanism into the Covenant or the Charter before such a consensus materializes is to put the cart before the horse. This is why collective security has remained strictly on paper. It is an ideal toward which nations may strive, but not a reality on which they can base their defense.

Collective Self-Defense

At this point, a note on terminology is necessary: According to the United Nations Charter there is a substantial difference between alliances and collective security even though statesmen and journalists mix both terms and refer to alliances as collective security arrangements. Semantically, of course, any device ensuring the security of more than one or two nations may indeed be called collective; nonetheless, according to the sections of the Charter that authorize alliances (Articles 51, 53, and 107), alliances should be referred to as *collective self-defense treaties*. (See Article 51 in Document 10.3.) The United Nations was to initiate a system of collective security (and therefore a system without alliances). But its Charter authorized defense treaties: first, to permit the continuation of wartime alliances against the enemies of the United Nations (that is, the fighting alliance against Germany and Japan) in case of their return to aggressive policies; and, second, to provide nations with a legitimate means of collective self-defense as a stopgap before the collective security mechanism, based on the unanimity of the five Great Powers, was organized. According to Article 51 of the Charter, a nation in the exercise of its legitimate and inherent right of individual self-defense may be assisted by other nations provided that the Security Council is notified of such group action and that it is understood that the group action remains subordinate to future United Nations collective action by the Security Council if and when it so decides; any action under collective self-defense arrangements—that is, alliances—would continue only until the Security Council took appropriate measures to restore peace and security. In view of the fact that the Security Council cannot decide on any measure without the concurrence of its five permanent members, no action based on an alliance involving any of the great powers or any of their allies could possibly be interrupted and taken over by the Security Council. A veto cast by a Great Power on its own or its ally's behalf would be sufficient to keep the continuation of an allied action legitimate.

Peace-Keeping Operations

In a few cases the United Nations General Assembly has resorted to a method of combating conflict that cannot be classified as either collective security or self-defense in the sense of the Charter: the peace-keeping operation, which, basically, means the interposition of the United Nations military presence between two hostile nations or between factions within a nation-state. The United Nations forces sent to the Congo, Cyprus, and the Middle East are examples. A peace-keeping operation differs from a collective security operation in four ways: 1) It is applied against a dangerous situation, not against an aggressor; it therefore avoids the difficult question of determining who is the aggressor and who the victim. (2) It is limited in application to a few geographically suitable situations, whereas collective security was to be applied to any threat anywhere to international peace. (3) As a rule, a peace-keeping military force can be agreed upon only if it is composed of small and more or less neutral nations with no forces from any of the five Great Powers participating, whereas the Charter envisioned a permanent military force for collective security predominantly composed of contingents from the five Great Powers; in 1974 the peace-keeping force policing the disengagement of Israeli and Egyptian armies on the Suez front was composed of 6,396 soldiers from eleven countries (Austria, 599; Canada, 1,097; Finland, 640; Ghana, 499; Indonesia, 549; Ireland, 271; Panama, 409; Peru, 497; Poland, 820; Senegal, 399; and Sweden, 616). (4) Instead of being the result of a binding order issued by the Security Council, as Chapter VII of the Charter assumed collective security operations would be, a peace-keeping operation is deemed to be essentially voluntary. It cannot operate unless the parties concerned agree to it, especially the governments on whose territory the peace-keeping operation is to take place. In contrast to the military sanctions envisioned by the Charter, a peace-keeping force is not instructed to use force, to win and to defeat an enemy, but rather to act as a mixed force of observers and policemen—soldiers without an enemy.[18]

The problem obviously is funding; if the operation is voluntary, can any nation, especially those who might have voted against the measure recommending the operation, be taxed through the budget of the United Nations and so forced to contribute? A resounding *nyet* from the Soviet Union and her allies was the answer when the argument concerning funding of operations approved by the General Assembly without a five-power agreement culminated in the early 1960s. The 1964-1965 session of the General Assembly proved finally unable to transact any business whatsoever except matters of pure routine, because of a deep financial crisis, largely caused by several collective actions—especially the costly peace-keeping operations in the Congo and the Gaza strip. Neither the Soviet Union nor France was willing to contribute financially to actions that they had not approved; being forced to finance what they politically opposed was viewed by them, more or less, as "international taxation without representation." A depressing financial and political crisis of the United Nations followed.[19]

THE UN: A MIRROR OF DISUNITED NATIONS

The United Nations Organization cannot reform the world. It can only reflect the world as it is, which is not too good and certainly not as it one day might be, whether better or worse (see Figure 10.1). In reporting on

FIGURE 10.1
THE UNITED NATIONS CANNOT
REFORM THE WORLD

"If they ever do beat those swords into ploughshares, they'll end up walloping each other over the head with them."

Drawing by Stan Hunt; © 1964 The New Yorker Magazine, Inc.

the state of the world to the General Assembly in 1973, Secretary-General Kurt Waldheim called the need for global concord "never so urgent." Inviting nations to "take a hard look at matters as they are," the secretary-general asked: "Do the majority of the member states really want an organization which is more than a conference machinery and a forum for the pursuit of national policies?"

To judge by the subsequent behavior and votes of the member-states their answer was "no," the time for change has not yet come.

At present the Charter cannot legislate out of existence two incongruities: the incompatibility between national sovereignty and effective international organization and the contradiction between the facts of inequality and the fiction of equality. "In the measure that an international organization is effective, it is bound to impair the freedom of action of its members," noted Hans J. Morgenthau in his "obituary" on the United Nations under Dag Hammarskjöld. "And in the measure that member states assert their freedom of action, they impair the effectiveness of the international organization."[20] The problem of unequal capabilities among nations is related: The theoretical freedom sovereignly to determine national goals is simply not matched by equality in the capacity to achieve them.

The United Nations is very often described by its well-wishers as a supranational body with a will and concept that might conceivably be different from the will and concepts of its national components. Sometimes, in fact, a portion of the international civil-service personnel employed by the United Nations is able to think and act in supranational terms. Under an internationally minded secretary-general such as Dag Hammarskjöld, the United Nations may almost gain, at least temporarily, its own momentum and detach itself from the original stimulus that was a vague compromise between different national policies. This, however, can last only until a major power, by its veto or by financial pressure, "calls" the United Nations back to order and forces the staff back into its role as an instrument of the will of nations and not their master.

An international organization is the sum of the good and bad will of member nations; these organizations are not, and cannot be, any better or worse than their members. As W. W. Kulski has noted:

> An association of states cannot achieve more than the member-states, in particular great powers, are willing to do. To submit a matter to the United Nations is not to refer it to an organization which can settle problems otherwise unsolvable for the member-states. It is merely to transfer the negotiations from the diplomatic chanceries to another forum where the same protagonists can be found.[21]

International organizations sometimes create a premature impression that they represent entities separate from, and placed above, their constituent members. In reality, they remain only international; they do not become supranational;they do not supersede national identities and separate, often antogonistic, interests. This fact tends to be overlooked, particularly in the United States. One reason is perhaps the United States's own historical experience in creating one nation out of many states and nationalities; this may lead Americans to be more optimistic about the United Nations than they would otherwise be. Furthermore, in 1944 and 1945, in order to avoid a repetition of the withdrawal of United States support, both congressional and popular, for the League of Nations in the 1920s, both the government and the mass media tended to oversell an idealized image of the new United Nations Organization to the public. Another contributing factor, perhaps, is the neat grammatical trick, so easy in the English language and impossible in most other languages,[22] that endowed the new organization with a more unified image than the mosaic of antagonistic nations warrants: the word "organization" was dropped from the title so that the official designation became *The United Nations*, which can give an impression of supranational unity and so obscure the reality of an organization of disunited nations.

This concludes Part III, which has dealt with the possible moral, legal, and social restraints on national behavior. Noting the deep divisions of humanity into nationalist and mutually suspicious nation-states as well as into various ideological blocs, a reader may be tempted either to manifest impatience or despair or, on the contrary, to plunge into wishful dreaming and search for a panacea, however it may be labeled: adherence to morality and law, world federation, total disarmament, or simply love. Such a temptation is understandable but should be resisted. Before any reform can be contemplated—and there is no doubt that reform is necessary—our analysis must include a study of the strategies and tactics that nations and their leaders adopt when they are forced to act in a framework whose complete overhaul they cannot reasonably expect in a foreseeable future. Thus, naturally, they contribute to the perpetuation of the system they say they deplore.

Notes

1. Andrei Voznesensky, *Antiworlds*. New York: Basic Books, 1966, p. 3.
2. Harlan Cleveland, *International Cooperation Year* (U.S. Department of State Publication No. 7638). Washington, D.C.: Government Printing Office, 1965, p. 3.
3. Charles de Vissher, *Theory and Reality in Public International Law*. Princeton, N.J.: Princeton University Press, 1957, p. 109.
4. Alexis de Tocqueville, *Democracy in America*, Henry Reeve translation as revised by Francis Bowen and further corrected by Phillips Bradley, Vol. 1. New York: Knopf and Vintage Books, 1954, pp. 269-270.

5. Harold Nicolson, "Diplomacy Then and Now," *Foreign Affairs*, 40:1 (October 1961), 40.

6. Robert Michels, *Political Parties*. New York: Dover, 1959, p. 401.

7. See Inis L. Claude, *Swords into Plowshares*, 3d ed. New York: Random House and Knopf, 1964. The whole book is an excellent analysis of the problems and progress of international organizations in our time.

8. Paul G. Hoffman, *Can Peace Be Won?* New York: Doubleday, 1951, p. 62.

9. David Mitrany, *A Working Peace System*. London: National Peace Council, 1946, p. 7.

10. Claude, *Swords into Plowshares*, p. 351.

11. Claude, *Swords into Plowshares*, pp. 353-354, 367.

12. Vernon V. Aspaturian, "The Union Republics and Soviet Diplomacy: Concepts, Institutions, Practices," *American Political Science Review*, 53:2 (June 1959), 383-411.

13. Arnold Wolfers, *Discord and Collaboration*. Baltimore, Md.: The Johns Hopkins Press, 1962, p. 171.

14. See Kenneth W. Thompson, "Collective Security Reexamined," *American Political Science Review*, 47:3 (September 1953), 753-766.

15. See the discussion of Nixon's Guam Doctrine in Chapter 13, a doctrine that in 1970 limited the United States's capability to the handling of only one major and one minor war simultaneously.

16. The United States permanent representative in the Security Council in the 1960s, Ambassador Charles Yost, typically entitled his book on international politics *The Insecurity of Nations: International Relations in the Twentieth Century*. New York: Praeger, 1968.

17. UN Document S/1511, June 27, 1950.

18. Marina S. Finkelstein and Lawrence S. Finkelstein, *Collective Security*. New York: Intext, 1973, pp. 259-261.

19. John G. Stoessinger *et al.*, *Financing the United Nations System*. Washington, D.C.: Brookings, 1964, pp. 191-246. The World Court's advisory opinion on the cost of peace-making operations is examined on pp. 140-156. See also Lincoln P. Bloomfield *et al.*, *International Military Forces*. Boston: Little, Brown, 1964.

20. Hans J. Morgenthau, "The UN of Dag Hammarskjöld Is Dead," *New York Times Magazine*, March 14, 1965, p. 32.

21. W. W. Kulski, *International Politics in a Revolutionary Age*. Philadelphia: Lippincott, 1964, p. 454.

22. In French, more realistically, the official title is *ONU, Organisation des Nations Unies*. In the author's native Czech it is *Organizace Spojených národů*.

Additional Readings

Additional readings on international organizations may be found in *Discord and Harmony: Readings in International Politics*, edited by Ivo D. Duchacek and published by Holt, Rinehart and Winston in 1972. Chapter 4, "Contacts and Cooperation among Nations (pp. 45-69), contains a study on the superpowers in the United Nations by John G. Stoessinger. See also "The Concept of Collective Security" by Kenneth W. Thompson, pp. 349-357.

IV

STRATEGIES
Destruction,
Domination,
Deterrence,
Diplomacy

11

Interventions: Violent and Nonviolent

When national leaders are confronted with what they perceive, correctly or incorrectly, as an opportunity to enhance national well-being and security or when, on the contrary, they see a threat to national safety or freedom of action, they usually adopt one or, to be on the safe side, a combination of the following options:

1. *War*   Its aim is to destroy the source of the threat or sometimes, when there is no threat, to build an empire for economic or ideological reasons.
2. *Interference*   Various penetrative techniques short of open warfare represent a gray and controversial category between violent and nonviolent or abnormal and normal interaction among nations; the purpose of such techniques, ranging from intervention and subversion to psychological warfare, is to weaken the enemy from within or to strengthen a sympathetic elite ruling a foreign state.
3. *Economic measures*   Political manipulation of international economic relations usually serves the aim of imposing one's national will on others or resisting foreign will.
4. *Deterrence or the balancing process*   The goal is to intimidate the adversary into acceptable behavior and the traditional method is to build up adequate counterpower by mobilization of national resources, especially armaments, and by alliances.

5. *Total Submission*   Total submission means the end of a nation-state as an independent unit; such a termination of national sovereignty may be due either to external coercion or to voluntary decision on the part of the submitting state, which may, for instance, conclude that joining a supranational community represents greater benefits and safety than going it alone. (Chapter 12 will deal with this relatively rare possibility in the context of our discussion of the possibility of world government.)

6. *Diplomacy*   Its goal is to compromise, its method negotiation.

For purposes of analysis, it is helpful to distinguish the categories listed above, but they overlap: Economic considerations are grafted onto political strategies and vice versa; armaments and alliances are developed for economic reasons and have economic consequences; international war and internationalized civil war may be difficult to tell apart—interference by radio propaganda may be the first phase of a major war; depending on our definition of violence not only war but also colonial rule, economic blackmail, and political manipulation of tariffs, credits, and currencies may be deemed to represent various forms of violent behavior, since they may result in intolerable damage to lives and property.

THE INEVITABILITY OF CONFLICT AND THE AVOIDABILITY OF VIOLENCE

With due consideration of the above categories as well as cautions, the present chapter and the three following are based on four working assumptions; they have emerged from the preceding analyses of the strength of territorial nationalism, the variety of individual and group interests, the frailty of human judgment, the resulting uncertainty and tentative nature of major national decisions, and, finally, the limited impact of moral, legal, and social norms upon national behavior.

The first and basic assumption is that conflict among nations is perceived by national leaders as inevitable. By conflict we mean "a struggle over values and claims to scarce status, power, and resources in which the aims of the opponents are to neutralize, injure or eliminate their rivals."[1] Among nations scarce values include not only power, resources, and status (only one nation can really be the number one superpower), but also freedom of action—and their characteristic sum total: national security, a subjective feeling rather than an objective fact. In Arnold Wolfers' words:

> Security points to some degree of protection of values previously acquired. . . . [which] rises or falls with the ability of a nation to deter an attack, or to defeat it; . . . security, in an objective sense, measures the absence of threats to acquired values, in a subjective sense, the absence of fear that such values will be attacked.[2]

The scarcity of values desired by individuals, groups, and nations seems, therefore, to lead inevitably to competition and conflict. However, what is scarce and what is highly desired is a matter of perception, analysis, feelings, and ideology—and these vary with different individuals, groups, circumstances, and times. The inevitability of conflicts of interest and concepts among individuals and groups can perhaps be simply traced to the basic fact that humans are humans and therefore have necessarily different and conflicting views, emotions, preferences, and needs with regard to those values they deem, rightly or wrongly, to be in short supply.

The second assumption is that the inevitability of conflict does not mean the inevitability of violence. A conflict may be solved by peaceful submission, negotiated or arbitrated compromise, or by "shelving" it—that is, by an agreement to continue to disagree without doing anything about the disagreement for the time being. Or solution of a conflict in favor of either side may be avoided by mutual deterrence.

It may be noted that the term "conflict" is used here to describe both the *state* of not being in harmony with one another (facts, viewpoints, goals, opinions, sentiments) and the *process* of solving that state of disharmony or incompatibility.

The third assumption is that the study of international conflicts necessarily encompasses not only *inter*national clashes of interests, that is, conflicts among nations; but also *inter*personal conflicts, such as possible personality clashes between national leaders; *intra*national conflicts, that is, domestic conflicts concerning the goals and methods of foreign policy; and *intra*personal conflicts, such as tensions or aggressive tendencies in the leaders' minds, some of which were discussed in Chapter 6.

Finally, the fourth working assumption is that the examination of the determinants of aggressive behavior in individuals can only partly explain aggressive behavior on the part of nations. The link between individual behaviors and collective-national behavior is extremely complex and often indirect. In the words of Herbert C. Kelman, professor of social ethics at Harvard University,

> The behavior of nations is the aggregation of a variety of behaviors on the part of many individuals, representing different roles, different interests, different degrees of influence on final decisions, and contributing in very different ways to the complex social processes that eventuate in a final outcome such as war. One cannot, therefore, expect that the behavior of a nation will be a direct reflection of the motives of its citizens and even of its leaders. While war does involve aggressive behavior on the part of many individuals, this behavior is not necessarily at the service of aggressive motives. Leaders may engage in aggressive behavior for strategic reasons, for example, and the population at large for reasons of social conformity.[3]

Admittedly, several aspects of our four working assumptions are controversial from a philosophical, sociological, or psychological point of view; in our context they seem generally confirmed by the behavior of that group of individuals—political leaders—who make foreign-policy decisions on behalf of their nations.

WAR AMONG NATIONS

War is one of the frequently used means by which nations either resist the imposition of a foreign will or, conversely, impose their own will on others. Those who have a pessimistic view of the nature of men consider the use of violence perhaps regrettable but human. Others with a more optimistic opinion of men and their capacity to use reason consider war the most uncivilized and inhuman way of dealing with conflicts of interest. Whatever our view of men and their future, we must record that despite numerous and persuasive admonishments to the contrary, armed conflict and bloodshed have characterized international relations since the dawn of history.

Threat to a nation's vital interest has usually served as a rational justification for war. We have already noted that a threat may be erroneously or exaggeratedly perceived; this is how many international wars begin. A threat or a need for conquest may also be "invented" by a paranoiac mind; expansionist conquerors have considered the mere existence of other territorial states a threat to their grandiose dreams. If all actual or potential rivals were eliminated, absolute freedom of action would be enjoyed by the conquering nation and its Caesar for as long as the undisputed dominion lasts. History has known several attempts to establish a world without rivals, that is, a world state by conquest. While occasionally dreaming about a world absolutely safe for their concept or nation, states and leaders have usually aimed at a more realistic target of relative, not absolute, freedom of action and security. This, one hopes, is the policy of nations in the age of superweapons.

In the preatomic age, the common opinion was that of the Prussian general and writer Karl von Clausewitz (1780-1831), who said: "War is only a part of political intercourse, therefore by no means an independent thing in itself. . . . War is a mere continuation of policy by other means."[4] This statement, frequently quoted in the last 150 years, is still correct in the sense that only policy makers determine whether a threat, real or imagined, to the existence of a nation should be just paralyzed by deterrence or eliminated by a military action. Unlike the balancing process as we shall see later a military action may give a nation a greater degree of security if it wins but a greater insecurity if it does not win. Defeat is always possible, victory never guaranteed.

In the atomic age, the decision to wage or not to wage a war remains in the hands of political leaders. The Roman razing of Carthage demonstrates that total destruction of a nation and a civilization is not an apocalyptic vision characteristic of our era; long before our time, nations, states, empires, and civilizations have risen and fallen through war. The real revolutionary change of our period that affects previous theories of war is not the nondefensibility of a state but the probability of total annihilation of both the "victor" *and* his defeated enemy in a global nuclear war. In such a context it seems to make sense to distinguish the possibilities of wars in the old as well as the new style (see Document 11.1).

Categories of Warfare

In Western literature wars are usually divided into the following categories:

1. *Civil wars* (including insurgency and guerrilla warfare), with a lower or higher degree of foreign support or involvement. There may sometimes be wars by proxy when the conflicting sides in a civil war represent—at the outset or at the end—the interests of major outside powers. The result of such a war determines the political orientation of a given country and so may decisively affect the overall international situation. The Spanish Civil War in 1936 is a good example.

2. *Limited wars* based on the following assumptions:

a. That the survival of a nation is not at stake. Neither side has unlimited goals (usually expressed in terms of "unconditional surrender"); therefore, both sides can accept a limited defeat.

b. That both sides will remain immune to irrational emotions that could change a war waged for a limited stake into one waged for an unlimited stake.

Limited wars (local or regional) have continually been waged by minor powers (also by major powers in the background or by only one major power in the foreground) ever since Hiroshima. Only conventional weapons have been used. Some authors maintain that a limited war could be waged even among the major powers and with minor-caliber atomic weapons, provided that the above two assumptions were adhered to.

The problem here is obviously how to distinguish in practice between minor-caliber atomic weapons and major atomic weapons. By present-day standards, the atomic bombs used against Hiroshima and Nagasaki were minor. Some writers have raised the controversial question whether in a military campaign the cheap and effective destruction of a bridge by a small nuclear device rather than by a dynamite squad would constitute a transmutation of a limited war into a nuclear one.

3. *Nuclear wars* in which weapons of mass destruction may be used by both sides. No such wars have ever been fought. The United States's use of atomic bombs against Japan was an atypical, "safe" case since Japan was subject to the atomic bombardment at the very end of a war she knew she had actually lost; and, above all, Japan had no atomic weapons to threaten or retaliate with.

DOCUMENT 11.1

WAR THEN AND NOW

Then

War and peace were regarded as clearly identifiable conditions in the relations among nations. War was war and peace was peace and the differences between the two were clear-cut. .·. .

A. The capacity for surprise attack was limited.

B. The initial blows struck against an enemy would not do catastrophic damage to the enemy nor crush its capacity to strike back or to continue the struggle.

C. When attacked, a nation usually had sufficient time to organize its defenses, militarily and politically.

D. The tempo of conflict was moderate.

E. Military weapons and skills seldom took major leaps forward. If the offense scored an advantage it was likely to be temporary, for the defense was presumed to be always capable of catching up with the offense.

F. The more military power a nation had, the greater was the security of that nation.

G. Although the ravages of war were acknowledged to be dreadful by all parties, they were not so dreadful that ambitious nations ruled out the possibility of war as a deliberate instrument of national policy.

Now

A. The capacity for surprise attack is now impressive. Warning time may be minutes, seconds, or even zero time.

B. The initial blows that one nation can now direct toward another may be catastrophic.

C. If full-scale warfare begins among the major powers, the nation attacked will have little time to ready its military and political defenses.

D. The tempo of the conflict, once begun, may be extremely rapid.

E. The rate of innovation in weaponry is very high, and new developments are often of the utmost importance.

F. National security can no longer be assumed to improve with each increase in the military power of a nation.

G. The destructive capabilities of the major nations are staggering. Because of the damage that can be done to a nation in the event of all-out war, and because of the danger that a small conflict might escalate into a large conflict, gains/cost calculations relating to war have been radically altered. As the probable costs of war rise, the circumstances that would justify a nation in resorting to full-scale war are harder to find.

Reprinted with permission from Andrew M. Scott, *The Functioning of the International Political System.* New York: Crowell-Collier-Macmillan, 1967, pp. 16, 24, 25.

In his *Thinking about the Unthinkable* Herman Kahn lists four categories of thermonuclear war:

1. *Inadvertent war*, which might occur almost unintentionally as a result of mechanical or human error, false alarm, self-fulfilling prophecy, or unauthorized access to the atomic trigger obtained by a terrorist, criminal, or insane person. Kahn places inadvertent war caused by mechanical or human error at the top of his list, especially if the weapons are allowed to proliferate and each country adopts its own never-perfect standards of safety. In December 1973 it was announced that the United States had begun a program to equip its tens of thousands of tactical nuclear weapons, maintained in many foreign countries, with advanced electronic controls designed to prevent their misuse even if terrorists, guerrillas, or hostile armies overrun an overseas base.

In this connection we should note that unauthorized use of conventional weapons is by no means unusual. One example is an order issued by a four-star general, John D. Lavelle, during the war in Vietnam in 1971. A year later at a congressional hearing General Lavelle admitted that he had authorized twenty air attacks against North Vietnamese airfields, radar sites, missile sites, and missiles on transporters after failing to obtain authority to begin attacking what he said was a substantial buildup of North Vietnamese forces. The attacks were falsely reported as "protective reaction" missions. General Lavelle admitted that "it was not very smart" for his subordinates to fake combat reports, "but that's how it happened. . . . I believe somebody someplace got overeager" (*New York Times*, June 13, 1972). Quite possibly, overeagerness on the part of a subordinate could play a role not only in subnuclear but also in nuclear confrontations, and therein lies the apocalyptic dimension of our future if we have one.

2. *War by miscalculation*, which may result from a policy maker's misperception, misunderstanding of a situation or his failure adequately to think through the consequences of his action (a leader might be overconfident).

3. *War by calculation*, which may be based on a rational study of available options. War may appear to be the least undesirable of choices. It is sometimes said that there is no alternative to peace. What if the choice were between fighting a madman (a new Hitler, for instance) for a faint chance of survival or submitting to his power with the certainty of mass extermination? One may perhaps project even into a nuclear age the alleged choice that some Russians had under the Nazi occupation of the Ukraine: to die by fighting the Germans or to die by living under them.

4. *Catalytic war*, which is based on the possibility that some third party or nation might for its own reason start a war between two major powers by, for instance, disguising its own attack as a Soviet attack against the United

States. Some ambitious power could conceivably hope to become the dominant nation by causing the mutual destruction of the two top superpowers.[5]

Today there are many conflicting theories on what actually would happen if a nuclear war between two or more atomic powers were ever to occur. For instance, would it start or end with the use of nuclear weapons?

In 1969 a nationwide controversy arose in the United States on the advisability of deploying at a multibillion-dollar cost an antiballistic missile system (Safeguard) in response to the 1967 Soviet deployment of giant intercontinental ballistic missiles (SS-9s) that were to contain multiple independently targeted reentry vehicles (MIRVs). The questions raised concerned not only the cost of the new weapons system and the probability of a new escalation of the Soviet-American-Chinese armament race but also the purpose and the efficacy of the proposed antiballistic missile, or ABM, system. Was the ABM to protect the cities or the United States's retaliatory power? Or was it to protect both the people and the nuclear arsenals? And against what was it to be a protection—a deliberate Soviet mass attack, an accidental war, or perhaps only a small suicidal Chinese attack? Many technicians and scientists attacked the project as unnecessary if the Soviet ICBMs were inaccurate, and ineffective if they were accurate.[6] (Chapter 12 will return to this issue in connection with the balance of terror.)

Nuclear wars have so far been waged only in human minds and electronic brains. Strategic theoreticians have tried, for example, to predict or advise which targets would be chosen unilaterally or on the basis of an implicit understanding between the nuclear rivals. In order to cause or threaten maximum devastation and suffering (in terms of "megadeaths"), cities and industrial centers could be picked as targets; such targeting is called *countervalue* or *countercity* targeting. The purpose of countercity targeting is to deprive the adversary of his *will* to retaliate by crippling his country so severely in the first strike that the use of his retaliatory power might seem pointless. An alternative to countercity targeting is *counterforce* targeting, the purpose of which is to deprive the atomic rival of his *capacity* to retaliate: the chosen target is not cities and people but the rival's second-strike capability, that is, his missile pads in fortified silos or submerged in the ocean.

If a nation could be certain that its adversary's will or capacity to retaliate could be eliminated by countervalue or counterforce strategy, such a certainty would, in fact, endow that nation with an *assured* first-strike capacity, by which is meant the possibility to strike first without fear of devastating retaliation. Such a "fearless" capacity to strike first has been referred to as "active deterrence" by the British and "Type II deterrence" by Herman Kahn and other American strategic analysts. Neither the United States nor the Soviet Union possesses today the capacity to initiate an assured first strike against the other. This is relatively reassuring; it should be noted that both superpowers still have such a first-strike capacity with regard to the other four nuclear powers, China, France, England, and India, as well as, of course, all the nonnuclear powers. Lacking, however, the capacity of an assured first strike against each other, neither the Soviet Union nor the United States can really protect its allies against the rival superpower since it cannot make its threat of punishment by an atomic strike credible: no nation can believe in the willingness of a nuclear superpower to initiate an atomic strike on behalf of its ally and so risk an atomic counterblow and thus the superpower's own devastation. The mutual paralysis of the two superpowers, caused by their respective retaliatory capacities, tends therefore to induce large, medium, and even small nations to ponder the desirability of producing their own countercity deterrent. By its first nuclear explosion in 1974 India may have begun a "poor man's" atomic deterrent race— a "nuclear chain reaction" of sorts—which, by 1985, as the United States Arms Control and Disarmament Agency estimated, may add 25 to 30 nations to the present nuclear club. By the 1980s the world's nuclear power stations are expected to produce not only huge quantities of electric energy for peaceful purposes but also, as a byproduct, about 100,000 kilograms a year of plutonium, which is the basic fissionable material required to produce a nuclear bomb. It is true that in 1969 a majority of nations approved a nonproliferation treaty, sponsored by the United States and the Soviet Union (but opposed by China), which was to prevent the spread of atomic weapons. Under the nonproliferation treaty, the nuclear powers pledged not to help other nations acquire nuclear weapons and those countries without such weapons in 1969 pledged not to develop them. By 1974 eighty-three nations had ratified the treaty, but sixty-two did not sign or ratify the treaty. And among the sixty-two, twenty-five countries are more or less industrially and technologically advanced enough to produce an atomic device should they decide to do so. The thirteen countries with either present or potential nuclear capacity which have not ratified the 1969 treaty are: Japan, West Germany, Italy, Belgium, the Netherlands, Switzerland, Turkey, Colombia, Egypt, Indonesia, South Korea, Libya, and Venezuela. The other twelve potentially nuclear powers which have not signed the treaty are: Spain, Israel, South Africa, Argentina, Brazil, Portugal, Pakistan, Bangladesh, Algeria, Chile, Saudi Arabia, and North Korea. In addition, several communist signatories of the nonproliferation treaty, such as East Germany, Poland, and Czechoslovakia (the latter with its own uranium deposits), are technologically and scientifically so developed that their present abstention from the nuclear deterrent race could be easily and very quickly altered should they ever decide that violation of rather than adherence to the nonproliferation treaty of 1969 would be in their and Soviet interest.

Communist Categories of Just and Unjust Wars

In official communist public statements and literature, the concept of "just" and "unjust" war has been superimposed on the distinctions identified previously. It was spelled out in a succinct statement by Khrushchev. His subsequent demotion and disgrace have not, so it seems, affected the basic validity of his analysis in the communist world (see Document 11.2)—the controversy is about the *application* of the theory.

Soviet and Chinese writings on the subject of war in the current era divide violent conflicts into from three to five seemingly neat categories:

1. Revolutionary conflicts between the proletariat and the bourgeoisie.
2. Liberation wars between colonial and capitalist countries.
3. Intercapitalist wars over the exploitation of our planet.
4. Local or regional wars between the socialist and capitalist countries.
5. General wars between the communist and capitalist camps, including a world thermonuclear war, which, the new Soviet Party Program (1961) admits, "can bring unprecedented destruction to entire countries and wipe out entire nations. The problem of war and peace has now become a life-and-death problem for hundreds of millions of people."

The last three types of war are deemed "unjust" by both the Soviet and the Chinese. They differ radically, however, in estimates of their avoidability.

Whereas the Soviet thesis assumes only the possibility and not the inevitability of an armed conflict among the capitalists or between capitalism and socialism, the Chinese consider wars an inevitable consequence of capitalism, private property, and the existence of classes. When in 1969 Peking issued a second Red Book by Mao Tse-tung on the subject of war, the first entry in the volume was: "*War* is the highest form of struggle for resolving contradictions, when they have developed to a certain stage, between classes, nations, states, or political groups, and it has existed ever since the emergence of private property and of classes."[7]

The first two types of war—revolutions and national-liberation uprisings—are deemed "just" and "unavoidable" by both the Soviet and the Chinese doctrines. This is not a point of major disagreement between Peking and Moscow. China, however, insists that the Soviet assumption of avoidability of both conventional and nuclear wars between capitalist countries and between socialist and capitalist nations not only diminishes the boldness of revolutionary and antiimperialist movements, but also leads to an antirevolutionary collusion between Soviet socialist imperialism and American capitalist imperialism. This was, for instance, the aggressively critical line that Peking adopted in 1973 and 1974, during the fourth Arab-Israeli war and the subsequent negotiations leading to a

DOCUMENT 11.2

ON JUST AND UNJUST WARS

In the present conditions we must distinguish the following kinds of war: world wars, local wars, and wars of liberation or popular uprisings. . . .

Let us begin with the problem of world wars. The Communists are the most resolute opponents of world wars, as they are of wars between countries in general. Only the imperialists need these wars in order to seize foreign territories and to enslave and plunder the peoples. . . . The imperialists can start a war, but they cannot do so without giving thought to the consequences. . . .

Now about local wars. There is much talk in the imperialist camp today about local wars, and the imperialists are even making small-caliber atomic weapons to be used in such wars. There is even a special theory on local wars. Is this mere chance? Not at all. Some of the imperialist groups fear that a world war might end in complete destruction of capitalism, and for this reason they are banking on local wars.

There have been local wars in the past and they may break out again. But the chances of starting wars even of this kind are dwindling. A small-scale imperialist war, no matter which of the imperialists starts it, may develop into a world thermonuclear and missile war. . . .

Now about national-liberation wars.

There will be liberation wars as long as imperialism exists, as long as colonialism exists. Wars of this kind are inevitable. . . . The peoples win freedom and independence only through struggle, including armed struggle. . . . It is a sacred war. We recognize such wars. . . .

Is there the likelihood of such wars recurring? Yes, there is. Are uprisings of this kind likely to recur? Yes, they are. But wars of this kind are popular uprisings. Is there the likelihood of conditions in other countries reaching the point at which the cup of the popular patience overflows and they take to arms? Yes, there is such a likelihood. What is the attitude of the Marxists to such uprisings? A most favorable attitude. These uprisings cannot be identified with wars between countries, with local wars. . . . The Communists support just wars of this kind wholeheartedly and with no reservations and they march in the van of the peoples fighting for liberations.[1]

1. Compare Mao's statement on the same subject: "Revolutions and revolutionary wars are inevitable in class society, and without them it is impossible to accomplish any leap in social development and to overthrow the reactionary ruling classes and therefore impossible for the people to win political power. . . . History shows that wars are divided into two kinds, just and unjust. All wars that are progressive are just, all wars that impede progress are unjust. We Communists oppose all unjust wars that impede progress, but we do not oppose progressive, just wars. Not only do we Communists not oppose just wars, we actively participate in them." Mao Tse-tung, *On People's War.* Peking: Foreign Languages Press, 1967, pp. 1-2.

From an address by Nikita Khrushchev reprinted in *Pravda,* January 6, 1961.

cease-fire and disengagement; the Chinese press accused Moscow and Washington of sacrificing the just Arab cause for the sake of furthering Soviet-American collaboration. In its November 16, 1973, issue the *Peking Review* said

> On October 6, 1973, Egypt, Syria, and the Palestinian guerrillas rose in action against the armed attack by Israeli troops. . . . [The Arab victories] exploded the myth that Israel was "invincible." . . . The two superpowers once again played an ignominious part in the entire event. By delivering only a small quantity of arms to the Arab countries, the Soviet Union, far from giving any real support for a counteroffensive against Israeli aggression, actually intended to contend with the other superpower in a vain effort to control certain Arab countries. Their aim was to make the Arab and Palestinian people stop fighting, bind them hand and foot and place them at their mercy. It was precisely at the time when the situation was very favourable to the Arab people that the two superpowers—the Soviet Union and the United States—rushed in with their proposal for a "ceasefire in place" on October 22, calling on the Arab countries to stop fighting.

Following the Sino-Soviet border clashes, a *sixth* category of possible war was discussed not only in the Western but also in the communist press: war between socialist states. A Czechoslovak communist writer, Stanislav Budín, reminded his readers that in Stalin's last work, *The Economic Problems of Socialism*, Stalin still maintained that the next great war would take place among the imperialist states; but, Budín added,

> . . . like many other ideas, this too has been disproved by reality. A war among the imperialists is today unthinkable. At the same time, a war among the socialist countries has become a real possibility, however surprising and disagreeable this realization may be.[8]

The Soviet thesis contains two paradoxes. The first paradox is the Soviet expression of the belief that a class war between socialism and capitalism is actually less probable at the present time than before because, as Khrushchev put it in his speech to the Twentieth Party Congress (*New York Times*, February 15, 1956), "there are powerful social and political forces, commanding serious means capable of preventing the unleashing of war by the imperialists, and—should they try it—of delivering a smashing rebuff to the aggressors." By the "serious means" at the command of the socialist camp Khrushchev evidently meant Soviet atomic bombs and missiles. Moreover, and this is the basis of the Soviet thesis that the capitalist reluctance to start major wars leads to the possibility of peaceful coexistence, "the principal feature of our epoch is the emergence of socialism from the confines of one country and its transformation into a world system," as Khrushchev expressed it in his famous speech of

February 14, 1956, adding: "Capitalism has proved impotent to hinder this world-historic process." The Soviet thesis about the new cautiousness and even reasonableness of capitalism endows the opponents of the communist system with much greater rationality and freedom of choice than the original communist theory of capitalism's blind subservience to profit and inevitable expansionism was willing to admit.

The second paradox inherent in the Soviet thesis on acceptable and inacceptable wars is the condemnation of all local and general wars fought by conventional weapons, for they could so easily escalate into thermonuclear conflicts. This is indisputably true. Yet the question should be asked whether the same escalation of war from a lower to a higher type cannot just as easily occur with regard to national-liberation wars or civil wars, which in terms of Soviet theory, the communists should "support wholeheartedly and without reservation." Addressing the International Convocation on Peace, held in New York in 1965 to discuss the practical implications of the encyclical *Pacem in Terris* of the late Pope John XXIII, a Soviet spokesman, Dr. Yevgeny Zhukov (director of the Soviet Institute of History of the Soviet Academy of Science), declared that a total ban on wars, including revolutions and wars of national liberation—as had been suggested by some other speakers—would be "absurd for it was impossible to reverse history."

If we look at Document 11.3 we may discover that Dr. Zhukov, though wrong, one hopes, about the future, was certainly right as far as world history since World War II is concerned. Although since Hiroshima there have been no wars, nuclear or conventional, between the superpowers, paralyzed by the prospect of mutual nuclear annihilation, there have been numerous subnuclear wars between nation-states, civil wars within nation-states, and, even more frequently, internal wars marked by foreign intervention.

INTERNATIONALIZED INTERNAL WARS

If the period since World War II is viewed as a mirror of probable wars to come, the lesson is clear: the nuclear stalemate has reduced the probability of major nuclear confrontations to a minimum (according to optimists, to zero) but it certainly has not eliminated local wars among nations and internal wars, to both of which superpower competition has usually been added. Thus the mutual nuclear paralysis of the superpowers tends sometimes to generate and at other times to intensify or prolong internal armed conflicts. The reason is evident: superpowers support sympathetic elites in the hope that they might seize (or keep) national power and so effectuate (or prevent) a change in their country's foreign and military policies that would benefit the supporting superpower. Or, as a student of the strategic uses of domestic violence put it:

DOCUMENT 11.3

A PARTIAL LIST OF LIMITED WARS IN THE
LAST THIRTY YEARS OF PEACE[1]

1945-1949	Indonesian war of independence
1946-1949	Greek civil war combined with Communist Yugoslav, Bulgarian, and Albanian interference
1946-1950	Chinese civil war combined with United States support of Chiang Kai-shek
1947-1954	War in French Indochina—internal/international
1947-1948	Arab-Israeli war I
1948-1958	Communist guerrilla war in Malaya—internal/international
1949-1955	Huk guerrilla warfare in the Philippines
1950-1953	Korean conflict—internal/international
1950-1951	Chinese Communist conquest of Tibet
1954-1962	War in Algeria
1956	Soviet military intervention in Hungary
1956	British-French-Israeli invasion of Suez area—Arab-Israeli war II
1957-1959	Revolution in Cuba
1958	United States military intervention in Lebanon
1959	War in Vietnam
1960-1963	Civil war and the United Nations intervention in the Congo
1961	Indian military action and conquest of Portuguese Goa
1961	Rebellion of Kurds in Iraq
1961-1962	Sino-Indian clashes on Himalayan borders; China's invasion of northern and northeastern India
1964	Civil war in the Congo (United States rescue operation)
1965	United States armed intervention in Santo Domingo
1965	Anti-Sukarno rebellion in Indonesia
1966-1970	Nigeria-Biafra war
1967	Arab-Israeli war III
1967	Greek-Turkish clashes on Cyprus
1968	Soviet armed intervention in Czechoslovakia
1969	San Salvador—Honduras War
1970	United States intervention in Cambodia
1971	Indian-Pakistani-Bangladesh war
1973	Arab-Israeli war IV
1974	Turkish invasion of Cyprus

1. Minor military clashes in the above period not specifically listed: revolutions in Paraguay, Bolivia, Colombia, Guatemala, Brazil, Iraq, Syria, and Yemen; uprisings or guerrilla activities in Indonesia, Thailand, West New Guinea, Angola, Kenya, Kashmir and the Naga district in India, and Laos; the Arab-Black warfare in Chad and the Sudan, the intertribal massacre in Burundi, and many others.

> Due to the unacceptable destruction that international war would in all
> likelihood bring today, the major contestants have turned to the
> manipulation of domestic revolutions as a means of maneuvering for
> power . . . [R]evolution is replacing war . . . the balancing of power has
> come to depend to a great extent on the outcome of domestic revolutions.[9]

In such a context state boundaries may prove, ironically, much more
stable than what is behind them. Characteristically, Khrushchev at one
point suggested that all existing boundaries should be internationally
recognized as unchangeable. The sanctity of boundaries, so confirmed,
was, of course, not meant to prevent the great powers from piercing them
by subversion, conspiracy, and psychological warfare.

Civil strife has always invited meddling. "When people have taken arms
against you," noted Machiavelli, "there will never be lacking foreigners to
assist them." Our age of revolutions perhaps offers greater opportunities
for intervention in states torn by civil strife than Machiavelli's. Today we
witness a proliferation of new states without national consensus; many are
polyethnic and polytribal, and internal tensions and violence are frequent.
All emerging nations are in the process of modernization, which uproots
individuals and groups and causes deep cleavages even in those new states
that are relatively homogeneous ethnically or tribally. Furthermore,
long-established states are also experiencing unrest and violence. Some
civil strife may be externally initiated or directed, but many more instances
are spontaneous and may, as it were, "suck in" one or the other of the great
powers; sometimes revolutionary groups and their leaders organize
revolutions or civil wars with the hope that the outside powers cannot
remain indifferent to their chances of success or failure. In Asia, Africa,
and Latin America, many revolutionary activities present themselves as
either pro-communist or pro-Western without being fully either, in the
expectation of substantial outside help to achieve victory and keep power.
Thus a great power's prestige or interest may become enmeshed in a civil
war by design, afterthought, or accident.

It is therefore not only nuclear stalemate but also global unrest in an
interdependent world that tends to internationalize many internal conflicts
that in a different age could perhaps have developed without provoking
foreign interest and interference.

And yet it would be incorrect to conclude that the great powers are
determined to rush into any civil strife wherever and whenever it may
occur. The use of interference in the domestic affairs (revolutionary or not)
of another country will probably remain selective. Several considerations
will affect any great power's answer to the question, To intervene or not to
intervene?

1. An involvement in civil war might lead to such an escalation in military
involvement that the world-war and nuclear level would be reached.

2. Precipitous intervention in favor of one side might provoke the rival great power to intervene and thus prevent the favored side, which could have won unaided, from winning. The simultaneous involvement of major antagonists in a civil war tends to transform the streets and the barricades of a fighting city into a mirror of the international balance of power—and lead to a costly stalemate. The experience and devastation of Vietnam may have sobering effects not only on the United States but also on China, Russia, and any revolutionary movements they may control.

3. There may be a situation in which the victory of either of the contending native sides will not be considered worth any great power's involvement. The distance or proximity of the would-be intervening powers may be one of the factors. Even in the present era of great mobility of weapons and personnel the problem of logistics is still considerable. A good illustration is the Brazilian Communist party plan for guerrilla warfare, which, when published in 1969, bore evidence of Chinese influence, if not authorship. It warned against any hope for "external logistics support" and gave the Brazilian guerrillas only a very vague promise of Latin-American "solidarity"—whatever that may mean:

> The liberation war of the Brazilian people will be a protracted one and no rapid victory should be expected. To win the victory of the revolution in the whole country, it is necessary to destroy the armed forces of the reactionaries, and the U.S. troops who are bound to be sent to Brazil. . . .
> The people will rely mainly on their own strength to carry on the war. No illusions about external logistics should be encouraged. But the Brazilian people are not alone. They have the solidarity of the revolutionary peoples and the support of the Latin American people. This will help them greatly in the struggle to be carried out through their own strength.[10]

4. As the United States and the Soviet Union have already learned, and as the People's Republic of China is bound to learn, foreign investment in internal strife may not pay significant dividends at all. Revolutionary leaders are not generally known for being sentimental about those who first gave them encouragement and help. In 1793 the United States did not feel particularly obligated to France when revolutionary Paris needed American help to combat the enemies of republicanism. Instead of honoring the alliance, the United States adopted a policy of neutrality, and Alexander Hamilton wrote a series of interesting articles in support of George Washington's decision, based on a nonsentimental concept of national interest. Similarly, the Soviet Union has no guarantee today that Cuba, North Vietnam, Egypt, North Korea, and the Palestinian Liberation Organization will always base their policies on gratitude for Soviet assistance.

The four impediments to precipitous decision to intervene are important, but naturally they do not guarantee self-restraint on the part of great powers. In international politics, as in daily life, there have always been and always will be gamblers who may consider intervention more effective, cheaper, and less risky than any other international balancing technique.

What are Interference and Intervention?

In our interdependent and intercommunicating world it is not easy to define the point at which social, cultural, economic, scientific, and legitimate diplomatic interaction among states ends and an unacceptable form of foreign interference begins. The difficulty of defining aggression, which should include different forms of indirect aggression, such as intervention and interference, has already been noted in Chapter 10. Certainly sending terrorist bands or an agent with an atomic minibomb in his suitcase across another nation's borders should be treated as aggressions, although they are less open and brazen techniques than sending hundreds of tanks and a thousand planes, as did the Soviet Union in August 1968 in order to stop the Czechoslovak democratization of communism or, as the Czechs called it, "socialism with a human face." But what about more subtle forms of indirect aggression, intervention or interference, such as the training of military and guerrilla personnel, radio broadcasts aimed at fomenting civil strife in the target nation, infiltration[11] and subversion,[12] granting asylum to political refugees and permitting them to engage in political, propaganda, or conspiratorial activities, and granting such exiled groups semidiplomatic recognition as governments-in-exile? Examples of the latter form of interference are numerous: European governments-in-exile in London during World War II, the Cuban anti-Castro National Committee in the United States in 1961, Palestinian offices and terrorist bases in Syria, Lebanon, Egypt, and Jordan, and the Palestinian Liberation Organization office in Moscow established by a joint communiqué of the Soviet Government and the Organization's leader, Yasir Arafat (August 3, 1974). Less conspicuous methods of interference are: subsidizing and manipulating foreign political parties, interest groups, mass media, scholars, and writers, or simply maintaining informal and informative contacts with the internal opposition to a foreign government. If the American ambassador in London wines and dines the leader of the opposition (who happens to be favorably disposed toward the United States) and if the ambassador wines and dines him more often than he does the prime minister (passing over the point whether this would be a wise behavior), is this subtle interference in the domestic affairs of the United Kingdom? What if the American ambassador in Prague wines and dines writers and artists more often than he does the Czech party bureaucrats? In 1966 political parties in Chile labeled then United States Ambassador Ralph A. Dungan's statement that "from a social viewpoint private property is not an unlimited right" a gross interference in their parliamentary debate on the merits of a proposed land reform. In the same year, United States Assistant Secretary of State Lincoln Gordon stated in Buenos Aires that "abuses of freedom on the Argentine campuses should be corrected through civilized and lawful means, not through violent police raids," and the Argentine government lodged a formal diplomatic protest against what it labeled illegitimate intervention in the domestic affairs of Argentina. In 1972, Roosevelt's wartime ambassador to the Soviet Union, W. Averell Harriman, wrote an article (*New York Times*, May 3, 1972) in which he gave support to West German Chancellor Willy Brandt's policy of rapprochement with the Soviet Union and Communist Poland, chided the Christian Democratic party for criticizing Brandt's policy as sacrificing too much for too little, and concluded:"Certainly the United States should bring strong pressure quietly but firmly on the Christian Democrats making plain our concern over their opposition to ratification [of two pending treaties]." This suggestion that American pressure be exerted within the German parliament (was it not interference?) was made when the parliament was about to vote on Willy Brandt's treaties with the Soviet Union and Poland. The German-Polish treaty recognized the Western frontiers of Poland as permanent; at the end of World War II these new Polish boundaries had been drawn in such a way as to compensate Poland for its loss to the Soviet Union of territories in the east by adding territories to Poland in the west at the expense of the territorial integrity of Germany.

Diplomatic pressure, indicating strong disapproval of domestic developments in Germany, was used by the United States in the wake of the Nazi enactment of anti-Semitic legislation (the Nuremberg Laws of 1935). Following several days of anti-Semitic pogroms in Berlin President Roosevelt recalled the United States ambassador to Washington. The Nazi government condemned Roosevelt's stand and viewed it as interference in a matter that was essentially within the domestic jurisdiction of Germany—administrative steps directed against German nationals of Jewish origin, viewed by the Nazis as a danger to the purity of the Aryan "race".

Today, concern with the civil liberties and human rights of people living in other nation-states than one's own is deemed justified and therefore is not considered to constitute an illegitimate interference in the domestic affairs of a nation-state, despite the obvious problems of definition, interpretation, verification, and possible enforcement in a world that basically still remains rigidly divided into sovereign territorial units. The United Nations resolution of October 24, 1970 on the Principles of International Law concerning Friendly Relations and Cooperation among States[13] enumerates principles that may appear mutually exclusive: on the one hand, there is a reaffirmation of sovereign equality and the rights inherent in sovereignty, the inviolability of frontiers, and nonintervention in internal affairs; on the other hand, there is a reaffirmation of the international respect for human rights and fundamental freedoms that in our era are still granted, protected, or violated by nation-states. The United Nations also reaffirms the right to self-determination of all peoples; but when some nations tried to exert pressure on South Africa to change its racial policies, its government labeled such efforts "inacceptable interference in its domestic affairs"; and the Soviet Union would most probably react similarly to any international inquiry or censure concerning the Soviet treatment of the Ukrainian, Moslem, and other non-Russian groups within its territory.

In an interdependent world it is difficult to draw a line between purposeful and deliberate intervention and unwitting interference, or simply influence. Thus, the sheer existence of a powerful nation may become a source of power emanation influencing, attracting, or antagonizing the rest of the world. Such an emanation of national might would make the United States and the Soviet Union participants in international politics even if the Soviet ministry of foreign affairs and the U.S. Department of State and all their embassies were abolished:

> We have grown so much that we are today like an awkward young giant in a crowded and cluttered room: whatever we do or do not do—whatever position we place ourselves in—we cannot help affecting others. . . . Our bigness and our economic might have taken us past the happy age of innocence in which we could say of the world around us: "We just work here."[14]

Sometimes a nation is suspected of using its power for the purpose of intervention even if its present leaders honestly assure the world of the contrary intention. At other times, despite the apparent lack of interest on the part of a mighty nation, an intervention may actually be hoped for. An intervention that has not been promised or contemplated may be called a "phantom intervention." However unrealistic the hope for or fear of a great power's intervention is, it may significantly affect the course of events. When in 1948 the Communist party seized political power in Czechoslovakia, its democratic opponents were hypnotized into passivity by the assumption that if they did not yield the Soviet Union would invade the country and impose the communist coup. It is possible that their assumption was correct, but there is no proof of it. In the Hungarian revolution of 1956 some individuals and groups quite unrealistically hoped for American counterintervention against the Soviet invasion. At one point a freedom fighter used the microphone of Radio Budapest to read slowly the American Declaration of Independence, thus creating a false impression that the United States could not, in the light of its history and power, remain passive when liberty anywhere in the world was engaged in a life-or-death struggle.

Several efforts have been made recently to categorize interventions as either legitimate or illegitimate. The task is not simple when one considers how many forms interaction among nations may assume in addition to the traditional intergovernmental or diplomatic forms. And some may argue that even the conduct of foreign policy within diplomatic channels represents interference in another country's foreign-policy decision-making processes; in this context recognition or nonrecognition of a territorial authority that has been challenged by a domestic opponent may constitute interference.[15] Where indeed is the line that could clearly separate the welcome and inevitable consequences of our world growing together despite the maintenance of national state boundaries and the unwelcome and condemnable activities that illegitimately and intolerably cross the same boundaries? One possible distinction, considered by Andrew M. Scott in his study of informal penetration, is the presence or absence of consent on the part of the government inside whose territories foreign agents or instruments operate (peace corpsmen or foreign-aid missions, for instance).[16] Another author, Richard W. Cottam, argues that the present strong trend away from the sovereign self-contained national state is one of the major reasons for the unprecedented growth of what he calls "competitive interference." His study suggests drawing a line between tolerated and nontolerated penetration of one national government's domain by another. He places diplomatic contacts in the category of the most commonly accepted form of interference while placing in the less tolerable or outrightly intolerable categories of interference activities such as (1) educational and propagandizing operations by declared agents of one government aimed at the citizenry of another, (2) public statements on the subject of policies made outside diplomatic channels, (3) public statements indicating approval or disapproval of official personnel or aspirants to official positions, (4) lobbying activities conducted on behalf of a foreign interest, (5) overt efforts to remove official personnel or to help elect a favored candidate, (6) subversion, and (7) direct use of force to alter policies or official personnel.[17]

The level of tolerance of one or another form of interference varies, of course, with time and with nations. Some nations protest only when the first Marine reaches the national shores. Others protest as soon as the first Coca-Cola bottle is opened.

Studies by James N. Rosenau and by Oran R. Young (see Document 11.4) took into account changes in technology and customs that may significantly alter the views on what is unacceptable interference. (Radio propaganda and satellite surveillance, for instance, have become such a general practice that they may be now considered an acceptable form of international interference.) Their studies therefore focused on (1) behavior that sharply breaks with existing forms of behavior, (2) the systematic and deliberate rather than haphazard or inadvertent character

DOCUMENT 11.4

DEFINITIONS OF INTERVENTION

Informal access or informal penetration . . . are means by which the agents or instruments of one country gain access to the population (or parts of it) or processes of another country.

From Andrew M. Scott, *The Revolution in Statecraft: Informal Penetration.* New York: Random House, 1965, p. 4.

Intervention occurs when a state's sovereignty is violated because another state forces it to act against its will by threatening severe damages to its vital interests, or engages in direct, unsolicited interference in matters which are traditionally left to the jurisdiction of individual states.

From Doris A. Graber, *Crisis Diplomacy: A History of U.S. Intervention Policies and Practices.* Washington, D.C.: Public Affairs Press, 1959.

Intervention is any action . . . that significantly affects the public internal realm of another sovereign state and which stops short of aggressive crossing of international frontiers.

From Manfred Halpern, "Morality and Politics of Intervention," in James N. Rosenau (ed.), *International Aspect of Civil Strife.* Princeton, N.J.: Princeton University Press, 1964, p. 252.

The behavior of one international actor toward another [is] interventionary whenever the form of the behavior constitutes a sharp break with then-existing forms *and* whenever it is directed at changing or preserving the structure of political authority in the target society.

From James N. Rosenau, "The Concept of Intervention," *Journal of International Affairs,* 22:2 (1968), 167.

Intervention refers to organized and systematic activities across recognized boundaries aimed at affecting the political authority structures of the target . . . activities . . . designed either to replace existing structures or to shore up structures thought to be in danger of collapse.

From Oran R. Young, "Intervention and International Systems" *Journal of International Affairs,* 22:2 (1968), 178.

of the behavior and (3) whether the target of interference is the political authority, its policies and structure.

In connection with the European Conference on Security and Cooperation the London-based European Cooperation Research Group (EUCORG) prepared a study that examined some of the specific problems which concerned the future relationship of the communist and noncommunist halves of Europe. Both sides insisted on the principle of noninterference, yet both were also confronted with the increased rate of mutual interpenetration and the increase in international concern about matters that, until recently, had been considered matters exclusively or essentially within the domestic jurisdiction of sovereign states. The study listed examples of manifest interventions in violation of international law and examples of interference not constituting a violation of the principle of nonintervention:

Impermissible Interventions	Permissible Interference
1. Armed intervention	1. External concern and procedures in matters concerning *human rights,* discrimination, and self-determination
2. Threats against the personality of the state such as blackmail and threats by means of troop maneuvers	2. External concern with and action against the practices of *environment-polluting* states
3. Attacks against diplomats and their families	3. External concern and programs for the preservation of *cultural heritage,* threatened by civil war, foreign occupation, or natural calamities
4. Economic or political threats, *except* where such threats serve the protection of human rights; refusal to deal commercially with racist regimes in Africa is such a legitimate exception	4. National protection of *migrant workers* in foreign lands
5. Assisting, inciting, financially supporting, or tolerating subversive military, terrorist, political, or economic activities directed against the integrity of the political, economic, or cultural foundations of another state.	5. External measures for the protection of the *right to reunite families*
	6. Reaffirmation of the right to grant *asylum* to political refugees as an expression of respect for basic human rights and not a hostile act toward the state from which the individual has fled.[18]

Since among nations, their leaders, and their lawyers there seems to be no agreement as to what exactly constitutes indirect aggression, intervention, or interference, we have to handle the definitional problem as well as we can—recognizing that in our interdependent world the line between legitimate international concerns and actions and the objectionable practice of armed or nonarmed interference is either blurred or shifting. Document 11.5 illustrates the definitional difficulty. In this book the term "intervention" is primarily used to describe a *military* action across recognized national boundaries in support of a government or its opposition in a target country; obviously, the interventionist views either the government or its opposition as legitimate, which may or may not be the case. The term "interference" is used to describe a continuous or repeated penetration of a target country's political processes or structure by other means than military crossing of national boundaries. Many authors use the terms "intervention" and "interference" interchangeably; in the contemporary definitional jungle they are as right as this study, which tries to differentiate between the two terms.

"Just" and "Unjust" Intervention

Much of what has been said about ends and means in politics (see Chapter 8) applies to the problem of intervention. Like everything else in international politics, interference and intervention have been praised or condemned according to the goals they were supposed to have attained. Military intervention is viewed as right or legal when undertaken by an international organization, especially if internal events threaten international peace (the United Nations intervention in the Congo, for instance) or when, according to Richard A. Falk, the internal arena of conflict "represents a struggle for certain minimum domestic rights that the world as an emerging and limited community is coming to recognize as mandatory."[19] Falk's justification of intervention by concern for human rights was directed to the situations in Rhodesia, South Africa, and, in the past, Nazi Germany—not to the situation in Vietnam, which, as an outspoken critic of the American intervention, he has subjected to other moral, legal, and political criteria.

In the 1930s a group of Polish colonels proposed an allied, armed intervention in Germany, after the expression of the sovereign will of the German people, recorded in free elections, had resulted in a majority for the coalition of the Nazis and nationalists. A military intervention by several foreign governments against an undesirable result of democratic elections seemed then unworthy of serious consideration. Today one might argue that such an unorthodox intervention in the domestic affairs of Germany—a preventive war for the sake of peace—might have given peace to humanity and prevented the 16 million casualties of World War II.

Other value judgments concerning some interventions that took place after World War II are also quite controversial. The West called the Soviet invasion of Czechoslovakia in 1968 a brutal interference in the domestic affairs of another socialist country, as did Communist China (see Document 11.9) as well as most communist parties in Western Europe, the French and Italian ones in particular. It was, however, defended as a legitimate and just intervention by the five interfering communist states (the Soviet Union, East Germany, Poland, Hungary, and Bulgaria). Subsequently, the so-called Brezhnev Doctrine (see Document 11.7) reaffirmed the right of Soviet intervention for the sake of socialism in the future.

In 1961 the American attempt to intervene in Cuba by means of an invasion by anticommunist Cuban exiles armed and trained by the Central Intelligence Agency was also condemned by many nations, not only communist states, but many American citizens and some foreign governments seemed to deplore the failure of the undertaking rather than the principle.

Another question is whether sending troops to fight in another country at the request of its legitimate government is an intervention or a legitimate implementation of a pledge between two allied or friendly governments. It would seem to be both legal and moral to help a friend in need, that is, for instance, an allied government confronted with foreign invasion or faced with serious civil disorder, especially if instigated or exacerbated by an outside power. The problem, of course, lies in determining which is the legitimate government: the one still in the capital though isolated from the rest of the country, the one in control of the countryside or the jungle, or the one in exile hoping to return with the assistance of an outside power?

In the Spanish Civil War (1936-1939) the fate of the freely elected republican government was sealed when France and England decided to adhere to the principle of nonintervention, while fascist Italy and Nazi Germany adhered to the same principle in words but not in acts. Franco's ultimate victory was based on massive German and Italian help; the Soviet assistance to the republic consisted mostly in sending communist political organizers rather than massive military help. In civil wars the delicate and explosive point is often reached when military intervention by different, mutually antagonistic outside powers is requested by both the existing government, whose power may have partly faded away, and the insurgents, whose political and administrative controls are limited to a portion of the territory. External intervention or nonintervention may decide the internal issue.

Even more complex is the problem of intervention in civil-war situations affecting nations whose territories have been internationally divided into two states, such as Korea, Vietnam, and Germany. Are such states really sovereign states or only organized territorial camps in an undecided and continuing civil war? In the controversies concerning the American massive involvement in Vietnam it has often been stressed that the American intervention had been requested not by a state but by an

American puppet, the government in Saigon. Furthermore, because both the communists and the anticommunists were Vietnamese, the war in Vietnam should have remained a purely internal affair despite the division of Vietnam into two states. There was naturally also the opposite argument. In the words of an American official,

> The communists are fond of saying that whether the Viet Cong are born in the North or South, they are still Vietnamese and therefore an indigenous revolt must be taking place. Certainly, they are Vietnamese, and the North Koreans who swept across their boundary in 1950 to attack South Korea were also Koreans. However, this did not make the Korean war an indigenous revolt from the point of view of either world security or in terms of acceptable standards of conduct. By the same token, if West Germany were to take similar action against East Germany, it is doubtful that the East Germans, the Soviet Union, and the rest of the communist bloc would stand aside on the grounds that it was nothing more than an indigenous affair.[20]

Finally, there is also the question whether defense against foreign intervention can justify counterintervention. Is that legitimate, moral, or wise? "Intervention to enforce non-intervention is always rightful, always moral, if not always prudent," wrote John Stuart Mill in the nineteenth century. "The doctrine of non-intervention to be legitimate must be accepted by all governments. The despots must consent to it as well as the free states. Unless they do," warned Mill, "the profession of it by free countries comes to this miserable issue—that the wrong side may help the wrong, but the right must not help the right."[21]

Intervention as a General Practice

Whatever our moral, legal, or political preference may be with regard to intervention in the domestic affairs of another country, we must record that all nations not only practice it but have done so for millennia. The ancient historian Thucydides introduces the history of the Peloponnesian War with an account of the attempt of the Greek city Corcyra to reinstall the exiled political leaders of Epidammus and the opposite effort of Corinthians equally to meddle in the domestic affairs of Epidammus. "It is indeed clear that the Greek city-states exploited civil strife to further their own policies," noted Max Beloff, "and that political parties existed within the Greek states which depended, or came to depend, upon foreign support."[22] Two thousand years ago the Indian philosopher and statesman Kautilya advised the Indian kings in detail how through bribery they should win over disaffected groups in neighboring kingdoms, capitalizing upon "anger, fear, greed, and pride—the most usual reasons for disaffection." The first appropriation of the first United

States Congress in 1789 contained a contingency fund for the purpose of bribery of foreign statesmen in the pursuit of the American national interest.[23]

The French Revolution, with its messianic commitment to republicanism—and the opposite commitment of European monarchies to suppress the French republican contagion—opened an era of unprecedented justification of the right to intervene in the domestic affairs of other countries for the sake of a supranational ideal. Although the first French Constitution of 1793 declared in Article 119 that the French people "do not interfere in the domestic affairs of other nations and will not tolerate interference by other nations in their affairs," the French revolutionary system and its heir, Napoleon, brazenly justified intervention against the monarchical system in the name of liberty and republicanism (which happened to coincide with French needs of defense and expansion). The Holy Alliance viewed counterrevolutionary intervention not only as an international right but as a duty. In the nineteenth century the Austrian statesman Metternich (1773-1859) observed of the Americans that

> . . . in fostering revolutions wherever they may show themselves, in regretting those which have failed, in extending a helping hand to those which seem to prosper, they lend a new strength to the apostles of sedition and reanimate the courage of every conspirator. If this flood of evil doctrines and pernicious examples should extend over the whole of [Latin] America, what would become . . . of our conservative system which has saved Europe from complete dissolution?[24]

In Latin America the record of the United States is one of numerous interventions in support of both revolutions and counterrevolutions, despite the original Adams "doctrine" that proclaimed the United States to be only the "well-wisher to the freedom of independence of all." (See Document 11.5.) Soon after, the American principle of noninterference was geographically qualified in the Monroe Doctrine, which interdicted European intervention in the domestic affairs of the Western Hemisphere and permitted United States counterinterventions in Central and South America. A British cartoon published in 1895 illustrates the implications of the American doctrine as seen by the competing British (Figure 11.1).

Commitments to Intervention

Ideological blocs openly commit themselves to intervention for the sake of what they consider a just cause. First, there is the Afro-Asian commitment to anticolonialism, which is shared by the communists insofar as it does not apply to the right of national self-determination within the Soviet bloc or within the communist polyethnic states. The pledge of intervention against the remaining colonial powers is usually implemented

---

DOCUMENT 11.5

THE UNITED STATES AND NONINTERFERENCE, 1821

America . . . has abstained from interference in the concerns of others, even when the conflict has been for principles to which she clings, as to the last vital drop that visits the heart. . . . Wherever the standard of freedom and independence has been or shall be unfurled, there will her heart, her benedictions, and her prayers be. But she goes not abroad in search of monsters to destroy. She is the well-wisher to the freedom and independence of all. She is the champion and vindicator of her own. She will recommend the general cause by the countenance of her voice, and the benignant sympathy of her examples. She well knows that by once enlisting under other banners than her own, were they even the banners of foreign independence, she would involve herself beyond the power of extrication, in all the wars of interest and intrigue, of individual avarice, envy, and ambition which assume the colors and usurp the standard of freedom. The fundamental maxims of her policy would insensibly change from *liberty* to *force*. The frontlet upon her brow would no longer beam with the ineffable splendor of freedom and independence; but in its stead would soon be substituted an imperial diadem, flashing in false and tarnished lustre, the murky radiance of dominion and power. She might become the dictatress of the world.

From John Quincy Adams, "Address" (July 4, 1821), *Niles' Weekly Register*, July 21, 1821, p. 331.

---

by propaganda, financial aid, or military assistance channeled to rebels and guerrilla movements in Portuguese colonies, Rhodesia, and South Africa. Since the late 1960s the Organization of African States has had a special budget for support of conspiratorial and guerrilla activities directed against the remaining white-supremacist regimes in Africa.

Second, there is the communist commitment to support wars designated by such terms as wars of national liberation, people's wars, progressive wars, or whatever terms may be used to describe the right and duty to intervene in the domestic affairs of noncommunist states. The trend, which the Comintern institutionalized in the twenties, did not end in 1943 with the close of the Third International.

In the United Nations General Assembly in 1965 (in connection with the second Congo crisis) the representative of the Soviet Ukraine reaffirmed the principles of both noninterference *and* interference; he argued that nations should not interfere in the domestic affairs of other nations but that the peoples' just struggle for national independence and freedom must never be interfered with. An external support for such a struggle was not interference, he said, but on the other hand, preventing such support from reaching the insurgents was interference.

FIGURE 11.1
A BRITISH VIEW OF THE MONROE DOCTRINE

Master Johnny Bull: ''Monroe Doctrine! what is the 'Monroe Doctrine' ?''
Master Johnathan: ''Wa-al—guess it's that everything everywhere belongs to us!''

Drawing from *Punch*, 1895.

In 1967, in Havana, the Three Continental Communist Conference on Intervention, attended by delegates from eighty-two underground and above-ground communist parties, resulted in the establishment of a Committee of Assistance and Aid for the Peoples Fighting for Their Liberation. The committee was presided over by a Russian, a Chinese, a Cuban, and nine other interventionists. Preceding the meeting, an editorial, entitled "Courageous Fighters for the People's Happiness" in *Pravda* (February 2, 1965) openly explained that the "Soviet Communists . . . feel bound in sacred duty to take an active part" in support of "the underground Communist parties that are actively and courageously doing their work." On May 18, 1967, the Central Committee of the Cuban Communist party admitted that it had been training and sending guerrilla fighters to Venezuela. Following the Venezuelan capture of three of Castro's men on Venezuelan soil, Havana Radio proclaimed (as reported in the *New York Times*, May 19, 1967):

> We are lending and will continue to lend aid to all those who fight against imperialism in whatever part of the world. . . . Imperialism never needs excuses to commit its crimes. Nor does the Cuban revolution need to ask its permission or for forgiveness to fulfill its duty of solidarity with all the revolutionaries of the world, among them the Venezuelan revolutionaries, because the justification of the acts of the revolutionaries is the system of imperialism itself.

In August 1958 Adlai E. Stevenson, twice a candidate for the United States presidency, discussed with Soviet Premier Khrushchev the Soviet interference in the domestic affairs of communist states, especially the Soviet armed intervention in Hungary and Stalin's attempt to curb Tito's independent policies. He described the discussion as follows:

> He let me have it. . . . "The trouble is [said Khrushchev] that Americans poke their noses where they should not. . . . I am sure that neither Tito nor Kadar authorized Mr. Stevenson to raise this question. If I wrote Comrade Tito [and he emphasized the word Comrade], he would undoubtedly be deeply shocked and all the more so would Comrade Kadar, for these are internal matters. . . . It would be better not to raise questions that relate solely to us and foreign Communist parties. We and Tito are Communists, and somehow we will settle this affair. It is an internal affair. . . . When I cited Hungary and Yugoslavia as examples of flagrant Soviet interference, [Khrushchev] sharply informed me that what went on in the communist part of the world was none of the United States' business. . . . However, he evidently considers everything that happens in the non-communist part a legitimate concern of the Soviet Union.[25]

The right of Soviet military intervention and political interference in the affairs of communist states was reaffirmed and fully developed in the wake

DOCUMENT 11.6

THE BREZHNEV DOCTRINE

In connection with the events in Czechoslovakia, the question of the relationship and interconnection between the socialist countries' national interests and their internationalist obligations has assumed particular urgency and sharpness. The measures taken jointly by the Soviet Union and other socialist countries to defend the socialist gains of the Czechoslovak people are of enormous significance for strengthening the socialist commonwealth, which is the main achievement of the international working class.

At the same time it is impossible to ignore the allegations being heard in some places that the actions of the five socialist countries contradict the Marxist-Leninist principle of sovereignty and the right of the nations to self-determination.

Such arguments are untenable primarily because they are based on an abstract, non-class approach to the question of sovereignty and the right of nations to self-determination.

There is no doubt that the peoples of the socialist countries and the Communist parties have and must have freedom to determine their country's path of development. However, any decision of theirs must damage neither socialism in their own country, nor the fundamental interests of the other socialist countries, nor the worldwide workers' movement, which is waging a struggle for socialism. . . .

The sovereignty of each socialist country cannot be opposed to the world of socialism, of the world revolutionary movement. . . . As a social system, world socialism is the common gain of the working people of all lands; it is indivisible and its defense is the common cause of all Communists. The weakening of any link in the world socialist system has a direct effect on all the socialist countries, which cannot be indifferent. Thus, the antisocialist forces in Czechoslovakia were in essence using talk about the right to self-determination to cover up demands for so-called neutrality and the CSSR's withdrawal from the socialist commonwealth. But implementation of such "self-determination," i.e., Czechoslovakia's separation from the socialist commonwealth, would run counter to Czechoslovakia's fundamental interests and would harm the other socialist countries. Such "self-determination," as a result of which NATO troops might approach Soviet borders and the commonwealth of European socialist countries could be dismembered, in fact infringes on the vital interest of these countries' peoples, and fundamentally contradicts the right of these peoples to socialist self-determination. . . .

Those who speak of the "illegality" of the allied socialist countries' actions in Czechoslovakia forget that in a class society there is and can be no such thing as non-class law. Laws and the norms of law are subordinated to the laws of the class struggle and the laws of social development. . . .

From "Sovereignty and International Duties of Socialist Countries," *Pravda*, September 25, 1968.

DOCUMENT 11.7

"THE USSR WILL NEVER IMPOSE ITS WILL ABROAD"

Members of the legal profession in the West. . . assert not infrequently that since the Soviet Union advocates, in conformity with Marxism, a world revolution, any means may suit the ends, including nonobservance of international law and armed intervention in the affairs of other states. It is not difficult to refute this contention. The Soviet State, supporting the concept of universally recognized international law, has been consistently defending the principle of noninterference in the internal affairs of other states; it strongly rejects the idea of imposing revolution from abroad; it will never send a soldier to impose its will on another country.

From a speech by Evgeny N. Nasinovsky, Legal Aviser of the Permanent USSR Mission to the United Nations, April 26, 1968. *Proceedings of the American Society of International Law at Its Sixty-Second Annual Meeting,* Washington, D.C.

---

of the Soviet military invasion and occupation of Czechoslovakia in August 1968. An article entitled "Sovereignty and International Duties of Socialist Countries," published in *Pravda* on September 25, 1968, became subsequently known as the Brezhnev Doctrine (see Documents 11.6 and 11.7). It was denounced by Communist China as a manifesto of socialist imperialism (see Document 11.8); clearly China feared that one day Moscow might wish to assure the purity of the communist faith in China by a military intervention of the kind ordered by Khrushchev in Hungary in 1956 and by Brezhnev in Czechoslovakia in 1968. The Brezhnev Doctrine was opposed by Yugoslavia and Rumania for similar reasons. In April 1974 a high-ranking Czechoslovak general who had defected to Austria in the wake of the Soviet occupation of his country revealed the Warsaw Pact contingency plan (code name "Polárka") allegedly calling for sending Czechoslovak troops through eastern Austria into Hungary after President Tito's death if his death and the subsequent succession crisis resulted in interethnic as well as ideological turmoil in Yugoslavia. It may be recalled that the Soviet concept of an "offensive defensive" formed the background for the Soviet decision to invade Finland in 1939 (see p. 154); in Khrushchev's words: "Finland represented a real threat to us because its territory could be used by more powerful governments." Brezhnev could argue that, in the case of internal disorder in Yugoslavia, its territory could be used by the United States for purposes hostile to the interests of the Soviet Union in its sphere of influence.

For obvious reasons, the Soviet claim to the right of armed intervention

DOCUMENT 11.8

CHINA OPPOSES SOVIET DOMINATION

Since Brezhnev came to power, with its baton becoming less and less effective and its difficulties at home and abroad growing more and more serious, the Soviet revisionist renegade clique has been practising social-imperialism and social-fascism more frantically than ever. Internally, it has intensified its suppression of the Soviet people and speeded up the allround restoration of capitalism. Externally, it has stepped up its collusion with U.S. imperialism and its suppression of the revolutionary struggles of the people of various countries, intensified its control over and its exploitation of various East European countires and the People's Republic of Mongolia, intensified its contention with U.S. imperialism over the Middle East and other regions and intensified its threat of aggression against China. Its dispatch of hundreds of thousands of troops to occupy Czechoslovakia and its armed provocations against China on our territory Chenpao Island are two foul performances staged recently by Soviet revisionism. In order to justify its aggression and plunder, the Soviet revisionist renegade clique trumpets the so-called theory of "limited sovereignty," the theory of "international dictatorship" and the theory of "socialist community." What does all this stuff mean? It means that your sovereignty is "limited," while his is unlimited. You won't obey him? He will exercise "international dictatorship" over you—dictatorship over the people of other countries, in order to form the "socialist community" ruled by the new tsars, that is, colonies of social-imperialism, just like the "New Order of Europe" of Hitler, the "Greater East Asia Co-Prosperity Sphere" of Japanese militarism and the "Free World Community" of the United States.

From *Peking Review*, Special Issue, April 28, 1969.

was endorsed by all communist countries, whose leaders correctly concluded that their staying in power depends on the presence of Soviet armed forces (East Germany, Poland, Czechoslovakia, Hungary, Bulgaria, and Mongolia) or on Soviet military, political, and economic support (Cuba, about whose leader it has been often said that while his heart tends to be in revolutionary Peking his stomach is definitely in sugar-consuming Moscow and East Europe).

Besides the Afro-Asian commitment to anticolonialism and the communist commitment to support "wars of national or class liberation," there is the concept of Arab unity, which the Arabs use to claim that any intervention or interference among Arab states is not an international matter but a domestic Arab matter. There are some similarities between the concept of the Soviet Union as a base of world communism and its right to lead all communist parties and the occasional Egyptian or Libyan claim to play a leading role in Pan-Arabism. This was particularly so when Nasser led Egypt and tried also to lead the rest of the Arab world. In 1961 (as quoted by *Al Ahram*, Cairo, March 31, 1961) Nasser referred to the Egyptian leadership of the Arab cause as a service and as a duty:

> We have borne the major burden of supporting Algeria's struggle for freedom, and we supported the independence of Tunisia, Morocco, Sudan, Iraq, Omar, the Arab South, Lebanon and even Jordan. . . . This we do as our duty, for we believe that our people as a result of its material and moral potentialities was placed by Fate at the head of the Arab struggle and forms its base. The role of the Base is not domination but service.

The same official newspaper wrote again the next year (December 29, 1962):

> As a state, Egypt deals with all Arab governments, whatever their forms or systems. . . . As a revolution, Egypt should only deal with people. This does not imply interference on our part in the affairs of others, since the fundamental premise of our struggle is that the Arab people are a single nation.

This thesis was reaffirmed time and again. In 1966 (*Al Ahram*, August 19, 1966) an article written by Mohammed Hasanayn Haykal, who then often voiced official views, asserted that Cairo "willingly or unwillingly was a party in the political and social struggle inside every Arab country"; this was so because Egypt was "the home of the most advanced revolutionary experience" and the Arab country most capable of "serving its own principles outside its borders."

The Arab thesis was voiced in an international framework at the United Nations General Assembly (August 16, 1958) during a debate over United States support of Lebanon's and Jordan's sovereignty and independence against Syrian attempts at overthrow and subversion. The spokesman of Saudi Arabia, Ahmad Shukairy, condemned what he termed the United States's intervention in the internal affairs of the Arab world:

> If the Arabs are treated as peoples or nations, a set of political considerations come into play. If they are treated as one single people, one single nation, then all those considerations will have to be reversed and reversed without mercy. . . . Arab imperialism [the spokesman had in mind the Western accusations against one Arab state that was attempting to subvert and annex another one] is inconceivable. It is unthinkable for one to enslave himself, to capture his own land, to subdue his own people, and to conquer his own fatherland. One can conceivably conquer others, dominate others, infiltrate in the territory of others. But no Arab is an alien to any Arab, and no Arab country is foreign to another Arab country. This is the main premise upon which we call the United Nations to act.[26]

Until 1973 the idea that there is one Arab nation was a matter of much talk and little action. After Nasser's death and, even more important, after Egypt's defeat in the 1967 Arab-Israeli war, the Egyptian claim to leadership over the united Arabs declined rapidly. Also other dynamic Arab leaders asserted their right to interpret and proclaim common Arab goals: Qadaffi of Libya and Boumedienne of Algeria, in particular. Nevertheless, in 1973, to the surprise of both Israel and her Western supporters, the Arabs proved able for the first time to act in relative unity and to use their main weapon, oil, effectively in connection with the joint Egyptian-Syrian action against Israel.

In addition to these open commitments, there is also, as noted previously, a growing consensus that interference in the domestic affairs of other countries is consistent with our interdependent age, and that the former rigid norms of international law permitting intervention only under a very exceptional set of circumstances cannot be applied today.

"The rigidity of nonintervention," writes Richard A. Falk, "is inappropriate for a world of growing interdependence, where the welfare of nations often depends upon foreign aid, technical assistance programs, guaranteed prices, and military alliances."[27] The old international law was based on the concept of defensible, impermeable, and self-contained territorial states. The previously high walls of national sovereignty have been substantially lowered by global economic interdependence and the evolution of mass media, travel, and weapons. Even the Iron Curtain could not resist and has now become an Iron Sieve. Perhaps Marshall McLuhan is right in his assertion that we are in the process of becoming a worldwide village. It is characteristic of a village that neighbors poke their noses in other people's business. Constantly.

The United Nations and Intervention

Open commitment to intervention on the part of some blocs and nations, the unreliability of restraints on the tendency of great powers to intervene, and the general practice of intervention have converged into a demand that the United Nations either prohibit or interdict illegitimate or immoral forms of intervention. The problem, however, is that the leaders of the United Nations are themselves the leading interventionists. Time and again the United Nations has passed resolutions prohibiting the fomenting of civil strife and other forms of aggressive intervention. They tend to become an almost annual ritual in international hypocrisy.[28] The resolution of 1966 (reconfirmed though partly rephrased in 1967) proclaims that "no state has the right to intervene, directly or indirectly, for any reason whatever, in the internal and external affairs of any other state."[29] All members but one voted for it. Positive votes were cast by the United States (then intervening in Vietnam), the Soviet Union (then presiding over the Three Continental Committee on Intervention in Favor of Peoples' Wars), Cuba, Egypt, and the rest. The only abstention was by Malta, whose delegate made the following statement:

> The draft declaration on the inadmissibility of intervention in the domestic affairs of States, contained in document A/6220, is being openly violated by several states that voted in favour of it in the First Committee; and it is not likely that these States will modify their policies in accordance with the draft declaration. In these circumstances, my delegation does not believe that the adoption of such a declaration at the present time will increase the prestige of the United Nations. Accordingly, my delegation will not participate in the vote.

This was the only honest stand and therefore a lonely one.

ROUTINE PENETRATIONS

Various forms of political interference in the domestic affairs of foreign nations have become so generalized, anticipated, and routinized that the issue that raises national eyebrows is not their mere existence, but only their brazenness, excessive scope, or high intensity. In the framework of the routinized practice of interference that occurs without the consent of the target state yet does not normally lead to passionate protests, two forms of unauthorized penetration deserve our attention: psychological warfare and espionage.

Psychological Warfare

Any verbal, written, or visual communication that aims at influencing future behavior or condemns or commends a past behavior may be labeled propaganda since it does propagate, or spread, the communicator's views, principles, intentions, anger, or praise. In this section we will be specifically concerned with psychological warfare or propaganda in the sense of interference in the domestic affairs of foreign states, that is, the use of mass communication media for the purpose of inducing the target audience to think and behave in a manner favorable to the designs of the originator of the messages and, usually, in a manner detrimental to the government of the target country. Frequently, the most immediate goal is to weaken the bonds of confidence or loyalty that bind the target audience (citizens, workers, soldiers) to their authorities. In wartime the tendency to desert can thus be encouraged; in peacetime, tensions and pressures directed at the national government can be increased. By propaganda messages, transmitted by radio, television, films, pamphlets, or cultural exchanges, a government may try to create a more favorable image of its power, performance, and goals than the rival government is willing to concede; on the other hand, the rival government's policies, power, and record are depicted by the other government's output in a much less favorable light. Constant jamming of all Western broadcasts by the communist governments up to the early 1960s indicated how much the Western messages praising the democratic way of life and debunking the communist one were feared. Radio propaganda which penetrates the sovereign territory of another country against the wishes of the authorities of the recipient country is, of course, an interference in the domestic affairs of other states; it is, however, a practice that all major states have adopted in our age of mass communication media. Washington, Moscow, Peking, London, Paris, Bonn, Rome, Cairo, Jakarta, Havana (Radio Free Dixie addresses itself especially to American blacks), all broadcast in one another's languages and a host of others. The Voice of America addresses its messages to enemy, neutral, and friendly worlds in some forty-odd languages, including several dialects of Indian and Chinese.

Apostles and then missionaries were only individual predecessors of the present mass communications and cultural and scientific exchanges. Tourists, cultural, scientific, business, and student delegations, films, books, magazines, television and radio programs, and telecommunication satellites pierce the walls of sovereignty; ideas and concepts seep through them from all directions, with or without the consent of governments. The revolutionary development of mass communication and mass transportation techniques has also placed at the disposal of totalitarian states unprecedented technical possibilities and devices by which such unauthorized contacts may be limited or discouraged. Improved police surveillance, for example, now includes all kinds of electronic devices, travel limitations, rigid censorship or direction of all creative activities, and effective radio jamming. Yet, to date, the techniques by which nongovernmental contacts between national communities can be limited seem to lag behind the ingenuity and elusiveness of the methods by which ideas and concepts can be made to circulate despite the contrary wishes of the governments concerned.

Informational activities carried over national boundaries by other than radio broadcasts often require and obtain the permission of the recipient country. It is usually granted on a reciprocal basis with a hope that neither will profit from the exchanges more than the other. This applies to educational and informational movies, television programs, and all types of printed materials, ranging from newspapers to scientific books. Only rarely can propaganda by the printed word reach its target without the permission of the recipient government, as is the case when printed material is smuggled into a country or sent in containers with the help of helium-filled balloons. The latter method was practiced by an organization funded by the Central Intelligence Agency, the Free Europe Committee, in the early 1950s. The balloons, launched from West Germany, were carried to different targets in Poland, Czechoslovakia, and Hungary by the winds, which conveniently blow more regularly from the west to the east than in the opposite direction. Special devices emptied the leaflet containers over predetermined target areas. In due course the communist governments protested against such a violation of their sovereign air space. The practice was discontinued.

The role of propaganda is a major one, but it can easily be overestimated. Three limitations on the effectiveness of any psychological warfare activities must be stressed:

1. In many instances it is technically possible partially to jam or otherwise block the stream of propaganda messages.
2. As everyone engages in propaganda activities on the international scene—the thin air high above our heads represents a veritable battlefield of shortwaves—the effects of propaganda messages tend to some degree to cancel one another out.
3. Discrepancy between words and acts can ruin even the most brilliant propaganda gimmick. A propaganda technique should never be allowed to acquire its own momentum and become a self-justified activity; psychological warfare is an auxiliary of political, military, or economic measures, not their master. President Eisenhower's policy of liberation of Eastern Europe, which had a great propaganda appeal, was, for instance, quickly deflated in 1956 when Hungary tried to liberate itself from communism and Russian domination. As the Hungarians were to learn, the policy of liberation was not a policy, but a wish, however sincere, for liberation by declamation.

Espionage

The general practice of mutual international spying represents a special form of interference, the purpose of which is to weaken the opponent and strengthen oneself by piercing the secrets of the enemy while protecting one's own wall of secrecy by means of counterespionage. Depriving the rival of the possibility of a surprise action and discovering his strengths and weaknesses may have decisive importance not only in an actual clash but also in peacetime, when only threats and counterthreats are being used and their credibility or a nation's success in bluffing is at stake.

By far the most sensitive spot a spy could conceivably capture is a top position in the enemy nation's intelligence agency, where top-secret information is gathered, evaluated, and transmitted with recommendation for action and where the whole network of national espionage and counterespionage is directed. Such a feat was accomplished by an Englishman, the Soviet master spy H. A. R. (Kim) Philby, who not only became the top British intelligence officer but was detailed to Washington to coordinate Britain's and America's anticommunist espionage network. In this capacity he was able to penetrate and influence some of the most sensitive operations of the Central Intelligence Agency and the Federal Bureau of Investigation. His contacts with Allen Dulles and J. Edgar Hoover were frequent and intimate. It was, in the words of the London *Sunday Times*, "the greatest professional coup in the twisted history of the espionage business." When Philby was about to be arrested in 1963 he fled to Moscow, where he wrote a book in which he describes his double life for thirty years and indulges in sarcastic remarks about the naiveté and ineptness of the chiefs of the United States intelligence and counterespionage services.[30]

In an essay Philby refers to the FBI's counterespionage efforts, with which he was closely associated, and finds conspicuous for its failure:

> If ever there was a bubble reputation, it is Hoover's. . . . Hoover did not catch [Donald] Maclean and [Guy] Burgess [two British diplomats and Soviet spies]; he did not catch Fuchs [the atomic spy], and he would not have caught the rest if the British had not caught Fuchs and worked brilliantly on his tangled emotions . . . he did not even catch me.[31]

In the light of Philby's revelations an exchange of "jokes" that took place in 1959 between Allen W. Dulles, then director of the Central Intelligence Agency, and Soviet Premier Khrushchev has acquired an added flavor. At a White House dinner, during Khrushchev's official visit, the Soviet statesman greeted Dulles with, "I know you. *I read the same reports you do.*" Mr. Dulles replied, "I hope you get them legally."[32] Khrushchev then jokingly proposed that the two countries save money by pooling their spy networks "so we don't have to pay twice for the same information." Who knows, he may have surmised Philby was a double agent. (Espionage as an element of decisive importance in leaders' perceptions was discussed in Chapter 6.)

POLITICAL USES OF ECONOMIC RELATIONS

Asymmetric distribution of natural resources among nations, great disparity in their respective development and wealth, and the growing economic, technological, and ecological interdependence have combined to create conditions under which practically all aspects of international economic relations can be and frequently are used by political leaders for the purpose of exercising pressure on or interfering in the domestic affairs of foreign nations. Punitive economic measures such as trade boycotts and discriminatory manipulation of tariffs, export licenses, credits and loans can be used for the purpose of decreasing the opponent's power, eroding hostile alliances, or blackmailing a faltering friend, a neutral, or a rival. Denial, termination, or reduction of credits, economic aid, or technical assistance often constitutes a prologue to a major political drama. In the Sino-Soviet dispute, for instance, the beginning of the open rift in the late 1950s was marked by the sudden Soviet recall of all Russian technicians from China; according to Peking, they not only abandoned their unfinished projects without prior notice (including the development of the atomic bomb) but took with them all the blueprints as well. The twenty-year period of American-Egyptian hostility began in 1956 with the American denial of financial support for the construction of the Aswan Dam; the move was calculated to bring about the downfall of Egypt's leader, Nasser. The result, however, was that Nasser immediately succeeded in obtaining financial and technical support from the United States's main rival, the Soviet Union. Neither the Soviet decision regarding China nor the American decision regarding Egypt was caused by economic considerations; the goal was political, economic pressure was the method.

Some of the measures mentioned above are sometimes referred to as "economic warfare"; in fact, many of them are taken in direct connection with either anticipated or actual war. The legal literature usually condemns the use of economic warfare under conditions of peace, semipeace, undeclared war, or cold war. Such condemnation evidently does not prevent the use of economic warfare, especially since the line between war in the traditional legal sense and other forms of intensive hostility among nations is quite often blurred. Economic warfare measures include:

1. *Blockade*, the purpose of which usually is to starve the enemy or prevent strategic materials from reaching its industry and military forces. During the Cuban missile crisis in 1962 President Kennedy ordered the United States Navy to impose a selective blockade to prevent any more Soviet missiles from reaching the Soviet base in Cuba—in deference to international law it was called a "quarantine" but it was a "blockade without war" just the same.
2. *Blacklisting* of neutral, enemy, and allied traders who engage in commerce with the enemy during wartime.
3. *Freezing foreign assets* and so preventing their use in wartime.
4. *Preemptive buying* of food, oil, and other strategic materials so as to preserve or increase strategic reserves for the allies while causing disruption in the economy of the enemy.

At the opposite end of the scale of economic measures we find economic rewards or lures that may influence the foreign policy of a neutral nation, compensate a friend for his help, or build up the power of an ally. The list of economic rewards and lures includes: technical assistance and training of specialists and a peace corps; long-term credits and low-interest short-term loans; lowering tariff barriers or utilizing other measures aimed at opening up markets for favored imports; stabilization or guarantee of prices for raw materials; and shipment of military equipment, from rifles to submarines, as gifts, loans, or low-price purchases. Transfers of weapons from nation to nation will be examined in more detail in Chapter 13 in connection with armaments, disarmament, and other balancing techniques. One of the most successful economic and financial aid programs was the Marshall Plan, begun in 1947, in which the United States, fearing the postwar economic collapse of West Europe and a Soviet exploitation thereof, promised and finally accomplished the economic reconstruction and revitalization of the West European economy. As often happens in relations between a giver and the recipient, some of the beneficiaries of the massive American aid (France, for example) accepted but resented American generosity, partly because of their national pride, partly because of their suspicion that the generosity was but a thin veil behind which was hidden American self-interest and a determination to expand the American economy abroad. The French and Italian communists coined the derogatory term "coca-colonization of Europe" to deride the goals of the Marshall Plan.

Is Imperialism Inevitable?

In our interdependent world innumerable economic, financial, and technological links, crossing national boundaries, have developed on the basis of purely private initiative: these enterprises' avowed purpose was private or corporate profit, not politics. Nevertheless, a private exporter's or importer's profit interest, if threatened by foreign political events, may generate political pressure on his part directed at his own government; his demand may simply be that his government conduct the kind of foreign policy that would protect or promote his private commerce. Evidently, the more powerful the profit-seeking individual or corporation is, the better chance he has to influence the foreign policy of his nation; we say "chance" because there is no guarantee that his government will yield to his pressure rather than to the many other pressures to which it is exposed. Chapter 3 took note of the power and role of modern multinational corporations which may pursue goals contrary not only to those of the host country but also to those of the home country.

The specter of overconcentrated power in the hands of manufacturing corporations and banks led Lenin to conclude in his study of imperialism, written in the middle of World War I, that modern nation-states would inevitably become puppets in the hands of capitalist monopolies and that this situation would inevitably lead to intercapitalist wars over access to markets, raw materials, and investment outlets. His theory was basically one that predicted total "economization" of international politics from below: capitalist monopolies were to rise from their assembly lines to become decisive masters of bourgeois states and therefore primary makers of their foreign and military policies. The nature of the economic system was assumed to determine the nature of a nation's foreign policy; Lenin's revolutionary remedy was a plan and a hope for a capture of the bourgeois state from within by the working class, which then, in a true international proletarian spirit, would create a warless, comradely, federal world state.

Like all one-factor analyses of complex social and human situations, Lenin's theory of imperialism (already discussed in Chapter 7 during the examination of the role of ideologies) was challenged by both events and critics who find Lenin's analysis inaccurate and outdated in the late 1970s.

One particular event is worth stressing: the emergence of communist, socialist, welfare, and fascist states in which the control of the national economy has passed from the hands of private entrepreneurs to those of party bureaucrats and government officials. The defense of the economic and social standards of the masses rather than those of the bourgeoisie became, in Edward Carr's words, "a concern of national policy to be asserted, if necessary, against the national policies of other countries,"[33] and perhaps even at their expense. In a world consisting of antagonistic communist and noncommunist states, political, ideological, and security considerations may induce both communist and noncommunist states to seek territorial expansion, economic domination or parity, satellites and other forms of spheres of influence, and to seek to keep some countries in the position of being suppliers of raw materials for advanced economies, basically a colonial situation. Thus, the United States tariff, currency, credit, and economic aid manipulations for the purpose of punishing or rewarding foreign nations have their exact counterpart in the Soviet tariff, credit, and technical assistance manipulations for the purpose of luring neutral nations or punishing socialist states for their excessive flirtation with the American dollar and American technology.

Analytical challenges to Lenin's thesis[34] are also worth pondering; they are summarized in the following section of this chapter.

Causes of Imperialism and Asymmetry

In his essay on "The Leninist Myth of Imperialism," the French sociologist and political writer Raymond Aron challenged Lenin's equation—advanced capitalism = imperialist expansion = intercapitalist wars—as a propagandistic oversimplification of a complex issue. While some wars may have been caused by the search for profit, many others have been caused by the will to power, the passion of the masses and their leaders, or simply by miscalculation. While wars are certainly possible under capitalism, with its search for financial profit, they are also possible under communism with its search for ideological, security, or territorial "profit."

Aron focused particularly on three challengeable points in Lenin's thesis:

1. The capitalist rivalries that have been established have not led and do not necessarily lead to wars; trade competitions between nations are one thing, and life-and-death struggles another.

2. While it is true that capitalism in crisis may try to seek a remedy through war, this is not necessarily the case: The economic crisis in the 1930s led the United States to Roosevelt and the New Deal; in contrast, the 1930 crisis led Germany to Hitler and rearmament.

We may add to Aron's argument that ten years before Lenin completed his book on imperialism, J. A. Hobson subjected British imperialism to a critical analysis. While Hobson agreed that British imperialism was the result of capitalism, unlike Lenin, Hobson concluded that the imperialist foreign policy of capitalism was not inevitable but could be avoided if a sufficient number of Englishmen realized that imperialism benefited only a few and that it represented the nation's export of social ills abroad. In a word, Hobson believed in the possibility that the English would vote themselves out of imperialism.[35]

Evidently, other than economic factors play a role in shaping a nation's foreign policy: the national history, traditions and political culture, the leading personalities, the geographic location, and even size—capitalist but small Switzerland, for instance, is not generally suspected of imperialism and colonialism. But if other than economic factors are taken into consideration, then the economic explanation of national policy cannot provide us with any reliable insights. Was it, for example, capitalism that caused Nazi imperialism? "We maintain," writes Aron, "that the Nazi Reich was not driven to imperialism by residues of capitalism in its structure. If the private entrepreneurs or managers had been replaced by government-appointed managers, if the Ruhr had been nationalized, if the planning had been total, the imperialist temptation would not have been mitigated."[36] Or, in other words, there can be such a thing as "state capitalism," that is, a politically directed national economy. Indeed, Peking maintains state capitalism is a fact in the Soviet Union—hence, the Chinese label for the Soviet Union's policy: "social imperialism."

3. Finally, as several authors argue, for example, Norman Angell[37] and John Strachey,[38] neither colonialism nor modern wars pay; the annexation of foreign territories in the past only occasionally increased the wealth of the conquering country. Considerations of prestige and me-tooism have often played a more important role in the colonial drives of Western nations than sound economic calculations; in fact, rather than causing imperial conquest the leaders' concern for national economic and political welfare has often led to ending colonialism. The *economic* and political cost of maintaining a colonial rule against the wishes of the native population was certainly one of the reasons that the military leaders of Portugal decided in 1974 to transfer power to the African leadership in its three African

colonies, Guinea-Bissau, Angola, and Mozambique. Belatedly, Portugal under General Spinola did what other countries of Western Europe (in particular France under General de Gaulle) had done before: got rid of its rebellious colonies without becoming economically any worse off. Another good example of the disproportionate cost of maintaining control over an explosive situation is the British presence and responsibilities in Northern Ireland in the 1970s. A London weekly *(Sunday Times,* July 5, 1974) estimated the annual cost at $400 million in 1974; this was the difference between the taxes and payments received from Northern Ireland and the payments (such as social security and national health payments) and price supports channeled from London to Ulster. In addition to the annual deficit of $400 million, $50 million a year were necessary for the maintenance of British troops in Northern Ireland. Given the preceding line of reasoning that colonialism and wars do not pay, a *nuclear* war and conquest would evidently pay even less than any war and conquest Lenin could have visualized in his lifetime (1870-1924).

Another critique of Lenin's thesis is based on a macrolevel analysis of the contemporary anarchic system of nation-states which concludes that the struggle for power and security is inevitable regardless of the economic system—fascist, socialist, capitalist, or communist—which a nation has adopted. This is another formulation of the "prisoner's dilemma," which also characterizes the vicious circle of the arms race (see p. 630): all nations would be better off if none of them expanded and tried to control additional markets and investment outlets; since one of them may become imperialistic for economic or ideological reasons, all others will try defensively to expand and so all will finally be worse off. Thus, imperialism may, however paradoxical this may sound, have a defensive motivation. In Lionel Robbins' words: "Not capitalism, but the anarchic political organization of the world . . . the existence of independent national sovereignties—is the root disease of our civilization."[39] Or, as Robert Art and Robert Jervis explain:

> However imperialism is defined, it is an outcome of two factors—the disparity in power among states and the ability of the more powerful to turn the disparity to their advantage. The anarchy of international politics means that only opposition from other nations can prevent the strong from using their power imperialistically. Power must be checked by countervailing power. Where countervailing force does not exist, imperialism may occur.[40]

Other critics use sociological and psychological explanations and ascribe expansionist drives to the madness of the ruling class, a leader's desire to fulfill his death wish, or an elite's "atavistic hangover." In his study of imperialism and social classes Joseph A. Schumpeter[41] argued that many wars in history have been waged without adequate reasons; according to

Schumpeter, imperialism is atavistic in character, it stems from pre-nineteenth-century, that is, precapitalist conditions characteristic of absolute monarchies rather than of present systems. Schumpeter concluded that psychological habits of emotional reaction would be replaced by the economic rationalism that is characteristic of pragmatic capitalism.

Continuing and elaborating on Schumpeter's basic arguments, modern critics of American interventionist policies in Vietnam and Latin America point their accusing finger at "national security managers" rather than capitalist monopolies as the main imperialistic culprits. Some of these critics stress the fact that the partly emotional and partly strategic United States support of Israel ran counter to the big oil companies' major interests in the Arab world; others note that directors or presidents of such industrial complexes as IBM, Du Pont, and Ford opposed the war in Vietnam as harmful to American business. According to one acid critic of American foreign policy, Richard J. Barnet, national security managers in the Pentagon, the Central Intelligence Agency, the State Department, and the White House feel compelled, for security reasons, "to control as much of the world environment as possible"[42]—a policy that often runs counter to rational economic interests. A similar national security bureaucracy with a vested interest in a large military budget can, of course, be found in Moscow or Peking: socialism does not eliminate but merely institutionalizes the military-industrial complex that presides over and runs the entire national economy. When at the 1974 summit meeting in Moscow President Nixon and Secretary Brezhnev failed to reach an agreement on a phased limitation of offensive missiles, the MIRVs, Secretary of State Kissinger explained the failure at a press conference, stating that "both sides have to convince their military establishments of the benefit of restraint, and that is not a thought which comes naturally to military people on either side."

Lenin's economic argument nevertheless lingers on because, politically speaking, it retains a marked advantage over the more complex and sophisticated counterarguments: it is simple and it sounds plausible, since all human decisions contain some economic motivation; also, there are always huge profits made in wartime (even though admittedly there is no clear proof that those who profit from wars have also caused them); and, above all, Lenin's thesis has, as noted previously in Chapter 7, one attractive quality for the revolutionaries: it depicts the opponent as an undiluted evil.

In the contemporary United States a return to Lenin's 1916 thesis is represented by Harry Magdoff.[43] Armed with statistical figures of the 1950s and 1960s, Magdoff admits that total United States exports are less than 5 percent of the gross national product and foreign investment much less than 10 percent of domestic capital investment, but maintains that a group of about one hundred of the largest corporations has a decisive impact on American foreign policy. Furthermore, he demonstrates that the annual flow of American capital invested abroad is additive: the volume of accumulated capital abroad (which reproduces itself there) has been increasing at a faster rate than exports; in addition, United States corporations abroad are able to mobilize foreign capital for their operations.

His critics point to the fact that the target of American exports and investments has never been and is not now the colonial world but the friendly, though highly competitive developed Western world. In 1968, for instance, U.S. *trade* exports constituted only about 4 percent of total gross national product ($34.7 billion of $860.6 billion in 1968); two-thirds of these exports went to West Europe, Canada, Australia, and Japan. As for direct *investments* abroad, of $64.7 billion in 1968, only 30 percent was invested in all the developing countries (mostly in petroleum) while 70 percent was invested in West Europe, Canada, Australia, and to a small extent, in Japan. The conclusion is that the American economy as a whole is not heavily dependent upon activities in low-income countries.[44]

The Poor World and the Oil World

The contemporary world scene does not quite correspond with Lenin's prediction: West European colonial expansion has ended and West Europe has enjoyed prosperity (until the oil crisis); capitalism has not been replaced by communism on a world scale—instead, the highly developed capitalist and communist states coexist, competing but also cooperating in the economic and technological fields; in 1973, for instance, the Soviet Union's trade with the communist states accounted for 58.4 percent of its global trade, while West Germany and the United States became Moscow's first top trading partners in the First World (the Western nations; the communist states constitute the Second World). Furthermore, in the 1960s and 1970s the gap in terms of standards of living and economic progress substantially widened between the highly developed North, which now includes the United States, the Soviet Union, Japan, West Europe, and Canada, on the one hand, and the underdeveloped South, the Third World, on the other. In the wake of her rift with Communist Russia, Communist China is trying to lead the Third World, although many an African or Asian country suspects that China, now possessing nuclear capabilities, might soon prove to be just another superpower with tendencies to dominate and control her spheres of influence in the framework of her competition with the Soviet Union and the United States. In addition, in the wake of the fourth Arab-Israeli war in 1973, the Third World was split into two sectors: the Oil or Fourth World, composed of mostly Arab, oil-producing mini-giants, and the really poor half of the world whose possession of such raw materials as bauxite, copper, or iron ore cannot quite parallel the strategic importance of possession of oil. The Third or Poor World came to realize that conflict as well as cooperation between the First (Western), Second (communist), and newly rich Fourth Worlds could often be detrimental to the Third World; both conflict and cooperation between the industrial and oil-producing nations might and did result in skyrocketing prices of industrial goods, food, and fertilizers, which the Poor World has to purchase in order to survive. In the case of India, for example, the 1973 oil price increases thwarted the Indian production of fertilizers and food in 1974, resulted in widespread hunger in various parts of India, and helped to create India's worst inflation in history, running at 30 per cent a year. Nevertheless India's Prime Minister Indira Gandhi defended the increase of oil prices because, as she emphasized, the Middle East nations were exploited by the West." The Third World was also bound to discover that the increased bargaining power of the Arab rulers, preoccupied with their feud with Israel, was of little help to the Poor World (nor was it of much help to the poor masses in the Arab countries, a fact that no amount of socialist or Third World rhetoric could alter). Cadillacs and palaces among the oil-rich sand dunes seemed only very distantly related to the drought crisis and mass starvation in Mali, Mauritania, Chad, Niger, Upper Volta, and other countries in sub-Saharan Africa. In this regard it is illuminating to note the gross disparity between the oil revenues of the Oil World, which in 1973 pushed up the price of oil by 400 percent, and the Arabs' contributions to the fund that was to provide food, money, and services needed by the drought-stricken Africans. Below are a few data comparing oil revenues of the Fourth World with its contributions to sub-Saharan Africa:

Country	Contributions	Oil Revenues (1973)
Saudi Arabia	Nothing in 1973 ($2 million in 1974)	$4.3 billion
Libya	$760,000	$2.2 billion
Iraq	nothing	$2.1 billion
Kuwait	$300,000	$2.1 billion
Iran	nothing	$4.0 billion ($15 billion projected for 1974)
Abu Dhabi	nothing	$1.0 (about $23,000 for each inhabitant)

"And meanwhile the oil flows out and the billions flow in. And life goes on, *for some,*" as Chester L. Cooper appropriately concluded in his article "Oil Billions for the Few: Sand for the Starving" (*New York Times,* April 8, 1974).

The Oil World and the Poor World clearly share resentment against the West and very little else. The gap between the two may be well illustrated by data that indicate the gross difference between the dollar value of goods produced by a person a year (per capita gross national product) in the Oil World and in the Poor World. The following data show per capita gross national product in a Third World and Fourth World country in Latin America, Africa, and Asia in 1970 are taken from (*The U.N. Statistical Yearbook*, No. 22, 1971):

The Fourth World		The Third World	
Venezuela	$ 944	Haiti	$91
Libya	$1412	Chad	$64
Singapore	$ 844	India	$84

Our differentiation between newly rich countries and the poor countries necessarily oversimplifies: there are profound differences in politics and development not only between but also *within* the Poor and Oil Worlds. Even the now famous oil cartel, the Organization of Petroleum Exporting Countries (OPEC)—consisting of thirteen nations and associated members—which is capable of dictating prices to the First World, is much less united in its approaches to the West, the Communist World, and the Third World than the thirteen nations' common interest in achieving fabulous profits would indicate. Venezuela and Iran, for instance, are evidently less interested in the Israeli question than are the Arab members.

These and many other differences and conflicting national interests necessarily complicated the decision-making process in the thirteen-nation Organization of Petroleum Exporting Countries (OPEC) despite its initial decision to set up a special fund, a "Marshall Plan" for the Poor World, to help the developing countries to catch up with the twentieth century. Some countries, like Saudi Arabia, argued that the best help for the Poor World would be a reduction of the price of oil which, in turn, would lower the cost of manufactured goods that the Third World needed from the First World; Iran, on the other hand, insisted on keeping the price at the post-Yom Kippur War level. Saudi Arabia also seemed to prefer the OPEC aid to the developing countries to be channeled through the World Bank rather than through OPEC's overpoliticized special fund. Some countries, like Indonesia (exporting 1.4 million barrels a day), argued that for them their own developmental needs constituted the first and only priority.

All that shows again that all the labels used by the speakers at the United Nations—and this book—though perhaps useful shorthand expressions, are quite misleading for the purpose of a meaningful analysis: the Third World is poor but not uniformly so, the Fourth (Oil) World has conflicting economic and political priorities, the Second World contains antagonistic communist nations, and the First World is marked by a deep rift between West Europe and the United States. In his speech to the special General Assembly in 1974 the Chinese spokesman, Deputy Premier Teng

Hsiao-ping, actually labeled the two superpowers, the Soviet Union and the United States, as the First World, competing for hegemonic exploitation of the whole planet; he placed West Europe and Japan in the Second World, and incorporated China with the rest of the developing world into the Third World.

Imperialism in the 1970s

In the context of recent developments the old labels of imperialism and colonialism mean different things to different people. In Asia and Africa these terms necessarily have a clear racial connotation: white capitalist expansion and exploitation of Asia and Africa—they view the "white man's burden" as a burden mercilessly dropped on black, brown, or yellow shoulders. In West Europe, itself guilty of imperialism and colonialism in Asia and Africa, imperialism in the present era is equated with the superimposition of the economic and technological supremacy of the United States on the advanced economies of West Europe, Canada and Japan; Henry Pachter[45] labeled such imperialism "superimperialism" (superpower hegemony over developed economies and established countries) as opposed to "territorial imperialism" (old fashioned conquest of and direct rule over primitive national economies), "naval imperialism" (exploitation of distant countries by settlers with subsequent support by governments), or "neocolonialism" (domination of newly independent countries by investors and traders without any visible political control). In the socialist world, China has condemned the Soviet Union for "social imperialism" (see Document 7.5), which has combined direct military control (Soviet armed forces are stationed in all of East Central Europe and Mongolia) with total economic control by means of Soviet-coordinated socialist planning as well as the so-called international socialist division of labor, which consists of assigning some socialist countries the task of supplying raw materials for the more advanced socialist countries, a typical feature of colonialism. The Soviet actions are, however, not considered colonialism by Asians and Africans because Soviet control of East Europe is an interwhite affair; the Asians and Africans do not regard domination based on other than a racial basis as colonialism. As for China, the Soviet Union has denounced her attempts at the leadership of the Third World as a "yellow peril" and a revival of the old Chinese imperialist tendencies, dating back to the ancient Middle Kingdom (see Document 12.1).

To sum up: The various controversies about the origins, practices, and consequences of imperialism point to a complex relationship between politics and economics rather than to a simplistic conclusion that the economy is the sole determinant of foreign policy. Extreme disparity in economic power (which, in turn, can be transformed into military strength) has often, but *not always* produced political domination of a mighty nation over a small one. It would certainly be wrong to conclude that every economic asymmetry among nations (often due to accidents of history, geography, geology, or climate) represents imperialism and neocolonialism. Perhaps, though, one should call the Arab nations the new imperialists. In the 1970s they did demonstrate and exploit the extreme vulnerability of the United States and Western Europe to Arab oil blackmail. Subsequently, the Arab nations succeeded in penetrating and influencing the politics and economics of the First World by means of the so-called petrodollars, that is, liquid funds of the oil states which were accummulated as a consequence of the quadrupling of oil prices after the fourth Arab-Israeli war. The first major "petrodollar" expansion occurred in 1974 when the Shah of Iran bought a 25 percent interest in the steelworks of the famous West German Krupp enterprise in West Germany. As Senator Metzenbaum of Ohio calculated at that time, it would cost the oil states only about 75 percent of their excess dollar earnings in a single year to acquire a controlling interest in eleven American megacorporations, including A.T.&T., Boeing, General Motors, I.B.M., I.T.T., U.S. Steel, and Xerox. The World Bank estimated in 1974 that the accumulated reserves of the thirteen members of the Organization of Petroleum Exporting Countries might rise to $650-billion by 1980 and $1.2 trillion by 1985 (that sum equals the value of all the goods and services produced in the United States in 1973). This is the framework in which an apocryphal story was born that Saudi Arabia would one day use its petrodollars to buy General Motors and then announce: "What's good for Saudi Arabia is good for the United States."

If the term "imperialism" were used to describe virtually any relationship across state boundaries between unequals that involves exercise of influence—such as the relationships between West Germany and Holland, India and Bangladesh, China and North Vietnam, Nigeria and Gambia, oil-rich Saudi Arabia and oil-poor Italy or the United States and Mexico—"imperialism would include," as a study on transnational politics warns, "most of politics among nations and thereby the term would become virtually devoid of analytic value: Focusing on 'assymetries' or 'inequalities' seems more useful to us than trying to employ older terms encrusted with many layers of ambiguous and contradictory meaning."[46] There is, of course, a psychological dimension to any asymmetric economic relationship among nations: If a poor country develops economic relations with a rich country, it hopes for mutual benefits but fears that the rich nation may try to control the poor country's development, internal politics, and foreign policy. Nations that possess superior economic power and technology can never quite escape the suspicion that, especially in their confrontations with other superpowers, they may use their power and technology not only for their immediate benefit but also at the expense of small nations. And in this suspicion more often than not a poor nation proves right.

A New International Economic Order?

In April 1974 a special session of the United Nations General Assembly was called to draft a common Declaration on the Establishment of a New International Economic Order. The initiative for the meeting came from Algeria, whose leadership in the use of Arab oil as a political weapon had resulted in the quadrupling of oil prices, thus causing serious discomfort for the First World and a survival crisis in the Third World. The underlying theme of this special session of the General Assembly was the desire of the developing countries to impose a somewhat less self-centered attitude on the First and Second Worlds: The hope was that the imperial and postimperial controls exercised by the industrial North over the countries that produce raw materials would be replaced by a new partnership between the North and the South. Following the example of the oil-producing countries, the nations possessing bauxite, copper, and deposits of other valuable minerals expressed the hope that they too could dictate prices by means of international cartels and nationalization of foreign investments and facilities. A great many speeches, which one delegate labeled a "talking marathon,"pointed, often convincingly, to the need for sharing and greater equality between the developed and developing countries. The problems to be solved were, however, so staggering as to demand much more from the United Nations General Assembly than its usual fine art of combining unresolved contradictions and conflicting interests into ambiguously worded proclamations of high principles, which usually lack plans for actual implementation or enforcement. Two major problems begging for global attention were excessive *population growth* combined with a *food-production* crisis which has resulted in undernourishment or famine for many millions. According to the United Nations Food and Agriculture Organization (FAO) 400 million people were undernourished in 1974. The Overseas Development Council estimated that in 1974 nearly one billion people suffered hunger at least part of the year. Food production is especially lagging behind the population increases in the Third World; in the three weeks the United Nations General Assembly was in session the number of human beings on earth was increased by four million, mostly in Asia, Latin America, and Africa. The world's farmers are like Alice in Wonderland, who had to keep running faster just to stay in the same place: calculating present population growth rates, scientists predict that food output must double in the next generation simply to maintain the nutritional *status quo*. The United Nations World Population Conference held in Bucharest in August 1974 was attended by virtually every nation in the world (Pope Paul

VI agreed to Catholic participation in the Bucharest population-planning meetings). Its major theme—how the world is to feed a population growing at a rate of seventy-five million a year (corresponding to one-third of the United States population)—was continued and debated at the World Food Conference organized by FAO and held at Rome in November 1974. Behind the frightening statistical projections there loomed also an ideological and political argument over whether the Poor World was to blame for overpopulation, in which case the remedy was family planning; or whether the rich First World was to blame, in which case the remedy was redistribution and perhaps global "socialization" of the world's economic resources. As the *New York Times* put it (July 5, 1974), the issue was "Birth Control versus Wealth Control." Intertwined with the population and food crises was the *energy crisis,* which had demonstrated the industrial nations' vulnerability but even more so the extreme vulnerability of the Poor World to the combined effects of increased prices of oil, fertilizers, food, and manufactured goods. Finally there was the problem of *military expenditures* which sap the energies of all the four worlds. As Secretary-General Kurt Waldheim bitterly noted at the April 1974 meeting of the General Assembly: "During the three weeks of this Assembly session some $14 billion will have been spent on armaments." Besides the problems discussed above, there were other dramatic contradictions and tensions at the General Assembly meeting. The developing nations said they wanted the developed nations to help them and share their wealth with the developing nations, but at the same time these nations insisted on the right of all developing nations to nationalize all foreign enterprises and to fix compensations as they saw fit. This, of course, was partly consonant with the United Nations Covenant on Economic, Social, and Cultural Rights, (Article 1):

> All people may, for their own ends, freely dispose of their natural wealth and resources without prejudice to any obligations arising out of international economic co-operation based upon the principle of mutual benefit, and international law. In no case may a people be deprived of its own means of subsistence.[47]

Another feature of the special session of the General Assembly, allegedly devoted only to economics, was the self-evident political and propagandistic effort by China further to undermine the position of the Soviet Union in the Third and Fourth Worlds and assert its own leadership. Peking sent Deputy Premier Teng Hsiao-ping, known for his previous anti-Soviet stand, to exploit the Soviet incapacity and unwillingness to provide mass aid to poorer countries or credibly promise these nations better trade and monetary terms from the industrialized world. His address to the General Assembly condemned both the Soviet Union and the United States as "the two superpowers that are vainly seeking world hegemony," attempting to "bring the developing countries under their control" and, at the same time, "to bully the developed countries that are not their match in strength." The Chinese spokesman also equated the capitalist multinational corporations and the Soviet socialist "joint enterprises" invoking the principle of international division of labor. In this connection the Chinese condemnation of Soviet imperialism contained more violent language than anything Teng Hsiao-ping had to say about the United States:

> The "joint enterprises" the Soviet Union runs in some countries under the signboard of "aid" and "support" are in essence copies of international corporations. [The Soviet Union's] usual practice is to bag a high price on outmoded equipment and substandard weapons and exchange them for strategic raw materials and farm produce of developing countries. . . . In profiting at others' expense, the Soviet Union has gone to lengths rarely seen even in the case of other imperialist countries. . . . Selling arms and ammunitions in a big way, the U.S.S.R. has become an international merchant of death.

On December 12, 1974 the U.N. General Assembly adopted a new *Charter of Economic Rights and Duties* by 120 votes against six (and ten abstentions), representing the opposition of the industrialized West and Japan. The 34 articles of the Charter combine the Third World's justified economic grievances with radical rhetorics, stressing each nation's right to nationalize or regulate foreign investment, supervise multinational corporations within its jurisdiction, and dictate prices by means of commodity cartels. The Third World supporters of the new Charter likened its significance with the Universal Declaration of Human Rights (1950). The analogy is not particularly encouraging: in the economic field, however, crude oil may give more substance to economic rights than an oil-less idealism of the 1950s could to human rights which today are even less respected globally than 25 years ago.

Economic Aid and Technical Assistance

As far as considering the political implications of any economic or technical aid are concerned, it may be noted that such represents a specific form of external involvement in the domestic economic affairs of the recipient country. Aid is not domination since foreign assistance is usually not only consented to but welcomed by the recipient. Nevertheless, two qualifications should be added: first, economic aid or technical assistance accepted by a foreign nation may have so many strings attached that the *administration* of the aid programs ultimately constitutes intolerable interference in domestic economic and political affairs. Second, even the original "consent" of the recipient government may be somewhat debatable in an era of decolonization which has produced a great number of states that are economically unviable and that cannot live without foreign assistance. The new nations cannot afford to refuse what in the light of the political strings attached amounts to interference.

The fear lest interdependence become dependence has led many a neutral nation to ask and receive aid from several contending parties simultaneously, thus preserving its relative independence from them. By intelligently playing the interfering donors against each other, a neutral nation can thus ensure a flow of aid and loans from opposite sides. Some African and Asian national leaders have developed this technique of balanced dependence into a fine art: Like the legendary princess, they accept betrothal gifts from many suitors but have no intention of marrying any of them.

The United States emerged from World War II as the wealthiest industrial state on earth and started a tremendous flood of economic resources first to Western Europe (the Marshall Plan), and then to Asia, to Africa, and to Latin America (the Alliance for Progress). In the first two decades following the war the American government distributed more than $100 billion in economic aid—an amount unequaled in history. By comparison, the Soviet economic aid was modest: approximately $14 billion in the same period.

It should, however, be reemphasized that in scope and intensity economic aid and technical assistance programs bear no comparison with trade activities. Trade represents a greater foreign penetration into the social and political fabric of small nations than foreign aid. In Marshall R. Singer's words:

> American foreign aid rarely accounts for more than 3 to 4 per cent of the Gross Domestic Product (G.D.P.) of any country, but private trade between corporations in the United States and corporations and/or individuals in other countries often accounts for between 10 and 20 percent of the weaker country's G.D.P. and in some cases has accounted for as much as 40 percent.[48]

The flow of American dollars abroad, more through trade activities and the operations of multinational corporations than through outright aid or the Peace Corps, is bound to be both resented as actual or potential interference and desired as a precondition for development, if not survival. Some developing nations engage in competitive bidding to attract multinational corporations to their soil. The Third World, especially, as many poor countries are themselves ready to admit, cannot quite do without the multinational corporations (that is, without the flow of investment capital and technological-managerial skills) and yet they feel quite uncomfortable having them in their midst and observing impotently their sometimes deliberate and often unwitting impact on domestic politics and development.

The reasons for which the donor governments engage in foreign aid and technical programs are primarily political or military. The economic aspects seem secondary, except perhaps in the sense that the misery of the overpopulated and underdeveloped Southern Hemisphere is politically so explosive as to ultimately affect trade exchanges and peace in the Northern Hemisphere. The political gains of economic aid programs are, however, controversial. For example, in the case of the United States, massive aid has not gained any significant sympathy or love for this country. Therefore, the American foreign aid program experiences increasing difficulties in passing through Congress, whose political and economic priorities are dominated by domestic rather than international considerations.

What about *humanitarian* concern? Humanitarian considerations certainly characterize many individuals who implement the technical assistance and economic aid programs in foreign lands but are rarely decisive, if ever, among those who determine the national budget and decide whether or not to give aid. If humanitarian aspects of the American, West German, Soviet, French, or Chinese aid programs were really as dominant as the speeches of their leaders seem to stress, the aid programs would be channeled through international agencies to avoid any suspicion of political strings attached to the money sent abroad. All the receiving nations would prefer multilateral to bilateral arrangements, but the economic aid and technical assistance programs sponsored and administered by the United Nations, for instance, represent a mere fragment of the total aid proffered by the wealthy nations.

Despite some protestation to the contrary, economic aid and technical assistance have been used predominantly as instruments of international politics with potential (and welcome) economic or humanitarian side effects. Because this is so, the giver should not count on the gratitude that sometimes answers an act of true generosity. The British author Edward Crankshaw, reviewing a book on Soviet foreign aid (*New York Times Book Review*, May 28, 1967), noted with bitterness: "Governments are not humanitarian. Peoples may be." Turning to the United States, he added: "One cannot be rich and beloved, a fact that the British philosophically accepted over 200 years ago."

Notes

1. Lewis A. Coser, *The Functions of Social Conflict*. New York: Free Press, 1956, p. 3.

2. Arnold Wolfers, *Discord and Collaboration: Essays on International Politics*. Baltimore, Md.: The Johns Hopkins Press, 1962, p. 150.

3. Herbert C. Kelman, "Social-Psychological Approaches to the Study of International Relations: Definition of Scope," in *International Behavior: A Social-Psychological Analysis*. New York: Holt, Rinehart and Winston, 1965, pp. 5-6. See also Irving L. Janis, *Victims of Groupthink: A Psychological Study of Foreign Policy Decisions and Fiascoes*. Boston: Houghton Mifflin, 1972. "Groupthink" is defined as "the psychological drive for consensus at any cost that suppresses dissent and appraisal of alternatives in cohesive decision-making groups." Janis' case studies include fiascoes such as the Bay of Pigs invasion, the Korean war, the attack on Pearl Harbor, and the U. S. involvement in Vietnam. An improved

decision-making pattern is illustrated by the Cuban missile crisis and the Marshall Plan initiative.

4. Karl von Clausewitz, *On War*. Baltimore, Md.: Penguin, 1968, pp. 119, 402.

5. Herman Kahn, *Thinking about the Unthinkable*. New York: Avon, 1962, pp. 41-61. See also Herman Kahn, "Issues of Thermonuclear War Termination," in *How Wars End, Annals of the American Academy of Political and Social Science*, 392 (November 1970), 133-172.

6. See Abram Chayes and Jerome B. Wiesner (eds.), *ABM: An Evaulation of the Decision to Deploy an Antiballistic Missile System*. Introduction by Edward M. Kennedy. New York: Harper & Row, 1969.

7. Mao Tse-tung, *On People's War*. Peking: Foreign Languages Press, 1967, p. 1.

8. Stanislav Budin, "The Conflict on the Ussuri River," *Reportér* (Prague), 13 (March 4, 1969).

9. Cyril E. Black, *Communism and Revolution: The Strategic Uses of Political Violence*. Princeton, N. J.: Princeton University Press, 1964, pp. 431, 446.

10. *Peking Review*, June 25, 1969.

11. By infiltration is meant the penetration by enemy agents of the political, administrative, or military structure of a nation for intelligence reasons or for subversion. Infiltrators of the political or administrative apparatus of a government are usually nationals who, for ideological reasons or for money, serve a foreign government's interests within, and in hostile opposition to, their own national government.

12. By subversion is meant the attempt to weaken, paralyze, or overturn a national government. It should be recognized that large-scale subversion with the aim of seizing political power is separated by an imperceptible line from indirect aggression, that is, giving aid to one side in a civil war or fomenting insurgency. In practice, subversive and subbelligerent activities differ from one another in degree rather than in kind. They are often combined with overt propaganda and agitation, directed from abroad, as well as with more or less open support of political opposition or subbelligerency.

13. U N Resolution 2625 (XXV), October 24, 1970.

14. George F. Kennan, "Foreign Aid in the Framework of National Policy," *Proceedings of the American Academy of Political Science*, 23 (1950), 104-105.

15. Compare Max Beloff, "Reflections on Intervention," *Journal of International Affairs*, 22:2 (1968), 201: "Nonrecognition is always a form of intervention and is rightly treated as a hostile act by any *de facto* government against which it is applied." On the other hand, recognition of an insurgent group may be treated as intervention by the incumbent. Before the conclusion of the Evian Accords of 1962, by which the French-Algerian war was concluded, more than twenty nations "intervened" in France's domestic affairs by according recognition to the rebels after they had formed the Algerian Provisional Government, which for some time had to operate in exile.

16. Andrew M. Scott, *The Revolution in Statecraft: Informal Penetration*. New York: Random House (paperback), 1965, p. 194.

17. Richard W. Cottam, *Competitive Interference and Twentieth Century Diplomacy*. Pittsburgh, Pa.: Pittsburgh University Press, 1967, pp. 38-42.

18. European Cooperation Research Group (EUCORG), *The Principle of Non-Intervention in Internal Affairs in the Context of the Conference on Security and Cooperation in Europe* (Report 3). London, November 1973, pp. 2-8.

19. Richard A. Falk, "The International Law of War," in James N. Rosenau (ed.), *International Aspects of Civil Strife*. Princeton, N.J.: Princeton University Press, 1964, p. 209.

20. Leonard Unger, "The U.S. Stake in Southeast Asia," *Foreign Affairs Outline* (Department of State Publication No. 13). Washington, D.C.: Government Printing Office, June 1965, p. 4. See also Gregory Henderson, Richard Ned Lebow, and John G. Stoessinger, *Divided Nations in a Divided World*. New York: McKay, 1974.

21. Compare Manfred Halpern, "The Morality and Politics of Intervention," in Rosenau (ed.), *International Aspects of Civil Strife*, p. 286: "If national sovereignty is threatened, or itself clearly threatens peace, freedom, or justice, wisdom demands intervention."

22. Beloff, "Reflections on Intervention," p. 199.

23. Paul W. Blackstock, *The Strategy of Subversion: Manipulating the Politics of Other Nations*. Chicago: Quadrangle Books, 1964, p. 351.

24. Quoted by G. D. Lillibridge, "The American Impact Abroad" *The American Scholar*, 34:1 (Winter 1965), 45.

25. *New York Times*, August 27, 1958.

26. *New York Times*, August 16, 1958.

27. Falk, "The International Law of Internal War," p. 238.

28. Compare the following resolutions. The United Nations Resolution "Essentials of Peace," December 1, 1949: "The General Assembly calls upon every nation . . . to refrain from any threats or acts, direct or indirect, aimed at impairing the freedom or integrity of any State, or at *fomenting civil strife and subverting* the will of the people in any State." (Italics added.)

The United Nations Resolution "Peace through Deeds," November 17, 1959: "The General Assembly . . . solemnly reaffirms that, whatever the weapons used, any aggression, whether committed openly, or by *fomenting civil strife in the interest of a foreign Power*, or otherwise is the gravest of all crimes against peace and security throughout the world." (Italics added.)

29. "Text of Resolution (A/RES/2131-XX)," *UN Monthly Chronicle*, 3:1 (January 1966), 29.

30. Kim Philby, *My Silent War*. New York: Grove, 1968, p. 262.

31. Kim Philby, "On J. Edgar Hoover and the FBI," *Evergreen*, 54 (May 1968), 22.

32. *New York Times*, September 17, 1956, p. 19. The report, written by Richard E. Mooney under the title "Visitor, Cameramen Up Early; Khrushchev Twits Allen Dulles," introduced the story as follows: "Premier Khrushchev greeted the director of the country's Central Intelligence Agency last night with what the capital hopes was a joke."

33. Edward H. Carr, *Nationalism and After*. New York: St. Martin's 1945, p. 24.

34. An interesting collection of conflicting views on the subject of imperialism may be found in Robert J. Art and Robert Jervis, *International Politics: Anarchy, Force, Imperialism*. Boston: Little, Brown, 1973. The conflicting views of J. A. Hobson, Lionel Robbins, Harry Magdoff, S. M. Miller *et al.*, Joseph Schumpeter, Richard J. Barnet, John S. Galbraith, and Robert W. Tucker are on pp. 289-429.

35. J. A. Hobson, *Imperialism: A Study*. London: Allen & Unwin, 1905.

36. Raymond Aron, *The Century of Total War*. Boston: Beacon, 1968, p. 72.

37. Norman Angell, *The Great Illusion*. New York: Putnam, 1933.

38. John Strachey in his *The End of Empire* (New York: Random House, 1960) argued that the costs of maintaining the Empire overshadowed the economic gains derived from it.

39. Lionel Robbins, *The Economic Causes of War*. New York: Howard Fertig, 1968, p. 99.

40. Art and Jervis, *International Politics*, p. 291.

41. Joseph Schumpeter, *Imperialism and Social Classes*. New York: August M. Kelley, 1951.

42. Richard J. Barnet, *Intervention and Revolution: The United States and the Third World*. New York: World Publishing, 1968, p. 19.

43. Harry Magdoff, *The Age of Imperialism*. New York: Monthly Review Press, 1969.

44. S. M. Miller, Roy Bennett, and Cyril Alapatt, "Does the U.S. Economy Require Imperialism?" *Social Policy*, September-October 1970, pp. 13-19.

45. See Henry Pachter, "The Problem of Imperialism," *Dissent*, September-October 1970, pp. 461-488.

46. Robert O. Keohane and Joseph S. Nye, Jr. (eds.), *Transnational Relations and World Politics*. Cambridge, Mass.: Harvard University Press, 1972, p. xxvi. See also Richard W. Sterling, *Macropolitics: International Relations in a Global Society*. New York: Knopf, 1974. Particularly relevant are Chapter on Imperialism, p. 203-231, and Part II, "The Macropolitical World."

47. Resolution 2200 A (XXI) of December 16, 1966.

48. Marshall R. Singer, *Weak States in a World of Powers: The Dynamics of International Relationships*. New York: Free Press, 1972, p. 3.

Additional Readings

Additional readings on the subject of war and intervention may be found in *Discord and Harmony: Readings in International Politics*, edited by Ivo D. Duchacek and published by Holt, Rinehart and Winston in 1972. Chapter 11, "Politics and Guns" (pp. 257-300), contains excerpts from studies of war by Karl von Clausewitz and Herman Kahn and a collection of Nazi diplomatic dispatches describing the Soviet-Russian negotiations preceding the outbreak of World War II. Also related are "Limits of Intervention" by Graham T. Allison, Ernest May, and Adam Yarmolinski (pp. 341-349), "Nuclear Stalemate: Cause of Stability or Instability," by John H. Herz (pp.335-340), "The Third World: Why Do We Interfere," by Richard J. Barnet (pp.335-340) and two short excerpts, "Are They Geese or Missiles" by Arkady S. Sobolev and "The U. N. Nuclear Strategy: Assumptions and Dangers," by Robert S. McNamara.

12

International Checks and Balances

The system of states, as we have seen, is neither a complete jungle nor an organized community based on global consensus and endowed with a rule-making and rule-enforcing authority. It is something in between. Occasionally the system of states is like a wilderness where might makes right; at other times it seems capable of civilized behavior. Only some clashes of national interests are marked by bloodshed; other conflicts are solved peacefully even though the stakes are important and passions run high. As among individuals, the use of physical violence among nations is frequent but neither constant nor inevitable. Ironically, the presence of violence is rarely a reliable indicator of the seriousness or irreconcilable nature of the conflict; misperception, irresponsibility, or irrationality often play a decisive role.

If nations are not ready to surrender their weapons and sovereignty to a supranational authority and yet still wish to avoid fighting a war or yielding to terror or blackmail, only two options are left. They may be broadly defined as *deterrence* of a hostile design and *negotiation* with the aim of seeking a compromise (Chapter 14 will deal with the various forms, problems, and goals of diplomatic negotiations among territorial states).

Deterrence of a hostile design may be, and often is, coupled with a simultaneous search for a compromise solution by means of diplomacy. Such negotiations are often referred to as negotiations from a position of strength or parity. By itself deterrence does not remove the cause of a threat of a clash of interests; it merely pushes it aside or underground. The conflict may surface again with vehemence as soon as the obstacles to the initial threat have been removed or have lost their efficacy. Of course it may be argued that nonsolution of a conflict is preferable to a solution by violence. Furthermore, deterrence even without a simultaneous effort at a compromise solution may result in a gain of precious time in which a compromise solution may be found, or the intensity of the conflict may wear off or be overshadowed by new developments—for instance, a new conflict in a different area of international contacts and competition.

DETERRENCE

If a state pursues or is about to pursue policies that another nation considers detrimental to its survival or other vital interests, the almost instinctive response is raising sufficient obstacles to the execution of the hostile design. When a nation is threatened by pressure, blackmail, or armed attack, opposition must be organized as quickly and as effectively as possible. In such a situation a nation usually relies primarily on self-help or on the assistance of other similarly concerned nations. By making the implementation of a hostile design appear extremely costly and risky in the light of available and mobilized counterpower, nations hope to preserve their interests, their existence, and also their peace. Such a method of dissuasion by means of intimidatory power is called the balancing process, balance-of-power system, international checks and balances, counterterror, or simply deterrence.

Preventing an undesirable action by a threat of punishment or unbearable risk is as old as humanity. It underlies the concept of criminal law in which punishment is supposed to deter criminal acts and so teach civilized behavior. Parents have always used the principle of deterrence to discipline their children. As Thomas C. Schelling noted, parental deterrence, not unlike nuclear deterrence, may result in a situation in which the threatened punishment will hurt the threatener as much as it will the one threatened, perhaps more.[1]

The merits of the balancing process among nations have often been overrated since peace and its stability are thus based on an intrinsically unstable foundation, for instance, the perceptions of two or more major powers concerning the approximate equilibrium of their means of mutual destruction. Such a shaky basis of peace is certainly not reassuring. On the other hand, how much less reassuring and, in fact, terrifying is a confrontation between aggressive might and peaceful weakness! This is the situation of which domination by terror or blackmail is made.

The purpose of the balancing process on both the national and international level is to preserve the existence and interests of autonomous units within a multiunit or polycentric system—that is, a system composed of coordinate rather than subordinate units. If in such a system one component is to be protected against absorption or domination by another, actual or potential ambition and growth at the expense of others must be kept in check. In this sense international restraints by means of intimidation do not substantially differ from the mechanism of checks and balances embodied in the United States Constitution. These, too, are meant to preserve and protect the necessary components of the constitutional system: the federal and state governments and the executive, legislative, and judicial branches of government. All these units of government are supposed to remain coordinate to one another and not subordinate one to the other. The difference between a relatively satisfactory performance of the balancing principle on the domestic scene and its less satisfactory record on the international scene does not lie primarily in the fact that checks and balances are part of the American Constitution while the international system has not graced itself with such a legal document. The fundamental difference lies in the contrast between the general consensus on the national scene and its absence on the international one. Within nations all the components more or less agree that the units to be preserved have the right to exist. On the international scene, however, nations and their leaders tend to believe as well as to act on the assumption that world peace and international life would be more secure if, for instance, the United States, China, Russia, Israel, or Pakistan ceased to exist.

As noted previously, the primary goal of deterrent checks is neither the solution of a conflict of interests nor the elimination of its causes. Both the conflict and its causes often remain after obstacles to an obnoxious design have been raised. Deterrence prevents only the implementation of a hostile design by means of war or blackmail; it emphasizes the impact which a countervailing force has on the adversary's mind and calculation rather than on his capabilities. We speak of the balance of power when the ability to implement policy is checked by the ability to prevent such an implementation, that is, when the desire to dominate or absorb others is viewed as checked by the will and capacity not to be dominated or absorbed. Balance of power is certainly not a mathematical or physical equation expressing an exact equilibrium of weapons; it is a political concept that includes the balance both of wills and of physical means in the context and under the impact of the international system as structured at a given moment. Arnold Wolfers has defined the balance of power simply as the "opposite to hegemony or domination."[2]

THE NATURE OF THE BALANCING PROCESS

On the international scene the balancing process usually involves two or more nations. Sometimes a superior power acts as a regulator among minor antagonists. This used to be the role of Great Britain with regard to the balancing process in Europe. And this is the role that the Third World would like to play now between the West and the East, but it lacks adequate power and unity to do so. When alliances or blocs are engaged in this process, opposition to domination may take place both between and within the blocs. In addition to the primary balancing between the communist and Western blocs, a secondary and multiple process also takes place between the United States and Western Europe, within Western Europe between England and continental Europe, and within continental Western Europe between France and Germany, and so on. Nations find that they have to resist not only domination by a major enemy but also excessive interference by a major ally. Similarly, in the communist bloc there is not only Chinese opposition to Soviet domination and political direction of the bloc but also an asymmetric balancing process going on between Soviet Russia and Eastern Europe. And within communist Eastern Europe underdeveloped communist countries such as Yugoslavia, Rumania, and Albania rely on help from outside Eastern Europe to oppose the actual or potentially dominant position of the more developed comrade republics such as Poland and East Germany. It is evident that the fear of and the opposition to domination characterize not only openly hostile but also relatively friendly relations among nations.

If all nations engaged in the balancing process had identical goals of self-preservation without domination and violence, and if all were convinced that this was their common goal, the result could indeed be peace and stability. Such an ideal set of circumstances, especially the absence of suspicion, is, of course, rarely present. As we have seen, the power of individual nations differs widely; the disparity of power by itself gives rise to suspicions, because it is thought that superior power allows or encourages even greater ambitions.

These and other suspicions introduce an element of uncertainty and instability into the balancing process, whose alleged purpose is to maintain stability by preserving the status quo. Paradoxically, the balancing process, which may produce and actually has produced prolonged periods of international stability, has done so at the cost of constant movement and occasional violent jerks.

There are two major reasons for the presence of what one may call a *perpetuum mobile* in the balance system:

1. Power defies exact measurement. Therefore, nations seek a margin of safety in case their comparative estimates of their own and other nations' power prove wrong. This is one of the causes of the arms race. It should be recalled how baffling is the task of comparing such incomparable ingredients of national power as one nation's superiority in land armies, defensible boundaries, and a planned economy with another nation's superiority in missiles, foreign bases, and alliances. In his *History of the Peloponnesian War*, Thucydides describes how 2500 years ago statesmen

engaged in an analysis of the comparative advantages of the naval power of Athens and the land power of Sparta and its allies. A Spartan magistrate, Sthelenaidas, matter-of-factly concluded: "Others may have a lot of money and ships and horses, but we have good allies." The question is and has always been whether good allies can really compensate for inadequacies of money, ships, missiles, horses, or tanks.

2. The second reason for the dynamic nature of the balancing process is the need to adjust constantly to present and anticipated changes in the international environment. One has to project the present estimate and probable changes into a more or less distant future. Often new armaments, new alliances, and new mobilization of one's own power underline the maintenance of the old order of things; constant changes and adjustments are supposed to guarantee that no major changes occur. Some people tend to conclude that this is a mere reflection of the dialectics of nature itself: Thesis produces antithesis, action produces counteraction, and power produces counterpower. There is nothing automatic, however, about peace and order based on a balance of power: As indicated earlier, it requires constant effort and action.

For the past three hundred years a great many books and polemical articles have been written on the subject of the balance of power. However, the practice is much older than the theory or the term itself. Actually the balancing process seems as old as mankind's recorded history. The theme of the balance of power runs like a red thread through many classical books on ancient history, politics, and philosophy. The ancient Indian writer Kautilya (300 B.C.) was concerned with the problem of domination and its prevention by adequate counterpower or counterstrategy even more than he was with moral values in politics. Polybius (205 B.C.) analyzed a triangular balancing process among Rome, Carthage, and Syracuse:

> Hiero [the king of Syracuse] during the whole of the present war had been most prompt in meeting the Carthaginian requests [for help] esteeming it requisite both in order to retain his dominions in Sicily, and to preserve the Roman friendship, that Carthage should be safe; lest by its fall the remaining power of Rome should be able, without control or opposition, to execute every purpose and undertaking. And here he acted with great wisdom and prudence: For that is never, on any account, to be overlooked; nor ought such a force ever to be thrown into one hand as to incapacitate the neighboring states from defending their rights against it.[3]

Over 2500 years ago the Spartan king Archidamus, according to Thucydides, suggested that Athens should be prevented from aggressive actions by the specter of unbearable and unnecessary destruction of Athenian possessions:

> When the Athenians see that our actual strength is keeping pace with the language that we use, they will be more inclined to give way, since their

land will still be untouched and, in making up their minds, they will be thinking of advantages which they still possess and which have not yet been destroyed.[4]

Both among and within territorial units peace and order have been based less on harmony and consensus than on effective obstacles to any unit's attempt to break the peace and impose its will unilaterally. An impressive ability to punish an attempt at domination or a violent solution of a conflict has often intimidated men and nations into civilized behavior.

Peace and order based only on intimidation without any consensus and regulatory force of government are admittedly extremely shaky. Such factors as misperception, irrationality, or an imbalance of power, surreptitiously established and favoring the forces of aggression, can never be excluded. Nor can we, of course, exclude the possibility that peace and order will be violated even in communities that have established governments on the basis of consensus. Social and political changes affect all relations among men and groups; and as the frequent occurrence of civil wars and other forms of domestic violence demonstrates, neither the regulatory effectiveness of the government's coercive power nor the intensity of general consensus is permanent.

DEMOCRACIES IN THE BALANCING PROCESS

The principle of checks and balances is one of the most glorified principles of the American Constitution and represents an observable practice in domestic politics. The power and interest of one group is constantly being checked by the power and interest of another group, sometimes with violence (labor-industry, black-white, students-faculty-administration, farmers-cities, and other clashes of interests and balances of power). But many Americans tend to condemn similar political processes on the international scene. They point to their dangers, cost, and failure to solve anything with finality—as if, on the domestic scene, anything had ever been solved and disposed of without cost and with finality. Looking back nostalgically to their 150 years of relative isolation and seeming unconcern with the European shifts in alliances that characterized the balancing process in the eighteenth and nineteenth centuries, many Americans tend to forget that, to a large extent, the security of the United States resulted from the European powers' preoccupation with one another (that is, a Europe-centered balancing process).

Some authors, such as Ernst B. Haas,[5] have also pointed to the disadvantages that plague democracies in contrast to dictatorships when, very much against their will, they must respond to changes in alignments and armaments, the two most characteristic instruments of the international balancing process. Unlike elected heads of state, dictators have no problems with parliamentary committees, an opposition party, or an inquisitive press. Since the balancing process requires prompt and rapid adjustments, the ease with which the dictator can make them seems to put him at a marked advantage.

While it is true that the absence of free inquiry and criticism may facilitate a dictator's rapid or secret preparation for sudden change, experience seems to indicate that democracies, too, are capable of both rapid response and secret decision in matters affecting national security. Neither the House of Commons in England nor the National Assembly in France has significantly inhibited its country's effectiveness in the international balancing process. Prior to its own entry into World War II, the United States was able to transform itself quickly into an arsenal of democracy. The decision to get involved in the conflict in Korea was reached by President Truman with speed and in secret; criticism and debate followed later. The ill-fated partial support of an invasion of Cuba in 1961, the successful solution of the missile crisis in Cuba in 1962, the dispatch of troops and marines to Lebanon in 1958 and to the Dominican Republic in April 1965, and participation in and then extension of the war in Vietnam amply demonstrate that a free press, congressional committees, an opposition party, and the voting public do not inhibit the democratic leader's capacity for secret and risky decisions as significantly as has sometimes been suggested by textbooks on American government.

Another criticism of the balance of power is that it causes wars while it aims at securing peace. The cause-and-effect relationship is more complicated than that. Only some wars were initiated on the basis of an estimate that the existing balance could be upset with impunity and transformed into an advantageous imbalance. Many more wars started not because there was a balance but because one side, rightly or wrongly, believed that the equilibrium had ceased to exist or might cease to exist. Aggressors usually initiate wars in the belief that their chances of winning are much greater than those of their enemies. Hitler began his war in 1939 confident that the Western democracies would not dare to oppose his conquest of Poland, or if they did, that they would immediately be crushed. His perception of favorable imbalance rather than balance was the decisive factor.

Critics of the balancing process are, of course, right in their warnings that the balance-of-power system does not guarantee a balance (or a correct perception of a balance or imbalance). It seems to guarantee only one thing: a continuous effort toward the goal of balance, which leads to the vicious circle of armaments and counterarmaments, alliances and counteralliances, ambitions and fears, suspicions and countersuspicions, intimidation and counterterror, with a probability of war. The theologian Reinhold Niebuhr once called international peace and order based on the balancing process without common consensus and without the regulatory force of government "a kind of managed anarchy."[6] He warned that such mitigated anarchy might overcome the management at the end.

While only a very few people today would praise the balancing process as an undiluted good (such praise could be heard until World War I), a great many accept it without praise or condemnation as a necessary and logical consequence of the present international system composed of sovereign states, in which most of the time nations cannot rely on anybody but themselves, a system in which no centralized guarantee of survival exists. As Kenneth Waltz expressed it: "Balance-of-power theory assumes that the desire for survival supplies the basic motivation of states and describes the expected outcome. . . . Perception of the peril that lies in unbalanced power encourages the behavior required for the maintenance-of-power system."[7]

One may wish for another world and a different nature of men and nations, but one cannot disregard the fact that critics of the balancing process fail to provide nations with advice as to an alternative course of action to be taken when they are threatened by a superior power that is neither willing to negotiate nor moved by Quaker-like declarations or unilateral actions of good will. Thus, even in the nuclear age, the familiar pattern of politics among nations seems to continue: Nations feel compelled constantly to react to real or imagined threats to their real or imagined interests. By diplomacy or by enhancing their military and economic powers, all states seek to obtain advantages for their people—frequently at the expense of their neighbors. Major nations impress their superior but limited capabilities upon their allies, neutrals, and enemies. In a word, every nation, as has always been the case, energetically promotes what it considers to be its national interest.

And yet, not everything in international politics today may be called "business as usual." International relations, in their eternal flux, have undergone a substantial change under the heat and shadow of the mushroom cloud, just as a liquid, placed over a fire, at a certain point changes not only its temperature but even its substance by becoming steam or gas.

BALANCING IN THE NUCLEAR AGE

In what way, if any at all, have the purpose and the consequences of the balancing process, which has been practiced for millennia, been affected by the existence of thermonuclear weapons? The *purpose* of nuclear balancing remains basically the same as the traditional process: to achieve an approximate equilibrium of power in order to prevent domination or blackmail. The goal is to prevent war, not to wage it. The *risk* that, intentionally or unintentionally, the balancing process may produce imbalance is also the same; no balancing process among nations can guarantee equilibrium as a result.

The consequences of quantitative imbalance among nuclear powers appears, however, somewhat less important than they used to be. The United States and the Soviet Union have today more firepower than all the armies in human history ever possessed. In 1969, on the eve of a new Soviet-American effort to bring the armament race down to a more reasonable level at the SALT (Strategic Arms Limitation Treaty) conference in Helsinki it was estimated that both superpowers had reached an approximate parity in intercontinental ballistic missiles. The Russians were credited with twelve hundred nuclear missiles in position or nearly so, while the United States had about a thousand Minutemen and sixty giant Titan II missiles. If the arsenals of one side were doubled, this would not put the opponent into a doubly disadvantageous position. As always, what really matters in armament mathematics is not the quantity but the *quality* of one's weaponry—and the *intentions* behind it. In the nuclear age the size of nuclear stockpiles is no indication of the net number of missiles or bombs that would actually hit the selected countervalue or counterforce targets (people or retaliatory missiles) despite the malfunction or inaccuracy of some of them and despite enemy defenses.

A marked superiority over the other side may still be achieved by a scientific or technological breakthrough that would result in improved range, penetration, and accuracy of the offensive ICBM missiles, in effective antiballistic missiles (ABM) defenses, or, in a never-ending vicious process, in the offensive missiles becoming immune to the ABMs. Such a quality race began in the late 1960s when both the Soviet Union and the United States developed the first generation of MRVs, multiple reentry vehicles; one of these is able to carry several atomic warheads that would fall like shotgun pellets on a target area. The United States and the Soviet Union then began developing MIRVs, multiple *independently* targeted reentry vehicles, that is, highly sophisticated missiles capable of releasing pretargeted atomic warheads on widely separated targets; for instance, one single Soviet missile could simultaneously pulverize New York, Washington, and Chicago, and one single American MIRV could do the same to Moscow, Leningrad, and Smolensk. In 1974 the United States developed an even more sophisticated multiple warhead missile, known in the Pentagon's acronymic slang as MARV—*maneuverable* reentry vehicle. This warhead, destined for the advanced Trident missiles, has a relatively simple terminal guidance system that causes it to "wiggle" or change course as it reenters the atmosphere, thus confounding any tracking radar equipment and constituting an antimissile missile system. Perhaps we are already approaching the climax anticipated by an American cartoonist in 1967 (see Figure 12.1).

The terrifying speed, cost, and sophistication of the nuclear missile, antimissile, and anti-antimissile race formed the background of the American-Soviet disarmament talks that started in Helsinki in 1969, led to the first agreement on the limitation of strategic arms in the nuclear age in

FIGURE 12.1
THE MISSILE RACE

"Our anti-anti-missile-missile just shot itself down, sir!"

Drawing by Huffine; Copyright 1967 Saturday Review, Inc.

1972,[8] and then, alternating between Vienna and Helsinki, continued throughout the first half of the 1970s. The United States invention of the MARV missile in 1974, at least initially immune to ABMs, could have been interpreted by the Soviet Union as giving the United States an assured first-strike capacity—and thus a tool of atomic blackmail. Chapter 13 will return to the problems of disarmament in the prenuclear and the nuclear age, especially the three main obstacles to agreement: (1) the mutual distrust which both necessitates and excludes foolproof on-site inspection (MIRVs and MARVs, for instance, cannot be detected by satellite inspection); (2) the difficulty in estimating parity in terms of the quality of weapons (for instance, the respective accuracy and ABM-immunity of Soviet and American offensive missiles); and (3) the ever-present fear of violation or open abrogation of a disarmament agreement by the other side.

Nuclear Miscalculations

In the past, error, accident, insanity, attainment of superiority, or, conversely, fear of potential inferiority often unleashed a war in which the total defeat of one nation was at stake. Total annihilation, however, was extremely rare, although Carthage was literally erased from the surface of the earth by the quite primitive weapons of the Romans. Even in this extreme case, however, only one side was punished by total destruction.

Today, on the contrary, a failure in the nuclear balancing process could unleash a war in which both the aggressor and his victim would be totally destroyed. Herein lies the substantial difference between the prenuclear and the nuclear balancing processes. It is this difference that endows the problems of possible misperception and miscalculation with truly apocalyptic proportions. In his Labor Day speech in 1964, President Lyndon B. Johnson illustrated the difference as follows: "In the first nuclear exchange 100 million Americans and more than 100 million Russians would all be dead. And when it was over, our great cities would be in ashes, and our fields would be barren, and our industry would be destroyed, and our American dreams would have vanished." In addition to the total or near-total destruction that the belligerents would inflict upon one another, thermonuclear weapons, if used to their full extent, could render a great portion of our globe uninhabitable; innocent bystanders would be devastated along with the participants. Such weapons could conceivably destroy mankind.

In terms of nuclear balancing, however, it is precisely the specter of potential universal annihilation that may render the process not less but more meaningful. Although nations continue to suspect or fear one another, they fear their own destruction even more. "It is on the fear of atomic apocalypse," concluded French sociologist and historian Raymond Aron, "that we must base our hope that the directors of the great powers will be wise."[9] The deterrent effects of the present-day balancing process are determined by the equality in the probability of national suicide as a consequence of international homicide, *if* both sides are capable of atomic retaliation and *if* the determination to retaliate is credible.

Second-Strike Capability

Second-strike or retaliatory capability refers to a nation's technical ability to inflict a devastating punishment even after the aggressor's initial attack has destroyed the attacked nation. The possibility of a devastating first strike can never be totally excluded from consideration when vital issues are at stake. Its occurrence could even be a rational possibility if the first strike could be viewed also as the last one, with no follow-up strike ("assured first strike"). But this becomes an unbearable proposition when the potential initiator of the first nuclear strike can rationally expect a devastating retaliatory strike. The second-strike capability is the first precondition for an effective balance of mutual terror. Thomas C. Schelling calls it "a massive modern version of an ancient institution, the exchange of hostages."[10] Both the Soviet Union and the United States may be viewed as "hostages" of each other. Pretargeted nuclear-tipped missiles and bombers are on an around-the-clock alert status. The reaction time is estimated to be from three to fifteen minutes. American nuclear submarines, equipped with Polaris and Poseidon missiles, are submerged in the oceans and beneath the polar icecap of the North Pole; they are all able to destroy the aggressor *after* he has already destroyed a major part of the United States. The Soviet Union is similarly well equipped with missile systems.

> For nearly two decades the strategic nuclear armaments of the Soviet Union and the United States have been great enough to hold the other's civilian population as hostage against a devastating nuclear attack. Living with this situation has not been and will not be easy: it has become, quite simply, one of the major tensions of modern life. Yet the mutual-hostage relationship has been given credit, and probably justly so, for the prevention of massive world wars.[11]

The importance of second-strike capability explains why so much of the thermonuclear arms race today is concerned with the protection of the retaliatory defenses; bombs and missiles are dispersed, placed on movable platforms, and are concealed or protected by hardened silos, the depth of the ocean, and an ABM system. Depriving the opponent of his second-strike capacity would make him extremely vulnerable to the first strike or blackmail based on it.

The technical capacity to deliver a vehement retaliatory blow conditions the deterrent quality of the balance of power only to the extent that the opponent is aware of it. Here total secrecy would defeat the purpose of policy. This fact leads to the curious phenomenon of constant public bragging on the part of major nuclear opponents about their secret weapons. One day, for instance, Nikita Khrushchev informed a Japanese delegation (September 15, 1964) that Russia had developed "the most terrible weapon." Two days after the Soviet hint that the doomsday machine had actually been completed, President Johnson in a speech in California (September 17, 1964) informed the world that the United States had so improved its radar protection that it could "see" beyond the curve of the horizon, and that, in addition, the United States now had ways of destroying orbiting satellites (presumably equipped with nuclear weapons). The nuclear "me-tooism" did not stop there. In 1965 Admiral Sergei G. Gorshkov, the commander in chief of the Soviet navy and a deputy defense minister, described the ineffectiveness of the American retaliatory devices. According to Admiral Gorshkov, the Soviet navy constantly monitors all the movements of American Polaris submarines, knows the regions where the submerged nuclear submarines are stationed, and has them all covered by missiles "capable of turning them into common graves for all American seamen."[12] In 1974 the coming of the

FIGURE 12.2
MISSILE BOASTING

"Oh, yeah? Well, we've got missiles we haven't even *counted* yet!"

Drawing by Ross; © 1969 The New Yorker Magazine, Inc.

third American generation of multiple warhead missiles, the MARVs, was announced by the Pentagon, not by Moscow, which perhaps could have learned about the MARVs from its spies.

This boasting will probably go on (see Figure 12.2). The secret of new weapons will, of course, never really be revealed, but enough—though not too much—will be said to inform the adversary of the existence of either retaliatory weapons or an effective defense against them. Ironically, even boasting, as a part of the balancing process, must be kept in balance, for excessive claims could lead to excessive responses and a panicky race. Nuclear powers actually keep one another informed with respect to military policy and strategy to avoid being underestimated or overestimated. Soviet military and political personnel study American strategic and military reports and vice versa. A recent volume on Soviet strategic thinking by Marshal V. D. Sokolovskii has become required reading for most NATO officers.[13] According to some skeptical observers the Soviet-American disarmament talks in the 1970s were not about disarmament but about intelligent armament and therefore served the primary purpose of exchanging strategic concepts and calculations concerning first- and second-strike capabilities.

Credibility of Retaliation

The second precondition for an operative balance of mutual deterrence is the technical capacity to retaliate; the second precondition is the *determination* to retaliate after the first surprise attack has already transformed the victim into a radioactive wasteland. The technical capacity to deliver a retaliatory blow would have little or no deterring effect if the potential aggressor were led to believe that his opponent had the weapon but not the will to use it. If the United States, one may justifiably ask, were transformed into heaps of ashes, would it make much sense to inflict the same fate on China after everything except the retaliatory submarines under the icecap of the North Pole had been pulverized? If this were our state of mind and the Chinese Communists *knew* it, then a dangerously high premium would be placed on the first surprise attack. Clearly, the determination to use the retaliatory power even in a completely hopeless situation should not exist in a secret spot of one's heart but should be made public and believable so as not to leave the opponent any shadow of a doubt that the retaliation threat is not a bluff. Only if the technical capacity to deliver the second strike is coupled with credible determination to do so may the opposing nuclear panoplies produce, in Inis L. Claude's words, "mutual cancellation rather than mutual ignition."

As we have seen, a peace based on nuclear brinkmanship contains several paradoxes: Its stability is partly the result of *certainty* concerning the adversary's technical capacity to deliver a retaliatory blow and partly the consequence of constant *uncertainty* concerning the determination of one's nuclear opponent; the rationale of such a peace rests basically on the assumption of an irrational decision.

In his analysis of the paradoxes of nuclear strategy, Hans J. Morgenthau has described the problem succinctly: "No nation can afford to yield to a threat of nuclear war that is only a bluff; nor can it stand up to a threat that turns out not to be a bluff." Miscalculation on either count could be fatal to the political or physical survival of a nation. "Yet a nation," as Morgenthau points out, "cannot determine with certainty when the other side is bluffing without the test of actual performance—a test which it is the very purpose of mutual deterrence to avoid."[14]

The destructiveness of modern weapons is so vast that no issue seems to justify their use. And yet, no government in possession of thermonuclear weapons can dispense with the threat of making use of them even when it would be senseless, as is their use following one's own total destruction. A former member of the Policy Planning Staff of the U.S. Department of State, Louis J. Halle, reached the conclusion that there is no occasion on which the United States would be rationally justified in firing its great nuclear weapons at the territory of an enemy. According to Halle, negotiation rather than retaliation in kind should rationally follow a massive nuclear attack on the United States.

> On the other hand, even though Washington should come to the conclusion that under no circumstances would it ever fire its nuclear warheads, its survival and the survival of its allies would still depend on the belief of any powerful enemy rival in the possibility that it would fire them. Any strategy devised for actually firing the great nuclear weapons must in some measure be irrational. And yet such a strategy has to be devised because it is now not possible to dispense with the contingent threat of actually firing such dreadful nuclear weapons. It is not easy to get out of this dilemma without resort to wishful thinking.[15]

Or as Raymond Aron expressed it: "It is neither honest nor advisable to insist that there is no alternative to peace. In strict logic, such a formula means capitulation. If war is 'impossible,' how can one threaten a possible aggressor with war?"[16]

FIVE SCHOOLS OF NUCLEAR THOUGHT

Analyses of the nuclear stalemate have produced five basic approaches, or schools of thought. They can be identified as advocates of preparation, advocates of disarmament, survival through terror, nonnuclear warfare, and the Chinese nonnuclear variant.

Advocates of Preparation

In accordance with the approach of advocates of preparation, the possibility of a nuclear war not only should not be placed in a category of unthinkable occurrences but on the contrary should be thoroughly studied and prepared for. Limited nuclear warfare for the purpose of blackmail, in particular, should not be ruled out; this includes such techniques as the bombing of military installations, of a city, or of a small region. Not to be prepared for such an occurrence would be to invite blackmail by those who would be prepared. According to this theory, limited nuclear warfare would not mean the end of society. In his study of thermonuclear war, Herman Kahn, the most articulate spokesman of this school of thought, points out that the damage of nuclear war need not be total or even very great; a large country could, according to his estimate, return to its prenuclear way of life within ten years after a medium-sized war. The U.S. Office of Civil Defense and Mobilization prepared an estimate of casualties, based on the 1950 Census, that could be expected in seventy-one "critical target areas" in the event of a *limited* thermonuclear war between the USSR and the United States. For its study the Civil Defense Office assumed that on a mid-October day, some 224 military and civilian targets in the United States were hit by 263 hydrogen bombs with a force of 1446 megatons, that is, the equivalent of 1.446 billion tons of TNT. The result would be the death of 48.9 million Americans. By far the heaviest toll would be in New York, with 3.364 million killed in the first twenty-four hours, and 2.634 million more fatally injured. Some 2.278 million persons would be injured but would survive. The calculations, carried out on computing machines, were designed to take into account "random bombing errors" and variations in wind patterns that would determine the distribution of radioactive fallout. The civil-defense estimate, submitted to the joint Congressional Atomic Energy Subcommittee (Chet Hollifield was the chairman), drew the conclusion that the nation could recover from such an attack, although approximately 25 percent of its population would have been killed.

These calculations are, of course, highly unreliable; such consequences as starvation, epidemics, large-scale fires, ecological damage, and societal breakdown cannot really be calculated by even the best computers. Nevertheless, those who think and calculate in the framework of this school of thought—and these include the top military experts in the United States, the Soviet Union, and China—suggest that a retaliatory strike following the first nuclear salvo does not need to be aimed at the enemy's cities (though threatening to aim at cities is an ideal posture for deterring an attack by a calculating aggressor) but may be directed selectively against an enemy's military and industrial targets, the pillars of the nation initiating a nuclear exchange.

The problem with this argument is that even a counterforce (as opposed to a countercity) nuclear attack will result in enormous civilian casualties; furthermore, no technological distinction can be created between nuclear weapons endangering the second-strike forces of the opponent in a first or preemptive strike and weapons designed to attack the same force in a retaliatory strike, nor is there a real difference between nuclear weapons designed for limited attacks and those designed for strategic retaliation. And this in itself precludes a disarmament agreement that would limit the superpowers' arsenals to only "defensive" (second-strike) or "limited" nuclear missiles.[17]

Advocates of Disarmament

The second school of thought considers the probability of unlimited nuclear warfare so great that it cannot find any use for the balancing process in the nuclear age. It advocates complete and total nuclear and conventional disarmament—if necessary, by unilateral action. Only disarmament, according to this view, is the logical step following the terrifying climax in the development of weapons of mass destruction. Such an approach focuses on arms as the main cause of tension rather than on the tensions and suspicions causing nations to arm. It relies mainly on the power of human appeal. In his *The Human Way Out* (Pendle Hill Pamphlet,

1958), Lewis Mumford expressed the hope that unilateral disarmament by the United States would prove so irresistible that others would follow. In their pamphlet *Speak Truth to Power: A Quaker Search for an Alternative to Violence* (1955), the American Friends Committee proposed methods of nonviolence in international relations; "military power is as corrupting to the man who possesses it as it is pitiless to its victims." In the Quaker view, only if nations recognize that the evil is in man and not in a particular system can peace and harmony follow.

Whatever view one may have of the practical effects of unilateral disarmament or action by humane example, the fundamental worry of those who search their way out of the nuclear impasse should not be underestimated. The worry is that the nuclear balance may get out of control more easily and with more catastrophic consequences than any other balance in the past.

Amitai Etzioni expresses this thought in a direct polemic with Herman Kahn in the following terms:

> If, in order to survive, we have to reach an agreement with the Communists despite all the armament and counterarmament, why not reach it without undergoing this wasteful, futile, perilous build-up? Does not the arms race itself create conditions preventing the kind of agreement which even the proponents of the arms race see as absolutely essential?
>
> Kahn's strategy—and the current military policy of the United States—yield us little besides an evergrowing pile of weapons which at best will never be used. Never has a non-war cost more: in money and resources as well as in energy, nerves, and intellect. All this sacrifice earns an illusion of an extra ounce of security in the shortest run, and in the process makes the world a vast field of powder kegs. It becomes more and more likely that at least some of the powder kegs will blow up, or be blown up.[18]

Even if one could exclude the initiation of nuclear war as a result of a rational decision, it could still occur as a consequence of (1) an escalation from civil, revolutionary, local, regional, conventional, or limited nuclear war; (2) proliferation of atomic weapons among more and more countries with the consequence that the number of leaders who could touch off nuclear war by miscalculation, brinkmanship, or accident would correspondingly increase; (3) an action by a third power that by dropping an atomic bomb on one of the superpowers may hope to profit from their mutual devastation; (4) human error, such as the wrong interpretation of a garbled code order; (5) mechanical failure, such as accidental self-triggering of a nuclear device; (6) unauthorized action, such as an order to fire issued by an insane officer; (7) false alarm, such as an incorrect interpretation of the image on a radar screen when a flock of flying ducks was mistaken for incoming missiles or bombers (this has already happened); and (8) an unauthorized use of the hot line between

Moscow and Washington (most improbable). (Kahn's four categories of possible nuclear war are described on pp. 401-402.)

Survival through Terror

The third approach actually welcomes the political and psychological effects of the potential universality of destruction with hope and confidence. In contradistinction to the disarmament proposal of the pacifists, this school of thought does not condemn or discard nuclear weapons but hopes to use their very destructiveness for a constructive purpose. "It may well be," said Winston Churchill (reported in the *New York Times*, March 2, 1955), "that we shall, by a process of sublime irony, have reached a stage in the story where safety will be the sturdy child of terror and survival the twin brother of annihilation." The intensity of universal horror may, for the first time in the history of nations, help to create a supranational community, one of fear. A common fear is a common interest of sorts—a common interest in survival among atomic powers first, and under their guidance among all the others ultimately. Around the community of fear, step by step, new forms of international relations may emerge, not starting with but perhaps ending with national disarmament. Thus the destructiveness of modern weapons may perhaps be converted into the first constructive steps away from the present anarchy of states toward some form of world commonwealth.

In one of his speeches in the House of Commons (November 3, 1955) Winston Churchill used the parallel of certain mathematical quantities that, passing through infinity, change their signs from plus to minus, and the other way round. The infinitely destructive weapons may produce a similar transformation in international relations; in Churchill's words "when the advance of destructive weapons enables everyone to kill everybody else, nobody will want to kill anyone at all."

Perhaps. But statistical or computerized horror may prove an insufficient brake; many people simply lack imagination, and others cannot be frightened by statistical descriptions. As Elton B. McNeil succinctly expressed it:

> Fear is a more personal experience and one not easily aroused in the abstract. With the increasing sophistication of all societies and the growing ease of communication, simple atrocity piled atop atrocity seems unable to evoke the emotional response it once did. Nuclear holocaust has grown beyond the realm of comprehension and thus has lost its capacity to inspire a continuing terror.[19]

If nuclear terror may lose its grip on the minds of average citizens, what about the mind of a madman who happens to be a national leader? Winston Churchill himself admitted that the nuclear deterrent "does not cover the case of lunatics or dictators in the mood of Hitler when he found himself in his final dug-out. This is a blank.'' It is perhaps appropriate to remind ourselves of Hitler's own words:

> We will never capitulate, never. . . . We might be destroyed, perhaps, but we will drag a world with us—a world in flames.

Nonnuclear Warfare

The fourth school of thought shares with the three previous ones the conviction that nuclear war is now unthinkable. But it reaches quite an opposite conclusion as to the advent of either a disarmed or a more closely knit world. It stresses the observable fact that the existence of nuclear weapons has so far not inhibited the use of practically all nonnuclear means of combat. Since the time of Hiroshima and Nagasaki, fighting on regional, local, revolutionary, or insurgency levels has been constant. The fourth school foresees not an expansion of peace and collaboration but, on the contrary, a more frequent occurrence of all types of violence other than nuclear. Under the umbrella of mutual nuclear cancellation, the struggle for influence and against domination will take the form of regional and local wars, wars by proxy, civil wars, and revolutions, more often than not supported from the outside by major powers. This probability was discussed in Chapter 11 under the heading "Internationalized Internal Wars."

The Chinese Nonnuclear Variant

In Peking's view, the existence of nuclear weapons did not affect China's own war; after all, in 1949, when the Communist conquest of the Chinese mainland was completed the American nuclear arsenal was already in its fourth year of buildup and the Soviet Union stood only on the threshold of its own nuclear era. In 1948, while the United States had an atomic monopoly and did not need to fear any retaliation in kind, it did not dare to blackmail Russia and force its way into blockaded Berlin; instead an elaborate airlift was organized.

Neither the Soviet boldness in Berlin nor the communist defeat of the American-supported Nationalist regime in China resulted in the use of American atomic power. Now, when American atomic power is frozen by the retaliatory power of the Soviet Union and China, the fear of escalation, as China publicly argues, should not influence the communist strategy and tactics of revolutionary warfare. It is in this context also that Peking refers to the American and Soviet atomic bombs as paper tigers that may roar but would never really dare to bite.

In the 1960s the Chinese nuclear thesis, defended in Peking's specific dispute with Moscow over the best communist strategy in our era (see

Document 12.1), had some obvious defects, most of which were related to the type of thinking that issued from the relative nuclear backwardness of China in the 1960s. With 600 to 700 million inhabitants and without MIRV and ABM systems, it made sense, of course, for China to stress and propagandize the human factor over hardware. As Brigadier General Samuel B. Griffith noted in his study of the military thinking of Mao Tse-tung,

> The historical experience of the Chinese leadership has confirmed them in the belief that man's dedication, imagination, courage and perseverance—under the infallible guidance of the Communist Party—can prevail against material and technical superiority. They saw this belief justified in Cuba, North Viet Nam and Algeria. They expect to see it justified elsewhere.[20]

A general review of the world situation in 1974, as seen and evaluated by China (issued by the Press Agency *Hsinhua* on January 9, 1974) was symptomatically entitled, "World in Great Disorder: Excellent Situation." It concluded with the following:

> The new year will be a year of still greater disorder. In this turbulent world, the people in their fight are, like stormy petrels flying high in the sky, harbingers of a rising storm. In this great disorder they have nothing to lose but their chains [a quotation from the Communist Manifesto of 1848] as they have a new world to win!

There is a controversy whether the Chinese variant of the fourth nuclear school is the closest to or the farthest from future probabilities (see Figure 12.3). "The revolutionary guerrilla wins civil wars, not international ones," notes one observer in disagreement, and adds:

> No civil war can change the balance of world power unless it takes place in America or Russia. . . . As for China, mesmerized by the magic of mere numbers, we have led ourselves to believe that 800 million people must be able to do something highly damaging to somebody. They have in fact hardly been able to do anything at all; and any increase in Chinese strength would anyway be first and foremost a worry for the Soviet Union, not for the United States.[21]

Besides some defects, the Chinese doctrine contains also some insights. In a limited way it shares the *optimism* of the third school of thought concerning the nuclear powers' inhibitions against using their nuclear panoplies, for the paper-tiger theory is basically an optimistic one. It also shares the fourth school's anticipation of frequent subnuclear violence in our century. Peking, however, looks forward to future occurrences of limited and revolutionary violence not with the anxiety of the fourth school of thought but with confidence and revolutionary hopes of capitalizing

DOCUMENT 12.1

"PSEUDOREVOLUTIONARIES WITH THEIR MASKS OFF"

Peking . . . galvanizes Trotskyite ideas about some sort of a "bourgeois degeneration of Soviet power" and puts a sign of equality between the United States imperialism and the Soviet Union, which is labeled "social imperialism". . . . Matters have gone so far that Hitler's ravings about the need to "save" the people from the "Slav" threat have been taken out of the mothballs. The people in Peking emulate the ringleaders of the Nazi Reich in attempting to portray the Soviet Union as a "colossus with feet of clay," clamoring about the Soviet "paper tiger" and threatening to "pierce it on the first attempt." . . . We cannot turn a blind eye on the fact that a militaristic psychosis is being stubbornly fanned in Peking and demands are made of the people "to prepare for hunger, to prepare for war." Even the recent launching of a satellite is being used to whip up nationalistic passions and for threats against our country. . . .

The Communist party has been smashed. . . . Bodies of power in China are patterned on a militaristic model inherited from the Chiang-kai-Chekists. All power is concentrated in the hands of the military. . . . By acting thus, Peking shows the imperialists that it does not intend to take concerted actions with the USSR and other socialist countries against imperialist quarters to carry out their antipopular designs and plans. The latest events in Indochina [U.S. invasion of Cambodia] being added proof of this.

By their actions the Peking leaders leave no doubt that they strive to use the heroic freedom struggle of the peoples in their global intrigues that stem from the Great Han dreams of becoming new emperors of "the Great China" that would rule at least Asia, if not the whole world.

From *Pravda*, May 18,1970, distributed in English by the Tass press agency.

---

upon the nuclear stalemate and the impatience of the underdeveloped portions of the world (see Chapter 1 on the explosive gap between the world's North and South).

Nevertheless, while talking big, China has so far acted with circumspection. Not Mao, but smiling Khrushchev dangerously challenged the United States in Berlin and in the sensitive Caribbean area by introducing medium-range missiles into Castro's Cuba. China's record in combining cautiousness with daring is not unimpressive. China fought the United States to a standstill in Korea and humiliated India in Assam and Ladakh without pressing the point further than was necessary. China has frightened or lured its neighbors, Burma and Pakistan, into cooperation and, at the same time, challenged Soviet political supremacy in the Communist and Third Worlds. It has not abandoned hope for an early extension of communist control over Taiwan, the Pescadores, and the offshore islands but it has not pressed the point to a dangerous climax; nor

FIGURE 12.3
THE CHINESE NUCLEAR VARIANT

"I've stopped worrying about what the Americans might do—now I'm worried about the Russians worrying about what the Chinese might do."

Drawing from *Punch*, London.

has Peking asked for an early return of Chinese Hong Kong from England and Macao from Portugal. After having exploded its first atomic bomb (1964) and hydrogen bomb (1967), China seems to have acquired not only nuclear technology but also greater nuclear sophistication in the matter of risks and strategies; thus, since 1969, the Chinese leaders have appeared much less certain about whether the Soviet and American nuclear arsenals—or any nuclear arsenal, for that matter—belong to the category of paper tigers who never bite, deliberately or accidentally. Although the Chinese press in the 1970s still propagandized and stressed the superiority of the human factor over nuclear hardware and anticipated drowning American and Soviet nuclear imperialism in a "vast ocean of people's wars," the current Chinese strategic doctrine may, in fact, echo the computerized calculations and fears of the Chinese counterparts to McNamara and Sokolovskii rather than the old Mao's emphasis on the glory of mass revolutionary warfare. And therefore the fifth, Chinese, school of thought may have transmuted itself into a mixture of the first approach, advocating preparation for limited and general nuclear exchanges, and the fourth view, which foresees frequent subnuclear warfare, local and/or revolutionary.

Mixtures of different schools of nuclear thought are not, of course, a Chinese speciality; they all overlap as well as conflict one with one another not only among and within nations but also within the mind of one and the same individual strategist and analyst. The preceding description represents only a crudely simplified list of the main trends of contemporary thinking about the thinkable and the unthinkable in the post-Hiroshima world (see Figure 12.4).

AFTER ATOMIC FISSION: POLITICAL FUSION OR POLITICAL ATOMIZATION?

The fundamental difference between the preatomic balancing process and the present one is not, as noted previously, in the purpose or in the uncertainties but in the cataclysmic consequences for all the balancing states in the case of a failure in the process. However imbalanced superpowers may be, they are equal in their ultimate vulnerability. Rationally, every one seems to agree that the cost of a thermonuclear war would necessarily be higher than any possible profit derived from it. No issue seems worth a center-to-center exchange of nuclear salvos. Yet no one can really be certain that the other side sees it in the same way. Peace rests, therefore, on a combination of destructive certainty and political uncertainty, a situation that Raymond Aron calls ''a game of menace and bluff in which the wills face one another without going to the ultimate test of

FIGURE 12.4
SCHOOLS OF NUCLEAR THOUGHT

Drawing by Richter; © The New Yorker Magazine, Inc.

arms."[22] Either a loss of nerve or an excessive display of it could lead to a disaster.

More than two millennia ago, the Indian philosopher-statesman Kautilya, quoted previously, noted, "While a fight with a stronger enemy is like that of a foot-soldier with an elephant, a fight between equals like the clash between two unbaked vessels brings ruin to both." Today nations endowed with thermonuclear capabilities have, in a sense, become fragile unbaked vessels that cannot risk a clash. Some therefore express a hope that the time has come for all to melt national vessels and remold the mixture into one world community. There are no convincing indications that this is soon to happen.

Superpowers Paralyzed, Small Powers Emboldened

Whereas the mightiest nations have become more clearly equal in their capabilities and fears as a result of nuclear stalemate, the great discrepancy of capabilities that separates the great powers from the small ones has politically become less meaningful. "Nuclear armament makes at once for gross inequality in the power of states and for substantial equality among all states through the inability of the most powerful to use force effectively."[23] The unprecedented concentration of destructive power has inhibited its possible uses, including, as smaller nations see it, the use of the great powers' arsenals for the purposes of either protection or punishment of a nonnuclear nation. As a result, the nuclear stalemate has increased, not decreased, the insistence of all nations on building their own lives independently, through their own national efforts, and within their own national shells, however potentially breakable these are. The new nationalism is due in part to the rise of many new nations whose nationalist preliberation fever continues unabated in their postliberation era, and in part to the very fact of the mutual nuclear paralysis among superpowers. While logically the common fear of mutual annihilation should unify the world in its common interest in surviving, the splitting of the atom has so far tended to further "atomize," not unite, humanity. "Having reached agreement that it would make no sense for the world to die of a nuclear thrombosis," noted Johnson's Assistant Secretary of State Harlan Cleveland (the *New York Times*, February 28, 1964), "the world seems to have broken out in a rash of smaller local disputes—each carrying the virus of general war." It is as if the nuclear stalemate had lifted the lid off the many incipient disputes among nations and within nations. Nations both fear the use of nuclear weapons and suspect that the same fear would inhibit their allies' use of them in behalf of their partners. In such a context it becomes attractive either to have one's own deterrent or not to be aligned at all. Also, as seen from the vantage point of superpowers bent on improving their long-range missiles, allies have become somewhat less necessary. The destructiveness and range of modern weapons, Henry

Kissinger noted, "have a tendency to produce extreme nationalism, and neutralism."[24] And modern, activist neutralism is only a specific form of nationalism, asserted against the magnetic pull of one or the other pole of the international system. Egypt's Sadat succinctly expressed the new strength of weak states caught between two mutually intimidated superpowers:

> My pride in taking the decision [to attack Israel on Yom Kippur in 1973] stems from the fact that it was a hundred per cent Egyptian decision made against the will of the two superpowers.

Nine months later (July 1974), the Turkish invasion of Cyprus, following a military coup apparently engineered by the then ruling junta in Athens, was another example of a small power's capacity to challenge the will of its main ally (the United States) and protect its freedom of action and the promotion of Turkish national interest by an implicit reliance on a potential Soviet support.

A noted Italian career diplomat, Minister Roberto Ducci, calls this emphasis on salvation through one's own effort "modern political protestantism" (*Foreign Affairs*, April 1964); it runs in the opposite direction to ecumenism, which in church matters is the result of a religious stalemate and, in political matters, the result of reciprocal nuclear paralysis. To date, political protestantism occupies the center of the world stage; political ecumenism is expected to compete with it—but only at a later date.

World Government?

Under what conditions do nations, small and large, find it expedient to submerge their sovereignty in a common pool of supranational authority? The past and the present offer us very few examples of voluntary total submission to a new supranational or other-national authority. More numerous are examples of terminations of national sovereignty by conquest: surrender and submission to a foreign authority that result from military defeat or such a persuasive threat that the nation and its leaders decide to accept absorption by another state rather than continue their opposition. Some may consider, especially in our era of thermonuclear missiles, that any life, even that of enslavement, is preferable to the death of an unbearably large portion of the nation. The question has already been raised but not answered in Chapter 10 as to the percentage of the population that may be sacrificed so that the state may live. The 1974 Constitution of Communist Yugoslavia (Article 238) prohibits any one from signing an act of capitulation, accepting or recognizing the occupation of the country, or preventing citizens "from fighting against the enemy." Such acts are "punishable as high treason." The

Constitution evidently reflects the Yugoslav experience and the glory of the anti-Nazi guerrillas fighting with and against the conventional weapons of World War II. How this article would be applied if the nation faced an atomic ultimatum, giving it a choice between national survival in slavery—which might not be permanent—or turning Yugoslavia into a quite permanent atomic dust bowl, is almost beyond conjecture.[25]

A nation might, however, willingly decide to cease to be a separate state if its leaders and its people conclude that a new community and authority such as a regional or a continental federation or a United States of the World is capable of ensuring a higher degree of order, peace, social justice, and prosperity than the present system of sovereign and antagonistic national states. This is the fervent wish of world federalists and similar groups. Hope is often expressed that under the shadow of thermonuclear missiles and as a consequence of the growing cultural, scientific, intellectual, and physical contacts among all nations of the world, men will begin to develop a rational allegiance to, and an emotional identification with, the transnational community of the human race. Nations are bound to find it preferable, so the argument goes, to solve their conflicts of interest in a civilized and peaceful fashion within the framework of a world community endowed with world authority. However tardily, nations will discover what many but not all individuals and groups within nations have known for some time—that order is preferable to chaos, and a peaceful solution of unavoidable conflicts is preferable to violence. Furthermore, now that total annihilation threatens the human race, the interests of nations and of the human race have become one: The end of mankind would mean the end of nations. Sentiment seems ready to endorse this hopeful argument, but reason, based on experience, cannot help challenging it on three points.

First, many individuals and nations do not believe that a third world war would really result in the end of life on earth. Scientists (see Einstein's words in Document 8.3) and strategists are quite divided on the issue. The Chinese Communists anticipate that "a thousand times more beautiful civilization" would follow a worldwide nuclear holocaust. To prove them wrong would give little satisfaction, except in the world beyond. In a less than total annihilation, the interests of the human race and those of nations are not automatically one; they could clash. An entire nation might be sacrificed for the sake of the rest of humanity. But also a major part of mankind might be sacrificed for the sake of one nation.

Second, the degree of emotional or rational identification of individuals and national groups with the transnational community of men, a "world nation," is still very low. Supranational humanism may be a subject of passionate sermons, books, and pamphlets, but it has not become a practical basis for political action. It has already been stressed how ambiguous and subject to opposing interpretations is the concept of national interest. What about the general interest of mankind? Who is to determine its contents? Quincy Wright once asked the following question: "Can there be a world society unless contact is made with some society in some other planet to which it can be opposed?"[26] We may safely assume that we would all become fanatic Earthlings when threatened by an invasion from Mars—except perhaps for some traitors or those nations that had secretly arranged for an alliance with the invaders.

In the absence of a common threat from outer space, can a common threat from within our planet force humanity to do what it has been reluctant so far to do voluntarily? Can the specter of a global Hiroshima cause nations to regard unity as the only alternative to suicide through disunity? Many observers believe so and point to the observable fact that the enormity of thermonuclear arsenals has not only inhibited direct confrontations among superpowers but prodded them into several cooperative agreements. Skeptics argue that the Soviet and American *rapprochement* has been caused not only by thermonuclear warheads but also, if not primarily, by the problem of domestic priorities and by the Chinese challenge to both nations. They also point to the frequency and intensity of subnuclear violence—local and regional wars or confrontations both among and within nations. "Undoubtedly, fear may be a creative force," writes the Protestant theologian Reinhold Niebuhr:

> The scared man can run faster from the pursuing bull than he ever thought possible. But the creative power of fear does not increase in proportion to its intensity. Fear, finally, becomes paralyzing. Furthermore, the fear of mutual destruction easily degenerates into a fear of a particular foe. Even now it may be regretfully recorded that the fear of Russia in the West and of the West in Russia seems more potent than the common fear of destruction.[27]

These lines were written in 1946 and may sound less convincing today than at the dawn of the nuclear age. Nevertheless, Niebuhr's emphasis on the difference of the effects of a threat from without and from within a community cannot be lightly discarded. Elsewhere we have already noted that many transnational unions (the European Economic Community, Pan-Arabism, Switzerland, the United States) have been formed in response to and often against other communities of men rather than as deliberate stepping-stones to a unity of mankind. Even on the occasions when people stop looking at mankind through national-ethnic glasses, they replace them with ideological, regional, or continental filters rather than simply using their eyes. This metaphor, most probably wrongly, assumes that there can be such a thing as undistorted, 20-20 vision.

Without a global consensus that would express the transformation of present nations into one community, one "world-nation," an agreement among the existing nations to proclaim a world state and even agree on its constitution would not be worth the paper on which the agreement and constitution were written. If the component units of a world federation were endowed with a veto, necessitating constant laborious negotiations or leading to stalemate or violence, we would essentially be where we are now and where we have been for many centuries. If, on the other hand, we think of some global democratic formula (some federal variant of the Connecticut Compromise, for instance), and if we also dismiss a world dictatorship as an undesirable variant of a world state, it is difficult to imagine how the Russians and the Americans, for instance, could accept a rule by majority in any important matter since they both would dread the possibility of the Chinese and the Indians creating a tyranny by permanent majority (1.5 billion Asians versus 450 million Caucasians). For instance, could such a "community" accept a decision by a majority with a margin of 0.5 percent (as was the case in the election of President Kennedy) that would give the position of utmost power, world presidency, to one nation?

Third, even if a world state or a world federation were established on the basis of an incipient world community in which the present national loyalties would really be replaced by a loyalty to the human race, such a state would not itself be a guarantee of peace and order. As we know, territorial states, albeit embodying a high degree of general consensus, have not been able to eliminate violence, including cruel civil wars, from the domestic scene. Loyalty to a state does not exclude violent disagreements on the method and goals of government. In a world state it would be possible to conceive of a civil war between communists, democrats, and fascists, or of an interracial conflict—both cutting across the present national divisions. A global civil war might be deadlier than the civil war between the North and the South in the United States. The emergence of a consensus, national or global, does not guarantee its permanency; secession from a world state would be at least as conceivable as from a nation-state.

The last two points—that man's allegiance to the world community is embryonic and that the state by itself has never been a guarantee of civilized behavior and permanency of consensus—should be seen not as an invitation to utter pessimism but as a warning against wishful thinking in inaccurate analogies. Terms such as "government," "federation," and "state" are often transferred from the national context, where they have proved their worth, onto the world scene, where their premature introduction could cause more harm than good. As we shall see in Chapter 14, nations may succeed in reducing violence and chaos among themselves by methods and formulas that have no exact counterparts on the hierarchically organized domestic scene. Finally, it should be recognized that peace and order *among* nations, when established under whatever formula, do not guarantee by themselves peace and order *within* nations. It is conceivable that class, racial, or student violence and civil wars could erupt within states while the states lived in international peace, respecting each other's boundaries.

Notes

1. Thomas C. Schelling, *The Strategy of Conflict*. Cambridge, Mass.: Harvard University Press, 1960, p. 10.

2. Arnold Wolfers, *Discord and Collaboration*. Baltimore, Md.: The Johns Hopkins Press, 1962, p. 118.

3. Polybius, *Histories*, I. "Here is the aim of modern politics pointed out in express terms," added the eighteenth-century English philosopher David Hume to the above.

4. Thucydides, *The Peloponnesian War*. Baltimore, Md.: Penguin, 1954, pp. 36-37.

5. Ernst B. Haas, "The Balance of Power as a Guide to Policy," *Journal of Politics*, 15 (August 1953), 370-398.

6. Reinhold Niebuhr, *The Children of Light and the Children of Darkness*. New York: Scribner, 1944, p. 174.

7. Kenneth N. Waltz, "International Structure, National Force, and the Balance of World Power," *Journal of International Affairs*, 21:2 (1967), 215.

8. The 1972 Soviet-American treaty limits each nation to two antiballistic missiles sites with 200 ABMs; thus the two nations agreed to leave themselves partly defenseless, and to rely on their offensive missiles for mutual deterrence.

9. Raymond Aron, "Political Action in the Shadow of Atomic Apocalypse," in Harold D. Lasswell and Harlan Cleveland (eds.), *The Ethic of Power*. New York: Harper & Row, 1962, p. 453.

10. Schelling, *The Strategy of Conflict*, p. 20.

11. Wolfgang K. H. Panofsky, "The Mutual-Hostage Relationship between America and Russia," *Foreign Affairs*, 52:1 (October 1973), 109.

12. *Pravda*, January 28, 1965.

13. Marshal V. D. Sokolovskii (ed.), *Soviet Military Strategy*. Englewood Cliffs, N.J.: Prentice-Hall, 1963.

14. Hans J. Morgenthau, "The Four Paradoxes of Nuclear Strategy," *American Political Science Review*, 17:1 (March 1964), 24.

15. Louis J. Halle, "Peace in Our Time—Nuclear Weapons as a Stabilizer," *New Republic*, December 28, 1963, pp. 18-19.

16. Raymond Aron, "Introduction," in Herman Kahn, *Thinking about the Unthinkable*. New York: Avon, 1962, p. 12.

17. Panofsky, "The Mutual Hostage Relationship," p. 118.

18. Amitai Etzioni, "Our First Manual of Thermonuclear War," *Columbia University Forum*, Fall 1961, p. 12.

19. Elton B. McNeil (ed.), *The Nature of Human Conflict*. Englewood Cliffs, N.J.: Prentice-Hall, 1965, p. 311.

20. Samuel B. Griffith II, "The Glorious Military Thought of Comrade Mao Tse-tung," *Foreign Affairs*, 42 (July 1964), 674.

21. Kenneth N. Waltz, "The Politics of Peace," *International Studies Quarterly*, 11:3 (September 1967), 205.

22. Aron, "Political Action in the Shadow of Atomic Apocalypse," p. 445.

23. Kenneth N. Waltz, "International Structure, National Force, and the Balance of World Power," *Journal of International Affairs*, 21:2 (1967), 215.

24 Henry A. Kissinger, "NATO's Nuclear Dilemma," *The Reporter*, March 28, 1963, p. 27.

25. This and other issues concerning "treason" by capitulation are discussed in greater detail in Ivo D. Duchacek, *Power Maps: Comparative Politics of Constitutions*. Santa Barbara: ABC-Clio, 1973, pp. 85-88.

26. Quincy Wright, "The Nature of Conflict," *The Western Political Quarterly*, 4:2 (June 1951), 203.

27. Reinhold Niebuhr, "The Myth of World Government," *The Nation*, March 16, 1946, p. 314.

Additional Readings

Additional readings on the subject of nuclear deterrence and balancing processes may be found in *Discord and Harmony: Readings in International Politics*, edited by Ivo D. Duchacek and published by Holt, Rinehart and Winston in 1972. The following four essays are directly related to the subject: "Never Has a Non-War Cost So Much" by Amitai Etzioni (pp. 307-315); "Nuclear Deterrence and Moral Considerations" by Philip Green (pp. 316-321); "The Modern Balance of Power: Duopoly at the Top" by Kenneth N. Waltz (pp. 328-334) and "Tacit Coordination of Expectations and Behavior" by Thomas C. Schelling (pp. 378-395).

13
Signaling and Balancing Techniques

Nations use a variety of techniques to communicate their intentions and the extent of their power to one another and thus influence one another's perceptions and behavior. These techniques are millennia old—they were known to the ancient Romans and Greeks and to generations of political leaders before them—and the unprecedented advances of modern science and technology have not fundamentally changed them. As to their form, communications among nations range from verbal messages and symbolic acts to demonstrations of military power and actual military operations. As to their purpose, communications among nations aim at eliminating or causing misperception and miscalculation, or disturbing or maintaining international stability, whether maintained by imbalance or balance of power.

These techniques may be divided into the following six major categories:

1. *Messages* (written or oral, transmitted by heralds, cables, or satellite hot lines) or symbolic gestures. Messages may affect behavior even if not preceded or accompanied by other acts.
2. *Armaments*, by which nations increase their power to impose their will on others or resist the will of others.
3. *Alliances*, coalitions, economic aid programs, and spheres of

influence, by which a nation increases its power to dominate or resist domination by adding the power of other nations to its own.

4. *Interference*, including efforts to undermine or dissolve rival coalitions and alliances, by which the power of the opponent may be decreased from within.

5. *Collective security*—so far only a theoretical concept—which aims at an extreme imbalance of power between all peace-loving nations, on the one hand, and the actual or potential aggressors, on the other.

6. *Disarmament proposals*, to reduce the arms race and stabilize it at a lower level that is politically and economically less costly than the previous level. Closely related are proposals for disengagement, which is a *geographically* determined form of arms limitation.

The first technique,[1] communication of views and intentions through messages or symbolic gestures, differs from the other techniques in that it affects the future *uses* of the existing capabilities, not their substance. Messages neither add to nor subtract from the existing distribution of material power among nations (balance of power in its narrower sense).

In contrast to communications in a narrow sense, armaments, intervention, and alliances are partly messages and partly acts whose aim is to alter or maintain the existing distribution of capabilities. These techniques are both signals of intentions and preparations for future contingencies; they represent mixtures of more or less publicity and secrecy. Arms, especially in the nuclear age, are propagandized for the purpose of deterrence, but their real effectiveness and strategic plans remain, of course, a tightly guarded secret. In intervention the element of publicity is limited to overt aggressive propaganda, the rest of the operations remaining covert. In alliances the element of publicity—"we shall go it together"—is often more important than the actual increase of collective power. Collective security has so far remained a theoretical concept; but if and when realized, its salient feature will be the global message that peace has become indivisible and that its breach any time, anywhere in the world will be prevented or punished by a grand alliance of all peace-loving powers. This message, inscribed in the United Nations Charter, has lacked credibility because it has remained only a communication without being backed up by an organized collective power. Disarmament proposals represent primarily messages; their credibility, however, has to be buttressed by such acts as reducing one's defense budget or agreeing to accept on-site inspection.

In all six categories of signaling and balancing techniques the link between communication of intentions and the capability to implement them is intimate and direct; these techniques are based on the assumption that only a credible ability and credible determination to bestow a benefit or inflict damage will induce the recipient nation to reorient its views and policies, desist from a planned action, or engage in an action that, in the absence of a lure or a menace, would not be undertaken. We do not say that a reasoned argument—for instance, in favor of general peace, order, or prosperity—has no effect, but evidently even an unconvincing argument may be transformed into an irresistible one by making the target nation fully aware of the communicating nation's ability and determination to back up the argument by a real advantage or sanction.

The process of persuasion and intimidation (deterrence) assumes both correct interpretation and rationality on the part of the target nation. The signaling and balancing techniques may, of course, be misread and lead to a misperception on the part of the recipient. Also, the signaling nation may deliberately bluff and lie. On the international scene, as noted in Chapters 5 and 6, deceit and misperception of an honest message are frequent. By the assumption of rationality on the part of the recipient is meant a reasoned calculation of acceptable losses or advantages in the case of compliance; for a madman is usually quite immune to an intelligent argument even if it is accompanied by a credible threat or promise of profit. If there is no real alternative—as, for instance, between total annihilation and total enslavement—an irrational response may be expected. In actual situations, as Thomas Schelling analyzed,[2] a recipient may sometimes rationally pretend irrationality, nonreceipt of the message, or its wrong interpretation. The strategy of explicit and implicit bargaining and its relation to game theory will be further discussed in Chapter 14, dealing with diplomacy and negotiations.

Each of the six categories of the signaling and balancing techniques will be described separately, but, in practice, nations usually employ several or all of them simultaneously, frequently in conjunction with diplomatic negotiations. Statesmen are never quite certain of the effectiveness of any of these techniques and tend to give them all a try.

MESSAGES

The focus here is on the deliberate messages—oral or written communications and symbolic gestures—by which states try to make their friends, their foes, and the neutral nations believe certain things about their intent and power and behave accordingly. Informing and misinforming other nations about one's will and power is an essential part of the international signaling and balancing process. As already noted, the effectiveness of any political communication is closely related to the capability of the communicating nation to take action should the argument go unheeded. Bearing in mind the relationship between intent and power, we will describe four types of communications among nations: declarations of involvement, declarations of strict neutrality, declarations of activist nonalignment, and diplomatic protest, which encompasses symbolic gestures and mob protest.

Declarations of Involvement

Announcement of active interest and participation in international politics usually takes the form of public solemn statements, addressed to both foreign and domestic audiences, or of secret communications from nation to nation through diplomatic channels. In the American context, declarations of national political goals are often referred to as doctrines.

Some of the typical American doctrines are:

1. The Monroe Doctrine (1823), which confirmed the isolation of the United States from Europe but proclaimed the United States's involvement in the Western Hemisphere.
2. Woodrow Wilson's Fourteen Points (1918), which proclaimed the American goal of making the world safe for democracy, based on the right of nations to determine their own governments and establish their own states.
3. The Truman Doctrine (1947), which announced the readiness of the United States to help Greece and Turkey against Soviet and communist pressures and to support "free peoples who are resisting attempted subjugation by armed minorities or by outside pressures."
4. The Marshall Plan (1947), which proclaimed the willingness of the United States to restore the economy of Western Europe, shattered by the preceding war. It was combined with a threat that "governments, political parties or groups which seek to perpetuate human misery in order to profit therefrom politically or otherwise will encounter the opposition of the United States."
5. The Johnson Doctrine (1965), which justified the intervention of the United States in Santo Domingo and proclaimed that "the American nations cannot, must not, and will not permit the establishment of another Communist government in the Western Hemisphere."
6. The Nixon Doctrine (1970), proclaimed at Guam, which emphasized the need to bring American policy objectives, strategies, and defense budgets into balance "with each other and with our overall national priorities." President Nixon further explained this doctrine of partial retrenchment:

> The stated basis of our conventional posture in the 1960s was the so called "2½ war" principle. According to it, U.S. forces would be maintained for a three-month conventional forward defense of NATO, a defense of Korea or Southeast Asia against a full-scale Chinese attack, and a minor contingency—all simultaneously. These force levels were never reached.
>
> In the effort to harmonize doctrine and capability, we chose what is best described as the "1½ war" strategy. Under it we will maintain in peacetime general purpose forces adequate for simultaneously meeting a general Communist attack on either Europe or Asia, assisting allies against non-Chinese threats in Asia, and contending with a contingency elsewhere.

Evidently, the Nixon Doctrine was explicitly based on the improbability of two simultaneous major attacks in the period of continuing Sino-Soviet rift.

The communication of national objectives or objections is not limited to formal and solemn declarations such as those just listed. Every hour of every day of international politics is marked by a constant flow of words that describe, elaborate on, refine, clarify, or obscure what each nation really wants on the international scene. The occasion for such a communication of policy may be a press conference by the chief of state, a debate in a national legislature, a political party meeting, a congressional hearing, an editorial in the government press, a radio or television program, a speech at a veterans' or housewives' rally, a banquet or cocktail party at a foreign embassy, a celebration on the occasion of the safe return of astronauts from the moon, or simply the beginning of a new calendar year. Briefly, whatever occasion presents itself may be used for the purpose of policy communication through some mass media. Some occasions are solely dedicated to the purpose of the international communication of national policies. Broadcasting in many foreign languages Radio Moscow Radio Paris, Radio Peking, Radio Cairo, and the Voice of America predominantly serve the purpose of promoting, explaining, and justifying national policy goals to foreign audiences. They usually have other goals too, such as widening the gap between unfriendly foreign governments and their people. This was discussed earlier in connection with interference techniques.

The Soviet or Chinese counterparts to American presidential doctrines are contained in speeches and proclamations made by the communist leaders, statements adopted by international gatherings of communist leaders, or editorials propagandized by all available mass media. One example of an international communist proclamation was the "Statement of the Meeting of Representatives of the 81 Communist and Workers' Parties," held at Moscow in December 1960, which proclaimed:

> Peaceful coexistence of countries with different social systems does not mean conciliation. . . . On the contrary, it implies intensification of the struggle of the working class, of all the Communist parties, for the triumph of socialist ideas. But ideological and political disputes between states must not be settled through war. . . . International developments in recent years have furnished many new proofs of the fact that U.S. imperialism is the chief bulwark of world reaction and an international gendarme, that it has become an enemy of the peoples of the whole world.[3]

An example of a programmatic policy statement in the form of an editorial, simultaneously reprinted in all Chinese Communist newspapers and broadcast by all China's radio stations, was the January 1, 1970, call for war-readiness in the 1970s, which described China's policy goals:

It has long been our consistent policy to develop diplomatic relations with all countries on the basis of the Five Principles of Peaceful Coexistence but on no account can we tolerate the invasion and occupation of our sacred territory by any imperialism or social-imperialism. We are determined to liberate Taiwan—the sacred territory of our motherland!

The mention of the Five Principles of Peaceful Coexistence refers to the principles that were first spelled out in the treaty between India and China regarding Tibet in 1954 and repeated the same year (June 1954) in a common declaration of policy by Nehru and Chou En-lai. They recur in the communiqué issued at the close of the Asian-African conference at Bandung (April 1955). The five principles are: (1) mutual respect for territorial integrity and sovereignty, (2) nonaggression, (3) noninterference in internal affairs, (4) equality and mutual benefit, and (5) peaceful coexistence.

In almost identical terms the themes of defense against intruders and determination to liberate Taiwan were repeated year after year each January 1. In 1974 (*Peking Review*, January 4, 1974), for instance, the pledge "We must step up the building of the people's militia especially in cities and border areas, and resolutely strike at the handful of class enemies engaged in sabotage" was accompanied by an appropriate woodcut (see Figure 13.1) And despite the détente with the United States, which still maintains diplomatic relations with the government on Taiwan, the *Peking Review* emphasized: "The liberation of Taiwan is the common aspiration and sacred duty of the people of the whole country, including the people in Taiwan Province."

Declarations of Strict Neutrality

Announcements of the national intention to abstain from active participation in international politics, especially in the arms and alliances race, represent the opposite of declarations of involvement. George Washington's Farewell Address of 1796 is a good example of a unilateral proclamation and justification of the desire of the United States for isolation from Europe and its entangling alliances. While a nation may cogently argue why it wants to be left alone and play no active role in the balancing process, its reasoned argument may go unheeded; a chasm may separate the nation's plea from its capability to implement it. The following four factors usually determine whether a nation's wish to go it alone will be, in fact, respected:

1. *Geographic inaccessibility*—a rare commodity in our age, but once an important factor. The Alps in one case and the Atlantic and Pacific Oceans in another for a long time contributed to the preservation of the neutralism

FIGURE 13.1
CHINA IS READY

"Ever ready to defend the motherland."

Woodcut by Chin Ho-teh, *Peking Review*, January 4, 1974.

and isolationism of Switzerland and the United States, once relatively weak countries.

2. *Acting as a buffer zone.* For instance, Austria's geographic location is extremely vulnerable, but since May 16, 1955, her neutrality has been successfully maintained by an agreement among the Soviet Union, the United States, Great Britain, and France. For over half a millennium the common interests of Germany, France, Italy, and Austria, combined with the geographic inaccessibility of Switzerland, preserved her neutrality. Similar interests in a neutral buffer created and preserved neutral Belgium until World War I. While the balance of power around the neutral country lasts, its status is respected and preserved. If the balance changes, neutrality ceases to be a protection. Belgium was invaded twice by Germany (1914 and 1940). Even Switzerland experienced an interruption of its independence and neutrality when the French Jacobins initiated revolutions in Rome, Naples, and Switzerland (1798-1799) and added the Roman, Neapolitan, and Helvetian republics to the list of French dependencies.

3. *An intensive preoccupation of the major powers with one another in distant geographic areas*. There is in this case little time and energy left for the isolated neutral. The success of the United States in its neutral isolation from Europe was predominantly due to the balancing process among the European nations and their preoccupation with one another, first in Europe itself and then, in the era of colonial expansion, in Asia and Africa.

4. *A modest degree of intimidatory power, an independent military strength*. The credible ability to defend one's neutrality adds to its successful maintenance. Making an attack on a well-armed neutral appear as costly as possible diminishes the aggressor's anticipated gain. Some neutral nations are known for the excellence of their military establishments. Following World War II, for instance, and before the birth of the Atlantic Alliance, the armies of the three European neutral states, Sweden, Switzerland, and Turkey, were the best trained and best equipped on the European continent west of the Soviet Union.

The history of the glories and failures of neutral isolation shows that it usually takes at least three nations—the candidate for neutrality and two major antagonists in a balanced situation—to make neutrality a success. Many present-day neutrals can indulge in the luxury of nonalignment because in many areas of the world the American, Soviet, and Chinese powers cancel one another out. Some neutral leaders who engage in nonneutral denunciations of the United States's power fail to realize that their freedom of denunciatory speech is due precisely to that power. Without a balance of power, a unilateral desire for or declaration of neutrality would be but a pious wish. The experience of Switzerland in the eighteenth century, and of several West and North European small nations in World War II, demonstrated that a unilateral declaration of neutral policy and a sincere desire to be left alone are no protection against domination whenever the balance of interests and power among major nations changes in favor of an expansionist power. Their experience with the illusion of neutrality forms much of the background for the Belgian, Dutch, Norwegian, Danish, and Luxembourg decisions of 1949 to protect their independence, not through neutrality and isolation, but through participation in the North Atlantic Alliance.

Declarations of Activist Nonalignment

The usual combination of isolation from and neutral attitude toward the international balancing process is generally described as *traditional strict neutrality,* in contrast to *activist neutralism* or *nonalignment*. Modern neutralism as practiced by many Asian and African nations is neither neutral to nor isolated from the major political conflict of our day. Modern declarations of nonalignment are actually declarations of maximum involvement. Unlike traditional neutralism, which was usually associated with a passive role in international politics or a narcissistic isolation, the modern form of activist nonalignment means a constant and dynamic effort to influence by words, example, or vote the behavior of major nations. Activist nonalignment is usually directed against any permanent entanglement with one or another of the great-power blocs. It is not necessarily opposed to alliances as such, but only to some of them. The Arab countries, for instance, are allied in the Arab League against Israel while condemning any other type of alliance. The Bandung Conference (1955) and other meetings of nonaligned countries from Asia and Africa represent an alignment of sorts against an alignment with Soviet Russia or the United States.

At the fourth meeting of nonaligned nations in Algiers (September 1973), for instance, the representatives of the 73 participating nations (see Document 13.1) agreed to apply diplomatic and economic measures against Israel, which was condemned for refusing to withdraw from occupied Arab

---

DOCUMENT 13.1

ALIGNMENT OF THE NONALIGNED

Participants in the 1973 Conference of Unaligned Nations

Afghanistan, Algeria, Argentina, Bangladesh, Bahrein, Bhutan, Botswana, Burma, Burundi, Cambodia, Cameroon, Central African Republic, Chad, Chile, Congo, Cuba, Cyprus, Dahomey, Egypt, Equatorial Guinea, Ethiopia, Gabon, Gambia, Ghana, Guinea, Guyana, India, Indonesia, Iraq, Ivory Coast, Jamaica, Jordan, Kenya, Kuwait, Laos, Lebanon, Lesotho, Liberia, Libya, Madagascar, Malawi, Malaysia, Morocco, Peru, Qatar, Saudi Arabia, Sierra Leone, Singapore, Somalia, South Vietnam (Viet Cong), Mali, Malta, Mauritania, Mauritius, Nepal, Niger, Nigeria, Oman, Sri Lanka, Sudan, Swaziland, Syria, Tanzania, Togo, Trinidad, Tunisia, Uganda, United Arab Emirates, Upper Volta, South Yemen, Yugoslavia, Zaire, and Zambia.

Observers and Special Guests at the 1973 Conference of Unaligned Nations

Observers: Barbados, Bolivia, Brazil, Colombia, Ecuador, Mexico, Panama, Uruguay and Venezuela, 14 African anticolonial movements, the Puerto Rican Socialist party, and the Palestine Liberation Organization. Special guests: Austria, Finland, and Sweden. Secretary-General Waldheim also attended.

First Five Summit Conferences

1. Belgrade, 1961 (25 members and 3 observers).
2. Cairo, 1964 (47 members and 10 observers).
3. Lusaka (Zambia), 1970 (52 members and 11 observers).
4. Georgetown (Guyana), 1972 (foreign ministers only).
5. Algiers, 1973 (73 members and 25 observers).

---

territories (this was a few weeks before the Yom Kippur war); to support insurgent movements in Portuguese Guinea, Angola, and Mozambique by starting a fund to help finance those movements' armed forces; to ask for a reorganization of the United Nations to give the Nonaligned Third World a greater voice, especially by eliminating or reducing the five big powers' supremacy in the Security Council, and to press for general world disarmament, including a ban on the construction and testing of nuclear weapons. In the economic field, these nations reemphasized their right to full control over natural resources and other themes concerning foreign investment and trade which were first articulated at the United Nations Conference on Trade and Development in 1964 (UNCTAD); in a more radical way these themes were finally expressed in the new Charter of Economic Rights and Duties of States (December 12, 1974).

While underdevelopment is the most important common denominator, of the nations of the nonaligned world, in the political field the opposition against alignment with one superpower or the other varies in intensity and leads to considerable tensions within the Nonaligned World. Among the 73 participants in the conference were a Soviet ally and customer, Castro's Cuba, and other nations or revolutionary groups clearly committed to one superpower rather than the other—pro-Soviet India, the Provisional Revolutionary Government of South Vietnam (the Viet Cong)—and among the observers were pro-American Bolivia and Brazil. The status of observer was also granted to 14 anticolonial guerrilla movements in Africa, the Palestine Liberation Organization, and the Puerto Rican Socialist party, which advocates secession from the United States. On the other hand, the four real European neutrals, Switzerland, Austria, Finland, and Sweden, were not even granted the status of observers; the last three were invited as "special guests"—whatever that means.

Modern neutralism is intimately connected with the new nations' domestic problems. "For a new state, foreign policy is domestic policy pursued by other means," notes the former director of the Office of Research and Analysis for Africa in the U.S. Department of State, Robert C. Good. "It is domestic policy carried beyond the boundaries of the state."[4] The proclamation of nonalignment combined with an almost febrile activity on the international scene "perpetuates the cohesive role of the revolution against colonialism" and helps to establish the new nation's identity, which, seen from within, appears an uncertain entity. In external relations the identity of the new state is fully recognized: It becomes a member of the United Nations, where it votes, speaks, criticizes the foolishness of the great powers, and thunders against its former colonial master. All this is duly reported in the local press, a useful point for the next election or for the discouragement of any opposition. The prime ministers or foreign ministers of the nonaligned states travel to Moscow, Peking, and Washington, where they are received with full honors and often succeed in playing one power bloc against another in order to receive economic aid from both sides. As Good concludes, a new nation's legitimacy is more easily asserted through its foreign policy than through its domestic policy. Domestic issues tend to divide a new state along tribal, linguistic, or religious lines, but the policy of activist neutralism tends to unite it, at the same time enhancing the prestige of the national leader.

As we have seen, some proclamations of foreign policy or communications of views on the international scene have a double function: to serve the needs of foreign policy and also, sometimes dominantly, the needs of internal unity and development. This is so not only in the case of newly developing nations but often also in the case of long-established nations. Such an old and highly developed democracy as Switzerland consciously connects its proclamations of strict, classic neutrality with its internal needs for unity. The director of the Graduate Institute of International Studies at Geneva, Jacques Freymond, frankly admits:

> [the] neutrality which the Swiss cantons have been led to adopt in order to maintain the federal link remains today the cement of their unity. . . one of the requirements of their domestic equilibrium. . . . A foreigner who observes from the outside the peaceful and prosperous country does not always grasp the effort required to insure its stability, to smooth out the inevitable tensions which crop up in a multilingual country, and compensate for the attractions exerted by various national cultures [German, French, and Italian] to which Switzerland belongs without being the homeland of those cultures.[5]

Diplomatic Protest

Unlike declarations of involvement or neutrality, which aim to influence the *future* behavior of states, a diplomatic protest refers to and objects to some past behavior, such as violation of territorial waters, air space, or contractual obligation, or an offensive statement in the press or in a public speech. Often the goal of a diplomatic protest is only to put the protesting nation's anger on record for future reference, domestic or international. No real response to the protest is expected. At other times the purpose of a diplomatic protest is to redress a past wrong or prevent a future one. The diplomatic protest has been defined by Joseph C. McKenna as "an intergovernmental communication expressing dissatisfaction with the offically approved policy or action of the recipient state on the grounds that the policy or action violates the complaining state's legal or moral obligation to the sender, and asking redress of grievance."[6] McKenna found that the diplomatic protests of the United States were unsuccessful in 20 percent of the cases he studied, uncertain in 25 percent, and successful in 55 percent. The successes of the 55 percent were occasionally due to the strength of the argument, but more often compliance was the result of an implicit threat of diplomatic chill or worse. A nation with less power than the United States to harm the interests of the recipient nation would show a much less satisfactory record in the effectiveness of its diplomatic protests.

The form of diplomatic protest is usually a diplomatic note transmitted from one government to another. Sometimes the protest assumes the form of symbolic gestures.

Symbolic Gestures Symbolic gestures are used to communicate friendly intentions or protest, displeasure, or hostility. Among the friendly gestures that otherwise do not affect the material balance of power we find naval visits, a deliberate care in attending the target nation's diplomatic functions, festivals, or exhibitions, respecting and honoring the foreign nation's days of national triumph or grief, raising the rank of a diplomatic mission from legation to embassy, and agreements on cultural exchanges or trade. The unfriendly gestures include diplomatic snubs, recall of an ambassador, appointing a diplomat or negotiator of a lower rank than the issue seems to warrant, severance of diplomatic relations, and such military gestures (display of weapons, military parades, or maneuvers) as "would have little impact on the outcome of hostilities should they occur."[7]

Mob Protest Since the late 1950s a new form of international protest has frequently appeared on the scene: protest against the policies of a nation by an engineered mob action, usually directed against its embassy, information offices, or tourist agency. Some such protests may be spontaneous, but most are sponsored and organized by the same government that originally authorized foreign activities on its soil and promised to respect and protect the building that the mob, imitating spontaneity, now attacks and often burns down. When in 1965 Tunisia's President Bourguiba suggested that the Arab states should at long last recognize the existence of the state of Israel on the basis of the original United Nations proposal of 1947 (which, if applied now, would mean a modification of Israel's boundaries in favor of Egypt and Jordan, an international status for Jerusalem, and repatriation of the Arab refugees), the United Arab Republic protested by sending a mob against the Tunisian embassy in Cairo; Tunisia replied by directing a mob against the United Arab Republic's embassy in Tunis. In connection with the war in Vietnam, American embassies, consulates, and Information Agency libraries and cultural centers were the favorite targets of pacifist, leftist, and communist mob protests. Some were spontaneous, many were not. It was calculated that within a ten-year period (1955-1965) American libraries abroad were the target of forty major mob demonstrations that took the form of smashing windows and furniture, burning books, and destroying exhibits. On one occasion in Cairo, in 1964, a mob burned 24,000 books as a protest against the role of the United States in rescuing white hostages in the Congo. The U.S. Information Agency maintains more than 150 libraries and reading rooms stocking a total of 2,400,000 books all over the world; unlike the embassies themselves, they are usually located in overcrowded downtown areas of major cities, and it is easy for professional agitators to direct crowds toward them. For many days after a mob protest, the ruins of a smashed library or burned cultural center remind the passerby of the successful mob action against the symbol of the power of the United States. The smashed symbol of American power is an image cherished by many an anti-American government, which explains why the government that had authorized an American library sometimes sends the agitators to destroy it and then pays with apologies for the damages done. Mob violence has thus become a noisy accompaniment to diplomacy's soft words, sometimes even supporting a government's request for aid or a loan (see Figure 13.2).

ARMAMENTS

Increasing one's power is the most frequent and often the most effective means by which a nation's intentions and capabilities are explicitly or implicitly communicated to other nations and by which its readiness for possible future contingencies, including violent confrontation, are materially enhanced. By this method a nation's will may be successfully imposed on others or the imposition of a hostile design may be discouraged and, in war, resisted. The crudest and the most usual form of increasing a nation's power is *armament*. It is an eloquent signal and, with the exception of secret plans and weapons, can hardly pass unnoticed by foreign nations; often, it is sufficient to read the arming nations' newspapers and national budget. (see Document 13.2).

Mobilization of Resources

Under the present world conditions of advanced technology and mass-based governments, an arms race is bound to entail much more than the building up of armies and arsenals; it also means a deliberate, publicized mobilization of many other ingredients of national power: industrial, technological, scientific, and agricultural resources, in combination with a psychological mobilization of the public. By an appropriate "hate campaign," public opinion is readied for hardship or a possible clash in case military, economic, and psychological mobilization fails to have the desired deterrent effect. Mobilization of the elements of national power may, of course, provoke identical efforts on the opposing side, whatever its original intentions may have been. We have already noted in another context that in the balancing process the vicious circle of measures and countermeasures, suspicion and countersuspicion usually leads to a dangerous and costly inflationary spiral. And yet the failure to respond to a potential enemy's increase in power—a unilateral disarmament of sorts—may lead to such an imbalance that war becomes inevitable. In the

DOCUMENT 13.2

THE ATOMIC ARMS RACE

Alamogordo, New Mexico (first test)	July 16, 1945
Hiroshima (20 kilotons, first use in war)	August 6, 1945
Nagasaki	August 9, 1945
First Soviet atomic test	September 23, 1949
First British atomic test	October 1, 1952
First United States hydrogen bomb (Eniwetok)	November 1, 1952
First Soviet hydrogen bomb	August 12, 1953
First Soviet orbiting satellite (Sputnik)	October 4, 1957
First American satellite	January 31, 1958
First French A-bomb (Sahara)	February 13, 1960
First Soviet manned spaceship	April 12, 1961
Soviet resumption of thermonuclear tests (explosion of superbombs with an explosive force equivalent to 20-100 megatons)	September 1, 1961
Test-ban treaty (U.S., U.K., and USSR)	August 5, 1963
Hot line agreement (Moscow-Washington)	August 31, 1963
First Chinese atomic test	October 16, 1964
First French satellite	November 26, 1965
First Chinese hydrogen bomb (Lob Nor)	June 18, 1967
First French hydrogen bomb (Mururoa Atoll)	August 29, 1968
First Chinese satellite	April 25, 1970
First American and Soviet MIRVs	1969-1974
First Indian Atomic Explosion	May 18, 1974

1930s this point was made by Winston Churchill and time and again by the critics of the pacifist and socialist agitation against rearmament in England and France. The pacifist mood and disarmament in Western Europe does indeed seem to have contributed to Hitler's belief that neither England nor France would dare to oppose his plan of world conquest or that both would be crushed if they tried to stand in his way.

Transfer of Weapons

A given distribution of power among nations may be affected by a geographic shift of arms without their quantitative increase or qualitative improvement. In 1947, for instance, the Truman Doctrine (military aid to Greece and Turkey) would have affected the balance of power in the eastern Mediterranean even if it had not mobilized an additional ounce of American resources, simply by redirecting and specifically retargeting the existing capabilities. In our time of mutual nuclear paralysis and superpower involvement in local and internal wars, a shift of weapons to either the insurgents or the incumbents profoundly affects international stability. Also, for instance, changing the targets of the existing MIRVs in Russia from locations in the United States to Peking, Shanghai, Canton, and Lob Nor (the site of China's atomic installations) would certainly greatly affect the world situation even if not a single bayonet were to be added to the Soviet arsenals. The issue of the transfer of nuclear technology became a major worry for the Soviet Union during the second phase of the Strategic Arms Limitations Talks (SALT) in 1973 and 1974, when Moscow was faced with a possibility it had long been determined to block: the construction of a full-fledged and independent European nuclear deterrent, including West German acquisition of control over nuclear weapons.[8]

FIGURE 13.2
THE NEW DIPLOMACY

"They want to borrow another 100 million."

Drawing by Roland Michaud in *Look*, 1965.

COALITIONS AND ALLIANCES

Resistance to domination may be increased either by a nation's own effort or by combining such an effort with that of other nations. The necessary precondition for cooperative effort among nations is the realization that a threat to their freedom of action, welfare, or survival is coming from the same source, whether it is the policy of one particular nation or a group of nations. The recognition of the existence of a threat does not mean that its intensity will be viewed as identical by all nations concerned. Their attitude will vary according to their own power of resistance and their geographic proximity to the source of the threat.

Alliances, bilateral or multilateral, are usually directed against an enemy identified in advance although not always mentioned by name in the treaty. None of the Western alliances mentions Soviet Russia or Communist China by name, but almost all these pacts have these countries and their potentially aggressive policies in mind. Only the ANZUS treaty of 1951 (an alliance between Australia, New Zealand, and the United States) was initially meant as an alliance against a possible renewal of Japanese imperialism. Most of the communist alliances mention as their target, in the words of the Soviet-Bulgarian Treaty, "Germany trying to resume her aggressive policy or any other State which directly or in any other form would be associated with Germany in a policy of aggression." Germany is mentioned; the United States is meant. (See Document 13.3.)

The Effectiveness of Alliances

In combination with armaments, alliances and counteralliances represent the most frequent and effective measures for maintaining, disturbing, or restoring a balance among nations. As with weapons, the sheer existence of an alliance is supposed to deter war by notifying and warning the potential aggressor about the increased power of resistance. The proclaimed and publicized community of interests implies the existence of a power pool, but there is often more publicity than real pooling of power. Many a meeting of allied councils is, in reality, a series of rituals, speeches, resolutions, ceremonial signatures of pacts, and diplomatic banquets and other pomp and circumstance. Showmanship is as much a part of public relations in alliances as it is in commercial activities.

The deterrent quality of alliances is primarily determined by two factors:

1. The community of interests, whether it is produced by a common fear, ambition, an ideology, a plan of expansion, or material profit.
2. The structure and performance of the alliance's organization, which may translate the common interest into more or less effective common action.

DOCUMENT 13.3

ALLIANCES

North Atlantic Treaty Organization (NATO)—April 4, 1949
Fifteen nations (the United States, Canada, Iceland, Norway, Britain, the Netherlands, Denmark, Belgium, Luxembourg, Portugal, France, Italy, Greece, Turkey, and West Germany) pledged to take such action individually and collectively as they deem necessary in case of an external armed attack on any of them, which they will regard as an armed attack on all. Armed forces are assigned to the NATO command prior to the outbreak of hostilities. Based on Article 51 of the United Nations Charter, which recognizes the "inherent right of individual and collective self-defense."

The Warsaw Pact—May 14, 1955
Seven nations (the Soviet Union, Bulgaria, Czechoslovakia, East Germany, Hungary, Poland, and Rumania) pledged mutual support in case of an external armed attack on any of them. The Pact's common command and political council parallel the structure of NATO. Pro-Chinese and anti-Soviet Communist Albania and neutralist Yugoslavia are not members. According to the Brezhnev Doctrine, the Warsaw Pact may also be used for the purpose of armed interference to protect communism against undersirable reform or rebellion. It was soused in 1968 to eliminate "socialism with a human face" in Czechoslovakia. Based on Article 51 of the United Nations Charter.

Organization of American States (OAS)—September 2, 1947
Twenty-one American republics (Canada is not a member) agreed to regard an armed attack or threat directed against the Western Hemisphere or any American state as an attack or threat directed against all. It is the only alliance that provides for action in case of attack coming not only from without but also from the Organ of Consultation, may order economic sanctions or recommend military measures. The area protected comprises the whole Western Hemisphere, including portions of the North and South polar regions, Canada, and the Galápagos. Based on Article 51 of the United Nations Charter.

Southeast Asia Treaty Organization (SEATO)—September 8, 1954
Eight nations (U.S.A., U.K., France, Australia, New Zealand, Pakistan, Thailand, and the Philippines) agreed to resist armed attack by collective action. The area protected by the treaty excludes Taiwan and Hong Kong. France and Pakistan are no longer members. Based on Article 51 of the United Nations Charter.

Central Treaty Organization (CENTO)—February–November 1955
Great Britain, Turkey, Iran, and Pakistan pledged to consult on measures of self-defense in case of a threat to the peace in the Middle East. The United States, although not a signatory member has provided funds and arms and participated in the work of CENTO's economic antisubversion and military committees. By 1974 CENTO was practically defunct. Based on Article 51 of the United Nations Charter.

Whenever a community of interest among nations has been expressed in a common machinery, such a superstructure may be viewed as a rudimentary international (regional or functional) government. Alliances often are loose confederations.

Only a very few alliances, as noted in Chapter 10, have succeeded in transforming themselves into federal unions. The defensive alliance of three German cantons in the Alps, for example, was the nucleus around which the Swiss federal state was finally built; from a rather loosely organized anti-British fighting league the American colonies transformed themselves into first a confederal and then a federal state.

The duration and the effectiveness of any alliance, like that of any state, are determined by the continuation and the intensity of common interests as well as by the performance and the responsiveness of the organization superstructure to the needs and claims of the members. If the consensus fades away or if the alliance's machinery is poorly led, an alliance may break up; it may become an alliance only on paper, endowed with no real power.

Erosion of Alliances

Contemporary alliances are highly asymmetric in terms of power: Either one or the other nuclear superpower is necessarily their leader. The inevitability of superpower leadership and asymmetry in international organizations as well as the members' inevitable resentment against asymmetry and superpower leadership has already been noted in Chapter 10 (see the section on "The Inevitability of Leadership and Resentment"). Without the nuclear and economic might of the leading superpower the alliance would be ineffective, but with it, it has problems. The superpower at the helm not only is a source of economic aid and sophisticated as well as costly weapons but also is the main fountain of political and strategic concepts. The superpower's leadership is easily criticized or resented on many counts: because it commits errors in the estimate of the situation or in tactics or strategy, errors that may ruin the alliance; or because it behaves in a domineering and arrogant fashion, even though its policy is correct and in the interest of all; or, finally, because the leading power acts or is suspected of acting in its own selfish interest instead of in the interest of the collective whole.

The suspicion of potential domination and exploitation has nothing to do with the real intentions of the leading power, which perhaps may wish to serve and not abuse its power. But the suspicion that great capabilities may lead to great abuses seems inevitable.

In 1965 a Canadian politician described the dilemma of a small ally who is the neighbor of a superpower in these terms:

We like the feeling of security and well-being that comes from living next door to the United States. But while we like you, we are also worried about you. American cultural, economic and political influence so pervade our way of life that we have begun to wonder if one relatively small nation can retain its independence in the face of the strong pressures by our giant neighbor to the south.[9]

Columnist James Reston, reporting on the speech in the *New York Times*, added the following comment: "The problem is that the United States is simply too big and powerful for the comfort of its associates, and the dilemma is that both the military security and psychological insecurity of the allies come from this same American source."

Both the Soviet and Western alliance systems suffer similar strains; they increase in proportion to the growth of self-confidence mixed with uncertainty on the part of medium-sized and small nations. Feeling that the nuclear stalemate perhaps makes a direct use of violence by superpowers less probable, the lesser powers tend to resent support, direction, or interference by the leading member of the existing alliance. Neutrality becomes an attractive alternative.

A brief summary of the "stresses and strains of going it" with other nations[10] in both the Western and Soviet alliances will illustrate the process of erosion. It is a consequence of changes in the international situation that have affected the community of interests in the foundations of the alliances and conditioned the attitude of the lesser allies to the superpower at the top of each alliance's structure.

The Atlantic Alliance

When the North Atlantic Alliance (NATO, the North Atlantic Treaty Organization) was established in 1949, the major interests of Western European nations and the United States were complementary.[11] Western Europe, exhausted after a long war, needed and eagerly accepted the massive support of the American economy. This was also the period of American atomic monopoly; the atomic and then hydrogen arsenals (the first H-bomb was exploded on November 1, 1952) of the United States were viewed as the only deterrent to the huge Soviet land armies, poised against Western Europe across the North European plain. In 1948 (the year of the communist conquest of Czechoslovakia and of the dangerous Berlin blockade), Stalinist Russia seemed, rightly or wrongly, bent on an ambitious expansion of communism by blackmail or force. Europe was still the primary area of conflict; events in Asia and Africa were shattering but secondary (the culmination of the civil war in China in 1949, conflict in Korea six months later, and the French and the British wars against the communists in Indochina and Malaya).

At that time, the West European allies entertained some doubts and suspicions, mostly on two accounts, about the leading power of the alliance, the United States: First, the United States might pay undue attention to the Asian theater at the expense of Western Europe and without consulting it. Second, the United States, viewed by many Europeans as an inexperienced and politically unsophisticated giant, might act perhaps too rashly in Europe and trigger the A-bomb prematurely or unnecessarily. The French expressed their hope for deterrence but fear of war by saying: "We cannot afford another liberation." Europe wanted to be protected by the atomic terror, not experience it on its own battlefield.

Twenty-five years later the situation had changed so profoundly that United States Secretary of State Henry Kissinger described the European-American relationship within NATO in rather bitter terms (March 11, 1974), subsequently slightly amended to soothe European nerves:

> The biggest problem American foreign policy confronts right now is not to regulate competition with its enemies—we have a generation of experience with that and with ups and downs we are going to handle it—but how to bring our friends to a realization that there are greater common interests than simply self-assertiveness.

Since the late fifties strong and prosperous Western Europe, working toward a confederal West European Community, has no longer needed the economic assistance of the United States and has begun to dread American domination and selfishness. While Western Europe and Berlin remained important issues between the West and the Soviet Union, problems in the Middle East, Asia, Africa, and Latin America asserted themselves with insistence. In the non-European areas the American and West European interests did not coincide; often they clashed. Since, as we have noted, nations cooperate more easily and effectively *against* rather than *for* something, the image of a more smiling Russia under the folksy Khrushchev, and later that of a pragmatic Russia under the dull and seemingly matter-of-fact trio of Brezhnev, Kosygin, and Podgorny proved a much less effective cement of Atlantic unity than did the image of Stalinist Russia. (It should be recalled that not only Truman but also Stalin was an architect of the Atlantic Alliance.) A nuclear stalemate replaced the former reliance on the atomic superiority of the United States. Those West Europeans who in 1949 might have feared an irresponsible triggering of the American atomic bomb began to doubt in the 1960s that Paris (or any other European city) could ever be considered by Washington worth an exchange of atomic salvos between the United States and the Soviet Union. From this background the French desire to have their own atomic deterrent power (*force de frappe*) also issued.

It would be wrong to present the stresses and strains in the Western alliance only as a result of a clash of personalities (De Gaulle versus Johnson or Giscard d'Estaing versus Ford) or of European and American interests in different parts of the world. There was also, inevitably, an honest difference of opinion about the best policy and strategy in the present era. Conditioned by different national histories and experiences, anchored in different geographic situations, Americans and Europeans were bound to interpret many events differently. This applied also to nuclear stalemate. The first two atomic bombs ever used in war and not on a test ground were directed against an enemy that, on the verge of defeat, had only conventional weapons to retaliate with. Therefore only speculation, some experience from testing, and the game of mathematical probabilities—but no real experience—color European and American thinking about the nature and consequences of a possible clash between nations possessing nuclear arsenals. The characteristic feature of NATO nuclear readiness is the so-called two-key system, which requires the consent of the member-nation from whose territory an American nuclear weapon is to be fired. There is no similar provision in the Warsaw Pact, where the Soviet nuclear dominance seems to be absolute. Also in contrast to NATO, where the presence of several American officers in key offices within the French or German ministries of national defense would be unacceptable, the penetration by Russian personnel of high, medium, and even low commands of the Warsaw Pact forces is general, thorough, and more or less public.

The Communist Alliances

A process of erosion has also affected the communist alliances. The reasons are similar. Like Paris, Peking began to wonder in the late 1950s under what circumstances Russia would be ready to use its atomic arsenal for the protection of some vital Chinese interests and thus risk the destruction of much that the Soviet Union has been building over the past forty years. There was also the clash of personalities, the clash of different national traditions, Asian resentment against European allies, and differences in geographic priorities. In analyzing stresses in alliances, Arnold Wolfers used the parallel of a wheel whose hub is formed by the leading power. Its allies are spread out along the rim, each occupying the end of a spoke. Danger to any allied country is communicated to the hub as a threat to the entire wheel and elicits a correspondingly defensive reaction. The estimate of the danger would vary according to the different perspective that a nation has when placed at the hub or at the rim, or, even more important, at the opposite point of the rim from a particular other nation.[12] This image, originally meant to illustrate the erosion of the Western allies, applies fully to the situation among the communist allies, including the Sino-Soviet competition as to who has the right to be at the hub. For Peking, the situation around Berlin presents a different set of priorities than the situation around the Chinese offshore islands of Quemoy and Matsu, around Taiwan, or in Vietnam.

We have noted that when the conciliatory image of the Soviet Union replaced the former militant one, it had an eroding effect on the Western allies. The same sort of change affects communist alliances. The "new look" of the United States, first John F. Kennedy's administration, then the period of Kissinger's diplomatic initiatives that led to the end of war in Vietnam, and then Nixon's state visits to Peking and Moscow and Ford's continuation of the détente in the Middle East, resulted in some new thoughts among the allies of the Soviet Union. Given the tightly centralized and authoritarian control that Moscow exercises over the structure and functioning of the Warsaw alliance system, no real weakening of the official ties took place; there was no development corresponding to France's, England's, or West Germany's assertions of diplomatic independence. Nevertheless, the new look of the United States had its effect on the popular mood of the Warsaw Pact nations, especially the mood of the young generation, which spread into the rank and file of the armed forces. How reliable, for instance, could be the loyalty of the Polish, Hungarian, Czechoslovak, and Rumanian contingents of the Warsaw Pact forces in any direct confrontation with other-than-German contingents of the NATO forces? Even in the Soviet Union itself the journal of the Soviet armed forces (*Kommunist vooruzhennikh sil*, October 1969) complained that the younger Soviet generation lacked "hatred" for the West, demonstrated "immature class feelings" and pacifism, and put forward "distorted notions about humanism." The journal advocated a better training of young recruits in "hatred for the enemy" lest they forget that "American ideologists and bourgeois propaganda have a pathological hatred toward socialism" and that in Vietnam "Yanks in uniform torture old men, women and children, drop bombs on peaceful cities and villages, and employ napalm and poison gases." If Soviet youth is in such need of reeducation in hatred against the adversary of the Warsaw Pact, how much more would reeducation be needed in present-day Rumania, Czechoslovakia, Hungary, and Poland.

Nonalignment as an Erosive Element

There is still another element that adds to the strains within both the Western and the Soviet alliances: the relative success of nonalignment. The leading powers have the capacity and willingness to increase the power and well-being not only of their allies but also of more or less friendly neutrals. The aim of many Soviet, American, and Chinese aid programs—often received simultaneously by the same country—is to prevent nonaligned nations from being lured or frightened into alignment. As noted previously, some recipients diligently play the superpowers against one another and get richer in the process. They hope that in this way their independence of power blocs will not only be preserved but actually be compensated for. The superpowers go along with this gambit, sometimes with the hope of gaining an ally, but always with the aim of denying the coveted neutral to the other side.

Whatever the reasons for economic or other assistance to a nonaligned nation, its neutral status does raise some questions in the minds of many allies. If advantages derived from an alliance with a mighty ally are being bestowed upon a neutral, including military assistance in case of need (such as the Anglo-American assistance to India when it was attacked by Communist China), the position of neutralism becomes very attractive. One has all the advantages and none of the disadvantages that result from an alliance among unequal partners. Yugoslavia in this respect is a particularly interesting example. This communist country has politically achieved what is physically impossible: It keeps its foot in three relatively open doors simultaneously—the Soviet, Western, and the Third World doors.

The erosive factor in the Western and the Soviet systems has also led to reinterpretations of their alliances that now occasionally permit an ally to seek an accommodation with the adversary against whom the alliance was initially directed. Communist Rumania, for instance, which has remained neutral in the Sino-Soviet and Soviet-Albanian conflicts, has asserted its economic independence of Russia by forming several important links with industries and banks in West Germany, the United States, and France. Rumania has placed a new emphasis on its Latin culture and replaced Russian with French as the most important language to be taught in schools. In August 1969, it was the first communist country to receive a President of the United States on an official state visit.

In Asia, local antagonisms are combined with the growing doubt of many Asian nations about the United States, in terms not of its willingness but of its capacity and skill to fight and win a guerrilla war in the context of revolutionary social reform. This has resulted in the efforts of some Asian countries to seek accommodation with Communist China or, at least, to create an impression of a lesser identification with the West by emphasizing their Asian orientation. Pakistan left the SEATO alliance in 1972 and sought a new accommodation with China in response to the United States and Soviet support of Pakistan's main enemy, India. And in the 1960s the Philippines, formerly one of the staunchest SEATO allies of the United States in the Pacific, became more concerned with domestic than external defense problems; a part of the internal problem was the desire to break the cultural identification of the Philippines with the United States and to reassert Asian and Malay identity of the Filipinos.

In our analysis of the erosive process in all alliance systems, the focus has been on the resentment and centrifugal tendencies on the part of other than the leading powers. The picture would not be complete if we were not to add that the erosive process may also start from the top, not only as a result of a superpower's impatience with reluctant or ungrateful allies, but also as a consequence of technological advancement, especially in the accuracy and range of nuclear-tipped missiles. Some allies and their geographic location that were an indispensable asset in the past, for example, because they provided missile bases, may become burdens or irrelevant entities in the future. The fall of any of the ill-defined and internally unstable states in Asia or Africa—compared by one scholar to "sponges"[13]—cannot affect the nuclear balance of power between Washington and Moscow. This view has been criticized by those theorists who contend that the passage of any small country from one camp to the other, though unimportant in itself, may initiate a chain of events—the domino theory—which, in the case of the United States, might begin in Saigon and via Taiwan, Japan, and Hawaii reach Washington or, in the case of the Soviet Union, might begin in Prague and via Poland and the Ukraine reach Moscow. Overreaction by the United States in Vietnam or the Dominican Republic and by the Soviet Union in Hungary or Czechoslovakia suggests, however, that even illusory dominoes are the stuff of which American and Soviet hawks may be made.

To sum up: In contrast to the traditional European balancing process in the nineteenth century, which developed between three or more major powers and was fundamentally affected by shifting alliances or allegiances of smaller nations, the present, basically bipolar balancing process is primarily characterized by both secret and publicized increases in the military and technological capabilities of the two superpowers.

Spheres of Influence

The term "spheres of influence" is old. It dates from the period when Western European nations, notably England, France, and Germany, were carving Asia and Africa among themselves and trying to determine the acceptable limits of their respective colonial slices. In the American context, strangely enough, the term has a bad connotation, just as do such other allegedly European terms as "alliances" or "power." In fact, however, starting with the Monroe Doctrine, the United States has always acted according to the "spheric" principle where it could, although it condemned the principle in speeches. The Soviet Union, on the other hand, has constantly and consistently acted according to and openly referred to the "spheric" principle. As Hans J. Morgenthau noted: "The Soviet Union and the United States have always regarded spheres of influence as consonant with their respective national interests, though the latter has denied this fact in its national rhetoric."[14] The Western Hemisphere was constantly viewed by the United States as its sphere of decisive influence. The Soviet Union now views Eastern Europe, part of the Baltic, and Northern Europe as its sphere. In both spheres we may note some loopholes: Cuba in the Caribbean, Austria in Eastern Europe, and Finland,

Sweden, Norway, and Denmark in Northern and Baltic Europe. Today, it seems that a sphere of influence is usually coextensive with the alliance system that one of the superpowers succeeded in establishing or imposing on that area and to which it has the overwhelming capability of denying the opposite power politico-military access. Nations outside the formal alliance systems are also outside the spheres of *decisive* influence and therefore in the gray zone of contending influences.

DECREASING THE RIVAL POWER

In all balancing processes, physical or political, an approximation of an equilibrium may be obtained not only by increasing the weight on one scale (in international politics by armaments or alliances) but also by decreasing it on the opposite scale or by doing both simultaneously.

The methods used to weaken the opponent's power are extremely varied. Some are lumped together under the heading of overt and covert intervention or interference in the domestic affairs of another nation, usually with the aim of affecting the target nation's policies or its capability to pursue them. Penetration of a nation's policy-making institution by agents or sympathizers, bribery of opinion makers, infiltration of the mass media, and open propaganda belong to the category of deliberate interference whose primary target is not the material substance of the national power but its future uses for the purpose of achieving national objectives. Before World War II, for instance, fascist Italy spent millions to influence the writings and editorial policies of the leading conservative dailies and weeklies in France.

The purposes and methods of interference were discussed in detail in Chapter 11, especially in the three sections dealing with internationalized internal wars, routine transnational penetration, and political manipulation of international economic relations.

COLLECTIVE SECURITY: GLOBAL IMBALANCE

The idea of collective security is to group all peace-loving nations in a grand alliance against any aggressor who may violate the peace at any time at any place in the world. The identity of the aggressor is not stated or implied, although in both the Covenant of the League of Nations and the United Nations Charter the assumption seemed to be that only autocratic monarchies or fascist dictatorships are capable of initiating a war. Theoretically, the collective security is supposed to protect all nations against hazards inherent in the nature of the international system itself.

The concept and practice of collective security was discussed in Chapter 10, which dealt with the United Nations and other international organizations.

DISARMAMENT

In an era of the rising destructiveness and cost of modern weapons, it is only natural that the problem of disarmament is one of the single most dramatic issues on the stage of international politics. Never before—thanks to modern communications and missiles—have the nations of the world been physically so close to one another and never before has their capacity completely to annihilate each other been so absolute. In the 1960s and 1970s, disarmament conferences between the major and smaller powers in Geneva, Vienna, and Helsinki have been practically continuous. The United States has created a special executive department for the sole purpose of the study and promotion of disarmament, the Arms Control and Disarmament Agency.

Some people take the disarmament efforts very seriously. Some are less convinced, feeling that while no major power today can afford not to pay at least lip service to the desirability of disarmament, the time to disarm has not yet come.

The Statistics of Overkill

So far not only great industrial powers but even the poorest nations of the Third World have continued to consider it in their national interest to divert their resources increasingly toward armaments. The United States Arms Control and Disarmament Agency, which has been compiling data on world military expenditures for 120 countries since 1964, has noted the unmistakable trend toward further rises in such expenditures. In 1969 total world military spending reached a record of $200 billion, an increase of 44 percent since 1964, when the agency began compiling the national data; over that six-year period more than $1 trillion was spent for arms and the armed forces.[15] This sum is more than twice as much as the yearly income of the world's 93 underdeveloped countries, in which more than 2.5 billion people live. The world's military budgets in this period took as much public money as was spent by all governments on all forms of public education and health care.

One of the most striking—and disturbing—aspects of the latest trends in world military spending is the "upward spiral of arms budgets in the poorer countries."[16] The military expenditures for developing nonaligned nations represent an increasing proportion of world outlays. While the world's economic standard of living in real terms has improved little, the diversion of resources to military purposes has expanded in step with the world's capacity to produce. The burden of military spending per capita has grown larger in the same period, the burden being greatest in the poorer countries. In 1964, a survey prepared by United Press International indicated that the nations of Africa take out of their meager resources a sum of $845 million a year for armaments. In some cases the percentage that the African nations are willing and able to spend on arms was well above 15 percent: the Congo, 25 percent; Mauritania, 21.5 percent; Morocco, 20.2 percent; Cameroon, 16 percent; and Ethiopia, 15.7 percent.

In absolute terms, of course, the most advanced industrial nations continue to dominate world outlays, especially the United States, the Soviet Union, the People's Republic of China, and France, which are also the biggest suppliers of weapons to the developing world.[17] In the 1970s, it was estimated that the world's stockpile of nuclear weapons was equivalent to twenty tons of TNT for every human being on earth. This is called the overkill capability. It was further estimated that the United States alone had the overkill capability of destroying 140 major Soviet cities at least 100 times and probably 2,000 times over. The overkill capacity appears to most people to be sheer folly. Nuclear strategic experts argue that adding up billions of tons of TNT and subdividing them by the total number of the world population does not tell the whole story. If peace is partly based on the atomic balance of power, including the possibility of deterring or retaliating against a surprise attack, atomic weapons that are not accurate would have to be used not only against cities but also against small military targets, many of which would be concealed, dispersed, or protected by hardened sites. In such a context many millions of tons of TNT would, so to speak, be wasted.

Arguments for Disarmament

The contemporary dimensions of the nuclear arms race among the superpowers and the conventional arms race in the rest of the world should induce all nations to take a hard look at what they have been doing and reconsider whether the present tempo and cost of the arms race will not, even without war, ultimately lead to economic near-suicide. (See Figure 13.3.)

In this context four of the many arguments in favor of international concentration on the issue of disarmament, or at least reduction and control of armaments, should be identified:

1. The armament race is not merely economically unproductive; it is a very costly economic waste. Equating the cost of sophisticated complex missiles with the cost of new hospitals, schools, or social welfare programs is especially depressing.
2. The sheer existence of weapons may induce their use. Allegedly, the existence of the atomic bomb was at least one of the reasons for its use against defeated Japan. General Leslie Groves, head of the supersecret Manhattan Project during World War II, writes:

FIGURE 13.3
THE SUICIDAL ARMS RACE

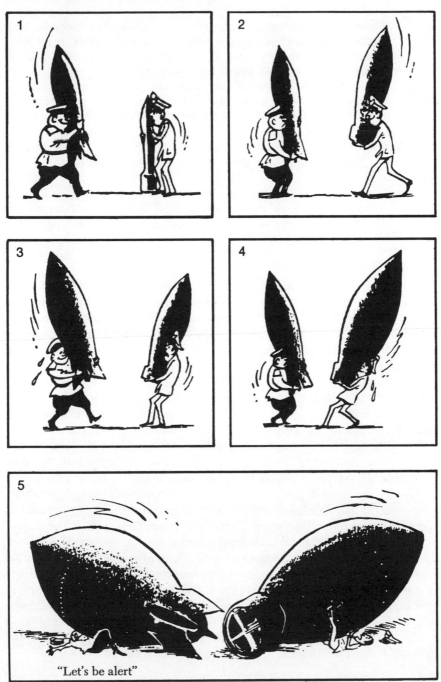

Drawing by Behrendt in *Het Parool*, Amsterdam, 1967.

> When we first began to develop atomic energy, the United States was in no way committed to employ atomic weapons against any other power. With the activation of the Manhattan project, however, the situation began to change. Our work was extremely costly, both in money and in its interference with the rest of the war effort. As time went on, and we poured more and more money and effort into the project, the government became increasingly committed to the ultimate use of the bomb.[18]

In 1974, commenting on the cease-fire in the Middle East with skepticism (*New York Times*, January 20, 1974), C. L. Sulzberger noted:

> The biggest threat to stability remains the fact that all nations in and around Palestine have been stuffed with arms. So many tanks and missiles stud the Middle East that, if a fuse short-circuits, another terrible conflict could explode.

One short-hand description of the constant flow of arms into the Middle East is "two tanks in every tent." The problem of peace based on arms balancing is how to make the antagonists aware of their respective relative strengths, knowledge of which is supposed to prevent an adventurous policy based on miscalculation. However paradoxical it may seem, such knowledge of relative strength, as Lewis Coser noted, "can most frequently be attained through [armed] conflict, since other mechanisms for testing the respective strength seem to be unavailable."[19]

3. The existence of weapons, even if it does not produce a tendency to use weapons before they become outdated, is bound to increase the role of the military strategist and weapons technician. Allegedly the military mind is more attuned to the concept of war and victory—and to past experiences[20]—than to negotiation and compromise.

4. Finally, total and general elimination of weapons would eliminate suspicion among nations because nations, having nothing to fight with, would no longer dread violence. This would promote peaceful, nonviolent solution of all conflicts. Like a pebble dropped into the international pond, disarmament would give rise to a series of circles of cooperation that would expand to the total circumference of international relations and culminate in a universal consensus and world state. (A similar hope and metaphor was expressed by Paul S. Reinsch, one of the proponents of a functional approach to peace, that is, an approach that begins with cooperation in social and economic fields and proceeds from there to cooperation in the political field. Functionalism is discussed in Chapter 10.)

There is evidently a close relationship between weapons and international tension. But the question may be asked, What in this relationship is the primary cause and what is the effect? Are weapons (or alliances, or military bases, or close physical contact) the initial causes of suspicion and fear? Or is it rather the other way around—that suspicion and fear or ambition cause the armament race, the pushing of strategic lines forward, and the building of bases in foreign lands?

Weapons are both the consequence and cause of political tension. Fear or ambition comes first; weapons follow as symptoms of offensive or defensive intentions. Then the armament effort, whatever its original cause, produces additional fears and suspicion. Increased armaments are taken as indicators of increased ambition; a never-ending spiral of armaments and counterarmaments begins. Weapons as such are neutral. They are neither unequivocally offensive nor unequivocally defensive. They are not feared primarily because of the metal and explosives from which they are composed but because of the intention that is assumed to lie behind them. The inanimate object becomes a deadly weapon because of the intention and the nature of its use. A stone used for building homes may become a deadly weapon. In a totally disarmed world, the 800 million Chinese could stone all the other nations out of their sovereignty.

In view of the fact that the armaments race is the symptom and consequence of political tension and conflict, it can hardly be stopped or even reduced unless the *cause* of the political tension is also eliminated. This is why all disarmament efforts so far have ended in failure. The success of the Atomic Test Ban should not blind us into believing that it was a disarmament agreement. Suspension of tests in the air, under water, and in outer space did not prevent the United States and Soviet Russia from continuing tests in the laboratories and underground, from improving the delivery system and conventional weapons, and from producing additional nuclear warheads in an effort to compensate with both quantity and quality for the partial freeze on above-the-ground testing.

If ever an international conference were to succeed in eliminating the political cause of an arms race (ambition, fear, and suspicion), a disarmament conference would not even be necessary. Without fear or ambition no nation would be prompted to spend the money to build and maintain costly arsenals. If, on the other hand, a technical disarmament conference were one day really to succeed, its success would actually be in the *political* field, not in that of disarmament as such. If nations were ever to agree on a substantial limitation or elimination of their arsenals, the agreement would not be the first step toward political reconciliation but its consequence and symptom. And this is perhaps the main argument for the continuing efforts toward disarmament: Their real goal, although ostensibly a decrease in weapons, is *political* disarmament.

Political suspicion (or its opposite, trust) overshadows in importance the largely technical questions of military hardware. This will be confirmed if we briefly examine three major obstacles over which many a disarmament conference has irretrievably stumbled. They are the problems of verification, parity, and possible violation of the disarmament agreement at some later date.

Verification

If it is true that nations arm because they do not trust one another and because they suspect one another's intentions, then nations cannot disarm unless they can be reasonably certain that the other parties will be unable to cheat. In a disarmament negotiation one possible outcome is dreaded the most: If the disarmament agreement is made without proper safeguards, one side that credulously disarmed might find itself at the mercy of the other fraudulent, and therefore well-armed, side. Any negotiation concerning inspection has encountered the following two problems:

1. Is a watertight inspection technically feasible? While an atomic test can be detected (only the underground, small-yield tests may be confused with natural tremors of the earth), detection of the production of bomb parts, work in the laboratories, and production of conventional weapons, distributed among several industrial plants, is practically impossible. This was well demonstrated by the secret German rearmament after World War I. In the 1970s when the Soviet Union and the United States were able to observe much of each other's nuclear armament efforts by spy satellites orbiting the earth in the nonterritorial outer space, the problem arose of how to agree on limitation and inspection of the production and testing of multiple independently targeted nuclear warheads (MIRVs), not detectable by the spy satellites. Multiple warheads are practically impossible to detect from above. Clustered atop launchers under a single cap, they form a complex that even from a moderate distance looks like a single warhead. The American argument was that MIRVs could truly be detected only by close on-site inspection methods, which the Soviet Union has always opposed. The 1972 treaty limiting defensive missiles actually referred to 1,000 land-based launchers and 710 sea-based launchers for the United States, while the Soviet Union was allowed 1,410 land-based launchers and 950 sea-based ones. The reason is simple enough: Orbiting spy satellites can spot the number of launching pads and submarine ports but cannot detect how many missiles have been hidden away. This is why in 1972 the Soviet Union and the United States agreed only to those limitations that they could mutually verify by means of orbiting spy satellites. In 1974 this problem of verification led the United States to insist that systematic testing of even very old missiles should be curtailed because, as was then discovered, the most modern sophisticated guidance systems and warheads can be fitted on outdated rockets in order to avoid detection of an improvement in the system that could be decisive. Another problem of verification in the late seventies will probably be the

development of an undersea long-range missile system, the so-called ULMS, capable of operating over millions of square miles of ocean area, not detectable from above, and conceivably able to reach the Soviet Union from the Mississipi River or New York from the Volga River.

2. If nations do not trust each other, they must insist on an inspection that will be as effective as possible. In practice, this means a more or less unlimited access to national territory by international (neutral or mixed) inspection teams. One of the studies on the problem of disarmament reminds us that "inspection has sometimes been called 'institutionalized distrust' and in fact that is what it is."[21] Here, inescapably, a vicious circle begins. If nations do not trust each other, they are reluctant, in Khrushchev's words, to "open all their doors and their secret places to outsiders or to anyone except closest friends." When President Eisenhower proposed mutual inspection from the air (the Open Sky proposal of 1956), the Soviet spokesmen called it a thinly disguised "capitalist plot to spy and select targets for the future atomic bombardment of the land of socialism and progress." The Soviet leaders have so far insisted on their thesis that inspection can *follow* but cannot precede the growth of intimacy and trust between East and West. For twenty-five years neither side has proved able to move beyond the circumference of their vicious circle: When nations do not trust each other, a more or less effective inspection is absolutely necessary. But as they do not trust each other, an effective on-site inspection cannot be accepted because of the suspicion of its being misused for intelligence purposes. When, on the other hand, nations trust each other, inspection, which would then be possible, is quite unnecessary, as is amply demonstrated, for example, by the strict adherence to local disarmament without inspection on the Great Lakes between Canada and the United States.

Admittedly, the problem of verification, when discussed between a free and a closed society, is delicate. If the Soviet Union were to engage in secret violation of a disarmament proposal, its system of highly centralized power, uncontrolled by a free press and an opposition party, would practically guarantee the secrecy of most of its transgressions. In the United States, where all major decisions are exposed to public scrutiny, very few deviations from the disarmament agreement would go undetected. It is often said that all that Soviet and Chinese spies in the United States need to do is to read the *New York Times* every day, including the Sunday *Book Review*. Also the Communist party of the United States and its press can be relied on to keep a watchful eye on everything that could be interpreted as a deviation from an agreement with the Soviet Union. There is no corresponding "Democratic Worker" in Russia to observe and comment on the Soviet scene in behalf of the United States.

On the other hand, as was frankly admitted by John J. McCloy, adviser on disarmament to the American President from 1960 to 1962, acceptance of international inspection would be a greater sacrifice on the part of the Soviet Union than the United States, which has very little to hide from an international inspector:

> An international inspectorate, operating freely within the Soviet territory, would run counter to the concept of Soviet secrecy as a military and political asset. . . . [A]n international inspector may also represent a threat to the insularity and secrecy which form part of the Soviet and Russian way of life. . . . Vast areas of government operations are simply not known to the masses of the Soviet people or to the world. Any external inspection might be considered as endangering the government's control.[22]

Parity

In all disarmament negotiations there arises the problem of equation, or parity. Nations have always found it extremely difficult to agree on a mathematical formula, or ratio, that would express either the top limit or a new lower level of their respective armament efforts. At the Naval Disarmament Conference in Washington in 1922, five powers were able to agree on such a formula only with respect to their battleships and aircraft carriers. The approximate formula was 5 (United States): 5 (Britain): 3 (Japan): 1.75 (France): 1.75 (Italy). At that time they failed, however, to agree on a similar ratio with regard to cruisers, torpedo boats, and submarines.

In 1934 Japan, planning her conquest of China and Southeast Asia, proposed a common upper limit for naval rearmament instead of the former ratio of 5:5:3. Its request was based on several arguments: that new conditions created by naval and air construction called for new arrangements, that the "inferior ratio" for Japan inspired in China a feeling of contempt for Japan, and that the combination of the British and American navies pushed Japan to a further position of inferiority. In opposition to the Japanese demand for mathematical equality, the United States emphasized "equality of security and equality of self-defense." Yielding to the Japanese demand for equal tonnage, as Washington saw it, would have amounted to its assent to Japan's overwhelming preponderance in the western Pacific.

Another example of complicated disarmament mathematics was the American acceptance in 1972 of a marked inferiority in missiles and launchers (roughly 1,800 for the United States as opposed to 2,400 for the Soviet Union in both land- and sea-based launchers). In view of anticipated technological breakthroughs the accord was concluded for five years only but with the hope that it might be converted into a permanent agreement in 1977. The United States accepted inferiority in numbers and throw-weight (that is, the amount of weight a missile can lift off the ground and carry to a target) on the then probably correct assumption that in 1972 Moscow's advantage in quantity was largely offset by the American superiority in quality, especially in MIRVs. Yet by 1973 the Soviet Union had already developed its own first generation of MIRVs and it seemed to be only a matter of a few years, if not months, before the Soviet Union too would develop the maneuverable reentry vehicles, the MARVs, relatively immune to antiballistic missiles. The Soviet advance in missile technology led the United States's nuclear strategists to present a request for a $19 billion budget for strategic forces and operations in 1974 in order to catch up with and surpass the Soviet improvements in missile quality. Most probably, the Soviet strategists directed a similar request to their political leaders and budget directors in the Kremlin.

A frightening yet simple fact emerges: In an atmosphere of distrust in disarmament mathematics, one does *not* equal one. This is the reason that not only attempts at general disarmament but even quite modest attempts at placing a top limit on a current arms race stumble over the problem of parity. Different nations' armies, navies, air forces, and missile systems cannot be equated in quantitative terms only; quality, a highly controversial issue, must be added to the ratio formula. An agreement on a quantitative limitation of the number of military personnel and their weapons (missiles, aircraft, bombs, ships, invasion barges, tanks, and guns) is actually quite meaningless; it may be easily distorted by one nation's success in improving the quality of a weapon within the quantitative limits. The quick tempo of modern technology, which may give a lead to different nations at different times (through a laboratory breakthrough, for instance), introduces an element of permanent instability into a parity formula, the purpose of which is to stabilize the armament situation on an acceptable level. Furthermore, the quality of weapons is usually the most jealously guarded secret: In the initial stages of any disarmament effort when nations do not trust each other, it is unrealistic to assume that nations would be willing to reveal and compare the real effectiveness of their respective arsenals.

There is still another problem affecting the disarmament ratio and the quantity-plus-quality issue: An existing military establishment, even if it could be reliably and comparatively measured, is only one element, however important, of a nation's military potential. The disarmament equation formula must reflect the analysis and agreement as to what the total power of different nations is and should be. (The problems and pitfalls of any comparative measurement of national power were stressed and analyzed in Chapter 5.) As the record of the United States during World War II shows, some nations may have small peacetime armies but also the capacity to improvise an effective war machine overnight, so to speak, thanks to their advanced technology, well-organized industry, and managerial skills. Other nations' huge manpower reserves or the relative defensibility of their national territory may compensate for the lesser quality of their industrial and military establishments. Such equations between different elements of national power may lead to the mathematically impossible but politically justifiable argument that in order for a particular nation to be militarily equal to another nation it must be, in fact, militarily superior.

Such was basically the French argument during the 1932 disarmament conference in Geneva. France pressed for a military establishment superior to that of Germany in order to compensate for what France considered its inferiorities: Germany had a manpower and industrial establishment superior to that of France; France lacked a defensible frontier in the north and the east; through the northeastern gap Germany had already twice invaded France. Thus the "tradition" of Germany's aggressive intentions toward France was brought into the disarmament calculation. It was not easy to answer the question as to how many French armored divisions should compensate for the history of Prussia's and the German Kaiser's aggressiveness. Germany, naturally, pointed to France's manpower reserves in its colonial empire as well as to the French allies, Poland and Czechoslovakia, which had encircled Germany and confronted it with the nightmare of fighting on two fronts.

With regard to fascist Italy, France argued that in order to be equal to the Italian navy the French navy, guarding both the Atlantic and the Mediterranean coasts, must be twice as strong as the Italian one. If Mussolini's Italy was to be prevented from transforming the Mediterranean into an Italian lake, the equation would have to be two equals one.

On September 17, 1959, in Khrushchev's address to the United Nations General Assembly, the Soviet government proposed that "over a period of four years all states should effect complete disarmament. . . . All armies, navies and air forces would cease to exist, general staffs and war ministries would be abolished, and military institutions closed." At the end of this period nations would be left only with *police forces*[23] to keep internal order. After that, according to the Soviet plan, international inspection would be established.

This proposal was criticized not only for its lack of realism and abundant cheap propaganda effects but also on the basis of parity. The proposal clearly favored nations with massive populations. The Chinese millions could trample neighboring nations into submission just by marching through. In a tongue-in-cheek letter geophysicist David Stone warned (*Time*, December 19, 1969) that 800 million Chinese could cause an earthquake of the magnitude of 4.5 on the Richter scale if at a given moment, obeying a command by Mao, all the Chinese were to leap downward from a 6½ foot platform. If the leap were so organized as to coincide with the peak of a barely perceptible natural ripple that sweeps around the earth's surface every 54 minutes, Peking could aim a ground wave along the Pacific-rim earthquake belt and possibly set off quakes in California more devastating than the original shocks in China.

Furthermore any disarmament proposal that leaves nations only with their police necessarily also opens the more serious question of police force parity. The size of a police establishment and the perfection of its weapons, especially in the case of a dictatorial regime, would have to be compared internationally.[24] One London bobby without a gun cannot be compared with a Soviet militiaman equipped with the latest model submachine-gun. One could actually visualize a conquest of the whole disarmed world by a Chinese police force equipped only with tear-gas bombs and submachine-guns, an image that would make not only the southern but also the northern neighbors of China think twice.

It is evident that in the case of any gradual, step-by-step disarmament the problem of an acceptable ratio would have to be solved at each of the successive disarmament phases. No nation would consent to finding itself, however temporarily, at a marked disadvantage (and potentially therefore exposed to blackmail) at any of the contemplated steps leading to a world without arms. The hope is, of course, that mutual trust would grow proportionally with the progress of disarmament, thus making the problem of parity a less explosive issue in the final phases of gradual disarmament.

Violation of Disarmament Agreements

Under the title "After Detection—What?" Fred Charles Iklé examined the problem of the measures that would have to be taken after one of the parties violated the disarmament agreement and was found out. Iklé noted that "detection deters only" if the violator fears that his gain from violation will be outweighed by the loss he may suffer from the victim's reaction to it."[25] There would first be the problem of ascertaining and proving to everybody's satisfaction that a violation of a disarmament treaty had indeed occurred. The violator could and perhaps would deny the validity of the proof; accusation of violation could easily be labeled by the violator as a pretext for a violation of the same treaty by the accuser. When, in 1965, the Soviet Union, perhaps unintentionally, violated the Atomic Test-Ban Treaty by performing an underground test at Semipalatinski (it had released more radioactive debris in the atmosphere than the treaty permitted), the American statement of facts was denied by the Soviet Union and world public opinion was not mobilized against it. It seemed that there was a suspicion that the American statement was either incorrect or a part of Cold War tactics.

But even if the violation were not controversial but open and admitted, the problem of an appropriate countermeasure or punishment would not be easily solved. Before World War II, for instance, Japan openly resumed its freedom of action and began naval rearmament after the Western powers had refused to grant a favorable revision of the original Naval Disarmament Treaty of 1922. Would the appropriate reaction on the part of the Western powers have been passive acceptance of the changed situation, a frantic arms race with Japan, or an immediate war that would prevent Japan from exploiting the advantage gained by violation of the disarmament treaty? In 1963 President Kennedy raised the question of an appropriate countermeasure in connection with a secret preparation for a series of atomic tests. The preparation of tests cannot be detected. But when such tests are secretly or openly begun and their result is a scientific breakthrough, the violator may have gained such an advantage that the opposite side may not have time to catch up with him, since complex atomic tests cannot be improvised overnight. This is why President Kennedy, recommending the ratification of the Atomic Test-Ban Treaty, tried to assure the Congress and warn the Soviet Union by stressing that the United States, while strictly adhering to the treaty, would stay ready to resume all types of atomic tests at short notice.

In the mid-seventies nuclear experts in the United States emphasized the possibility that in the future the Soviet Union would denounce arms limitation agreements and resume its freedom of action; these warnings were used to press the President and the Congress for more substantial appropriations. The reason for the new pressure was the development of "accurate" multiple-warhead missiles that in the event of a Soviet attack on the Minuteman force (second-strike capacity) could be used to strike back at Soviet missiles (counterforce strategy) rather than at Soviet cities (countercity strategy). Basically, the demand for "unlimited" funds was based on the concept of a possible "limited" nuclear war—that is, limited, thanks to highly accurate warheads, to missile sites and sparing the population centers.

What was previously said about the durability of all compacts among sovereign nations applies fully to all present and future treaties concerning arms control or disarmament. In the words of former Assistant Secretary of State for Policy Planning (1953-1957) Robert R. Bowie,

> No arms-control plan will remain effective and dependable unless it continues to serve the national interests of each of the parties, as its leaders conceive their interests. In reaching their judgment, however, they will appraise the alternatives. The main function of inspection and of the remedies available to the other parties is to make evasion unattractive as an alternative course. To achieve this result, the inspection system should confront the potential violator with risks of detection and counter-measures outweighing the significance of the violation for the relative capabilities of the participants. The system as a whole must be designed to offer benefits to all participants which they are likely to prefer not to jeopardize.[26]

Disengagement

Like plans for disarmament, proposals for disengagement—a geographically determined disarmament of sorts—aim at reducing international tension by a cure of the symptoms rather than of the initial causes. The purpose of disengagement is to keep two nations that do not want to disarm physically separate, usually by creating a buffer zone between them, and so limit the possibility of friction and incidents; generally speaking, geographic closeness between two heavily armed hostile camps is potentially explosive. Disengagement plans have so far been less numerous than disarmament plans. One reason is simply that in many cases it is impossible to alter the facts of geographic contiguity, such as those that have characterized the Soviet-Chinese or German-French enmity.

After World War II disengagement proposals assumed different forms: creation of an atom-free zone in Europe and in Asia; withdrawal of both the American and Soviet armed forces from Berlin, Germany, and Eastern Europe; elimination of the American bases adjacent to the Soviet Union; the end of the Soviet presence in Cuba; and withdrawal of troops from disputed areas along the Sino-Soviet borders. The creation of demilitarized zones was supposed to improve the international atmosphere. Another type of disengagement effort is the effort to prevent a relatively demilitarized area from being remilitarized by the presence of competing superpowers. A good example is the Indian insistence that the Indian Ocean be kept demilitarized, that is, free of the presence of superpower navies. Speaking to the Lok Sabha (the lower house of the parliament), India's Foreign Minister Swaran Singh complained of the presence of the United States's nuclear-powered aircraft carrier *Kitty Hawk* in the Indian Ocean since, as he put it (*India News*, March 22, 1974),

> any large-scale presence of the navy of one big power is bound to attract navies of other big powers. Such rivalry would create problems for littoral countries, the overwhelming majority of whom desire to maintain the Indian ocean as an area of peace.

Although debated in detail, none of the disengagement proposals mentioned above has ever reached the point of being seriously prepared for implementation.

One example of a successfully negotiated disengagement (combined with a buffer zone in which a United Nations peace-keeping force was stationed) is the Arab-Israeli agreement of January 17, 1974. See Document 13.4.

A more difficult—and shakier—disengagement agreement between Syria and Israel was signed in Geneva on May 31, 1974. It also established a

DOCUMENT 13.4

EGYPTIAN-ISRAELI DISENGAGEMENT, JANUARY 17, 1974

Egypt and Israel will scrupulously observe the ceasefire on the land, sea and air called for by the U.N. Security Council and will refrain from the time of the signing of this document from all military or paramilitary actions against each other.

The military forces of Egypt and Israel will be separated in accordance with the following principles:

1. All Egyptian forces on the east side of the canal will be deployed west of the line designated as line A on the attached map. All Israeli forces including those west of the Suez Canal on the Bitter Lakes will be deployed east of the line designated as line B on the attached map.

2. The area between the Egyptian and Israeli lines will be a zone of disengagement in which the United Nations Emergency Force will be stationed. The U.N.E.F. will continue to consist of units from countries that are not permanent members of the Security Council.

3. The area between the Egyptian line and the Suez Canal will be limited in armament and forces.

4. The area between the Israeli line, line B on the attached map, and the line designated as line C on the attached map, which runs along the western base of the mountains where the Gidi and Mitla passes are located, will be limited in armament and forces.

5. The limitations referred to in paragraphs 3 and 4 will be inspected by U.N.E.F. Existing procedures of the U.N.E.F., including the attaching of Egyptian and Israeli liaison officers to U.N.E.F., will be continued.

The detailed implementation of the disengagement of forces will be worked out by military representatives of Egypt and Israel, who will agree on the stages of this process. These representatives will meet no later than 48 hours after the signature of this agreement at Kilometer 101 under the aegis of the United Nations for this purpose. They will complete this task within five days.[1] Disengagement will begin within 48 hours after the completion of the work of the military representatives, and in no event later than seven days after the signature of this agreement. The process of disengagement will be completed not later than 40 days after it begins.

This agreement is not regarded by Egypt and Israel as a final peace agreement. It constitutes a first step toward a final, just and durable peace according to the provisions of Security Council Resolution 338 and within the framework of the Geneva Conference.

For Egypt: Mohammed Abdel Ghany al-Gamasy, Major General

For Israel: David Elazar, Lieut. Gen., Chief of Staff of Israel Defense Forces

1. They did.

United Nations buffer zone and three separate zones of decreasing military importance on both the Israeli and Syrian sides of the UN buffer area: zone "A" with a limited number of military forces; zone "B," where no heavy artillery could be installed; and zone "C," where no antiaircraft missiles could be present.

Another example of disengagement, following military engagement and combined with a United Nations interposition between the two sides, was the compromise reached in August 1974 by Greece, Turkey, Cyprus, and its former ruler and subsequent guarantor, England. In fact, however, the disengagement agreement guaranteed Turkish military presence and Turkish *involvement* in shaping the future of Cyprus.

As a *preventive cure* (in contrast to an agreement reached at the conclusion of hostilities) disengagement has been criticized on four counts:

1. As in any other disarmament proposal, the problem of parity in disengagement is very delicate and controversial. When, in the late 1950s, Polish Foreign Minister A. Rapacki proposed the demilitarization and possible neutralization of Germany and Eastern Europe (in practical terms, "de-Sovietization" and "de-Americanization" of that area), it was quickly pointed out that such a measure would be to the advantage of the Soviet Union, whose armed forces would withdraw a few hundred miles to the east, ready to come back at a moment's notice (as they did with efficiency and speed to suppress the Hungarian revolution in 1956 and Czechoslovak liberal communism in 1968), while the American counterforce would be pushed several thousand miles back over the Atlantic. The net result would be a shift of the balance of conventional military forces in Europe in favor of the Soviet Union. In view of the Brezhnev Doctrine (which after all reflects the Soviet view of the politico-military unreliability of the Soviet Union's Eastern European allies), it is unlikely that a United States withdrawal from West Germany and Europe could really be matched by a similar Soviet withdrawal from Poland, Czechoslovakia, and Hungary. Of course, even if, hypothetically, such a demilitarized and "disallied" zone from the Rhine to, say, Brest Litovsk could be created, the political orientation of its various components would not be immune to possible internal changes with external consequences; for instance, Poland, Czechoslovakia, and Hungary, once free of the Soviet military presence, might conceivably opt for a true neutral status à la Austria, which the Brezhnev Doctrine forbids. It is also not difficult to imagine the panic in Moscow or Washington if, again hypothetically, in a demilitarized Europe the government of a neutral and unified Germany fell into the hands of a strongly pro-American political party as a result of elections or, on the contrary, into the hands of an all-German Communist party as a result of a *coup d' état*. It should be noted that in these two hypothetical situations—Germany adopting a Western or Eastern orientation or East

Europe pulling out of the Warsaw Pact—the geographic situation would give the Soviet tanks a marked advantage in annulling by force any undesirable developments within the zone of disengagement.

2. The critics of proposals for disengagement between the nuclear superpowers also point to the fact that in the age of missiles geographic proximity is of secondary importance. Through their respective offensive and defensive missile systems the United States and the Soviet Union have become neighbors all over the world.

3. Critics have argued that it has never really been demonstrated that the physical closeness of two armed camps leads per se to conflicts. Wars do not start by frontier incidents but by hostile intent. Where there is no desire for conflict, accidental frictions on the boundary lines will not be allowed to escalate to any serious level. But where there is a hostile intent, either frontier incidents may be prefabricated or genuine skirmishes may be blown into major confrontations. When in October 1969 Communist China proposed to the Soviet Union a mutual disengagement from the disputed areas along the Sino-Soviet borders, the proposal was generally welcomed as an indication of détente. This was in contrast to the preceding major crisis, marked by persistent rumors about an impending Soviet attack on China and at least a Soviet preemptive raid on the Chinese atomic installations at Lob Nor, a desert lake in Chinese Turkestan (Sinkiang-Uighur Autonomous Region) at which most of the Chinese nuclear tests have been conducted. The reasons for the temporary détente, however, could be found in Peking and Moscow rather than in the Sino-Soviet border regions. The same applies to the 1974 Arab-Israeli disengagement: it resulted from rather than caused the political détente between Moscow and Washington and from the impact of détente, as translated by Kissinger, on Cairo, Damascus and Tel Aviv.

4. As the preceding examples indicate, disengagement proposals tend to confuse cause and effect as disarmament proposals often do. "Engagement," that is, pushing one's military line as far as one can (for instance, the American presence in Berlin, West Germany, South Vietnam, Laos, or South Korea, or the Soviet presence in East Berlin, East Germany, Czechoslovakia, and Cuba), is the result of mutual distrust: disengagement would therefore result from, rather than cause, a détente. The often-quoted observation by Salvador de Madariaga, made on the subject of disarmament in the late 1920s, applies also to the disengagement proposals in the 1960s and 1970s: "The solution of the problem of disarmament [and now we add "of disengagement"] cannot be found within the problem itself but outside it."[27]

ARMAMENT AND WORLD COMMUNITY

In conclusion we may note that in a disarmed world two nightmares would still remain. In a substantially disarmed world, a shift of the remaining weapons from one area to another could have a profound effect. In our discussion of interference we mentioned the consequences of supplying arms to the insurgents or to the incumbents in a civil strife—a few tanks could make a difference. In a totally disarmed world the danger of a secret or open violation of a general disarmament agreement would be quite considerable, as a violation would give a tremendous advantage to the violator and severely penalize those who had been complying with the agreement in good faith. The knowledge of how to make weapons would remain even in a totally disarmed world; as one scholar correctly warned, "short of universal brain surgery, nothing can erase the memory of weapons and how to build them."[28]

For these reasons, any serious disarmament proposal should combine the concept of a gradual disarmament of nations with a simultaneous armament of the world community, that is, the establishment of a supranational police force and authority. No nation would ever deprive itself of a police establishment to protect its law-abiding citizens against the criminal or insane fringe of the national society. Similarly, a world whose national compartments are disarmed would have to arm itself internationally to protect its law-abiding citizens against a potentially criminal or insane fringe of the world community. Disarmament, even if agreed upon, would not transform men into angels. A supranational police force would have to protect the nationally disarmed world against the blackmail or conquest that one well-concealed or rapidly produced atomic bomb could ensure. It should not be overlooked that the peaceful use of atomic energy results in by-products that can be rapidly, easily, and cheaply converted into weapons.

If a supranational force and authority appear as logical corollaries of the disarmament of nations, the problem has ceased to be that of weapons and has clearly become that of political agreement as to who would control, and how and for what purpose they would control, the worldwide monopoly of coercion, that is, world government and its police force. "In fact the problem of disarmament is not the problem of disarmament," noted Salvador de Madariaga in 1929. "It really is the problem of organization of the World Community."[29] If ever such a stage of international development is reached (at present it seems a utopia; see Document 13.5), and nations agree on total disarmament, it would be a political compact resembling the political agreement of the original thirteen American colonies. Thomas C. Schelling expressed this parallel when he wrote:

> If militarily superior to any combination of national forces, an international force implies (or is) some form of world government. To call such an arrangement "disarmament" is about as oblique as to call the Constitution of the United States "a Treaty for Uniform Currency and Interstate Commerce." The authors of the Federalist papers were under no illusion as to the far-reaching character of the institution they were discussing and we should not be either.[30]

DOCUMENT 13.5

PROGRAM FOR GENERAL AND COMPLETE DISARMAMENT IN A PEACEFUL WORLD

[Introduced by the United States Government at the Sixteenth General Assembly of the United Nations, 1961.]

The last stage (III) of a progressive and inspected disarmament of nations simultaneously with the armament of the world community is described as follows:

By the time Stage II has been completed, the confidence produced through a verified disarmament program, the acceptance of rules of peaceful international behavior, and the development of strengthened international peace-keeping processes within the framework of the UN should have reached a point where the states of the world can move forward to Stage III. In Stage III progressively controlled disarmament and continuously developing principles and procedures of international law would proceed to a point where no state would have the military power to challenge the progressively strengthened UN Peace Force and all international disputes would be settled according to the agreed principles of international conduct.

The progressive steps to be taken during the final phase of the disarmament program would be directed toward the attainment of a world in which:

A. States would retain only those forces, non-nuclear armaments, and establishments required for the purpose of maintaining internal order. They would also support and provide agreed manpower for a UN Peace Force.
B. The UN Peace Force, equipped with agreed types and quantities of armaments, would be fully functioning.
C. The manufacture of armaments would be prohibited except for those of agreed types and quantities to be used by the UN Peace Force and those required to maintain internal order. All other armaments would be destroyed or converted to peaceful purposes.

From *Freedom from War* (Department of State Publication No. 7277). Washington, D.C.: Government Printing Office, September 1961.

In view of the preceding observations the question should now be asked, Why have two great powers such as the Soviet Union and the United States invested so much money, time, energy, and propaganda output on the issue of disarmament? There are several reasons. One is the remaining hope that through disarmament discussions some outstanding political issues may be solved in the light of mutual realization that both sides are armed to such a formidable point that a solution by arms is unimaginable. Another reason is mutual nuclear education, as was previously noted; disarmament talks are more about what weapons could do than about doing without them. In the words of the Director of the United States Arms Control and Disarmament Agency, Fred Charles Iklé:

> By relying on nuclear deterrence, the major powers are presuming a certain harmony between their own strategic views and those of other nuclear powers. While Americans and Russians have sought to understand each other's views, they have treated their differences as errors in thinking to be corrected in long disarmament conferences and numerous informal talks by patient and persistent education. In the meantime, the views of both sides have undergone considerable evolution; and now, indeed, each side sees errors in ideas that it firmly defended in the past.[31]

Still another reason is certainly the Soviet and American need to pacify their own and international public opinion, which tends to confuse cause and effect and to view disarmament not as a result but as a precondition for political détente. "The concept of disarmament has achieved such ideological sanctity," writes Inis L. Claude, "that international organizations are as little likely to strike it off the agenda of debate as churches are to eliminate prayers from their Sunday services."[32] Finally, the disarmament proposals, often formulated with a view to their unacceptability, are "an integral part of the arms race" and the Cold War, as is suggested by a recent book on Soviet-American gamesmanship in disarmament by John W. Spanier and Joseph L. Nogee. Spanier and Nogee forecast that "the future will witness the continuation of disarmament diplomacy as both the Soviet Union and the United States continue to dance their almost courtly 'disarmament minuet.' "[33] As captives of their own system of states, nations find themselves engaged in a paradoxical game, often referred to as "prisoner's dilemma,"[34] for which there seems to be no satisfactory purely rational solution:

> The prisoner's dilemma in a sense governs all forms of the social contract, where each party has the choice of being either "good" or "bad." If they are all good, they will all be better off; and yet if they are all good it may pay one of them to be bad, in which case it pays all of them to be bad and they all end up worse off.[35]

Game Theory: The Imprisoned Nations Dilemma

The term "prisoner's dilemma" comes from an anecdote used to illustrate a model of conflict and cooperation in game theory. Despite its name, suggestive of recreation or sport, game theory is nothing playful but is instead a mathematically based method of studying and analyzing, but not predicting, rational decision making; as we have learned, many decisions among nations and men are irrational or even insane. According to Thomas C. Schelling, game theory "is concerned with situations—games of 'strategy,' (in contrast to games of skill or games of chance)—in which the best course of action for each participant depends on what he expects the other participants to do.''[36] A game is therefore a situation in which two or more players make decisions as to (1) the sequence of their (2) moves in the light of natural limitations and anticipated decisions and their impact on the sequence of countermoves. Another term for the "players" is the decision-making units, that is, nation-states; another term for "moves" is decisions for or against a particular action (to start or not to start a war, blackmail, interference, or negotiation); and "strategy" is another term for a rational sequence of moves.

Game theory examines various conflict situations. One of them is a *zero-sum game* between two sides, A and B, in which what A wins, B loses; chess, two-person poker, a two-candidate election, a dog-fight between two fighter-jets, or a battle over a hill are examples of zero-sum games. Another conflict situation is a *nonzero-sum game* (or variable-sum and mixed-motives game) which represents a case in which the interests of conflicting parties partially diverge and partially coincide; collective bargaining between workers and management and conflicts and bargaining among nations are examples of nonzero-sum games. A further distinction is made between games involving two or several players; the latter are called *N-person games*, in which often but not always a subset of N players form a coalition while the remaining group forms a countercoalition. The result is basically a two-person game of one collective actor against the other.

Game theory cannot and does not attempt to describe how rational participants in conflicts behave or prescribe how they ought to behave. It uncovers the logical structure of various conflict situations and describes the structure in mathematical terms. The potential contribution of game theory to the study of international conflicts, which usually involve many more than two antagonists, was expressed by Anatol Rapoport as follows:

> The theory of the N-person game with its labyrinthine analyses and inconclusive "solutions" should impress the participants in multilateral conflicts with the immense complexities of the situations in which they find themselves. The greatest lesson is that purely strategic considerations are not sufficient for a basis of "rational decision," indeed that the very concept of rational decision becomes diffuse in most real-life situations. This lesson should serve to direct the attention of would-be rational decision-makers to other than strategic problems of conflict—to psychology, to problems of communication, and to ethical questions, all of which are sadly neglected in our technique-worshipping and competition-dominated age.[37]

The previously mentioned prison analogy is useful for illustrating a situation in which two sides whose interests are partly in conflict and partly in harmony decide their conflict and cooperation according to largely predictable rational arguments. According to the anecdote, two prisoners, charged with a grave crime, are held in prison; they are both kept in solitary confinement and *cannot communicate* with each other. If neither confesses, both will go free because of lack of evidence. If both confess, they will go to jail for ten years. If only one confesses, the other will go to jail for twenty years while the one who betrayed the other, that is, turned state's evidence, will receive a two-year commuted sentence. Expressed in terms of game theory, this is a typical case of a nonzero-sum game, that is, a situation in which the participants win something competitively from each other but may also collectively gain or lose. For the two prisoners the optimum strategy is evidently to deny all allegations and keep silent. But since they cannot communicate, they can only think and anticipate what the other prisoner may or may not do. Prisoner A knows that he will be released if he remains silent and *if B also remains silent*, but that he will get the maximum sentence of twenty years in jail *if the other speaks first and confesses*. If, on the other hand, A confesses, A will get a two-year commuted sentence or a ten-year sentence, depending on whether B remains silent or also confesses. By confession A assures himself of a lesser sentence, two years or ten years, instead of the twenty years he would receive if he risked trusting B's silence and himself denied everything while B spilled the beans. Therefore, both A and B, discarding the chance that the other might keep silent, choose what appears to them a safer course, and so both are finally worse off than if they had both kept silent.

Arms control agreements, disarmament treaties, and détente between distrustful nations all bear resemblance to the game-theory anecdote. In the prisoner's dilemma the penalty the silent and loyal A suffers from being betrayed by B (while tacitly and trustingly cooperating with him) is evidently worse than the penalty A suffers if he betrays B. Similarly, in arms control arrangements or détente between distrustful adversaries such as the United States and the Soviet Union, Israel and Egypt, China and Russia, India and Pakistan, and France and Germany before World War II, both sides could reap considerable gains from mutual trust and cooperation, but "these gains are outweighed by the rewards for successful cheating and by the penalties of being trustful and cheated."[38] In other words, if all nations disarmed totally, and were therefore more secure and economically better off, it might profit one of them to rearm and exploit all the disarmed ones, in which case it might pay all of them to be armed, and so they all end up worse off—which is exactly the situation the world has been in for centuries.

Notes

1. The first category also has been called "signals" and techniques 2-5 "signs" by Robert Jervis in his paper on "The Logic and Paradoxes of Signaling Conflict." presented to the 1966 Annual Meeting of the American Political Science Association in New York, p. 2. It

now forms part of Robert Jervis' book *The Logic of Images in International Relations*. Princeton, N. J.: Princeton University Press, 1970.

2. Thomas C. Schelling, *Arms and Influence*. New Haven, Conn: Yale University Press, 1966. See also Thomas C. Schelling, *The Strategy of Conflict*. New York: Oxford, 1963.

3. The Washington Center of Foreign Policy Research, *Two Communist Manifestoes*, 1961, p.61.

4. Robert C. Good, "State-Building as a Determinant of Foreign Policy," in Laurence W. Martin (ed.), *Neutralism and Nonalignment*. New York: Praeger, 1962, pp. 3-13.

5. Jacques Freymond, "European Neutrals and Atlantic Community," in Francis O. Wilcox and H. Field Haviland, Jr. (eds.), *The Atlantic Community: Progress and Prospects*. New York: Praeger, 1963, p. 86. The book contains very valuable articles by Rupert Emerson, Marshall D. Shulman, Arnold Wolfers, and others.

6. Joseph C. McKenna, *Diplomatic Protest in Foreign Policy*. Chicago: Loyola University Press, 1963, p. 17.

7. Jervis, "The Logic and Paradoxes of Signaling in Conflicts," p. 2.

8. Andrew J. Pierre, "Can Europe's Security be 'Decoupled' from America?" *Foreign Affairs*, 51:4 (July 1973), 771.

9. James Reston, "Ottawa: America and Its Allies," *New York Times*, March 14, 1965, p. E-10.

10. See Arnold Wolfers (ed.), *Alliance Policy in the Cold War*. Baltimore, Md.: The Johns Hopkins Press, 1959, pp. 1-15. The symposium contains very useful analyses by Paul H. Nitze, Erich Hula, Hans J. Morgenthau, Charles Burton Marshall, and others.

11. Alvin J. Cottrell and James E. Dougherty, *The Politics of the Atlantic Alliance*. New York: Praeger, 1964, p. 264.

12. Wolfers, *Alliance Policy in the Cold War*, pp. 210-211.

13. Kenneth N. Waltz, "The Politics of Peace," *International Studies Quarterly*, 11:3 (September 1967), 205. Waltz writes: "We are misled by the vision of dominoes. States in the area of fighting lack the solidity, shape, and cohesion that the image suggests. Externally ill-defined, internally fragile and chaotic, they more appropriately call to mind sponges; and sponges, whatever their other characteristics, do not from the transmission of impulses neatly fall down in a row."

14. Hans J. Morgenthau, "Spheres of Influence." Paper presented at the United Nations Institute at the City University of New York, February 1, 1969, p. 12. In this context see also Ned Lebow and John G. Stoessinger (eds.), *The Divided Nations*. New York: St. Martin's, 1974.

15. U. S. Arms Control and Disarmament Agency, *World Military Expenditures, 1969, and Related Data for 120 Countries*. Washington, D. C.: Government Printing Office, December 1969.

16. U. S. Arms Control and Disarmament Agency, *World Military Expenditures, 1969*, p.2.

17. According to a report published in June 1972 by the Stockholm International Peace Research Institute (financed by the Swedish government and headed by Professor Gunnar Myrdal), the Soviet Union has now become the largest supplier of conventional weapons to Third World countries. The chief recipient of Soviet arms, the report said, was Egypt, which received weapons valued at $250 million in 1970 and $420 million in 1971, obviously in preparation for the 1973 war against Israel. See also the Chinese condemnation of the Soviet Union as an "international merchant of death," p. 446.

18. Leslie R. Groves, *Now It Can Be Told*. New York: Harper & Row, 1962, p. 265.

19. Lewis Coser, *The Function of Social Conflict*. New York: Free Press, 1956, p. 137.

20. See General James M. Gavin's article, "The Weapons of 1984," *Saturday Review*, August 31, 1968, which begins: "Although war is as old as humanity itself, man has shown an amazing inability to understand its changing character from one era to the next. Governments have been toppled and 'good' nations have been conquered and destroyed, all because they followed the advice of their military experts. Generals, all too often remembering their last war nostalgically, have sought to distill from their memories the ideas that would win the next war. . . . Unhappily their efforts at divination have yielded little."

21. Donald G. Brennan (ed.), *Arms Control, Disarmament, and National Security*. New York: Braziller, 1951, p. 37.

22. John J. McCloy, "Balance Sheet on Disarmament," *Foreign Affairs*, 40 (April 1962), 353-354.

23. Compare Woodrow Wilson's Fourth Point in his Fourteen Points address in 1918: After the victory in World War I "national armaments will be reduced to the lowest point consistent with *domestic safety*" (italics added). Even the pacifist Quaker program, *Speak Truth to Power: A Quaker Search for an Alternative to Violence* (Philadelphia: American Friends Service Committee, 1955, p. 62), speaks in terms of disarmament that is "universal in character, enforceable in practice, and complete down to the level *needed for internal policing*" (italics added).

24. India with a population of 550 million (estimated at 580 million by 1975), for instance, had 717,173 policemen (official statement, July 18, 1970). This is six times more policemen than is the total population of one of India's "neighbors" in the Indian Ocean, the Maldive ministate—sovereign, independent, and a member of the United Nations.

25. Fred Charles Iklé, "After Detection—What?" *Foreign Affairs*, 39 (January 1961), 208.

26. Quoted in Brennan, *Arms Control*, p. 53.

27. Salvador de Madariaga, *Disarmament*. New York: Coward-McCann, 1929, p. 56.

28. Thomas C. Schelling, "The Role of Deterrence in Total Disarmament," *Foreign Affairs*, 40:3 (April 1962), 400.

29. Madariaga, *Disarmament*, p. 56.

30. Schelling, "The Role of Deterrence in Total Disarmament," pp. 401-402. See also Thomas C. Schelling and Morton H. Halperin, *Strategy and Arms Control*. New York: The Twentieth Century Fund, 1961, p. 143.

31. Fred Charles Iklé, *Every War Must End*. New York: Columbia University Press, 1971, p. 128.

32. Inis L. Claude, *Swords into Plowshares*. New York: Random House, 1959, pp. 303-304.

33. John W. Spanier and Joseph L. Nogee, *The Politics of Disarmament: A Study in Soviet-American Gamesmanship*. New York: Praeger, 1962, p. 200.

34. Anatol Rapoport and Albert M. Chammah, *Prisoner's Dilemma: A Study in Conflict and Cooperation*. Ann Arbor, Mich.: University of Michigan Press, 1965, p. 258.

35. Kenneth E. Boulding, "The Learning and Reality-Testing Process in the International System," *Journal of International Affairs*, 21:1 (1967), 11.

36. Schelling, *The Strategy of Conflict*, pp. 9-10. The pioneering work in the field of game theory is John von Neumann and Oskar Morgenstern, *Theory of Games and Economic Behavior*. Princeton N.J.: Princeton University Press, 1953.

37. Anatol Rapoport, "Game Theory and Human Conflict," in Elton B. McNeil (ed.), *The Nature of Human Conflict*. Englewood Cliffs, N.J.: Prentice-Hall, 1965, p. 225.

38. Karl W. Deutsch, *The Analysis of International Relations*. Englewood Cliffs, N.J.: Prentice-Hall, 1968, p. 121.

Additional Readings

Additional readings on the subject of balancing techniques may be found in *Discord and Harmony: Readings in International Politics*, edited by Ivo D. Duchacek and published by Holt, Rinehart and Winston in 1972. Chapter 14, "Conflict and Compromise," contains Thomas C. Schelling's application of game theory to tacit bargaining among unfriendly nations (pp. 378-395). Chapter 13, "Balance and Imbalance of Power," which contains essays on the subject of balance of power by Kenneth N. Waltz, John H. Herz, Graham T. Allison, and others, has already been recommended in relation to the preceding chapter.

14
Coexistence and Diplomacy

Balancing techniques and negotiations represent two possible separate or combined responses to an actual or potential conflict of interest among nations. The main purpose of most signaling and balancing techniques is to resist or to curb foreign will and power; the purpose of diplomatic negotiations among nations is to reach a compromise by bargaining. The characteristic feature of negotiations is the communication between policy makers of their respective estimates that the conflict is negotiable and of what the terms of an agreement, based on mutual concession, might be. If concessions are excluded *a priori*, no negotiation in a real sense is possible or advisable. If, for instance, both the Soviet Union and the United States are determined to add the whole of Germany to their respective military and political systems, no negotiation is possible, as no concession can be granted in one or the other direction. The result would be, as it has been, that Germany must remain divided. If one side wants what the other side cannot concede even in part, as Hans J. Morgenthau noted,

> no amount of talk will make either party yield. The two women who came before King Solomon, each claiming the baby as her own, raise an issue which in its very nature could not be settled through negotiations. The

issue itself called for all or nothing and the wise King, by giving it the appearance of treating it as though it could be settled by a compromise, demonstrated that it could not.[1]

Ideally, the result of successful negotiation is an agreement based on mutual accommodation. The result is usually incorporated into a treaty or communiqué (see the example in Document 14.1). "There is no durable Treaty which is not founded on reciprocal Advantage," wrote François de Callières, the well-known author of a book on the best manner of negotiating with sovereigns in the eighteenth century, "and indeed a treaty which does not satisfy this condition is no treaty at all, and is apt to contain the Seeds of its own dissolution."[2] The satisfaction deriving from the agreement must therefore be more or less evenly distributed; agreements may sometimes be based, so to speak, on a balance of mutual dissatisfaction. The reciprocity of advantages and disadvantages is the first precondition for a durable agreement.

The second condition is the awareness of both parties that, in spite of their present conflict of specific interests, they also have something in common: a shared interest in survival, a need for order based on a precise definition of mutual rights and duties that they consider preferable to living in uncertainty or chaos, or a clear and present common danger. The emergence of a common enemy may create a feeling of sudden harmony between nations that have previously known only mutual suspicion and hatred; the Churchill-Stalin military partnership against Hitler is a good example. In international bargaining the contending parties must be aware of some common interest that makes them mutually dependable to some degree. This is not dissimilar to collective bargaining between industry and labor, in which the success of the negotiation depends on the explicit or implicit recognition of both sides that neither can quite do without the other. Negotiations necessarily fail when nations believe that they not only can do without one another but can survive in total opposition to one another.

CONFLICTS AMONG FRIENDS AND COOPERATION AMONG FOES

In international politics the term "cooperation" is usually associated with an atmosphere of trust and friendship. By contrast, the term "international conflict" evokes the opposite image of suspicion, hatred, and bloodshed. Such a contrast is too rigid in actual practice. In international politics the dividing line between cooperation and conflict, or friend and enemy, is quite fluid; nations move from one category to another with much greater ease and less embarrassment than individuals do in interpersonal relations. In fact, it is sometimes difficult to ascertain at what exact point the process of solving a conflict has transformed the contending parties into cooperating partners or at what point an intimate partnership has been replaced by suspicion or outright enmity. A pessimistic view of such fluidity dreads the ease with which amity can become enmity. An optimist hopes for the contrary movement. Neither the pessimistic nor the optimistic view should be excluded from our consideration.

In the course of promoting its own interests, a nation will find that some of its interests are in harmony with those of other nations, that some are in conflict, and that some are neither in harmony nor in conflict. Sometimes the sheer fact of geographic distance precludes either competition or cooperation, and negotiations are not necessary. This is less and less true in our shrinking and interdependent world. Still, a very limited amount of diplomatic activity would mark, for instance, the relations between Costa Rica and Mongolia. Sometimes interests are in competition but do not contain any element of urgency or threat of violent solution and may therefore be shelved, so to speak, without an attempt at compromise.

Hostile Allies

Very rarely, if ever, is there either total harmony or total conflict of personal or national interests. As mentioned earlier (Chapter 11), men being men, and nations being nations, perfect and permanent harmony among them is difficult to imagine. Conflicts of interest break out among relatives, neighbors, allies, and intimate friends and often require arduous negotiations, adjustments, mutual accommodation, explicit or tacit compromises, or arbitration by a third party. Allies may often have profound disagreements on trade and tariff policies while their political and military cooperation flourishes. An alliance may continue even though its functioning has been seriously hampered by political or strategic disagreements. A book published in 1964 on the subject of the wartime relations between the United States and fighting France, so closely associated in their then common struggle against Germany and for the liberation of France, was entitled *Hostile Allies: FDR and Charles de Gaulle*.[3] In the 1970s, on the other hand, we could imagine this title: *Mao and Nixon–Nixon and Brezhnev: Cordial Enemies*. Of course, in a case of conflict, a tradition of friendship and mutual trust makes a compromise solution easier than a tradition of enmity; if parties trust each other they can anticipate that despite their conflicts of interest the agreed-upon solution will be adhered to by all parties concerned.

Cooperating Rivals

While it is true that no two nations can be expected to have all their interests in harmony with one another all the time, it is equally true that rarely do two nations, however angry they may be with each other, have all their interests in conflict all the time. Enemies have often proved quite capable of granting each other mutual concessions, reaching working compromises, or engaging in a limited cooperation in one sector while uncompromising enmity and total distrust prevail in a different, usually more sensitive, sector of their relations.

History shows that even in an actual war the interests of the belligerents are not always in total conflict; some common interests may manifest themselves. While enemies are aiming at the annihilation of their opponents, they customarily respect the life and the immunities of their respective diplomatic missions, which, following the outbreak of hostilities, are usually repatriated through neutral countries. Even such revolutionary regimes as Communist Russia and Nazi Germany considered it mutually advantageous to arrange for the orderly repatriation of their respective missions from Berlin and Moscow after hostilities had begun on the eastern front. Some enthusiastic believers in the power of international law and morality tend to see in such manifestations a proof of the strength and universality of international law and customs. This is exaggerated, but such instances do point to the community of some interests even while the majority of vital interests are viewed as irreconcilable. While the chances of victory and defeat appear about equal, belligerents usually respect the Geneva international legal conventions concerning the treatment of the wounded and of prisoners of war, although simultaneously the belligerents engage in the merciless killing of each other's military personnel and the civilians in industrial cities and other target areas. In the no-man's-land between the French and German trenches of World War I, the hatred and fire between both sides was sometimes temporarily suspended to permit the removal of the wounded and the burial of the dead.

All these incidents seem to indicate that the period of implacable enmity does not preclude the manifestation of common interests in some areas, however limited and marginal they may be. Political conflict rarely appears to include the totality of all interests, both political and nonpolitical, and constitute the so-called pure conflict in which one side aims at winning everything while the opponent fears he may lose everything; Rome's total destruction of Carthage—a zero-sum game in terms of game theory—seems to be the exception rather than the rule. And it is the simultaneity of compatible and conflicting interests which permits nations to coexist and negotiate compromises on some conflicts of interest while using deterrence and occasionally violence to prevent a unilateral solution of other conflicts.

DIPLOMACY AND BALANCING TECHNIQUES

The important distinction between negotiations, whose primary purpose is compromise, and balancing techniques, whose primary purpose is deterrence, should not obscure the fact that there is an intertwining connection between the balancing process and negotiation. Diplomacy is usually a part, a form, or a special technique of the balancing and signaling process. Chapter 12 already noted that in international politics the search for influence and control over men and events usually represents an admixture of signals, acts, persuasion, intimidation, and coercion. The use of violence and the balancing, signaling, and negotiating techniques analyzed in four separate chapters in this book represent a cluster of interlaced political activities whose purpose is to influence decision makers and shape situations. Whether deliberately or unwittingly, a threat of the use of violence is present in many a peaceful diplomatic negotiation.

In the balancing process the power of each balancing nation is the subject of careful though rarely accurate measurement. In diplomatic negotiations the evaluation of each other's power and intentions is an equally cautious process. National leaders prepare their contacts with foreign leaders with extraordinary care so as not to prejudice but in every way enhance their bargaining position at a conference table even before the negotiation starts. Many diplomatic conferences have been delayed for months by arduous preliminary negotiations on the subject of the agenda and the sequence of the items to be negotiated in the future. The placing of an item on the agenda, its exact wording and position, could conceivably indicate a premature willingness to yield or limit the elbowroom for bargaining maneuvers. No diplomatic conference can start unless the preliminaries are settled first; although they strike an outside observer as futile, purely formal, or prestige-oriented, their settlement is actually part of diplomatic bargaining. Among the preliminaries are such issues as when and where the meeting should take place (often neutral countries such as Switzerland are chosen since coming there has an equal effect on the prestige of all concerned), what should be the order of precedence in entering the conference room or sitting around the table, what shape the table should have, who should be the first to speak, and other matters of protocol that in reality are serious calculations of the respective power and prestige of the negotiating parties.

At the last Big Three Conference of World War II at Potsdam (August 1945), Truman, Churchill, and Stalin agreed to enter the conference room through three different doors simultaneously so as not to create an impression of hierarchy of either power or merits in the common struggle against Nazi Germany. The importance of prestige and status and even the respective personal heights of the Big Three remained a part of the Potsdam conference while other vital issues were being discussed. In his memoirs President Truman noted that both Stalin and Churchill always took precautions not to look smaller in photographs than Truman: "I was surprised at Stalin's stature—he was not over five feet five or six inches tall. When he had pictures taken, he would usually stand on the step above me. Churchill would do the same thing. They were both shorter than I."[4]

The issue of respective tallness did not seem to plague the 1968-1970 Paris conference on Vietnam, where Ambassador Averell Harriman, and then Henry Cabot Lodge, both six-footers, had to negotiate with diminutive Vietnamese leaders. But the shape of the conference table and the sitting order delayed the opening of the conference for more than ten weeks. An incredible haggling went on and on as to whether the table should be square, oblong, rectangular, oval, round, or any number of imaginative mutations.

A round table flanked on two sides by smaller rectangular tables for secretariat personnel was finally agreed on. This shape allegedly left intact the vital interests of all parties and permitted each to view the conference in whatever way it chose. It satisfied the communist delegations, since it made it possible for the National Liberation Front (NFL) to sit down as an equal partner in a four-party meeting. The two rectangular stenographers' tables, on the other hand, satisfied the United States and South Vietnam, since the two tables could be interpreted as an indication that the conference was really only between the communists on one side and the anticommunists on the other (see Figure 14.1).

FIGURE 14.1
ROOM DESIGN FOR VIETNAM PEACE TALKS IN PARIS

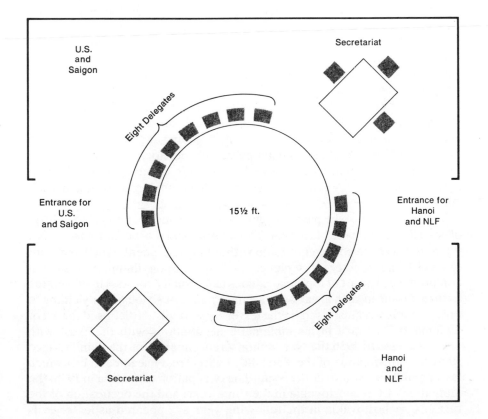

"Rectangular tables produce cliques or sides, and if the sides are already chosen, you tend to get a fixity of position," was one of the arguments for an oval or round table in general, as voiced by Dr. Robert Sommer, chairman of the psychology department of the University of California at Davis (*New York Times*, January 17, 1969). "Space around a circular table is undifferentiated and cohesive—it tends to draw people toward the center," was his conclusion, based on the apparent theory that every table shape exerts its own psychological pull on discussions. It is still to be demonstrated whether a rectangular table would have made the Paris negotiations any longer and any more difficult than they were. When finally in January 1973 Henry Kissinger and Le Duc Tho conferred for a total of thirty-five hours over six days in Paris, neither the shape of the table nor the size of the two chief negotiators seemed to be the issue; on January 24 Kissinger and Tho initialed the Vietnam cease-fire agreement sitting opposite each other at a normal oblong conference table.

VIOLENCE, BLACKMAIL, AND DECEIT

If, as it is said, violence begins where the diplomatic art of persuasion and compromise leaves off, the line between the two is a thin one.

The diplomatic conference in Paris between the United States, North Vietnam, South Vietnam, and the National Liberation Front was a typical case of nations engaged simultaneously in violence and diplomatic bargaining (see Figure 14.2). In December 1972, for instance, when the October agreement between Kissinger and Le Duc Tho appeared stalemated and both sides were accusing each other of procrastination, President Nixon ordered a renewal of the bombing attacks above the 20th parallel in North Vietnam, including round-the-clock B-52 raids in the Hanoi-Haiphong area. After twelve days of raids, bombing above the 20th parallel was halted. A general cease-fire in Vietnam began on January 27, 1973.

Violence may also be part of negotiations in an indirect way, in the form of so-called diplomatic blackmail. The favorite and most common form is a threat to leave the conference table without an agreement, which is meant to evoke the specter of violence to follow upon failure to reach a compromise. The art of diplomatic blackmail usually consists in presenting a current issue in such a way as to seem so minor or so local that yielding to prevent violence appears to be the lesser of two evils. Hitler used the art of diplomatic blackmail in his diplomatic negotiations with the West with great success. In 1936 the Nazi military reoccupation of the demilitarized Rhineland in violation of the Versailles Peace Treaty seemed to be a much lesser evil than a war over the issue. The occupation of Austria in 1938, the mutilation of Czechoslovakia in the same year, and the occupation of the rest of Czechoslovakia in the following year all appeared as lesser evils than a major war. Only on September 3, 1939, did the Nazi diplomatic technique of extreme blackmail fail: At that time a world war appeared a lesser evil than condoning another in Hitler's series of "last territorial demands."

The following instance of diplomatic blackmail under the shadow of the A-bomb occurred in postwar Japan. In 1946, during the American-Japanese negotiations concerning the revision of the old imperial constitution, the Japanese representatives did all they could to delay or dilute the United States proposal for its democratization. As there was a danger that in the newly constituted Far Eastern Commission the Soviet Union might influence the shape of the new Japanese constitution to serve the interests of the Japanese Communist party, the impatient General Douglas MacArthur set a deadline for the Japanese acceptance of the American draft. Characteristically, he selected February 22, George Washington's birthday. The Japanese government was under extreme pressure: The institution of the emperor was threatened. Furthermore, General MacArthur also suggested that he would bypass the constitutional framework and political parties and propose the American draft directly to the Japanese people for approval by a plebiscite. In a final discussion with

FIGURE 14.2
TNT "STAMPS" ON DIPLOMATIC MESSAGES

Editorial cartoon by Pat Oliphant. Copyright 1969, *The Denver Post*. Reproduced with permission of the Los Angeles Times Syndicate.

the Japanese representatives General MacArthur's closest associate and spokesman, General Courtney Whitney, gave the Japanese government twenty to sixty minutes to examine the draft and accept or reject it with all the consequences that have been suggested. It is interesting to read General Whitney's words (remember, however, that this negotiation was conducted by military, not diplomatic personnel):

> At the end of about one hour, I decided that we should rejoin our hosts [members of the Japanese government had been considering the draft in a neighboring room] and we were rising as Mr. Shirasu, the Secretary of the Minister of Foreign Affairs, reappeared. He seemed flustered by the drastic changes in our draft, and it occurred to me that this was an opportune moment to employ one more psycholgical shaft. I did not know the impressive support that I was about to receive from an unexpected quarter. As he mumbled apologies for keeping us waiting, I replied with a smile: "Not at all, Mr. Shirasu. We have been enjoying your atomic sunshine." And at that moment, with what could not have been better timing, a big B-29 came roaring over us. The reaction upon Mr. Shirasu was indescribable, but profound.[5]

The inferior bargaining position of post-Hiroshima Japan could hardly be more impressively brought home. The American draft of the Japanese constitution was accepted with only minor changes.

The above historical examples show the deliberate use of a combination of diplomacy and the threat of violence. Even more numerous are instances where violence forms an integral part of the negotiations without anybody purposefully introducing it into the process. If a representative of an atomic power entertained a representative of a lesser power and in his technique of persuasion sincerely relied only on his rational arguments, engaging smile, and excellent cook (see the eighteenth-century recipe for successful diplomacy on page 550), would the guest dissociate all these charming approaches from the shadow of tremendous atomic or economic power that looms so large behind the banquet silver? Or, in a less dramatic but more facetious context, if the United States embassy were suddenly to serve tea rather than the usual coffee after dinner, would there be a panic in the country dependent on exporting coffee to the United States?

And then there is something else to consider: Like any other technique of international politics, the technique of diplomatic negotiation may be perverted or misused. Instead of serving the purpose of peace through compromise, it may serve the purpose of conquest through diplomatic blackmail—as the example of Hitler's "diplomacy" has shown. By such perverted diplomacy or diplomatic deceit a nation may be weakened, humiliated, and subjugated by a "negotiation" that does not aim at a real compromise based on mutual concessions but at a phony one based on real concession by one party and deceit by the other. Many nations throughout history have been "negotiated" down from a position of security into one of insecurity, leading finally to defeat. Three times in modern history, for example, Czechoslovakia has lost either her territorial integrity or her independence through what was presented by her expansionist neighbors as diplomatic "negotiations": Czechoslovakia's agreement to the cession of the fortified border regions of the Sudetenland to Germany (the Munich Agreement of 1938), the Nazi division and occupation of rump Czechoslovakia (on the basis of an agreement signed on March 14, 1939, by the Czech President), and the Soviet occupation of Czechoslovakia in 1968 (based on an invitation allegedly issued by a pro-Soviet wing in the ruling Czechoslovak Communist party).

The danger of a false compromise is particularly severe in disarmament negotiations when the aim is apparently general disarmament, but in reality the goal of one side or both is to produce the unilateral disarmament of the opponent power. The United States viewed with suspicion the Soviet proposal for elimination of all atomic weapons at the time when it had a clear supremacy in this field. This seemed tantamount to placing the United States in a greatly inferior position in comparison with Russia's huge land armies, the central position of Russia in Eurasia, and the projection of Soviet power to Berlin. In 1949 Russia viewed with equal suspicion an American proposal that suggested the scrapping of all land armies; its navy, air force, and atomic arsenal would have given the United States superiority over Russia. Frequently only with the benefit of hindsight is it possible to clearly distinguish diplomatic deceit from diplomatic negotiations undertaken for the purpose of reaching a compromise and strengthening peace. Fred Charles Iklé has warned that

> . . . in the nuclear age, when a single battle can bring total disaster, negotiation has acquired the nimbus of Salvation that will protect the world from destruction and eventually deliver it from the terrible engines of war. But negotiation is only an instrument; it can be used on the side of the angels as well as by the forces of darkness.[6]

Acquisition of information about the nature and intensity of interests in conflict must precede and be fed into the process of searching for a solution by compromise. E. A. J. Johnson expressed well the two aspects of diplomatic activity:

> Although diplomacy might be described as a complex and delicate instrument that measures the forces working at the epicenters of international relations, unlike the physicist's seismographs—which can only record disturbances—the subtle machinery of diplomacy can be used to arrest, meliorate, or reduce the discord, misunderstandings, and disagreements which precipitate international crises.[7]

FOUR PURPOSES OF DIPLOMACY

As to their specific purposes, diplomatic negotiations among nations may be divided into four categories of bargaining:

1. Resolving a conflict of interests peacefully.
2. Preventing a clear and immediate danger of violent solution (or a risk of yielding to rival pressures).
3. Restoring peace after a clash of national interests has led to violence.
4. Establishing an atmosphere, framework, system, or permanent organization for the peaceful solution of potential future conflicts.

Diplomatic bargaining during severe international crises necessarily differs from diplomatic negotiations in a period of relative calm. A recent study on bargaining during international crises pointed out, for instance, that during such major crises as Berlin in 1961 and Cuba in 1962 the contending powers tried "to shake the resolve of opposing decision makers so as to undermine the credibility of their bargaining position," projecting the responsibility for a given crisis onto the opponent and "emphasizing the negative or dangerous aspects of a situation" as a prelude "to offers for positive rewards that would, in effect, change the character of the whole confrontation."[8] This would lead subsequently to a negotiated agreement and an end of crisis.

An attempt to solve a conflict frequently leads to an agreement on the methods of solution of future conflicts. Sometimes, even without a conflict but in anticipation of a future one, nations try through preliminary negotiations to build an institutional framework for future negotiated solutions of conflicts. This is the fountainhead of international law and international organizations (analyzed in Chapters 9 and 10).

When national leaders talk and write to each other and negotiate agreements, their contacts and communications may be explicit and *direct*, as in summit meetings and international conferences, and, potentially, in any future use of the hot line between Moscow and Washington. The contacts and communications may also be explicit and *indirect*, that is, through professional diplomats or personal emissaries. And then there is the process of implicit or *tacit* bargaining, that is, "negotiations" without contact and without exchanges of verbal messages. Logic and the art of guessing sometimes replace communication when nations are not on speaking terms but are aware of their conflicts of interest as well as some of their common interests. The concluding portion of this chapter will return to the problem of tacit bargaining.

Whatever form of international bargaining is chosen—explicit or implicit, direct or indirect—the stream of signals, messages, arguments, proposals, counterproposals, lures, and threats is primarily addressed to those who have the authority to make decisions, that is, to those who can offer concessions or accept counterconcessions (or engage in the art of diplomatic guessing) in behalf of their nations. The public is usually unaware of the febrile diplomatic calculations and exchanges of proposals. In this sense also, negotiations may be seen as distinct from those balancing techniques, such as propaganda, subversion, economic pressures, and military action, that are primarily directed against the public or the lower levels of government and through them against the top leadership. If the public is seduced or frightened by psychological warfare, if the state machinery is subverted, or if the people are suffering under economic privations or are being decimated by an effective military action, their discontent and despair may weaken or break the will of their leaders; and this is the very purpose of such "nondiplomatic" measures.

In theory, national governments, depending on their policy goals and circumstances, have a choice between deterrence and diplomacy. In practice, they usually choose a combination of the two, mostly because they can never be certain whether diplomatic negotiations will result in a compromise solution or whether deterrence or a test of force will ultimately be necessary. As a consequence, negotiations—even those that sincerely aim at compromise—are often preceded or accompanied by a propaganda barrage, by economic pressures, or by military threats in order to ensure diplomatic success or to ensure the nation against diplomatic failure.

On the other hand, in war, which represents the opposite of peaceful compromise by diplomacy, informal contacts and some tacit bargaining are maintained in spite of the formal severance of political and diplomatic relations. A limited war, as Thomas C. Schelling has shown,[9] remains limited only if the fighting nations, although no longer on speaking terms, tacitly recognize and agree that it is in their mutual interest to prevent the war from escalating.

It seems that in most situations the choice of violent means does not eliminate all traces of diplomatic bargaining, nor does the use of diplomacy eliminate all traces of potential or actual violence.

DIPLOMATIC MISSIONS

A diplomatic mission—an embassy or legation—is a symbol and an instrument of peaceful accommodation, that is, peaceful solution of conflicts through the understanding of mutual positions and the willingness to negotiate on this basis. An embassy (presided over by an ambassador) or a legation (presided over by a minister plenipotentiary) is manned by men and women professionally trained for international negotiation, for legitimate gathering of information about the intentions and power of the nation to which they are accredited, for communicating and interpreting their nation's policies, perceptions, beliefs and actions, and for ceremonial as well as legal representation of their own nation's interests abroad.

When nations are not on speaking terms because of war or extreme hostility or because they do not recognize each other's legitimacy, no diplomatic missions are exchanged. For fifteen years the United States did not recognize the Soviet government as a legitimate one; there were many official and nonofficial contacts between the two countries, but no diplomatic ones. Similarly, after World War II, the United States and many other countries denied diplomatic recognition to the government of Communist China. In the same period, Franco's Spain and the communist countries had no diplomatic relations with each other; in 1972 East Germany became the first communist state to establish diplomatic relations with Fascist Spain.

When one nation grants diplomatic recognition to another and establishes diplomatic missions, the act implies the recognition not only of the government's legitimate authority over its territory, its institutions, and its people, but also—and this is the core of the matter—of the capacity to negotiate international agreements and abide by them. An ambassador is accredited (that is, sent with letters presenting his credentials) to a foreign government; the foreign government receives him, treats him with respect, and provides him with immunities and privileges. Thus the ground is prepared for future contacts and negotiations. Although both the sending and the receiving governments anticipate some future clashes of interests, by establishing their missions they also give expression to their hope that future conflicts can and will be solved by peaceful methods, that is, by negotiations. Logically, when diplomacy fails to provide for a peaceful solution of a vital conflict and war ensues, diplomatic relations are severed. Diplomatic missions are closed, and the ambassadors and their staffs are sent home. Once all direct diplomatic communication ceases, mutual contact is limited largely to physical contact on the battlefield and indirect contact through a third party. Following the severance of diplomatic relations, it is customary for the embassy of a nation uninvolved in the conflict to act as a go-between and accept the duty of maintaining the minimum necessary contacts between the two hostile countries. From the 1950s to the 1970s, for instance, Communist Czechoslovakia was in charge of the indirect representation of Cuba in Washington, while Switzerland did the same for the United States in Havana. In 1960 Indonesia and her former colonial ruler, Holland, severed their diplomatic relations over the question of West Irian. The indirect representation of Indonesian interests at The Hague was taken over at Indonesia's request by the United Arab Republic; the indirect representation of the Dutch interests in Jakarta was taken over by the United Kingdom. One year later a most unusual step was taken: Even the customary indirect representation by a third party of now extremely hostile countries was suspended, an act which even the enemies in World War II had not adopted. After West Irian became part of Indonesia in 1963, diplomatic relations between Indonesia and Holland were resumed.

Summit Meetings and Professional Diplomats

Many books have been written in favor of a continuous and professional form of diplomatic negotiations, as can be conducted only by ambassadors and their staffs accredited to foreign governments and fully acquainted with the leading personnel as well as the capacities and limitations of the foreign nation. Other books and articles, on the contrary, favor occasional dramatic meetings of heads of state at the summit.

The contrast between the two forms is more apparent than real. Even if at various occasions a summit meeting of chiefs of government takes place, it is preceded by negotiations through diplomatic channels. The summit meeting often only ratifies or proclaims agreements reached through diplomatic channels. Personal contacts between national leaders may be useful, of course, and this is the most valid argument for summit meetings. There is, of course, also a counterargument: the Kennedy-Khrushchev summit meeting in Vienna in 1961 seemed to have resulted in the Soviets' underrating the determination and courage of John F. Kennedy, mostly on account of his youth and lack of experience. The consequences of some summit meetings warn us against hasty improvisations and agreements that have not been carefully prepared in advance. Harry S. Truman referred in his memoirs to the agreement on the occupation zones in Europe made at the summit in Quebec in 1944: "This shows conclusively that heads of state should be very careful about horseback agreements, because there is no way of foretelling the final result."[10] Twenty-five years later, a similar caution with reference to hasty agreements at the summit was voiced by Soviet Minister of Foreign Affairs Andrei A. Gromyko, who said in his speech to the Supreme Soviet (July 10, 1969):

> Our countries are divided by profound class differences. But the Soviet Union always believed that the USSR and the USA can find common language on questions of maintaining peace. It stands to reason that arguments on these questions can be achieved only when they are in keeping with the mutual interests, including the interests of our allies and friends. . . . The Soviet Union, naturally, noticed the statements of the President of the United States [Nixon] in favor of a *well-prepared* Soviet-American summit meeting. [Italics added.]

Unprepared solutions or improvisations made at the summit may indeed have disastrous consequences and threaten peace more than if the meeting had not taken place.

Modern experience with grand summit meetings is, to say the least, mixed. The past four decades have witnessed a series of summit meetings: They include the Munich summit in 1938 (England, Nazi Germany, France, and Fascist Italy) and the Soviet-Nazi summit in Moscow in August 1939, both of which paved the way to World War II; the Teheran (1943), Yalta (February 1945) and Potsdam summits (July-August 1945) between Stalin's

Russia, the United States, and England, which were to prepare for common victory in World War II and for a durable peace after the war; and, following the period of the Cold War, a series of summit contacts[11] between Russia and the United States (at Geneva in 1955, the Kennedy-Khrushchev meeting in Vienna in 1961, and the Johnson-Kosygin meeting in Glassboro, New Jersey, in 1967), culminating in Nixon's summit meetings with the Chinese leaders in February 1972 and with the Soviet leaders in Moscow in May 1972 and then again in June 1974. In contrast to the sense of accomplishment which marked the summit meeting in Moscow in 1972, the results of the second Nixon-Brezhnev summit meeting (held in the wake of the Watergate impeachment procedures) were disappointing: the two superpowers merely agreed to limit both countries to a single deployment area for ABMs instead of two, as agreed in 1972, and prohibit underground tests exceeding fifty kilotons (corresponding to the explosive force of more than two Hiroshima bombs).

Subsequently, however, President Ford and Secretary Brezhnev agreed at their first summit meeting at Vladivostok (November 25, 1974) to put a ceiling on their arsenals of nuclear weapons for the next decade. Under the new agreement the United States and the Soviet Union may each have about 2,400 offensive vehicles (missiles or bombers); about one half of the missiles may be MIRV'ed. Thus Russia and America will acquire the capability to destroy each other 15 times by 1984; they promised to have another look at their respective overkill capabilities in 1981 when new talks on a possible gradual reduction of the arms race may begin. According to the critics of the Vladivostok deal, the agreement simply ratified the present scope and tempo of the arms race, at best preventing its acceleration. According to Kissinger, the Vladivostok accord represented a "breakthrough" since it has put a "cap on the arms race."

The series of summit meetings between heads of states in the period from 1938 to 1973 illustrates well the point made previously, namely, that the great world powers are indeed able to convert their enmity, reflecting their conflicting national interests and ideologies, into *temporary* partnership. Can we, should we, ask humans in our temporal world to achieve more than temporary partnerships? It is true that in connection with World War II some of the conversions of enmity negotiated at the summit into relative amity were of extremely short duration. Another feature that characterizes the five World War II summits (Munich, Moscow, Teheran, Yalta, and Potsdam) is that the main reason for the change of enmity into relative amity was an external threat—we have already observed that nations more readily cooperate against an outsider than for some common good: for instance, nations are usually quite ready to combine to promote one ideology *against* another ideology, the common defense of some nations *against* another group of nations, or the economic and technical progress of a selected few (for example, the Oil World and the First World, leaving the rest of the world behind and in an inferior position). All the five accords of

World War II represent a typical example of what is meant by negotiations among adversaries, that is, a mutual search for accommodation and compromise in the areas where it is possible, while leaving conflicts in other areas unsolved, to be resolved by future negotiation or conflict. None of the five agreements can be therefore classified as a compact between friends or a purely deceitful instance of gamesmanship between enemies. Elements of deceit as well as tentative trust were present in all of them.

A pessimist can draw a depressing conclusion from these five cases by pointing to the short duration of these cooperative arrangements, their close connection with fighting an outsider viewed as a dangerous common enemy, and the ease with which, in international politics, one's friend today may become one's worst enemy tomorrow. An optimist, on the other hand, may stress the reverse and point to the ease with which the enemies of yesterday may become the partners of tomorrow, often quite able to establish their cooperation on a durable basis; after all the relative cordiality now prevailing between France and England and France and Germany, former enemies, points to the possibility of positive results from contacts and negotiations among those who only yesterday seemed implacable foes.

Which estimate, the optimist or pessimist, should be applied to contemporary negotiations, at the summit and below it, among the superpowers? It is too early to say; unlike the previous five cases of summitry the post-Cold War ones are not fully documented—conclusive evidence is not yet in nor will it be in for some time to come. But one difference between the World War II meetings and agreements and the contemporary ones should be noted: the awesome difference between the prenuclear and the thermonuclear age. The possibility of mutual annihilation may endow contemporary diplomatic negotiations between adversaries with greater urgency and perhaps with a greater hope for durable success than could have been the case before, during, and at the end of World War II. Through regular contacts and negotiations, occasionally leading to a well-prepared summit, nations in general and superpowers in particular may discover that some of their seemingly nonnegotiable conflicts (those concerning Vietnam, Korea, Germany, the Middle East, advanced missile systems, East Central Europe, and others) are negotiable after all, while other conflicts that really exclude any compromise for the time being are not worth the risk of violent solution or that they can, with duly publicized protests, be shelved without any present solution. A good example of such a frankly mixed result of summit diplomacy is the final communiqué issued by Chou En-lai and Kissinger at the conclusion of the Mao-Nixon summit meeting in Peking in February 1972. Both sides agreed that their social and ideological differences should not hinder the gradual development of closer trade, cultural, and political links between the two countries, including permanent diplomatic representation, which, however, could not attain the status of a full-fledged ambassadorial representation while, as China saw it, the province of Taiwan, with American support, remained under the control of the enemy the Chinese Communists had defeated in civil war, the Nationalist party.

Recording agreement on many general points, both parties also frankly recorded their areas of disagreement: China reaffirmed its support of North Vietnam, North Korea, and revolutionary movements in general, and the United States reaffirmed its support of South Vietnam and South Korea and its opposition to any violent solution of the Taiwan issue, although recognizing the principle according to which Taiwan was a part of China. Excerpts from the Sino-American communiqué are reproduced in Documents 14.1 and 14.2.

Between negotiations through normal diplomatic channels and a summit meeting, there may occur a conference of foreign ministers. Unjustly perhaps, such conferences of top experts in foreign policy who do not have the ultimate responsibility for agreement or disagreement have the reputation of rarely being successful. This, perhaps, is what led former Soviet Premier Nikita S. Khrushchev, the noted phrasemonger, to comment caustically: "A foreign ministers' conference is like a deep freeze. You put meat into it and after a while you take it out. It is neither better nor worse. Nothing happens." This was meant to imply that, unlike the overcautious conference of foreign ministers, a summit meeting of presidents and prime ministers either spoils the diplomatic "meat" beyond redemption or cooks it into a palatable meal. However, it is understandable that foreign ministers prove extremely cautious in committing themselves and their leaders to anything. Their business is to think through all the implications of any agreement, and their experience has taught them a great deal about the unpredictability of men and nations.

Functions of Diplomats

A diplomatic mission, usually called an embassy, represents the national leadership abroad both politically and legally vis-á-vis the receiving nation. In this capacity, it negotiates a great number of agreements, some of which may be of vital importance to the nation and to the entire international community. Ambassadors and their staffs may, for instance, prepare specific agreements that a future summit meeting will only ratify and publicize. They prepare political and military agreements of such importance as NATO and the Warsaw Pact and also negotiate agreements on trade, tariffs, copyrights, scientific and cultural exchanges, economic aid, and technical assistance. Some of the agreements have importance only for individuals or interest groups, not for the whole nation. Consular officers, in particular, deal with promotion of trade, extradition of criminals, issuance of visas, and the legal problems that may be created by a death, birth, or inheritance of their citizens in a foreign country.

Negotiation is not the only role of diplomatic missions abroad. They have to fulfill two other important roles connected with the balancing aspects of international politics.

1. Diplomats are "the eyes and ears" of their nations abroad. Their intimate knowledge of the host country and its politics should enable them to evaluate the intentions and power of that nation, especially any significant changes in its strength or goals. They report their findings and estimates to the central office. The reporting duty usually occupies 80 percent of the time and energy of top diplomatic personnel abroad. In

---

DOCUMENT 14.1

U.S.-CHINESE COMMUNIQUÉ, FEBRUARY 27, 1972: AGREEMENTS

The leaders of the People's Republic of China and the United States of America found it beneficial to have this opportunity, after so many years without contact, to present candidly to one another their views on a variety of issues. They reviewed the international situation in which important changes and great upheavals are taking place and expounded their respective positions and attitudes . . .

There are essential differences between China and the United States in their social systems and foreign policies. However, the two sides agreed that countries should conduct their relations on the principles of respect for the sovereignty and territorial integrity of all states, nonaggression against other states, equality and mutual benefit, and peaceful coexistence.[1] . . .

With these principles of international relations in mind the two sides stated that:

Progress toward normalization of relations between China and the United States is in the interest of all countries.

Both wish to reduce the danger of international military conflict.

Neither should seek hegemony in the Asia-Pacific region and each is opposed to the efforts by any other country or group of countries to establish such hegemony . . .

Neither is prepared to negotiate on behalf of any third party or to enter into agreements or understandings with the other directed at other states.

Both sides are of the view that it would be against the interests of the peoples of the world for any major country to collude with another against other countries, or for major countries to divide up the world into spheres of interest. . . .

The two sides agreed that it is desirable to broaden the understanding between the two peoples. To this end, they discussed specific areas in such fields as science, technology, culture, sports and journalism in which people-to-people contacts and exchanges would be mutually beneficial.

---

1. These are the five principles of peace known in Asia as *Panch Shila*. They were spelled out in the treaty between India and China regarding Tibet in the spring of 1954 and repeated in the Nehru—Chou En-lai declaration of June of the same year. They are also part of the Preamble of the Chinese Constitution of 1954.

---

principle, diplomats are supposed to obtain their information by legitimate means, not by any cloak and dagger techniques. There has always been and perhaps always will be a controversy about the exact line separating diplomatic reporting from spying. In communist and fascist countries the concept of legitimate access to information differs from that prevailing in countries with a free press and a relatively unhindered circulation of news.

DOCUMENT 14.2

U.S.-CHINESE COMMUNIQUÉ, FEBRUARY 27, 1972: DISAGREEMENTS

The sides reviewed the long-standing disputes between China and the United States:

The Chinese side reaffirmed its position: The Taiwan question is the crucial question obstructing the normalization of relations between China and the United States; the Government of the People's Republic of China is the sole legal government of China; Taiwan is a province of China which has long been returned to the motherland; the liberation of Taiwan is China's internal affair in which no other country has the right to interfere; and all U.S. forces and military installations must be withdrawn from Taiwan. The Chinese government firmly opposes any activities which aim at the creation of "one China, one Taiwan," "one China, two governments," "two Chinas," an "independent Taiwan" or advocate that "the status of Taiwan remains to be determined."

The U.S. side declared: The United States acknowledges that all Chinese on either side of the Taiwan Strait maintain there is but one China and that Taiwan is part of China. The United States does not challenge that position. It reaffirms its interest in a peaceful settlement of the Taiwan question by the Chinese themselves. With this project in mind, it affirms the ultimate[1] objective of the withdrawal of all U.S. forces and military installations from Taiwan. In the meantime, it will progressively reduce its forces and military installations on Taiwan as the tension in the area diminishes.[2] . . .

The Chinese side stated: Wherever there is oppression, there is resistance. Countries want independence, nations want liberation and the people want revolution--this has become the irresistible trend of history. . . . The Chinese side stated that it firmly supports the struggles of all oppressed people and nations for freedom and liberation. . . . All foreign troops should be withdrawn to their own countries.

The U.S. side stated: Peace in Asia and peace in the world require efforts both to reduce immediate tensions and to eliminate the basic causes of conflict. . . . The United states supports individual freedom and social progress for all the peoples of the world, free of outside pressure or intervention. . . .

1. "Ultimate" may, of course, still be a number of decades off.
2. Partial withdrawal is related to a decrease of tension; how substantial the decrease is will most probably be estimated by the United States, not China.

In the early 1950s the Eastern European communist countries considered the possession of a tourist map of their capital cities or a railroad timetable as illegitimate and therefore in the category of spying. (The problem of accuracy and timeliness of diplomatic reporting was discussed in Chapters 5 and 6.)

2. Diplomats are also spokesmen and interpreters of their country's past and present. An ambassador and his staff transmit confidential material such as a proposal, a threat, or the preliminary draft of a treaty, and also answer all sorts of inquiries concerning their country's policies, economics, history, literature, and art. Such questions are raised not only by governmental officials but also by the opposition leaders and students who may be the government of tomorrow and by intellectuals, newspapermen, businessmen, and labor and industrial leaders. As all of them directly or indirectly may influence their government's policies, it is useful to keep them informed and to answer their inquiries as well as possible. There are, of course, problems. An American diplomat may be called upon to explain the rise of unemployment in the United States to a communist economist, the misery of the Appalachians to a country that has received a generous food-for-peace program, America's friendly relations with Israel to a representative of the Arab League, the situation in the black ghettos to an African diplomat, and a series of anti-French articles in the American press to a French president. A Soviet diplomat also has a great deal of explaining to do: Why, for example, in view of the alleged superiority of the Soviet economic system over the decaying American one, does the USSR allow itself to be assessed for the purpose of contribution to the regular United Nations budget at less than half the United States's capacity? How can he explain that the allegedly superior political system of communism could produce, in constant succession, such controversial or criminal leaders as Stalin, Molotov, Beria, Malenkov, and Khrushchev, leaving only Lenin and the present leader, whoever he may be, beyond controversy? Why, in view of the Soviet support of the right of national self-determination in Asia, Latin America, and Africa, have the Ukrainians or Soviet Moslems not been granted the same right? What is the difference between the Soviet concentration camps for class enemies and the Nazi camps for racial enemies? Or, finally, why after fifty years of the allegedly superior system of the communist economy has the USSR so often been obliged to feed its people capitalist food? This, of course, is a question that not only diplomats but Soviet citizens may ask.

Qualities of a Diplomat

The functions of a diplomat assigned to a foreign country are as varied and multifaceted as are the political, economic, social, and cultural features of both his own and the host country. The diplomatic career calls not only for professional training and a lifelong dedication but also for some specific qualities that are essential for a successful discharge of diplomatic duties. The classic manual of diplomacy, written in 1716 by François de Callières and entitled *On the Manner of Negotiating with Princes*, described the qualities that a good negotiator should possess. Although the forms of international life and communications have profoundly changed in our era, the eighteenth-century concept of the successful diplomat still largely applies today; the sixteen major qualifications as analyzed in detail by Callières in 1916, may be summarized as follows. A good negotiator must be quick, resourceful, a good listener, courteous, and agreeable, and he must have (1) an observant mind, (2) a sound judgment that takes the measure of things as they are and that goes straight to the goal by the shortest and most natural paths without wandering into useless refinements and subtleties, (3) the gift of penetration such as will enable him to discover the thoughts of men and to deduce from the least movement of their countenances what passions are stirring within, (4) sufficient self-control to resist the longing to speak before he has thought out what he shall say (this should particularly apply to debates in the United Nations), (5) courage in danger and firmness in debate, (6) the tranquil and patient nature of a watchmaker, (7) equable humor, (8) the ability to suffer fools gladly (again this applies particularly to multilateral parliamentary diplomacy at the United Nations), (9) a knowledge of history, foreign institutions, and habits, (10) the ability to tell where, in a foreign country, the real decison-making power lies, (11) the presence of mind to find a quick and pregnant reply to unforeseen surprise, (12) knowledge of foreign languages (in Callières' time the emphasis was naturally on Latin and, in addition, German, Italian, Spanish, and French), (13) some knowledge of literature, mathematics, science, and law, (14) the ability to simulate dignity even if he does not possess it, (15) a spirit of application that refuses to be distracted by the pleasures of frivolous amusements such as gambling, drinking (drugs, we may now add), or women (a diplomat should not neglect women, since sometimes "the greatest events have followed the toss of a fan," but he should not lose his heart to them—"love's companions are indiscretion and imprudence"), and (16) good manners and a good cook, who is often an "excellent conciliator."

This is, then, the eighteenth-century concept of a diplomatic superman. What about honesty, one may ask? Sir Henry Wotton's well-known definition, "a diplomatist is an honest man sent to lie abroad for the good of his country," does not correspond with Callières' concept of a good negotiator:

> The good negotiator will never found the success of his mission on promises which he cannot redeem or on bad faith. It is a capital error, which prevails widely, that a clever negotiator must be a master of the art of deceit. . . . No doubt the art of lying has been practiced with success in diplomacy; but unlike honesty which here as elsewhere is the best policy,

a lie always leaves a drop of poison behind, and even the most dazzling diplomatic success gained by dishonesty stands on an insecure foundation, for it awakes in the defeated party a sense of aggravation, a desire for vengeance, and a hatred which must be always a menace to his foe.[12]

THE STYLE OF DIPLOMACY

The style of diplomacy necessarily reflects the political customs, unity, and cleavages of its time. Many authors today deplore the decline of the diplomatic style, and especially deplore the frequent use of deceit, violent language, or uncivilized manners, such as former Soviet Premier Khrushchev's surprising decision to take off his shoe and pound the desk in protest during the debate at the sixteenth United Nations General Assembly in 1961. Some express the hope that a change in the diplomatic style might produce a change in international politics and look back with nostalgia to the period of 1815-1914, which was marked by a prolonged period of peace among the major powers as well as generally good manners in international diplomacy. This is why many authors tend to refer to the hundred years separating the Congress of Vienna from the beginning of World War I as the Golden Age of Diplomacy; the conduct of foreign affairs was then in the hands of a relatively small international elite. Their background was largely similar; and so was their concept of the world to be preserved. This certainly does not apply to present-day diplomats, whose background and concept of the world to be established profoundly differs from continent to continent and from one ideological bloc to another.

"In its time of celebrity professional diplomacy was a bureaucratic expression—elegant but still bureaucratic—of a political concord seemingly firm and universal but actually neither," noted Charles Burton Marshall in his penetrating study of the Golden Age of Diplomacy.

> Diplomacy is the expression of political customs, not itself determinative of the character of political relations. The technique of diplomacy did not create the Golden Age. Rather the conditions of the time—with Europe ascendant and superficially tranquil for the time being—provided opportunity for diplomacy and its practitioners to seem prodigious. The circumstances, while they lasted, were bound to be flattering to diplomats. Elements of success were in the environment, like a rainy spell for forest rangers or the abundance of duck for hunters.[13]

As we have noted elsewhere, the international scene and the actors on it are intricately intertwined; like policy makers, diplomats both shape and reflect their environment, and so does their style.

The role of professional diplomats has been underestimated as often as it has been overrated. In the era of worldwide rapid communications, of jet travels undertaken by prime ministers and foreign ministers, and of occasional summit meetings, ambassadors and their staffs have sometimes been described as messenger boys whose only role is to transmit a message from the policy maker to the appropriate address. Such a view completely overlooks the informational and reporting activities of the diplomatic personnel and their share in policy making: many a diplomatic note apparently originating at the office of a head of state only reflects the ambassador's suggestions or his previous estimates of another nation's power and intentions; the embassy often delivers what it had initiated or at least greatly influenced. Furthermore, the skill and manner of the ambassador is often directly related to how well the ground has been prepared for the receipt of the note.

On the other hand, the personal role of the ambassador and his staff may easily be overrated if his role as an instrument of national policy is confused with policy making. Although it is true that administration and execution of policy sometimes represents more than half of the policy, the final responsibility, accountability, and capacity to act remain with the policy makers in the capital city: The ambassador only projects the will and the intentions of his national government abroad.

Open Diplomacy versus Quiet Diplomacy

Every negotiation among men is composed of two stages: the delicate bargaining stage and the final stage, in which the result is made known to all concerned. Delicate interpersonal negotiations leading to betrothal, marriage, or divorce are usually confidential; the result, for good reasons, is publicly announced. A similar principle applies to diplomacy. It should be confidential and quiet, but its results "should never be secret in the sense that the citizen should on no account be committed by his government to treaties or engagements of which he has not been given full previous knowledge."[14]

The issue of the open versus the secret aspects of foreign policy was confused by the appealing but rather naive statement that President Wilson made the first of his Fourteen Points, namely that nations emerging from the nightmare of World War I should commit themselves not only to "open covenants" but to "covenants openly arrived at after which there shall be no private understandings of any kind but diplomacy shall proceed always frankly and in public view."

The English historian Sir Harold Nicolson, a former member of the British diplomatic service and a Member of Parliament from 1935 to 1945, wrote later,

> President Wilson was an idealist, and what was perhaps more dangerous, a consummate master of English prose. . . . He possessed, moreover, the gift of giving commonplace ideas the resonance and authority of biblical

sentences, and, like all phraseologists, he became mesmerized by the strength and neatness of the phrase he devised.[15]

But was Wilson in his practice of diplomacy really so mesmerized by his own phrase "covenants openly arrived at"? It does not seem so. Nicolson tells us:

> . . . on reaching Paris, President Wilson decided that by "diplomacy" he had not meant "negotiation," but only the results of negotiation, namely treaties. He also decided that the phrases "openly arrived at" and in "public view" were relative only and contained nothing that need to deter him from conducting prolonged secret negotiations with Lloyd George and Clemenceau, while one American marine stood with fixed bayonet at the study door, and another patrolled the short strip of garden outside. I can well recall how startled I was, on first being admitted to the secret chamber, to discover how original was the President's interpretation of his own first rule. Today, being much older, I realize that the method he adopted was the only possible method which, in the circumstances, could have led to any result.[16]

Bilateral and Multilateral Diplomacy

Diplomatic negotiations are usually conducted on a bilateral rather than a multilateral basis. Even when a diplomatic conference such as the Congress of Vienna in 1815, the League of Nations in the 1920s, or the United Nations in our time creates the impression of multilateral diplomacy in the full sense, most of the negotiations in such a gathering are conducted on a bilateral basis; a multilateral agreement issues from an intricate complex of bilateral negotiations, interconnected and interlaced. The confidential nature of diplomatic bargaining usually imposes a limit on the number of participants.

There are of course numerous times when more than two nations participate in actual negotiations. When they are more or less equal and equally interested, we can speak of multilateral diplomacy in the fullest sense of the word. It should be differentiated from multilateral negotiations that are presided over by two major powers without whose consent the multilateral agreement is impossible. Such a negotiation is really a bilateral one, for the others play the role of diplomatic kibitzers. Unlike their counterparts in card games, they are not always expected to keep silent; occasionally they are permitted and sometimes even encouraged to voice their preferences.

Diplomacy by Parliamentary Procedures

If by parliamentary diplomacy or diplomacy by conference we mean speech making and subsequent counting of votes in the United Nations General Assembly or other international conferences, parliamentary diplomacy is a contradiction in terms. Diplomatic negotiation is, by definition, contact and communication between policy makers with a view toward coming to terms. The search is for harmony and unanimity, not victory. The parliamentary method, on the contrary, is sometimes the opposite to the search for unanimity; matters are decided by a majority of votes to which the defeated minority is supposed to bow, not agree.

If, on the other hand, by parliamentary diplomacy we mean confidential bilateral or multilateral negotiations that may occur in the lobbies or corridors surrounding the parliamentary chambers of the United Nations, then this is a very useful form of modern diplomacy which, however, does not essentially differ from the classical forms. It may be either bilateral or multilateral, occasional or continuous, conducted by professional diplomats or by policy makers. Since the United Nations lobbies provide for constant and continuous contacts and communications among more than 130 nations, lobby diplomacy tends to be continuous, since some of the parliamentary organs of the United Nations, the General Assembly, its committees, the various councils, and the specialized agencies are more or less permanently in session. Insofar as nineteenth-century diplomacy has been praised for its continuous character, lobby diplomacy may be praised for the same reason. In addition, present-day lobby diplomacy has the advantage of being exposed to multilateral influence and scrutiny and thus being global in scope.

In the General Assembly The Assembly hall is a less appropriate place than the delegate's lounge for sampling reaction to policies or reaching agreements. At best, it is a forum for "expressing views and hopes," as General de Gaulle expressed it in his talk to Secretary-General U Thant in 1964. Some less kind observers of the United Nations debates have called the General Assembly a forum for the exchange of insults. Even when a debate is concluded by majority vote, no issue is settled and no dispute solved. In a world that lacks a basic consensus, no important issue can be decided by majority vote. A democratic counting of positive and negative votes among nations rarely results in a binding and enforceable decision as it does within nations; it merely produces a lineup of the majority against the minority. In addition, as previously demonstrated in Chapter 10, both terms, "majority" and "minority," are questionable on the basis of population and actual power. As the vote counting is usually preceded by an acrimonious debate, the purpose of such a procedure is not to persuade one another and find a common ground, but to convince the rest of the world that the opposite side is the quintessence of evil. Furthermore, there is a marked tendency to use the speeches delivered at the United Nations for the purpose not of convincing other national leaders of the correctness of a particular view, but of indirectly addressing a domestic audience. Statesmen from democratic countries, especially on the eve of general elections, find the adoption of a posture of crusader or mediator during a United Nations debate a useful domestic vote-getting device. Leaders of the developing countries sometimes misuse their dramatic speeches at the United Nations for the purpose of shifting the attention of their citizens from some pressing domestic issues to international and distant ones. Assuming the position of wise men, giving advice to both the Western and communist major powers on how to compose their differences, is a rather frequent device employed by some Asian and African leaders. Thus, too often the goal of the so-called parliamentary form of diplomacy is not conciliation but a cheap propaganda effect, not search for a common ground but an overemphasis on differences, not respect for the opposite viewpoint but extreme denigration of the other side with the hope that the world press will not fail to report it. Diplomacy by debate and voting is then no diplomacy at all, for it diminishes rather than increases the chances of negotiation and conciliation.

Third-Party Techniques Up to this point, our focus has been on negotiations involving only two parties, two nations, or two blocs. There are also forms of peaceful solution of an international conflict in which a third party is added to the parties to a dispute. While often less effective and less resorted to than diplomatic negotiations, third-party techniques such as mediation, conciliation, arbitration, and judicial settlement (all described in Chapter 10 under the heading "Peaceful Settlement of Disputes") are useful under some circumstances. The effectiveness of most third-party techniques presupposes, of course, some preliminary negotiation concerning the identity, role, and authority of the third party—the mediator, the arbiter, or the International Court of Justice. One may therefore wonder why third-party techniques are used at all, since some preliminary diplomatic contact and agreement is necessary.

In many cases a nation that desires either a positive or a negative decision concerning a dispute in which it is involved may prefer an expert decision based on objective findings; in other cases, a government finds it easier to yield to a third party than to its direct opponent. Losing a case by a decision reached by a disinterested party may also be less easily construed by the government's domestic opposition as a diplomatic defeat and proof of political ineptness. On vital issues, of course, a nation is usually not willing to yield to anybody—whether the adversary or a third party. For this reason, third-party techniques have been used and have proved successful in solving conflicts of much less than vital national interest, that is, marginal matters.

A simple fact seems to emerge: If nations are willing to compromise on important issues and assume the corresponding willingness on the other side, they rarely need a third party, whose mediating or arbitrating role would have to be based on the agreement of the contending parties. This fact reemphasizes the importance, desirability, and perhaps ultimate inevitability of direct diplomatic negotiations between nations in serious conflict.

BARGAINING WITHOUT COMMUNICATION

Some authors, Thomas C. Schelling in particular, have brought important insights to the process of bargaining among unfriendly or hostile nations when communication is incomplete or impossible, as it is in hot or cold wars. The behavior of nations in the process of tacit bargaining was analyzed in terms of strategy games (nonzero-sum games) in which conflict is mixed with common interest or mutual dependence. This is in contrast with the so-called pure conflict (zero-sum games) in which there is no dependence or common interest between the would-be total winner and the would-be total loser. As was explained in the concluding section of the preceding chapter, game theories in international politics focus on the decision-making process in which two or more participants ("players") make decisions as to the sequence of their moves (strategy) in the light of their limitations and anticipated countermoves.

We have already recorded the view according to which most international conflicts are, in essence, bargaining situations—nonzero-sum strategy games—in which there is a common interest in reaching outcomes that, at least, are not so disastrous for one side as to prompt it to take desperate, nihilistic action. According to Schelling, most international conflicts, including the violent ones, belong to the category of situations in which the element of conflict provides the dramatic interest, but

> mutual dependence is part of the logical structure and demands some kind of collaboration or mutual accommodation, tacit, if not explicit—even if only avoidance of mutual disaster. . . . Though secrecy may play a strategic role, there is some essential need for the signaling of intentions and the meeting of minds. . . . They are games in which what one player *can* do to avert mutual damage affects what another player *will* do to avert it, so that it is not always an advantage to possess initiative, knowledge or freedom of choice. . . . [17]

Schelling compared the coordination of national policies without communication to a driver jockeying in heavy traffic where all the drivers have some interests in common (movement and survival) and other interests in conflict (to reach the parkway exit first) and where skill, logic, and the art of guessing play an important role. In Schelling's words:

> People *can* often concert their intentions or expectations with others if each knows that the other is trying to do the same. Most situations. . . provide some clue for coordinating behavior, some focal

point for each person's expectation of what the other expects him to expect to be expected to do. Finding the key, or rather finding *a* key—any key that is mutually recognized as the key becomes *the* key—may depend on imagination more than on logic; it may depend on analogy, precedent, accidental arrangement, symmetry . . . casuistic reasoning, and who the parties are and what they know about each other.[18]

War and Peace by Computers

Some scholars have voiced the hope that the constant effort and countereffort to improve the quality of weapons tends to transform nuclear threats into a kind of game for the highest stakes, in which the military are being increasingly replaced by scientists, civilian strategists, political scientists, psychologists, and computing machines. In her study on the inevitability of revolutions in a period of nuclear stalemate, Hannah Arendt has noted, for example,

> It is as though the nuclear armament race has turned into some sort of tentative warfare, in which the opponents demonstrate to each other the destructiveness of the weapons in their possession; and while it is always possible that this deadly game of ifs and whens may suddenly turn into the real thing, it is by no means inconceivable that one day victory and defeat may end a war that never exploded into reality.[19]

Some observers have since argued that the Cuban missile crisis was in fact the first nuclear "war" so fought between the two nuclear superpowers. During the thirteen days of crisis, the ICBMs were targeted and nuclear bombers and conventional armies were on the move, while the risks and gains of this game for the highest stakes were calculated by human computers, that is, by Kennedy's and Khrushchev's minds, "programmed" by their respective advisory and intelligence staffs, the Executive Committee of the National Security Council in the American case, and the Politburo in the Soviet case.

It would be comforting to think that a sophisticated and computerized study of all the implications of national strategy could lead to "wars"—and victories and defeats—not through several volleys of ICBMs but through a diligent manipulation of IBM cards, provided, of course, that we could assume rational or predictable behavior on both sides. By rational behavior we mean that the policy makers have well-defined and mutually consistent objectives following an order of preferences and that they are capable of calculating the losses and gains of their strategy. But can we assume such rational behavior even on the part of an intelligent leader? An assumption of such behavior may be seriously upset by the leader's wrong information, false analogy, bewitchment by history or creed, sickness, insanity, and other factors that cause misperception (see Chapters 5 and 6). So far the computers seem to digest IBM cards indicating GNP (Gross National

Product) more readily than cards indicating GLN (Gross Loss of Nerve) or GTG (Gross Tendency to Gamble).

Quincy Wright examined the hope for peace through computers and found it wanting:

> Under suitable conditions, war might be decided by highly intelligent generals without bloodshed. Each would calculate the best utilization of materials and manpower, the best strategy and maneuvers of armed forces both for himself and the enemy, each assuming—as in playing a game of chess—that the other would similarly calculate and would follow the plan most in his own interest. According to such calculations, victory for one side and defeat for the other might be certain, and the defeated would surrender without any hostilities. However, it is highly improbable that war will ever be so conventionalized that incalculable factors like courage, morale, faulty intelligence, accidents of weather, and new inventions can be eliminated. The party whose defeat seems certain by logical calculations will not surrender without a trial of strength unless indeed the disparity of strength is very great as in interventions by a great power in the territory of a very weak power.[20]

Or, to return to Schelling's analogy, a driver's imaginative and logical calculations in a traffic jam may be completely upset by one single driver who is drunk, high on LSD, or struck by a heart attack. Or the high-risk (yet expert) driver might simply prove unable to withstand the stress and thus commit a primitive driving error.

Moreover, as Karl Deutsch convincingly argues, the game theory of deterrence and tacit bargaining often neglects to calculate *cumulative risk*:

> Schelling's reckless driver is likely to get the right of way at the first intersection, and thus to pass it quickly alive. Let us suppose that his chances of survival are 0.9 or 90 per cent. Let us then suppose that he continues his reckless tactics and that his chances of survival and success at every following encounter at intersections are likewise 90 per cent. In that case, his chances of being alive after two encounters are 90 per cent of 90 per cent, or 0.9^2, which is 81 per cent. . . . 21 successive encounters would offer our high-risk player only one chance out of eight to stay alive, . . . and 70 would leave him less than once chance in 1,000. The fact that each single encounter offered him nine chances out of 10 to live is almost irrelevant compared to the deadly effect of cumulative risks. The foreign affairs of nations and states which intend to continue for long periods of time must be governed by methods that more likely than not will let them survive for generations and centuries.[21]

THE SEPARABILITY OF ISSUES

From the understanding that nations can cooperate in some areas while their conflict in others may continue unresolved, one may deduce that the task of diplomacy should be to enlarge the area of cooperation or reduce the area of conflict; it would be wrong, however, to imagine that the enlargement of one area necessarily leads to the reduction of the other. Conflict and cooperation often occur on different levels that may or may not be interconnected: Political conflict may be accompanied by economic or humanitarian cooperation. Political cooperation in one sphere does not exclude conflict in another. One thousand agreements on marginal issues cannot balance one single conflict of vital security interests that both sides consider worth a war. The respective quality, not quantity, of common or conflicting interests is what ultimately counts.

Two basic approaches have emerged in response to the interconnection between international conflict and cooperation. One is called functionalism, that is, the effort to shift international contacts and negotiation away from political and military matters toward basically economic, social, and cultural issues such as the common fight against pollution, illiteracy, overpopulation, underdevelopment, drug trafficking, ill-health, and so on with the hope that nations, accustomed to cooperation in social "workshops," antipollution agencies, and health centers will prove able to transfer their habit of cooperation to the political arena. The hopes and frustrations of the functional approach to peace were discussed in more detail in Chapter 10.

In contrast to functionalism, another school of thought recommends concentration on what really matters among nations, politics, but maintains that nations should tackle only one issue at a time. We may call such an approach the "one-at-a-time technique" or simply the "single-issue technique"; this has some undeniable merits but also some serious limitations.

The single-issue technique, as we noted, concentrates primarily on the political scene. Basically all negotiations and agreements among nations are, of course, single-issue affairs; it is inconceivable that nations could try to solve all their vital and less vital conflicts of interests, so to speak, at one sitting. What is meant here is focus either on the single issue that is the most immediately dangerous, such as the Middle East, Berlin, Cuba, or Vietnam, or on the one that is the most immediately negotiable, such as the neutrality of Austria (1955) or the suspension of those atomic tests that do not require international inspection (1963). By separating the most negotiable issue and concentrating on its solution, nations may succeed in removing at least one irritant from the international scene. And this is useful per se, for at least the quantity of interest conflicts has been reduced.

In addition, however, single-issue diplomacy is often accompanied by an assumption similar to that of functionalism, namely, that issues pitting one nation against another are separable yet so connected as to allow only the positive influence to proceed in the desired direction (that is, from the resolution of a marginal conflict to the central problem of hostility and suspicion) while preventing the negative influence of the core problem from spoiling peripheral compromises. Following the successful conclusion of the Atomic Test-Ban Treaty, many people expressed the hope that the good will created around the first agreement might branch out and favorably affect a whole array of less negotiable and more vital issues, including a general reduction of Soviet-American armaments. When later some new cooperative agreements were concluded, such as the nonproliferation treaty, was the point of the beneficial separability of political issues proved? Perhaps so. But some have argued that the continuing détente between Moscow and Washington was not a result of the successful resolution of a single issue such as the ban of detectable atomic testing but a consequence of several less specific factors: (1) the Soviet-American fear of nuclear confrontation; (2) the pressure of their domestic problems, the handling of which demanded more money and energy than the existing level of arms race permitted; and (3) the emergence of a *triangular* (Russia-China-United States) or *pentagonal* (Russia-China-United States-Japan-West Europe) power relationship, which opened a broader area for diplomatic maneuvers and occasional alignments of "two-to-one" or "three-to-two." In such a framework moderate détentes and cooperative arrangements among former antagonists became possible and useful; new flexibility replaced the previous rigidity of the basically bipolar relationship, in which the two antagonists faced each other in a narrow alley, unable to move sideways and capable only of advancing or yielding in direct confrontation, almost as in the game theorists' zero-sum model.

In general, all negotiations that focus on a single issue—be it disarmament, disengagement, a geographically limited area of conflict, or the so-called nonpolitical (economic, social, or cultural) functional issues—always involve some danger that both the negotiators and their observers will become overwhelmed by the self-propulsion of the negotiating technique or get so enmeshed in the specifics or technical details (such as the number and accuracy of missiles) as to lose sight of not only the broader political perspective but also the original purpose of the negotiations and the posssible consequences of either disagreement or agreement. Negotiations, which, after all, are only instruments of policy, may thus acquire a life of their own and such a momentum as to detach themselves from the political reality; then, of course, the result, while technically perfect, would hardly be worth the paper on which it is written.

SYMPTOMS OR CAUSES?

Nations and men have various views of the conflicts that separate them: All nations refer to their security as their primary concern but differently combine this fundamental concern with their estimates of foreign threat, with protection of their economy, ideology, prestige, and moral values, and with such specific issues as weapon systems or geographically determined conflicts such as those concerning Berlin, Germany, the Middle East, Vietnam, Cuba, Taiwan, Laos, or Turkey.

What in this web of international conflicts and tensions appears central to one observer seems peripheral to another; what seems negotiable though central to one nation may be viewed as nonnegotiable although marginal by another. The nations' conflicting opinions on what the international conflict is really about and what the causal connection is between the identifiable issues necessarily color their approaches to their resolution. In the analysis in Chapter 13 of the failures of many disarmament efforts we have pointed out that arms are both consequences *and* causes of international tension. So are security concerns, political and ideological goals, and geographically delineated issues.

From the practical point of view a theoretical dissection of international conflicts, while fascinating, is perhaps unnecessary because nations cannot really be expected to agree, first, on what is the primary cause and the effect that, in turn, may cause other effects, and, second, on what is a peripheral and what is a central issue, and at what point either the peripheral solution affects the central issue or the central issue casts such a long and dark shadow that even a marginal trifle cannot be successfully handled. However, in a system that insists on remaining divided into competing nations without merging into higher unity, nobody has as yet devised a better way than to try to look for compromise solutions by mutual accommodation and to keep on trying in whatever order or causal connection.

RIVALRY WITHOUT NUCLEAR VIOLENCE?
A CONCLUDING NOTE

When we try to peer into the last quarter of the twentieth century, the major features that characterize politics among and within nations in the mid-1970s do not seem to justify excessive optimism about nations' and men's capacity to solve their conflicts in a cooperative, or at least civilized, fashion. In the preceding chapters we have analyzed seven major features of contemporary conflict and cooperation among nations:

1. The *nuclear stalemate* is the dominant characteristic of our era. Its positive aspect is the reduction of the probability that any of the five major nuclear powers would unleash a thermonuclear catastrophe.

2. The *balancing process* with all its dangers of instability and miscalculation continues as it always has among nations. In addition to the extremely costly nuclear arms race between Russia and the United States, and increasingly also China, the balancing process proceeds on three levels:

   a. The conventional arms race among large and small nations. This race includes the large, competitive and dangerous traffic in arms to the Oil and Poor Worlds.

   b. Local and regional limited wars, made possible by the arms traffic and the direct interest of the superpowers in the outcome of such wars.

c. Competition for relative political influence in various areas of the world by means of interference in the domestic affairs of nation-states. One dimension of mutual penetrability of nation-states is the growing power of multinational megacorporations, which challenge nation-states and in turn are challenged by the political power of nation-states.

3. The *triangular relationship* between the Soviet Union, the United States, and People's Republic of China has to some extent replaced the decades-old Russian-American duopoly. In the new triangle each member is antagonistic to the other two, although precisely because it is a triangle, their antagonisms may acquire varying degrees of intensity or moderation in different sets of circumstances. Moreover, the antagonism and power relationship between Moscow and Washington are not of the same kind as those between Moscow and Peking or Washington and Peking. While both Moscow and Washington have an assured first-strike capacity with respect to Peking, neither Moscow nor Washington has such a capacity with regard to the other. "As long as the key to thermonuclear war, " as Michel Tatu noted, "is in the custody of the Soviet Union and the United States alone, possessing a first-strike capacity against every other nation, Washington and Moscow have no alternative but to carry on a private dialogue to the exclusion of China and other secondary powers."[22] The disequilibrium of the three parties is therefore still too great in the 1970s for a genuinely triangular situation to develop. Nevertheless, several assumptions about probable behavior in the framework of this imperfect triangle can be made: Each of the three powers aims at reducing a combination between the others to a minimum, although it is also in the interest of each to bluff or blackmail one rival by threatening collusion with the other. It is too early to say whether the present imperfect triangularity will soon be replaced by a real triangle or by a *pentagonal* relationship among the five present and potential power centers: Russia, China, the United States, West Europe (which is not united), and Japan (which is not armed).

4. The *future role of China* is even more unpredictable than that of any other major nation. By the 1980s China may acquire a credible nuclear delivery system and increase its industrial base; by that time its population will grow to 900 million or one billion. Roughly in the same span of time China will have lost its aging leaders, Mao and Chou, and so will face for the first time since her birth in 1949 a series of succession crises, never an easy matter in an authoritarian country. The future domestic changes in China naturally preoccupy the United States (see Figure 14.3), the Soviet Union, Japan, Western Europe, and China's immediate neighbors from Pakistan, India, and Bangladesh to North Vietnam and North Korea—and, of course, many others, including the younger as well as the old cadres in the Chinese Communist party and army.[23]

5. The *planetary management* crisis has four major ingredients: insufficient production of food, excessive production of people, scarcity

and high cost of energy, and pollution of our planet. All four underline the search for some modicum of coequal partnership between the developed North and developing South. In the last decades of the twentieth century peace and progress will continue to be directly related to success or failures in replacing the North-South tensions and misunderstandings with global agreements on new currency and pricing systems and on exploitation of the dwindling world resources (including a new law of the sea), increases in food production, and curbs on excessive population growth. As to the latter, the 1974 statistics show that world demand for food is increasing by thirty million tons a year, partly because of rising population in the Third and Fourth Worlds (two-thirds of the developing countries fell short of meeting their food needs in 1973) and partly because of increased protein consumption in the First and Second Worlds. In 1974 the world population reached nearly four billion persons, almost double what it was at the end of World War II; if the present growth rate of seventy-six million persons a year continues, the world will have over seven billion people by the year 2000. It seems inevitable, as Robert G. Wirsing argues, that the food/population/resources problem will intrude itself upon the international scene in ever-increasing magnitudes, regardless of whether its spiraling implications are granted "equal time" with the more traditional concerns of the study of politics among nations.[24]

Moreover, the global mobilization of industrial, scientific, manufacturing, chemical, and energy resources is expected to be combined with a "solemn responsibility to protect and improve the environment for present and future generations," as the universal ecological declaration, adopted by the UN conference on the Human Environment (Stockholm, 1972), proclaims, assigning to the nation-states "the responsibility to ensure that activities within their jurisdiction or control do not cause damage to the environment of other states or areas beyond the limits of national jurisdiction."[25] The North-South gap naturally permeates also the views of future planet management held by the First, Second, Third, and Fourth Worlds. The West tends to view the Planet Earth, in Maurice P. Strong's words, as "seen from outer space—that exhilarating yet sobering sight of a small finite Spaceship Earth with its living cargo sustained by a unitary, limited and vulnerable life-support system."[26]

By contrast, the Third and Fourth Worlds tend to regard the preoccupation of the industrialized countries with the environment as a "fad," rather remote from the interests and concerns of those who see salvation in rapid, even reckless, industrialization. As Strong described his experience during his travels in Asia, Africa, and Latin America,

> To a man faced with immediate starvation and other diseases of poverty, the risks he runs from contamination of the seas and the atmosphere seem so remote as to be irrelevant. To him factory smoke smells of money—and of jobs and needed consumer goods. And what if fly ash and sulphur dioxide afflict the surrounding area![27]

FIGURE 14.3
AFTER MAO—WHO?

"Whom would you prefer to be Mao Tse-tung's successor—Chou En-lai, Yeh Chien-ying, Li Teh-sheng, Chang Ch'un-ch'iao, or Wang Hung-wen?"

Drawing by Dana Fradon; © 1973 The New Yorker Magazine.

6. A general *malaise*, partly due to the uncertainty about the shape of things to come, reflects the five features already mentioned. This malaise, present in varying degrees in both the developed and developing nations, manifested itself in the 1960s and 1970s in large-scale riots, mass protest movements, ethnic and tribal frictions, terrorism, and urban and rural guerrilla movements. By a major twist of irony, alienated individuals and groups claim power (peasant power, proletarian power, ethnic, racial, or

black power, tribal power, student power) and invoke the right of revolutionary violence for the sake of reforming the contemporary power-conscious and violence-oriented national systems and the international system of states. The 1974 Chinese propaganda slogan gleefully proclaimed: "World in Great Disorder: Excellent Situation."

7. The conflict between *universalism* and ethnonational *parochialism* is the fundamental feature of our era, permeating and conditioning all the other tensions and clashes. It is a conflict between the existing system of self-centered territorial states and the incipient practice of transnational cooperation in disregard of national boundaries. One group of scholars seems to detect the promise of true universalism in the unifying tendencies of modern technology and economic and ecological interdependence; other scholars point with skepticism to the new tensions, chasms, and ethnonational barriers which, despite its unifying aspects, modern technology also produces among and within nations, continents, and the industrial North and the developing South. These skeptics occasionally warn against replacing the present anarchic system of sovereign territorial states—admittedly chaotic, but familiar and bearable—with a new chaos, unfamiliar and perhaps worse than the present one.

Although the interests of humanity and the interests of its territorial or ethnic subdivisions can be viewed as complementing each other, nations and states have often asserted their interests against what others have deemed the interests of mankind, both nations and humanity suffering as a consequence. Many observers warn today that territorial divisions, useful in the seventeenth century as a solution to violent interreligious conflict, are unnatural in our era of unprecedented economic and technological interdependence and mass exchange of goods, persons, and ideas. If territorial states have ceased to become defensible, self-contained, self-sufficient, and self-justified, then the time for territorial states and nationalism—each other's cause and effect—to pass away is now. Men everywhere should begin to feel, think, act, plan, and organize in supranational and human terms; territorial nationalism should be submerged by the irresistible tide of universalism. "Now that destruction threatens everybody, national interests are bound to recede behind—or at least *compete with*—the common interest of mankind in sheer survival," is the cautious hope expressed by John H. Herz in his important study[28] on the rise and anticipated demise of territorial states. How hopefully this sentence begins, only to be suddenly interrupted by a scholar's reservation stressing universalism's possible competition with nationalism rather than victory over it! In a new study entitled "The Territorial State Revisited," published in 1968, the author recognized the continuing need for territorial states to provide group identity, protection, and welfare but expressed a new hope that at long last the territorial state would emerge as "that which the philosophers of early nationalism had expected it to be: the custodian of cultural diversity among groups mutually granting each other their peculiar worth."[29]

The hope that an advanced technology might do for men what they cannot do for themselves is not new. In the revolutionary year of 1848, which was very much like 1969 in its student unrest, its revolutionary confrontations, and its hopes, Victor Hugo expressed the hope that technical innovations, and in particular the revolution in transportation (based on the steam engine), might bring about a brotherly commonwealth between a united Europe and a united America, "facing each other and stretching out their hands across the seas in close cooperation." To the thundering applause of the 1849 peace congress in Paris, Hugo concluded in the same way that many a speaker concludes today: "What do we need? To love each other."[30] But instead of love, the following hundred years were marked by hatred, revolutionary violence, and war. Nations and men continued to divide humanity into an ever-increasing number of territorial compartments of diminishing size and viability; in the 1960s and 1970s microstates appeared on the international scene, most of them becoming members of the United Nations.

The time may come when the "mystique" of broader continental or intercontinental structures, such as the Atlantic Community or a one-world community, evokes positive emotional reactions on the part of the presently nationalistic masses and their leaders. The time is not yet; we should warn against premature hopes and wishful thinking in this respect. The trend toward larger regional or even continental groupings (such as the European Economic Community, Pan-Africanism, Pan-Arabism, and the communist system) does not necessarily point toward a world state. Instead of being stepping-stones toward mankind's unity, regional, ideological, or racial supranationalism is often only old nationalism writ large. When West European nations (six in 1957 and nine as of 1973) began to forge their economic unity, one of their underlying motives was to assert European destiny and independence against the Americans and the Russians. African unity is being asserted *against* Western Europe and Arab unity, *against* Israel and her supporters. The free world and communist communities have been organized and maintain some degree of unity insofar as they feel threatened by each other.

Furthermore, every single polyethnic structure, be it empire, multinational federation, supranational regional organization, or international ideological movement, experiences the eroding force of nationalism. In spite of many speeches on the merits of Pan-Africanism and Pan-Arabism, both movements have made little headway. The assertion of national interests by many communist states against the Soviet concept of their collective interest is another significant illustration of the weakness of supranationalism and of the strength of nationalism. The European Economic Community represents the most integrated and most advanced form of supranational regional structure; its integrated economy and its political manipulation have proved capable of evoking both emotional responses and the incipient mystique of West European supranationalism. Yet European unity is more of a reality when asserted against the United States, the Soviet Union, or Eastern Europe than it is within the Community itself. One of its dominant architects, Charles de Gaulle, realistically referred to it as *L'Europe des patries*, "the Europe of Fatherlands," that is, a loose confederation of separate and nationalistic communities, united for some purposes but not for all. His successors, Presidents Pompidou and Giscard d' Estaing, continue to stress the same concept of French nationalism within the larger concept of Western European Community.

Although the atomic dimension of international relations has, we hope, reduced the likelihood of global wars, it has not perceptibly reduced the potency of territorial nationalism. On the contrary, the atomic stalemate appears to have given a new lease on life to virulent nationalism all over the globe.

Small and medium-sized nations tend to assert their independence and promote their national interests in a self-confident and sometimes cocksure way; they seem to feel reasonably confident that the great powers' hands, have, so to speak, been tied by their mutual fears and by their resulting cautiousness. As seen from the vantage point of nonatomic powers as well as small states and ministates, the great powers have actually become less great by becoming too big in their reciprocal awesome destructive capabilities. The Arab use of the oil embargo in 1973 as a political weapon demonstrated another weak spot in the nuclear and industrial armor of major powers.

It does require a special type of optimism to see in the reassertion of nationalism under the nuclear umbrella and in the misuses of advanced technology for parochial rather than universalistic goals merely the natural birth pains of an old world pregnant with a new one. It is not easy to see the world in the last quarter of the twentieth century as, basically, pulling together (See figure 14.4). And yet, two redeeming features may be noted: First, the dedication and belief of some who are not discouraged by the past and the present and who, as Max Weber once wrote, "in the face of all this can say 'In spite of all!' " and keep on trying. In Kissinger's words: "World politics is not a conjurer's business."[31] Second, on a more down-to-earth level, we can record that this world, at least so far, has shied away from the use of the doomsday weapons it has invented and now holds in terrifying readiness.

Since World War II major wars have been prevented and peace among the superpowers has been preserved by mutual terror and negotiations or by tacit bargaining that has resulted in some degree of self-restraint on the part of the superpowers. In the unstable, revolutionary, and nuclear world in which we live, moderation seems to be difficult but not entirely impossible.

FIGURE 14.4
WILL THEY?

"Basically, of course, we've got to pull together."

Drawing by Le Pelley. Reprinted by permission from *The Christian Science Monitor*; © 1966 The Christian Science Publishing Society. All rights reserved.

Raymond Aron succinctly characterized our era when he wrote:

> Inexpiable rivalry of states on all levels and with all means, but without the supreme weapon and collective catastrophe—such is the universe in which we live. I do not think we can escape this universe. I do not think we must resign ourselves to it. . . . I do not hide from myself the virtual contradiction between the realism of the short term and the hope in the long term of passing beyond international politics as they have been for millennia. It is perhaps our historic situation to be placed at the center of this contradiction.[32]

Placed between the world as it is and the world as we wish it to be, our vision is inevitably distorted by our involvement in the process of change; we have no sufficient distance. We know the past and the present, and we wish the future to be different, but we cannot forecast in what ways and by what means the present system will be transformed nor what the results of a transformation will be. If our history of men acting singly and collectively contains any valid lesson for the future, it shows that livable life—not a paradise, of course—has never been the result of a single sweeping stroke or of a utopian program such as "World Government" or "Federation Now." Consensus and order within nations have been only gradually built by constant, patient, often tedious negotiations, interrupted by passion, irrationality, and violence. We can hardly expect that consensus and order among nations can be established by any other than such a slow and gradual method, including the interruptions. Many a reader will therefore agree with Aron's short-term gloom tempered by his long-term hope that nations and men can perhaps learn.

The process of gradual learning is both hopeful and full of extreme risks. Because of lack of effort or of foresight, tomorrow may be canceled any day. Modern technology, which can end mankind's progress and life itself, can also speed up the evolution toward reason. Among men and nations anxiety about the present tempered by a hope for a better future is not new. With eyes turned toward the future humanity has always lived dangerously. In the last decades of the twentieth century it will keep on living not less dangerously but more so.

Notes

1. Hans J. Morgenthau, "What the Big Two Can and Can't Negotiate," *New York Times Magazine*, September 20, 1959, p. 9.
2. François de Callières, *On the Manner of Negotiating with Princes; on the Uses of Diplomacy; the Choice of Ministers and Envoys; and the Personal Qualities Necessary for Success in Missions Abroad*, translated by A. F. Whyte. Notre Dame, Ind.: Notre Dame University Press, 1963, p. 110. Originally published in Paris in 1716.
3. Milton Viorst, *Hostile Allies: FDR and Charles de Gaulle*. New York: Crowell-Collier-Macmillan, 1965.
4. Harry S. Truman, *Year of Decision* (*Memoirs*, Vol. 1). New York: Doubleday, 1955, p. 342.

5. Major General Courtney Whitney, *MacArthur, His Rendezvous with History*. New York: Knopf, 1956, p. 25.

6. Fred Charles Iklé, *How Nations Negotiate*. New York: Harper & Row, 1964, p. ix.

7. E. A. J. Johnson (ed.), *The Dimensions of Diplomacy*. Baltimore, Md.: The Johns Hopkins Press, 1964, p. xi. The volume contains articles by McGeorge Bundy, Henry A Kissinger, W. W. Rostow, James R. Killian, Jr., Adolphe A. Berle, and Livingston Merchant.

8. Oran R. Young, *The Politics of Force: Bargaining during International Crises*. Princeton, N.J.: Princeton University Press, 1968, pp. 412-413.

9. Thomas C. Schelling, *The Strategy of Conflict*. New York: Oxford, 1963, p. 53.

10. Truman, *Year of Decision,* p. 213.

11. One summit meeting in Paris did not take place in 1960; Premier Khrushchev canceled it when he was able to prove American intelligence overflights of the Soviet territory by shooting down the U-2 spy plane. President Eisenhower's visit to the Soviet Union was then also canceled.

12. Callières, *On the Manner of Negotiating with Princes*, p. 31.

13. Charles Burton Marshall, "The Golden Age in Perspective," *Journal of International Affairs*, 17:1 (1963), 13. The entire issue, on diplomacy in transition, is recommended.

14. Harold Nicolson, "Diplomacy Then and Now," *Foreign Affairs*, 40:1 (October 1961), 40.

15. Harold Nicolson, *The Evolution of Diplomatic Method*. London: Constable, 1957, p. 84.

16. Nicolson, *The Evolution of Diplomatic Method*, pp. 85-86.

17. Schelling, *The Strategy of Conflict*, p. 83.

18. Schelling, *The Strategy of Conflict*, p. 57.

19. Hannah Arendt, *On Revolution*. New York: Viking, 1963, p. 7.

20. Quincy Wright, "The Nature of Conflict," *Western Political Quarterly*, 4:2 (June 1951), 205.

21. Karl W. Deutsch, *The Analysis of International Relations*. Englewood Cliffs, N.J.: Prentice-Hall, 1968, p. 128.

22. Michel Tatu, *The Great Power Triangle: Washington-Moscow-Peking*. Paris: The Atlantic Institute, 1970, pp. 21-22.

23. An article describing the downfall of Mao's heir-apparent, Lin Piao, in 1971, contained the following information: "In 1963, in a mood of dark pessimism, Mao was reported to have expressed a foreboding that China would 'change color'—in other words, cease to be Red—after his death. In 1966, in a letter to his wife, Mao voiced the premonition that 'rightists' would take power in China when he died. In 1971, on the inspection trip from which he was returning when the attempt was allegedly made on his life, he predicted that struggle like the Lin Piao affair would occur in China "10, 20, 30 more times." Joseph Lelywed, "The Ghost of Lin Piao," *New York Times Magazine*, January 27, 1974, p. 26.

24. Robert G. Wirsing in his comment on the current revision of this book.

25. Maurice F. Strong, "One Year after Stockholm: An Ecological Approach to Management." *Foreign Affairs*, 51:3 (July 1973), 690-691.

26. Strong, "One Year after Stockholm," p. 691.

27. Strong, "One Year after Stockholm," p. 691.

28. John H. Herz, "Rise and Demise of the Territorial States," *World Politics*, 9:4 (1957), 493.

29. John H. Herz, "The Territorial State Revisited," *Polity*, 1:1 (1968), 34.

30. Quoted by Hans Kohn, *The Twentieth Century*. New York: Crowell-Collier-Macmillan, 1950, pp. 5-6.

31. Raymond Aron, "Political Action in the Shadow of Atomic Apocalypse," in Harold Lasswell and Harlan Cleveland (eds.), *The Ethic of Power*. New York: Harper & Row, 1962, p. 458.

32. Kissinger made this statement in his talk in Cairo with Hassanein Heykal, then the editor of *Al Ahram* and an influential journalist; he was subsequently dismissed by Sadat. *New York Times*, December 5, 1973.

Additional Readings

Additional readings on the subject of diplomatic negotiations may be found in *Discord and Harmony: Readings in International Politics*, edited by Ivo D. Duchacek and published by Holt, Rinehart and Winston in 1972. Chapter 14, "Conflict and Compromise," contains the following essays: "What is Negotiation" by Fred Charles Iklé, "Open Covenants Secretly Arrived at" by Harold Nicolson," and the controversy about the Pentagon Papers, as reflected in the opinions of Justice Potter Stewart, Byron R. White, John M. Harlan, Hugo L. Black, and Harry A. Blackmun.

Index

Abel, Elie, 169n
Abernathy, Ralph, 47
Abu Dhabi, 10
Accidents, role of, 175, 401
Acheson, Dean, 169n, 199, 217n; on defense perimeter, 152; on Korean War, 152
Act. *See* Action
Action: conflicting interpretation of, 164-65; and credible messages, 160-62; ideology as a guide for, 219-70; moral values as a guide for, 273-81
Active deterrence, 402
Actors, in international politics: ethnic groups as, 6, 66-67; foreign-policy-promoting groups as, 74; functional interest groups as, 6, 67-74; international organizations as, 6, 355-56; leaders as, 175-78; migrant workers as, 66-67; multivocal, 63; multinational corporations as 7,8, 68-69; oil world as, 439-42; political opposition as, 6, 66-67; public as, 74-75; states as, 5-6; third world as,5

Adams, John Quincy, on interference, 421
Adebo, S.O., on tribalism, 81
Africa: Pan-Africanism movement in, 566; tribalism in, 80-82
Aggression, indirect, 411; unprovoked, 330, 332; U.N. definition of, 332; See also Interference, Wars
Agnew, Spiro, 193
Agreement, polyethnic states resulting from 82-83
Alapatt, Cyril, 450
Albania, dispute with England, 349, 351
Alien groups, elimination of, 94-98
Alienation: as a cause for interference, 84; and ethnic groups, 83-84; and political strife, 84-87; as a cause of polyethnicity, 83-84
Alliance for Progress, 447
Alliances: and balancing process, 497-506; CENTO (Central Treaty Organization), 498; communist, 502-3; effectiveness of, 497, 499; erosion of, 499-500; NATO (North Atlantic Treaty Organization), 498; OAS (Organization of American

States), 498; purpose of, 482-83, 497; SEATO (Southeast Asia Treaty Organization), 498; Warsaw Pact, 498, 502-3. *See also* Soviet-Nazi Pact

Allies, conflicts between, 532. *See also* Nonalignment, Oil World, Third World

Allison, Graham T., 207, 217n, 451n, 529n

Almond, Gabriel A., 134n

Alperowitz, Gar, 217n

American Civil War; casualties in, 299; hostility in, 88; and national self-determination, 88

American Society of International Law, 129, 340

Amin, Idi, 98, 305

Anarchy, 115-16

Angell, Norman, 450n; on cost of colonialism and war, 436

Antarctic Treaty (1959), 339

ANZUS Treaty, 497

Appeasement; definition of, 149; policy of, 148-49;and Munich Agreement (1938), 148, 289-90

Arab States: league of, 441-43; relations with Israel, 20, 154; unification of 427-28; *See also* Oil World, Petrodollars, Third World

Arafat, Yasir, 411

Arbitration, 379; defined, 343; international, 343-47; judicial settlement distinguished from, 343

Ardrey, Robert: on territoriality, 16

Arendt, Hannah, 570n, on revolutions, 557;

Armaments: in conventional balancing, 482, 494; cost of, 507-8; computerized, 557; naval, treaty for limited, 514; in nuclear balancing, 459-64, 496; race, 495; verification, 512-14; world community and, 522-27; world military expenditures for, 507-8

Arms. *See* weapons

Aron, Raymond D., 311n, 450n, 462, 480n, 569n, 570n; on imperialism, 435-36; on morality, 283; on nuclear war, 462

Art, Robert J., 450n; on imperialism, 437

Arthasastra, 275

Aspaturian, Vernon V., 391n

Asset freezing, 433

Assimilation, for ethnic homogeneity, 95

Astakov: Soviet-Nazi Pact, 292

Asymmetry: as a cause of international tension, 241-44; in economic capabilities, 442-44, 499; and imperialism, 442-44; and interdependence, 413; in political power, 244, 499-500; and resentment 244, 367; *See* also Communism; International organizations; Alliances

Aswan Dam, 433

Atomic weapons: balancing process and, 459-66; communism and, 255, 470-75; Einstein on 301; international relations and, 459-64, 496; nationalism and, 255, 475, 567; Nonproliferation Treaty (1969), 403; Test-Ban Treaty (1963), 38, 511, 559. *See also* Missiles; Nuclear balancing; Nuclear stalemate; Nuclear warfare

Atrocities: in Burundi, 305; in Nazi Germany, 296-97; in Uganda, 305; in Vietnam, 305-9. *See also* Genocide; War crimes

Attlee, Clement, 97, 153

Augsburg Peace Conference (1555), 35

Austrian Neutrality Treaty (1955), 164

Authority, list of territorial units of, 9-10; and nation-building, 33-39; need of, 21; and territorial state, 20-22

Autonomy and interethnic tension, 89-94

Awolowo, Obafemi, 81

Background, effect of leader's 187-89

Bainbridge, Kenneth, 304

Balance of power: defined, 453-54; international law and, 324. *See also* Balancing process

Balancing process, 395, 452-80; and alliances, 497-506; in antiquity, 455-57; and armaments, 466-69, 494, 495-96; and communications of view and intentions, 465; critique of, 458-59; decreasing rival power in, 483, 506; definitions of, 453-54; democracies in, 457-59; and diplomacy, 533-36; by economic